COMMERCIAL AGENTS AND THE LAW

LLOYD'S COMMERCIAL LAW LIBRARY

Arbitration Law
by Robert Merkin
(looseleaf)

Force Majeure and Frustration of Contract
second edition
edited by Ewan McKendrick
(1995)

The Mareva Injunction and Related Orders
third edition
by Mark Hoyle
(1997)

Arbitration Practice and Procedure: Interlocutory and Hearing problems
third edition
by D. Mark Cato
(1997)

Practice and Procedure of the Companies Court
edited by Alan Boyle QC and Philip Marshall
(1997)

Illegal Transactions
by Dr Nelson Enonchong
(1998)

Interests in Goods
second edition
edited by Norman Palmer and Ewan McKendrick
(1998)

Limitation of Actions
by David W. Oughton, John P. Lowry and Robert Merkin
(1998)

The Practice and Procedure of the Commercial Court
fifth edition
by The Hon Sir Anthony Colman, Victor Lyon and Philippa Hopkins
(2000)

Privity of Contract: Impact of the Contracts (Rights of Third Parties) Act 1999
by Robert Merkin
(2000)

Sale of Goods
edited by Ewan McKendrick
(2000)

Arbitration Law
by Robert Merkin
(2004)

Civil Jurisdiction and Judgments
fourth edition
by Adrian Briggs and Peter Rees
(2005)

Arbitration Act 1996
third edition
by Robert Merkin
(2005)

COMMERCIAL AGENTS AND THE LAW

BY

SÉVERINE SAINTIER
Ph.D
Lecturer, School of Law, University of Sheffield

JEREMY SCHOLES
Solicitor
Lecturer, School of Law, University of Sheffield
Consultant, Director of Competition Law, Commercial Group, Walker Morris

|L|L|P|

LONDON SINGAPORE
2005

Informa Professional
(a trading division of T&F Informa (UK) Ltd)
Mortimer House
37–41 Mortimer Street
London W1T 3JH
professional.enquiries@informa.com

EAST ASIA
Informa Professional Asia
No. 1 Grange Road
#08–02 Orchard Building
Singapore 239693
professional.asia@informa.com

First published 2005

British Library Cataloguing in Publication Data
A catalogue record for this book
is available from the
British Library

ISBN 1–84311–3279

Text set in 10/12pt Times
by Interactive Sciences Ltd
Gloucester
Printed in Great Britain by
MPG Books,
Bodmin, Cornwall

To François, Martine and Allen
SS

To my parents, Eric Scholes (1928–1977) and Evelyn Scholes
JPS

FOREWORD

The authors are to be congratulated for tackling the implementation of the EC Directive on Self-Employed Commercial Agents in the UK by means of the Commercial Agents (Council Directive) Regulations 1993. It has always been an ambitious undertaking to write on the law of agency. It is a broad subject, drawing on all aspects of the law and touching all areas of commercial activity; and it has been a well-traversed area of academic comment. In recent years, in common with so many parts of English law, the position has become more complicated. In particular, the European dimension has expanded, the tentacles of European Community law spreading throughout domestic law. Its reception into and effect on English law cannot be ignored. Nor should they be marginalised, for a proper appreciation of modern English law does not allow the European contribution to be treated as an alien exception to our domestic law. We need to understand both its European origins and exactly how it has now become a fully functioning component of the ever-changing kaleidoscope that is our own law.

The value of a dedicated treatment of commercial agency law, as opposed to simply integrating the discussion into a general treatment of agency law, is that it provides the opportunity for detailed, in-depth exploration of the background to and peculiarities of the Regulations. Moreover, the publication of this book a decade or so after the Regulations have come into force has meant that there has been time for reflection and a greater opportunity to appreciate their impact and limitations.

Naturally, the authors examine in detail the novel phenomenon of the "commercial agent" and the Regulations' shift from the common law practice of safeguarding the interests of the principal to protecting the agent. They approach their task critically, highlighting the inadequacies of verbatim implementation of the Directive and the gaps which that leaves. The task is done comparatively, with reference not only to the laws of France and Germany but usefully—and helping to remedy a common deficiency in much traditional comparative UK legal scholarship—to the divergence in practice between English and Scottish courts. A particularly useful feature of this book is its attention to issues of agency and competition law. The authors have also sought to offer guidance on how uncertainties might be resolved in the future.

We can be grateful to the authors for providing a point of reference for anyone seeking guidance in this now major area of the law of agency.

Francis Rose
Professor of Commercial Law
University of Bristol

9 October 2005

FOREWORD

PREFACE

This book seems like the culmination of a strand of work that has been running through our respective independent professional lives for many years. Séverine's PhD was an in-depth comparative and empirical treatment of commercial agency in English and French law, various articles arose from that, and her subsequent book, *Commercial agency law: a comparative analysis* (Ashgate, 2002) was derived from the PhD. Jeremy first wrote about this subject in the PLC journal in 1993, and has since been through a number of updates to his Chapter (with precedent etc) in the PLC *Commercial Contracts Manual.* The fruits of our combined efforts here are greater than the sum of the parts taken in isolation, and neither of us could have written this book on our own. We hope that it will be a useful source of guidance on the subject.

Marketing and sales agents buying and selling goods on behalf of their principals are, of course, a very long-standing feature of business life. Along with the classics of different forms of distribution and newer ideas such as logistics services agreements, they are one of a number of ways in which businesses can get their products to market. In our practical experience, the number of situations when a marketing or sales agency ought, in principle, to be attractive to a manufacturer or supplier are perhaps more numerous than one might imagine.

When the 1986 EC directive on self-employed commercial agents was implemented in the UK through the Commercial Agents (Council Directive) Regulations 1993 and the parallel secondary legislation for Northern Ireland, there was considerable uncertainty as to what the Directive meant. Apart from the indemnity option on lump sum payments on termination, however, the prevailing view (led, it must be said, by the DTI) was that it would probably not involve very much change from the pre-existing English common law and equitable rules.

How wrong this view was. Much as many English lawyers might well wish that the Agency Regulations could be consigned to the sidings, if not wished away entirely, it is clear to us that, in the choice of tools in the toolbox for getting goods to market, where agency is concerned, it is the hybrid regime of the Agency Regulations and such of the pre-existing law as remains applicable, the body of law with which we deal in this book, which is the mainstream now. That there was a need for a book that attempted to dovetail the two influences together (some might say, to seat the Agency Regulations in context, but we think that description risks underestimating the continued importance of the common law and equitable rules) seemed clear to us.

The 11 years since the Agency Regulations came into force have seen perhaps less reported case law than one might have expected (though we are conscious, of course, that the great majority of possible disputes between principal and commercial agent never get anywhere near a court). There is next to nothing on the mutual duties of good faith which we consider are fundamental in the Agency Regulations; somewhat more on the commercial agent's rights on termination. The latter case law (though much of it is inconclusive) reveals a surprising willingness by the courts (particularly in Scotland, somewhat less so in England and Wales) to be guided by the French and German law principles which were the inspiration for much of the EC Directive; and at least the beginnings of a reaction, at least from the lower courts in England and Wales, that there must be another way of interpreting the commercial agent's rights on termination which treats him fairly and gives him recompense for the loss of his notional share of the notionally jointly owned goodwill (thus giving him the fundamental protection which the Directive requires English law to provide), while not giving him an unmerited windfall at the same time. The latter trend is, we believe, welcome.

We detect an increasing reluctance on the part of business in the UK to use commercial agency as a means of getting goods to market, driven largely by uncertainties arising from the Agency Regulations and concerns about the liabilities of the principal on termination. It would be a shame for commercial agency, which is useful in business terms more often than one might think, to be left off the list of possible options for that reason. We hope that that will not happen. The commercial "toolbox" for getting goods to market will be the poorer if it does.

Nobody is an island in this world, and it is customary at this stage for authors to thank all the people who have helped out in some way in the production of their book. We do this in no particular order. We are indebted to Professor Francis Rose for agreeing to write the foreword. We would also like to thank our much-appreciated colleague Professor Robert Bradgate in the School of Law at the University of Sheffield, Professor Malcolm Clarke of Cambridge University and Professor Ewan McKendrick of Oxford University, for commenting on first drafts of chapters. In relation to the German law parts of the book, we should like to thank Merih Altay, a former student of ours from Germany (now a trainee solicitor at DLA Piper Rudnick Gray Cary in London) for some excellent research work in Münster, and our much appreciated colleague in Sheffield Annette Nordhausen (a sometime Rechtsänwaltin in Lower Saxony) for her invaluable help at a later stage. Jeremy would like to thank his colleagues in the Commercial Group at Walker Morris for some interesting ideas and discussions on this subject down the years. We should like to thank Maître Jean-Marie Leloup, Docteur en Droit, avocat of the Cour d'Appel at Poitiers and former bâtonnier of the Ordre des Avocats in Poitiers and author of the leading French text on this subject (*Les agents commerciaux: statuts juridiques, stratégies professionnelles*: Delmas, currently in its 5th edn, 2001) for some invaluable insights on how the French system actually works. All of that said, though, there are no shoulders other than our own to bear the responsibility for this book.

We are grateful for the permission from the editors of Ashgate and from Legal & Commercial Publishing Ltd for their consent to our using some of the previously published material contained in Séverine's *Commercial agency law: a comparative analysis* and the PLC *Commercial Contracts Manual* respectively. The staff in the libraries of the law faculties in Rouen and Bordeaux IV were very helpful to Séverine: we thank them.

We should like to thank The British Academy for the funding for a research visit for Séverine to France, and the School of Law at the University of Sheffield for partially funding a research assistant for the German law part of the book. A special mention must go to Eleanor Taylor, our editor at Informa/LLP, for her patience and skilful coaxing, and helping us overcome our nervousness, in getting this book first into a completed manuscript and then into a completed book. Jeremy would like to thank Séverine for her patience in bearing with him in the writing of this when he had many pressures upon him from different directions.

On a more personal note, Séverine wishes to thank her husband Allen for bearing with her when writing the book. Jeremy would like to thank Annette for her support, encouragement and patience during a very busy writing period over the summer of 2005.

If there is anyone we have forgotten, please accept our apologies (but please let us know).

Except for Chapter 7 (where we have managed to include the CFI judgment of 15 September 2005 in *DaimlerChrysler AG* v. *Commission*), we have sought to state the law as at 2 August 2005.

SEVERINE SAINTIER
JEREMY SCHOLES
Leek and Bamford,
November 2005

TABLE OF CONTENTS

TABLE OF CASES

English and Scottish Courts

European Cases

French Cases

German Cases

Australian Cases

Canadian Cases

TABLE OF LEGISLATION

Northern Ireland

EC LEGISLATION

Directives

Regulations

Conventions

Treaties

LEGISLATION OF OTHER EC MEMBER STATES

France

CHAPTER 1

GENERAL INTRODUCTION

The Commercial Agents (Council Directive) Regulations 1993[1] (to which we shall refer hereinafter as "the Agency Regulations"), implement Directive 86/653 on the Coordination of the Laws of the Member States relating to Self-Employed Commercial Agents.[2] The Directive was enacted for the double purpose of (1) reinforcing the protection of commercial agents, and (2) harmonising the laws relating to commercial agents across Europe in order to facilitate trade within the European Union.[3] The goal of a reinforced protection has undeniably been met, since the Directive provides commercial agents with considerable cover at various stages of the commercial agency relationship. Yet, harmonisation has not been as successful, principally because the Directive leaves a considerable amount of freedom to Member States[4] in their implementation.[5] However, considering the huge disparity which existed between national rules on commercial agency prior to the Directive, this freedom was inevitable and compromises had to be made. Harmonisation is undeniably important within a European law context. It is less so however for the purpose of this book, which concentrates on the study of the Agency Regulations and their impact on the common law rules of agency and contract. As a consequence, in its analysis

1. SI 1993/3053 applies in Great Britain, i.e. England, Wales and Scotland. SI 1993/3053 was amended by SI 1993/3173 which corrected an error in SI 1993/3053 by adding the words "indemnity or"after the opening word of the first line in regulation 17. The text was the object of a more substantial amendment in 1998 (SI 1998/2868) in order to bring the jurisdictional provisions in line with the Directive. A consolidated version appears in Appendix 2. A separate (but substantially identical) statutory instrument applies for Northern Ireland: the Commercial Agents (Council Directive) Regulations (Northern Ireland) SR 1993 No 483 amended by SR 1999 No 201 (reproduced as Appendix 3). Ireland has of course separate implementing legislation. It is very different from that of Great Britain and Northern Ireland. See the European Communities (Commercial Agents) Regulations 1994, SI 1994/33 and the European Communities (Commercial Agents) Regulations 1997, SI 1997/31, reproduced as Appendix 4. In this book, reference to "the Agency Regulations"should be understood as a reference to the implementing text applying to Great Britain.

2. OJ L. 382/17, 31 December 1986.

3. See preamble of the Directive, OJ L. 382/17, 31 December 1986.

4. "Member States"is meant to be understood as the then 15 Member States. For the states which have become Member States of the EU after that date (the most recent being the accession of the 10 new Member States on 1 May 2004), and for the Member States of the European Economic Agreement, no such freedom was given.

5. Articles which give freedom of implementation to Member States are as follows: article 2(2) gives the option to Member States to leave outside the scope of the Directive commercial agents whose activities are regarded as secondary by national laws; article 7(2) leaves the choice to Member States in the implementation of the accrual of indirect commission; article 13(2) leaves the option to Member States to provide that the commercial agency contract shall not be valid unless evidenced in writing; article 15(3) gives Member States the option to extend the mandatory periods of notice to six months; article 16(b) and finally, article 17 gives Member States the choice between two kinds of termination rights, an indemnity or compensation for damage suffered. To see the choice of the various Member States, see the European Commission 1996 Report on the implementation of Directive 86/653 COM(96)364, final, reproduced as Appendix 9.

of the Agency Regulations, this book will focus on the protective stance of the Directive.

1.1 BACKGROUND AND SCOPE OF THE BOOK

It is well known that, when the Agency Regulations came into effect on 1 January 1994, they caused considerable uncertainty. This uncertainty is primarily attributable to the fact that the Agency Regulations implement the Directive, which is based on the civilian rationale that commercial agents are the weaker party within the relationship. As such, the Agency Regulations contradict the fundamental common law assumption that, because of the fiduciary nature of the agency relationship, principals are the ones in need of protection. Moreover, prior to the implementation of the Directive, the starting point of the law of agency at common law was the usual one of freedom of contract. In fact, "agency agreements were almost entirely regulated by agreements between the parties upon the general basis of the relevant laws of contract".[6]

This stark contrast was recognised by the EU institutions and the UK was consequently given additional time to implement the Directive.[7] However, the government has not used this additional time to the full since the Agency Regulations are almost a reproduction of the Directive. This near-verbatim implementation, which seems to be the more recent "copy out"[8] manner in which the UK implements directives, is nevertheless regrettable as it is a major, yet under-reported, cause for uncertainty surrounding the Agency Regulations.

1.2 THE NEAR-VERBATIM IMPLEMENTATION AND THE LEGAL PARADOX OF THE AGENCY REGULATIONS

In fact, the near-verbatim implementation of the Directive introduces a double layer of uncertainty. Directives only aim to provide a set of guidelines on a particular issue. As a consequence, directives are not generally drafted with the attention to detail which is appropriate in a piece of national implementing legislation.[9] By almost reproducing the text of the Directive, the Agency Regulations therefore introduce a drafting style which is very different from that of English legislation. This represents the first layer of uncertainty, which could be termed as the "internal uncertainty".

This problem is further exacerbated by the fact that the Directive, and consequently the Agency Regulations, are not meant to be a complete code regulating every aspect of the

6. Christou, *International Agency, Distribution and Licensing Agreements*, (2003), 4th edn, para 3.1, p 86.

7. Article 22 of the Directive.

8. This method of implementation seems to have been adopted following the successful contention by the European Commission before the European Court of Justice that the English government failed to correctly implement certain Directives. See for instance *EC Commission* v. *UK* [1994] ECR I2435 where the ECJ held that regulation 2 of the Transfer of Undertakings (Protection of Employment) Regulations 1981 (SI 1981/1794) had incorrectly implemented the Acquired Rights on Transfer of Business Directive 77/187. This required correction by the UK through the passing of amending provisions under the Trade Union Reform and Employment Rights Act 1993. For more on this, see Bercusson, *European Labour Law*, (1996), 3rd edn, pp 236–237.

9. Christou, *International Agency, Distribution and Licensing Agreements*, (2003), 4th edn, para 3–07, p. 87.

relationship between commercial agents and their principals. As a result, the Agency Regulations not only apply alongside the common law rules of agency and contract, but the latter therefore also play the crucial role of filling the gaps left by the implementing legislation. However, considering that the two sets of rules are based on opposed rationales (see section 1.1), the relationship between the Agency Regulations and domestic law is sometimes fraught with tension. This second layer of uncertainty can be referred to as the "external uncertainty".

This double layer of uncertainty is regrettable as it creates what could be termed as a "legal paradox". On the one hand, the Agency Regulations undeniably reinforce the protection of commercial agents by providing them with rights throughout the commercial agency relationship, the most important ones being the right to require the principal to behave at all times with good faith and the right to a lump sum payment on termination. On the other hand, the near-verbatim implementation means that many of the weaknesses of the directive, for example the lack of definition of crucial terms such as good faith and the calculation of compensation or indemnity, ambiguity over the status of certain articles, and even plain silence over the meaning of termination, are also present in the Agency Regulations. Domestic law must therefore step in, in order to fill gaps left by the implementing legislation. However, because the Agency Regulations are based on a civilian ethos which is directly opposed to the traditional common law position, domestic law is not always well equipped to explain concepts which are alien to English lawyers. This double layer of uncertainty therefore jeopardises the very protection that the Agency Regulations set out to put in place, and hence creates the legal paradox.

The primary aim of this book is to solve this double layer of uncertainty in order to provide the reader with as complete an understanding as possible of the workings of the relationship between a commercial agent and his principal. This will be done first by undertaking an in-depth and critical analysis of the Agency Regulations themselves in order to see what they entail for each party. However, because the Agency Regulations do not regulate all the facets of the commercial agency relationship, they must be studied alongside the common law rules of agency and contract. Only by studying the Agency Regulations and domestic rules on contract and agency side by side will we be able to see how the two set of rules dovetail, thereby allowing the readers to have a complete picture of the commercial agency relationship.

1.3 THE STRUCTURE OF THE BOOK

In relation to the organisation of the book as a whole, it will start with a certain element of "scene setting". This will be done in Chapter 2, which will provide an overview of the "legal map", which is important in order to understand the impact of the Agency Regulations on the more traditional common law rules of contract and agency. Considering that the Agency Regulations emanate from a European source, it is necessary to place them in their European context (section 2.2). Chapter 2 will also briefly refer to the laws of France and Germany which are part of the protective stance of the Directive,[10] in order to help

10. The French rules regulating the commercial agency relationship prior to implementation of the Directive were contained in Decree 58/1345 of 23 December 1958, D 1959, L 132. For details, see S Saintier *Commercial agency law: a comparative analysis*, (2002), Chapter 1, especially pp 6–48. In Germany, the rules were created in 1953 and inserted in the German Commercial Code the Handelsgesetsbuch (HGB).

us understand why the Directive considers the (commercial) agent to be the weaker party within the (commercial) agency relationship.

Chapter 2 will then concentrate on looking at the scope of application of the Agency Regulations (section 2.3). First, their territorial and jurisdictional scope of application. Secondly, considering that the Agency Regulations apply only to commercial agents as defined, to understand who they are and what kind of commercial function they serve is therefore important in order to differentiate them from other commercial intermediaries. This section, which represents the core of the chapter, will show that the courts in this country demonstrate a good understanding of who commercial agents are. Considering that prior to the implementation of the Directive the notion of commercial agent was a "legal category unknown to the common law"[11] this is very good. This section will however show that the situation is not perfect, since there are problems in relation to sub-agents and, most seriously in relation to the issue of "secondary activities". Following the choice left in the Directive, the UK has opted for the possibility to exclude from the scope of the Agency Regulations, commercial agents whose activities are secondary. Member States were therefore left with the task of defining the criteria by which a person's commercial agency activities are to be treated as "secondary" for the purpose of the Diretive. The Agency Regulations have done so in a schedule. The drafting of this schedule is far from clear and the review of case law shows that the schedule is applied so widely that it could jeopardise the protective stance of the Agency Regulations. The problem at the moment is such that we propose that the schedule be reviewed.

The following five chapters will provide an in-depth analysis of the core parts of the Agency Regulations. This analysis will chronologically consider the four areas where the impact of the Agency Regulations is at its most crucial in terms of the commercial agent's reinforced protection: performance of the commercial agency relationship in Chapter 3, remuneration arrangements in Chapter 4, termination of the relationship in Chapter 5 and, finally, the calculation of the two termination rights, the French-based compensation and the German-based indemnity in Chapter 6.

The provisions of the Agency Regulations dealing with performance of the contract are contained in Part II ("Rights and Obligations") and Part III ("Remuneration"). Of the two, Part II is undeniably the more important. It represents a very substantial improvement on the commercial agent's protection from the traditional common law rules, since it establishes mandatory and reciprocal rights and duties, which place the parties on a much more equal footing than was previously the case under the common law rules. The most significant change is undeniably the introduction of the civil-law based obligation of good faith for both parties. Yet, the precise impact of the notion of good faith is unclear since the Agency Regulations, by doing no more than in effect almost copying the Directive, fail to explain what it means and what it entails for the parties. This is a regrettable illustration of the "legal paradox" mentioned above and will consequently be considered in detail in Chapter 3 (section 3.4). That chapter will, however, show through the review of the limited case law on the matter but also through analogies with other areas of English law, particularly employment law, that the substance of such good faith obligations is not so alien to English lawyers as we might have thought. Such analogies will provide a source of guidance on what the mutual obligations of good faith under the Agency Regulations mean, hence ensuring that the protection of commercial agents is reinforced. However,

11. Reynolds, *Commercial Agents Directive* [1994] JBL 266.

since commercial agency agreements are contracts, Chapter 3 will also set out key express terms for such an agreement, seen from the viewpoint of the commercial agent and the principal (sections 3.2 and 3.3). In order to assess the true impact of the Agency Regulations on the common law rules, they will be reviewed in the light of the commercial agent's common law and fiduciary obligations.

In relation to the rules on remuneration provided by the Agency Regulations, Chapter 4 will show that they largely (though not entirely) yield to contrary agreements. However, it will also show that remuneration is an area where the highly pervasive quality of the mutual obligation of good faith should not be underestimated (section 4.2).

Chapter 5 will concentrate on the issue of termination. Termination is undoubtedly the stage of the commercial agency relationship where the protection of commercial agents has been the most substantially reinforced by providing commercial agents with the right to claim compensation or indemnity on termination. However, illustrating the "legal paradox" mentioned above, even at this most crucial stage of the Agency Regulations, the near-verbatim implementation jeopardises the efficiency of the level of legal protection which they provide to the commercial agents. The first threat to the protection of the commercial agent is the fact that the Agency Regulations pose as a mandatory rule that compensation and indemnity are due on "termination" and yet they fail to define the process by which, and the circumstances in which, termination will occur. This is regrettable since understanding what constitutes termination and how it can occur is as important as understanding how the termination rights function. In the first part of Chapter 5 we will therefore consider the process of termination itself by looking at the various methods by which and circumstances in which a commercial agency agreement can come to an end (section 5.2). We will see how, thanks to the interpretation of the Agency Regulations by the courts of this country, protection of commercial agents has indeed been substantially reinforced. However, we will also see that the situation is not perfect, and the reinforced protection is threatened by problems of incompatibility between the Agency Regs and the common law rules of contract in relation to summary termination of contract for serious breach. We have proposed a solution which, because it has not been tested by the courts in this country, is somewhat uncertain.

The second part of Chapter 5 will then study the consequences that termination has for the parties; the right for all commercial agents to claim, one of two kinds of termination payments, a French-law based "compensation" or a German-law based "indemnity" (section 5.3). Such a right is undoubtedly the most substantial enhancement of the protection of commercial agents. Prior to the implementation of the Directive, commercial agents in English law were only entitled to receive damages if, by termination the contract, the principal was acting in breach of contract and normal contract law rules of causation, mitigation, etc. This Chapter will show that it is now accepted by the courts in this country that the two termination payments have a meaning which is very specific to the commercial agency relationship and must therefore not be confused with the more traditional common law concept of compensation for loss. The scope of application of the two termination payments themselves is also well understood.

Chapter 6 will complement Chapter 5 by concentrating on the contentious issue of the calculation of the two termination rights. This Chapter will show that the lack of details in the Agency Regulations as to how the two termination rights should be calculated provides the last illustration of the "legal paradox" mentioned above. The lack of details is most serious in relation to the French-law based "compensation". Because of the way the Agency Regulations implement the Directive, "indemnity" will only apply in English law when the parties expressly opt for it; "compensation" therefore applies as the default position and most case law in the UK consequently involves "compensation". The lack of details in the Agency Regulations means that the task of calculating such payments is left to the judiciary. This is however where the problem lies. The problem is that the English and the Scottish courts are divided on the issue. Whereas the Scottish courts are generally inclined to look at French law for guidance, the English courts refuse to do so. In the first part of this chapter, we will therefore consider the question whether the courts in this country must follow what their French and German counterparts do (section 6.2). We will then look at compensation (section 6.3) and indemnity (section 6.4). Following the continental origins of such termination payments, Chapter 6 will contain more substantial reference to the relevant laws of France and Germany. Such references will not be made as illustrations of how the Agency Regulations should be interpreted, but merely as examples of how France and Germany apply concepts which sometimes still elude English lawyers. A comprehensive review of the case law to date will reveal how the English and the Scottish courts have coped with these alien notions of compensation and indemnity. We shall see that the reluctance of the English courts to follow the French courts' evaluation of the amount due to the commercial agent is due to the fact that they perceive the French award of two years' worth of commission to be a tariff. The more recent cases show that the English courts are trying to devise their own methodology that can be used to provide a consistent and fair assessment of the loss of the commercial agent.

In general, commercial agency agreements will not give rise to competition law concerns. However, because the position in EU law is not as straightforward as it might be, the matter must still be considered. This will be done in the last substantial chapter of the book, Chapter 7. Chapter 7 will begin by looking at Regulation 20 of the Agency Regulations, the specific provision on post-termination restraint of trade clauses binding on the commercial agent, which, although not technically competition law, is driven by similar priorities. It will go on to consider whether a commercial agent is to be treated as a business independent of the principal for competition law purposes. If the commercial agent is not to be so treated, the commercial agency agreement will not be an agreement between independent undertakings at all and in many (but not all) respects will not be caught by competition law. We shall then examine what happens when the commercial agent has to be treated, for competition law purposes, as an independent trader rather than as an appendage of the principal. In such situations (which are common in practice) the principles are very much akin to those applicable to distribution agreements since, economically, the functions of commercial agent and distributor are seen as being very similar.

Finally, Chapter 8 will round off the book as a general conclusion.

CHAPTER 2

COMMERCIAL AGENTS AND COMMERCIAL AGENCY AGREEMENTS: AN OVERVIEW OF THE LEGAL MAP

2.1 INTRODUCTION AND ROAD MAP OF THE CHAPTER

Agency is of immense importance in business and professional life, and indeed everyday life. All manners of people act as agents from time to time. Agents for buying and selling goods are perhaps the most obvious example, but agency is the basis of estate agency, company directors, partners, insurance broking, the activities of financial intermediaries, ship management, many roles in the transporting of goods, the co-ordination of syndicates of lending banks etc. In each of these "special" situations, the law is found in the generally applicable common law rules of agency and in a further body of law (generally a combination of statute and case law) particular to the activity in question.

In the case of the agent buying or selling goods on behalf of his principal, there was in the UK, prior to the implementation of EC Council Directive 86/653[1] by the Commercial Agents (Council Directive) Regulations 1993 and the similar delegated legislation in Northern Ireland,[2] (to which we shall refer hereinafter as "the Agency Regulations"), no specific legal regime. Commercial Agents, which should now be seen as a special class of agents with a specific legal regime applicable to them, were in law no different from any other kind of agents. The relationships they had with their principals were regulated by the general common law rules of agency.[3]

The starting point of the law of agency in English law is the usual one of freedom of contract, that the agent and the principal should be free to agree between themselves what terms they want. At common law, the agency contract will therefore usually be the primary source of the parties' rights and obligations. However, to this there has traditionally been added a very important qualification, based upon the fiduciary nature of the agency relationship. Because the agent has the power to affect the legal relationship of the

1. Directive 86/653 on the co-ordination of the profession of self-employed commercial agents, OJ L. 382/17, 31 December 1986. See Appendix 1.

2. For England Regulations 1993, SI 1993/3053 as amended by Commercial Agents (Council Directive) Amendment Regulations 1993, SI 1993/3173 and Commercial Agents (Council Directive) Amendment Regulations 1998, SI 1998/2868. Reg 215 of the Agency Regulations states that they do not apply in Northern Ireland. Separate but substantially identical rules apply there: the Commercial Agents (Council Directive) Regulations (Northern Ireland) 1993, SR 1993/483 as modified by SR 1999/201.

3. The English Law Commission, in its 1977 report, stated that they were unable to identify commercial agents per se, they nevertheless acknowledged that "there exists a class of persons who may be described as manufacturers' selling agents". See Law Commission Report on the Proposed EEC Directive on the Law Relating to Commercial Agents, No 84, (1977), para 19, p 166.

principal in more ways than one, the underlying assumption is that agents are in a position to take advantage of their favoured position *vis-à-vis* their principal by taking bribes, misappropriating their principals' money, assets and business opportunities, getting into positions of conflicts of interest and generally looking after their own interests better than those of their principals. Accordingly, the traditional assumption in English law has been that principals need to be protected against their agents and one finds a (consistently) strong judicial bias in favour of principals and against agents.[4]

The general law consequently imposes several fiduciary obligations on the agent[5] so as to protect the principal from potential misuse of power by the agent though, as we shall see in Chapter 3 (section 3.3.1.2) in the commercial context, the terms of the contract can almost certainly override the general fiduciary obligations implied by law. The fiduciary rules are significantly different from the Agency Regulations, because they are based on a totally different rationale; they do not recognise the particular needs of commercial agents and therefore provide them with very few rights.[6] The common law rules are nevertheless still relevant, since the Agency Regulations do not apply to all commercial agency agreements[7] and even where they do apply, do not regulate the whole content of commercial agency contracts. In fact, as was made clear in the case of *Roy* v. *MR Pearlman Ltd*,[8] the common law rules of contract are not displaced by the Agency Regulations. The two will therefore co-exist. Consequently, the relationship between the two sets of rules must be defined.

In light of the above, the main aim of this chapter is scene-setting, i.e. to provide a general overview of the area of (commercial) agency in relation to both domestic and European law in order to provide readers with the necessary information to help them understand what follows and appreciate fully the impact of the Agency Regulations on the traditional common law rules. This aim will be carried out in three stages:

(1) Much has been said about the civil law origin of the Directive as being in direct contrast to the traditional common law rules of agency, but no detail has been provided about this. A brief review of the civil law basis of agency, alongside the common law rules of agency,[9] will therefore be carried out in order to understand why the civil law rationale of the agency relationship is so different from the common law rationale of the English rules of agency (section 2.2).

4. The bias is most apparent in cases where the agent in breach is liable even if he acted in good faith. See for instance *Boardman* v. *Phipps* [1967] 2 AC 46, HL affirming sub nom *Phipps* v. *Boardman* [1965] Ch 992 CA affirming [1964] 1 WLR 993.

5. The traditional fiduciary duties include the following: a duty not to delegate, a duty not to put himself into positions of conflict of interest, a duty not to make a secret profit, a duty not to accept payments, bribes and finally, a duty to account. Such duties are considered in more detail in Chapter 3, see section 3.3.1.2.

6. It must be noted that recent cases such as *Kelly* v. *Cooper* [1993] AC 205 and *Yasuda Fire and Marine Company of Europe Ltd* v. *Orion Marine Inc Underwriting Agency Ltd* [1995] QB 174 show a certain relaxation of such duties in commercial contexts. For a discussion of the relationship between fiduciary duties and good faith, see Chapter 3, section 3.4.1.15.

7. The Directive applies only to the national laws, regulations and administrative provisions governing the relations between commercial agents and their principals: article 1(1) of the Directive.

8. [1999] 2 CMLR 1155.

9. We will review only such of the domestic rules as are strictly necessary to understand the impact of the Agency Regulations, as a fuller account of such rules is beyond the scope of this book. For a comprehensive work on the law of agency, see generally FMB Reynolds, *Bowstead and Reynolds on Agency*, (17th edn, 2001).

(2) A review of the wider European framework will also be carried out. Considering that the Agency Regulations emanate from a European source,[10] it is consequently crucial to place them in their European context (section 2.3).
(3) We will then be able to study the crucial preliminary issues of the Agency Regulations to find out when and to whom they apply (section 2.4).

The main aim of this book being an in-depth analysis of the Agency Regulations, the third and final part represents the core of this chapter and will consequently be the most detailed.

2.2 THE COMMON AND CIVIL LAW AGENCY RULES: THE PRELIMINARY SCENE SETTING

In both common and civil law systems, commercial agents are first and foremost "agents" in law since they act on behalf of and in the name of the principal. Yet, the traditional agency rules applicable to them in common and civil law systems differ in two main ways.

(1) The law of agency in a common law country such as England is of a general nature and embraces a very wide range of legal areas; commercial agents, up until the implementation of the Directive, were therefore not recognised as a separate category. In a civil law system such as France or Germany, on the other hand, although the fundamental rules are of general application, they tend to isolate different types of agent according to function, and develop specific rules for each type, as is the case for commercial agents.
(2) The two sets of legal rules are based on different rationales; whereas French and German laws regard commercial agents as the weaker party, English common law regards the principal as deserving protection.

Considering that the Agency Regulations implement the Directive, which is based on the civil law rationale, it is important to understand why civil law considers the (commercial) agent as the weaker party within the (commercial) agency relationship. This will be done by looking first at the agency rules in general and, secondly, at the commercial agency rules more specifically.

2.2.1 The nature and object of agency agreements

The fact that civil and common law systems regulate the agency relationship in such a drastically different manner seems to be explained when looking at the origins of the general rules of agency. In civil law countries such as France and Germany, the rules of agency are based on the Roman law concept of "mandate", which clearly distinguishes, on the one hand, the relation that the agent has with his principal and, on the other hand,

10. Directive 86/653 on the Coordination of the Laws of the Member States Relating to Self-Employed Commercial Agents, OJ L. 382/17–21, 31 December 1986.

the relations the agent can have with third parties.[11] This is what has been called the theory of separation.[12] This means that in civil law, the default position in terms of authority is that the agent has only a limited power of negotiation, i.e. no authority to conclude contracts on behalf of the principal. Such an authority only exists when expressly granted by the principal.[13] The agent can therefore only bind the principal when the latter has expressly authorised him to do so in the contract.

This therefore explains why in France, for instance, the law of agency isolates different types of agents depending on the extent of their authority and power.[14]

In common law countries such as England, however, the position is very different, since there seems to be fusion between the person of the agent and that of the principal.[15] Even though the extent of the agent's "authority" usually depends on what has been agreed with the principal, most authors now agree that the essence of an agency relationship is the "power" that the agent has to affect the position of the principal. In fact, at common law, the agent has the power to bind the principal in situations when he acts beyond the authority expressly granted to him as well as in situations when there is no authority given by the principal at all.[16] It has therefore been argued that the default position at common law is that the agent has the power to bind the principal *vis-à-vis* third parties whether the principal has consented to it or not.[17] The latter can therefore be bound by acts of the agent, even though there is no express provision for it in the contract. Such a short analysis of the agency relationship helps to explain why, at English common law, principals are the parties seen as being in need of protection.

The Directive, which is inspired by the civil law tradition, clearly seems to reflect the restrictive concept of the authority of the commercial agent, since it defines him as having "the authority to negotiate (. . .) or negotiate and conclude contracts for the sale and/or purchase of goods".[18] Under the Directive, the default position for the commercial agent therefore appears to be the limited authority to negotiate only.[19] This is reinforced by the fact that one of the mandatory obligations of the principal is to let the commercial agent

11. Müller-Freinfels, *Legal relationships in the law of agency: power of the agent and commercial certainty*, (1964) 13 Am J Compa Law, p 193.

12. Pothier, *Traité sur les obligations*.

13. Article 1998–1 of the French Civil Code stipulates that the principal is only bound to perform the transactions that the agent has made on his behalf providing that they conform with the power granted. The Civil Code adds that the principal can only be bound by acts of the agent done outside his authority if he has ratified them, expressly or impliedly (article 1998–2 CC). For an English translation, see the French government legal database website, www.legifrance.gouv.fr

14. In France, the main categories of intermediaries are distributors, employed sales representative, commission agent, brokers and franchisee. They all have different status and different rules apply to them. It would be beyond the scope of this work to review them all in detail. For details, see C Diloy, *Le contrat d'agence commerciale en droit international* (2000) pp 32–33.

15. C Diloy, op cit, para 35, p 32.

16. The most common examples are implied and apparent authority. To discuss such rules would be beyond the scope of this book. For details, see article 27, para 3–021 and Chapter 8, article 74 respectively in FMB Reynolds *Bowstead an Reynolds on Agency*, (17th edn, 2001).

17. C Diloy, op cit, para 35, p 33.

18. Article 1(2) of the Directive. The default position was much more apparent in the first and second proposals of the European Commission, which stipulated that "the commercial agent shall have authority to negotiate transactions for account of the principal. He shall have authority to conclude agreements in respect thereof only where the principal empowers him to do so" as per article 9(1). See OJ C. 56/5, 2 March 1979.

19. But the Directive does not exclude implied authority to contract.

know whether he accepts or refuses the transactions procured by the commercial agent.[20] In such a situation, commercial agents do not have the power to bind the principal, unless it has been expressly granted; hence, they are the weaker party. This certainly was a fair assessment of the commercial agency relationship at the time of the first EU Commission proposal[21] and still seems to be the case in more recent times, at least, for England,[22] as case law on the Agency Regulations seems to corroborate.

Such an explanation for the need to protect commercial agents is based on the general rules on agency. Even though such rules are even now applicable to commercial agents, they must be linked to the economic need for protection specific to commercial agents and upon which the Directive is also based. We therefore turn to this economic need in order to understand why commercial agents require this additional protection.

2.2.2 The economic civil law rationale of the Directive for protecting commercial agents

The Directive is based on the mainland European civil-law rationale whereby commercial agents are in need of protection.[23] A commercial agent is generally used as a marketing tool by a manufacturer or trader who want to expand his business at home or abroad.

The other point which is absolutely fundamental to an understanding of the Directive is that mainland European civil law also considers the commercial agency relationship as a quasi-partnership whereby the commercial agent and the principal both enter into the relationship for the same purpose of creating or developing a customer base, i.e. goodwill for the goods (and services) of the principal.[24] The commercial agent brings his marketing skills, contacts, trade connections etc. to the relationship in order to develop a market for the principal's goods (and services). The principal, for his part, brings the goods and services to be sold. During the life of the relationship, both parties, so the thinking goes, will benefit equally from the customer base—i.e. the goodwill created—the commercial agent through the commissions earned, and the principal through the sales of his goods and services. During the life of the relationship, there is therefore a perfect balance between the parties.

However, the commercial reality is that the commercial agent does not act for himself but for the principal. As a result, as remarked by Lord Drummond Young in the Scottish case of *Lloyd Gailey* v. *Environmental Waste Controls*,[25] "the goodwill created by the

20. Article 4(3) of the Directive.

21. The Law Commission in its 1977 report stipulates that "by far the majority of commercial agents in the Member States in the present time are authorised only to negotiate on behalf of their principals, the conclusion of an actual agreement for the transaction being a matter for the principal itself". Law Comm Report on the proposed EEC Directive on the law relating to commercial agents, LC 84.

22. F Randolph and J Davey, *Guide to the Commercial Agency Regulation* (2nd edn, 2003), p 47.

23. See the preamble of the Directive, OJ L. 382/17, 31 December 1986.

24. This is particularly true for France which defines the commercial agency relationship as a relationship entered into for the common interest of the parties, article L 134–4 al 1 of the French commercial code. For an English translation of this article, see Appendix 5. For details of this notion of common interest mandate, see Chapter 6, section 6.3.1.1. In Germany, the commercial agent is only entitled to receive indemnity if the principal benefits from the customer base created and the commercial agent suffers a corresponding loss of commissions. For details, see Chapter 5, section 6.4.1.

25. [2004] Eu LR 423.

agent is attached to the goods sold and not to the agent himself". He adds that "the goodwill therefore accrues to the principal who supplied the goods".[26]

Consequently, mainland European civil law is very sensitive to the risk that once the customer base is established by the commercial agent, the principal may terminate the relationship with the commercial agent in order to sell directly to customers, and thus cut out the "middle-man". This would not only cause the commercial agent to suffer a financial loss but would also create an imbalance in the relationship, since the principal alone would then continue to benefit from the customer base. The commercial agent, so the civil law thinking goes, must be protected from such a loss, hence he needs protection in the event of termination. The rationale behind this need for protection on termination is therefore of a purely economic nature and derives from the civil law conception that the commercial agency relationship is a quasi-partnership.[27]

This need for economic protection, which is specific to commercial agents is undoubtedly the driving force behind the termination payments contained in the Directive.[28] Both French and German laws have recognised this "economic" need to protect commercial agents on termination for some time. Both countries provide commercial agents with a right to claim termination payments when termination occurs.[29] However, French and German law each provide protection from such financial loss in very different ways; France concentrates on the loss suffered by the commercial agent following termination. Germany concentrates on the goodwill, or enhanced goodwill, that the principal receives from the commercial agent's efforts.[30] The Directive incorporates these two systems, requiring that Member States provide in their law for one or other of them, but leaving the choice between the two to each Member State.[31]

From the above, it should now be clear that the main role of the commercial agent is to create, develop or simply maintain a customer base for the principal's goods and services. Using commercial agents is therefore a valuable strategy for manufacturers who look to create, develop or simply maintain their business both at home and abroad. Commercial agents are in other words used as "marketing tools" by their principals. Yet they are not the only "marketing tool" available. Manufacturers of goods can choose a wide variety of ways in which to distribute their goods to customers. Apart from commercial agency agreements, the choice is usually between distributorship or some variation on that theme (with selective distribution or franchising, if brand image or consumer experience at the point of sale or provision of after-sales service are seen as important); and the manufacturer selling direct through an employed sales force, perhaps setting up a branch;

26. *Ibid*, at para 24.

27. Once again, this is especially true for France. For details, see Chapter 6, section 6.3.1.1.

28. The economic aspect of this need was better emphasised in the preamble of the first and the second EU Commission proposals than in the final text of the Directive. The last recital of the preamble stipulated that "(. . .)whereas in many cases commercial agents are, as a rule, though in differing degrees, economically in a weak position *vis-à-vis* their principals (. . .)". See OJ C. 56/6 of 2 March 1979. In its report on the first EU Commission proposal, the House of Lords Select Committee doubted such an assertion by referring to statements by the Confederation of British Industry and the Association of British Chambers of Commerce. See para 6 of the 51st Report of the HL Select Committee. HC 36–I of 12 November 1996.

29. The first legislative protection for commercial agent in France came in 1958 (Decree 58/1345, D 1959, L 132), Germany formally protected them in its commercial code in 1953 (Handelsgesetzbuch or HGB).

30. For more details, see Chapter 6, section 6.3.1 for France and section 6.4.1 for Germany.

31. Article 17 of the Directive.

and all with the possible intervention of a logistics service provider to operate the supply chain.[32]

The main factors for choosing between the various possibilities are, in principle, simple. We discuss these briefly, as to rehearse them in detail would be beyond the scope of this book.[33]

2.2.3. Commercial agents and other marketing tools: how to choose?

When choosing which marketing tool is the most appropriate to a trader's needs, the decision is based on commercial and legal considerations.

Commercial considerations

The two main commercial considerations are the control of the business and financial risk. An agency agreement, or even an employment one, is in principle, the preferred choice when the manufacturer wishes to retain a high level of control over various aspects of the business (sales price, terms of sale, choice of customers, the goods themselves etc), though the degree of flexibility and discretion to be given to the commercial agent can be whatever the parties agree. Imposing resale price maintenance on a distributor (i.e. insisting that the distributor may not re-sell the product down the supply chain at less than a minimum price established by the supplier) will generally be illegal in competition law, and this, regardless of whether the parties have any position of strength in their market or not.[34] The ability of a supplier to control its distributors in their choice of customer or sales area, while permitted within limits in competition law terms, can be difficult.[35] With a commercial agent, however, in the great majority of cases, the principal can validly (and almost always will) retain the freedom to decide these issues.

As a general proposition, a supplier may well prefer agency over distributorship where close control of the methods of marketing is important (for example, because brand image is a crucial factor), or where direct contract between a manufacturer-supplier and the customer, once initial contact has been established by the agent, is important (perhaps

32. "Logistics, [in the past], has been contemplated in the context of the value-added services associated with express delivery (e.g. track-and-trace, proof of delivery, destination change in transit, etc). However, logistics, as it is more generally understood nowadays in the sector, is a product which comprises the planning, implementation and control of the flow and storage of goods, and as such it constitutes a distinct service offering . . . The logistics offering includes a combination of different services such as warehousing, inventory control, just-in-time management and financial management, and has evolved in response to a very distinct customer-demand, arising from the growing trend for companies to outsource certain non-core activities" (European Commission merger decision in *TNT Post Group Jet Services*, IV. M. 1405, 15 February 1999, CELEX 31999 M 1405 and see merger decision *Ocean Group/Exel(NFC)*, IV.M.1895 of 3 May 2000, CELEX 3200 M 1895 paras 7–9). Further helpful information about contract logistics services and their role appears on the websites of logistics services providers, such as Exel (www.exel.com) and Caterpillar Logistics (www.catlogistics.com).

33. For additional detail, see R Christou, *International Agency, Distribution and Licensing Agreements*, (4th edn, 2003), Chapter 18.

34. See principally the EU block exemption for vertical agreements, Commission Regulation 2790/99, art 4(a), OJ L. 336/21 of 29 December 1999 and commentary in Commission Guidelines on Vertical Restraints, paras 46–48 (OJ C.291/1 of 13 October 2000). For an example of what happens when things go wrong, see *Argos Ltd* v. *OFT* and *Littlewoods Ltd* v. *OFT*, judgment of the Competition Appeal Tribunal of 14 December 2004 [2004] CAT 24.

35. See European Commission Reg 2790/99, art 4(b) and the qualifications contained therein (some of which are complicated), and the commentary thereon in Commission Guidelines on Vertical Restraints, paras 49ff. [See for more details (ed) P Roth, *Bellamy & Child, European Community Law of Competition* (5th edn, 2001), Chapter 7, and of course Chapter 7 below.

because of user requirements necessitating bespoke design or manufacturing or because of very specialised after-sales service which only the manufacturer-supplier can provide).[36]

Financially however, the manufacturer appears to take a greater risk with an agency agreement since ownership of the goods, and generally the credit risk, remains with him. This may however be offset by lower commissions than a distribution margin, depending, of course, on what the parties have agreed.

Appointing a distributor allows the manufacturer to share the risk and offload some of the expenses to the distributor. This comes at the price of a reduction in control by the principal and a reduction in the manufacturer's margins (because of having to allow a higher margin to a distributor than the commission one would pay to a commercial agent). However, this is not always the case, since a distribution agreement where the supplier allows very long or "back to back" credit terms to the distributor means that "the principal is taking the credit risk on all the distributor's customers, without having any control over the extent of the risk which the distributor takes".[37]

If it appears that the manufacturer's main preference is financial, a distributorship is better since the distributor buys and resells the goods himself and therefore the manufacturer does not have to pay him commission.[38]

Legal considerations

On a pure legal aspect, the main advantage with a distribution agreement is that the tax position is also simpler, but there may be some competition issues. For an agency agreement, the position in competition law will generally be more permissive.[39]

In tax terms, though, in a cross-border context, an agency agreement may involve the principal in foreign tax liabilities which would not arise if another marketing tool were used.

Now that the Directive has been implemented by the Agency Regulations, an additional factor must be taken into account: that of compensation and indemnity payments when the commercial agency contract is terminated pursuant to Regulation 17(1). This is a crucial factor. Termination payments will be due each time the commercial agency relationship ends, which includes the situation when the commercial agency contract expires by effluxion of time in the normal course of events and is not renewed,[40] even when there was no expectation of renewal.[41] The right to payments therefore does not depend on whether the principal is committing a breach when terminating the relationship. The width of the

36. See further on this *Scholes*, Agency, in (ed.) Battersby, Commercial contracts (Legal & Commercial Publishing Co Ltd, 2004), Vol. 1, pp 1.2.3–1.2.5.

37. R Christou, *International Agency, Distribution and Licensing Agreements*, (4th edn, 2003) p 569.

38. The distinction between a commercial agent and a distributor can sometimes be slim. Compare and contrast *AMB Imballagi Plastici SRL* v. *Pacflex* [1999] 2 All ER (Comm) 249 and *Mercantile International Group Plc* v. *Chuan Soon Huat Industrial Group Ltd* [2001] 2 All ER 632.

39. For the discussion of issues of competition law in relation to the commercial agency relationship, see Chapter 7 hereof.

40. *Whitehead* v. *Jenks and Cattell Engineering Ltd* [1999] Eu LR 827; *Frape* v. *Emreco* [2002] SLT 371, [2002] Eu LR 10 and *Tigana Ltd* v. *Decoro Ltd* [2003] EWHC 23, [2003] Eu LR 189. For discussion of these cases, see Chapter 4, section 4.2.1.1.

41. *Light and others* v. *Ty Europe Ltd* [2003] EWCA Civ, 25 July 2003, [2003] All ER (D) 445. For a discussion of this case, see Chapter 5, section 5.2.1.1.

right to such payments is such that when the Agency Regulations came into effect, it was predicted that this would cause the death of commercial agency agreements. Anecdotal evidence suggests to us that fewer new commercial agency relations are being set up now than was the case prior to the Agency Regulations.[42] This shows that choosing between agency, distributorship or other forms of marketing arrangements should first and foremost be driven from a business viewpoint and not "with a view to worrying first about legal issues".[43]

2.3 COMMERCIAL AGENTS AND THE EUROPEAN DIMENSION: THE 1986 DIRECTIVE

The Agency Regulations implement Directive 86/653,[44] which was enacted primarily in order to reinforce the protection of commercial agents. The fact that the Agency Regulations are of EU inspiration is of crucial importance since, to ensure that commercial agents are adequately protected by the national implementing legislation, the English and Scottish courts must apply the Agency Regulations in a 'purposive' manner, i.e. in conformity with the terms of the Directive implemented.[45] In the light of such an obligation, a rapid overview of the background to the Directive is therefore relevant for a deeper understanding of the Agency Regulations.

The drafting of the Directive was a long process spanning a ten-year period.[46] The first proposal of the European Commission was produced in 1976.[47] Following a three-year consultation process, a second proposal was published in 1979.[48] The final and current text of the Directive is significantly different from the two European Commission proposals. It would go beyond the scope of this work to review these two proposals in great detail, and would by this stage not be a very useful exercise either. Moreover, even though the two European Commission proposals contained some positive features, it is believed that the current and final text of the Directive is, on the whole, more satisfactory even though

42. There is nevertheless a need for empirical research to see whether principals in England would now insist that on termination the commercial agent will receive the German-based indemnity as it is cheaper than the French-based compensation. For details of the differences in calculation between the two termination payments, see Chapter 6, section 6.3.1 for France and section 6.4.1 for Germany.

43. R Christou, *International Agency, Distribution and Licensing Agreements*, (4th edn, 2003) p 570.

44. Directive 86/653 on the Coordination of the Laws of the Member States Relating to Self-Employed Commercial Agents, OJ L. 382/17–21, 31 December 1986.

45. For authority for the need for purposive interpretation, see amongst others, case 14/83 *Von Colson* v. *Land Nordrhein-Westfalen* [1984] ECR 1891; *Litster* v. *Forth Dry Dock & Engineering Co Ltd* [1990] 1 AC 546. This is so even where the national implementing legislation was adopted prior to the Directive in question: case C–106/89 *Marleasing* v. *La Comercial International* [1990] ECR I–4135. The issue here is the EU law priority of ensuring effective enforcement of a directive. For a useful short explanation of the issues involved in the principle of the "indirect-direct effect" of a directive, see Steiner and Woods, *Textbook on EC Law*, (8th edn, 2003), pp 105–111.

46. The delay is no doubt explained by the huge difference in national laws relating to self-employed commercial agents. Another explanation might be that, at the time the Directive was enacted, voting could not be done through qualified majority. See Randolph and Davey, *Guide to the Commercial Agency Regulations*, (2nd edn, 2003), p 18.

47. Doc Com (76) 670 submitted on 17 December 1976 and published in OJ C. 13/2 of 18 January 1977.

48. Submitted on 29 January 1979, published in the OJ C. 56/5 of 2 March 1979.

not perfect.[49] Reference to the two European Commission proposals will therefore be made only as and when necessary for interpretation purposes.

2.3.1 From the Council Directive to the Agency Regulations: a near-verbatim implementation

Prior to the Directive, there was no specific law covering the commercial agency relationship; the traditional common law rules of agency applied to agents for the sale of goods as they applied to all classes of agents and without any special features. The UK government was consequently granted additional time to implement the Directive.[50] After several years of drafting, the Agency Regulations 1993[51] were finally enacted. The current text is however quite different from the various drafts issued by the DTI.[52] The UK government could be said not to have used the additional implementing time granted to the full, since the current Agency Regulations merely replicate the Directive almost word for word. Such a near-verbatim implementation is not satisfactory not only because the Directive was not meant to be implemented in this manner but also because, as a result, the various weaknesses contained in the Directive are simply carried straight over into the Agency Regulations.[53]

This creates a series of problems. First, it creates a clash of drafting styles. EU directives are traditionally very general in their drafting. English legal texts are however a lot more detailed and precise. Secondly, the Directive, being the result of political compromise, is consequently vague on some matters and remains silent as to detail on crucial issues such as the status of the commercial agent, good faith and the calculation of the two termination payments. The Directive itself is therefore the source of a number of difficulties.

By copying the Directive, the Agency Regulations introduce such weaknesses into the English legal system. This is very unfortunate because such weaknesses bring uncertainty which jeopardises the very protection of commercial agents that the Agency Regulations have set out to put in place.

49. The two European Commission proposals contained 37 articles as opposed to 23 in the current text of the 1986 Directive. The main advantage of the two EU Commission proposals is that they regulated the commercial agency relationship in a more detailed manner. For instance, it was clear that the commercial agent, as an independent businessman, could organise his activities as he saw fit (article 2), delegation and sub-agency were also expressly allowed (article 5(3)). The two proposals also contained more details as to what good faith entails (article 5(2)). The details contained in the two EU Commission proposals had the advantage of providing clarity. However, the rules on termination were not as protective as the current ones, since they only allowed for indemnity payments (article 28). For a more in-depth analysis of the two EU Commission proposals, see S Saintier *Commercial agency law: a comparative analysis*, (2002), Chapter 3, especially pp 89–96.

50. Article 22 of the Directive.

51. SI 1993/3053 as amended. See fn 2 for details.

52. For an interesting review of the differences, see Randolph and Davey, *Guide to the Commercial Agency Regulations*, (2nd edn, 2003), pp 24–27.

53. The main weaknesses of the Directive are as follows: (1) the status of some articles is not so clearly defined, as a result, it is not immediately obvious whether they can be derogated from; (2) there is a lack of details as to what good faith entails; (3) it is not clear what constitutes termination or when termination may occur or in which circumstances it may occur; and (4) the method of calculation of the two termination payments is not defined. For a more in-depth critical analysis of the Directive, see S Saintier *Commercial agency law: a comparative analysis*, (2002), Chapter 3, especially pp 136–140. Since such weaknesses are present in the Agency Regulations, such questions will be specifically addressed in the relevant chapters of this book. For the issue of good faith, see Chapter 3, section 3.4.1, for the meaning of termination, see Chapter 5, section 5.2 and for the calculation of the two termination payments, see Chapter 6, sections 6.3.1 and 6.4.1.

Near-verbatim implementation and the legal paradox

In fact, this uncertainty creates what we refer to as a "legal paradox". On the one hand, the Agency Regulations undeniably significantly reinforce the protection of commercial agents by (1) giving them a special status, and (2) providing them with rights throughout the relationship, the most important ones being a mutual and mandatory duty of good faith[54] and the right to be compensated or indemnified on termination.[55] On the other hand, because of the near-verbatim implementation, many crucial terms such as good faith and the two termination rights are left undefined. This creates uncertainty, which jeopardises the protection of commercial agents. This uncertainty could be termed as "internal uncertainty" since it is due to the way the Directive, and therefore the Agency Regulations, are drafted.

This "internal uncertainty" is exacerbated by the fact that the Agency Regulations are not meant to be a complete code regulating the commercial agency relationship, so they apply alongside the common law rules of agency and contract. However, because the Agency Regulations and the common law rules are based on two opposed rationales, the relationship between the two sets of rules is not easy. This could be termed the "external uncertainty", which in turn further accentuates the "legal paradox".

As a result, much depended on the English and Scottish courts' interpretation of the Agency Regulations to clarify their scope of application and ensure their effectiveness in protecting commercial agents. After a slow and uncertain start, there is now a small but growing body of case law, which shows that the English and Scottish courts are broadly succeeding in both tasks by reinforcing the protective stance of the Agency Regulations in their interpretation. This is of crucial importance as it balances out some of the weaknesses created by the near-verbatim implementation.

2.3.2 Implementation in France and Germany

As previously mentioned, the Directive is mostly inspired by the French[56] and German rules,[57] which have protected commercial agents for a considerable time. Implementing the Directive was therefore not as big a shock in these two Member States as it was for England. The fact that the current French and German rules are the result of the implementation of the Directive is important in terms of interpretation. In fact, even though the French and German implementing rules have not changed their respective existing laws as dramatically as in England, the current French and German rules are nevertheless now based on an EU directive and must consequently be interpreted as such. This means that any judgment of a national court in any Member State as to the meaning of the Directive, can potentially be persuasive authority in the courts of France and Germany, or, for that matter, in any other national court in the EEA. As a consequence, the English and the

54. Regulation 3(1) for the commercial agent and regulation 4(1) for the principal. For details as to what this entails for each party, see Chapter 3, section 3.4.1.

55. Regulation 17(1).

56. The influence of the French decree is mostly related to the definition of the commercial agent (article 1(2)), compensation on termination (article 17(3)) and the pattern that the rule is that on termination, payments are due as a rule (article 17) and the exclusion is the exception (article 18).

57. Several articles of the German code have been quoted almost verbatim, § 85 HGB is transposed to article 13 of the Directive, § 86(a) HGB to articles 4(2)(a–b) of the Directive; § 87 HGB to article 8 of the Directive, § 87(a) HGB to article 11 of the Directive and § 89(b) HGB to article 17(2)(a) of the Directive.

Scottish courts may look at France and Germany for help when interpreting the relevant parts of the Agency Regulations, but the reverse is therefore also true.[58]

In other words, while the Directive draws for its inspiration largely on the pre-Directive French and German laws, the treatment post-Directive of commercial agency agreements in those legal systems, being from then on based on the Directive should logically take account of developments under the Directive around Europe (including even the UK!), and may not necessarily be the same as it was before.

Implementation in France was done through legislation,[59] which has now been incorporated *in extenso* in the new French commercial code.[60]

The German rules are also contained in a commercial code.[61] The most important legacy of the French and German laws of commercial agency, as far as the Agency Regulations are concerned,[62] is the two termination payments of compensation and indemnity respectively. Reference to how the French and German courts calculate compensation and indemnity payments respectively will consequently be made at a later stage when reviewing the calculation of the termination payments within the Agency Regulations.[63] This is so because we think it is better to incorporate the French and German rules into the body of the book as and when they are relevant rather than place them in a separate chapter.

Yet, it cannot be emphasised enough that reference to French and German law is not meant as an example of how the courts in this country should apply the Agency Regulations but merely as an illustration as to what happens or what could be done in situations where the Directive, and therefore the Agency Regulations remain silent or are vague.

Now that we have seen the European and civil-law basis of the Agency Regulations, we shall consider the scope of application of the Agency Regulations themselves.

2.4 THE AGENCY REGULATIONS: PRELIMINARY ISSUES: TO WHOM THEY APPLY AND WHEN

As previously mentioned, the Agency Regulations undoubtedly reinforce the protection of commercial agents by providing them with a special status and giving them substantial rights at each stage of the relationship: conclusion, performance and termination.

58. This is of crucial importance in relation to termination payments and will accordingly be covered in Chapter 6, para 6.2.

59. Statute 91–593, Journal Officiel de la République Française, JO 27 June 1991, p 8271 complemented by the Decree 92–506 of 10 June 1992, D 1992, L 320 which modifies the decree 58/1345 of 23 December 1958 and the arrêté of 9 January 1993 which replaces the arrêté of 22 August 1968. See the French government database legifrance.gouv.fr.

60. Articles L 134–1 to L 134–17 French commercial code. For an English translation, see Appendix.

61. §§ 84–92 c HGB.

62. Most EU Member States have opted for the German option, England and Northern Ireland are the only Member States where the French-based compensation option also applies. By EU Member States, the authors refer to those 15 countries forming part of the EU as then was when the Directive was enacted. Since then, the Directive also applies to Member States of the European Economic Area to which no freedom was given. The authors do not know what the situation is for the 10 additional Member States which joined on 1 May 2004. It is thought that the new Member States will be required to implement the Directive with effect from the date of accession.

63. See Chapter 6, see section 6.3.1 for the French-based compensation and section 6.4.1 for the German-based indemnity.

The relationship between the Agency Regulations and the common law rules

The Agency Regulations do not cover all commercial agreements.[64] Nor are the Agency Regulations a complete code of what a commercial agency agreement should include.[65] The common law rules of agency and contract are therefore not displaced by the Agency Regulations;[66] the two sets of rules will consequently co-exist. However, this co-existence is not as simple as it seems for two reasons:

(1) The rationale underlying the Agency Regulations, that commercial agents need protection,[67] is in direct contrast to the traditional common law perception that principals are the weaker party.

(2) Even though the Agency Regulations are not meant to replace the common law rules, because of the near-verbatim implementation, they are merely superimposed on the common law rules of contract and agency with no real explanation as to how the two sets of rules are meant to relate one to another. However, considering that the status of some regulations is not clearly defined, the relationship between the two sets of rules is not easy.

We know that the common law rules apply where (i) the Agency Regulations remain silent on a particular issue,[68] or (ii) when the Agency Regulations specifically allow it.[69] This is so, provided that the common law rules are not inconsistent with the Agency Regulations.[70] Likewise, we also know that the Agency Regulations will take precedence where the common law rules are (i) less protective of commercial agents than the Agency Regulations, or (ii) remain silent on a given issue.

Even though thus far the position seems fairly obvious, there are nevertheless some grey areas. For instance, when the common law rules applicable to the commercial agent are more lenient than the Agency Regulations, it is not clear which set of rules should prevail. Similarly, when the Agency Regulations remain silent on something which is permitted at common law, should the provisions at common law nevertheless be controlled by the protective stance of the Agency Regulations? This will be relevant for the consequences of the independence of the commercial agent for instance. Following the doctrine of "indirect-direct effect" mentioned earlier,[71] the English and Scottish courts are clearly under an obligation to interpret the national provisions (including the common law rules) in the light of the Directive.[72] Yet, how far this obligation should go is not immediately obvious, especially in relation to the choice of the English government to exclude

64. For the restrictions, see regulation 2. For details, see section 2.4.2.2 below.

65. For a discussion as to whether this should be the case, see Chapter 6, section 6.3.2.2 especially footnotes 232–235 and associated text.

66. *Roy* v. *Pearlman Ltd* [1999] 2 CMLR 1155.

67. The underlying idea is not dissimilar, in very broad terms, to the "floor of rights" given to employees in English employment law by the reforms of the 1960s and 1970s (right to redundancy payment, the statutory concept of unfair dismissal, property in the job etc), currently contained in the Employment Rights Act 1999.

68. For instance, the meaning of "termination", when and in which circumstances termination may occur. For details, see Chapter 5, section 5.2.

69. This will be the case for summary termination (regulation 16(a)).

70. *Roy* v. *Pearlman Ltd* [1999] 2 CMLR 1155. This is in line with what was expressly stipulated in the two European Commission proposals (article 1(2)). OJ C. 56/5 of 2 March 1979.

71. See fn 45 above.

72. Case 14/83 *Von Colson* v. *Land Nordrhein-Westfalen* [1984] ECR 1891; *Litster* v. *Forth Dry Dock & Engineering Co Ltd* [1990] 1 AC 546.

from the scope of the Agency Regulations those commercial agents whose activities are secondary.[73]

Studying the scope of application of the Agency Regulations is therefore of crucial importance, since it will provide some answers to these questions. This will be done in two steps: first, by reviewing the conditions under which the Agency Regulations apply, and secondly, by considering to whom they apply.

2.4.1 The scope of application of the Agency Regulations

The Agency Regulations came into force on 1 January 1994.[74] Their scope of application must be assessed with reference to chronological and territorial restrictions.

2.4.1.1 Application of the Agency Regulations in point of time

In chronological terms, the situation is reasonably straightforward. The Agency Regulations apply instantaneously[75] as they not only apply to all commercial agency contracts entered into after 31 December 1993 but also to all such contracts entered into before 1 January 1994 that existed at that date "unless rights and liabilities have already been accrued".[76] For such contracts, the Agency Regulations therefore apply *retrospectively*, since any rules in pre-existing contracts inconsistent with the Agency Regulations will be automatically ineffective. Such an overriding effect has been held not to contravene the principle of non-retroactivity.[77]

The effect of the application in point of time can be most particularly witnessed at the stage of termination. In fact, the expression "unless rights and liabilities have already been accrued" is taken to refer only to commercial agency contracts, which have been terminated and where the parties are not in a contractual relationship any more. Accordingly, if a commercial agency contract, entered into before 1 January 1994, had been terminated before the Agency Regulations came into effect but another contract was entered into on 1 January 1994 in order to comply with the Agency Regulations, the period before 1 January 1994 will nevertheless still be relevant. Such periods will be taken into consideration for the calculation of minimum notice periods and termination payments as the cases of *Moore* v. *Piretta Ltd*[78] and of *Ingmar GB Ltd* v. *Eaton Leonard Technologies Inc*[79] illustrate. This is in line with the protective stance of the Directive.

The Agency Regulations apply from day one of the agreement

Still in relation to the chronological impact of the implementing legislation, it is important to mention that the Agency Regulations apply in full as soon as the commercial agency agreement is entered into. Commercial agents therefore get the full protection of the

73. Regulation 2(4). The matter will be discussed in more details in section 2.4.2.2.
74. Regulation 1(1).
75. The lack of transitional period in the Agency Regulations can be explained by the fact that the UK was given additional time to implement the Directive (article 22). It has been said that legal certainty has suffered because of this. See F Randolph and J Davey, *Guide to the Commercial Agency Regulations*, (2nd edn, 2003), p 33. We can argue that legal certainty has suffered more because of the near-verbatim implementation of the Directive by the Agency Regulations.
76. Regulation 23.
77. See comments of Mitting J in the case of *Moore* v. *Piretta Ltd*, [1999] 1 All ER 174, at p 181c.
78. [1999] 1 All ER 174. For a discussion of this case, see Chapter 6, section 6.4.2.
79. (1999) Tr LR 333.

Agency Regulations from day one of the contract. As such, commercial agents are better protected than employees who, generally, only acquire protection against unfair dismissal after one year of employment and redundancy payment after two years of employment.[80]

This application in point of time would also seem to indicate that the principal cannot, at least insofar as rights and benefits arising under the Agency Regulations are concerned, impose a probationary period on the commercial agent. This is therefore another respect in which commercial agents are better protected than employees. In fact, to impose a probationary period would probably be regarded as a breach of the mandatory nature of termination rights as defined by the European Court of Justice[81] and against the protective stance of the Agency Regulations, or even against the requirement of good faith.

2.4.1.2 Territorial scope of the Agency Regulations: conflict of laws

In terms of the territorial scope of the Agency Regulations, the situation is more complicated, as it raises issues of governing law and jurisdictions.

The Agency Regulations implement a directive. As such, their territorial scope of application extends across the European Economic Area[82] (to which we shall hereinafter refer as the EEA), irrespective of any cross-border element. Accordingly, the Agency Regulations apply equally to purely domestic relationships where both parties are in the same Member State as well as where one of them is in another EU Member State[83] or, an EEA Member State, or even, following the European Court of Justice ruling in *Ingmar Ltd* v. *Eaton Leonard Technologies Inc*[84] where one party is outside the EU altogether, if the place of performance of the commercial agent's obligations is within the EU and/or the EEA. The latter decision has the advantage of eliminating the issue of forum shopping. Yet, this ruling does not solve all the conflict of law issues. The situation is exacerbated by the deliberate silence of the Directive[85] on the matter. The rules must therefore be critically considered.

When the Agency Regulations first came into effect, most unusually, they defined their application by reference to the place of performance since the initial text only applied to commercial agents whose activities were performed in Great Britain.[86] Presumably that meant that the canvassing and finding of customers, negotiating with them and (if appropriate) entering into contracts with them by the commercial agent on the principal's behalf

80. Comment by F Randolph and J Davey, *Guide to the Commercial Agency Regulations*, (2nd edn, 2003), p 49.

81. Case C–381/98 *Ingmar Ltd* v. *Eaton Leonard Technologies Inc* [2001] 1 CMLR 9.

82. The members are the members of the EU and Iceland, Liechtenstein and Norway (Switzerland having decided not to ratify).

83. Case C–215/97 *Barbara Bellone* v. *Yukohama SpA* [1998] ECR I–2191. See also case C–456/98 *Centrosteel Srl* v. *Adipol GmbH* 13 July 2000, [2000] ECR I–6007 where the ECJ held "the Directive is intended to harmonise the laws of the Member States governing the legal relations between the parties to a commercial agency contract irrespective of any cross-border elements. Its scope is therefore broader than the fundamental freedoms laid down by the EC Treaty". See para 13.

84. Case C–381/98, [2001] 1 CMLR 9. The case is discussed in more detail below. See fnn 101–107 and associated text.

85. The Directive expressly stipulates that "the rules on conflict of law do not, in the matter of commercial representation, remove the inconsistencies (. . .) nor would they even if they were made uniform . . . ". See recital 3 of the preamble, OJ L. 382/17, 31 December 1986.

86. Regulation 1(2). Great Britain includes England, Wales and Scotland. Northern Ireland has separate implementing legislation: Commercial Agents (Council Directive) Regulations (Northern Ireland) 1993 as amended. For details, see fn 2 above.

must take place in Great Britain if the Agency Regulations are to apply. Such a restriction, which did not exist in previous drafts, was criticised on the ground that it was unclear and inconsistent with international conventions.[87]

Following the criticisms made by the European Commission, the Agency Regulations were amended in 1998.[88] The position now is that

— the Agency Regulations apply (as before) "in relation to the activities of commercial agents in Great Britain" (Regulation 1(2));
— but, where the commercial agent is performing in Great Britain, the English court, in proceedings before it, must apply the law of another EEA Member State in place of the Agency Regulations if principal and agent have agreed that their agency agreement is to be governed by that "foreign" law (Regulation 1(3)(a));
— where the commercial agent is performing somewhere in the EEA outside Great Britain, the English court, in proceedings before it, *must* apply the Agency Regulations to the agency agreement if the parties have agreed to its being governed by English law, but only where the law of the other EEA Member State which is the place of performance allows parties to agency agreements which are to be performed there to choose to have their agency agreement governed by what is there a foreign law (Regulation 1(3)(b)).

Even though such rules are better than what went before, they are not perfect and must be reviewed. We must distinguish those situations when the parties expressly make a choice of law from those when the parties remain silent, as the rules will differ.

The contract stipulates that English law should apply

When the commercial agent acts in Great Britain and the parties stipulate that English law should apply to their relationship, then the Agency Regulations will apply.[89] Following the 1998 amendment, the Agency Regulations can apply even when the contract is performed outside Great Britain, in which case the relevant courts or tribunals will be required to apply English law on condition that the law of that Member State allows the contract to be governed by the law of a different Member State.[90] This amendment undoubtedly improves the situation. Yet, it is not entirely satisfactory, since the Agency Regulations will apply only if the law of the other Member States contain similar rules allowing for a choice of law clause[91] and they only work when there is an express choice of law clause in favour of the law of another Member State.

87. See below.

88. The Commercial Agents (Council Directive) (Amendment) Regulations 1998, SI 1998/2868, which came into force on 16 December 1998 and in Northern Ireland by SR 1999/201. The amendment take effect in relation to disputes being dealt with by the English courts after that date, regardless of when the disputed agreement was made: *IFR Limited* v. *Federal Trade SpA*, 19 September 2001, QBD (unreported).

89. With the exception of Northern Ireland to which a separate text applies as per regulation 2(5). See fn 2 above.

90. New regulation 1(3)(b).

91. Christou remarks for example, that this therefore would not work in Portugal, since Portuguese law only permits the application of a foreign law to an agreement if this foreign law is more favourable to the commercial agent. Christou, *International, Agency, Distribution and Licensing Agreements*, (4th edn, 2003), para 3.214, p 147.

However, following the unreported case of *IFR Limited* v. *Federal Trade SpA* (QB Comm Court 19 September 2001), the 1998 amendment

> is not confined to agency contracts which are entered into on or after 16th December 1998, but extend to proceedings which came before the court on or after that date, even if they relate to a contract already existing on that date.

The contract stipulates that the law of another EEA Member State should apply

Following the 1998 amendment of the Agency Regulations, when the parties to a commercial agency agreement for performance by the commercial agent in Great Britain choose to subject their relationship to the law of another EEA Member State, the Agency Regulations will not apply.[92] However, the amended text is most peculiar in this respect since it says that the law of the other Member State concerned will apply "in place of Regulations 3 to 22". This is rather strange because it seems to mean that, even when the parties have chosen the law of another Member State to regulate their relationship, Regulations 1, 2 and 23 will nevertheless apply. The matter is quite serious, especially in relation to Regulation 2, which deals with the definition of commercial agents. It is not clear why this is the case and it does not seem to add anything to the protection of commercial agents. If anything, considering that in relation to the definition of who is a commercial agent, the UK has opted to exclude from the scope of the Agency Regulations a number of activities, which are deemed secondary,[93] it complicates the situation.

It seems rather strange that the law of another Member State needs to have reference to English law in order to decide whether its own national implementing legislation applies in a situation where that was clearly the parties' intention. We do not think that that is right.

The point could simply be that the choice of law provision only applies if the choice is made by a commercial agent as defined. Likewise, it could be simply explained by the way the Agency Regulations are drafted: Part I (which contains the definition) is defined as "General" and therefore it is considered that the substance of the Agency Regulations does not start until Part II. This certainly seems to be corroborated by the comments of Tuckey LJ in the case of *Light and others* v. *Ty Europe Ltd.*[94]

Problems remain after the 1998 Amendment

There is a further point to consider in this situation. The new Regulation 1(3)(a) works on the unstated assumption that the law of the other EEA Member State which implements the Directive can, on its terms, apply to the activities of commercial agents operating in an EEA Member State outside the relevant national territory if the parties have agreed that it should so apply. That is fine if the relevant non-UK law does indeed have such effect in territorial terms. If it does not, then, on the face of it, the commercial agent would remain unprotected even after the 1998 amendment to the Agency Regulations. That cannot be what was intended under the Directive, but this situation remains unresolved. One cannot say that, as the implementation of the Directive by the UK is apparently defective in this respect and results in a gap in the protection of commercial agents, the commercial agent can avail himself of directly enforceable rights under the Directive (the

92. New regulation 1(3)(a).
93. Regulation 2(3). See section 2.3.2 below.
94. [2003] EWHC 174 (QB), [2003] 1 All ER (Comm) 568. For discussion, see section 2.4.2.1.

time for the Member States to implement the Directive having long since passed, etc). On general principles, an unimplemented EC directive cannot affect relations between private parties (that would be to give a directive "horizontal direct effect" which the ECJ rejected in *Marshall* v. *Southampton and S.W. Hampshire Area Health Authority*[95]). The courts may, however, be able to interpret the Agency Regulations in some way to fill the gap (thus giving them "indirect direct effect", which, as mentioned earlier, is permitted in EC law[96]).

If this is not possible, the commercial agent may have a claim against the UK (on the basis of the ECJ's judgment in *Francovich*[97]) for damages for incorrect implementation of the Directive.[98]

In the situation where (1) the agent is to act in Great Britain, (2) the parties have chosen the law of another EEA country to govern the agency agreement, but (3) the legislation of the relevant EEA country implementing the Directive does not apply when the commercial agent is to act outside that country's territory, it would be reasonable to assume that the English courts would find a way of deciding that the Agency Regulations applied to it, though quite what the reasoning would be to reach that conclusion remains to be seen.

The contract stipulates that the law of a non-Member State will apply

The new rules are nevertheless welcome, because they seem to comply with the principle of party autonomy, which is a fundamental tenet of conflict of laws, i.e. that as a rule, the parties are free to choose the legal system by which their relations are to be governed and the courts will respect that, at least where the choice of law is made in good faith.

However, following the very important European Court of Justice ruling in the case of *Ingmar GB Ltd* v. *Eaton Leonard Technologies Inc.*,[99] the principle of party autonomy can be overridden when it conflicts with the protective stance of the Agency Regulations. In this case, Ingmar, a commercial agent incorporated in the UK, represented a Californian principal, Eaton in the UK and in Ireland. The contract was expressly stipulated to be covered by the laws of California. When the contract was terminated, Ingmar instituted proceedings against the principal to recover unpaid commission and seek compensation pursuant to Regulation 17. At first instance, it was decided that the Agency Regulations only applied when the parties to an agreement were nationals of a Member State and that in any event, the Agency Regulations did not express a principle of public policy which overrode the choice of Californian law as the choice of applicable law.

The Court of Appeal held that Ingmar could not be protected by the Agency Regulations because of the choice of law clause (Californian law) but also made a reference to the European Court of Justice in order to determine the applicability of the Directive in such a situation.[100]

The European Court of Justice decided that the Agency Regulations could apply to the contract, regardless of the choice of law clause, even though the principal was in a non-EU

95. ECJ case 152/84, [1986] 2 All ER 584.
96. ECJ 14/83 *Von Colson* v. *Land Nordrhein-Westfalen* [1984] ECR 1891. See fn 45 above.
97. ECJ cases C–6/90 and C–9/90 *Francovich* v. *Italy* [1991] ECR I–5357.
98. For more on this, see the reference to Steiner and Woods earlier, fn 45 above.
99. Case C–381/98 [2001] 1 CMLR 9.
100. (1999) Tr LR 333.

Member State, since termination rights under the Directive were mandatory.[101] The European Court of Justice reached its decision in two steps. First, the court held that since the purpose of articles 17 and 18 of the Directive (which contain the commercial agent's rights to payments on termination) was to protect commercial agents on termination and article 19 of the Directive says that the parties may not derogate from those articles to the commercial agent's detriment, the regime was therefore mandatory in nature.[102] Secondly, relying on the purpose of harmonisation, the court held that for the protection to be effective, the provisions could not be evaded by "the single expedient of a choice of law clause".[103] To allow this would lead to an uneven (or potentially uneven) application of the Directive in different EU Member States.

The ruling of the European Court of Justice is undoubtedly in line with the protective stance of the Directive. Its scope of application therefore seems to have a wider impact than binding purely the EU and EEA Member States.[104] However, does the ruling not attribute an extra-territorial effect to the provisions of the Directive, as Eaton submitted? The European Court of Justice was very careful on the issue and followed the Advocate General's opinion by insisting that the rules on termination are applied if "the situation is closely connected with the Community, in particular where the commercial agent carries on his activities in the territory of a Member State".

By eliminating the possibility of forum shopping for contracts concluded outside the EU as long as they are performed within the EU, the European Court of Justice ruling is of crucial importance for the protection of commercial agents. However, this case also undermines the principle of party autonomy, for which it has attracted criticism.[105]

The agency agreement is expressed to be governed by English law, but the place of performance of the agent is outside the EEA

In this situation, the Agency Regulations are irrelevant. This was always the intention. The Agency Regulations do not prohibit the parties in a case like this from choosing to contract on terms that proceed *as if* the Agency Regulations or certain parts of them were applicable, even though they are not (though it would be a very odd thing to do). As a matter of contract, there is no reason why such an arrangement should not be effective (though one would obviously in addition want advice on the relevant foreign law).

When the contract remains silent on choice of law

When, in a cross-border situation, the parties have not specified a choice of law clause in their commercial agency agreements, the general choice of laws rules will of course apply by default. They are the 1980 Rome Convention on the Law Applicable to Contractual Obligations and the Contracts (Applicable Law) Act 1990 which implements the Rome Convention in the UK, the Convention appearing as Schedule 1 to the 1990 Act.

101. Case 381/98 [2001] 1 CMLR 9.
102. *Ibid*, para 21.
103. *Ibid*, para 25.
104. See however the French case where the supreme civil court took the opposite view to that of the ECJ: *Cass Com 28 November 2000 SA Allium* v. *Société Alfin Incorporated*, JCP G 2001, II, 10527. This case seems to be accepted as an anomaly and accordingly, should not be followed.
105. See Verhagen, The tension between party autonomy and the European Union law: some observations on *Ingmar GB Ltd* v. *Eaton Leonard Technologies Inc*, [2002] ICLQ 135–154.

The text stipulates that, in the absence of a choice of law clause, the contract will be governed by the law of the country with which the contract is most closely connected (article 4).

The presumption in article 4(2) of the Convention is that this will be the law of the country where the party who provides "the performance which is characteristic of the contract" has its principal place of business (which may or may not, of course, be the same place as where that "performance" has to take place under the contract). That would mean, for example, that where a commercial agent established in France represents a Belgian principal in the UK and the commercial agency agreement is silent on choice of law, the governing law would be French law not English law.

There are three reasons, it seems to us, why an English court could and would find that English law (in the form of the Agency Regulations) governed the agreement rather than French law, viz:

(1) The fact that the Agency Regulations state that they would apply here, and that, on the face of it, is the default provision (regulation 1(2));
(2) Article 4(5) of the Rome Convention provides a justification for disregarding the presumption in article 4(2) if it appears from the circumstances taken as a whole that the contract is more closely connected with some other country than with that of the agent's principal place of business (though if the commercial agent was appointed by the Belgian principal to act both in the UK and France, rather than just the UK, it would be more difficult to argue that English law should apply to the commercial agent's activities in the UK; and
(3) Article 20 of the Rome Convention gives priority over Convention principles to EU provisions establishing choice of law rules, and there is a strong argument that Regulation 1(2) is such a provision.[106]

When the commercial agent performs in more than one country

So far, the rules reviewed were based on the assumption that the whole contract was performed in one country only. It is of course possible for the commercial agent to represent the principal in more than one country, both within and outside the EU. The final point to mention is therefore that of the situation where the commercial agent exercises his activities in two or more countries. In such a situation, should the parties be entitled, within the same contract, to decide that different laws will apply, depending on the place of performance? Advocate General Léger in the case of *Ingmar GB Ltd* v. *Eaton Leonard Technologies Inc*[107] seems to think so, but the point was not taken by the European Court of Justice. It has been remarked that such a position is incompatible with principles of private international law.[108] To try to avoid problems it is therefore advisable for the parties to enter into a separate agreements for each state that the commercial agent works in, or at least in such a situation to set out a clear choice of law regime in the commercial agency agreement.

106. For details, see Dicey and Morris, *Conflict of Laws*, (13th edn, 2000), pp 1464–1473. See also *Scholes*, Agency in (ed) *Battersby*, Commercial Contracts (Legal and Commercial Publishing Ltd), 2004, Vol. 1, pp 1.2.9 and 1.2.10.

107. [2001] 1 CMLR 9, at para 37.

108. F Randolph and J Davey, *Guide to the Commercial Agency Regulations*, (2nd edn, 2003), p 36.

2.4.2 To whom the Agency Regulations apply: Regulation 2

The Agency Regulations only govern the relations between commercial agents as defined[109] and their principals. The Agency Regulations do not define who the principal is. Considering the protective stance of the text towards commercial agents, this silence is not surprising. There is nevertheless an indirect reference to the principal in the Schedule of the Agency Regulations where the principal is referred to as "the manufacturer, the importer or the distributor of goods".[110]

The definition of commercial agents provided by the Agency Regulations is of crucial importance not only to know whom they will apply to, but also to understand who commercial agents are and what functions they perform.

In everyday commercial usage, the term "agent" is applied very loosely, and often not accurately.[111] On that aspect, the Agency Regulations are therefore welcome, since they provide a definition of who commercial agents are[112] and what functions they perform. They create a categorisation that did not exist under the common law rules. However, following the near-verbatim implementation, the definition is not as precise as may first appear, and must be reviewed in detail.

The Agency Regulations define commercial agents in two steps. First, they give a definition of commercial agents and, secondly, they give a list of agents who are to be excluded from the protection of the implementing text. The same plan will be followed.

2.4.2.1 Definition

A commercial agent is defined as "a self-employed intermediary who has continuing authority to negotiate the sale or purchase of goods on behalf of another person (the principal), or to negotiate and conclude the sale or purchase of goods on behalf of and in the name of that principal".[113]

If we disassemble the definition provided by Regulation 2(1), we can see that it contains four important elements. The commercial agent is:

(1) A self-employed intermediary,
(2) who has continuing authority
(3) to act in the name and on behalf of the principal
(4) for the purpose of negotiating and/or concluding the sale or purchase of goods.

The first three elements of the definition relate to the characteristics that a commercial representative must have in order to be regarded as a "commercial agent" for the purpose of the Agency Regulations. The last element relates to the role and functions of a commercial agent. The definition therefore serves two purposes:

109. Regulation 1(2).
110. Para 3(a) of the Schedule.
111. A car dealer for instance may be described as the "sole agent" for a particular manufacturer. This is technically incorrect since the dealer is not the agent of the manufacturer but a distributor. R. Bradgate, *Commercial law*, (3rd edn, 2000), para 3.2.2, p 130.
112. Regulation 2(1).
113. *Ibid.*

(a) By providing the three cumulative characteristics necessary to be regarded as a commercial agent, the definition creates a categorisation, which did not exist under the traditional common law rules of agency. As a result, it provides commercial agents with a distinct status, which differentiates them from other commercial intermediaries, representatives and employees and other "non-commercial agents";

(b) By defining the role of a commercial agent, this part of the Agency Regulations helps us to understand what kind of commercial function they serve, which in turns helps to define further the scope of application of the Agency Regulations.

Even though the definition appears complete, problems arise. By following the Directive to the letter, the Agency Regulations fail to define the meaning of certain civil-law-based concepts,[114] which are alien to English lawyers. Given that commercial agents as such were not recognised at common law, this is regrettable, as it creates uncertainty. This is yet another illustration of the legal paradox mentioned earlier.

Let us therefore take each element of the definition in turn so that we can appreciate its full impact.

(1) Who commercial agents are:

Prior to the implementation of the Directive, commercial agents were generally referred to as manufacturers' agents,[115] but because the general common law rules of agency applied to them, there was never any need to define that term with precision. The Agency Regulations therefore provide a welcome change.

(a) A self-employed intermediary . . .

The description of a commercial agent as a "self-employed intermediary" raised a few queries; whereas the word "employee" is familiar, the expression "self-employed" is not so usual in common law terms.[116] The phrase however simply means that the commercial agent is an independent businessman, i.e. he is a separate entity from his principal. The matter was quickly understood by the High Court of England and Wales in the case of *AMB Imballagi Plastici SRL* v. *Pacflex Ltd*[117] where Judge Raymond Jack QC looked at the meaning of "self-employed" in the Treaty of Rome[118] and concluded that the expression was more akin to the English expression "independent contractor".[119]

The independence of the commercial agent is of crucial importance. As a separate entity from the principal, the commercial agent enjoys a certain freedom in the way he sets up his business, i.e. the commercial agency, and more importantly, in the way he conducts his

114. As mentioned earlier, the definition is loosely based on French law.

115. The two main organisations which look after the interests of commercial agents in the UK are the Professional Sales Association (www.salespeople.org.uk) and the Manufacturer's Agents Association (www.the-maa.co.uk). The latter is the UK representative in the International Union of Commercial Agents and Brokers. For detail of the IUCAB, see www.iucab.nl.

116. Surprisingly, the House of Lords Select Committee did not find it to be a problem at all. They said, in their 1977 report that a commercial agent is broadly "an independent person ". See para 1 of the 51st Report of the HL Select Committee, HC 36–I of 12 November 1996.

117. [1999] 17 Tr LR 557.

118. The DTI in its Guidance Notes had already stated that the expression is derived from (the then) articles 52 and 57 of the Treaty of Rome.

119. [1999] 17 Tr LR 557.

commercial agency functions. Such consequences of the commercial agent's freedom are reasonably straightforward and in line with the rules at common law relating to independent contractors.[120] However, two more controversial consequences of the commercial agent's independent status are, in principle at least, the freedom to act for other principals and the freedom to act for himself.

The four consequences of the commercial agent's freedom must therefore be considered in turn.

Freedom to set up the commercial agency business as he sees fit

This freedom essentially refers to the legal status of the commercial agent and is reasonably simple.

As an independent contractor, the commercial agent is free to set up his commercial agency business as he sees fit. As a consequence, he can trade as a sole trader or establish a company for the purpose and still be protected by the Agency Regulations.

Such a possibility is obvious when looking at the two proposals of the European Commission,[121] other regulations[122] or even the 1977 House of Lords Select Committee Report.[123] However, in the early days of the Agency Regulations, the meaning of "self-employed" was not entirely clear to English lawyers, and there was a body of opinion which seriously contended that the implementing legislation could not apply to a commercial agent who was established as a company.[124] The question was therefore raised in court and was resolved in the case of *AMB Imballagi Plastici SRL* v. *Pacflex Ltd*[125] where the High Court of England and Wales held that a limited company can be a commercial agent and still be protected by the Agency Regulations. A similar position was taken in no uncertain terms in the more recent case of *Bell Electric Ltd* v. *Aweco Appliance System GmbH & Co*,[126] where Elias J held that "the argument that the concept of self-employed intermediary could not be intended to refer to a corporate body but only a natural person is (. . .) wholly unsustainable".[127] The matter is now settled, which not only reinforces the protection of commercial agents but also ensures harmonisation with Member States where the same rule applies.[128] The two aims of the Directive are therefore met.

Freedom to conduct the commercial agency business as he sees fit

This freedom is also reasonably straightforward, but is nevertheless essential in order to differentiate commercial agents from employees.

120. The main relevant case which distinguishes employees from independent contractor is that of *Ready Mixed Concrete (South East) Ltd* v. *Minister of Pensions and National Insurance* [1968] 2 QB 497.

121. Article 33(1) stipulated that it was possible for the parties to derogate from certain provisions when the commercial agent was a legal person whose paid-up capital exceeded a certain turnover. OJ C 56/5 of 2 March 1979.

122. Regulation 22.

123. The report stipulates that "it becomes clear, at a late stage in the draft that (it) the Directive is intended to cover companies acting as agents as well as individual so acting". See para 2 of the 51st Report of the HL Select Committee, HC 36–I of 12 November 1996.

124. The DTI Guidance Notes indicate that the expression is understood as including, for example, companies as well as self-employed individuals.

125. [1999] 17 Tr LR 557.

126. [2002] EWHC 872, [2002] Eu LR 443.

127. *Ibid*, at para 50.

128. In France and Germany, commercial agents can be legal entities as well as individual entities. For France, this is expressly stipulated by article L 134–4 al 1 commercial code, for Germany, this is expressly stipulated by § 84 commercial code HGB.

In the silence of the Agency Regulations,[129] the common law criteria which are used to distinguish employees from independent contractors will apply.[130] As the case of *Smith* v. *Reliance Water Controls Ltd*[131] shows, it essentially boils down to an issue of control.[132] In fact, as an independent contractor, the commercial agent has "the power of deciding the thing to be done, the way in which it shall be done, the means to be employed in doing it, the time and the place where it shall be done".[133] The freedom to conduct the commercial agency business as the commercial agent sees fit is therefore one of the defining characteristics of the commercial agent, a legal incident of his status as an independent contractor.

This freedom means that the commercial agent has a right to delegate some of his tasks and use sub-agents.[134] This is so, we would say by necessary implication, even though the Agency Regulations do not expressly allow it.[135] However, the freedom that the commercial agent enjoys need not be unrestricted.[136] Even as a legal incident of his status as an independent contractor, the freedom to delegate must be compatible with the commercial agent's obligations under domestic law. Both at common law[137] and under the Agency Regulations,[138] the commercial agent must act in the interests of the principal. As a consequence, the commercial agent must choose the sub-agent carefully. Moreover, the freedom to delegate need not be unrestricted and it can even be excluded, provided that there is a clear and express exclusion. As such, this freedom can therefore easily be reconciled with the fiduciary rules.

Freedom to act for other non-competing principals

The third legal incident of the commercial agent's status an independent contractor is his freedom to represent several principals simultaneously. The commercial agent might need to do so for financial reasons when he is granted very short-term contracts as was the case

129. The only reference in the Agency Regulation is that of regulation 3(2)(c) which requires the commercial agent to comply with the reasonable instructions of the principal. The first and second EU Commission proposals were better on that aspect since they stipulated that the commercial agent must comply with the instructions of the principal "provided that they do not affect the commercial agent's independence" (article 5(2)(f)), OJ C. 56/8 of 2 March 1979.

130. In *Ready Mixed Concrete (South East) Ltd* v. *Ministry of Pensions and National Insurance* [1968] 2 QB 497, MacKenna J, at p 515c, stipulated that there were three conditions to differentiate between a contract of service and a contract for service, namely, (1) whether the person received wages rather than some other form of remuneration commission, (2) whether the person is subject to the employer's control, and (3) whether the provisions of the contract are in accordance with a contract of services.

131. [2003] EWCA Civ 1153, [2003] Eu LR 874.

132. Scott Baker LJ, relying on well-established common law principles, looked primarily at the control exercised by the principal but he also looked at other factors such as whether the commercial agent was remunerated through commission, whether the commercial agent was entitled to take up non-competing agencies, whether he was liable for promotional expenses and whether he was responsible for the main tools for carrying his tasks, e.g. a car and a mobile phone. [2003] Eu LR 874, at para 26.

133. *Ready Mixed Concrete (South East) Ltd* v. *Ministry of Pensions and National Insurance* [1968] 2 QB 497, MacKenna J, at p 515f.

134. However, just because the commercial agent has implied authority to delegate, it does not mean that he has implied authority to create sub-agency contract binding on the principal.

135. This was expressly allowed in the two European Commission proposals, article 5(3). See OJ C. 56–5 of 2 March 1979.

136. McKenna J in *Ready Mixed Concrete (South East) Ltd* v. *Ministry of Pensions and National Insurance* [1968] 2 QB 497 at p 515g.

137. For details of fiduciary duties, see Chapter 3, section 3.3.1.2.2.

138. Regulation 3(1).

in *Cooper, Watkins, Bartle* v. *Pure Fishing (UK) Ltd*[139] where the nine claimants were bound by a series of six-month contracts.

However, similarly to the previous legal incident, it need not be unrestricted and must be seen in the light of the commercial agent's obligation to act in the principal's interest. Accordingly, it is clear that the commercial agent may represent several principals at the same time, at least if they are non-competing principals. This is mentioned indirectly in the Schedule to the Agency Regulations.[140]

In the case of *Smith* v. *Reliance Water Controls Ltd*,[141] the commercial agency contract allowed the appellant to work for other non-competing principals. Scott Baker LJ took this fact into consideration as evidence that the commercial agency contract was not a sham and that the appellant was really an independent contractor and not an employed sales representative. This is interesting since it suggests that not only is a commercial agent free to take up other non-competing agencies but that such a freedom is one of the defining characteristics of the commercial agency.

Whether, in English law apart from the Agency Regulations, the commercial agent may act for a number of competing principals is, surprisingly perhaps, not clear[142] (see Section 3.3.1.2 below). As we mention below, the express or implied terms of the contract will be crucial in this respect, as it is plainly open to a principal to agree to this. It is thought that for the commercial agent under a commercial agency agreement to which the Agency Regulations apply to act for a competing principal or principals without the consent of the first principal will amount to a breach of his duty of good faith,[143] entitling the first principal to summarily terminate the relationship and not pay compensation or indemnity pursuant to regulation 18(a). However, in reverse, in the light of the principal's obligation of good faith,[144] it is thought that the principal cannot unreasonably refuse the commercial agent's request to act for a second principal.[145]

Freedom to work for himself alongside the commercial agency

The last legal incident of the status of the commercial agent as an independent contractor is his freedom to choose to work for himself alongside the commercial agency. This freedom was expressly allowed in the first and second EU Commission proposals,[146] and is not unrelated to the previous one. As a consequence, the commercial agent may entirely properly work for himself, at least in so far as such a commercial activity does not compete with that of the principal, the position as to competing activities being as just noted. This, arguably, is required both at common law[147] and by his duty of good faith in the Agency Regulations.

139. [2004] EWCA Civ 375, [2004] 2 Lloyd's Reports 518.

140. Para 3(c) of the Schedule stipulates that a commercial agent who devotes substantially the whole of his time to representative activities, can do so for one principal or for a number of principals whose interests are not conflicting.

141. [2003] EWCA Civ 1153, [2003] Eu LR 874.

142. Article 7(1), OJ C. 56/8 of 2 March 1979.

143. Regulation 3(1).

144. Regulation 4(1).

145. For more details over the fiduciary duties, see Chapter 3, section 3.3.1.2.

146. Article 7(1), OJ C. 56/8 of 2 March 1979.

147. As a fiduciary, the commercial agent must not place himself in a position where his own interests conflict with those of the principal: *Aberdeen Rly Co* v. *Blaikie Bros* (1854) 1 Macq 461.

The freedom undeniably exists, yet it is not clear how widely it should be used since the freedom may create problems for the commercial agent. In fact, when the commercial agent uses his freedom and spends less time representing the principal than he does on his own activities, this raises the question whether his commercial agency activities are secondary, in which case, the Agency Regulations do not apply.[148] The matter must therefore be considered more fully when dealing with secondary activity later in this chapter.[149]

In spite of his independence, the commercial agent nevertheless remains a representative since he acts on behalf of the principal. As such, the commercial agent must comply with, and remain within the terms of, the authority given to him by the principal.

(b) ... Who has continuing authority...

The Agency Regulations stipulate that the commercial agent has "continuing authority", yet they remain silent as to what this means. The silence has raised two significant problems, namely, it is not clear (i) what "continuing" means precisely, and (ii) whether "authority" bears the same meaning that it has under traditional common law rules.

Meaning of the term "continuing"?

It is obvious that the expression "continuing" does not imply that the commercial agent must have an unlimited duration contract, since the Agency Regulations clearly cover long-term and short-term contracts alike.[150] The term "continuing" simply refers to an element of "durability" in the relationship, e.g. that the commercial agent must act for the principal continuously over a certain period of time. There is therefore permanence when the parties are linked by a series of short-term contracts.[151]

The requirement of "durability" is a characteristic which differentiates commercial agents from intermediaries who only act on a one-off basis, such as brokers. It is normal not to protect such intermediaries, since a commercial agent instructed to act for a one-off transaction does not build goodwill for the principal and therefore does not have the economic need for the protection on termination highlighted earlier.[152] We however face the problem of quantification: how many transactions does it take for the authority to be "continuing"? The DTI suggested that, if a commercial agent is appointed for a specified number of transactions, then the Agency Regulations do not apply. This looks incorrect.[153] It appears to mean that a commercial agent appointed for three specific transactions is not protected; and presumably the same will apply if he is appointed for one hundred transactions. However, if a commercial agent is appointed for three weeks, three months or three years, he would be. It is therefore thought that specifying a number of transactions will not

148. Regulation 2(3).

149. For details, see section 2.4.2.2.

150. See Regulations 14 and 15 for the rules on termination for fixed and indefinite duration contracts. For details as to what these entail, see Chapter 5, section 5.2.1.2.

151. See *Duncan Moore* v. *Piretta* [1999] 1 All ER 174 and *AMB Imballagi Plastici SRL* v. *Pacflex* [1999] 2 All ER (Comm) 249. In both cases, the commercial agency relationship had started a long time before the Agency Regulations came into effect.

152. For details, see section 2.2.2.

153. For similar viewpoint, see F Randolph and J Davey, *Guide to the Commercial Agency Regulations*, (2nd edn, 2003), p 40 who use the rules relating to the commission and exclusivity to make their point.

prevent the commercial agent from being covered by the Agency Regulations, at least if their number is more than one.

It has been said that when a principal uses the same commercial agent on an ad hoc basis for a number of one-off transactions, the latter should be protected by the Agency Regulations since continuing authority will arise through a course of dealing.[154] This seems accurate. However, it was also suggested that this can be avoided if each ad hoc appointment is made under a written agreement stating that no continuing authority was granted.[155] In the light of the protective stance of the Agency Regulations and the mandatory nature of termination payments as defined by the European Court of Justice,[156] this suggestion is thought to be incorrect.

The fact that the authority must be "continuing" raises another question over the status of commercial agents who are appointed on a seasonal basis, such as Christmas. Arguably they are not covered by the Agency Regulations since their authority with the principal is not "continuing" but intermittent. Yet, is there a difference between a commercial agent who is appointed for three months and a commercial agent appointed for the Christmas season? Moreover, what if a commercial agent has been working for the same principal every Christmas over a period of ten years for instance? Is he not protected by the Agency Regulations? Arguably, he has not continuously been working for the principal, hence, he might not be protected. The DTI argued that the activities of commercial agents selling Christmas hampers would be likely to be found to be secondary, in which case, they are not protected by the Agency Regulations.[157] We shall therefore address this question later, when dealing with secondary activity.[158]

Meaning of "authority": are sub-agents protected?

We have seen earlier that a consequence of the commercial agent's independence is his freedom to delegate some of his duties as he sees fit. As delegation is possible, this raises the question whether sub-agents are themselves regarded as commercial agents for the purpose of the Agency Regulations, i.e. do they have "authority" from the principal? The DTI stated that the Agency Regulations are in principle capable of applying to sub-agent agreements. Such a statement is vague, since it is not clear whether the DTI means that a commercial agent can delegate or whether a sub-agent will be protected by the Agency Regulations. Here, the two European Commission proposals are of no help either, since even though they allow the commercial agent to delegate,[159] they remain silent on the liability (if any) between sub-agents and principals. In the silence of the Agency Regulations, the question therefore needs to be reviewed in the light of the common law rules.

At common law, authority is often, but not always, derived from a contract. Common law recognises that sub-agency is permitted with the express or implied consent of the

154. Christou, *International Agency, Distribution and Licensing Agreements*, (4th edn, 2003), para 3.43, p 98.

155. *Ibid.*

156. Case 381/98 *Ingmar GB Ltd* v. *Eaton Leonard Technologies Inc* [2001] 1 CMLR 9. This case is discussed earlier, see fnn 101–103 and associated text.

157. Regulation 2(4).

158. For details, see section 2.4.2.2.

159. Article 5(3). OJ C. 56/8 of 2 March 1979.

principal.[160] However, even when sub-agency is permitted, there is, in principle,[161] no direct agency relationship between the principal and the sub-agent.[162] Nonetheless, a tort action between the principal and the sub-agent would still be possible since the sub-agent owes the principal a duty of care.[163]

Given that the main interest of the sub-agent will be to know whether he can claim termination payments from the principal, the pressing question is whether there is a need for a direct relation between the principal and the sub-agent before the latter can be protected by the Agency Regulations. The issue arose in the case of *Light & Others* v. *Ty Europe Ltd*[164] which involved nine claimants. The facts are important. Before 1 June 1997, Ty UK Ltd, a company partly owned by Mr Swallow, was the sole UK distributor of toys designed and manufactured by Ty Inc. Ty Inc, who grew dissatisfied with Ty UK Ltd, persuaded the latter to relinquish its rights by giving Mr Swallow sole selling rights for Ty products in the UK for three years as of 1 June 1997.

To this end, Ty UK Ltd was liquidated and a new company, Ty Europe Ltd, entered into a selling rights agreement with a new Swallow company, Swallow Corporate Sales Ltd (SCS). The agreement was for only three years and when the contract expired at the end of May 2000, SCS dropped out. SCS has since ceased trading and has no assets. Before June 1997, some of the nine claimants had worked as commercial agents for Ty UK Ltd. Following the change from Ty UK Ltd to Ty Europe Ltd, the claimants entered into commercial agency agreements with SCS with effect from the same date of 1 June 1997. It was clear from the start that the contracts would end on 31 May 2000 to match the duration of SCS' commercial agency agreement with Ty Europe Ltd.

Shortly before the contracts in question ended, Ty Europe Ltd offered employment as sales representatives to some of the claimants, with effect from 1 June 2000. The representatives declined and shortly after that date, started proceedings against Ty Europe Ltd for compensation under Regulation 17 on the basis of the sub-agency agreement between SCS and themselves. Ty Europe Ltd's defence submitted that the claimants were not its commercial agents, because their authority only came from SCS and authority for the purpose of the Agency Regulations could only be derived from an agency contract with the principal. There was no direct contract, and the Agency Regulations could therefore not apply.

Decision of the first instance court

Judge MacGonigal, sitting in the Leeds Commercial Court, rejected this argument and interpreted "authority" in Regulation 2(1) in the light of traditional common law rules. He stated that the claimants had "continuing authority" pursuant to Regulation 2(1) on the

160. Originally, at common law, the first fiduciary duty of the agent was that of non-delegation as imposed in *De Bussche* v. *Alt* (1878) 8 Ch D 286. The principle of non-delegation is now subject to such a number of exceptions that it is more accurate to say that an agent is not allowed to delegate performance of his obligations unless delegation is authorised by the principal. For a brief discussion, see Chapter 3, section 3.3.1.2.4.

161. In the case of *Prentis Donegan & Partners Ltd* v. *Leeds & Leeds Co Inc*, Rix J emphasised that privity between the principal and the sub-agent would only arise in exceptional circumstances, [1998] 2 Lloyd's Rep 326 at p 334.

162. This therefore means that the sub-agent cannot obtain remuneration for services rendered from the principal: *Schmaling* v. *Tomlinson* (1815) 6 Taunt 147 and the principal cannot recover money from the sub-agent: *Calico Printers Association* v. *Barclays Bank Ltd* (1931) 145 LT 51, CA.

163. *Henderson* v. *Merret Syndicates Ltd* [1994] 3 WLR 761.

164. [2003] EWCA Civ 1238, [2004] 1 Lloyd's Rep 693.

basis that authority does not necessarily derive only from a contract directly between the sub-agent and the principal. Judge MacGonigal added that authority can be delegated to a sub-agent with the express or implied consent of the principal,[165] and further stated that it did not matter, for the purpose of Regulation 2(1) that the authority was received when Ty Europe Ltd accepted the orders negotiated or that it was delegated by SCS.[166] Judge MacGonigal finally considered whether the expression "continuing authority" in Regulation 2(1) bore a special meaning and answered it negatively, but gave permission to the principal to appeal.

Judgment of the Court of Appeal

The Court of Appeal reversed the decision of Judge MacGonigal. Tuckey LJ, who gave the leading judgment in the Court of Appeal, agreed that the claimants were undoubtedly commercial agents, as they negotiated the sale of goods on behalf of the appellant, i.e. the principal, and that the authority was continuing.[167] However, Tuckey LJ decided that this was only a starting point and that the more important question was whether there had to be a direct contract between the sub-agent and the principal before the substantive provisions of the Agency Regulations could apply.[168] To this, Tuckey LJ answered positively in no uncertain terms by stating "the conclusion that such a contract is required is inescapable" since "the substantial rights and obligations laid down in the Regulations were only intended for those in a contract relationship".[169] Tuckey LJ reached his decision by looking at other provisions of the Agency Regulations, which make reference to an "agency contract", including Regulation 17.[170] Because there was no direct contract between the claimant and the appellant, the claimants were not protected by Regulation 17 and therefore could not claim compensation.[171]

Following such an analysis, it was not enough that the main principal had accepted the sub-agent, or at least knew about him, to impose obligations on the principal towards the sub-agent, since authority between the principal and the sub-agent cannot be implied under the Agency Regulations unlike the position at common law. This means that even if the "head" commercial agent has an implied right to delegate under the Agency Regulations, this does not give him implied authority to create a sub-agency contract binding on the principal. As Ward LJ stated, the sub-agents did not have actual authority.[172] Tuckey LJ was so adamant in his position that he said that there was no need to refer the matter to the European Court of Justice for clarification.[173] He added that "if the

165. [2003] EWHC 174, [2003] 1 All ER (Comm) 568, at para 26.
166. *Ibid*, at para 19.
167. [2004] 1 Lloyd's Rep 693, at p 697, para 19.
168. *Ibid*.
169. [2004] 1 Lloyd's Rep 693, at p 697, para 23.
170. *Ibid*, para 21. Tuckey LJ also looked at Regulation 13 which gives the parties the right to request a signed written document setting out the terms of an agency contract; Regulation 4 which imposes on the principal an obligation of disclosure. Finally, looking at the obligation of the principal to allow the commercial to see extracts from his books pursuant Regulation 12, Tuckey LJ concluded that such obligations are "what one would expect in a contract between an agent and principal but not in a relationship at one remove such as that of a principal and a sub-agent", at para 23.
171. *Ibid*, at para 20.
172. [2004] 1 Lloyd's Rep 693, at para 51.
173. *Ibid*, at para 28.

regulations had been intended to cover such a relationship, they could have said but they do not".[174]

If the position of the Court of Appeal is correct, this would seem to indicate that a sub-agent can never be protected by the Agency Regulations against the main principal. A sub-agent cannot claim compensation or indemnity against the "head" commercial agent either because, even though he acts as the agent of the "head" commercial agent, he does not act as his "commercial agent" since he acts in the name of the principal and not in the name of the "head" commercial agent. This point was well understood by Tuckey LJ in *Light & Others* v. *Ty Europe Ltd.*[175]

Does that mean that sub-agents will never be entitled to claim compensation or indemnity from the principal? Following the reasoning of the Court of Appeal, it seems so. Yet, this cannot be right, as to do so could allow a principal to set up a sham structure in order to avoid liability to its commercial agent. Thankfully, this will not be possible as such a hypothesis was also considered by Tuckey LJ who said that, in such a situation, the court would be entitled to ignore the structure.[176]

More seriously, if the Court of Appeal is correct, this means that a whole category of commercial agents is left unprotected. Can this be right? Considering it is against the protective stance of the Directive, it seems doubtful. Yet, the argument that a direct contract is necessary between the sub-commercial agent and the principal is not easily defeated. Incidentally, this argument was already made in the earlier case of *AMB Imballagi Plastici* v. *Pacflex Ltd*,[177] where Waller LJ also stated that the need for an agency contract can be seen both "by implication from the nature of the obligations" and "expressly" when looking, for instance, at Regulation 4(2)(b).[178]

In *Light & Others* v. *Ty Europe Ltd*,[179] when deciding that the sub-agent could not claim compensation from the principal, Lightman LJ's reasoning seems to have been influenced, at least in part, by the fact that the sub-agent must not be a financial burden on the principal. Lightman LJ said that to confer the right on the sub-agent to claim compensation from the principal "would expose the principal to double liability both to his commercial agent and to any (often unknown) sub agents".[180] A solution which would protect the sub-agent without financially burdening the principal would be to share any compensation or indemnity payments between the head commercial agent and the sub-agent in the same manner that commission for transactions concluded after termination occurs are apportioned between a new and an old commercial agent.[181]

In fact, Tuckey LJ himself said "I can see no reason why as agents, they [the claimants] should not be able to establish a stake in SCS's compensation claim".[182] The problem with this solution is that the sub-agent is at the mercy of the "head" commercial agent. If the "head" commercial agent does not make a claim for compensation or indemnity, as

174. *Ibid*, p 697 at para 23.
175. *Ibid*, see comments by Tuckey LJ, at para 26.
176. Para 27, p 698. One must not however deny that there is a similar power to ignore sham arrangements in other areas. Courts are slow to label an arrangement a sham, see for instance *WDA* v. *Exfinco* [1992] BCC 270.
177. [1999] All ER (Comm) 249.
178. *Ibid*, at p 252b.
179. [2004] 1 Lloyd's Rep 693.
180. *Ibid*, at para 45.
181. Regulation 9. For details, see Chapter 4, section 4.10.2.
182. [2004] 1 Lloyd's Rep 693 at p 698, para 26.

happened in *Light & Others* v. *Ty Europe Ltd*,[183] the sub-agent is left without protection. Likewise, if the head commercial agent is insolvent, the compensation or indemnity will be shared between general creditors.

The fact that in *Light & Others* v. *Ty Europe Ltd*,[184] the refusal by Lightman LJ to apply the Agency Regulations to sub-agents seems to have been motivated by the fact that sub-agents must not be a financial burden for the principal at the stage of termination[185] is, interestingly, in line with the reasoning of the French courts. Sub-agency is expressly permitted under the French implementing text,[186] since the main commercial agent is allowed to delegate. Yet, the French implementing statute does not provide sub-agents with any express protection. Any right that they may have against the principal is defined through French common law principles and French sub-agents fare no better than their English counterparts.

In fact, in France, the Civil Code gives the principal a direct right of action against the sub-agent[187] but nothing to the sub-agent. In 1960, the French Supreme Court interpreted the Civil Code article in question widely, stating that a reciprocal right should also be granted to the sub-agent against the principal.[188] This interpretation was crucial for sub-agents since it gave them the right to sue the principal for money owed on commission and even for compensation on termination. However, French case law shows that this direct right of action has never been applied because the sub-agent must not be a financial burden for the principal.[189]

Following *Light & Others* v. *Ty Europe Ltd*,[190] the position of sub-agents under the Agency Regulations seems fragile. It is therefore advisable for commercial agents not to act as sub-agents, as their right to compensation or indemnity looks very thin.

(c) . . . To act in the name of and on behalf of the principal

The fact that the Agency Regulations require the commercial agent to act in the name and on behalf of the principal is not surprising. It simply reiterates that the commercial agent is an agent in law, i.e. he does not act in his own name. This final characteristic marks the essential difference between commercial agents and distributors who buy and resell goods in their own names.[191]

UNDISCLOSED AGENT AND COMMISSION AGENTS ARE NOT PROTECTED

The double requirement that the commercial agent must not only act on behalf of the principal, but also in the name of that principal, shows that undisclosed agents are not

183. [2004] 1 Lloyd's Rep 693.
184. *Ibid.*
185. See fn 185 above.
186. Article L 134–1 al 1 of the French commercial code. For an English translation, see Appendix.
187. Article 1994–2 cc. For an English translation see www.legifrance.gouv.fr
188. Cass 27–12–1960, D 1961, 491; RTDCiv 1961, 700.
189. J. M. Leloup, *Les agents commerciaux, statuts juridiques, stratégies professionnelles*, (5th edn, 2001), p 256.
190. [2003] EWCA Civ, 25–7–2003, [2003] All ER (D) 445.
191. The distinction between both activities can sometimes be very fine, as it is now accepted that the fact that a commercial agent is remunerated through a mark-up is not incompatible with the Agency Regulations. Compare and contrast *AMB Imballagi Plastici Srl* v. *Pacflex* [1999] All ER (Comm) 249 where the relationship was found to be a distributorship and *Mercantile International Group* v. *Chuan Soon Huat Industrial Group Ltd* [2002] 1 All ER (Comm) 788 where the relationship was found to be a commercial agency. On the facts, the decisions are satisfactory.

covered by the Agency Regulations. This is so presumably because undisclosed agents do not build up goodwill for the principal.

The double requirement also shows that commission agents are not covered either. This was made clear by the European Court of Justice in the case of *Mavrona & Sia OE* v. *Delta Etaireia Symmetochon AE*.[192] The case was heard by the European Court of Justice following a request by a Greek court for a preliminary ruling. Prior to the implementation of the Directive, Greek law drew no distinction between commission agents (paid by commission and contracting on behalf of the principal but in the agent's own name) and commercial agents. The Greek court asked the European Court of Justice whether this could still be the case after the implementation of the Directive.[193] The argument of the Italian claimant was that it was possible for commission agents to be protected since the decisive point in the definition provided by the Directive is that the commercial agent acts on behalf of a principal, which commission agents do.[194] The European Court of Justice rejected such an argument, on the basis that there was no reference in the Directive to persons who, while acting on behalf of a third party, do so in their own name. Since commission agents as understood in this sense and commercial agents do not have the same need for protection, commission agents do not come within the scope of the Directive.[195] Interestingly, the European Court of Justice also held that, provided this is not prohibited by Community provisions, it is possible for a Member State to introduce national rules inspired by the provisions of the Directive in order to protect commission agents.[196]

Intermediaries or representatives?

From the above, it should be clear that commercial agents act on behalf of their principal. Consequently, the fact that they are defined as "intermediaries" in regulation 2(1) seems a little strange as the term "representative" would have been more accurate. The use of the term "intermediary" can nevertheless be explained on the ground that it reflects more the variety of tasks that a commercial agent can do, in addition to the representative activities.[197] For instance, a commercial agent may also be required to store goods, to act as a del credere agent etc. The use of the term "intermediary" could also be explained by the fact that the default position is the restricted power of negotiation as opposed to the power to conclude contracts for the principal. When a commercial agent merely has authority to negotiate, arguably, he has no representative power, hence he is not an "agent" in the true sense of the word, but simply an intermediary.

(2) The role and commercial functions of commercial agents:

Regulation 2(1) stipulates that the role of commercial agents is to "negotiate the sale or purchase of goods on behalf of the principal or to negotiate and conclude the sale or purchase of goods on behalf of the principal". The definition indicates that the Agency Regulations apply equally to purchasing and selling agents[198] and also to commercial

192. Case C–85–03, order of 10 February 2004, [2004] ECR I–1573 CELEX document 6200300085.
193. Paras 8–9.
194. Para 14.
195. Para 21.
196. Para 20.
197. F Fournier, *L'agence commerciale*, (1998), para 243, p 134.
198. Looking at the case law, the former category seems to be in the minority since of the reported cases so far, only *Graham Page* v. *CST Ltd* [1997] 3 All ER 656, involved a purchasing agent.

agents who have a limited authority to "negotiate" contracts for the principal, i.e. marketing agents and those who have a wider authority to "negotiate and conclude" contracts for the principal, i.e. sales agents.

Even though the definition appears complete by protecting a wide array of commercial agents, it is not perfect and raises two problems. First, there is a clear emphasis on the negotiating function of the commercial agent, yet the Agency Regulations fail to define what "negotiate" entails. Secondly, the Agency Regulations only mention commercial agents who deal with goods, the position of commercial agents who deal with goods and services is therefore not clear.

(a) What the negotiating function of the commercial agent entails:

The emphasis on the negotiating function seems to indicate that it is central to the profession. The failure to define what "negotiate" means or what it entails precisely is therefore surprising. Considering that the majority of commercial agents established in the UK appear only to have authority to negotiate,[199] the matter must be clarified.

To understand what "negotiate" involves is important for the scope of application of the Agency Regulations on two respects. First, to understand the marketing role that commercial agents play helps us to differentiate them from other intermediaries. Secondly, to understand "how far the agent needs to be authorised in order to be negotiating"[200] is important to see what the "negotiation threshold"[201] is.

"To negotiate" is part of the commercial agent's marketing role

Following the Court of Appeal in the case of *Parks* v. *Esso Petroleum Company Ltd*,[202] it is now clear that to "negotiate" for the purpose of the Agency Regulations requires more than merely haggling over the price of the goods.[203] This is accurate since most commercial agents cannot negotiate the price at which they promote and/or sell the goods of the principal.[204]

In this case, Mr Parks operated as agent at a petrol station owned by Esso, but ran the shop there as an independent contractor. In May 1997, Esso gave notice of immediate termination of the agency agreement on the ground of an alleged breach of contract by Mr Parks. Amongst other claims, which are not directly relevant here, Mr Parks claimed he was entitled to an indemnity payment under the Agency Regulations.

The central question was therefore whether Mr Parks was a commercial agent for the purpose of the Agency Regulations. Morritt LJ, who gave the leading judgment, said that Mr Parks was not a commercial agent because he did not have any negotiating power, nor did any negotiation actually take place since "Mr Parks did not 'deal with, manage or conduct' the sale of petrol to his customers, for he took no part in the customer's choice

199. Randolph and Davey, *Guide to the Commercial Agency Regulations*, (2nd edn, 2003) p 45.

200. Randolph and Davey, op cit p 46.

201. Expression borrowed from R Christou, *International agency, distribution and licensing agreements*, (4th edn 2003), p 92.

202. [2000] Tr LR 232.

203. The Court of Appeal decision corrects the High Court decision which stated that Mr Parks had not negotiated the sale of fuel because the price at which motor fuel is sold is fixed by the principal, [1999] 1 CMLR 455 at 478, para 86.

204. As mentioned earlier, the ability of the principal to control the price at which his goods are sold is usually a crucial factor in deciding whether to use commercial agents or distributors. For details, see section 2.2.3.

and self-service".[205] Morritt LJ added that "in so far as the definition indicates the need for skill or consideration, Mr Parks provided none".[206] The reasoning of Morritt LJ seems to show that he understood that to "negotiate" is a skill which forms an integral part of the marketing role of commercial agents and that such a skill requires commercial agents to take active steps towards obtaining customers for the principal's goods.

This case is important as it shows that Morritt LJ understood the difference between "agents" and "commercial agents" for the purpose of the Agency Regulations. Mr Parks was an "agent" for the sale of fuel since he was a self-employed intermediary with continuing authority to conclude sales on behalf of the principal (Esso) and was remunerated by commission. However, he was not a "commercial agent" for the purpose of the Agency Regulations since he was not *negotiating* the sale of fuel i.e. he was not actively promoting the fuel on behalf of the principal. The impact of this case must not be underestimated. To decide that Mr Parks was not a commercial agent is dangerous from a social viewpoint, because it narrows down the application of the Agency Regulations.[207] Yet, the outcome of the decision is nevertheless thought to be correct, since it shows that the process of negotiation is central both to the marketing function of commercial agents and to their need for protection, which is in line with the economic rationale for protection of commercial agents underpinning the Directive.[208]

What is the negotiation "threshold"?

Following *Parks* v. *Esso Petroleum Company Ltd*,[209] a commercial agent will "negotiate" if he plays some part in getting the customer to buy the goods of the principal. Yet, what is not clear is how active must the commercial agent be in this respect. As mentioned by the DTI, the important question is whether canvassing/introducing commercial agents who merely promote and market the principal's goods by soliciting orders from third parties are covered by the Agency Regulations.[210] A positive answer was provided by the Court of Appeal in the case of *Tamarind International Ltd & Others* v. *Eastern Natural Gas (Retail) Ltd & Another*.[211] The negotiation "threshold" of the Agency Regulations is therefore quite low. Considering the protective stance of the Agency Regulations, this seems correct.

However, as remarked, the central question remains whether the commercial agent is *authorised* to negotiate and not whether he actually negotiates.[212] The question is important when comparing new and mature commercial agency agreements. When a commercial agent is appointed with the specific task of breaking into a market, he will be very active in promoting the goods of the principal, and the amount of actual negotiation and the level of negotiation anticipated by the parties will be very high. In mature commercial agency agreements most of the sales might well be repeat orders, in which case, there will

205. [2000] Tr LR 232, at p 238h.
206. *Ibid*, at p 239a.
207. The social argument for affording protection to the likes of Mr Parks was emphasised by his counsel, see [1999] 1 CMLR 455 at 479, para 86. In Germany, petrol station attendants are protected. See Chapter 6, section 6.4.1.
208. For details, see section 2.2.2 above.
209. [1999] 1 CMLR 455.
210. The DTI said that the matter was to be decided by the courts. See DTI Guidance Notes, published in September 1994, p 7.
211. [2000] Eu LR 708.
212. Randolph and Davey, *Guide to the Commercial Agency Regulations*, (2nd edn, 2003), p 46.

probably be very little negotiation going on. Yet, this does not mean that the commercial agent ceases to be a commercial agent, since he still has *authority* to negotiate.

Is the negotiation and/or conclusion of contracts the only function that a commercial agent may perform?

Regulation 2(1) appears to simply make the distinction between sales agents and marketing agents. Even though such functions are the essence of the commercial agent's representative activities, they do not illustrate the full spectrum of the powers that a commercial agent can be granted by the principal.

In that respect, the two EU Commission proposals provided a lot more detail by stipulating that the commercial agent could, for instance, be required to look after the principal's property,[213] indicating that he was in charge of the stock or to act as a del credere agent.[214] The fact that the final text of the Directive does not contain such detailed information is logical, since it would have been impossible to harmonise the laws of the Member States in such detail. Moreover, it would not really have added anything to the level of protection of commercial agents.

Providing that an intermediary has the minimum negotiating powers "to look for clients, to promote and negotiate the sales of certain goods in a given territory",[215] he will be considered as a commercial agent for the purpose of the Agency Regulations. It is therefore thought that the Agency Regulations do not prevent the parties from imposing additional obligations on the commercial agent as they see fit. To ask the commercial agent to look after the principal's stock is for instance necessary when the commercial agent is empowered by the principal to break into a foreign market.[216]

(b) Are commercial agents dealing with services and commercial agents dealing with goods and services protected?

Regulation 2(1) stipulates that commercial agents are appointed to negotiate and/or conclude the sale or purchase of "goods". Since services are not mentioned in the implementing text, it is not clear whether commercial agents who provide services only and commercial agents who handle on their principal's behalf contracts for combined supplies of goods and services (e.g. the sale and fitting of replacement windows (a sector in which the use of self-employed sales agents is common)) are covered by the Agency Regulations. Following the near-verbatim implementation, the Directive is of no help on that matter. The first and second EU Commission proposals are ambiguous on this point; they only mention "goods" in their definition of the commercial agent and yet other articles refer to "goods and services",[217] indicating that commercial agents dealing with combined

213. Article 5(2)(e). See OJ C. 56/5 of 2 March 1979.

214. Article 21, reference as above.

215. P Crahay *Les contrats internationaux d'agence et de concession de vente*, (1991), para 90, p 62.

216. See *Page* v. *Combined Shipping & Transport Co Ltd* [1997] 3 All ER 656.

217. See for instance article 7 on the possibility for the commercial agent to carry on business for his own account or to represent other principals aside the commercial agency, providing that "the business is in goods or services which do not compete with those for which he was appointed with the principal"; article 8(1) on the claims brought against the commercial agent's possible breaches over the "goods and services forming the subject matter of the contract"; article 10(2)(a) on the obligation of the principal to give all the relevant documents relating to the "goods and services for which the commercial agent has been appointed". See OJ C 56/5 of 2 March 1979.

supplies of goods and services could be protected. We consider that that is the better view.

The meaning of "goods"

The uncertainty in this area is exacerbated by the absence of a definition of "goods" in the Directive. According to the DTI guidance notes of 1994, "goods" clearly has to be interpreted in accordance with the EC Treaty, which explains why the Agency Regulations do not define the word. The DTI then adds that the definition provided by the Sale of Goods Act 1979, s 61(1) is a "reasonable" guide, without "necessarily being absolutely co-extensive with the Directive meaning".[218]

It has been suggested that the definition of "goods" in the EC Public Procurement Directive implemented in England by the Public Supply Contract Regulations 1995 could provide some help on the grounds that an EC law definition in one directive is at least persuasive for the interpretation of the same term in another.[219] It stipulates that "goods" includes electricity, substances, growing crops and things attached to and forming part of the land which are agreed to be severed before the purchase or hire under the supply contract and any ship, aircraft and vehicle. In the case of *Tamarind and Others* v. *Eastern Natural Gas and Eastern Energy*,[220] gas was treated as goods, which is in line with common law, since gas would be treated as goods under the SGA 1979.

In relation to commercial agents dealing with computer products, especially software, following the case of *St Albans City and District Council* v. *International Computers Ltd*[221] software is likely to be seen as "goods" if the software is supplied via a physical medium, but not if it is supplied by email attachment or by download from a website.

Commercial agents who deal only with services

Because services are not expressly mentioned in regulation 2(1), it seems very clear that commercial agents who deal only with services are not covered by the Agency Regulations.[222] This certainly seems to be the view of Lord Drummond Young in the Scottish case of *Lloyd Gailey* v. *Environmental Waste Control*.[223] Yet it is not clear what the justification under the Directive is for not protecting such commercial agents. In *Lloyd Gailey* v. *Environmental Waste Control*,[224] Lord Drummond Young proposed, as a possible reason for the distinction, that principals who provide services are more likely to come into direct contact with the customers than principals who sell goods, and thus the goodwill can be more readily accepted as belonging morally to the principal rather than

218. SGA, s 61(1) stipulates that for England, "goods" include all personal chattel other than things in action and money and for Scotland, "goods include all corporeal moveable except money".

219. R Christou, *International agency, distribution and licensing agreements*, (4th edn, 2003), para 3.47, p 99.

220. [2000] Eu LR 708.

221. [1996] 4 All ER 481. See also the Scottish authority *Beta Computers (Europe) Ltd* v. *Adobe Systems (Europe) Ltd* (1996) SLT 604.

222. See also regulation 4(2)(a) which refers to the obligation of the principal to provide the commercial agent with "the necessary documentation on goods"; regulation 6(1) which defines that remuneration is for "the goods forming the subject of the agency contract". Similarly, paras 2(a), 2(b)(ii), 3(a)(b)(d) and 4(c) of the Schedule also only refer to "goods".

223. [2004] Eu LR 423. Lord Drummond Young stated "like the Directive, the Commercial Agents (Council Directive) Regulations 1993 are confined to agents who engage in the sale or purchase of goods" at para 25.

224. [2004] Eu LR 423.

the agent.[225] Lord Drummond Young then gave the example that for a financial intermediary, it will normally be the reputation of the principal that is relied upon by the customer rather than the reputation of the intermediary.[226]

This is interesting, but does not explain why in France, for instance, commercial agents who deal with services are protected.[227]

Commercial agents who have mixed contracts for the supply of goods and services

If it is correct that commercial agents who deal purely with services are not covered by the Agency Regulations, the more pressing question is to know what happens to commercial agents who are appointed to represent the principal for the supply of goods and services.

Several arguments can be brought forward showing that such commercial agents could nevertheless be covered by the Agency Regulations:

> First of all, the second draft of the Agency Regulations expressly excluded services. Since the current text does not contain such an exclusion, it is arguable that commercial agents who deal with goods and services are not excluded.
>
> Secondly, considering that one of the aims of the Directive is to improve the protection of commercial agents as a profession, to deny the application of the Agency Regulations to commercial agents who deal with mixed goods and services contracts would be pointless. Additionally, this is not satisfactory for harmonisation since in France for instance, commercial agents who will deal with pure services contracts are expressly protected (even though the Directive does not oblige France to protect them).[228]
>
> Thirdly, it has been mentioned that the reference to goods in the definition is only a matter of defining the status of the commercial agent; commercial agents who deal with goods and services could consequently be covered.[229] This argument is further reinforced by the fact that other relevant regulations such as the regulations on commissions[230] simply refer to "transactions" and are not specific to goods. However, arguably, this simply goes back to the definition of commercial agents where there is no mention of services.

In the absence of a judicial answer, it has often been suggested that if the commercial agency contract relates to the supply of goods with provision of ancillary services, the contract should be covered by the Agency Regulations.[231] However, if the contract relates to the supply of services and the provision of products is merely ancillary, then the Agency Regulations do not apply.[232] This is a possibility; however, it is not clear what happens when the parties expressly agree that the commercial agency which is for the sale of goods and services should be covered by the Agency Regulations. Can they do so? In the light

225. *Ibid*, at para 24.
226. *Ibid*.
227. Article L 134–1 al 1 of the French commercial code. For an English translation, see Appendix 5.
228. *Ibid*.
229. Randolph and Davey, *Guide to the Commercial Agency Regulations*, (2nd edn, 2003), p 43.
230. Regulations 7, 8.
231. R Christou, *International agency, distribution and licensing agreements*, (4th edn, 2003), para 3.49, p 99.
232. *Ibid*.

of the protective stance of the Agency Regulations, it is thought that if both parties agree that the contract is subject to the implementing text, then the Agency Regulations should apply.

Until recently, the debate over the status of commercial agents who provide goods and services was purely academic. The question was however raised in the Scottish case of *Lloyd Gailey* v. *Environmental Waste Control*,[233] where Lord Drummond Young stated that the question was to be decided on the basis on the activities of the principal. Lord Drummond Young stated that "if that business is not predominantly one involving the sale of goods, I am of the opinion that the agents' activities are necessary secondary",[234] in which case, the Agency Regulations do not apply. Lord Drummond Young based his decision on the Schedule of the Agency Regulations. The case will therefore be analysed in detail in the next section. The important question is whether the same conclusion would be reached by an English court.

Even though the situation is at the moment not entirely clear in relation to the Agency Regulations, special attention must be drawn to Member States where commercial agents who deal with goods and services are protected. Should an English principal appoint a commercial agent in such Member States and stipulate that the contract is subject to English law, the local law may nevertheless apply if it has an overriding effect.

2.4.2.2 The categories of agents expressly excluded from the Agency Regulations

Following the Directive, the Agency Regulations exclude three distinct categories of intermediaries.

First, certain "agents" cannot be regarded as "commercial agents" for the purpose of the Agency Regulations. They are officers of a company, an association or a partnership who have power to bind that company, association or partnership and insolvency practitioners and their equivalent in any other jurisdiction.[235]

Secondly, unpaid commercial agents, commercial agents who operate on commodity exchanges or in commodity markets and the Crown Agents for Overseas Government and Administrations or its subsidiaries,[236] are also expressly excluded from the scope of the Agency Regulations.

Thirdly, opting for the choice left in the Directive,[237] the Agency Regulations do not apply to "persons whose activities as commercial agents are regarded as secondary under English law".[238]

Whereas the first two sets of exclusions are self-explanatory and raise no real problem, the same cannot be said about the exclusion of persons whose activities as commercial agents are regarded as secondary. The main problem with this exclusion is that the Directive fails to define what amounts to a "secondary activity"; the matter is therefore left to be defined by the Agency Regulations.

233. [2004] Eu LR 423.
234. *Ibid*, at para 39.
235. Regulation 2(1).
236. Regulation 2(2).
237. Article 2(2) of the Directive.
238. Regulation 2(4).

A Schedule within the Agency Regulations serves that purpose.[239] However, the Schedule, which is "unhappily worded",[240] raises two distinct problems. First, there is no clear definition of what a secondary activity is. As a result, it is not immediately obvious what it means or how it should be assessed. This is serious as the precise scope of the Schedule is consequently uncertain. Secondly, there is some doubt as to whether the Schedule should be evaluated in the light of the protective stance of the Directive.

The meaning of "secondary activities" and how they should be assessed

The schedule

At first sight, the drafting of the Schedule looks very logical; it is composed of five paragraphs, each one serving a particular purpose.

Paragraph 1 appears to provide a general definition of what a secondary activity entails by stipulating that "the activities of a commercial agent are to be considered secondary where it may reasonably be taken that the primary purpose of the arrangement with his principal is other than as set out in paragraph 2 below".

Then, paragraph 2 provides a definition of agreements which are presumed to be non-secondary providing that certain criteria are met. They are as follows:

(a) the business of the principal is the sale, or as the case may be purchase, of goods of a particular kind; and
(b) the goods concerned are such that:
 (i) transactions are normally individually negotiated and concluded on a commercial basis, and
 (ii) procuring a transaction on one occasion is likely to lead to further transactions in those goods with that customer on future occasions, or to transactions in those goods with other customers in the same geographical area or among a group of customers, and that accordingly it is in the commercial interests of the principal in developing the market in those goods to appoint a representative to such customers with a view to the representative devoting effort, skill and expenditure from his own resources to that end.

Paragraph 3 complements paragraph 2 by providing a list of factors to help determine whether the activities of the commercial agent are secondary or not. If such factors are present, they are an indication that the commercial agent is covered by the Agency Regulations. If any factor is missing, that is an indication that the agreement is secondary. The factors are:

(a) the principal is the manufacturer, importer or the distributor of the goods;
(b) the goods are specifically identified with the principal in the market in question rather than, or to a greater extent than, with any other person;
(c) the agent devotes substantially the whole of his time to representative activities (whether or not for one principal or for a number of principals whose interests are not conflicting);
(d) the goods are not normally available in the market in question other than by means of the agent;
(e) the arrangement above is described as one of commercial agency.

239. Regulation 2(3).
240. *AMB Imballagi Srl* v. *Pacflex Ltd* [1999] 2 All ER (Comm) 249 at p 256c *per* Peter Gibson LJ.

Paragraph 4 provides a list of criteria indicating that an arrangement is secondary. They are as follows:

(a) promotional material is supplied direct to potential customers;
(b) persons are granted agencies without reference to existing agents in a particular area or in relation to a particular group;
(c) customers normally select the goods for themselves and merely place their orders through the agent.

Finally, paragraph 5 provides that the activities of mail order catalogue agents for consumer goods and consumer credit agents are presumed to be secondary. It is, however, a simple presumption.

The problems with the Schedule

The way the Schedule is drafted seems to mean that if an agreement falls within paragraph 2, using the indications under paragraphs 3 and 4 purely for the purpose of making the assessment, then it must be taken that the business is not secondary.[241] Paragraphs 2, 3 and 4 are therefore the core of the Schedule. However, paragraphs 2, 3 and 4 relate more to the nature of the trade in question, which is "a wholly different concept to whether the agent's activities as agents are primary or secondary".[242] This is a serious problem since the Schedule is therefore very difficult to apply.

The word "secondary" gives the impression that the determining factor to assess whether the activities as commercial agents are primary or secondary is purely numerical. However, certain case law seems to consider that the Schedule goes much further. The two possibilities must therefore be assessed in turn.

Secondary activities: a numerical assessment?

Following Regulation 2(3), the sole purpose of the Schedule is to determine when a person's activities as commercial agents are regarded as secondary. This will arise when the said commercial agent, alongside his representative activities also has other non-representative activities. Applying a numerical test therefore requires us to carry out some kind of comparison between the commercial agent's various activities in order to see which of the activities is predominant.

This is however where the weakness of the Schedule lie. As remarked obiter by Waller LJ in *AMB Imballagi Srl* v. *Pacflex Ltd*,[243]

> paragraphs 3 and 4 suggest pointers (. . .) as to whether an arrangement is within para 2, but provide no assistance as to what is being compared with what for the purpose of deciding what might be secondary as compared with what might be primary, nor any assistance as to whether other factors are excluded.[244]

Paragraph 1 of the Schedule seems to make the assessment by comparing the commercial agents' agency activities with other non-agency activities that he may have with a given principal, i.e. what has been termed as the vertical approach.[245] Yet, the DTI seemed

241. *AMB Imballagi Srl* v. *Pacflex Ltd* [1999] 2 All ER (Comm) 249, Waller LJ at p 254h.
242. *Ibid*, *per* Judge Raymond Jack QC at first instance in the QBD, unreported.
243. [1999] 2 All ER (Comm) 249.
244. *Ibid*, at p 254d.
245. See Morison J in *Tamarind International Ltd* v. *Eastern Natural Gas (Retail) Ltd* [2000] Eu LR 708.

to suggest that the comparison should be made between the commercial agent's agency activities and the rest of his other non-agency activities, i.e. what has been termed as the horizontal approach.[246] The question is which of the two approaches should apply. The choice between the two is important for the scope of the Schedule in order to see what it does not exclude.

If we apply the so-called vertical approach, the Schedule can only be used to exclude commercial agents who have, aside from their commercial agency activity, other non-agency activities with a given principal. This would arise, for example, if the principal appoints an intermediary to represent him as agent for the sale of certain goods and also appoints him as a distributor for other goods. This test is advantageous to the commercial agent since it considerably narrows down the scope of the Schedule. In fact, a commercial agent who represents several non-competing principals and does nothing else only carries out agency activities and consequently is not covered by the exclusion. This argument seems to be reinforced when looking at para 3(c) of the Schedule, which gives as a factor showing that the activities of a commercial agent are primary that "the agent devotes substantially the whole of his time to representative activities, whether or not for one principal or for a number of principals whose interests are not conflicting".

Likewise, under this vertical approach, the Schedule cannot apply to a situation where a commercial agent represents a given principal but also works for himself. This should not however be prejudicial to the principal because if the commercial agent spends more time on his own activities than he does on his commercial agency activities and this is to the detriment of the principal, then the commercial agent fails to act in the principal's interest. Failing to act in the principal's interest is a breach of the commercial agent's obligation of good faith, which would allow the principal to terminate the relationship without having to pay termination payments as per Regulation 18(b)(i).

If we apply the so-called horizontal test, then the scope of the Schedule is wider, since it can encompass the two scenarios mentioned above.

Even though we accept that the test to decide whether the activities of the commercial agent are secondary or not is numerical, other questions remain unanswered. First, at what point should it be considered whether the activities of the commercial agent are secondary, at the beginning of the relationship the commercial agent has with the principal or when the relationship ends? It has been argued that the test should be a continuing one.[247] We agree. Secondly, the Schedule provides no yardstick by which to measure what is secondary; should the assessment be carried out according to the time that a commercial agent spends on his representative activities or the amount of business he brings? Neither is very satisfactory, but it is thought that the latter should be taken into consideration.

There is very little conclusive case law on the Schedule, but in *Hunter* v. *Zenith Windows*[248] it was held that the question was to be decided by looking at the relationship between the principal and the agent rather than according to the whole of the agent's business. The same position was adopted obiter, in the case of *AMB Imballagi Plastici SRL* v. *Pacflex*.[249] It is thought to be correct as this test is in line with the protective stance of the Agency Regulations, which is important since it will prevent an unscrupulous principal from appointing several commercial agents and trying to use the Schedule to

246. DTI Guidance Notes, published in 1994. See Appendix 8.

247. F Randolph and J Davey, *Guide to the Commercial Agency Regulations*, (2nd edn, 2003), p 56.

248. Unreported but see appendix of S Singleton, *Commercial Agency Agreements*, (1998).

249. [1999] 2 All ER (Comm) 249.

avoid the Agency Regulations on the pretext that each commercial agent's activities are secondary. On that aspect, the outcome of the case of *Tamarind International Ltd* v. *Eastern Natural Gas (Retail) Ltd*[250] was right.

Following all these criticisms, the Schedule seems to create problems rather than solving them. In the case of *Lloyd Gailey* v. *Environmental Waste Control*,[251] Lord Drummond Young advocates that "the word 'secondary' may have a wider signification than a mere numerical comparison of the agent's activities as a commercial agent and his other activities".[252] Lord Drummond Young adds that, by such an evaluation, most of the criticisms of Waller LJ in the case of *AMB Imballagi* v. *Pacflex Ltd*[253] disappear and the Schedule becomes "reasonably intelligible".[254]

Secondary activities: more than a numerical evaluation?

In the case of *Lloyd Gailey* v. *Environmental Waste Control*,[255] the claimant was appointed to act as a commercial agent in order to sell waste handling and compacting equipment, for which he was entitled to receive a 50 per cent commission. The claimant also negotiated contracts called Facilities Management Contracts whereby the principal both supplied (but did not sell) the equipment to the customers and agreed to make a set number of collections of waste uplifts per annum. The claimant also received a 50 per cent commission on the net profit made by the defendants on such contracts. When the defendant terminated the relationship, the claimant sought compensation under Regulation 17(6).

The Outer House of the Court of Session rejected the claimant's plea, on the ground that his activities as a commercial agent were secondary and the Agency Regulations consequently did not apply. To decide that the word "secondary" had a wider meaning than a mere numerical comparison, Lord Drummond Young looked at the purpose behind the Directive. He stated that the "underlying mischief" of the Directive for protecting commercial agents is that they build up the goodwill for the principal. Since they cannot realise this goodwill for themselves, commercial agents are therefore in a vulnerable position, and hence they require protection.[256]

Lord Drummond Young added that the expression

> "activities as commercial agents" in article 2.2 (of the Directive) seems to point to activities that involve the underlying mischief. Where, accordingly this mischief is absent or of relatively limited significance, it is open to the legal system of a Member State to deem the agent's activities as a commercial agent to be secondary.[257]

Lord Drummond Young further stated that the essential test to decide whether commercial agents were protected by the Agency Regulations was to see whether the goodwill built by the commercial agent had accrued to the principal.[258] According to Lord Drummond Young "whether that occurs depends on the nature of the principal's business rather than

250. [2000] Eu LR 708.
251. [2004] Eu LR 423.
252. *Ibid*, at para 26.
253. [1999) 2 All ER (Comm) 249.
254. *Ibid*, at para 28.
255. [2004] Eu LR 423.
256. *Ibid*, at para 26.
257. Para 26.
258. *Ibid*, at para 39.

the agent's activities".[259] Lord Drummond Young finally stated that "it is the nature of the principal's business that should determine whether the agent's activities are primary or secondary. If that business is not predominantly one involving the sale of goods, I am of the opinion that the agent's activities are necessarily secondary".[260] Lord Drummond Young said so because he thought that commercial agents who deal with services do not build goodwill in the same sense as commercial agents who deal with goods.

A not dissimilar position was reached earlier by the Court of Appeal in the case of *Tamarind International Ltd* v. *Eastern Natural Gas (Retail) Ltd*.[261] In this instance Morison J, who gave the leading judgment, looked at the way the Agency Regulations dealt with the issue of secondary activities and concluded that in order to apply the Schedule, the court was required to enquire into the primary purpose of the commercial agency agreement and that this purpose was to be judged by reference to criteria defined in paragraph 2 of the Schedule through the help of indicators in paragraphs 3 and 4.[262] Morison J stated that he had to look at the nature of the commercial bargain between the parties. Morison J concentrated on whether the primary purpose of the agreement was to develop a defined market for the goods of the principal and concluded that, in this case, the purpose was met, that the commercial agents had substantially developed the market for Eastern Natural Gas, and hence the purpose was primary and the commercial agents could therefore claim protection of the Agency Regulations.

With respect, the positions taken by Morison J in *Tamarind International Ltd* v. *Eastern Natural Gas (Retail) Ltd*[263] and by Lord Drummond Young in *Lloyd Gailey* v. *Environmental Waste Control*[264] are thought to be incorrect. As mentioned earlier, the purpose behind the exclusion of persons whose activities as commercial agents are secondary arises when a commercial agent works for a principal in several different capacities besides the agency, as a distributor or even as an employee for instance. If this person spends more time on the other activities, then his commercial agency activities become secondary and therefore he is not protected by the Agency Regulations. This lack of protection is explained by the fact that, by spending more time on his own activities, the commercial agent does not act towards developing the customer base for the principal's goods, hence, does not deserve protection on termination.

In the two aforementioned cases of *Tamarind International Ltd* v. *Eastern Natural Gas (Retail) Ltd*[265] and *Lloyd Gailey* v. *Environmental Waste Control*,[266] the claimants were only working for the principal in one capacity, that of commercial agents. The question whether the activities were secondary should therefore not have arisen. The fact that in both instances the courts considered that to decide whether the commercial agent's representative activities were secondary depended purely on whether the principal's goodwill had been developed or not is too narrow a criterion (if indeed it is relevant at all). It is true that the rationale behind termination payments is that commercial agents use their marketing skills to develop the goodwill for the principal but this is not the purpose behind the exclusion of commercial agents whose representative activities are secondary activities.

259. *Ibid.*
260. *Ibid.*
261. [2000] Eu LR 708.
262. *Ibid*, at para 28.
263. [2000] Eu LR 708.
264. [2004] Eu LR 423.
265. [2000] Eu LR 708.
266. [2004] Eu LR 423.

To decide that the activities of a commercial agent are primary or secondary purely on whether he builds goodwill for the principal's goods will lead to too many commercial agents being excluded from the protection of the Agency Regulation. This goes against the protective stance of the Agency Regulations. Morison J himself in *Tamarind International Ltd* v. *Eastern Natural Gas (Retail) Ltd*, said that the exclusion provided by the Schedule must not go so far as "to remove the protection that the provisions of the Directive are intended to guarantee".[267] This brings us to the next question: does the Schedule have to be interpreted in the light of the protective stance of the Directive?

(ii) Is the Schedule interpreted outside the protective stance of the Directive?

As we have seen, the Schedule is an "almost impenetrable piece of drafting"[268] and seems the only one of its kind within the EU. The Directive provides no guidance on the meaning of the Schedule. It is in principle not possible for a national court, in litigation between private parties, to use the preliminary reference procedure under Article 234 of the EC Treaty to seek from the ECJ a preliminary ruling on whether national legislation purporting to implement an EC directive does indeed correctly implement the latter. The only way in which the ECJ could directly answer that question would be in proceedings brought by the EU institutions (i.e. the European Commission) under Article 226 of the EC Treaty (or conceivably by another Member State under Article 227) against the relevant Member State for failure to fulfil an obligation under the EC Treaty.

On the other hand, the questions posed by the national court in the request for the preliminary ruling can be phrased in such a way that the ECJ's answer should make it very easy for the national court to make such a finding (something along the lines of "Article X of the directive has been implemented by regulation Y of the national implementing legislation. The drafting of regulation Y indicates that the national legislator thinks Article X means (a . . . b . . . c . . .). Is that the (or a) correct interpretation of Article X?"). The ECJ, for its part, if it considers the questions posed to it in the reference from the national court are impermissible, will reformulate them if necessary. Further, the ECJ is often not averse to dropping some pretty strong hints in its Article 234 preliminary rulings that a particular provision of national legislation is not compatible with EC law.[269] So it should be possible, in practice, to persuade the ECJ to express a view as to whether the Directive permits the UK to include the Schedule in the Agency Regulations. In the Scottish case of *Lloyd Gailey* v. *Environmental Waste Control*,[270] Lord Drummond Young said that there is no obligation to interpret the Schedule in the light of EU legislation at all.[271] Lord Drummond Young's argument is that the provisions of the Schedule were enacted following the provisions of article 2(2) of the Directive whereby Member States can exclude from their national implementing legislations commercial agents whose activities are regarded as secondary by domestic law. Lord Drummond Young adds that provided that the relevant domestic legislation does not go beyond the scope of article 2(2) of the

267. [2000] Eu LR 708, at para 21(3).

268. *AMB Imballagi Plastici* v. *Pacflex Ltd* [1999] 2 All ER (Comm) 249, at 250h, *per* Waller LJ.

269. See, for example, ECJ case C–221/89 *R.* v. *Secretary of State for Transport, ex p. Factortame Ltd ("Factortame (No. 3)")*, [1992] QB 680, [1991] ECR I–3905. See further J Steiner and L Woods, *Textbook on EC Law* (OUP, 8th edn, 2003), pp 548–551 and, for more detail, DWK Anderson and M Demetriou, *References to the European Court* (Sweet & Maxwell, 2nd edn, 2002), Ch. 4.

270. [2004] Eu LR 423

271. Para 30.

Directive, Member States have complete discretion as to how they define what is secondary.[272]

With respect, this is not entirely true. As remarked by Morison J in *Tamarind International* v. *Eastern Natural Gas Ltd*,[273] "article 2(2) (of the Directive) permits Member States to derogate from the protection which the Directive is intended to confer on commercial agents".[274] However, relying on the European Court Ruling in the case of *Barbara Bellone* v. *Yokohama*,[275] Morison J adds that "such a derogation must not substantially frustrate the purpose of the Directive itself and in practice remove the protection that the provisions of the Directive are intended to guarantee".[276] This is important as it seems to mean that if the Schedule removes the protection of the Agency Regulations from too wide a category of commercial agents, then this frustrates the purpose of the Directive itself.

On that basis, the Schedule must be interpreted in the light of the protective stance of the Directive. A better solution still would be to have a complete overhaul of the Schedule.

2.4.3 The making of a commercial agency agreement

At common law, a commercial agency relationship will invariably be created by a contract.[277] The relevant contract law rules will therefore apply.[278] The Agency Regulations have not brought any changes to such rules since they require no specific formality; a relationship will still be valid only through the consent of the parties. However, it seems that a direct contract is required, which excludes sub-agents.[279]

The existence of a commercial agency contract is nevertheless accepted even when entered into orally, in which case the commercial agent is protected. This was made clear by the European Court of Justice in the case of *Centrosteel Srl* v. *Adipol GmbH*.[280] The lack of formality is in line with the protective stance of the Directive and the Agency Regulations will consequently apply from the first day of the contract.[281] Should the parties wish, they can of course enter their contract in writing, and it will invariably be prudent to do so, but the choice is theirs.[282] Regulation 13 allows either party to require the other to provide a signed written document setting out the terms of the agreement including any variation. It is crucial to note that post-termination restraint of trade clauses binding on the commercial agent will be valid only if they are "concluded in writing", which is something different from a written statement of orally agreed terms.[283] It is therefore strongly advised to the parties to enter the contract in writing.

272. *Ibid*.
273. [2000] Eu LR 708.
274. *Ibid*, para 21(3).
275. [1998] ECR I–2191.
276. [2000] Eu LR 708, para 21(3).
277. See FMB Reynolds, *Bowstead and Reynolds on Agency*, (17th edn, 2001), article 7, p 44.
278. For details of rules on formation of contracts, see the relevant chapters in G H Treitel, *The law of contract*, (11th edn, 2003).
279. *Light and others* v. *Ty Europe Ltd* [2003] EWCA Civ, 25 July 2003, [2003] All ER (D) 445. For details, see section 2.4.2.1.
280. Case C–456/98 [2000] ECR I–6007.
281. This means that the principal cannot impose a probation period for instance.
282. Regulation 13.
283. Regulation 20(1)(a). For details, see Chapter 7, section 7.1.

2.5 CONCLUSION

The Commercial Agents (Council Directive) Regulations 1993[284] implement EC Council Directive 86/653.[285] The Directive is based on the civil-law rationale that commercial agents are in need of protection against their principals. When the Agency Regulations came into effect on 1 January 1994, they created considerable confusion because they contradict two of the most fundamental tenets of the common law rules of agency; (1) that commercial agents had not until that point been recognised as a separate category from other agents, and (2) that because agents are in a fiduciary position towards their principals, the latter are the ones perceived to be in need of protection.

The confusion was considerably heightened by the fact that the Agency Regulations copy the Directive almost word for word. The near-verbatim implementation causes serious problems at two different levels.

First, it creates what we refer to as an "internal uncertainty", i.e. uncertainty within the Agency Regulations themselves. Council Directives are not legislation *per se*, they are not directly applicable and their purpose is simply to provide a set of guidelines on a particular issue.[286] As a result, Directives are not "drafted with the attention to detail and the need to avoid ambiguity and inconsistency which is required in a piece of legislation".[287] This "internal uncertainty" is exacerbated by the fact that the Directive, being the result of political compromise, is full of vague and imprecise terms. By almost replicating the Directive, the Agency Regulations incorporate such weaknesses.

Secondly, the Directive, and therefore the Agency Regulations, are not a complete guide regulating every aspect of the relationship between commercial agents and their principals. The common law rules of agency and contract are not displaced and will consequently still apply. Yet, the Agency Regulations and the common law rules being based on two opposed rationales, the relationship between the two sets of rules is not easy. This is what we refer as the "external uncertainty".

Such a double layer of uncertainty which surrounds the Agency Regulations is serious since it undermines their protective stance. The main purpose of this chapter is therefore twofold: (1) to understand the content and scope of the Agency Regulations themselves in order to (2) see how such rules dovetail with the more traditional position of the common law rules of agency. Only then can we have a complete picture of the impact of the Agency Regulations.

By applying specifically to commercial agents, the Agency Regulations effectively create a separate legal category of agents where none existed before. To understand who commercial agents are and what they do is therefore of crucial importance in order to delineate the scope of application of the Agency Regulations, but also, more importantly, to help us understand why commercial agents need the level of protection that the Agency Regulations provide them with. This chapter therefore first had to place the Agency Regulations in their European and civil law context. To that effect, this chapter has shown that the civil law rationale for protecting commercial agents on termination is essentially

284. SI 1993/3173. For details, see fn 2 above.

285. Directive 86/653 on the co-ordination of the profession of self-employed commercial agents, OJ L 382/17, 31 December 1986.

286. R Christou, *International agency, distribution and licensing agreements*, (4th edn, 2003), para 3.07, p 87.

287. *Ibid.*

based on an economic consideration.[288] Commercial agents are professionals who are used by manufacturers or importers who want to create, expand and/or merely maintain a market for their goods. Commercial agents therefore do not act for themselves, but for a principal, hence, the goodwill they create, expand or merely maintain for the principal's goods remains with the latter. Commercial agents are consequently financially weaker than their principals and therefore, so the reasoning goes, in need of protection on termination. This chapter shows that, although the civil law rationale behind the termination payments was not understood when the Agency Regulations first came into effect, they are now well understood by the courts of this country.[289]

To understand who commercial agents are and what commercial function they perform[290] is also of crucial importance in order to differentiate commercial agents from other commercial intermediaries. This consequently further refines the scope of the implementing legislation. In this context, this Chapter has shown that commercial agents are first and foremost independent contractors, which distinguishes them from employees. Their independent status gives commercial agents a considerable level of freedom in the way they set up their commercial agency business and the way they conduct such a business. We have seen that by applying traditional common law rules, the courts in this country decided that commercial agents can be a legal entity as well as a physical person and still be protected by the Agency Regulations.[291] As independent contractors, commercial agents enjoy a certain amount of control over the way they conduct their business. They can therefore decide to carry out all the representative activities themselves if it is a small venture, or they can choose to delegate some of their tasks if the size of the agency demands it. This chapter has shown that, so far, the relationship between the common law rules and the Agency Regulations are reasonably compatible and therefore do not raise problems.

In relation to the commercial role that commercial agents play, the Agency Regulations only stipulate that they will "negotiate and/or negotiate and conclude transactions on behalf of the principal" as per regulation 2(1). However, the Agency Regulations did not provide details as to what "to negotiate" entails in practice. Thanks to the courts' interpretation, it is now clear that this refers to the marketing function of the negotiation and promotion of the principal's goods. However, in the absence of a clear definition, neither was it clear where the negotiation "threshold" stood. Case law shows that the threshold is quite low since canvassing and introducing agents are covered by the Agency Regulations.[292] In addition, it is also clear that commercial agents must play some kind of active role towards the creation and/or the development of a customer base for the principal.[293] Mere order-takers are consequently not covered by the Agency Regulations.

Even though so far the impact of the Agency Regulations seems to have been reasonably smooth, this chapter has also shown that the situation is not perfect. The near-verbatim implementation of the Directive has raised several questions. First, in relation to

288. For details, see section 2.2.2.

289. See the comment of Lord Drummond Young in *Lloyd Gailey* v. *Environmental Waste* [2004] Eu LR 423, at para 24.

290. See section 2.3 generally.

291. *Tigana Ltd* v. *Decoro Ltd* [2003] EWHC 23, [2003] Eu LR 189.

292. *Tamarind International Ltd and others* v. *Eastern Natural Gas Ltd* [2000] Eu LR 708.

293. *Parks* v. *Esso Petroleum Company Ltd* [2000] Tr LR 232.

sub-agents, following the case of *Light and Others* v. *Ty Europe*,[294] they seem not to be protected by the Agency Regulations.

Secondly, in relation to commercial agents who deal with combined supplies of goods and services, they appear to be in a similar weaker position following the Scottish case of *Lloyd Gailey* v. *Environmental Waste*.[295]

Thirdly, the most serious problem seems to be in relation to the issue of secondary activities. Following the choice left in the Directive, the UK has opted for the possibility to exclude from the ambit of the Agency Regulations, commercial agents whose commercial agency activities are secondary. However, the Agency Regulations do so by adding a Schedule, which is an "almost impenetrable piece of drafting".[296] As a result, it is far from clear what secondary means or how it is to be assessed. The word "secondary" seems to indicate that a numerical evaluation between agency and non-agency activities of the commercial agent could be used. However, recent decisions by the English[297] and Scottish[298] courts seem to apply the Schedule in a much wider manner than a numerical assessment. The courts essentially look at whether the primary purpose of the arrangement between the commercial agent and his principal is to develop a customer base for the principal's goods, in which case, the commercial agent will be protected. If this interpretation is correct, it raises the question whether the Schedule, by potentially excluding from the Agency Regulations a whole category of commercial agents, is not in fact frustrating the protective purpose of the Directive. We have advocated certain solutions, but, as they have not been tested by the courts, they are still surrounded by uncertainty.

For the commercial agents who are covered by the Agency Regulations, they must comply with the obligations as defined in their contract. However, following the rules on performance as defined in the Agency Regulations, the commercial agents are also bound by an obligation of good faith.[299] This obligation binds their principals with the same strength.[300] This is the first time that such an overriding requirement is introduced in the common law,[301] its impact is therefore unclear. Considering that the Agency Regulations fail to define what it means or what it entails for each party, it must be reviewed in the next chapter.

294. [2003] EWCA Civ, 25 July 2003, [2003] All ER (D) 445.

295. Unreported.

296. Waller LJ in *AMB Imballagi Plastici* v. *Pacflex Ltd* [1999] 2 All ER (Comm) 249, at 250h.

297. *Tamarind International Ltd and others* v. *Eastern Natural Gas Ltd* [2000] Eu LR 708.

298. *Lloyd Gailey* v. *Environmental Waste* [2004] Eu LR 423.

299. Regulation 3(1).

300. Regulation 4(1).

301. Even though good faith is present in the Unfair Terms in Consumer Contracts Regulations 1999 (SI 99/2083), implementing Directive 93/13 on Unfair Terms in Consumer Contracts, OJ L. 95/29, it is only used as a tool by the courts in order to decide whether a term is unfair or not.

CHAPTER 3

PERFORMANCE OF THE COMMERCIAL AGENCY CONTRACT

3.1 INTRODUCTION

The law in England and Wales in this area currently represents a rather complicated amalgam.

First and foremost, since the relationship of commercial agency is one of contract, what the contract says, through its express and implied terms, will be the essential starting point. As we shall show, however, the Agency Regulations (where they apply) imply some crucially important terms of a mandatory nature and are very capable of overriding express contract terms, especially where the exercise of discretions by either party is concerned. In our view, accordingly, where the Agency Regulations apply, it is no longer prudent to assume that one can rely on a commercial agency agreement to be necessarily fully enforceable in accordance with its terms.

There is a significant body of law pre-dating the Agency Regulations dealing with the relationship of agent and principal generally (i.e. not specific to the commercial agency context, which, of course, prior to the Agency Regulations, was not recognised as a separate category of agent at all[1]). That includes both rules established at common law and equitable rules based on the classification of the agent as fiduciary. This body of law is what will apply as the default rules in those situations where or to the extent that the Agency Regulations (for whatever reason) do not apply. To those agency relationships to which the Agency Regulations do apply, this body of law remains relevant, since the obligations of principal and agent to each other set out in the Agency Regulations are phrased in very general terms and certainly leave gaps. The relationship between this continuing body of law and the Agency Regulations has, in most respects, not been worked out. In situations where the Agency Regulations apply, a degree of caution similar to that appropriate to evaluating express terms in commercial agency agreements is called for when considering the application of these rules.

The provisions of the Agency Regulations dealing with performance of the commercial agency contract are in Part II ("Rights and obligations") and Part III ("Remuneration"). Of the two, Part II is by far the more important. Part III largely (though not entirely) yields to contrary agreement (and the parties, if they have agreed on little else, will generally have agreed on the rate of commission, on which transactions it is to be paid, and when it is to be paid).[2] As Part III is the more discrete of the two in its application, we shall deal with it separately in Chapter 4 and make no preliminary comment on it at this point.

1. See Chapter 2 above.
2. See Chapter 4 below.

Part II represents a very substantial improvement on the commercial agent's protection from the traditional common law rules, since it establishes mandatory and reciprocal rights and duties, which place the parties on a much more equal footing than was previously the case in English law. The most significant change is undeniably the introduction of the civil-law inspired obligation of good faith, imposed on the principal as well as on the commercial agent. This change is fundamental for the latter's protection compared with his position under the traditional common law rules. Yet the precise impact of the notion of mutual good faith is unclear as the Agency Regulations, by copying the Directive word for word, fail to explain what it means and what it entails for the parties. The DTI Guidance Notes on the Agency Regulations of September 1994[3] simply say, in relation to the agent's duty of good faith, that it "in effect restates the duties owed at common law by an agent to his principal" and, in relation to the principal's duty of good faith, that "it is thought that these duties merely amplify the position at common law".[4] While there is a degree of truth in that statement in relation to the commercial agent's position, it is pretty clear that the position of principals is very different where the Agency Regulations apply as opposed to where they do not. The highly pervasive quality of the mutual obligations of good faith, throughout all aspects of the commercial agency relationship, should not be under-estimated. We consider that their full impact has yet to be recognised in the UK. There has to date been hardly any judicial consideration of the mandatory obligation of good faith under the Agency Regulations. As we shall show, however, we consider that analogies with other areas of English law (especially individual employment law) provide a very fruitful source of guidance on what the obligations of good faith under the Agency Regulations mean. This is not the only aspect of the Agency Regulations where analogies with employment law are helpful, as, taking a "high level" view, the lump sum payments to which the commercial agent is entitled on termination in some ways resemble (rather loosely, it must be said) compensation for unfair dismissal pursuant to statute.[5]

It will be interesting to see in the future whether and, if so, to what extent the rules now applicable to commercial agents where the Agency Regulations apply percolate out into applying to agency in situations where the Agency Regulations do not apply. Such a development, bit by bit, would not surprise us.

For the present, however, since commercial agency agreements are contracts, we shall first set out typical key express terms for such an agreement. We shall then examine the English law applicable apart from the Agency Regulations, and then consider those parts of the Agency Regulations which apply to performance of the agency agreement, and then consider the relationship between the two.

3.2. KEY EXPRESS TERMS OF A COMMERCIAL AGENCY AGREEMENT (OTHER THAN AS TO REMUNERATION)

The following, by way of example only, is a typical starting point for the obligations of the parties under a commercial agency agreement for the sale of goods in a territory

3. Appendix 8
4. *Ibid.*
5. See Scholes and Blane, "Agency agreements: new protections for commercial agents", PLC, IV(10) (October 1993), 31 at p 42.

outside the principal's normal area of trading. It is somewhat pro-principal, but a typical starting point. There are many such agreements in use which have terms along these lines.

3.2.1 The agent's express obligations

The Agent undertakes and agrees with the Principal at all times during the term of the agency agreement:

To act towards the Principal conscientiously and in good faith and not to allow its interests to conflict with the duties that it owes to the Principal under this agreement and the general law.

Except as authorised by the Principal, not to act in any way which will incur any liabilities on behalf of the Principal nor to pledge the credit of the Principal.

To comply with all reasonable and lawful instructions of the Principal from time to time concerning the marketing and sale of the products in the allocated territory, and generally to carry out its agency in such manner as it thinks best to promote the interests of the Principal.

To use its best/reasonable endeavours to promote and sell the products in the allocated territory with all due care and diligence, to seek to improve the Principal's goodwill in the allocated territory, and (but only on the Principal's standard terms and conditions of sale unless specifically authorised otherwise by the Principal) without prior reference to the Principal to [negotiate][negotiate, conclude and enter into] contracts for the sale of the products in the name of and on behalf of the Principal.

To act in accordance with sound commercial principles in its relations with customers and potential customers in the allocated territory (including as to assessing, and where appropriate obtaining independent assessments of their creditworthiness) and to do nothing which the Principal considers could be prejudicial to its goodwill or commercial interests.

To describe itself in all dealings with the products and in all associated advertising and promotional material and (if any description is provided there) at its premises as "sales agent" or "selling agent" of the Principal.

To maintain at its own expense appropriate offices, stores and display and administration facilities and systems as may be necessary for the effective performance of its duties under this agreement.

To employ a sufficient number of suitably qualified dedicated personnel to ensure the proper fulfilment of the Agent's obligations under this agreement, including without limitation attending (on reasonable notice) meeting with the Principal to discuss the marketing and selling of the products in the allocated territory, attending trade exhibitions and other sales outlets as appropriate, and making regular and sufficiently frequent calls on customers or potential customers to promote the products.

To keep the Principal fully informed of its activities concerning the promotion and sale of the products and to provide the Principal with reports on request.

To keep the Principal fully and promptly informed of conditions and developments in the market for and use of the products in the allocated territory (whether advantageous or disadvantageous to the Principal), of competing products and the activities of the principal's competitors in the allocated territory and to perform market research accordingly.

To keep the Principal fully and promptly informed of its anticipated volumes of sales of the products so that the Principal may supply to the Agent sufficient volumes of stock of the products to meet customers" requirements in a timely manner.

Promptly to inform the Principal of any order or enquiry concerning orders for the products received for supply outside the allocated territory.

To inform the Principal promptly of any complaint or after-sales enquiry concerning the products received by the Agent.

To maintain a list of customers and potential customers for the products in the allocated territory from time to time, and on request to supply the Principal with an up-to-date copy of that list.

To use any samples of the products only for disposal free of charge to customers or potential customers for the products in the allocated territory and for the purpose of promoting sales of the products there.

To keep all stocks of the products which it holds or which are under its control in conditions notified to and approved by the Principal or (in the absence of such notification) which are appropriate for their storage and security all at its own cost, stored separately from other goods and clearly indicated as belonging to the Principal.

At its own expense to insure and keep insured all of the Principal's property which may at any time be in the Agent's possession, custody or control with a reputable insurer to its full replacement value against all the risks for which a prudent trader would insure his own property of the same type, to show to the Principal on demand the policy document and the most recent receipt for premium, to perform any obligation required of it under the terms of such insurance, to do nothing which could invalidate any such insurance, and to pay to the Principal promptly on receipt the proceeds of any insurance claim made in respect thereof, holding the same pending such payment in the trust bank account referred to below.

To issue invoices to customers (in a form suitable for value added tax or other sales tax purposes) in respect of the sale of products under this agreement, and to receive payment for the same.

To take such action as the Principal may from time to time request to seek to collect the debts owing to the Principal by customers in the allocated territory or to assist the Principal in taking such action, but not to take any such action without the Principal's prior instructions.

To collect and hold as trustee in a separate bank account [in the name of the agent but designated as a trust account for the Principal's benefit] all moneys due to the Principal in respect of sales or otherwise (except for any remitted directly by the customer to the Principal), to transfer the same to the Principal [with/without deduction of commission and reimbursable expenses] on the agreed dates, and to account on demand to the Principal for any interest earned on credit balances from time to time in that account.

Not without prior reference to the Principal (and then only acting on the Principal's express instructions) on behalf of the principal to take part in any dispute or commence or defend any court or other dispute proceedings or settle or attempt to settle or make any admission concerning any such proceedings.

To indemnify the Principal against any liabilities incurred by the Principal as a result of the Agent breaching any law from time to time in force in the allocated territory or the incurring of which is otherwise not authorised by the Principal.

To allow the Principal's authorised representative at any reasonable time to have access to the Agent's premises (or to arrange for the Principal's authorised representatives to have access to other relevant premises) for the purposes of inspecting the Agent's books and records and for inspecting or taking stock of or possession of any of the Principal's property which is in the Agent's possession, custody or control.[6]

3.2.2 The principal's express obligations

The Principal undertakes and agrees with the Agent during the term of this agreement:

To act at all times in its relations with the Agent dutifully and in good faith.

To pay the commission calculated in the agreed manner and on the agreed dates.

Subject to the following, and provided the Agent performs its obligations under this agreement, to indemnify the Agent against any liabilities which the Agent may incur as a result of acting with reasonable care and skill within the scope of its authority under this agreement as agent for the Principal. Everyday expenses, costs and charges incurred by the Agent in performing this agreement will be reimbursed by the Principal up to a maximum of £[x] per quarter against production by the Agent of appropriate invoices and receipts in support. Before incurring any expense, cost or charge which would result in that threshold being exceeded, the Agent shall seek the Principal's express approval.

To supply to the Agent:

At the Principal's own expense, such samples sales literature and other documentation and information and such technical market and other support as the Agent may from time to time

6. Taken with some adaptation (and with consent) from Scholes, Agency, in (ed.) Battersby, *Commercial Contracts*, Vol 1: *Marketing contracts and sales finance*, (Legal & Commercial Publishing Ltd, 2004)

reasonably require for the purposes of promoting and selling the Products and to enable it properly and efficiently to discharge its duties under this agreement; and

Stocks of the products delivered to the Agent's premises at the Principal's expense in such volumes as the Principal may decide and (subject to causes not within the Principal's control) to replenish that stock as necessary.

Within a reasonable period of becoming aware of the same, and subject to its rights hereunder, to perform any contracts for the sale of products made on its behalf by the Agent under this agreement.

Promptly and efficiently to deal with any complaint, dispute or after-sales enquiry relating to the products raised by a customer in the allocated territory.

Where appropriate, to inform the Agent within a reasonable time if any contract concluded on its behalf by the Agent will not be performed by it, and of the reason for such non-performance.

To give the Agent reasonable notice if at any time it expects that the volume of sales of the products will be significantly lower than the volume that the Agent would expect under normal circumstances.[7]

3.3 THE RIGHTS AND OBLIGATIONS IN ENGLISH LAW OF THE PARTIES TO A COMMERCIAL AGENCY AGREEMENT, APART FROM THE AGENCY REGULATIONS

These rules exist apart from the Agency Regulations, though, as noted above and as will be expanded below, they are to some extent affected by them. They remain relevant in those situations where the Agency Regulations do not apply to the relationship at all,[8] and, in situations where the Agency Regulations do apply, are there to fill the gaps (though one should be aware that they may be affected by the Agency Regulations, particularly given the highly pervasive and mandatory mutual obligations of good faith in Regulations 3 and 4). Given that the common law and equity, prior to the Agency Regulations, did not recognise commercial agents (nor, for that matter, any other type of agent) as a special class of agent, all the legal rules are of general application and can therefore only be dealt with in very general terms.[9]

As a general comment, in "classical" English law, the agent owes the principal important obligations but enjoys relatively few rights in return.

3.3.1. The agent's obligations to the principal in English law, apart from the Agency Regulations

In most cases, as noted above, the agency contract will be the main source of the rights and obligations of the parties. Unlike in the case of, for example, employment contracts, at common law relatively few terms are generally taken as implied into an agency agreement,[10] but the same tests for implying a term apply as in contract law generally.[11] To the extent that provable express terms of the agreement do not specifically regulate matters (and in the case of an oral agency agreement, that would be to a very large extent), the applicable rules are as follows. We shall first deal with those that arise from the

7. *Ibid.*
8. See Chapter 2, in particular section 2.3.2.
9. In this vein, see FMB Reynolds, *Bowstead and Reynolds on Agency*, (17th edn, 2001), para 6–001
10. R Bradgate, *Commercial Law*, (3rd edn, 2000), p 176.
11. As to which see *Chitty on Contracts*, (ed) H Beale (29th edn, 2004), ch 13.

common law, and then deal with those having their origins in the rules of equity, i.e. the fiduciary rules.

3.3.1.1 At common law

The common law rules of agency impose two main duties on the agent:

— the duty to perform according to the terms of the contract and to obey instructions; and
— the duty to exercise reasonable care, skill and diligence.

3.3.1.1.1 The agent's duty to perform according to the terms of the contract and to obey instructions

The first common law duty requires the agent (1) to act only within the limit of his actual express and implied authority, and (2) to obey instructions.[12] The latter part applies to express and implied instructions as long as they are lawful[13] and reasonable. Reasonable instructions are instructions which would not take the agent outside the scope of what he had originally contracted with the principal to do, unless he has subsequently agreed a variation to the scope of the contract (e.g. an instruction to act outside the territory allocated to him under the agency agreement or an instruction to handle a type of product not within the product range on which he was originally instructed). There could conceivably be instructions which, even though they are within the scope of the original mandate, would nevertheless be unreasonable (e.g. an instruction by the principal to the agent to visit a potential customer who is within the allocated territory but where going there would involve the agent in great personal danger because the customer's location has become a war zone). Beyond these fairly obvious limits, what is reasonable depends on all the circumstances, including in particular on market practice in the sector concerned.

Failing to obey the principal's lawful and reasonable instructions, the agent will be contractually liable to the principal. What of the situation where the principal gives the agent an instruction which, although within the scope of what the agent has agreed to do, the agent considers unwise or misguided? The agent may well be under a duty to advise and to warn the principal of what he sees as the pitfalls (especially if he was chosen as agent in the first place because of some particular expertise or, perhaps, if during the term of the agency relationship the agent has habitually given advice to the principal so that a duty to advise may have become part of the contract by a course of dealing when it was not part of the relationship at the start). But if the principal nevertheless repeats the instructions, disregarding any advice or warnings from the agent, the agent must follow the instructions (provided always that they are reasonable and lawful) or be in breach of contract and risk (depending on the terms) either a damages claim or a termination.[14] One could envisage circumstances where for the principal to persist in an instruction in the face of very serious warnings from the agent could be unreasonable, but one would have thought they would have to be extreme.

12. *Turpin* v. *Bilton* (1843) 5 Man & G 455.

13. See for instance cases on placing bets: *Cohen* v. *Kittel* (1889) 22 QBD 680 on the non-liability of an agent sued by the principal for failing to place bets; *Tatam* v. *Reeve* [1893] 1 QB 44 on the non-liability of the principal for failure to reimburse expenses of an agent who had placed a bet.

14. *Bowstead and Reynolds on Agency* (17th edn, 2001), para 6–003.

The agent will similarly be in breach of contract if (which, as noted above,[15] is possible in English law) he enters into a transaction which binds the principal where he had no actual authority to do that. This can arise where he had no such actual authority but a reasonable person dealing with him has the impression that he did have authority to conclude the transaction (e.g. because the agent had actual authority from the principal to enter into transactions up to a certain value only, the agent nevertheless enters into a transaction of a greater value, and the person dealing with the agent knew he had some actual authority from the principal but was not aware of the limitation[16]).

If the instructions are ambiguous, the agent must ask the principal to explain.[17] However, should the agent fail to ask for clarification, the principal will nevertheless be bound by a fair and reasonable interpretation of his instructions by the agent.[18] In an age of modern communications, it would be reasonable to expect the agent to question ambiguous instructions more than in the past. While the former part of the obligation applies equally to paid and unpaid agents, the latter varies when the agent acts gratuitously.[19] Considering that the Agency Regulations do not apply to unpaid agents,[20] this aspect of the common law rules will, of course, have no impact on commercial agents.

Where the Agency Regulations apply, it is hard to see that the agent's obligation under Regulation 3(2)(c) (a subset of the agent's obligations of good faith thereunder) "to comply with reasonable instructions given by the principal", is any different from the agent's obligations at common law.

3.3.1.1.2 The agent's duty to exercise reasonable care, skill and diligence

The duty to use skill, care and diligence when performing the duties is a rare example of an implied obligation of the agent[21] when the relationship is contractual. Such a duty is of extreme importance and its operation is closely regulated at common law[22] and by statute.[23] As such, this duty applies equally to all agents regardless whether they are paid or not since both types of agent must act with reasonable care.[24] On general principles, the duty of care and skill can be enforced against the commercial agent either in contract or in tort.[25] Any exclusions of the duty of care or exclusions or limitations of liability for breach of it will, in the normal way, need to meet the requirements of the Unfair Contract Terms Act, i.e. that liability for death or personal injury caused by negligence cannot be excluded and that liability for other types of loss can only be excluded or restricted if and to the extent that the exclusion meets the UCTA requirement of reasonableness.[26]

15. See Chapter 2, section 2.2.1.

16. R Bradgate, op cit, fn 10, pp 144/145.

17. *Woodhouse AC Israel Cocoa Ltd SA* v. *Nigerian Produce Marketing Co Ltd* [1972] AC 741 affirming [1971] 2 QB 23; *European Asian Bank AG* v. *Punjab & Sind Bank (No 2)* [1983] 2 All ER 508.

18. *Ireland* v. *Livingstone* (1872) LR 5 HL 395.

19. For an example of a variation of liability when the agent acts gratuitously, see *Chaudry* v. *Prabakhar* [1988] 3 All ER 178.

20. Regulation 2(2)(a).

21. *Turpin* v. *Bilton* (1843) 5 Man & G 455.

22. See *Henderson* v. *Merrett Syndicates Ltd* [1995] 2 AC 145 where a contract between names at Lloyd's and their agents who managed underwriting business contained a term giving the agent "absolute discretion" for the performance of his functions. The HL held that such a clause did not exclude the agents' obligation to act with reasonable care.

23. Unfair Contract Terms Act 1977, s 2.

24. However, what is reasonable may vary with the circumstances, *Chaudry* v. *Prabakhar* [1988] 3 All ER 178.

25. *Midland Bank Trust Co Ltd* v. *Hett Stubbs & Kemp* [1979] Ch 384.

26. As to which, see s 3 and Sched 2 UCTA 1977.

The standard of care and skill required of the agent is what would be reasonable to expect of an agent in all the circumstances of the particular case. He must take reasonable steps, for example, to check on the creditworthiness and reliability of potential customers and to perform market research if this is expected of him; must take reasonable steps to establish what the best price for the principal's products reasonably obtainable from time to time in the market would be; etc. He is not, however, strictly liable if things go wrong. He does not, unless the agency is of the del credere type, guarantee that the customer will perform the contract between customer and principal. His obligation is to take reasonable care, no more than that.

Where the Agency Regulations apply, it is hard to see that the commercial agent's obligation "to make proper efforts to negotiate and, where appropriate, conclude the transactions he is instructed to take care of" adds anything to the agent's common law duties in this respect.[27]

3.3.1.2 Fiduciary duties

3.3.1.2.1 Generally

Fiduciary duties are different from common law ones; they are far more stringent since an agent can be liable even though he was acting in good faith.[28]

The crucial feature of agency in English law is the fiduciary nature of the relationship, based on the premise (in marked contrast to the starting point in mainland European civil law, where the assumption is that at least a commercial agent is the weaker party in the relationship) that the principal is the vulnerable party and the party in need of protection. As noted in Chapter 2, this follows from the apparent fusion in English law of the persons of the agent and the principal and the ability in English law of the agent to bind the principal even where the agent is acting beyond the scope of his authority.[29] The concern about the principal's vulnerability is very clearly articulated by Mason J in the High Court of Australia in his judgment in *Hospital Products Ltd* v. *United States Surgical Corporation*. Although this is an Australian case (and so, strictly of persuasive authority only in England and Wales) we consider it to be a correct statement of much relevance to the law here. Mason J took the minority view that an exclusive distributor could have fiduciary obligations to its supplier of goods, at least insofar as the supplier's goodwill was concerned:

> The accepted fiduciary relationships are sometimes referred to as relationships of trust and confidence or confidential relations (cf. *Phipps* v. *Boardman*), viz, trustee and beneficiary, agent and principal solicitor and client, employee and employer, director and company, and partners. The critical feature of these relationships is that the fiduciary undertakes or agrees to act for or on behalf of or in the interests of another person in the exercise of a power or a discretion which will affect the interests of that other person in a legal or practical sense. The relationship between the parties is therefore one which gives the fiduciary a special opportunity to exercise the power or discretion to the detriment of that other person who is accordingly vulnerable to abuse by the fiduciary of his position . . . It is partly because the fiduciary's exercise of the power or discretion can adversely affect the interests of the person to whom the duty is owed and because the latter is at the mercy of

27. Regulation 3(2)(a)

28. See however recent developments which seem to show a relaxation of the rules in agency in commercial contracts: *Kelly* v. *Cooper* [1993] AC 205 and *Yasuda Fire and Marine Company of Europe Ltd* v. *Orion Marine Inc Underwriting Agency Ltd* [1995] QB 174.

29. For details, see Chapter 2, section 2.1.

the former that the fiduciary comes under a duty to exercise his power or discretion in the interests of the person to whom it is owed . . . [30]

A classic general formulation of fiduciary obligations is that of Lord Herschell in *Bray* v. *Ford*:[31]

. . . a person in a fiduciary position . . . is not, unless otherwise expressly provided, entitled to make a profit; he is not allowed to put himself in a position where his interest and duty conflict.

For present purposes, the following important qualifications need to be added to this.

Firstly, the precise scope and content of fiduciary obligations take their colour from their context, and have to be viewed as part of the particular relationship in question. In the words of Lord Upjohn in *Phipps* v. *Boardman*:[32]

Rules of equity have to be applied to such a great diversity of circumstances that they can be stated only in the most general terms and applied with particular attention to the exact circumstances of each case.

Accordingly, the simple use of the label "fiduciary" says nothing precise about the nature of the fiduciary duties which will arise in the relationship. The point is clearly made by Lord Browne-Wilkinson in *Henderson* v. *Merrett Syndicates Ltd*:[33]

The phrase "fiduciary duties" is a dangerous one, giving rise to a mistaken assumption that all fiduciaries owe the same duties in all circumstances. That is not the case.

Secondly, a relationship between parties can be at one and the same time both fiduciary and based on a contract, and in that event, at least if the context is commercial, the contract will prevail. Thus, as Mason J said in *Hospital Products Ltd* v. *United States Surgical Corporation* in the High Court of Australia:[34]

. . . the existence of a basic contractual relationship has in many situations provided a foundation for the erection of a fiduciary relationship. In these situations it is the contractual foundation which is all-important because it is the contract that regulates the basic rights and liabilities of the parties. The fiduciary relationship, if it is to exist at all, must accommodate itself to the terms of the contract so that it is consistent with, and conforms to, them. The fiduciary relationship cannot be superimposed upon the contract in such a way as to alter the operation which the contract was intended to have according to its true construction.

The point is reiterated by Lord Browne-Wilkinson in *Henderson* v. *Merrett Syndicates Ltd*[35] in the following terms:

The extent and nature of the fiduciary duties owed in any particular case fall to be determined by reference to any underlying contractual relationship between the parties. Thus, in the case of an agent employed under a contract, the scope of his fiduciary duties is determined by the terms of the underlying contract . . . The existence of a contract does not exclude the co-existence of concurrent fiduciary duties (indeed, the contract may well be their source); but the contract can and does modify the extent and nature of the general duty that would otherwise arise.

Bowstead and Reynolds on Agency, on the other hand, expresses a rather more hesitant view about the power of the contract to displace or regulate the fiduciary obligations.[36]

30. (1984) 156 Commonwealth Law Reports 42, 96–97.
31. [1896] AC 44, 51–52.
32. [1967] 2 AC 46, 123.
33. Fn 22 above, at p 206A.
34. Fn 30 above, at p 97.
35. [1995] 2 AC 145, 206.
36. See F Reynolds, *Bowstead and Reynolds on Agency*, (17th edn, 2001), paras 6–034ff.

Thirdly, not only can there be different "degrees" of fiduciary relationship (as Lord Browne-Wilkinson envisages in the passage from *Henderson* v. *Merrett Syndicates Ltd* quoted above); it is entirely possible for a particular relationship to be of a fiduciary nature in some respects or for some purposes, but not for others. This is clearly envisaged by Lord Wilberforce, giving the composite judgment of the Privy Council in *New Zealand Netherlands Society "Oranje" Inc* v. *Kuys*.[37] In *Hospital Products Ltd* v. *United States Surgical Corporation*,[38] Mason J (in a minority of one on this point, the other judges being of the opinion that there was, on the facts, no fiduciary relationship between supplier and distributor at all) was of the view that although HPI, the Australian distributor of USSC's surgical stapling products, carried on (and was entitled to carry on) its business generally for its own benefit and not in any sense as a trustee or fiduciary for USSC, it had nevertheless, through the fact of USSC entrusting HPI with the responsibility for protecting and promoting the market for its products in Australia, in effect made HPI the trustee of the goodwill of USSC's business in Australia.[39] In such a situation, labelling the relationship simply as a fiduciary one emphatically does not tell the whole story; there is a danger of further erroneous assumptions. In relation to commercial agency, where the mutual non-excludable duties of good faith imposed on principal and agent by the Agency Regulations have to co-exist with the existing fiduciary obligations of the agent in English law, this is important, as we shall comment later.

An important point to bear in mind at all times concerns remedies for breach of duty. In the event of a breach of a fiduciary duty, the key remedy for the beneficiary of the duty will be an action for an account of profits, i.e. for the payment over to the beneficiary of all the profits the defaulting fiduciary has earned from his breach (in principle receipts less any costs of earning them and perhaps also less an allowance for the fiduciary's efforts in earning them (if the fiduciary's breach of duty has been an honest one)), whether or not the beneficiary could itself have earned the profit and whether or not the beneficiary has suffered a loss as a result of the fiduciary's breach. By contrast, if the duty breached is a contractual one, the person to whom the duty is owed will (apart from the possibility of terminating the contract if the other party's breach has been a very serious one) only be able to recover damages if and to the extent that he has suffered a loss as a result of the breach (and provided further that the loss is not too remote, that the breach was the actual cause of the loss, that he has taken reasonable steps to mitigate his loss, etc). There is a danger that courts may describe a duty as a fiduciary duty purely as a means of enabling themselves to impose the equitable remedies in circumstances where they think those remedies would be appropriate, though the English courts are very conscious of this danger and regard that as wrong.[40]

3.3.1.2.2 The agent's fiduciary duty not to put himself into positions of conflict of interest

The main fiduciary duty, the fiduciary duty of fidelity, requires the agent not to put himself in a position where his duties to the principal could conflict with his own interests. In the

37. [1973] 1 WLR 1126, 1131.

38. Fn 30 above, at p 101.

39. See, in similar vein, *University of Nottingham* v. *Fishel* [2000] ICR 1462.

40. See *Attorney-General* v. *Blake* [1998] Ch 439, quoting with approval from the Canadian case of *Norberg* v. *Wynrib* (1992) 92 DLR (4th) 449, 481: "Fiduciary duties should not be superimposed on . . . common law duties simply to improve the nature or extent of the remedy."

words of Deane J in the High Court of Australia in *Chan* v. *Zacharia*[41] (talking about the liability to account):

> . . . the principle of equity is that a person who is under a fiduciary obligation must account to the person to whom the obligation is owed for any benefit or gain . . . which has been obtained or received in circumstances where a conflict or significant possibility of conflict existed between his fiduciary duty and his personal interest in the pursuit or possible receipt of such a benefit or gain.

This is a very important duty and is very strictly applied by the courts since, as Deane J says, a significant possibility of a conflict rather than an actual conflict will be sufficient for a breach.[42] The highest risk of conflict arises in relation to property. If the agent is in breach of the duty, the principal can choose whether to allow the agent to act or not[43] and in principle for financial compensation the principal can choose between a breach of contract claim for damages for loss of profits etc, or a claim based on breach of fiduciary duty requiring the agent to account for the profits made.

The following qualifications to the strictness of this duty should, however, be noted.

Firstly, an agent, like any other fiduciary, is not obliged to subordinate his own interests to those of the principal in activities outside the scope of and unrelated to the activity in which he holds the fiduciary obligation and will not be liable to account for profits he earns from activities outside that context. Thus, for example, a partner in a firm of solicitors who also owns a racehorse will not be accountable to his partners for profits he makes from racing.[44] The same would, of course, apply to an agent.

Secondly, a fiduciary wishing to enter into a transaction which would otherwise be a breach of duty and who wishes not to be liable for breach can protect his position by making a full disclosure to all the persons to whom the fiduciary obligation is owed of all relevant information known to him and obtaining the consent of those persons. *Phipps* v. *Boardman*[45] shows the extent of the disclosure required and the impossibility for the fiduciary to avail himself of this safeguard if there are persons amongst the class of beneficiaries who are, for whatever reason, unable to give a valid consent. In the commercial situation, however, the person to whom the fiduciary duty is owed will generally, of course, be competent to give consent.

Thirdly, where the fiduciary relationship arises under a contract, the terms of the contract will, as noted above, be crucial in establishing the extent of the fiduciary duties and what the fiduciary is entitled to do without breaching them.

For the agent to act for more than one principal, where this does not put him into any risk of conflicting interest and where the agency agreement does not require his full-time exclusive efforts, will be unobjectionable. The Schedule to the Agency Regulations confirm that such is the position when the Agency Regulations apply (see Chapter 4, section 2.4.2.1).

Plainly an agent may not, however, in the absence of very clear contractual provision to the contrary, act for both sides in the same transaction or dispute. Such is clear from

41. (1984) 154 CLR 178, 198–199.
42. *Aberdeen Railway Co* v. *Blaikie Bros* (1854) 1 Macq 461.
43. *Oliver* v. *Court* (1820) 8 Price 127.
44. See *Aas* v. *Benham* [1891] 2 Ch 244.
45. *Boardman* v. *Phipps* [1967] 2 AC 46 HL affirming sub nom *Phipps* v. *Boardman* [1965] Ch 992 affirming [1964] 1 WLR 993; see the penetrating analysis of this case in R Meagher, D Heydon and M Leeming, *Meagher Gummow and Lehane's Equity: doctrines and remedies* (4th edn, 2002), at paras 5–050–5–070.

North and South Trust Co v. *Berkeley.*[46] The claimant was the policyholder under an insurance policy that had been made through insurance brokers as agents for the policyholder. The claimant made a claim under the policy; the brokers then accepted instructions from the insurer to obtain a report from insurance assessors which the brokers then refused to disclose to their original client, the policyholder, on the basis that it had been commissioned in confidence for the insurer. Donaldson J held that this was a breach of fiduciary duty by the brokers, and that there was absolutely nothing in the circumstances to form the basis of any implied term that the brokers were free to act for the other side in the claim.

May, however, an agent, under the general law and in the absence of any contractual restriction upon him, act for competing principals?

Strangely, the position seems unclear. The treatment of the issue in *Bowstead and Reynolds on Agency*[47] is somewhat equivocal. One would have thought on first impression that, given the general strictness of fiduciary duties, the answer must be no. Certainly such is the default position in relation to partners. Under the Partnership Act 1890 (a codification of the previous century's case law), section 30 (which, as for all the "internal" provisions of that act, applies in the absence of contrary agreement between the partners) provides that if a partner carries on any business *of the same nature as and competing with* that of the firm without the consent of the other partners, he must account for and pay over to the firm all profits made by him in the other business. There is Australian case law that a senior employee may not carry on a business which directly competes with the employer's business, but only if there is actual competition between the two businesses (there would apparently be no problem there if the other business could compete with the employer but in practice does not actually do so).[48] Yet, on the other hand, the authors of the current edition of *Meagher Gummow and Lehane*, the leading Australian textbook on equity, make the bald statement (without citing any authority for the proposition) that "it clearly is not the law that an agent—or for that matter, a solicitor—cannot act for two principals engaged in similar businesses".[49] There is long-established English case law to the effect that company directors are under no such prohibition under the general law.[50] The Scottish Court of Session has said (in a case predating the Agency Regulations) that there is no general principle that an agent is not entitled to handle competing products (though in that case it was not entirely clear whether the so-called agent was really an agent or rather a distributor).[51] It is interesting that it would appear to be a breach of the commercial agent's duty of good faith in French contract law for the agent to handle the products of a competing supplier without the informed consent of the principal.[52]

Given that the relationship of commercial agency will always be based on a contract, what the contract says on this issue will be crucial. Given the uncertainties in the legal position, it is for principals to raise the issue and establish an agreed position with their

46. [1971] 1 WLR 470.

47. F Reynolds, *Bowstead and Reynolds on Agency* (17th edn, 2001), para 6–021.

48. *Blyth Chemicals Ltd* v. *Bushnell* (1933) 49 CLR 66.

49. Op cit, para 5–145, p 185.

50. *London and Mashonaland Exploration Co Ltd* v. *New Mashonaland Exploration Co Ltd* [1891] WN 165, approved by the House of Lords in *Bell* v. *Lever Bros Ltd* [1932] AC 161. See further on the position of directors, (ed) G Moise, *Palmer's Company Law*, Part 8.

51. *Lothian* v. *Jenolite Ltd* 1969 SC 111.

52. As to the position where the Agency Regulations apply, see section 3.4.1.6 below.

agents. *Kelly* v. *Cooper*,[53] an appeal to the Privy Council from the Court of Appeal of Bermuda, emphasises the importance of the contract as providing a solution to this problem. The case concerned a dispute between client and estate agent. The client had instructed the estate agent to sell his house; the owner of the adjoining property instructed the same agent to sell his house as well. The estate agent showed the neighbour's house to a potential purchaser, whose offer to buy that property was accepted, and the same purchaser then offered to buy the claimant's house as well, as the two houses together had effectively exclusive access to an attractive beach and the purchaser was keen to acquire both houses for use by different members of his family. Neither purchase was made conditional on the other taking place, and the client was never told, until after the purchase of both properties had been completed, that the same purchaser had been keen to buy both. The client, considering that if he had known the attraction for this particular purchaser of having the two together he would have held out for a higher price, sued the estate agent for damages for breach of duty in failing to disclose material information to him and for putting himself in a position where his duty and his self-interest conflicted. In finding for the agent, the Privy Council said that estate agents invariably acted for many principals at once, some of whom might well be selling competing properties and who would have conflicting interests. The court took the view that the client would have been well aware of the possibility that the agent might be acting for vendors of similar properties at the same time and that in so doing would receive confidential information in relation to those other vendors. In such a case, it was appropriate to imply a term into the contract to the effect that the agent was entitled to act for other principals selling competing properties and to keep confidential the information obtained from each of those principals (even though that information might well have been material to the client). Any other conclusion, said the Privy Council, would have made it impossible for estate agents to trade. The case is a very important confirmation of the principle that, in the commercial context, the terms of the contract are the fundamental basis of the relationship and can override or vary such fiduciary obligations as would otherwise have been implied.

3.3.1.2.3 The agent's fiduciary duty not to make a secret profit, not to accept secret payments, bribes etc

Somewhat similar to the duty of fidelity is the duty which requires the agent not to gain undisclosed economic benefit from his position as fiduciary. Again, Deane J in *Chan* v. *Zacharia*[54] sums up the principle very clearly:

> . . . the principle of equity is that a person who is under a fiduciary obligation must account to the person to whom the obligation is owed for any benefit or gain . . . which was obtained or received by use or by reason of his fiduciary position or of opportunity or knowledge resulting from it.

One aspect of this involves the misuse by the agent of the principal's property, i.e. money or confidential information or business opportunities which come under the agent's control or come to the agent's knowledge in the course of the agency relationship. This principle is also applied very strictly by the courts, which regard as irrelevant the fact that the agent acted in good faith or that the principal benefited from what the agent did.[55] In general, the agent will be required to account for the profit and will hold resulting assets

53. [1993] AC 205.
54. See fn 41 above.
55. *Boardman* v. *Phipps* [1967] 2 AC 46 HL affirming sub nom *Phipps* v. *Boardman* [1965] Ch 992 affirming [1964] 1 WLR 993.

on constructive trust for the principal, though in appropriate circumstances the courts will make an allowance to the agent if he has acted in good faith and invested significant effort in the venture.[56]

The other aspect of this duty is the obligation of the agent not to accept undisclosed payments from third parties or secret commissions or bribes in connection with his role as agent. The key cases concern company directors[57] and employees,[58] but the principle applies to agents in the same way. Here the agent is not misusing property belonging to the principal, but, rather, is misusing his position as agent. A bribe has been judicially defined as "a commission or other inducement which is given by a third party to an agent as such, and which is secret from his principal".[59] The agent will be in breach of duty if he accepts such a payment. The position would be different with the principal's fully informed consent.

The two aspects of this duty have traditionally been treated as separate, because until fairly recently the remedies available to the claimant in a secret commissions/bribe case were more limited than those available in a "misuse of property" case. The source of this distinction was the judgment of the Court of Appeal in *Lister & Co* v. *Stubbs*,[60] where an employee who had accepted secret commissions from one of his employer's suppliers in respect of the purchase of goods for the employer had invested the moneys received from the supplier and the investments had done well. The employer wanted to recover not the amount of the secret commissions, but the resulting investments or their value. The Court of Appeal said that, as there had been no misuse of property by the fiduciary, the commissions had never been money belonging to the employer (being the person to whom the fiduciary duty was owed) until the court declared that to be the case, so the remedy available had to be personal only and the resulting investments or their value were not held on constructive trust for the employer. This reasoning has now been strongly disapproved by the Privy Council in *Attorney-General for Hong Kong* v. *Reid*.[61] Here, a senior government lawyer in Hong Kong had accepted bribes in return for obstructing criminal prosecutions, in breach of what was held to be his fiduciary duty as a civil servant. He had invested the money in three freehold properties in New Zealand, which had increased in value. The Privy Council held that he was constructive trustee of the properties for the Crown, on the basis that the bribes should have been paid over on receipt to the Crown and that it was wrong to let him keep any profit at all from his breach of duty, but said that if the value of properties had been less than the amount of the bribes received he would still have been personally liable to pay over the amount originally received by way of bribe.

Criminal sanction in respect of secret commissions, bribes etc

Over and above more general criminal offences such as conspiracy to defraud which could be relevant in this context, it is worth noting in passing that there is a specific criminal offence under the Prevention of Corruption Act 1906 aimed at the bribing of agents. Under

56. *Hippisley* v. *Knee Bros* [1905] 1 KB 1; *Boardman* v. *Phipps*, fn 55 above.
57. *Boston Deep Sea Fishing and Ice Co* v. *Ansell* (1888) 39 Ch D 339.
58. *Lister & Co* v. *Stubbs* (1890) 45 Ch D 1.
59. *Per* Leggatt J in *Anangel Atlas Compania Naviera SA* v. *Ishikawajima-Harima Heavy Industries Co Ltd* [1990] 1 Lloyd's Rep 167, at 171.
60. See fn 58 above.
61. [1994] 1 AC 324.

section 1 of the Act, it is an offence for an agent, *inter alia*, corruptly to accept or to attempt to obtain "any gift or consideration as an inducement or reward for doing or for forbearing to do" any act in connection with his principal's affairs or business. The word "agent" is defined as including "any person employed by or acting for another" and is extended to include various types of public official; "principal" is defined as including an employer. The person who corruptly gives or offers the "gift or consideration" to the agent also commits an offence under section 1.

Section 1(4) states that it is immaterial under the Act if the principal's affairs or business have no connection with the UK and are conducted in a country or territory outside the UK or if the agent's functions are not connected with the UK and are performed outside the UK. It is an essential element of the offence that the act or omission by the agent which the bribe induces or is aimed at inducing has to be intended to influence or affect the affairs of the principal.[62]

In England and Wales, prosecutions can only be commenced with the Attorney-General's consent. Whilst it might be thought that the Act would more often be applied in respect of corruption by public officials, prosecutions in respect of bribery of agents in the private sector do take place.[63]

3.3.1.2.4 The agent's fiduciary duty not to delegate

The third fiduciary duty is that of non-delegation[64] unless permitted (expressly or impliedly). Delegation is of crucial importance in terms of liability. When delegation is authorised by the principal, the agent will be liable to the principal for the acts of the sub-agent and the sub-agent's rights will be against the agent and (in the absence of a direct contract between principal and sub-agent) not against the principal.[65] In such a case, even though there is in principle no privity between the principal and the sub-agent,[66] the impact of the Contracts (Rights of Third Parties) Act 1999 must not be underestimated. Moreover, tort actions are also available since the sub-agent owes a duty of care to the principal.[67]

In relation to the Agency Regulations, part of what distinguishes a commercial agent from an employee is the freedom of the former to organise the running of his business as he sees fit, consistently with his obligations to negotiate or conclude sales, which may involve appointing appropriate personnel and perhaps some delegation. The default position on delegation, where the Agency Regulations apply, is probably somewhat more relaxed than when they do not apply. We have dealt in Chapter 2 with the question of against whom the sub-agent has rights under the Agency Regulations on termination of his sub-agency agreement.

3.3.1.2.5 Other fiduciary duties of the agent

Agents have other fiduciary duties to their principals, to keep the principal's property separate from other property, to transfer it over to the principal when demanded (including

62. This emerges from the Privy Council case (on appeal from the Court of Appeal of Hong Kong) of *Commissioner of the Independent Commission against Corruption* v. *Ch'ng Poh* [1997] 1 WLR 1175.

63. See, for example, *R* v. *Archer* [2002] EWCA Crim 1207.

64. *De Bussche* v. *Alt* (1878) 8 Ch D 286.

65. *Mackersy* v. *Ramsays, Bonars and Co* (1843) 9 C&F 818.

66. This means that the sub-agent cannot get paid by the principal for the services rendered as in *Schmaling* v. *Tomlinson* (1815) 6 Taunt 147. Vice versa, the principal cannot recover money from the sub-agent *Calico Printers Association* v. *Barclays Bank Ltd* (1931) 145 LT 51, CA.

67. *Henderson* v. *Merrett Syndicates Ltd* [1994] 3 WLR 761. Compare and contrast with *Balsamo* v. *Medici* [1984] 2 All ER 304.

interest earned on it), to keep up-to-date accurate accounts and records of business transacted in the course of the agency and to produce those records to the principal when required.[68]

3.3.1.2.6 The relationship of the agent's fiduciary duties with the mutual duties of good faith under the Agency Regulations

It does not seem to us that breach of the mutual duties of good faith under the Agency Regulations is intended to give access to the equitable remedies available in English law for breach of fiduciary duty. We shall deal with this issue in more detail below.[69]

3.3.2 The principal's duties to the agent in English law, apart from the Agency Regulations

3.3.2.1 Generally

In sharp contrast with the numerous obligations of the agent, and subject to any additional ones expressly created defined in the agency contract, at common law the principal has only two duties towards the commercial agent, neither of which is fiduciary. They are:

- to pay remuneration to the agent; and
- to indemnify the agent in respect of liabilities he incurs while acting within the scope of his authority.

It is appropriate to mention at the same time the agent's lien over the principal's property, which in practice operates as a means of securing performance of the principal's duties.

In English common law to date, there is no support for the idea that the principal has a general duty towards the agent to co-operate in order to facilitate the agent in performing his obligations, to refrain from unreasonable interference in the agent's performance or, more generally, to act reasonably towards the agent.[70] This is very different from developments in certain other areas of English law, especially with developments in the last 30 years in the law of the contract of employment, where the courts (including the highest courts) have, in marked contrast with the usual hesitation about implying terms into contracts, been rather enthusiastically elaborating an implied contractual obligation of mutual trust and confidence between employer and employee.

As we shall make clear in section 3.4, we consider that the mandatory mutual obligations of good faith incorporated into commercial agency agreements by reason of Regulations 3, 4 and 5 of the Agency Regulations are intended to achieve in the commercial agency context something very similar to the mutual obligations of trust and confidence and co-operation which in English law are implied into the contract of employment and which are probably in practice implicit in the contract of partnership although, for reasons which we shall explain, there is only very limited law on the latter. It seems to us that, far

68. For a detailed summary of those duties, see F Reynolds, *Bowstead and Reynolds on Agency* (17th edn, 2001), paras 6–088–6–107.

69. Section 3.4.1.15.

70. A careful reading of the introductory part of Chapter 7 of F Reynolds, *Bowstead and Reynolds on Agency* (17th edn, 2001), pp 231–232 is enormously beneficial for an overview at this point.

from Regulations 3, 4 and 5 being mysterious, English law, through analogies with areas other than the law of agency, already has the ingredients in its larder with which to work out the answers to the issues which those Regulations pose.

3.3.2.2 The principal's duty to remunerate the agent

In the commercial context, it would be rare for an agency agreement not to specify the way that the agent's remuneration is to be calculated, in respect of what transactions it is to be payable, and when and how it is to be paid.

If the contract contains express provision on remuneration, then, at common law, that it what the court will enforce, and on normal English contract law principles, in accordance with the terms of the contract, whether that leads to a result which might seem unduly generous or unduly mean towards the agent.[71]

Somewhat unusually, given the usual hesitation of English courts about implying terms into contracts, the courts are willing to imply a right to reasonable remuneration in favour of an agent if they decide, in a particular case, that it was the common intention of the parties that the agent should be paid but that the contract has not said in what way this should happen. The courts are also willing to decide in such cases what reasonable remuneration should be and how it should be paid.[72] In such circumstances, the normal rules of construction of contracts will apply.[73] Implied payment must be reasonable according to the circumstances, and payment can also be implied from trade usages or customs of the area where the agent works. A restitutionary claim by the agent for the payment of reasonable remuneration by way of a *quantum meruit* may be possible as a last resort.

On this aspect, the Agency Regulations bring much change[74] since they do not apply to gratuitous agents.[75] We will therefore argue that, where the Agency Regulations apply, payment of remuneration has to be a right of the commercial agent and therefore is closely regulated especially in the light of the principal's obligation of good faith under Regulation 4. In fact, in the case of *Bell Electric Ltd* v. *Aweco Appliance Systems GmbH & Co KG*,[76] Elias J in the High Court at first instance held that a continuing failure to pay the due commission amounted to a repudiatory breach and as such entitled the commercial agent to terminate the relationship "for circumstances attributable to the principal" per Regulation 18(b)(i) and claim compensation (the appeal[77] was on different grounds).

71. When the contract leaves the sum of remuneration at the sole discretion of the principal, the court cannot, at common law, imply a right to be paid. See *Kofi Sunkersette Obu* v. *Strauss (A) Co Ltd* [1951] AC 243. This case would almost certainly be treated differently under the Agency Regulations. See below.

72. In *Way* v. *Latilla* [1937] 3 All ER 759, Lord Atkin said "while there is no concluded contract as to remuneration, it is plain that there existed . . . a contract of employment . . . in circumstances which clearly indicated that the work was not to be gratuitous", at p 762. The position of the commercial agent is thought to be even better since although the Agency Regulations do not apply to gratuitous agents, commercial agents have a right to be paid.

73. For details, see G H Treitel, *The Law of Contract* (11th edn, 2003) and (ed) H Beale, *Chitty on Contracts* (29th edn, 2004), Ch 12.

74. See Regulation 6, for details, see below.

75. Regulation 2(2).

76. [2002] EWHC 872, 8 May 2002 (QBD).

77. [2002] EWCA Civ 1501, 31 October 2002 (CA).

This is a welcome change compared to the common law rules where the right to sue the principal for having been deprived of an opportunity to earn a commission is only possible if expressly agreed or if such a term can be implied in the contract.[78]

Where, however, the contract states that the agent's right to remuneration will only arise if some future event happens, then if that event does not happen the agent will earn no remuneration and will have no right to a *quantum meruit* in that situation either (even though he may have tried very hard to bring that event about). Even if the contract is not specific on that point, there will be a strong presumption that that is intended to be the case, as the normal expectation would be that the agent's remuneration would be payable out of the moneys received by the principal under the contract with the third party, rather than out of the principal's other resources.[79] If the reason why the contract with the third party does not take place is that the principal decides, for reasons of his own, that he no longer wishes to enter into it, at common law the agent will have no right to remuneration.[80] The position under the Agency Regulations would, because of the mutual obligations of good faith, be very different.[81]

Furthermore, even if the contract between principal and third party is entered into, then unless the agency agreement says something different (expressly or by necessary implication), if that future event is (as it very often will be) the making of the contract between principal and third party, the agent will, at common law, be entitled to his remuneration only if his work was the effective cause of that contract being made. There is detailed and complicated case law on this concept of effective cause, nearly all of it concerning estate agents,[82] but as English law does not traditionally differentiate between different types of agent depending on their function, the principles are of more general application.

The agent will not be entitled to remuneration in respect of unauthorised transactions which he concludes, unless the principal decides to ratify them. If the agent is in serious breach of duty in respect of particular transactions (e.g. if he negligently understates the principal's price to the third party, a contract between principal and third party is entered into at that low price as a result of which the principal suffers), at common law the agent can validly refuse to pay the remuneration on that transaction (in addition to any possible damages claim he may have).

3.3.2.3 The principal's duty to indemnify the agent

The second duty owed by the principal is to indemnify the agent against losses and liabilities and to reimburse him in respect of the expenses incurred whilst performing the duties, provided always that he acts lawfully and within the limits of the authority given to him. In cases where the agency agreement contains no express right to indemnity, it will be treated as implied in the absence of some very clear indication to the contrary. The Agency Regulations remain silent on that aspect. Accordingly, the common law rules will therefore still apply.[83]

78. On that aspect, see S Saintier, *Commercial agency law: a comparative analysis*, (2002), Chapter 2, especially pp 65–67.

79. *Dennis Reed Ltd* v. *Goody* [1950] 2 KB 277.

80. *Luxor (Eastbourne) Ltd* v. *Cooper* [1941] AC 108.

81. See the discussion of *Page* v. *Combined Shipping and Transport Co Ltd* [1997] 3 All ER 656 below.

82. See F Reynolds, *Bowstead and Reynolds on Agency* (17th edn, 2001), paras 7–013–7–031, pp 239–258.

83. A more detailed study of the rules would be outside the scope of this book. For more details, see F Reynolds, *Bowstead and Reynolds on Agency*, (17th edn, 2001), paras 7–056ff.

3.3.2.4 The agent's lien over the principal's goods

A lien in English common law is a passive right to retain possession of property belonging to someone else until some debt or obligation owing to him by that person is paid or performed. At common law the creditor has no power to seize goods (they must already be in the creditor's lawful possession), and the creditor has no power of sale (though one is created now, in many cases, by statute[84]) and no property right in the goods that can be transferred to a third party. It is in the nature of a security interest, though not conceptually one. Liens can arise by contract or by long-established trade custom which the law recognises. They can be general or particular. A general lien is one where the creditor is entitled to retain possession of the debtor's goods until all and any debts or obligations of the debtor to him are performed. A particular lien, in contrast, only allows the creditor to retain possession of goods in respect of debtor's liabilities directly related to those particular goods.[85]

At common law, an agent has a particular lien on those of his principal's goods from time to time in his possession, in respect of any lawful claim he may have as agent against the principal in respect of those goods (remuneration or indemnity).[86] However, such a right is conditional on (a) the agent having lawfully obtained the possession of the goods in his capacity as agent and (b) there being no agreement or other understanding between principal and agent which is inconsistent with the agent having a lien.

The Agency Regulations being silent in this area but one of the two key aims of the Directive being to improve the position of commercial agents *vis-à-vis* their principals,[87] the common law rules must therefore still apply. The impact will depend on the terms of the contract.

3.4 PERFORMANCE: THE IMPACT OF THE AGENCY REGULATIONS: MATTERS OTHER THAN THE AGENT'S REMUNERATION

The Agency Regulations, in those cases where they apply, make a fundamental difference to the obligations of principal and agent to each other by comparison with the English common law rules. The relevant parts of the Regulation are Part II ("Rights and obligations") and Part III ("Remuneration"). Although the former have an impact (and sometimes a significant impact) on the issue of the agent's remuneration (so that Part III does not tell the whole story so far as the effect of the Agency Regulations on remuneration is concerned), it is sensible for the purposes of exposition to examine them separately, which we now do.

84. Torts (Interference with Goods) Act 1977, s 12. This will principally be relevant where the bailor is in breach of an obligation to take delivery of goods which are in the bailee's possession. An agent will thus potentially have a power of sale under his particular lien where he bought goods on the principal's behalf and is holding them for the principal. In the absence of contrary agreement, however, a selling agent holding his principal's goods will have no power of sale under his particular lien.

85. See further R Bradgate, *Commercial Law* (3rd edn, 2000), pp 512–517.

86. F Reynolds, *Bowstead and Reynolds on Agency* states (para 7–074, p 283) "clear authority for the general proposition as to the lien of an agent is difficult to find", but the proposition is universally accepted. For more detail on the specific application of liens in the context of agents, see *ibid*, 7–070–7–098.

87. See the recitals to the Directive 86/653.

3.4.1 The mutual and non-excludable obligations of good faith[88]

In Part II and before defining the other rights and obligations of the parties, the Agency Regulations impose reciprocal and compulsory obligations of good faith on each party. The place given to this duty in the Regulations seems to indicate that they are of paramount importance and that they must be reviewed on their own before the other obligations. Let us first see how the good faith obligations are imposed in the Agency Regulations before trying to explain what they mean and what kind of impact they have on the parties.

Reported UK cases to date involving the duties of good faith under the Agency Regulations are, to put it mildly, scarce, and such as there are tend to be inconclusive. They amount merely to the following.

Page v. *Combined Shipping and Trading Co Ltd*,[89] which was an interlocutory application by a UK commercial agent against his principal for a freezing order, as part of an action claiming compensation for termination under Regulation 17. The commercial agent alleged that the commission figures on which the calculation of compensation would be based were artificially depressed, as the principal, in breach of his duty of good faith, had, he alleged, deliberately starved him of opportunities to earn commission with a view to minimising his obligations to pay him. All that the court had to decide at this interim stage was whether the applicant commercial agent had an arguable case (nothing more conclusive than that) that he was entitled to compensation. In the course of giving judgment for the commercial agent and granting the freezing order, Millett LJ in the Court of Appeal, construing Regulation 17, said that he thought there was a good arguable case that "proper performance of the agency agreement" in Regulation 17(7) should be construed in the light, *inter alia*, of Regulation 4(1), and that that could well mean that the principal was not allowed to operate the agency relationship so as deliberately to minimise the amount of commission the agent could earn (even though the express terms of the agency agreement allowed the principal to do that).

Parks v. *Esso Petroleum Co Ltd*,[90] an appeal against a strike-out order, where the agent ran the argument that the principal, in allegedly misrepresenting to him before entering into the agency agreement an exaggerated level of profitability for the agency business, had acted in breach of his duty of good faith under Regulation 4. In the event, though the court accepted that a pre-contractual misrepresentation by the principal based on an untrue statement of current opinion could be a good cause of action for misrepresentation in "mainstream" contract law, Mr Parks was held not to be a commercial agent within the Agency Regulations at all,[91] and said nothing about Regulation 4.

Bell Electric Ltd v. *Aweco Appliance Systems GmbH & Co KG*,[92] where part way through the life of the commercial agency agreement the principal had stopped paying the agent's

88. Some of the following details are inspired from the contents of PhD thesis, later amended for publication: S Saintier, *Commercial agency law: a comparative analysis* (2002), Ashgate, see especially pp 118–132 and 224–230. The authors are grateful for Ashgate for permission to reproduce some of the material.
89. [1997] 3 All ER 656 (CA).
90. [1999] 1 CMLR 455 (Ch D).
91. See Chapter 2, section 2.4.2.1.
92. [2002] EWHC 872 (QB), 8 May 2002, Elias J.

commission entirely, and several months later announced that it was unilaterally varying the basis of the commission calculation to the agent's considerable disadvantage. In reaction to that, the commercial agent had purportedly terminated the agency agreement for repudiatory breach by the principal. The case could have been pleaded as a breach of the principal's duty of good faith as well as or instead of a "straightforward" breach of contract claim for repeated failure to pay commission, but was pleaded purely as the latter, with a claim for a compensation payment (on termination) under Regulation 17 in the alternative. In deciding that the commercial agent had, on the facts, indeed terminated the agency agreement for serious breach by the principal and had not affirmed the contract, and that such termination by the commercial agent was "justified by circumstances attributable to the principal" (so as to preserve, by reason of Regulation 18(b)(i) the commercial agent's right to a compensation payment, which he said in the circumstances added nothing to the breach of contract damages claim (which is at best debatable)), Elias J seems to rely purely on the repeated failure to pay commission as the serious breach of contract and not on any breach of Regulation 4. The Court of Appeal judgment[93] does not deal with the issue.

Cooper and others v. *Pure Fishing (UK) Ltd*,[94] where the claimant commercial agents handled one manufacturer's (M1's) limited range of fishing tackle, and also acted as sales agents for another manufacturer (M2) who produced complementary, not competing, products. Their commercial agency agreement with M1 did not preclude them from acting for other manufacturers of fishing tackle; their agreements with M2 apparently prevented them from handling competing products. M1 and M2 had discussed the situation and were content with it. M1 subsequently decided to add to its range of products a number of products which competed with those of M2, and to force the commercial agents to handle them. The latter objected, saying this would put them in breach of their agreements with M2, whom they wished to continue to represent. The defendant principal then alleged that their refusal to handle the new products was a repudiatory breach by them of their commercial agency agreements, entitling him to terminate them. The judge at first instance (Judge Kershaw in the Queen's Bench Division, Manchester District Registry) regarded this as a breach of the principal's duty of good faith, seeing it as an attempt to engineer a situation where the commercial agents would find it impossible to continue to act, because the principal wanted to replace them with direct employees. The finding on this point was not appealed.

The general view, which is one to which we subscribe, is that the duty of good faith imposed on the commercial agent under Regulation 3 does not add appreciably to the obligations imposed on an agent by the pre-existing English law, and in most cases is unlikely to add to a commercial agent's express obligations towards his principal under a reasonably fully drafted written agency agreement. The innovation, of course, is the duty of good faith imposed by Regulation 4 on the principal.

The absence of reported litigation on Regulations 3 and 4 is, in one sense, not surprising. One would have expected that pursuing damages claims for breach of these duties to the stage of trial in litigation would be rare. If principal and commercial agent have reached that degree of enmity in their relationship, then surely an effective working

93. [2002] EWCA 1501, 31 October 2002.
94. [2004] EWCA Civ 375, 18 March 2004.

relationship is, for all practical purposes, at an end and the case becomes one of termination and negotiating exit terms and the lump sum payment of compensation or indemnity due on termination (which of course could be accompanied by a damages claim in respect of breaches of contract while the contract was still in existence). Alternatively, under Regulation 18(b) one of the situations where, on termination, the commercial agent has no right to a lump sum payment is, logically enough, where he himself has terminated the agency contract. But he will nevertheless still be entitled to a lump sum payment even if he himself terminated the contract if "such termination is justified by circumstances attributable to the principal" (Regulation 18(b)(i)). A breach, or at least something more than a trivial breach, of the principal's duty of good faith would certainly be such a "circumstance". (We deal in more detail with this in Chapter 6.) One might therefore have expected a case law on the principal's duty of good faith to have developed under the Agency Regulations in that context, as is the case in UK employment law.[95] That this has not developed is perhaps somewhat surprising.

Given the lack of authority on which to work, we shall first consider why English law has to date not accepted any general duty of good faith in contract law. We shall then consider the mutual duties of good faith between commercial agent and principal as they exist in French law (which may give some clues as to what Regulations 3 and 4 of the Agency Regulations are intended to achieve). We shall then examine areas of English law which appear to provide analogies (some more useful than others) with the position of commercial agent and principal. We shall, finally in this section, consider some consequential issues. In the current state of English law, significant parts of what follows are of necessity, therefore, somewhat speculative.

3.4.1.1 The obligations themselves

3.4.1.1.1 The commercial agent's obligations

Copying the Directive almost to the letter, the Agency Regulations start with the commercial agent, for whom they stipulate that:

> "in performing his activities a commercial agent must look after the interests of his principal and act dutifully and in good faith.[96]
> In particular, a commercial agent must make proper efforts to negotiate and, where appropriate, conclude the transactions he is entrusted to take care of;
> communicate to his principal all the necessary information available to him[97] and comply with reasonable instructions given by the principal."[98]

3.4.1.1.2 The principal's obligations

In relation to the principal, the Agency Regulations stipulate:

> "In his relations with his commercial agent, a principal must act dutifully and in good faith.[99]

95. See section 3.4.1.5.3 below.
96. Regulation 3(1).
97. But note in this respect Regulation 21.
98. Regulation 3(2).
99. Regulation 4(1).

In particular, a principal must:

(a) provide the commercial agent with the necessary documentation relating to the goods concerned;

(b) obtain for the commercial agent the information necessary for the performance of the agency contract[100] and in particular notify his commercial agent within a reasonable period once he anticipates that the volume of commercial transactions will be significantly lower than which the commercial agent could normally have expected[101] and

(c) the principal shall, in addition, inform the commercial agent, within a reasonable period of his acceptance or refusal of, and any non-execution by him of, a commercial transaction which the commercial agent has procured for him".[102]

The obligation of good faith is mandatory, as the Agency Regulations stipulate that the parties may not derogate from their respective obligations[103] and that the consequences of any breach will be governed by the law applicable to the contract.[104] We shall say more about the consequences of breach in section 3.4.1.15 below.

3.4.1.2 Why are the mutual obligations of good faith important?

To require an obligation of good faith of both parties is of crucial importance for two main reasons.

First, because, in doing so, the Agency Regulations are the first EC-based legislation to introduce an overriding requirement of this type into English contract law.

Secondly, to impose a mandatory requirement of good faith on the principal as well as on the commercial agent is a very significant change for the latter's protection. In fact, under the traditional English law rules, because of the fiduciary aspect of the relationship, principals are not bound by such a duty. In fact, at common law, agents have very few rights compared to the panoply of obligations imposed upon them. The fact that the Agency Regulations require such a duty from both parties therefore highlights what is now the peculiarity of the commercial agency relationship compared with other types of agency agreement and, indeed, with other types of commercial contracts more generally. Most importantly, the reciprocal duty of good faith brings about a certain symmetry and reciprocity and balance between the parties, which, as will be seen, is central to the relationship.

In spite of the apparent importance of this reciprocal duty, the situation is less than satisfactory. By copying the Directive almost to the letter, the Agency Regulations fail to define what this concept of good faith, an import from mainland European civil-law legal systems, entails. This vagueness is particularly unfortunate for the UK, given that English common law does not have a general duty on contracting parties to behave towards each other in good faith. This is another illustration of the legal paradox to which we referred in Chapter 1, section 1.2.

100. But note in this respect Regulation 21.
101. Regulation 4(2).
102. Regulation 4(3).
103. Regulation 5(1).
104. Regulation 5(2).

3.4.1.3 Why does English contract law not contain a general duty of good faith?[105]

While English courts have long been familiar with the concept of good faith in the narrow sense as meaning honesty,[106] in mainland European civil law the concept is much wider, as an overriding obligation to deal fairly.[107] Despite some early signs that it might take root,[108] this wider continental concept was never adopted into English common law.[109]

Its absence is traditionally explained by the impact of the subjective classical doctrines of freedom and sanctity of contract which prevailed during the nineteenth century.[110] Although more and more commentators argue that English contract law should recognise such a duty to deal fairly,[111] some English lawyers remain hostile to the idea of incorporating a general requirement of good faith into English contract law.[112] The resistance basically takes two forms:

(1) a body of opinion totally opposed to such incorporation[113] and
(2) a body of opinion which considers that similar results to those of a general duty of good faith are (already) achieved in English contract law through different routes.[114]

The position of "total opposition" to a duty of good faith can be summarised in five arguments[115]:

105. This section draws heavily on Saintier, *Commercial agency law: a comparative analysis* (Ashgate, 2002), pp 224–230.

106. See the Sale of Goods Act 1979, s 61(3). For details of English legal history, see *Halsbury's Laws of England* (4th edn). Reissue (Butterworths 1998), Vol 9(1), para 612 (p 349) ("Halsbury's"); also A F Mason, *Contract, good faith and equitable standards in fair dealing* (2000) 116 LQR 71–74; R Harrison, *Good faith in sales*, Sweet & Maxwell, 1997, pp 4 and 7; and R Powell, *Good faith in contracts* (1956) 9 CLP 16, 24–25.

107. See the comments of Bingham LJ in *Interfoto Picture Library Ltd* v. *Stiletto Visual Programmes Ltd* [1989] QB 433, 439.

108. During the 18th century, the English common law courts looked as though they were about to receive into the law of contract the civil law notion of good faith. In fact, judicial attempts were made to incorporate such notions into English contract law, which went wider than requiring mere honesty. In *Carter* v. *Boehm* (1766) 3 Burr 1905, 1910, Lord Mansfield referred to good faith as "the governing principle applicable to all contracts and dealings". See also *Mellish* v. *Motteaux* [1792] Peake 156, 157 where Lord Kenyon said "In contracts of all kinds, it is of the highest importance that the courts of law should compel the observance of honesty and good faith.".

109. The good faith principle was firmly rejected in the 19th century. See *Baglehole* v. *Walters* (1811) 3 Camp 151 by Lord Ellenborough at p 171, where the courts insisted that in a sale of goods, it was up to the buyer to look after his own interests (caveat emptor) by express provisions in the contract. See also *Smith* v. *Hughes* (1871) LR 6 QB 597.

110. See AF Mason, *Contract, good faith and equitable standards in fair dealing* (2000) 116 LQR at p 70.

111. The number of advocates of the introduction of a duty of good faith has grown since Powell. For academic work, see generally R Brownsword, NJ Hird and G Howells (eds), *Good faith in contract, concept and context* (Aldershot, Ashgate, 1999). See also Beatson and Friedman (eds), *Good faith and fault in contract law* (Clarendon Press, 1995). See Staughton LJ, *Good faith and fairness in commercial law* (1994) JCL 193. For a practitioner's book, see Furmston (ed) *The law of contract* (Butterworths, 1999), pp 67–85.

112. See M Bridge, *Does Anglo-Canadian contract law need a doctrine of good faith?* (1984) Can Bus LJ 385, and for a more recent version, *Good faith in commercial contracts* in Brownsword, Hird and Howells (eds), (op cit, fn 111 above). See also Teubner, *Legal irritants: good faith in British law or how unifying law ends up in new divergences* (1998) 61 MLR 11–32.

113. In Furmston (ed), op cit, fn 111, this is referred to as "the sceptical view" (pp 69–73, paras 179–184).

114. In Furmston (ed), op cit, fn 111, this is referred to as "the neutral view" (pp 73–75). The routes referred to there are economic duress, promissory estoppel, misrepresentation, mistake and frustration.

115. Presented in Furmston (ed), op cit, fn 111, pp 69–73.

(1) that an obligation to deal in good faith requires the taking into consideration of the legitimate interests of the other party, which goes against the individualist ethics of English contract law.[116] Indeed, whilst English contract law is based on a self-interested method of dealing, a contract law which incorporated a duty of good faith would be based on an "other-regarding" method of dealing. The notion is regarded as being *unworkable in practice*,[117] since the judges would have to interfere with the will of the parties, which would in effect restrict the pursuit of self-interest.

(2) That good faith is a hollow and vague notion placed on "too high a moral plane".[118] In fact, an obligation of good faith means to impose a set of moral standards against which contracting parties will be judged. Yet it is not clear against what moral standards they are to be judged. That represents a lack of calculability and predictability.[119]

(3) To decide whether a party has or has not acted in good faith would imply looking at his/her reasons for contracting, which would be problematic.

(4) Good faith interferes with the terms of the contract, which goes against the principle of party autonomy and is inconsistent with the fundamental principle of freedom of contract.[120]

(5) Good faith, if applied to all contracts alike, fails to recognise the different contexts of contracting.[121] The main aspect of this concern is that good faith cannot apply in markets where opportunism is high.

The essence of such hostility towards a general duty of good faith can perhaps be explained by a lack of understanding of how the notion works.[122] In fact, the main problem for English commentators seems to be to know what would be the content of a general duty of good faith. As appears below, French law has developed this very far.

The second view, that English law already covers most of the ground that a general duty of good faith would cover, but in a piecemeal fashion and calling it different things in different places, appears more compelling, because these piecemeal solutions are varied

116. Lord Ackner stated in *Walford* v. *Mile* [1992] 2 AC 128, 138 that the notion was "inherently repugnant to the adversarial position of the parties". Lord Ackner had already expressed such an opinion earlier in *Banque Kayser Ullman SA* v. *Skandia (UK) Insurance Co Ltd* [1990] 1 QB 665, 772. For a similar view, see also Slade LJ who held "the law cannot police the fairness of every commercial contract by reference to moral principles" (*Banque Financière de la Cité SA* v. *Westgate Insurance Co Ltd* [1989] 2 All ER 952, 1013, and May LJ in *Bank of Nova Scotia* v. *Hellenic Mutual War Risks Association (Bermuda) Ltd: The Good Luck* [1989] 3 All ER 628, 667. See also the more recent case of *Regalian Properties PLC* v. *London Docklands Development Corporation* [1995] 1 All ER 1005.

117. See Lord Ackner in *Walford* v. *Mile*, fn 116 above.

118. See R Powell, *Good faith in contracts* (1956) 9 CLP 16, 31.

119. In Furmston, op cit fn 111, it is stated that it raises several questions such as whether good faith does anything to regulate bad faith; whether good faith regulates the stages of the contract as well as the substance; and whether good faith acts only for positive acts or whether it also acts as support and prevention of exploitation.

120. In *Union Eagle Ltd* v. *Golden Achievement Ltd* [1997] 2 All ER 215, Lord Hoffmann held that equity would not intervene since it was against the freedom of contract. This is, however, a different concept from that of good faith.

121. M Bridge, *Good faith in commercial contracts*, in R Brownsword, NJ Hird and G Howells (eds), *Good faith, concept and context* (Ashgate, 1999), p 147.

122. Lord Steyn, *Contract law: fulfilling the reasonable expectations of honest men* (1997) 113 LQR 438.

and cover a wide range of areas.[123] A strong argument is that of Lord Steyn who states that as long as English contract law respects "the reasonable expectations of the parties",[124] there is no need for an overriding requirement of good faith in it, because "there is not a world of difference between the objective requirement of good faith and the reasonable expectations of the parties".[125] There is, as will be seen, an element of truth in this argument as far as French law is concerned, because when the French courts use good faith as an interpretative tool, they have to uphold the true intentions of the parties as per Article 1156 CC.[126]

We shall see below that the duty of good faith in French contract law essentially requires loyalty and co-operation from all parties. This means that the parties are required to take into account each other's interests.[127]

3.4.1.4 The contractual duty of good faith in French law

Looking at French law, where an obligation of good faith in contract law has existed since the inception of the Civil Code in 1804[128] might help us to understand what good faith entails. We will look at how French law has applied good faith generally, and also specifically in relation to the commercial agency relationship.

Reference to French law will, however, be made purely as an informative element, in order to try to understand what good faith could mean and how it could apply, as a rule of conduct, and what kind of repercussions it could have on other parts of the Agency Regulations. We are not in any sense urging that this approach should be adopted as the model in the UK. There is certainly no requirement to do that. As a matter of EU law, there is no presumption that EU law intends to define legal concepts by reference to the national law of one or more Member States, unless the relevant EU legislation makes an express statement to that effect.[129] If anything, rather on the contrary, as we shall explain in section 3.4.1.5, we consider that English law already has a number of analogous ideas, particularly in other types of long-term "relationship" contracts, which could be applied to some advantage to make sense of the mutual good faith obligations now forming part of commercial agency.

In France, the duty of good faith is imposed by the Civil Code. It is mandatory and applies to all kinds of contracts. Good faith in France binds in an equal manner all the parties to the contract. Yet, similarly to the Directive, the French Civil Code did not contain and does not contain any detail as to what the duty precisely entails nor the standards by which it is to be judged.[130] It fell to the French courts to fill the gap.

123. Economic duress, promissory estoppel, misrepresentation, mistake, frustration, implied terms and abusive termination. See also Mason, who argues that English law already contains some aspects of a duty of good faith. He argues that English law is moving away from the traditional adversarial concept of contract towards "a conception of contract, which places more emphasis on conduct, which takes account of the interests of the other party" (AF Mason, *Contract, good faith and equitable standards in fair dealing* (2000) 116 LQR 72).

124. *Per* Lord Steyn, op cit fn 122, p 439. For an earlier comment, see *First Energy (UK) Ltd* v. *Hungarian International Bank Ltd* [1993] 2 Lloyd's Rep 194, 196.

125. *Per* Lord Steyn, op cit, fn 122, p 439.

126. See section 3.4.1.4.

127. See sections 3.4.1.12 and 3.4.1.15.

128. Article 1134–3 stipulates that parties must perform the contract in good faith.

129. ECJ case 64/81 *Corman* v. *Hauptzollamt Gronau* [1982] ECR 13, 14 January 1982, para 8; ECJ case C–296/95 *R* v. *Customs & Excise Commissioners, ex p. EMU Tabac SARL* [1998] ECR I–1605, 2 April 1998.

130. These were some of the lacunae of the French system highlighted by Professor Powell in his article, R Powell, *Good Faith in Contract* (1956) 9 CLP 16, p 31.

In relation to the commercial agency relationship, France has implemented the Directive in a way that is consistent with its pre-existing law and which appears not to have involved changing the rationale.[131] Where the Directive requires the parties to behave with good faith towards each other, the French Commercial Code stipulates that the relationship is entered into for the common interest of the parties.[132] So far as we are aware, in French law this consequence of the mutual obligation of good faith as making the contract one of "common interest" is unique to commercial agency agreements. Looking at how the notions of common interest and good faith have been applied in French law could therefore be useful to illustrate how good faith is intended to work in the sphere of the commercial agency relationship.

Looking first at French contract law generally (i.e. the Civil Code), good faith acts as a rule of conduct, which essentially requires duties of loyalty, fidelity and co-operation from each party when performing their respective obligations. French contract law classifies the parties to the contract in respect of each obligation as either the creditor (*créancier*) or debtor (*débiteur*) of that obligation i.e. the promisee and the promisor. Depending on the role of the party in question, the obligation of good faith varies slightly and each must be considered in turn.

Good faith and the promisor

In relation to the promisor of an obligation, loyalty requires him to perform his contractual duties honestly and faithfully, and also conscientiously and diligently. In order to complete these contractual duties, the promisor must by implication take all reasonable steps in the particular circumstances to perform the contract in the most useful manner for the promisee. Those steps are what a reasonably prudent and conscientious *commerçant* (trader) or *gérant* (manager of a business) would take: he is not obliged to put his own business at risk. A promisor would therefore be in breach of his duty of loyalty, should he, on purpose, fail to complete the contractual obligations by, for instance, placing himself in a situation where it would be impossible to perform.[133] Any action by the promisor intended to prevent the promisee from acquiring the expected contractual profits would be regarded as disloyal and in breach of good faith.[134] Finally, loyalty also prevents the promisor from taking advantage of the situation for his sole profit.[135]

131. In France, commercial agents have been protected since 1958 through a decree (Decree of 23 December 1958, D 1958, L). France implemented the Directive through a statute in 1991. The statute has since been incorporated *in extenso* in the commercial code. We will therefore refer to the articles of the commercial code.

132. Article L 134–4 of the French Commercial Code. See Appendix 5 for a translation.

133. For the commercial agent, this would be a breach of a loyalty, by, for example, acting for competing principals without the knowledge and consent of the first principal. CA Rennes, 1 April 1998, *Sté Lambert* v. *Loiret*, mentioned in Chapter 6 fn 113. The position in English law is curiously not clear (see section 3.3.1.2.2 above). The Schedule to the Agency Regulations, para 3(c), suggests that in commercial agency agreements there may now be an implied obligation not to act for principals "whose interests are . . . conflicting", at least where the first principal is not aware of and has not consented to it. See further Chapter 2.

134. *CA Paris, 22 January 1995*, D 1995, J, 128 where an author who wanted to get out of a *contrat de préférence* with a publishing house deliberately submitted two manuscripts of a very mediocre quality, hoping that they would be rejected by the publisher who would then terminate the contract (publishers in France have a statutory right to terminate a contract with an author when they have refused two consecutive manuscripts). The court held that the author was still contractually bound and had to submit two novels and write them to the best of his abilities.

135. *Cass Com, 25 June 1991*, Bull IV, 236 where the distributor under a distribution agreement had kept for his sole benefit a copy of the customer list when the contract ended was held to have acted in bad faith. See also *Civ 1ère, 26 November 1996*, Bull I, No 415 where an insurance company was held to be in breach of the duty

The meaning of good faith as a duty of diligence/conscientiousness seems to be explicitly present in the Agency Regulations since they require the commercial agent, when promisor, to use *proper efforts* to comply with his contractual duties.[136] It seems therefore possible to say that the "in particular" additional duties imposed on the commercial agent in Regulation 3(2) are just an illustration of what good faith means in practice. It simply means that the commercial agent must make all reasonable efforts when performing his contractual obligations. So far, this seems no different from the traditional obligation at common law.

Good faith and the promisee

In relation to the promisee of an obligation, his duty of good faith under French law is slightly different. It essentially obliges him to allow the promisor to perform his contractual obligations conscientiously and as the promisor should do, assuming that the promisor himself is complying with his obligations of good faith. The promisee must render the promisor's performance easier, or, at the very least, must not make it any harder than it inherently is. In other words, he must abstain from being disloyal. A promisee would be disloyal were he to act in such a manner so as to render the promisor's performance impossible[137] or simply more difficult.[138]

This aspect of the duty of good faith seems to be present in the Agency Regulations, though it is not at all clearly spelt out. Regulation 4(2) contains what we see as particular examples of the principal's obligation to act "dutifully and in good faith" to allow or facilitate the commercial agent to perform his contractual obligations,[139] for example, by requiring the principal to inform the commercial agent of various facts which are relevant for the performance of the contract such as, amongst others, information on the products and the market.[140] Similarly to the conclusion reached for the commercial agent, it seems clear that these "additional duties" which the principal must perform "in particular" are merely examples of a wider, more general duty of co-operation imposed on the principal. These applications of the general principle, in Regulation 4(2), must definitely not be seen as an exhaustive list. Arguably, the obligation of the principal, as a promisee, to give the commercial agent the means to perform his obligations and not to place obstacles in his way also extends to paying him the due commission on time. This seems to be what transpires from the case of *Bell Electric* v. *Aweco Ltd*,[141] in which Elias J in the High Court

of loyalty when it remained *maliciously silent* on the payment of an insurance claim in order to try to avoid having to pay it because of the imminent expiry of a limitation period.

136. Regulation 3(2)(a).

137. F Terré gives the example of a creditor who sends the debtor a seven-day formal demand for payment before starting legal proceedings, knowing perfectly well that the debtor is away for two weeks and therefore unable to respond to the demand. See F Terré, Ph Simler and Y Lequette, *Droit Civil, les Obligations*, (1996), para 415, p 348.

138. *Cass Com 3–11–1992*, JCP 1993, II, 22164 where in an exclusive distribution contract, the oil company was held to be in breach of good faith when it prevented the distributor from charging a competitive price with no just cause to do so on grounds of *force majeure*.

139. Regulation 4(2). It is to be noted that the two proposals of the European Commission were closer to the French law notion since they required the principal to "make available to the commercial agent all the assistance he needs, having regard to the circumstances for the performance of the contracts" *per* article 10(1): OJ C. 56/9, 2 March 1979.

140. Regulation 4(2)(a).

141. [2002] EWHC QBD 8 May 2002. For details, see Chapter 5, section 5.2.1.3.2, especially fnn 99–101 and associated text.

held that for the principal to stop paying the commercial agent's commissions for no valid reason was a serious breach of contract, entitling the commercial agent to terminate for "reasons attributable to the principal"[142] and not depriving him of his right to claim compensation.

So far we have concentrated mainly on only one aspect of the duty of good faith as it exists in French contract law, that of loyalty/fidelity. Good faith in France can also require a duty of positive co-operation and collaboration for certain types of contracts, where each party must in effect look after the other's interests as well as his own. This aspect of the duty of good faith is not required for all types of contracts, but it is particularly relevant in commercial agency contracts, which, in France, are, as noted earlier, considered to be entered into for the common interest of the parties.[143] As will be seen later, this characteristic of the commercial agency relationship is of crucial importance since it is thought to implement the good faith requirement in the Directive. This notion, which was first created by the French courts as a tool to protect commercial agents on termination, is now more important than that. It not only forms the basis of the lump sum payable on termination, in French law,[144] the compensation award, but also acts as the fundamental guiding principle for the obligations of the parties while the relationship is alive. This notion of common interest highlights the symmetry of the parties, which is so crucial to the commercial agency relationship.

The co-operation aspect of the duty of good faith in French contract law requires a more proactive stance from the parties than the loyalty/fidelity one. It requires, for instance, the promisor to refrain from acting in a way which would jeopardise the promisee's interests. As for the promisee, he would be disloyal if he failed to provide such support for the promisor as a reasonably prudent businessman, having proper regard to his own interests, would do.

In relation to the principal, the rules provided by the Agency Regulations are very different from the English common law rules, which of course left (and, where the Agency Regulations do not apply, still leave) principals a great freedom to behave towards their agents however they think fit, subject only to compliance with a literal interpretation of the terms of the agency agreement (which in practice will often have been drafted mainly by the principal in the first place) and to some very limited further controls (as to which, see below, section 3.4.1.5.1).

But the co-operation aspect of the duty of good faith seems to have been very well understood by the English Court of Appeal in the case of *Page* v. *Combined Shipping and Transport Ltd*,[145] where the court looked at a clause giving the principal absolute discretion as to how much business he put the agent's way and therefore how much commission the commercial agent would have the opportunity to earn. The court decided that there was at the very least a good arguable case that to leave the principal free to use such a clause according to its express terms, so as to ensure that the commercial agent earned no commission at all or only a minimal commission where such had not been the parties' original intentions, would be a breach by the principal of his duty of good faith. It will be recalled that this case was an application for an interlocutory injunction to freeze the defendant's assets pending trial (so that all the claimant had to show was that he had a

142. Regulation 18(b)(i).
143. Article L 134–4 of the French commercial code. See Appendix 5 for a translation.
144. For details, see Chapter 6, section 6.4.1.
145. [1997] 3 All ER 656.

good arguable case that he was entitled to a substantial sum), and therefore the decision is not conclusive. Yet, it is nevertheless interesting as an example of what good faith means, as a rule of conduct over the parties' behaviour. This case is reviewed in more detail later on.

We are not, as explained earlier, advocating that the concept of good faith as it applies in French contract law should be adopted in the UK. However, in the light of the protective stance of the Agency Regulations, it seems logical to consider the good faith obligation as a requirement that permeates the relationship as a whole. Furthermore, Regulations 3(2) and 4(2) should not be seen as an exhaustive list of what good faith entails, but only as examples. This logic seems to have been adopted by the Court of Appeal in the case of *Page* v. *Combined Shipping and Transport Co Ltd* and by the judge at first instance in *Cooper and others* v. *Pure Fishing (UK) Ltd.*[146] The mutual obligations of good faith as a means of controlling the behaviour of the parties are especially important in relation to the rights of each party to summarily terminate the relationship, as will be seen in Chapter 5.

3.4.1.5 English law analogies with the duty of good faith: obligations of trust and confidence, co-operation etc

We shall start by looking at such analogies as exist in contract law generally, and then focus on two specific "relationship" contracts, those of partnership and employment, which we consider (particularly the latter) to be helpful in trying to understand what the mutual obligations of good faith contain.

3.4.1.5.1 The law of contract generally

We have commented above on the absence of a general duty of good faith on contracting parties in English contract law. There are, nevertheless, limited examples of English law implying a term into commercial contracts that the parties must co-operate with each other to achieve the larger purpose of the contract.[147] Being based on the usual principles for implying terms into contracts (that a term cannot be implied unless both parties must necessarily have intended it, so that, if an officious bystander had suggested it to them during the course of their negotiations both would immediately have answered "Oh, of course",[148] or that the term is "necessary for business efficacy"[149]), such instances are, accordingly, rare. They depend on all the circumstances, and are based not on what might seem reasonable but on the express terms of the contract and on what is needed to bring those about,[150] and unlike the mutual duties of good faith in the Agency Regulations, will yield to contrary intention.

Mackay v. *Dick*,[151] a House of Lords judgment on appeal from the Scottish Court of Session, is taken as one of the leading cases in this area. The obligation to co-operate is, at face value, phrased in very powerful language and the standard of co-operation required seems to be pitched at a high level. It is a sale of goods dispute between buyer and seller

146. [2004] EWCA Civ 375, Court of Appeal, 18 March 2004.

147. See in particular JF Burrows, "Contractual co-operation and the implied term" (1968) 31 MLR 390.

148. *Hamlyn* v. *Wood* [1891] 2 QB 488, 491, *per* Lord Esher.

149. *The Woodcock* (1889) 14 PD 64, 68 *per* Lord Bowen.

150. See Lightman J in *Evans* v. *SMG Television Ltd and others* [2003] EWHC 1423 (Ch), 26 June 2003, para 192.

151. (1880–91) LR 6 App Cas 251.

of a large piece of tunnelling machinery. The (written) contract was made conditional upon the machine fulfilling performance criteria at "a properly opened-up" excavation at the site where the buyer, a contractor building a railway, was working. The specified test conditions were never made available by the buyer, who, when the machine had failed to perform at an excavation on site which was not "properly opened-up", nevertheless refused to give it any further trial and refused to pay the price. In ordering the buyer to pay the price, Lord Blackburn (giving the principal judgment of the court) made the general statement:

> where in a written contract it appears that both parties have agreed that something shall be done, which cannot effectually be done unless both concur in doing it, the construction of the contract is that each agrees to do all that is necessary to be done on his part for the carrying out of that thing, though there may be no express words to that effect. What is the part of each must depend on circumstances . . . [152]

This is, on the face of it, demanding language, requiring the parties to do *all* that is necessary to achieve the agreed objective. The substance of the case leads, however, to the considerably less startling proposition that, the contract having been made expressly conditional on the machine meeting performance criteria, there was a necessary implication that the buyer would make the agreed test conditions available and that, he having failed to do that, he was estopped from saying that the machine did not fulfil the condition which he had himself imposed.

Subsequent cases in the area of general commercial contracts have confirmed the view that the degree of co-operation required of the promisee by reason of the *Mackay* v. *Dick* implied term is very limited and, where it does arise, certainly not very demanding.

This comes most clearly from the judgment of Devlin J (as he then was) in *Mona Oil Equipment and Supply Co Ltd* v. *Rhodesia Railways Ltd*,[153] which concerned an agreement for the sale and purchase of a number of second-hand oil storage tanks which the seller did not yet own. Payment was expressed to be conditional on issue of a written confirmation by the buyer's shipping agent that the tanks were at the buyer's disposal. The seller approached the buyer's agent to seek that confirmation, but the agent, who had received no formal instructions from the buyer to act in the matter and took a rather officious position, refused to issue any confirmation. On the same day as hearing from the seller that its agent was proving unco-operative, the buyer formally instructed its agent to act. A technical inspection of the tanks then took place, some parts were found to be defective, the buyer refused to pay the price until the good parts had been segregated, and there was a general breakdown of communications between the parties. Finally the actual owners of the tanks concluded that the deal between seller and buyer was "off" and cancelled their contract with the seller. The seller accordingly sued the buyer for breach of contract, pleading that the contract impliedly put upon the buyer the duty to ensure their agents ascertained that the tanks were at the buyer's disposal and more generally a duty to do nothing to prevent or obstruct payment of the price. Devlin J, in refusing to award damages, accepted that the buyer was under an implied obligation to co-operate with the seller, but said that that went no further than what was absolutely necessary to make the contract workable in accordance with its express terms; that the buyer had performed such implied obligation as it had by instructing its agent in accordance with the contract to

152. *Ibid*, p 263.
153. (1949–50) 83 Ll L Rep 178.

proceed, and that it was not under any obligation to do anything further to inform the seller of the position or to try to clear up the misunderstanding (even though the buyer could very easily have done that). In effect, performance of the implied obligation to co-operate amounted to doing no more than the contract obliged the buyer to do in any event.

Such implied duties of co-operation, even in the fairly rare instances where they have been implied, are, accordingly, not at all demanding. In general, they will at most amount to a duty on each party to refrain from taking active steps to obstruct or make more difficult the performance by the other party of his obligations under the contract, rather than a duty to take positive steps to help the other party perform. In some situations, particularly where the party to whom performance is owed is exercising his property rights or is trading with other people, not even a term to refrain from taking active steps obstructive to the other party's performance will be implied.[154]

As Burrows says,[155]

> The law . . . stops short of demanding co-operation merely because that would be reasonable. The English law does not require a degree of conduct equivalent to the Roman "good faith". By and large, the motto seems to be "each man for himself", and a party is not required to interrupt his own activities merely to help the other if he sees him getting into difficulties . . . A party must perform his express promises to the letter; he must refrain from certain acts which substantially impede either the other party's performance or his enjoyment [of the subject-matter of the contract], in particular if those acts are done without any reasonable excuse. But this does not go very far. He may be allowed to get away with positive acts of obstruction if he was merely going about his business with others. He is seldom required actually to do a positive act which is not provided for in the express terms; he need only do that if there is something approaching a necessity for the act to render the express parts of the contract workable.[156]

Except for certain specific "relationship" contracts, this remains a fair representation of the position. The apparently wider statements by Lightman J in *Evans* v. *SMG Television Ltd. and others*[157] (a case about implied duties of co-operation in a contract for services between an effectively self-employed radio presenter and a broadcasting company) should not be taken as applicable outside those contexts.

Implied terms restricting the exercise of contractual discretions

What appears to be a separate strand of judicial authority establishes, however, that where under a commercial contract one party has a discretion the exercise of which is, on the face of it, unlimited, there may, in some circumstances, be implied into the contract some (admittedly fairly modest) limitations on the exercise of that discretion. Lord Mance in *Gan Insurance Co Ltd* v. *Tai Ping Insurance Co Ltd*[158] was emphatic that this is not an automatic implication in every case, and that it all depends on the circumstances. In *The Product Star*,[159] Leggatt LJ indicated that the courts are willing to read into contractual discretions in commercial contracts the implied term that "not only must the discretion be

154. E.g. *Luxor (Eastbourne) Ltd* v. *Cooper* [1941] AC 108, where the estate agent introduced a prospective purchaser to the client but the client subsequently decided not to sell his property, and the agent was held not entitled to any commission, contrast with *Alpha Trading* v. *Dunnshaw Patten* [1981] QB 290. See fn 80 above.

155. Op cit fn 147 above, pp 404–405.

156. As, indeed, there was in *Mackay* v. *Dick*, above.

157. [2003] EWHC Ch 1423 (26 June 2003), Ch D.

158. [2001] EWCA Civ 1047.

159. *Abu Dhabi National Tanker Co* v. *Product Star Shipping Ltd, The Product Star* [1993] 1 Lloyd's Rep 397, 404 (CA).

exercised honestly and in good faith, but, having regard to the provisions of the contract by which it is conferred, it must not be exercised arbitrarily, capriciously or unreasonably". In *Gan Insurance*, Mance LJ, while sounding the note of caution just mentioned, was in no doubt that, on the facts (the case concerned a reinsurance contract containing a claims co-operation clause whereby the reinsured was to co-operate with the reinsurers in the investigation and assessment of any loss, and no settlement was to be made nor liability admitted without the prior approval of the reinsurers, and the relevant issue was whether the reinsurers could withhold that approval if there were no reasonable grounds for so doing), there was an implied term in the contract prohibiting "unreasonableness in the sense of conduct or a decision to which no reasonable person having the relevant discretion could have subscribed". Despite repeating with approval the words used in *Gan Insurance*, Leggatt LJ in *The Product Star* warned strongly against taking too literally the apparent analogy with unreasonableness in the *Wednesbury Corporation* sense[160] in public law judicial review. The use of such words by the courts in these cases, though, is surely no accident; it is indicative of a judicial desire to maintain a relatively uninterventionist, "hands-off" role in such situations, only intervening in the most extreme cases: the courts cannot, of course, take the commercial decision in place of the parties.

Similarly, in *Paragon Finance plc* v. *Nash*,[161] the Court of Appeal held that a mortgagee's contractual power under a mortgage deed to vary the interest rate was not completely unfettered. The reasonable expectations of the parties, held the court, required that a term be implied to the effect that that discretion would not be exercised dishonestly, for an improper purpose, capriciously, arbitrarily or in a way that no reasonable lender, acting reasonably, would ever do.

Summing up, in *Horkaluk* v. *Cantor Fitzgerald International*,[162] Potter LJ said that:

> . . . in cases of this kind, the implication of the term is not the application of a "good faith doctrine, which does not exist in English contract law; rather it is a requirement necessary to give genuine value, rather than nominal force or mere lip-service, to the obligation of the party required or empowered to exercise the relevant discretion. While, in any such situation, the parties are likely to have conflicting interests and the provisions of the contract effectively place the resolution of that conflict in the hands of the party exercising the discretion, it is presumed to be the reasonable expectation and therefore the common intention of the parties that there should be a genuine and rational, as opposed to an empty or irrational, exercise of discretion. Thus the courts impose an implied term of the nature and to the extent described".[163]

The implied restrictions on the exercise of discretionary powers under contracts fit very well into the scheme of Regulations 3 and 4, to the extent that such apparently unfettered discretions cannot now be regarded as exercisable in accordance with their terms.

Accordingly, whilst the duties of co-operation normally implied in English law into a general commercial contract and the restrictions sometimes implied into the exercise of contractual discretions go some way to illustrating the possible effects of Regulations 3

160. *Associated Provincial Picture Houses Ltd* v. *Wednesbury Corporation* [1948] 1 KB 223 (a decision "so unreasonable that no reasonable authority could ever have come to it . . . to prove a case of that kind would require something overwhelming" (*per* Lord Greene); "a decision of the council . . . so outrageous that no right thinking person could support it" (*per* Griffiths LJ in *R* v. *Greenwich London Borough Council, ex p. Cedar Transport Group Ltd*, [1983] RA 173).

161. [2001] EWCA Civ 1466, para 41.

162. [2004] EWCA Civ 1287, 14 October 2004.

163. *Ibid*, para 30.

and 4 (and certainly seem to be consistent with those provisions), they do not provide a sufficient analogy to explain what Regulations 3 and 4 mean.

3.4.1.5.2 The mutual obligations of trust and confidence between partners in a partnership

Given the symmetry under the Agency Regulations of the duties of good faith of commercial agent and principal and the on-going "relational" nature of the arrangement, it is worth exploring whether the English law of partnership could be seen as a source of guidance as to their content.

Partnership in English law works by way of a matrix of reciprocal agency agreements between each partner and his co-partners generally creating similar obligations. By contrast, the obligations of the parties under a commercial agency agreement, though reciprocal, are not similar. The analogy with partnerships is perhaps not the easiest, given the traditional unwillingness of the English courts to intervene in disputes between partners other than with a view to the "nuclear" solution of dissolving the partnership altogether.[164] That is based on the view that, in the absence of allegations of dishonesty, disputes between partners are matters of internal management, and that the courts should not involve themselves in those. Partners being assumed to be capable of looking after themselves against their fellow partners, the assumption is that parties are capable of resolving their own differences about the running of the firm without judicial interference, except where the differences are terminal, and then the possibility of an application to the court to seek an order for dissolution is always there. The attitude is that the relationship of partnership requires a significant degree of "give and take" from all concerned. The current edition of *Lindley and Banks on Partnership* quotes the following statement of Lord Lindley's:

> . . . it is no part of the duty of the court to settle all partnership squabbles: it expects from every partner a certain amount of forbearance and good feeling towards his co-partner; and it does not regard mere passing improprieties, arising from infirmities of temper, as sufficient to warrant a decree for dissolution, or an order for an injunction, or a receiver.[165]

The assumption in the partnership relationship of a broad equality of bargaining power between partners is, admittedly, very different from the "downtrodden race" of commercial agents to whom Staughton LJ referred in *Page* v. *Combined Shipping and Transport Co Ltd*, but the French "mandate of common interest" idea and the notionally joint-ownership of the goodwill means that, in our view, it is an analogy worth pursuing nevertheless.

The issue of whether one partner can recover damages from his co-partners for breach of the partnership agreement is described in the leading text in this field as "one of the most difficult and unresolved areas of partnership law".[166] It would seem, however, that, not unlike the position in English law as to damages claims for breach of directly effective provisions of competition law prior to the Court of Appeal judgment in *Crehan* v. *Inntrepreneur Pub Company*,[167] people invariably proceed on the basis that a damages remedy is available. There is, by contrast, no question that breach of the mutual duties of good

164. See R I'Anson Banks, *Lindley and Banks on Partnership* (Sweet & Maxwell, 18th edn, 2002), para 23–14ff.

165. *Ibid*, para 23–16.

166. *Ibid*, para 23–206ff.

167. [2004] EWCA Civ 637, 21 May 2004.

faith in the Agency Regulations can give rise to a liability to pay damages (though, for the reasons noted above, such claims will understandably in practice be very rare unless and until the agreement terminates). In that sense, given that breaches of the reciprocal duties of good faith in the commercial agency agreement are likely to be treated as serious,[168] the analogy is perhaps more useful than at first sight appears. We do not consider that the *obiter dicta* comments of Lord Millett in *Hurst* v. *Bryk*,[169] to the effect that partnership agreements are different from other types of contract and that the Partnership Act has the effect of denying to a partner in a firm the right unilaterally to bring about the automatic dissolution of the partnership by acceptance of a repudiatory breach of the partnership agreement by other partners, limiting him instead to an application to the court for a (discretionary) order for dissolution, makes the analogy inappropriate (as those comments appear to go only to remedies and not to breach).

The partners in a partnership have relations of mutual trust and confidence towards each other.[170] They are, after all, "persons carrying on a business in common with a view to profit",[171] which presupposes that they are carrying on the business for their common benefit and that they have, in relation to the business, accepted expressly or by implication at least some level of mutual rights and obligations towards each other.[172]

The body of English law referred to as partners' duties of good faith towards one another is concerned exclusively with partners' central obligations of honesty,[173] the obligation on each partner to provide full information to any of his other partners about the firm's affairs,[174] and the partner's conventional fiduciary obligations not to benefit himself at the expense of his partners and not to use partnership property, opportunities etc for his own advantage.[175]

In addition to these "classic" fiduciary duties of good faith towards each other, partners owe each other a duty to act, when concerned with the firm's affairs, with reasonable care and not to incur avoidable liabilities for their partners. Losses resulting from a breach by one of the partners of those duties have to be borne, in the absence of contrary agreement, by the relevant partner,[176] thus forming an exception to the general principle that a partnership's losses are to be borne equally between the partners.[177] *Lindley and Banks on Partnership* makes the comment that this might be regarded as one aspect of or as an extension of the partner's duty of good faith, but that this idea has not been widely accepted in the partnership context.[178]

On the standard of care required, as between partners the traditional attitude in England has been to take a subjective approach, requiring of each partner the standard of care he would apply to handling his own personal affairs. In other words, the partners in a firm have to take each other very much as they are, with all their inherent strengths and

168. See the limited case law to date referred to in section 3.4.1 above.
169. [2000] UKHL 19 (30 March 2000).
170. *Whywait Ltd and Mays* v. *Davison* [1996] QCA 178, [1997] 1 Qd.R. 225 (Supreme Court of Queensland, Court of Appeal).
171. The statutory definition of a partnership in the Partnership Act 1890, s 1(1).
172. See R I'Anson Banks, op cit, fn 164, para 2–06.
173. See *Carmichael* v. *Evans* [1904] 1 Ch 486, 492, *per* Byrne J.
174. See, in the absence of express provision, Partnership Act 1890, s (28).
175. See, *inter alia*, Partnership Act 1890, s 29.
176. *Bury* v. *Allen* (1845) 1 Colly 589, *per* Lord Lindley.
177. Partnership Act 1890, s 24.
178. R I'Anson Banks, op cit, fn 164, para 20–11.

weaknesses, and the real protection lies in not taking an incompetent person into partnership in the first place. A partner who claims or is regarded as having special skills will, however, even on the traditional approach, be subject to a higher standard of care[179] An important recent Scottish case, *Ross Harper & Murphy* v. *Scott Banks*,[180] takes a rather different approach, indicating that the standard of care expected of the partner will be what is reasonable in "all the relevant circumstances", including (importantly) the nature of the business of the partnership in question (and including any risks inherent in that) and the way the partners in the firm in question normally conduct their affairs, but accepting that the relationship of partnership "may import some mutual tolerance of error" (though how much tolerance is not spelt out).[181] It is not clear whether this hybrid subjective/objective approach is a reliable statement of English law.

Whether mutual obligations between commercial agent and principal to take reasonable care in their doings within their relationship are part of the mutual duties of good faith in Regulations 3 and 4 of the Agency Regulations remains to be seen. From the commercial agent's side, such an obligation would in effect duplicate the agent's common law obligation to exercise reasonable skill, care and diligence in performing his duties. Given the symmetry which the mutual obligations seek to bring to the relationship, it would seem not unreasonable for the principal, for his part, to be under similar obligations towards the commercial agent to act with reasonable care (e.g. as to the provision of market information under the specific duty in Regulation 4(2)(b), though this example may be covered by general principles of liability for negligent advice in tort law anyway).

Given the traditionally limited intervention of the courts in the partnership relationship mentioned above, one does not, outside the areas of fiduciary duties and the reciprocal duties of care referred to above, find judicial statements in English law about the general obligations of partners to one another during the life of the partnership. English partnership law simply does not work in that way. By looking at certain of the grounds on which, under the Partnership Act 1890, the court may dissolve a partnership on the application of one or more of the partners, it seems possible, however, to deduce some general obligations by a process akin to reverse engineering. The grounds for dissolution of a partnership could thus be said to form a sort of negative code of behaviour; this is not the behaviour of partners behaving properly or normally. It is not, of course, a complete code: it only represents the most serious, extreme breaches of partners' obligations to each other, those of a gravity such as to justify a dissolution of the firm. We suggest, nevertheless, that the principles thus deduced cast some helpful light on the reciprocal duties of good faith between commercial agent and principal, or at least on the serious examples of what principal and commercial agent should not do. Since the duties of the commercial agent to his principal are much more fully developed in English common law generally, we believe that these analogies will be of more use in trying to establish the meaning of the principal's duty of good faith to the commercial agent.

Section 35 of the Partnership Act 1890 provides:

> On application by a partner, the court may decree a dissolution of the partnership in any of the following cases:
> (a) [repealed by the Mental Health Act 1959];

179. *Winsor* v. *Schroeder*, (1979) 129 NLJ 1266.

180. 2000 SLT 699 (Outer House of the Court of Session).

181. R I'Anson Banks, op cit fn 164, para 20–12, n 51 reports that, on the appeal, the Inner House did not appear to support this formulation but made no conclusive comment either way.

(b) when a partner (other than the partner suing) becomes in any other way permanently incapable of performing his part of the partnership contract;
(c) when a partner (other than the partner suing) has been guilty of such conduct as, in the opinion of the court, regard being had to the nature of the business, is calculated to prejudicially affect the carrying on of the business;
(d) when a partner (other than the partner suing) wilfully or persistently commits a breach of the partnership agreement, or otherwise so conducts himself in matters relating to the partnership business that it is not reasonably practicable for the other partner or partners to carry on the business in partnership with him;
(e) when the business of the partnership can only be carried on at a loss; or
(f) whenever in any case circumstances have arisen which, in the opinion of the court, render it just and equitable that the partnership be dissolved.

The pertinent points here are section 35(c) and the second limb of section 35(d), and there may well be a significant overlap between the two. There is only very limited reported case law on these provisions.

What is conduct "calculated to prejudicially affect the carrying on of the business"? In the partnership context, it is thought that this would include the commission of a serious criminal offence by a partner, at least (but perhaps not only) where it arose directly from the partnership business. Equally, conduct which amounted to breach of some professional rules might well have this effect, although again one would have thought that the breach must be a serious one. The main concern for the other partners will, of course, be for the commercial reputation of the firm.[182] *Quaere* whether there would only be a breach by one party of its duty of good faith if the other party were entirely innocent of any wrongdoing. But, moving into the agency context, what if the principal, against well-reasoned advice in the strongest terms from the commercial agent, launches and requires the commercial agent to handle a new range of products which the agent considers will be a commercial disaster, not only making huge losses but also likely to cause serious damage to both their reputations, and that prediction is fulfilled? Such conduct by the principal would then have prejudicially affected the carrying on of, certainly the commercial agent's business, if not that of the principal too. Would the principal be in breach of its duty of good faith to the commercial agent here?

Examples from the partnership context of behaviour which could make it "not reasonably practicable for the other partners to carry on the business" in partnership with one of their number could include behaviour that very seriously damaged the commercial credibility of the firm; continual quarrelling and having reached a degree of animosity where there is no realistic chance of friendly co-operation being restored in the future; or, perhaps, one partner taking major steps in relation to a very significant matter of partnership business on which he knows that the other partners will have strong and differing views but does nothing to consult them (e.g. finalising and serving the defence in a major piece of litigation against the firm; taking on the lease of new premises, perhaps dismissing a key employee etc); or persistent refusal by a partner to attend partnership meetings

182. Cf. the supportive attitude of the House of Lords to the ex-employees' claims in the joined cases of *Malik* v. *Bank of Credit and Commerce International* and *Mahmud* v. *BCCI* [1998] AC 20 that the stigma attaching to them as a result of their ex-employer's collapse and the revelations that the latter had operated its business for many years in a systematically, institutionally fraudulent and corrupt manner (of participation in which they were treated as entirely innocent) had made them unemployable. The House of Lords was emphatic that it would not regard a similar stigma worthy of compensation attaching to an employee by reason of the fact that the employer's business had simply failed or not been very successful.

or to take part in important decision-making; or simply (at least in an extreme case) "not pulling one's weight" (at least if he has warnings, a chance to improve, etc).[183]

All of these ideas could have an application, by analogy, in the reciprocal duties of good faith between principal and commercial agent in Regulations 3 and 4 of the Agency Regulations.

3.4.1.5.3 The mutual implied obligations of trust and confidence between employer and employee under the contract of employment[184]

Individual employment law is the major exception to the hesitation of English law about implying obligations of co-operation, trust and confidence etc into contracts. In this area, the courts have been doing exactly that for many years, and with an enthusiasm which, considering their approach generally, seems really nothing short of remarkable.

The origins of this principle lie in the statutory protection against unfair dismissal introduced by the Industrial Relations Act 1971 (now contained in the Employment Rights Act 1999). A pre-requisite for the employee bringing a claim for unfair dismissal is that he must have been dismissed by the employer, and for the employee to terminate the contract of employment of his own motion, by way of resigning from his job, is not a dismissal by the employer. The 1971 Act incorporated the concept of constructive dismissal, that termination by the employee will nevertheless be treated as a dismissal by the employer where the employee's termination is caused by some act of the employer justifying the employee in regarding the contract as having been brought to an end by the employer. *Western Excavating (ECC) Ltd* v. *Sharp*[185] was a judicial cutting-back on the range of behaviour by the employer which would allow a resignation by the employee to be treated as constructive dismissal. The Court of Appeal said that a resignation by the employee could only be treated as a constructive dismissal if what the employer had done amounted to a material breach by him of some contractual obligation of his under the contract of employment: allegedly unreasonable behaviour less than a breach of contract was not enough. The courts, having taken away with one hand, then proceeded, to a large extent, to give back with the other hand, expanding the range of the employer's contractual obligations by developing the mutual implied duties of trust and confidence, which did not add very much to the pre-existing implied duties on the employee's part[186] but were a material addition to the employer's obligations.

In *Malik* v. *Bank of Credit and Commercial International SA (in voluntary liquidation)*,[187] the House of Lords confirmed that the mutual obligations of trust and confidence are a crucial implied term in the contract of employment. Lord Steyn summed up the obligation, seen from the employer's viewpoint, thus:

> It is . . . an obligation that the employer shall not without reasonable and proper cause conduct itself in a manner calculated and likely to destroy or seriously damage the relationship of confidence and trust between employer and employee.

He further emphasised that, in the employment context at least, it adds far more to the employer's obligations than it does to those of the employee (where there were already

183. See further R I'Anson Banks, op cit fn 164, paras 24–70ff.

184. See D Brodie (1996) 25 Industrial Law Journal 121, (1998) 27 Industrial Law Journal 79, (2001) 117 LQR 604.

185. [1978] ICR 221, CA.

186. Though note the predictions of D Brodie ((1998) 27 ILJ 79) that the courts may well in the future start to add to the employee's obligations through the implied term.

187. Fn 182.

implied obligations to serve the employer loyally and not to act contrary to the employer's interests).

The following introductory statements on the subject from leading employment texts give more of the general flavour:

> It is incumbent upon an employer and employee to facilitate performance of their mutual obligations under the contract. This is a general contractual principle, particularly relevant to the employment relationship, which takes effect as an implied term in the contract.[188]

> The duty of mutual trust and confidence is a mutual duty, owed by both employer and employee, to one another. It affects every aspect of the employment relationship, often determining the manner in which other express or implied terms of the contract are to be exercised by the parties or determining the limits of the rights and duties imposed by those terms . . . . .The duty of mutual trust and confidence is implied into all contracts of employment, obliging the parties to do nothing to undermine the mutual trust and confidence which is regarded as the cornerstone of the relationship of employment.[189]

In *Donovan* v. *Invicta Airways Ltd* [1969] 2 Lloyd's Rep 413, Wrangam J referred to the duty of each of the parties to the contract of employment "to treat each other with such a degree of consideration and courtesy as will enable the service to be carried on". Put another way, is the employer's behaviour, taken as a whole and judged reasonably and sensibly, something that the employee could not be expected to put up with?[190]

The emphasis in the passages just quoted upon the pervasiveness of this implied obligation in the employment relationship and on how it bears upon the performance of other terms (express and implied) of the contract of employment is very important for present purposes. The policy of English individual employment law since the early 1970s of seeking to even out an imbalance of power between employer and employee is exactly the same as the second aim of the Directive, the "motive of social policy, that commercial agents are a down-trodden race [who] need and should be afforded protection against their principals".[191] Its essence is to strike a balance between the employer's interest in managing his business as he thinks fit and the employee's interest in not being unfairly and improperly exploited.[192]

The obligations which these mutual duties impose on employers are, as already identified, particularly relevant for present purposes. Although there are some differences between the two as to the situations when they respectively apply (the complications arising at the time of the termination of the relationship: see below), we consider that the implied mutual obligations of trust and confidence in the individual contract of employment are the closest that English law has come to achieving an outcome similar to that intended to be brought about by Regulations 3 and 4 of the Agency Regulations, and form very useful indications as to how Regulations 3 and 4 should be understood and interpreted.

It is also important that, in employment law, the mutual obligations appear to go beyond a passive obligation on each party not to do anything to prevent or obstruct the performance by the other of its obligations,[193] but rather are an obligation to take positive steps

188. BA Hepple, *Hepple and O'Higgins: Employment Law* (Sweet & Maxwell, 4th edn, 1981), p 134.

189. D Peyton, in *Encyclopaedia of Employment Law* (Sweet & Maxwell, loose-leaf), para 2I–1.1.

190. J Gaymer, *The Employment Relationship* (Sweet & Maxwell, 2001), p 172.

191. *Per* Staughton LJ in *Page* v. *Combined Shipping and Trading Co Ltd*, [1997] 3 All ER 656, 660.

192. *Per* Lord Steyn in *Malik* v. *BCCI*, fn 182.

193. Such as "working to rule" or "going slow": *Secretary of State for Employment* v. *ASLEF (No 2)* [1972] 2 All ER 949.

to help the other party achieve the purposes of the employment relationship.[194] It appears that they cannot be contracted out of.[195]

There are uncertainties about how fundamental the mutual duties of trust and confidence are, in the employment relationship. According to the Employment Appeal Tribunal, a breach of that duty will always amount to a repudiatory breach of the contract of employment (if a breach is not serious enough to amount to a repudiation, it will not be a breach of the implied duty).[196] On the other hand, the House of Lords in *Malik* v. *BCCI* was clear that there is no reason why it should be unlike any other contract term such that breach would (subject to proving causation and satisfying the normal rules on remoteness and mitigation) give rise to a right to damages.

Nevertheless, the courts have emphasised from a relatively early stage that the obligation does not amount to a duty on the employer to behave reasonably.[197] While the effect that the employer's behaviour has on the particular employee is important, it is clearly established that to be a breach of the implied term the employer's conduct does not have to have been specifically targeted at the employee in question.[198] Furthermore, breach could be established by a series of smaller acts cumulating over a period rather than a single large one.[199]

The sorts of behaviour by employers which have been found to amount to a breach of the implied duty of trust and confidence, and where similar issues can arise between commercial agents and principal include:

> a failure to inform employees of their pension rights and possible ways of enhancing these,[200] but not to the extent that the employee is or should have been aware of them already.[201] There has been a further important judicial effort to cut back on the obligations of the employer in this respect, with the Court of Appeal signalling, in a dispute about long-term disability insurance rights following from an employee's resignation after a nervous breakdown, that there is generally no implied term that the employer must take reasonable care of the employee's overall economic well-being.[202] This qualification is likely to be important in relation to the commercial agency relationship;
>
> significant changes to working hours, methods of working and the place of work, at least if these are imposed without warning or only with very little warning and without reasonable assistance, and this even if the employer has the express right under the contract to introduce such changes unilaterally[203];
>
> humiliating treatment of one employee in front of other employees;

194. See BA Hepple, op cit, fn 188, p 135 and discussion above.
195. See D Brodie, *Beyond exchange: the new contract of employment* (1998) 27 ILJ 79, 83–86.
196. *Morrow* v. *Safeway Stores plc* [2002] IRLR 9.
197. *Post Office* v. *Roberts* [1980] IRLR 347.
198. *Malik* v. *BCCI*, fn 182 above, where the employer's behaviour complained of had been the systematically fraudulent and corrupt manner in which it had run its business generally.
199. *Lewis* v. *Motorworld Garages Ltd* [1986] ICR 157.
200. *Scally* v. *Southern Health Board* [1991] ICR 771 (HL).
201. *University of Nottingham* v. *Eyatt* [1999] IRLR 87 (Ch D).
202. *Crossley* v. *Faithful & Gould Holdings Ltd* [2004] EWCA Civ 293, 16 March 2004 (CA).
203. E.g. *United Bank* v. *Akhtar* [1989] IRLR 507, where an employee was required to move his place of work from Leeds to Birmingham without warning, even though his contract of employment contained a mobility clause entitling the employer to require him to relocate temporarily or permanently to any of the employer's places of business within the UK.

the employer calling in the police at short notice to investigate allegations of theft against an employee without first putting its suspicions to the employee directly[204];

(possibly) a failure, if the employee is issued with a disciplinary warning, to provide reasonable support to the employee in rectifying the problem which has been identified to him[205];

applying an employment sanction for misconduct by an employee which, while being permitted to the employer under the contract of employment, is disproportionate to the gravity of the employee's relevant acts or omissions[206];

using intimidating, misleading tactics with a view to persuading employees to accept a new variable bonus scheme rather than their existing guaranteed salary package[207];

applying excessive levels of abusive language and anger in discussions with employees (which are to be judged against the overall standards of the relevant sector)[208];

failing to explain to an employee the consequences of agreed changes to the terms and conditions of employment, at least where there was important relevant information in the employer's possession which the employee did not have[209];

doing nothing to help and showing an apparent lack of concern, when an employee barman who was Catholic but working in a public house in a strongly Protestant area of Belfast was threatened with personal violence[210];

discriminating between employees in a similar position in not offering them the same redundancy terms[211];

a blanket refusal, on a change of control, to consider identical amendments to the company pension scheme to those which had been considered and approved annually for the previous 20 years and which would benefit employees[212]; and

a persistent refusal to disclose to a senior employee (a salaried partner in a firm of solicitors) financial information about the firm, where the employee had been promised a bonus and the employer had not paid it but kept referring to its financial problems.[213]

In a similar way to the principle developed in relation to commercial contracts more generally,[214] but probably more often in this context, the employer's implied duty of trust and confidence has been taken to operate as a limit on the exercise of apparently unfettered express discretionary powers under the contract of employment in a number of instances, most importantly in relation to the awarding and calculation of bonus payments. In

204. *Fyfe & McGrouther Ltd* v. *Byrne* [1997] IRLR 29.
205. *Associated Tyre Specialists Ltd* v. *Waterhouse* [1976] IRLR 387.
206. *BBC* v. *Beckett* [1983] IRLR 43.
207. *Cantor Fitzgerald International* v. *Bird* [2002] IRLR 867 (High Court QBD).
208. *Ibid.*
209. *Hagan* v. *ICI Chemicals* [2002] IRLR 31 (QBD).
210. *Smyth* v. *Croft Inns Ltd* [1996] IRLR 84.
211. *Transco plc* v. *O'Brien* [2002] IRLR 444 (CA).
212. *Imperial Group Pension Trust Ltd* v. *Imperial Tobacco Ltd* [1991] 1 WLR 589 (Ch D).
213. *Farrell Matthews & Weir* v. *Hansen* [2005] ICR 509, 26 October 2004 (Employment Appeal Tribunal); but in the commercial agency context, note Regulation 21 of the Agency Regulations. The presentation of the examples in this way is modelled on D Peyton, op cit, fn 189, para 2.1.1.8.
214. See section 3.4.1.5.1 above.

Horkulak v. *Cantor Fitzgerald International*[215] (a claim for damages for wrongful dismissal including compensation for loss of a valuable bonus), the Court of Appeal said that where under a contract one party has the power to exercise a discretion, the court would read into the contract an implied term that there would be a genuine and rational exercise of that discretion. As the ultimate decision-maker as to bonus was the president of the employer's parent company, it was implicit (said the court) that he would pay due regard to the interests of both employer and employee, rather than simply seeking to achieve the minimum cost to the company. The analogy with the Court of Appeal's comments in the commercial agency relationship in *Page* v. *Combined Shipping and Trading Co Ltd* seems obvious. *United Bank* v. *Akhtar* and *BBC* v. *Beckett* are further examples of this trend to regulate the exercise of apparently unfettered contractual discretions.

In one important respect, the implied obligation of trust and confidence in the employment contract is more limited than the reciprocal obligations of good faith between commercial agent and principal. This is in relation to the termination of the contract, and is motivated by a judicial desire to prevent employees circumventing the statutory maxima on the amount of compensation for unfair dismissal by adding collateral common law claims. The House of Lords in *Johnson* v. *Unisys plc*[216] rejected the idea that the manner of dismissal (e.g. without a fair hearing and in breach of an employer's contractual disciplinary procedures)[217] gives rise to a breach of the implied term. It took the view that Parliament, in providing a statutory right to compensation for unfair dismissal (with statutory financial limits as to amount) under what is now the Employment Rights Act 1999, had provided (apart from damages for wrongful dismissal at common law, being the amount of wages to be paid during a valid period of contractual notice, subject to the duty to mitigate, the incidence of which is taken account of under the statutory remedy) a complete remedy for the employee in respect of the termination of the contract and that to add a further common law remedy would be contrary to Parliament's intentions in legislating with statutory maxima. This outcome has been criticised from many directions and the House of Lords itself has subsequently expressed concerns about it, stating that the difficulties need resolving by legislation.[218] The commercial agent's rights to compensation or indemnity on termination of his agreement not being limited in this way, and furthermore the principal's obligation of good faith under Regulation 4 of the Agency Regulations being expressed to apply "in relations with his commercial agent", it seems clear that the principal will be subject to this obligation in respect of the manner, fact and consequences of terminating the contract, as well as during the life of the agreement.

While the employment law case law shows a certain tendency (as one might expect) to concentrate on matters of courtesy and on the insistence that the individuals on each side behave decently towards each other in a personal sense (which may be less important in the context of commercial agency, at least where the agent is corporate[219]), the end outcome of the employment contract is the provision of services of an economic nature,

215. [2004] EWCA Civ 1287 (14 October 2004).

216. [2001] UKHL 13, 22 March 2001.

217. Being a different point from possible damages claims in respect of "stigma" resulting from the employer's dishonesty, as in *Malik* v. *BCCI*.

218. See the judgments of Lords Nicholls and Steyn in *Eastwood* v. *Magnox Electric plc* [2004] UKHL 35, 15 July 2004.

219. Though as Elias J correctly points out at first instance in *Bell Electric Ltd* v. *Aweco Appliance Systems GmbH & Co KG* [2002] EWHC 872, 8 May 2002, para 50, there is no difference in the treatment under the Agency Regulations between natural persons and legal persons.

just like the commercial agency contract. The analogy between the mutual duties of good faith in commercial agency and the mutual obligations of trust and confidence in the employment contract are likely to be closer where the commercial agent is an individual or an individual trading as a company than where the commercial agent is a larger business. But in the current absence of judicial authority on the meaning of Regulations 3 and 4 of the Agency Regulations, we consider that the implied term in the employment contract is a useful source of guidance which commercial agents and principals should certainly bear in mind.

3.4.1.6 An overview

As this chapter shows, English law has a number of possible sources of guidance as to the effect of the mutual obligations of good faith in Regulations 3 and 4. Of those examined, we consider that the mutual obligations of trust and confidence in the contract of employment are likely to prove the most helpful. We consider further that breaches of the principal's obligations (other than trivial ones) are likely to amount to "circumstances attributable to the principal"[220] such that a resulting termination by the commercial agent would not deprive him of the right to a compensation of indemnity payment on termination.[221]

3.4.1.7 The mutual duties of good faith: consequential issues

A number of consequential issues need to be considered.

— The mutual obligations of good faith as a key requirement in the commercial agency relationship, and the status of the "in particular" obligations in Regulations 3(2) and 4(2) of the Agency Regulations.

— Whether the mutual obligations are binding to the same extent on commercial agent and principal.

— Whether the mutual obligations apply to pre-contractual discussions and negotiations.

— Whether the mutual obligations apply to termination and the consequences of termination.

— Assuming the mutual obligations amount to a positive obligation to help, co-operate and facilitate the other in performing his obligations under the contract, rather than merely an obligation to refrain from preventing or obstructing performance by the other, what degree of help, co-operation and facilitation may be required?

— The mandatory nature of the mutual obligations.

— The effect of the mandatory obligations on the express terms of the commercial agency agreement.

— The relationship of the mandatory obligations to the "traditional" obligations of principal and agent in English law, including, on the agent's side, the fiduciary obligations.

220. Regulation 18(b)(i). Note however that Regulation 18(b)(i) may apply in the absence of a breach by the principal. See Chapter 5, section 5.2.1.3.2, fnn 117–120 and associated text.

221. Regulation 18(b).

— The consequences of breach of the mutual obligations.

We shall deal with each in turn.

3.4.1.8 Good faith as a key requirement, and the "in particular" obligations

The failure of the Agency Regulations to define good faith as a notion and the standards by which it is to be judged is undoubtedly the most serious problem caused by the verbatim implementation of the Directive. It is not made clear whether the mutual obligations of good faith are to act as a key requirement. Considering that, within the Member States which have a concept of good faith, the notion seems to vary from one state to another, the lack of details is therefore not so surprising. Yet, the lack of details is nevertheless regrettable in relation to the UK, which, until the implementation of the Directive, of course, had no such general requirement.

The positioning of Regulations 3 and 4 in the "architecture" of the Directive, the fact that Regulation 5 states them to be mandatory, and the origins of the good faith obligations in the contract law of the mainland European civil-law Member States (where the obligation binds the parties during the entire performance of the contractual relationship and permeates the entire relationship[222]) are extremely strong indications (notwithstanding *Corman* v. *Hauptzollamt Gronau*[223]) that Regulations 3 and 4 are intended to be fundamental to the commercial agency relationship in English law.[224] To the extent that there has been judicial consideration of them in the UK (which to date has been almost non-existent[225]), the courts appear to be proceeding on this basis. The courts have certainly taken the mutual implied obligations of trust and confidence in the employment relationship to be over-riding and all-pervasive. It would be entirely reasonable to expect them to do the same with Regulations 3 and 4 once those come to be judicially considered in any depth, albeit, perhaps, with a certain reluctance, given the English lawyer's "reflex" perception of the principal/agent relationship as a "classical" commercial one with the principal being the vulnerable party. It is clear to us that, on this basis, commercial agency agreements in English law are now, to this extent, different from other types of commercial agreement and from other types of agency agreement.

On this basis, the "in particular" obligations of principal and commercial agent under Regulations 3(2) and 4(2) respectively are merely examples of what the "umbrella" obligation of good faith includes on each side. We consider that that is the meaning of those provisions.

An altogether different meaning could perhaps be given to Regulations 3(2) and 4(2), namely that they are all that the mutual obligations of good faith are intended to encompass. The European Commission's two published proposals for the Directive give no real support either way, and the final text of the Directive is, as has been noted earlier, a watered-down version of those. In fact, the duty of good faith imposed on the commercial

222. Article 242 of German Bürgerliches Gesetzbuch (BGB, the Civil Code), article 1375 of the Italian civil code, article 1134–3 of the French civil code.

223. See fn 129 above.

224. This is very obvious when looking at the commercial agent who is bound by good faith when *performing his activities* (Regulation 3(1)). It is less so when looking at the principal who is only bound *in his relations with the commercial agent* (Regulation 4(1)).

225. See *3.4.1* above.

agent under the published proposals if anything resembled more closely the traditional fiduciary duties of an agent in English law[226]; by contrast, for the principal, the obligation of good faith in those drafts was closer to an obligation of cooperation.[227]

We are entirely unconvinced that the latter is the intention in the final version.

3.4.1.9 Whether the mutual obligations are binding to the same extent on commercial agent and principal

The terminology used to define the duty of good faith for the principal and the commercial agent is subtly different in each case.[228] It may not, therefore, be obvious whether the duty of good faith binds the commercial agent and the principal to the same extent.

Regulation 3(1) requires the commercial agent to act dutifully and in good faith *when performing his activities*. Regulation 4(1) however, requires the principal to act dutifully and in good faith *in his relations with the commercial agent*. Although this might be an accident of drafting, looking at the final text of the Directive,[229] looking at the proposals of the EU Commission[230] and other regulations,[231] it is more likely to be deliberate. It therefore seems unlikely that the two different forms of wording are meant to say the same thing. Yet, the reason for such a difference is not so obvious.

There are possible explanations for the difference in vocabulary. A simple explanation would be that the different expressions merely highlight the fact that the commercial agent may be required to undertake extra duties such as to stock and deliver goods for the principal, to provide after sales services etc, which represent other "relations" that the commercial agent has with the principal as opposed to the core activities of the commercial of negotiating or negotiating and concluding contracts.[232] The word "relations" might therefore simply emphasise the fact that the commercial agent receives or could receive an additional remuneration for such activities performed.[233] This interpretation seems to be strengthened by the fact that the commercial agent is bound when performing his "activities" as opposed to "obligations".[234]

226. Article 5(1) of the first and second proposals stipulated that the commercial agent gad to act fairly and in good faith when carrying out his activities *vis-à-vis* the principal and third parties. This included the obligations to make proper efforts when negotiating or concluding the transactions, to supply information on clients, duty to account, duty to keep separately moneys belonging to the principal etc. See OJ C. 56/8 of 2 March 1979.

227. Article 10(1) of the first and second proposal stipulated a general obligation to act fairly and in good faith. Then, article 10(2) added additional duties which were "without prejudice to the general duty specified in para 1".

228. The commercial agent must "look after the interests of his principal and act dutifully and in good faith when performing his duties" (Regulation 3(1)) whereas the principal must act "dutifully and in good faith in his relations with the commercial agent" (Regulation 4(1)).

229. Articles 3(1) and 4(1) of the Directive.

230. Articles 5(1) and 10(1) of the two drafts of the European Commission for the duties of the commercial agent and the principal respectively. See OJ C. 56/9 of 2 March 1979.

231. Regulation 17(1) defines the right of the commercial agent to claim compensation or indemnity "after termination of the agency contract". Regulation 17(6) stipulates that the commercial agent can claim compensation for the damage suffered at the end of *his relations* with his principal.

232. It is possible to say that such activities are the "core" agency activities when looking at the definition of the commercial agent under Regulation 2(1). For details, see Chapter 2, section 2.4.2.1.

233. This is the case in French law for instance.

234. This is even clearer when looking at article 5(2) of the previous proposals where the commercial agent had in addition to the normal "activities" of an intermediary i.e. negotiating and concluding transactions, could also be required to get the money from third parties, look after the property entrusted to him etc, which can be regarded as additional "activities". See OJ C. 56/8 of 2 March 1979.

A further explanation might be that it highlights the fact that the parties may choose to enter into a series of fixed-term contracts. As a consequence, instead of being an accident of the text, the difference in drafting is deliberate in order to show the diversity of the functions that a commercial agent might give his principal and ensure that principals cannot use potential loopholes to deprive commercial agents of their protection. In the light of the protective stance of the Agency Regulations, it is unlikely that the obligation of the principal is lighter than that of the commercial agent.

3.4.1.10 Do the obligations of good faith apply at the stage of pre-contractual negotiation between principal and would-be commercial agent?

As previously mentioned, Regulation 3(1) imposes a duty of good faith on the commercial agent when he "performs his activities". This would seem to suggest that good faith does not extend prior to the conclusion of the commercial agency contract. Regulation 4(1) however, imposes a duty of good faith on the principal "in his relations with the commercial agent", which is clearly wider. Could it be that this indicates that the principal, but not the commercial agent, is subject to a duty of good faith during the antecedent negotiations?

To impose a duty of good faith on the principal at this stage could be said to make some sense, since the principal normally dictates the terms of the contract. Furthermore, he will invariably have more information about his own business and its products than the intending commercial agent has. Whether he will have more information than the commercial agent about the sector is less obvious. Sometimes he will. In other cases, the principal's very reason for wishing to appoint X as its commercial agent is precisely because of X's knowledge of the sector, trading contacts, established reputation for acting for principals who are suppliers of good products, etc (an extreme example of which would be Mr Coleman, the individual behind the corporate selling agent in *Tigana Ltd* v. *Decoro Ltd*,[235] upon whose views as to what foreign-produced leather furniture would sell well in the UK most UK furniture retailers, his principals' main customers, appear to have relied).

To require good faith of the principal in pre-contractual negotiations with the commercial agent would prevent the principal from taking advantage of the commercial agent, rather like the Unfair Terms in Consumer Contracts Directive does,[236] and a similar duty to disclose information rather like the duty of disclosure placed on the insured in insurance law in English law. To impose such a duty on the principal would especially make sense when the commercial agent assigns his commercial agency to another commercial agent, as it would protect the latter.[237] This issue arose, but was not dealt with by the court, in *Parks* v. *Esso Petroleum Ltd*[238] where the claimant agent alleged, *inter alia*, that the

235. [2003] EWHC 23 (QBD), 3 February 2003.

236. The Council Directive 93/13 EEC of 5 April 1995, OJ L. 95, 21 April 1993, pp 0029. In the recitals of the Directive, it is stated that in making an assessment of good faith, "particular shall be had to the strength of the bargaining power of the parties, whether the consume had an inducement to agree the terms (. . .) the requirement of good faith may be satisfied by the seller or supplier where he deals fairly and equitably with the other party whose legitimate interests he has to take into account ".

237. For more details on assignment, see Chapter 5.

238. [2000] ECC 45 (CA).

principal had been in breach of his duty of good faith in exaggerating in the pre-contractual negotiations the likely profitability of the petrol station which the claimant agent was going to operate. The court (having decided that Mr Parks was not a commercial agent within the Agency Regulations at all) understandably expressed no view on this point, though noted that an untrue statement in the negotiations by the principal of its then current opinion as to profitability would amount to misrepresentation, actionable in the normal way.

If it is right that the principal's duty of good faith operates prior to the making of the agency agreement, then why should the commercial agent not also be bound by the same duty of disclosure? Such would certainly make sense in the light of the reciprocity and symmetry mentioned earlier. Even though the primary aim of the implementing text is to reinforce the protection of commercial agents, the reciprocity of the duty of good faith must not be overlooked. Under the traditional common law rules, such a duty arises.[239] In the light of the case of *Roy* v. *M R Pearlman Ltd*,[240] common law rules are not displaced by the Agency Regulations, so long as the former are consistent with the latter. In the event of an inconsistency, the Agency Regulations prevail. In this area, there does not seem to be any inconsistency between the two sets of rules. There would seem, at the very least then, to be a reasonably strong arguable case that both parties are bound to negotiate in good faith.

Equally, if the negotiations are unsuccessful, presumably the mutual duty of good faith would, in the absence of an express confidentiality agreement, operate to impose on each party a duty to keep confidential confidential information each has received from the other in the process.

3.4.1.11 Does a duty of good faith apply when terminating the relationship and dealing with the consequences of termination?

According to the same argument, both parties should also bound by their duties of good faith when terminating the relationship and also in dealing with the consequences of termination (e.g. as to finalising the financial settlement between them and as to the operation of any post-termination restrictive covenant as referred to in Regulation 20).

3.4.1.12 What degree of co-operation is each party required to provide to the other in order that both parties can perform their respective obligations?

We have referred earlier[241] to the general position taken by English law that, on the rather rare occasions where an obligation on one party to co-operate with the other so that the other may perform its contractual obligations will be implied, it is generally limited to an obligation to refrain from doing anything to prevent or obscure performance by the other, rather than an obligation to take positive steps to assist the other. The exception is the mutual implied duties of trust and confidence in the contract of employment, where each party is obliged to take positive steps to help the other in performing its part of the bargain.

239. *Arklow Investment* v. *MacLean* [2000] 1 WLR 594 PC.
240. [1999] CMLR 1155.
241. Section 3.4.1.5.1.

Given the mainland European inspiration of the Directive, the mutual obligations of good faith now in Regulations 3 and 4 of the Agency Regulations clearly include, at the very least, an obligation on commercial agent and principal not to prevent or obstruct performance by the other, whether that involves a restriction on the freedom of each party to use his property as he considers best suits himself or not.[242] Regulations 3 and 4, however, may well, however, go further than these two requirements, implying (in a way, of course, that cannot be excluded[243]), an obligation to take positive steps, to some extent at least, to help the other party to achieve performance of its contractual obligations.

On the assumption that such is indeed the case, can any guidance be offered as to how far the obligation to take positive steps to assist and facilitate may go? Given the pro-principal starting point of English law, the main uncharted waters, it seems to us, are what support the commercial agent can expect from his principal to facilitate the performance by the commercial agent of his obligations, express and implied. Predictably, there is a total absence of judicial discussion of this issue, so again one is forced to draw on more general principles.

We are inclined to think that, in the commercial agency context, the courts would expect somewhat less from the principal under a commercial agency agreement than an employer would have to do pursuant to his implied obligations under the contract of employment. Such an approach would be consistent with the traditional view of agency as an arm's length relationship between two commercial parties. There is likely to be a very significant qualification of "what is reasonable in all the circumstances" and, we believe, a very significant degree to which it will be acceptable for the principal to look after its own interests.

We take this view on the basis of the way English courts have interpreted express (and implied) obligations in commercial agreements to "use best endeavours" or to "use reasonable efforts" to bring about a particular outcome. At first sight, an obligation to "use best endeavours" sounds extremely exacting for the obligor, and would be likely to give the promisee of such an obligation significant comfort; an obligation to "use reasonable efforts" inevitably represents a lower requirement. The case law on such terms suggests, however, that the standard of performance required of the obligor in such a case is materially less demanding than might at first sight appear, and that, even into a "best endeavours" obligation the courts are willing to imply very significant qualifications of reasonableness in favour of the obligor.[244]

An obligation to "use best endeavours" has been said to be certainly "not the next best thing to an absolute obligation or a guarantee".[245] Rather, such an obligation is limited to doing what can reasonably be done in the circumstances, judged by reference to the facts existing at the time of performance of the obligation, not at the time of entering into the

242. As the Court of Appeal recognised in *Page* v. *Combined Shipping and Trading Co Ltd* [1997] 3 All ER 656, accepting that there was a good arguable case that "proper performance" by the principal meant something very different from allowing him, as the contract apparently did, to reduce the trading routed through the agent to nil or nearly nil for the balance of the contract term with the effect of depriving the agent of almost all commission. The contrast with *Luxor (Eastbourne) Ltd* v. *Cooper* could scarcely be greater.

243. Regulation 5.

244. For statements very supportive of this position, see the very powerful dissenting judgment of Mason J in the High Court of Australia in *Hospital Products Ltd* v. *United States Surgical Corporation*, fn 30 above, pp 91–92.

245. *Midland Land Reclamation Ltd and Leicestershire CC* v. *Warren Energy Limited* (1997), unreported, but referred to in www.practicallaw.com/5-100-8007?tab=5&jurisfilter=.

contract. In *Terrell* v. *Mabie Todd & Co*,[246] the reasonableness qualification was expressly built into the defendant's obligation from the start (obligation on the licensee of IP rights to use best endeavours to procure the manufacture and sale of as many products incorporating the licensor's invention as reasonably possible). In *Rackham* v. *Peek Foods Ltd*[247] it was not, but the court readily implied it. *Rackham* concerned an agreement to purchase all the shares in a property company, the agreement being conditional on approval by the purchaser's shareholders. The agreement contained an obligation on the part of its purchaser and its merchant bank to use best endeavours to procure such approval. After exchange of contracts, the boards of the purchaser and its merchant bank accordingly issued a circular to the purchaser's shareholders recommending that they vote in favour of the purchase. Before the shareholders' meeting at which the resolution was to be put, however, the government announced new legislation aimed, *inter alia*, at increasing the tax burden on property companies' profits. The purchaser's board adjourned the EGM, issued a further circular saying that, in the light of this, it was no longer recommending the acquisition to shareholders, and at the re-convened shareholders' meeting the directors of the purchaser and their merchant bankers used their shares in the purchaser to ensure that the resolution to approve the purchase was not put. Templeman J said there was no breach of the "best endeavours" obligation, which did not oblige the directors of the purchaser or their bankers to give bad advice; they were, in the circumstances, under a duty to the shareholders in the purchaser to ensure the acquisition was not approved, and the "best endeavours" obligation certainly did not oblige them to take any action not in the interests of the purchaser. Even within a "best endeavours" obligation, it was open to the obligor, on a material change of circumstances like this, to let its own interests prevail over those of the obligee. In similar vein, Deane J in *Hospital Products Ltd* v. *United States Surgical Corporation* says that an obligation to "use best efforts" to bring about a particular outcome (the usual US language for "best endeavours") does not make the obligor a fiduciary and obliged to prioritise the interests of the promisee to the exclusion or detriment of his own.[248]

Similarly, it seems that the steps which the obligor under the "best endeavours" obligation is required to take pursuant thereto will be limited to what is practical, given the aims of the parties and the timetable within which they intend those to be achieved. *Hargreaves Transport Ltd* v. *Lynch*[249]concerned a sale and purchase of land, where the vendor sold the property with the benefit of a pending application for outline planning permission for a change of use to a transport depot, the sale being conditional on the purchaser obtaining "planning permission" for use as a transport depot and for running a road haulage business. After exchange of contracts the outline planning permission was granted, an application for detailed permission was lodged by the purchaser, the latter was rejected by the local planning authority, and the purchaser, in consequence, rescinded the contract. The Court of Appeal said that there was an implied obligation on the purchaser to use all due diligence and to take all reasonable steps to obtain a detailed planning permission, but that, the detailed permission having been refused, that did not extend to an obligation to

246. [1952] 69 RPC 234 (QBD).
247. [1990] BCLC 895 (Ch D, Templeman J).
248. *Ibid*, fn 30 above, p 122.
249. [1969] 1 WLR 215 (CA).

take an appeal against the refusal to the Secretary of State. The latter was likely to take between 6 and 12 months to be resolved, the purchaser was wanting to develop the site and to re-locate its business there well within that period, and the vendor was well aware of that. On the other hand, in *Sharneyford Supplies Ltd* v. *Edge*,[250] the vendor of land was held not to have used his best endeavours to obtain vacant possession of the property which he had agreed to sell in that condition (but which was occupied by third parties) where he had begun negotiations with the occupiers to seek to agree to pay them to leave but which negotiations had broken down; he had not served them with notice to quit on the basis of counsel's advice that proceedings for possession were unlikely to succeed.

It would seem, therefore, that even an obligation to "use best endeavours" includes the very significant qualification that the obligor need do only what is reasonable in all the circumstances, taking account of the cost and degree of difficulty involved; that he is not obliged to do anything which would put his financial stability at risk or which would undermine his own commercial standing or goodwill; that, if the obligor of such an obligation is a company, the directors must act in the interests of their company and not subordinate those to the interests of the promisee; and that any expenditure incurred must go no further than what is reasonable.

An obligation to "use reasonable efforts" or to "take reasonable steps" to bring about a particular outcome implies an even lower standard of activity on the part of the obligors in *UBH (Mechanical Services) Ltd* v. *Standard Life Assurance Co*,[251] it was described as "appreciably lower than best endeavours". The obligor could balance its obligation against all other relevant commercial issues, including the cost of compliance, the uncertainties and practicalities of compliance, and the prospects of success. It would appear, therefore, that if using reasonable efforts to bring about the outcome would result in some financial or other commercial disadvantage to the obligor, it is free to take no action.[252]

In *Pagnan SpA* v. *Tradax Ocean Transportation SA*,[253] Bingham LJ (as he then was) referred to the general principle that, where the courts are implying an obligation into a contract, they will imply the least onerous obligation necessary to give business efficacy to the contract. We believe that that idea would also be influential in this context.

We consider, therefore, that, whilst it is likely that the principal under a commercial agency agreement to which the Agency Regulations apply is under an obligation to provide positive support to the commercial agent to facilitate the latter in performing his obligations under the agreement, the obligation is unlikely to be found to be an onerous one. We would not want commercial agents to build up exaggerated hopes in this respect.

3.4.1.13 The mandatory nature of the obligations

It is crucial to remember that Regulation 5 states that the parties may not derogate from the mutual obligations of good faith, at any time.

250. [1987] Ch 305 (CA).
251. *The Times*, 13 November 1986.
252. See also *P&O Property Holdings Ltd* v. *Norwich Union* [1993] EGCS 69; *Phillips Petroleum Co UK Ltd* v. *Enron Europe Ltd* [1996] EWCA Civ 693 (10 October 1996).
253. [1987] 2 Lloyd's Rep 342, 348.

3.4.1.14 The effect of the mutual obligations of good faith on the express terms of the commercial agency agreement

We began this Chapter by saying that, where the Agency Regulations apply, it is no longer prudent to assume that the commercial agency agreement will necessarily be enforceable in accordance with its terms. By now, the pervasiveness of the mutual obligations of good faith into all aspects of the principal/commercial agent relationship should have become apparent. An effort needs to be made to map the limits of the propensity of Regulations 3–5 to alter the express terms of the relationship the parties have agreed.

We cannot see, for example, that Regulations 3–5 can have the effect of altering the scope of the commercial agent's authority (for example, giving him authority to conclude contracts on the principal's behalf rather than just negotiating and leaving the final decision to the principal); nor the identification of the transactions on which commission is to be earned; nor the agreed rate of such commission; nor the duration of the agency agreement[254]; nor to convert a power to terminate summarily into a power only to terminate on giving a period of reasonable notice. Equally, if termination by the principal at a date later than the actual date of termination would have meant that the commercial agent got some benefit which was not available on the actual date of termination, we do not see that Regulations 3–5 mean that the commercial agent must be deemed to have had his contract terminated on that later date.[255]

On the other hand, following from the lines of authority identified above, both in relation to the contract of employment and in commercial contracts, where a party to a commercial agency agreement (it will invariably be the principal) has a contractual discretion which is on the face of it unlimited (e.g. a power to terminate the agreement without cause; a power to vary the territory or range of products or customers allocated to the commercial agent; a power to dilute the agency from being exclusive to being non-exclusive, etc), the exercise of the discretion must satisfy the limited "hands-off" "reasonableness" test which the courts have developed (and which, as noted, bears a resemblance to the very high threshold for judicial intervention in administrative law which is *Wednesbury Corporation* unreasonableness). It would appear that a failure to observe that standard will be a breach of contract by the principal justifying the commercial agent in treating the contract as being at an end and, through Regulation 18(b)(i), his termination not depriving him of the right to a lump sum payment on termination; an exercise of a discretion which does not reach that level of unreasonableness seems unlikely to have that effect. If the principal is minded to take "disciplinary" measures against the commercial agent, it seems to us that he must discuss them fully with the agent and give the agent proper opportunity to put its side of the argument; that there may well be a requirement that the commercial agent be given a chance to improve its performance, and that any reaction to a change of circumstances be proportionate.

Equally, if the principal is not performing its obligations under the agreement, the commercial agent's reaction must be measured and proportionate, and it must not precipitately rush to claiming that behaviour by the principal justifies it in terminating the agreement because it wishes to claim a lump sum payment on termination.

254. See in this respect the comments of Lord Millett in *Reda* v. *Flag Ltd* [2002] IRLR 747, 753, in general doubted by Potter LJ in *Horkaluk* v. *Cantor Fitzgerald International* [2004] EWCA Civ 1287 (14 October 2004), but which in these specific respects still seem to hold good.

255. Cf. *Harper* v. *Virgin Net Ltd* [2005] EWCA Civ 271.

3.4.1.15 The relationship of the mutual obligations of good faith to the "traditional" implied obligations of principal and agent in English law, including, on the commercial agent's side, the fiduciary obligations

The court in *Roy* v. *M R Pearlman Ltd* was of the view that, to the extent that they are not inconsistent with the Agency Regulations, the "traditional" implied obligations of principal and agent to each other remain.

It should by now be clear that we take the view that, despite the views expressed by the DTI in 1994,[256] the mutual duties of good faith imposed on principal and agent under the Agency Regulations are different from the agent's fiduciary duties in English law.

The essence of fiduciary obligation is that the fiduciary has to put the interests of the person to whom he owes the duty ahead of his own interests and, if the situation arises, pursue the other's interests at the expense of and to the detriment of his own. Breach of fiduciary duty, of course, gives the person to whom the duty is owed access to a range of equitable remedies.

Under the mutual duties of good faith under the Agency Regulations, by contrast, it seems clear that each party must act so as to best advance the joint interests of both parties. This approach is certainly consistent with the French idea of commercial agency as the mandate of common interest: the idea that the parties are notionally co-owners of the goodwill attaching to the commercial agent's activities, which is the basis of the commercial agent's right to a lump sum payment on termination, can be said to be the natural and logical consequence of an obligation to co-operate in this way during the life of the commercial agency agreement. Accordingly, it is permitted for each party to take account of his own interests as well as those of the other party (whether in equal weight in all circumstances remains to be seen). Thus, in matters within the scope of the agreed activities to which the mutual obligation of good faith applies, it is not permitted for either party to have regard to its own selfish interests and nothing more; but a party is not obliged to put the other side's interests to the exclusion of his own either. Each party has to achieve a balance and have regard to both.

The traditional obligation of the agent to hold property and money of the principal as fiduciary for the principal seems to us to be unaffected by the Agency Regulations. The principal's money is the principal's money: it is not jointly owned.

Beyond that, it seems to us that the result of the mutual obligations of good faith is that, in those respects in which the commercial agent is a fiduciary in English law, he is now fiduciary not exclusively for the principal but for the principal and himself jointly, and has to act in the best interests of both of them. Such would seem to be the case, for example, in relation to the goodwill (his quasi-proprietorial interest in which is of course acknowledged through the right to compensation or indemnity on termination). Regulation 5 seems to have the effect that this arrangement cannot be varied by contract. To this extent, Regulations 3 and 4 of the Agency Regulations (which are mandatory) thus seem to "trump"[257] the traditional fiduciary obligations on the agent implied into the agency relationship (which can, in English law, be varied by contrary agreement), and commercial agency in English law now seems to be different from other types of agency arrangement. Though it does not arise under the Agency Regulations at all, there is a similar analysis

256. DTI Guidance Notes 1994, Appendix 8.

257. To use the words of Langley J in a different context in *Days Medical Aids Ltd* v. *Pihsiang Machinery Manufacturing Co Ltd and others* [2004] EWHC (Comm) 44, 29 January 2004, para 254.

(in the context of an exclusive distributorship agreement) in Mason J's very powerful dissenting judgment in the High Court of Australia in *Hospital Products Ltd* v. *United States Surgical Corporation*.[258] How this principle is to be applied in each situation remains to be seen.

3.4.1.16 Consequences of a breach of the mutual duties of good faith

Regulation 5(2) says that the consequences of breach of Regulations 3 and 4 are to be governed by the law applicable to the contract (which, of course, may be a different legal system from that of the place of performance[259]). That resolves the conflict of laws issue, but says nothing more specific about how breaches should be treated substantively.

The mandatory nature of Regulations 3 and 4 is not inconsistent with their operating by way of contractual terms implied by statute.[260]

Randolph and Davey[261] consider, without reaching a conclusion, the question of whether the duties arising under Regulations 3 and 4 are contractual in nature (noting that no clear statement is made in the Agency Regulations as to whether they are a condition (breach or other than trifling breach of which would, without the need for express provision to be made in the Agency Regulations to this effect, entitle the other party to terminate and/or claim damages) or a warranty (giving rise to a right to damages only)) or statutory (in which case the various hurdles to proving an actionable tortious breach of statutory duty would have to be surmounted,[262] and for which, in the absence of specific statutory provision, only a damages remedy would be available).

We consider that all the indications are that the mutual duties of good faith are contractual in nature. This would seem to fit with the preservation of the commercial agent's right to a lump sum payment on termination if he terminates the contract where "such termination is justified by circumstances attributable to the principal", which appears to acknowledge, at least indirectly, a right for the commercial agent to repudiate the contract for serious breach by the principal (though "circumstances attributable to the principal" (words taken verbatim from Article 18(b) of the Directive) could include other events as well) (see further on this in Chapter 5). Though it does not give an answer to the question in English law, the ECJ's preliminary ruling in *Arcado SPRL* v. *Haviland SA*[263] provides support for treating the obligation as contractual. The point at issue here was whether litigation in a Belgian court claiming unpaid commission and a lump sum compensation payment on termination of a commercial agency agreement was "proceedings in matters relating to a contract" for the purposes of the jurisdiction rules in Article 5(1) of the 1968 Brussels Convention on Jurisdiction and the Enforcement of Judgments in Civil and Commercial Matters. The ECJ said that both claims were "matters relating to a contract"

258. Fn 30 above, pp 91–97.

259. See Chapter 2 on conflict of laws issues in this area generally.

260. The best example of this is the implied terms as to title in sale of goods contracts under the Sale of Goods Act 1979, s 12, taken together with UCTA 1977, s 6.

261. Randolph and Davey, *Guide to the Commercial Agents Regulations*, Hart Publishing (2nd edn, 2003), pp 62–63.

262. The claimant has to prove (i) that the statute in question was intended to provide a private law remedy in tort to individuals who suffer loss as a result of breach of the duty in question, (ii) that he is within the class of people to whom the duty is owed, (iii) that the loss he suffered is of the type of damage the statute was intended to prevent, (iv) that the defendant's breach of the statutory duty was the cause of the claimant's loss, and (v) that the loss suffered is not too remote to be recoverable. See further, *Clerk and Lindsell on Torts*.

263. ECJ case 9/87, [1988] ECR 1539, judgment of 8 March 1988.

(the court seeing the basis of the right to the compensation payment as being "the failure to comply with a contractual obligation"[264]). Slynn AG (as he then was) said in his opinion "It seems to me that, if proceedings are brought which, as an essential element of the claim, allege the existence of what it is agreed would be a contract if it was made (even if the existence of the contract is in dispute), then they are to be regarded as covering 'matters relating to a contract' ". In *Bell Electric Ltd* v. *Aweco Appliance Systems GmbH & Co KG*,[265] Elias J appears to treat the claim for compensation, as well as that for damages for breach of contract, as contractual.

If, as strongly appears to be the case, the reciprocal obligations of good faith permeate all aspects of the commercial agency relationship as a whole and are thus of fundamental importance to it,[266] it would seem to follow that failure (or at least a non-trivial failure) to comply with such a requirement should be treated as a repudiatory breach, allowing the victim to terminate the relationship immediately. A breach by the principal of his duty of good faith would entitle the commercial agent to terminate the agreement and still have his right to his lump sum payment of compensation or indemnity (on the basis that his termination was "justified by circumstances attributable to the principal"[267]). A breach by the commercial agent of his duty of good faith would entitle the principal to terminate and to pay no lump sum on termination (pursuant to Regulations 18(a) and 16). Such severe consequences would seem to be consistent with the importance of good faith as a mandatory requirement. They would also be consistent with the symmetry approach of the Agency Regulations.

264. *Ibid*, para 13 of the judgment.

265. [2002] EWHC 872.

266. As is borne out by *Page* v. *Combined Shipping and Transport Co Ltd*, where the Court of Appeal suggests that the right to a compensation payment on termination must be approached in the light of the parties' good faith obligations while the contract was alive.

267. Regulation 18(b)(ii).

CHAPTER 4

THE COMMERCIAL AGENT'S REMUNERATION

4.1 GENERALLY

It would, obviously, be rare for the parties to a commercial agency agreement not to have agreed with reasonable precision (i) the basis of calculation of the commercial agent's remuneration, (ii) the transactions on which that remuneration is to be payable, (iii) the date when the remuneration accrues and, if different, the date on which it is to be paid, and (iv) the mechanics of payment.

Over and above an initial statement of general principle, the Agency Regulations provide detailed rules as to (i), (ii) and (iii), but the detailed rules only apply where the commercial agent is remunerated, in whole or in part, by "commission" as defined. The general (but not universally held) view,[1] being the one to which we subscribe, is that the detailed rules on (i) and (ii), and the bulk of the rules on (iii) are non-mandatory, and so will yield to contrary agreement. By contrast, for the commercial agent's protection, there are "backstop" dates as to (iii), an exclusive list of the circumstances in which the commercial agent can lose his right to commission, and a right for the commercial agent to receive relevant financial information from the principal, which are stated to be mandatory.

4.2 THE REMUNERATION ARRANGEMENTS IN A TYPICAL COMMERCIAL AGENCY AGREEMENT, AND THE IMPACT UPON THEM OF THE MUTUAL DUTIES OF GOOD FAITH UNDER THE AGENCY REGULATIONS

Generally, the commercial agent will be remunerated by a commission, being a percentage of the net invoice price of the products sold through him or of the cash ultimately received by the principal from those sales (reflecting the English common law idea that, in the absence of contrary agreement, an agent is only entitled to commission where his intervention has been the effective cause of the transaction between principal and third party[2]). Sometimes a commission (typically at a lower rate) may also be granted in respect of the

1. Scholes and Blane, *Agency agreements: new protection for commercial agents*, PLC, IV(10) (October 1993), 31; F Randolph and J Davey, *Guide to the Commercial Agents Regulations* (Hart Publishing, 2nd edn, 2003), para 8–12; and Advocate-General Cosmas in ECJ case C–104/95 *Kontogeorgas* v. *Kartonpak* [1997] 1 CMLR 1083, para 23 and fn 13 of the opinion, although the ECJ expresses no view on the point in the judgment. Contrast Christou, *International agency, distribution and licensing agreement* (4th edn, 2003), p 124. And note also S Singleton, *Commercial Agency Agreements: Law and Practice* (1998), p 51.

2. See Chapter 3, section 3.3.2.2 above.

principal's sales to customers based within the sales territory allocated to the commercial agent but which have not been concluded through the commercial agent. The agency agreement may provide for different rates of commission on different types of transaction (e.g. on different products within the principal's product range, a higher rate on newly launched products, a higher rate on sales to new customers than on repeat sales to existing customers etc) or for a higher rate if the commercial agent exceeds sales targets etc. The agency agreement may provide for a minimum commission payable in any event (in effect, a retainer), or (though it would be unusual) for a maximum commission.

Where such a commission structure is present in clear terms in the commercial agency agreement at the inception of the relationship, and particularly where it has been the subject of negotiation between the parties (with or without professional advice), it is inconceivable that recourse to arguments about possible breach of the principal's duty of good faith under Regulation 4 give any means for a commercial agent to seek variations to that structure once the agreement is up and running. That, surely, is not the role of Regulation 4. The attitude in England and Wales would surely be that the commercial agent had his chance to negotiate his commission arrangements before the event, and if he did not like the arrangements as finally negotiated then he should never have entered into the agreement in the first place.

The commercial agency agreement as drafted may, however, give the principal the right in certain situations and at his discretion unilaterally to vary, say, the rate of commission or the range of transactions on which it can be earned or the range of products allocated to the commercial agent or some other discretion. Here, the limited case law on the Agency Regulations to date suggests that the position is different, and that, on the basis of his duty of good faith under Regulation 4, the principal may only exercise such power to vary (or at least to vary other than in a *de minimis* way) or some other discretion if he pays due regard to the position of the commercial agent as well as to his own position.

The first case in which this issue was raised under the Agency Regulations, *Skingsley* v. *KJC Carpets Ltd*,[3] is really of no help at all. The unilateral reduction by the principal of the agent's rate of commission was a plain breach of the express terms of the contract. The principal, quite simply, had no right to make it at all. As has been noted earlier, the Court of Appeal in *Page* v. *Combined Shipping and Transport Co Ltd*[4] said there was an arguable case (strong enough to justify the imposition of a interim freezing order on UK assets of the defendant principal) that starving the commercial agent of opportunities to earn commission such that the agent would earn nothing, with a view to the principal minimising his liabilities to pay commission, was a breach of the principal's duty of good faith under Regulation 4 (even though the agency agreement expressly allowed the principal to do this), and that this was relevant to the calculation of the compensation lump sum due to the commercial agent on termination. In *Bell Electric Ltd* v. *Aweco Appliance Systems GmbH & Co KG*,[5] Elias J at first instance opined that the principal's repeated and prolonged failure to pay any commission even though it had been earned, followed by the "high-handed" purported imposition of a new regime for calculating commission which would be far less favourable to the commercial agent than the previous one, amounted to repudiatory breach of the commercial agency agreement by the principal such as to entitle

3. Bristol County Court, 4 June 1996; unreported, but there is a transcript in S Singleton, *Commercial Agency Agreements: Law and Practice* (1998), pp 181–184.
4. [1997] 3 All ER 656, CA.
5. [2002] EWHC 872, 8 May 2002.

the commercial agent to treat the principal as having brought the contract to an end and that the commercial agent did not, by resigning in these circumstances, lose his right to a lump sum on termination (because of the combined effect of Regulations 16 and 18(b)(i)). The agency agreement in *Bell Electric* contained no power for the principal unilaterally to vary the commission arrangements, but in the light of *Page* v. *CST* it seems unlikely that the presence of such a clause would have helped the principal.

Given the pro-commercial agent stance of the Agency Regulations, it seems likely that the level of "unreasonableness" in the actual variation under an apparently unfettered contractual power unilaterally to vary, which a court would regard as a breach by the principal of Regulation 4, will be lower than the level at which an English court, in a case where the Agency Regulations did not apply, would intervene. In the latter case, the level of unreasonableness required for judicial intervention at common law in relation to the exercise of an apparently unfettered contractual discretion is phrased in language similar to that of *Wednesbury Corporation* unreasonableness in administrative law, i.e. a very high standard of unreasonableness indeed.[6] How much lower than that standard it is, remains to be seen.

All of that does not mean, however, that the principal, in exercising contractual powers unilaterally to vary the commission arrangements, must look to the position of the commercial agent and to nothing else. He has to consider the position of and act in the interests of both parties. If the contract gives him the power to vary the remuneration arrangements, and if, taking proper account of the interests of both sides, there are valid reasons for the principal to do that, he has the right to do that and will not be in breach of contract by so doing. If rewards are to be shared, then the symmetry to which we have referred earlier suggests that risks must be shared too. If there is a downturn in the market, varying the agreement to achieve a reasonable sharing between principal and commercial agent of the consequences of that downturn seems entirely right and proper in terms of, and is entirely consistent with, the principal's obligations under Regulation 4. If the commercial agent is, on any objective measure, underperforming (and has been given a fair chance and appropriate support to do better but continues to underperform), but the principal nevertheless wishes to retain his services, it is reasonable and not in breach of the principal's duty of good faith for the principal to vary the commercial agent's terms, at least to an extent proportionate to the problem (albeit that translating that into practical action is fraught with uncertainty). It would no doubt be a breach of the commercial agent's duty of good faith under Regulation 3 for him to be too greedy (under the mutual obligations, he, for his part, has to have regard to his principal's legitimate interests as well as his own). That should be a useful counterbalance to commercial agents getting exaggerated ideas of the potency of the threat of claiming the equivalent of constructive unfair dismissal as a bargaining counter in such situations.

4.3 PART III OF THE AGENCY REGULATIONS: REMUNERATION

Part III, the part of the Agency Regulations which deals specifically with the commercial agent's remuneration, consistently with other parts of the Agency Regulations, follows the

6. See the discussion in Chapter 3, section 3.4.1.5.1.

terms of the Directive very closely. As the reader of this book will by now be very well aware, uncertainties inevitably follow.

4.4 THE BASIC SCHEME: REGULATION 6

Regulation 6 sets out the basic scheme of the Agency Regulations' rules on remuneration of commercial agents. This is that:

(1) if there is an agreement between principal and commercial agent as to remuneration, then (subject to (a) the mandatory rules for the commercial agent's protection in parts of Regulations 10–12 (which are applicable (like the rest of Regulations 7–12, only if and to the extent that the remuneration consists of "commission" as defined in Regulation 2(1)), and (b) (inevitably) to the parties' mutual duties of good faith) that will be respected;

(2) if there is overriding legislation or case law concerning the level of remuneration, that will apply in priority to Regulation 6(1).[7] There is no such legislation or case law in England and Wales, not so far as we are aware in any other parts of the UK;

(3) in the absence of any agreement as to remuneration between the parties (a rare state of affairs, to put it mildly), the commercial agent is entitled to "the remuneration that commercial agents appointed for the goods forming the subject of his agency contract are customarily allowed in the place where he carries on his activities and, if there is no such customary practice, a commercial agent shall be entitled to reasonable remuneration taking into account all the aspects of the transaction".[8]

A right to be remunerated

At first sight, then, the "basic scheme" rules provided by the Agency Regulations do not appear to modify, to any appreciable extent, the common law rules on remuneration, under which an agent of a commercial nature is, in the absence of contrary provision, entitled to reasonable remuneration.[9] On further examination, though, an important difference between the two sets of rules emerges. The Agency Regulations, consistently with the protective stance of the Directive, provide the commercial agent with a right to be remunerated *which cannot be taken away from him*. This is implicit from the fact that the Agency Regulations do not apply to "commercial agents whose activities are unpaid",[10] and explicit from the fact that Regulation 11 (which, by Regulation 11(3), is stated to be mandatory) restrictively defines the situations in which the commercial agent's right to commission will be lost.[11]

The fact that the commercial agent has an inalienable right to receive remuneration of some sort has four important consequences.

7. Regulation 6(2).

8. Regulation 6(1).

9. The courts will usually award remuneration on a *quantum meruit* basis. For a case where the payment was agreed on a commission basis, see *Withy Robinson (A firm)* v. *Edwards* (1985) 277 Estates Gazette 748.

10. Regulation 2(2)(a).

11. Regulation 11. Regulation 11(3) stipulate that the parties cannot derogate from such situations to the detriment of the commercial agent.

(1) As a right of the commercial agent established by secondary legislation, the matter will not be decided any more as a matter of construction by the courts or by implications of terms, as it is the case under the common law rules.[12]

(2) The commercial agent's right to be remunerated is consequently an obligation of the principal, and the fact that the Agency Regulations provide detailed default and mandatory rules about this obligation highlights its importance. As an obligation of the principal under the contract, it is therefore (whether based on express contractual provision or on Regulations 7–12) subject to the mandatory duty of good faith. If the principal fails, for no valid reason, to pay the commercial agent (at least if it is more than a "one-off" mechanical "blip"), this, it appears, will be regarded as a serious breach, entitling the commercial agent, if so minded, summarily to terminate the relationship for "circumstances attributable to the principal" and preserving his right to claim compensation or indemnity.[13] This was the interpretation reached by the High Court in the case of *Bell Electric Ltd* v. *Aweco Appliance Systems GmbH & Co KG*.[14] By deciding that the principal cannot prevent the commercial agent from having his remuneration once earned, the High Court emphasises the protective stance of the Agency Regulations. Interestingly, this interpretation is similar to what a French court would have done in the light of the mandate of common interest (as to which, see Chapter 6, section 6.3.1.1).

(3) Because commercial agents have a right to be remunerated, the remuneration, or at least the principles for calculating it, must be determined beforehand and, more importantly, cannot be left to the sole discretion of the principal. If it is, the principal must take account of the interests of both parties. This is the arguable case identified by the Court of Appeal in *Page* v. *CST*.[15] We commented on these situations above.

(4) It is worth repeating that, even though such rules are clearly very protective of the commercial agent, the principal should be entitled to vary the commission rate etc provided there are valid reasons for it.[16]

4.5 THE DETAILED SCHEME: REGULATIONS 7–12, APPLICABLE ONLY WHERE THE COMMERCIAL AGENT IS REMUNERATED (IN WHOLE OR IN PART) BY "COMMISSION" AS DEFINED

Regulations 7–12 apply only where the commercial agent is remunerated, in whole or in part, by commission as defined.[17]

Where that is the case, the rules set out in the Agency Regulations are detailed. They cover the commercial agent's entitlement to receive commission (Regulations 7–9), the moment when commission is earned and due for payment (Regulation 10), the instances

12. See especially *Alpha Trading Ltd* v. *Dunshaw-Patten Ltd* [1981] 1 All ER 487 and *Luxor (Eastbourne) Ltd (in liquidation) and others* v. *Cooper* [1941] 1 AC 108.

13. Regulation 18(b)(i).

14. [2002] EWHC 872, 8 May 2002.

15. [1997] 3 All ER 656.

16. This is what happens in French law. See Chapter 6, section 6.3.1.1, especially fn 73 and associated text.

17. Regulation 6(3).

when the right to claim commission is lost (Regulation 11) and the right for the commercial agent to check the books of the principal (Regulation 12). Each rule must be assessed in turn.

As noted above, the general (but not universally held) view, being the one to which we subscribe, is that the Agency Regulations rules on the basis of calculation and the transactions on which remuneration are payable (being Regulations 7–9) and most of the rules on when commission is to fall due and be paid are non-mandatory, and so will yield to contrary agreement. By contrast, for the protection of the commercial agent, the "backstop" dates for the accrual due and payment of commission, the circumstances where the commercial agent can lose his right to commission and the commercial agent's right to an explanatory statement from the principal as to the calculation of his commission (Regulations 10(2)–(4), 11 and 12) are mandatory, and cannot be derogated from to the commercial agent's detriment.

4.6 "COMMISSION": THE DEFINITION IN REGULATION 2(1) OF THE AGENCY REGULATIONS

The fact that Part III applies only where the commercial agent is remunerated, in whole or in part, by commission as defined is not surprising, as commission is the most common method of payment of commercial agents. It would be rare for a commercial agent not to be remunerated, at least in part, by commission as defined. Indeed, commission is usually regarded as the method of payment which differentiates commercial agents from distributors, an essential "badge" of the relationship.

Commission is defined in Regulation 2(1) "any part of the remuneration of a commercial agent which varies with the number or value of business transactions". *Mercantile International Group Plc* v. *Chuan Soot Huat Industrial Group plc*[18] concerned a contract which the courts were satisfied was in substance commercial agency, but where the agent's remuneration made it look like a distribution agreement. Conceptually confused hybrids like this are nowhere near as rare in practice as one might imagine. Here the commercial agent would conclude a sale contract with the principal's customer at one price, but would inform the principal that the sale was proceeding at a lower price, the difference between the two, the "mark-up", being retained by the commercial agent as his remuneration. The principal was aware of and entirely happy with this arrangement, but did not know how much the "mark-up" was and did not seem to care nor to seek to control it in any way. The courts were satisfied that there was no element of the commercial agent withholding information or moneys which it should have provided to its principal. The Court of Appeal, confirming Andrew Smith J at first instance, said that the "mark-up" was not "commission" within the Regulation 2(1) definition. Other than as to the commercial agent's remuneration, however, the contract documentation and the way the parties operated their relationship were entirely consistent with the arrangement being a commercial agency and not a distributorship. Being satisfied that the arrangement was not a sham, the courts said that the remuneration term did not prevent the arrangement being a commercial agency for the purposes of the Agency Regulations (the commercial agent being within the Regulation 2(1) definition of "a self-employed intermediary who has continuing

18. [2002] EWCA Civ 288, 8 March 2002.

authority to negotiate the sale or purchase of goods on behalf of anther person or to negotiate and conclude . . . "). Accordingly, the commercial agent was entitled to claim a lump sum compensation payment following termination of the agreement. The only effect of the remuneration term was that the provisions of the Agency Regulations concerning commission did not apply to the agreement.

It is hard to see why the "mark-up" did not fall within the definition of "commission" within Regulation 2(1), but Regulation 2(1), and thus indirectly, Regulation 6(3), must now be taken as qualified to that extent.

This case confirms the earlier decision of *AMB Imballagi Plastici SRL* v. *Pacflex Ltd*,[19] where the Court of Appeal had held that, for the purpose of the Agency Regulations, the concept of remuneration does not include the circumstances in which a representative is paid through a mark-up. It is important, since it shows that the courts will look at the contract as a whole, rather than only at the method of remuneration, in order to define its nature.

The fact that it is not a pre-requisite to the application of the Agency Regulations that the commercial agent be paid solely by commission is, nevertheless, positive for the commercial agent, as it gives the parties the freedom to agree on a different method of termination if that suits their needs better, whilst remaining within the coverage of the Agency Regulations for other purposes. When, for instance, a principal appoints a commercial agent to break into a market, the commercial agent will often face significant initial expense.[20] It may take some time before the commercial agent can get appreciable orders from customers and start to earn commission, and he will probably want some remuneration in the meantime. A better method of payment in such a case, from the commercial agent's point of view, is therefore a retainer, as the case of *Duffen* v. *FraBo SpA (No 1)*[21] illustrates. While such an arrangement plainly does not amount to "commission" (so that Regulations 7–12 will not apply to it), the method of remuneration will not prevent the application of the other rules of the Agency Regulations.

4.7 THE COMMERCIAL AGENT'S ENTITLEMENT TO COMMISSION: REGULATIONS 7–8

The commercial agent's right to receive commission is, under the Agency Regulations, rather wide. He is entitled to receive commissions on commercial transactions concluded between the principal and the third party, both for certain transactions concluded during the life of the commercial agency contract (Regulation 7) and also for certain transactions concluded after the commercial agency contract has terminated (Regulation 8). The two must be reviewed separately, as they are the object of different rules.

4.8 COMMISSIONS ON TRANSACTIONS CONCLUDED DURING THE LIFE OF THE COMMERCIAL AGENCY CONTRACT: REGULATION 7

The predominant view, being the one to which we subscribe, is that Regulation 7 is non-mandatory. Accordingly, even where the commercial agent is remunerated in whole or in

19. [1999] 2 All ER (Comm) 249.
20. S Singleton, *Commercial Agency Agreements: Law and Practice* (1998), p 8.
21. [1999] ECC 58; (No 2) [2000] Lloyd's Rep 180.

part by commission as defined (so that Regulations 7–12 in principle apply), the parties may validly exclude Regulation 7 if they wish.[22] We consider that, generally, they will wish to do that. It is prudent, when drafting, to do so expressly (lest it be later argued that the parties intended some retained vestigial role for Regulation 7 in filling gaps in the express terms).

Regulation 7 lists three situations where the commercial agent will be entitled to commission on a transaction concluded during the life of the agreement. They are where the transaction between principal and third party is:

- concluded as a result of his action;[23]
- concluded with a third party whom he has previously acquired as a customer for transactions "of the same kind";[24] or
- concluded with a customer "belonging" to any specific geographic area or group of customers to which the commercial agent has been given "an exclusive right" under the commercial agency agreement.[25]

The first two of these we shall refer to as "direct transactions"; the third of these we shall refer to as "indirect transactions".

What does "concluded" mean"? It is thought to mean when the contract between the principal and the third party is entered into.[26]

How does the word "concluded" work where the commercial agency is for marketing only, i.e. the commercial agent has no authority to conclude transactions on the principal's behalf, but only to negotiate? Interpreting that word literally, if the commercial agent, under a marketing-only agency, introduces the potential third-party customer to the principal but the principal then decides (for whatever reason) not to contract with that third party, no contract will have been "concluded". In the light of the protective stance of the Directive, it is thought that it includes both types of commercial agent. However, for the sake of clarity, it would have been appropriate to add "or when the third party is introduced by the commercial agent".

4.8.1 Direct transactions

Regulation 7(1)(a) ("concluded as a result of his action") is "first time business". Regulation 7(1)(b) ("concluded with a third party whom he [the commercial agent] has previously acquired as a customer for transactions of the same kind") is "repeat business".

First-time business

In relation to the "first-time business", the fact that the entitlement to commission is dependent on whether the transaction is concluded "as a result of [the commercial agent's] action" appears to be similar to the common law requirement of *effective cause*.[27] On that basis, there could be scope for the argument by the principal that, if the customer would

22. See fn 1 above and the authorities cited.
23. Regulation 7(1)(a).
24. Regulation 7(1)(b).
25. Regulation 7(2).
26. FMB Reynolds, *Bowstead and Reynolds on Agency*, (2000), para 11–025.
27. *Millar, Son & Co* v. *Ratford* (1903) 19 TLR 575; and section 3.3.2.2. above.

have searched him out in any event and dealt with him regardless of the commercial agent's involvement, the commission is not due. However, in *Moore* v. *Piretta Ltd*[28] the Court of Appeal held, in relation to Regulation 17, that the requirement that the commercial agent must have "brought in" the customer is satisfied if the commercial agent has been "instrumental" in obtaining the new customer. It is not limited to the situation where the commercial agent "brought in" the customer single-handedly. It suffices for Regulation 17 purposes that the commercial agent has played an active part of some sort in "landing" the customer (e.g. by contacting customers on a list of "targets" provided to him by the principal), That being the case under Regulation 17, it would seem to follow that, in those circumstances, for the purposes of Regulation 7(1)(a) the transaction between principal and third party will be treated as having been "concluded as a result of [the commercial agent's] action". It seems, therefore, that the test of causation is less demanding than the "effective cause" requirement at common law.

On the other hand, there seems to be no objection to the commercial agency agreement providing in clear terms from its inception for a lower rate of commission to be payable on transactions where the commercial agent's efforts have been less than single-handed, though one could envisage practical problems in identifying the different levels of involvement. Any effort by a principal, once the agreement is operating, to vary the commercial agent's commission according to his perception of the commercial agent's contribution to "landing" the customer, whether under a discretionary power to do so contained in the agreement or not, would be subject to the mutual obligations of good faith referred to earlier.

Repeat business

In relation to "repeat business", commission is only due to the commercial agent on "repeat business" "of the same kind" as that for which he originally acquired the customer. Regulation 7(1)(b) is considerably more generous to the commercial agent than the common law rules, where, in the absence of an express agreement to this effect, the agent receives no commission on "repeat business".

What is a transaction "of the same kind"? A competition-law style analysis of the relevant market (substitute products, substitute sources of supply) may well be what is intended here,[29] though taking too narrow a view may risk discouraging cross-selling by the commercial agent (e.g. if the principal has a varied portfolio of products).

It has been suggested[30] that the entitlement to "repeat business" commission under Regulation 7(1)(b) is not limited to the situation where the commercial agent acquired the customer for a transaction "of the same kind" for the current principal, and that it might be enough that the commercial agent had, in an earlier existence as a commercial agent (or, for that matter, distributor or employee) for, for example, the current principal's main competitor, secured this customer as a customer for similar goods. If that is right, it could give the commercial agent an entitlement to commission on all manner of transactions with which he has had no connection at all. We consider that that very literal interpretation

28. [1999] 1 All ER 174.

29. See the European Commission *Notice on the definition of relevant market for the purposes of Community competition law*, OJ 1997 C. 372/5; UK Office of Fair Trading Competition Act guideline *Market Definition*, OFT 403; S Bishop and M Walker, *The economics of EC competition law* (Sweet & Maxwell, 2nd edn, 2002), ch 4.

30. Randolph and Davey, *Guide to the Commercial Agents Regulations* (2nd edn, 2003), p 70.

is not correct, taken in context, and especially in the light of Regulation 7(2) (see below). By implication, Regulation 7(1)(b) should be limited to commission on "repeat business" transactions where the commercial agent had previously acquired the customer for transactions "of the same kind" with the same principal. However, since regulation 7 is not expressly stipulated to be mandatory, nothing seems to prevent the parties agreeing a lower rate of commission for "repeat business" transactions than for "new business" transactions. This would make sense in the light of the symmetry between the parties.

4.8.2 Indirect transactions

Regulation 7(2) entitles the commercial agent to commission on transactions concluded by the principal during the term of the commercial agency agreement with customers "belonging to" any specific geographical area or customer group to which the commercial agent has been given "an exclusive right" under the commercial agency agreement.

This is a much wider range of transactions than "direct" transactions. It entitles the commercial agent to commission on transactions with customers falling within these categories even if he has never heard of the customer, let alone never had any contact with him. That Article 7(2) of the Directive and therefore, in the light of its near-verbatim implementation, Regulation 7(2) do indeed have this far-reaching effect was confirmed by the ECJ in its Article 234 preliminary ruling in *Kontogeorgas* v. *Kartonpak*[31] and reiterated in the UK in *Moore* v. *Piretta Ltd*,[32] where Mitting QC, sitting as a deputy judge of the Queen's Bench Division, commented that "the first sub-regulation [i.e. Regulation 7(1)] requires some action on the part of the agent to earn the commission, the second [i.e. Regulation 7(2)] does not".[33]

In Regulation 7(2), the UK has, however, adopted the most restrictive of the options offered by the Directive, since the commercial agent will only be entitled to commissions on such transactions on two conditions: he must have an exclusive right to a specific geographic area or group of customers,[34] and the transaction must have been concluded with a customer belonging to that group or area.[35]

The verbatim implementation raises three key questions.

(1) What does "an exclusive right" mean?

Agents (sales and marketing) will usually have either exclusive, non-exclusive or sole rights in their defined territory, which are generally understood by English lawyers to mean the following:

> *Exclusive rights* prevent the principal from himself actively seeking sales in the commercial agent's territory and from appointing other commercial agents or distributors there. Under the EC competition law regime for vertical agreements, only a rather qualified form of exclusivity is permitted.[36] The principal may, however

31. Case C–104/95 [1997] 1 CMLR 1083, [1996] ECR I–6643.
32. [1999] 1 All ER 174.
33. *Ibid* at p 178a. Emphasis added.
34. The UK has therefore opted for the most restrictive option offered by the Directive. For the choice, see article 7(2) of the Directive.
35. It is to be noted that the words "concluded" and "entered into" are used interchangeably but mean the same thing. The same mistake appears in article 7(2) of the Directive.
36. See Commission Regulation 2790/1999, OJ L 336/21 of 29 December 1999, especially article 4(b), and the Commission Guidelines on Vertical Restraints, OJ C 291/1 of 13 October 2000.

(subject to possible competition law concerns) reserve certain rights to himself, such as the right to continue to supply certain identified customers or classes of customers in the territory without involving the commercial agent.

Sole rights prevent the principal from appointing another commercial agent for the territory and (depending on the drafting) other distributors and other types of resellers, but will not prevent the principal himself from actively seeking sales in the territory or making passive sales at the level of customers (wholesaler/retailer/end-user) at which the commercial agent is operating.

Non-exclusive rights leave the principal free to appoint other commercial agents and resellers and himself actively to seek sales in the territory at the same level of customers as the commercial agent.

The Agency Regulations do not define "exclusive" for this purpose. Presumably it must include "exclusive" in the qualified sense permitted under the block exemption for vertical agreements. It is not clear whether a commercial agent with sole rights, rather than exclusive rights, can benefit from Regulation 7(2). Even if Regulation 7 was ultimately held to be mandatory, the commercial agent's right to commission under Regulation 7(2) could be overcome altogether by a clause denying the commercial agent an exclusive right to any specific area or group of customers in the first place (though note the possible double commission problem referred to below) or at least reduced significantly by excluding from the commercial agent's group of exclusive customers in an area those customers of the principal with whom the principal wishes to deal direct ("house accounts").

In *Duffen* v. *FraBo SpA (No 1)*,[37] the Court of Appeal upheld the commercial agent's right to commission on direct sales by the principal in the commercial agent's exclusive sales area, but on the basis that that was what the commercial agency agreement in question, as drafted, provided for, rather than on the basis of Regulation 7(2). Considering that the text stipulates that the commercial agent will be entitled to commissions regardless of his involvement, this seems to indicate that sole rights are meant to be included in the concept of "an exclusive right".

It has been suggested further that, since Regulation 7(2) does not expressly require the exclusivity to have been expressly agreed in the commercial agency agreement, there is a danger for principals who have not granted any exclusive or sole rights to their commercial agents but who in practice have only one commercial agent in charge of a particular area or group of customers, that their commercial agent will be able to claim under this regulation.[38] There is no authority on this proposition either way, but we are somewhat doubtful about it.

(2) What does "belonging to" a particular geographical area or customer group mean?

This is a particular difficulty where the customer is a legal person and where the customer operates in a number of locations, some within the commercial agent's exclusive territory, others not. This was the other point addressed by the ECJ in *Kontogeorgas* v. *Kartonpak*.[39] The court said that:

37. [1998] 17 Tr LR 460.
38. Randolph and Davey, *Guide to the Commercial Agents Regulations* (2nd edn, 2003), p 70.
39. Case C–104/95 [1996] ECR I–6643.

— where the customer is a company, the crucial location is where it actually carries on business, and not (if different) where the registered office or corporate seat is;
— if a company carries on business in a number of different places, one has to look at "the centre of gravity of the transaction effected" between the principal and the third party. The ECJ did not lay down a single test for that, but referred, by way of examples, to the place from which the customer placed the order for the goods, the place where any negotiations took place, and the place where the goods were delivered to the customer.

(3) The possible liability of the principal to pay commission to two commercial agents in respect of the same transaction

There may be a concern for principals in that, if they have more than one commercial agent, they could become liable to pay commission twice (or, indeed, thrice) over on the same transaction: once, to the commercial agent who actually concludes the transaction with the customer; and again, to a different commercial agent or agents if the conditions of Regulation 7(1)(b) or 7(2) are fulfilled. There is no provision in the Agency Regulations dealing with this possibility.

The uncertainties outlined here highlight the importance of dealing expressly with the issue of commission in a commercial agency agreement.

4.9 COMMISSION ON TRANSACTIONS CONCLUDED AFTER TERMINATION: REGULATION 8

To grant commercial agents an express right to commission on transactions concluded after the termination of the commercial agency agreement is a significant improvement on their protection. Once again, however, uncertainty surrounds this right because of the verbatim implementation of the Directive into the Agency Regulations. As with Regulation 7, the predominant view is that Regulation 8 is non-mandatory. It will not apply if there is express provision in the commercial agency agreement as to commission, though it would be sensible to add that the express provisions of the agreement represent the entirety of the commercial agent's right to commission.

Under Regulation 8, the commercial agent is entitled to commission on transactions concluded by the principal after termination of the commercial agency agreement if either:

— the transaction is "mainly attributable" to the commercial agent's efforts while the commercial agency agreement was on foot, and was entered into "within a reasonable period" after it terminated;[40] or
— the customer's order reached the commercial agent or the principal before the commercial agency agreement was terminated, but the order was only accepted and the contract made after the commercial agency agreement had terminated (always assuming that, if the agency agreement had not been terminated, commission would have been payable under Regulation 7).[41]

40. Regulation 8(a).
41. Regulation 8(b).

There is no explanation of what "mainly attributable" means. It seems to include causation more indirect than "as a result of", and to be more generous to the commercial agent than the common law "effective cause" requirement.

Equally, no clues are given as to what a "reasonable period" after termination of the commercial agency agreement might be. If one was wanting to include in one's agreement a right for the commercial agent to commission pursuant to Regulation 8, one could always, since Regulation 8 is considered to be non-mandatory, spell that out and that would almost certainly be effective. Otherwise, one would want to consider such matters as the duration of the commercial agency agreement that has been terminated, any earlier agreements between the same parties (presumably to include pre-1994 ones as well as those after the coming into force of the Agency Regulations), the frequency with which contracts have been negotiated or concluded during it, the nature of the goods, and the typical length of time it takes for enquiries about this sort of product to this principal's commercial agents to turn into firm orders.

In *Tigana Limited* v. *Decoro Ltd*,[42] the two requirements in Regulation 8(a) were confirmed as being cumulative.

As to the "mainly attributable" point, the court said (uncontroversially enough) that this is a causal link between the agent's activities and the making of the contract with the third party. In this case, the court found that without the commercial agent's efforts the principal would have had virtually no customer base in the contract territory (the UK). The principal had started as a new entrant to the UK market, and had engaged this commercial agent because he had a quarter-century's experience of acting as commercial agent for importing the very specific type of product (leather upholstered furniture) into the UK, he was very well connected in the UK furniture trade, and customers (UK furniture retailers) often relied very heavily on this commercial agent's views as to whether particular new products would sell well in the UK or not. It was because this commercial agent had what Davis J described as "real standing and real clout in this particular business", and apparently almost entirely because of that, that major customers had become interested in the principal's products at all. On the "mainly attributable" point, then, the commercial agent here was in an unusually strong position.

Davis J pointed out that, with the passage of time, sooner or later transactions entered into by the principal after the termination of the commercial agency agreement will cease to be "mainly attributable" to the commercial agent's efforts, so that there is a connection between "mainly attributable" and "within a reasonable period". He decided that, on the facts, 9 months after termination of the commercial agency agreement was a "reasonable period". Until that point, the replacement commercial agent had done no more than administer and consolidate relationships with customers which the original commercial agent had brought in; only then had the new commercial agent started to bring in customers of his own; at that point a major trade fair had taken place at which new models of the product had appeared; and the commercial agent had only been agent for this principal for a year in any event.

The circumstances of *Tigana Ltd* v. *Decoro Ltd* were, accordingly, unusually favourable to the commercial agent for claiming commission under Regulation 8. Generally, a claim for commission thereunder is likely to be significantly more speculative than this one was.

42. [2003] EWHC 28, [2003] Eu LR 189.

Regulation 8 has been criticised for overlapping with the lump sum indemnity payment on termination. The argument is that it allows the commercial agent to be paid twice.[43] With respect, this criticism is unfounded. The indemnity payment is based fundamentally on the uplift in the volume of anticipated future business that results from the commercial agent's efforts during the period of the commercial agency. The case of *Tigana Limited* v. *Decoro Ltd*[44] shows that it is accepted that such payments do not overlap with the compensation alternative either.

4.10 CHANGE OF COMMERCIAL AGENT: APPORTIONMENTS OF COMMISSION: REGULATION 9

Finally, in order to avoid the principal having to pay commission twice for the same transactions, the Agency Regulations provide rules in Regulation 9 (which, like Regulations 7 and 8, are generally assumed to be non-mandatory) to apportion the commission between a new commercial agent and his predecessor.

The position is that, where both incoming commercial agent and outgoing commercial agent are each entitled to commission on a transaction, the new commercial agent has no right to such commission unless he can show that it is "equitable because of the circumstances" for it to be shared between the two of them.[45] The Agency Regulations give no clue as to the proportions in which the commission should be shared in that event, so presumably it is equally. The presumption is, accordingly, very much in favour of the outgoing commercial agent. This rule was tested for the first time in the case of *Tigana Limited* v. *Decoro Ltd*.[46] The text further adds that any commission unduly received by a commercial agent must be refunded to the principal.[47]

When a principal terminates a commercial agency agreement to which the Agency Regulations apply and Regulation 8 is applicable, he will want to be sure, before agreeing the final account with the outgoing agent, that any incoming commercial agent has no claim to commission in respect of those transactions on which the outgoing commercial agent could have a claim to commission under Regulation 8. The agreement of the new commercial agent not to seek commission in respect of any such transactions should be obtained. There is no reason to think that such an agreement would not be valid and binding.

4.11 WHEN COMMISSION IS OBTAINED AND DUE FOR PAYMENT: REGULATION 10

Under Regulation 10, the commercial agent obtains the right to be paid a commission as soon as and to the extent that:

(i) the principal has "executed" the transaction;[48] or

43. S Singleton, *Commercial Agency Agreements: Law and Practice* (1998), p 53.
44. See fn 42.
45. Regulation 9(1).
46. See fn 42.
47. Regulation 9(2).
48. Regulation 10(1)(a).

(ii) the principal should, according to the agreement with the customer, have "executed" the transaction; or

(iii) when the customer has "executed" the transaction.

The term "executed" is not known in English law parlance. However, following examples provided by the DTI as to what "execute" means for the principal and the third party alike,[49] it seems clear that the term merely means "to perform". So, "the principal executing the transaction" means the principal performing his part of the transaction. Under an English law sale of goods contract, the essential obligations of the seller are to transfer ownership to and deliver to the buyer goods that are in conformity with the contract description. The key duties of the buyer are to take delivery of and accept the goods (provided they are in conformity with the contract description) and to pay the price.

The use of the words "to the extent that" shows that, where the contract with the customer provides for delivery and payment by instalments, the commercial agent's entitlement to commission will arise pro rata.

The parties remain free to decide which of these three circumstances will apply. Furthermore, while Regulation 10(4) states that any attempt to derogate from the provisions of Regulations 10(2) and 10(3) to the commercial agent's detriment is stated to be void, Regulation 10(4) says nothing about the status of Regulation 10(1). Accordingly, it is assumed that Regulation 10(1) is non-mandatory, so that, subject to the mandatory "backstop" provision in Regulation 10(2), parties could agree other events entirely which would trigger the commercial agent's entitlement to be paid commission.[50]

Where the Agency Regulations apply, there are, as mentioned earlier, mandatory[51] "backstop" dates for the accrual due of commission[52] and its subsequent payment,[53] though the parties can of course agree earlier dates for these events if they wish.

Under the mandatory Regulation 10(2), the commercial agent's commission must accrue due at the latest when the customer "executes" his part of the transaction or when the customer should have done that if the principal had "executed" his part of the transaction on time. This is intended as an anti-avoidance device for the protection of the commercial agent, to ensure that he cannot be kept waiting for his commission to accrue due by the principal simply delaying performance of his obligations under the relevant sale contract.

The effect of Regulation 10(2) appears to be that, in commercial agency agreements within the Regulations, the agreement must provide that:

(a) in the normal situation, where the customer takes delivery, accepts the goods and pays the price on the due date under the sale contract, the commercial agent's commission must fall due by that date at the latest. If those events are split in point of time, commission must fall due no later than the latest of them (only then has the customer completely "executed" its part of the sale contract). Thus the

49. DTI said that the principal has executed when he has accepted, delivered the goods. For the third party, execute means to accept or pay for the goods. See DTI Guidance Notes published in September 1994, p 15, reproduced as Appendix 8.

50. It has even been said that it would be wise for principals to derogate from this regulation: J Schrire, *Commercial agents, a fundamental change*, (1994) 15 BLR, p 174.

51. Regulation 10(4).

52. Regulation 10(2).

53. Regulation 10(3).

commercial agency agreement can validly provide that, in the normal situation, the commission will only fall due when the principal has himself been paid (or perhaps been put in a position where he definitely will be paid), though it is always open to the principal to agree to the commission accruing due at some earlier stage.

(b) if the customer does not take delivery and accept the goods and pay the price on the due date under the sale contract, then

— if the principal is in breach of the sale contract (e.g. because the goods delivered did not meet the contract specification), the commercial agent's commission must fall due no later than the later of the contractual delivery date and the contractual payment date (i.e. not later than the date when the customer would, in the normal way (and assuming the principal had performed his part of the sale contract) have taken delivery, accepted and paid); and

— if the principal has performed his part of the transaction (i.e. has transferred and delivered or is ready to transfer ownership of and deliver goods which meet the contract specification) and his customer is, in breach of contract, refusing to take delivery, accept and/or pay for them, the commercial agent can be made to wait for his commission to accrue due until the customer actually takes delivery and pays the price.

The Agency Regulations even provide a time-limit for the principal to actually pay the commission (which must presumably mean paid for immediate value). It cannot be paid later than on the last day of the month following the quarter in which it became due.[54] Neither can such a rule be derogated from to the commercial agent's detriment.[55]

4.12 WHEN THE RIGHT TO COMMISSION IS LOST: REGULATION 11

Regulation 11 provides tight regulation of the circumstances in which the commercial agent can lose his right to commission. By Regulation 11(3), any agreement to derogate from its provisions to the commercial agent's detriment is void. It is therefore very good for the protection of commercial agents, since the principal cannot avoid paying the commission for any other reason.

The only situation when the commercial agent will lose the right to commission is if and to the extent that it is established that the transaction between the principal and the third party will not be "executed"[56] and that the principal is "not to blame" for the lack of performance.[57] Any commission which the commercial agent has already received has to be refunded if the right to it is extinguished.[58] The verbatim implementation is obvious here.

As mentioned above, "execute" means "perform".

54. Regulation 10(3), quarters running from the date the agency agreement takes effect.
55. Regulation 10(4).
56. Regulation 11(1)(a).
57. Regulation 11(1)(b).
58. Regulation 11(2).

"Not to blame", however, is a new idea for English lawyers. If the principal was in breach of contract with his customer, one would have thought he was pretty clearly "to blame" for the fact that the sale contract had not been performed. Such an interpretation would make sense in the light of Regulation 10(2).[59] But what if the reason for the principal's non-performance is that, in breach of an upstream contract with him, a components supplier has failed to deliver components on time where there was no breach by the principal of that contract? Is the principal "to blame" for his non-performance then? At the other extreme, one would have thought that the principal will not be "to blame" if the sale contract has not been performed because the buyer of the goods is in breach of contract or has ceased trading through insolvency. But what if, anticipating the impending insolvency of its customer, the principal terminates his contract with the customer under a power in the contract between them allowing him to do that? Plainly the termination of the sale contract by the principal is not a breach of contract by him; but is he "to blame" for the non-performance of that contract where he could simply choose to take no action and "wait and see"? There must be an arguable case that, if the principal has acted as a reasonable prudent businessman, he will not be "to blame" for his non-performance, whether he is in breach of contract or not. There is no law on these questions in England and Wales or any other parts of the UK at present.

Regulation 11 says nothing about the possibility that it may not be known, at the date for commission to become due, whether the contract between principal and his customer will be performed or not, and, if not, whether the principal is or is not "to blame" for the non-performance. As there is no specific provision made for the falling due of commission to be deferred in that event, the commission must accrue on that date regardless. If that results in commission being paid to the commercial agent which it ultimately transpires is not due to him, he is obliged under Regulation 11(2) to refund it. If principal and commercial agent have "fallen out" in the meantime, this may be troublesome for the principal.

4.13 DISCLOSURE OF INFORMATION ON THE METHOD OF CALCULATION OF COMMISSION: REGULATION 12

In addition to the principal's obligation to pay the commercial agent the commission due, the principal also has a (non-excludable) obligation under Regulation 12 to disclose to the commercial agent information related to the commission. This represents a significant improvement on the level of protection of commercial agents, since no such obligation exists at common law, except if litigation has been begun, when the disclosure rules in litigation procedure come into play.

The obligation imposed on the principal is quite substantial. He must provide the commercial agent with a statement of the commission due, no later than the last day of the month following the quarter in which the commission in which the commission became due.[60] Such an obligation is therefore a repeat one. The contents of the statement are also

59. Regulation 10(2) stipulates that commission is due at the latest when the third party has executed his part of the transaction or should have done so if the principal had executed his part.

60. Regulation 12(1).

closely regulated, since the principal must set out the "main components" used in calculating the amount of commission due.[61] Should the principal fail to provide the statement, the text then gives the commercial agent a right to demand any relevant information and in particular, an extract from the principal's books for the purpose of checking the amount of the commission due to him.[62] On this right to information, the DTI has confirmed that the principal is only required to provide the relevant extracts of the book and not all of them.[63] This is, once again, a significant improvement to the commercial agent's position by comparison with the common law.

There is a gap, however, in that the Agency Regulations, while giving the commercial agent this non-excludable right to information, remain silent as to any confidentiality obligation. However, at common law an agent is almost certainly under an obligation to keep his principal's confidential information confidential, and an obligation of confidentiality can probably be implied by virtue of the commercial agent's duty of good faith under Regulation 3. A well-drafted commercial agency agreement will, of course, contain a confidentiality clause. As a practical matter, principals, in performing their obligations under Regulation 12, will want to ensure that no superfluous information is inadvertently made available to the commercial agent.

61. *Ibid.*
62. Regulation 12(2).
63. DTI Guidance Notes, published in September 1994, p 17.

CHAPTER 5

TERMINATION OF THE COMMERCIAL AGENCY CONTRACT AND ITS CONSEQUENCES FOR THE PARTIES

5.1 INTRODUCTION AND ROAD MAP OF THE CHAPTER

Termination is undoubtedly the area where the Agency Regulations have made the most substantial changes to the level of legal protection for commercial agents, by giving them the right to a lump sum payment on termination, being in the language of the Directive either "compensation" or "indemnity".[1] Yet it is also the area that has caused the most controversy, because of the silence of the Agency Regulations on various issues such as what constitutes termination, what is the rationale behind the two termination payments, and also how some of the new rules relate to the traditional common law rules of agency and contract law. This silence can be explained by the fact that the Agency Regulations have almost replicated the Directive, which was not meant to be implemented in such a manner. Even though this appears typical of the more recent "cop-out" manner in which the government seems to implement directives,[2] the lack of details is nevertheless unsatisfactory, as this is yet another illustration of the legal paradox that such a method of implementation creates. Such questions therefore need to be addressed in order to assess and appreciate the full extent of the impact of the Agency Regulations on the traditional common law rules in this area.

Under the Agency Regulations, there are two main elements to termination: (1) the process of termination itself, and (2) the consequences it has on the parties, i.e. the right of the commercial agent to claim compensation or indemnity. Whereas a lot of attention has been paid to the latter, very little has been said about termination itself. This is disappointing because understanding what constitutes termination and how it can occur is as important as understanding how the termination rights function. This chapter aims to remedy this silence by studying these two complementary aspects of termination in turn.

— First, we will consider the process of termination itself by looking at the various methods by which and circumstances in which the commercial agency agreement can come to an end (section 5.2). Because of the silence of the Agency Regulations on this aspect, this will be done by reference to the traditional common law

1. Regulation 17(1).

2. Such an approach is explained by the fact that the European Commission has on occasion successfully sued the government in the ECJ for wrong implementation of directives. See for instance *Dr Sophie Redmond Stitching* v. *Bartol* [1992] IRLR 366, where the European Court of Justice decided that regulation 2 of the Transfer of Undertakings (Protection of Enployment) Regulations 1981 (SI 1981/1794) had incorrectly implemented the EC Acquired Rights Directive 77/187. Example borrowed from R Christou, *International Agency, Distribution and Licensing Agreements*, (4th edn, 2003) para 3.07, p 87.

rules of agency and contract. This is necessary mostly to fill the gaps left by the Agency Regulations but also to understand how the two sets of rules relate one to another.

— Secondly, we will study the consequences that termination has on the parties; the right for the commercial agent to claim compensation or indemnity (section 5.3). The civil-law rationale behind the need for such a right will first be considered before turning to its scope of application.

5.2 THE DIFFERENT METHODS AND CIRCUMSTANCES OF TERMINATION

Termination is *the* event that triggers the right of commercial agents to claim compensation or indemnity.[3] In spite of the importance of such an issue, the Directive and consequently the Agency Regulations remain silent as to what constitutes "termination".[4] The Agency Regulations refer only indirectly to possible causes, in relation to the exclusions the right to claim termination payments[5] or in case of immediate termination.[6] This silence seems to indicate that the common law principles of contract apply. This was confirmed by the case of *Roy* v. *MR Pearlman Ltd*,[7] where it was held that the principles of domestic law are not displaced by the Agency Regulations. This is entirely normal and correct.[8] Yet, as will be seen, because the Agency Regulations import into English law civil-law-inspired principles which are alien to the traditional common law rules, the co-existence of the two sets of rules is sometimes fraught with tensions.

At common law, an agency contract can be terminated through a deliberate act of the parties (section 5.2.1) or by operation of law (section 5.2.2). Our study of the Agency Regulations must therefore follow the common law model to fill the gaps left by the Agency Regulations, and consequently to appreciate how the traditional common law rules and the Agency Regulations dovetail.

5.2.1 Termination by the parties

At common law, an agency relationship may be terminated by mutual consent (section 5.2.1.1) or by the unilateral act of either party (section 5.2.1.2). The Agency Regulations lack serious detail in this matter. Not only do they fail to deal with termination by mutual consent but also, in relation to unilateral termination, they only seem to cover indefinite duration contracts. The one area covered by the Agency Regulations is that of summary termination. However, as will be seen, it is not perfect either, since the rules lack details,

3. Regulation 17(1).

4. Interestingly, in its 1987 Explanatory and Consultative Note, the DTI gave a non-exhaustive list as to what constituted termination. This included frustration, breach by the principal, including shorter notice periods; principal giving notice or early termination of fixed-term contracts and expiry of a fixed-term contract through passage of time. See Randolph and Davey, *Guide to the Commercial Agency Regulations*, (2nd edn, 2003), p 91.

5. Regulation 18.

6. Regulation 16.

7. [1999] 2 CMLR 1155.

8. The Directive applies to the national laws, regulations and administrative provisions governing the relations between commercial agents and principals (article 1(1)).

which raises issues of compatibility between the Agency Regulations and the common law rules (section 5.2.1.3).

5.2.1.1 Termination through mutual consent

Termination through mutual consent is not expressly provided for in the Agency Regulations. It is however indirectly referred to as an exception to the entitlement to a payment on termination when the commercial agent assigns the right to be the commercial agent, with the consent of the principal.[9]

Interestingly, the Agency Regulations remain silent on the issue of the principal selling his business, including his business interests under the commercial agency agreement. Considering that the question does not, at first sight, really advance the protection of commercial agents, since a change in the identity of the principal should be neutral, the silence is not surprising. Yet, the issue is nevertheless important, as it has serious consequences for the commercial agent and must consequently be looked at.

5.2.1.1.1 Transfer and/or assignment of the commercial agency relationship

The question must be looked at for each party separately, as the situation of each party raises very different issues.

Assignment by the commercial agent

Regulation 18(c) expressly stipulates that the commercial agent may assign the commercial agency to a third party. However, as this is merely defined as an exception to the commercial agent's right to claim compensation or indemnity, the Agency Regulations clearly lack detail. For instance, the Agency Regulations stipulate that the commercial agent may assign the commercial agency only with the consent of the principal.[10] This is not surprising, given that in English law a commercial agency contract is a contract of a personal nature, being one for the provision of services that involve personal skill and qualifications,[11] so that on general principles it would not be assignable at all except with the consent of the principal and incoming agent, thus making a new contract between principal and new agent by way of novation.

The problem is that the Agency Regulations remain silent as to what happens if the commercial agent purports to assign the commercial agency *without* the consent of the principal. There is the further question as to the reasons for which the principal is entitled to refuse to accept as substitute the assignee proposed by the commercial agent. The two must therefore be considered separately.

The commercial agent assigns without consent of the principal

If the commercial agent purports to assign his interests under the commercial agency without the consent of the principal, whether he does so by failing altogether to ask the

9. Regulation 18(c).
10. Ibid.
11. See *Chitty on Contracts*, Vol. I, paragraphs 19–054ff and cases there cited. Note the fact that if one party to such an agreement is a company, this does not necessarily make the contract into a non-personal (and thus assignable) one: *Griffiths* v. *Tower Publishing Co* [1897] 1 Ch 21.

principal's consent or by ignoring a justified refusal by the principal to consent to the assignment, the commercial agent fails to respect the principal's legitimate interests and therefore is in breach of his duty of good faith as per Regulation 3(1). This is a very serious breach of that duty, such as to allow the principal to summarily terminate the relationship without having to pay compensation or indemnity to the commercial agent, pursuant to Regulation 18(a). Furthermore, as the commercial agency contract is a contract of a personal nature, the principal cannot be obliged to enter into a new contract with the would-be new commercial agent against his will. The commercial agent would thus have lost on both counts.

Since the freedom to assign the commercial agency is a *prima facie* right of the commercial agent, the principal can only refuse to give his consent to this assignment for a valid reason. If the principal refuses consent for an invalid reason, he will be in breach of his duty of good faith to the commercial agent as per Regulation 4(1). This is a very serious breach, allowing the commercial agent to terminate for "circumstances attributable to the principal" pursuant to Regulation 18(b)(i) and still claim compensation or indemnity.

Legitimate reasons for the principal to refuse consent to assignment by commercial agent

What would be a legitimate reason for the principal to refuse consent to an assignment? In the light of the *prima facie* right of the commercial agent to assign his interest in the commercial agency, it is thought that the principal's duty of good faith to the commercial agent is the key to this. The principal is presumably obliged to take into account the commercial agent's desire to hand over to someone else and the circumstances of that, as well as his own interests in the efficient continued running of his business: for him to focus solely on the latter, however, and completely ignore the commercial agent's interests, would seem to be a breach of his duty of good faith. Valid reasons from his own point of view must be reasons relevant to the relationship between principal and commercial agent and not extraneous reasons, and presumably focussed on the proposed assignee's lack of ability or experience or trustworthiness, or perhaps the fact that he acts for competitors of the principal's.

The principal selling out his business

Where the principal is a company, then on general principles the sale by the shareholders of their shares in the principal is neutral so far as the legal relationship between principal and commercial agent is concerned. The identity of the principal has not changed on a share sale, albeit that the identity of the people who control the principal has. Whilst that may in the future lead, in practice, to the relationship between principal and commercial agent operating in a very different way from that before the change of control, we see nothing in the Agency Regulations to indicate that a change of control of the principal is intended of itself to give the commercial agent any rights at all.

THE PRINCIPAL SELLS THE BUSINESS AS A GOING CONCERN

The question arises where, on the other hand, the principal sells his business by way of a sale of the assets as a going concern. Normally a transfer of a business by way of assets sale will include the on-going trading contracts insofar as they are capable of assignment, or, if they are not, vendor and purchaser will often wish to achieve novation of them so that a new contract is formed on the same terms between purchaser and the continuing contractor. The commercial agency contract being a personal contract, an effective transfer can only be achieved by way of novation, i.e. by obtaining the consent of the co-contractor to the substitution of purchaser for vendor.

The question is whether this amounts to a termination of contract such as to entitle the commercial agent to a lump sum payment of compensation or indemnity. The Agency Regulations are silent about this. In the light of the symmetry of the relationship brought on by the reciprocal and mandatory obligations of good faith,[12] we consider that it should be possible for the principal to transfer his position under the commercial agency agreement to the purchaser of his business without triggering the obligation to pay compensation or indemnity to the commercial agent. If the commercial agency agrees a novation with the purchaser, so that he will then have a new commercial agent agreement with the purchaser of the original principal's business, and in principle on the same terms as the original agreement, then the commercial agent is no worse off. The consent of the commercial agent to the substitution of purchaser for vendor would be readily implied by conduct: there are no particular formalities to be followed, and such novations can be very "low-key" and still effective. However, this does raise problems when the "new" principal later wishes to terminate the contract. It is not clear whether for the calculation of the termination payments of the commercial agent, one should only take into consideration the relationship with the "new" principal or not.

Reasons for the commercial agent to refuse the principal's right to sell his business

What if the commercial agent refuses to enter into a novation, releasing the old principal and contracting with the new? Here, the key seems to be the commercial agent's reasons for refusing to deal with the would-be new principal, and the commercial agent's duty of good faith to the principal comes into play. He cannot just think about his own selfish position; he has to have proper regard for the legitimate interest of the principal to sell his business, and so far as considering his own interests is concerned must focus on relevant factors and not irrelevant ones, and his reaction must be reasonable and proportionate. As for the principal, the circumstances at the time of the transfer will be very important and it seems impossible to lay down any hard-and-fast rules. But if the commercial agent refuses, without a valid reason, to enter into a novation, then it seems to us, in view of the symmetry, that he then terminates the relationship with no just cause to do so and therefore loses his right to claim compensation or indemnity as per Regulation 18(b)(i).

The issue of assignment aside, there is no doubt that a commercial agency relationship can of course be terminated through mutual consent, since, in the silence of the Agency Regulations, common law rules apply.[13] At common law, termination through mutual consent will discharge the contract so that there can be no liability for breach of contract. However, under the Agency Regulations, even in the event of termination by mutual consent, assignment aside, the issue of compensation or indemnity arises. This is where

12. Regulations 3, 4 and 5.
13. *Roy* v. *MR Pearlman Ltd* [1999] 2 CMLR 1155.

the failure to determine what constitutes termination and when it may occur is regrettable. The question is mostly acute in relation to fixed-term contracts.

5.2.1.1.2. The expiry of a fixed-term commercial agency agreement by effluxion of time
It is trite law that fixed-term contracts expire with the passage of time, unless renewed, so the lack of such a mention in the Directive and therefore in the Agency Regulations was never considered to be a problem. However, since the right of the commercial agent to claim compensation or indemnity is linked to "termination", it soon became clear that to determine whether the coming to an end of a fixed-term commercial agency contract could be equated to "termination" was a crucial issue for the purpose of the Agency Regulations.

It also soon became important to see how the fixed-term contract ended, whether it was through the simple passage of time or whether it could be said to have ended because the parties had failed to renew it. At first sight the distinction seems irrelevant, since the effect is the same: the contract comes to an end either way. Yet, following the argument[14] that in the wording of the Agency Regulations "termination" implies a positive act by one of the parties, the distinction is important. When not renewing the contract, the principal, arguably, does a positive act, hence the contract can be treated as having been "terminated". With expiry through passage of time however, there is no such act and, arguably, no "termination". We will see that the two are treated as the same by the English and Scottish courts and will therefore be considered together.

Non-renewal and/or expiry of a fixed-term contract amount to termination

The issue of non-renewal of a fixed-term contract was indirectly touched upon in the case of *Moore* v. *Piretta Ltd*[15] where the Court of Appeal held that "it is to be noted that the grounds upon which the right to indemnity or compensation can be excluded do not include the expiry of the term of the agency contract or the expiry or non-renewal of the agency contract".[16]

The first case to expressly deal with the issue was that of *Whitehead* v. *Jenks and Cattell*[17] and was heard the same year. In this instance, on 1 January 1993, the commercial agent had entered into a commercial agency agreement with the defendant principal for a period of five years, with a notice period of six months. In accordance with the agreed notice, six months before the end of the contract, the defendant principal wrote to the claimant commercial agent stating that when the contract expired, it would not be renewed on the same terms, but indicating the possibility of renewing it on different terms, which the principal knew would be unacceptable to the commercial agent. The latter refused the proposed new terms and started legal proceedings claiming compensation for "termination". In the first instance Court, Deputy Judge Alton decided that "termination" embraced the ending of a fixed-term contract by effluxion of time. The judgment of Deputy Judge Alton has been heavily relied upon in later decisions and therefore calls for comment.

14. This was the argument adopted by the counsel of the defender in the Scottish case of *Frape* v. *Emreco* [2002] SLT 371, para 8.
15. [1999] 1 All ER 174.
16. *Ibid*, at p 179b.
17. [1999] Eu LR 827.

Deputy Judge Alton reached her decision by not only construing Regulation 17 in the light of other regulations where the word "termination" appears, but also by taking into consideration the protective stance of the Directive. First, looking at the Agency Regulations as a whole, Deputy Judge Alton agreed that the word "termination" meant something different depending on which regulation one is looking at, since "it may be focusing on the precise time of cessation of the relationship or it may be focusing on the mechanism by which termination occurred". Deputy Judge Alton also noted that the Agency Regulations allow the commercial agency contract to be terminated through, for instance, death, fundamental breach, and matters of national law such as frustration.

Deputy Judge Alton further stated that it did not make sense to consider that termination did not include the expiry of a fixed-term contract through passage of time, as otherwise some restrictions in the Agency Regulations could not apply to such instances. In particular, she referred to Regulation 20 on restrictive covenants and said that "there would be no sense in applying such restrictions where the contract is terminable on notice or terminated by reasons of frustration (. . .) and yet, not to a contract terminated by effluxion of time". As a consequence, Deputy Judge Alton concluded that "the word 'termination' as it appears in Regulation 17 (. . .) clearly covers not simply termination by deliberate act of a party but also a termination by the expiry of a fixed term". Then, relying on the protective stance of the Directive, deputy Judge Alton stated that not to consider effluxion of time as constituting termination would be against the aim of the Directive, as it would only protect commercial agents who have contracts of indefinite duration.

A similar position was adopted in the Scottish case of *Frape* v. *Emreco*[18] where the Court of Session also followed a purposive interpretation of the Agency Regulations.[19] The High Court of England and Wales provided an analogous answer in the case of *Tigana Ltd* v. *Decoro Ltd*[20] in no uncertain terms.[21] Davies J stated that to decide otherwise would not be in line with the regulation that allows the commercial agent to receive compensation on termination on grounds of retirement, ill health or age, and would also negate the protective stance of the Directive.[22]

Expiry by effluxion of time still amounts to termination, even when there is no expectation of renewal

A thread common to all these cases is that to differentiate between commercial agents depending on whether they are bound by fixed-term or indefinite duration contracts would be contrary to the protective stance of the Agency Regulations[23] and therefore that of the

18. [2002] SLT 371.

19. In this case, the contract stipulated that the relationship would end when the commercial agent reached 65 or on 31 May 1997, whichever was the earlier. Frape turned 65 on 13 April 1997 and the principal ended the contract.

20. [2003] EWHC 23, [2003] Eu LR 189.

21. Davis J referred to the submission of a counsel that the entitlement to termination rights does not apply to agency contracts, which have expired by effluxion of time as "plainly wrong". [2003] Eu LR 189, para 74.

22. *Ibid*, para 75.

23. Such cases therefore follow the argument by Professor Reynolds that the right to a termination payment should arise when fixed-term contracts expire not only in order to protect commercial agents who wanted a long-term contract but might not have managed to negotiate it but also because the principal, by not renewing the contract, does something akin to termination. See FMB Reynolds, *Bowstead and Reynolds on Agency*, (17th edn, 2001), p 603, para 11.041.

Directive. All these cases also have in common the fact that there was an expectation from the parties that, although entered into on a short-term basis, the contracts were to be renewed.

This therefore raises the question: What if there were no such expectations? What if it were clear to both parties, from the start, that the commercial agency contract would never be renewed? Does expiry, in such a situation, still amount to termination? This very question was considered in the case of *Light* v. *Ty Europe Ltd*,[24] even though the main issue was that of sub-agency.[25] Counsel for the defendant principal "suggested"[26] that, in this instance, the High Court of England and Wales was not bound by the reasoning of decisions such as *Whitehead* v. *Jenks and Cattell*[27] and others, since such cases could be explained on the basis that the parties had expectations that the contract would be renewed and such was not the case in this instance. This suggestion was considered and rejected both at first instance and on appeal in no uncertain terms,[28] therefore upholding once again the protective stance of the Agency Regulations.

The constant repetition[29] is of importance, as it brings some certainty to the whole issue: "termination" includes expiry of a fixed-term contract by effluxion of time, whether renewal was expected or not. The certainty of the answer is further reinforced by the fact that in both cases of *Tigana Ltd* v. *Decoro Ltd*[30] and *Whitehead* v. *Jenks and Cattell*,[31] the question of a reference to the European Court of Justice was raised. Yet, both Davies J[32] and Deputy Judge Alton respectively, were adamant that the issue was so clear to them that it did not warrant reference to the European Court of Justice.

The position of the English and Scottish courts is in line with the two European Commission proposals[33] and with the French[34] and German[35] systems. This is good for harmonisation, even though the same conclusion is reached in slightly different ways.

Even though the decisions are of a relatively low value in precedent terms and the issue consequently not firmly settled, the conclusion reached by the English and Scottish courts

24. [2003] EWHC 174 QB, [2003] 1 All ER (Comm) 568 for first instance. For the CA decision, [2003] EWCA 1238, [2003] Eu LR 858.

25. For the facts, see Chapter 2, section 2.4.2.1, especially fn 164 and associated text.

26. The emphasis on the word "suggest" is important since both in the Queen's Bench Division and in the Cout of Appeal, the judges remarked that although the counsel for the defendant had raised the issue, his main argument was that the claimants were not entitled to any payment on termination since they had suffered no damage. See comments of Judge McGonigal at para 58 in the Queen's Bench Division and comments of Tuckey LJ in the Court of Appeal at paras 33 and 34.

27. [1999] Eu LR 827.

28. In the Queen's Bench Division, Judge McGonigal, at para 60 and in the Court of Appeal, see Lord Tuckey, para 33.

29. See even more recently, *Cooper, Watkins, Bartle* v. *Pure Fishing (UK) Ltd* [2004] EWCA Civ 375, on whether the contract was "terminated" under Regulation 18(a). For details, see section 5.2.1.3.2 below, see especially fnn 121–123 and associated text.

30. [2003] EWHC 23 (QB), [2003] Eu LR 189.

31. [1999] Eu LR 827.

32. [2003] Eu LR 189, para 73.

33. Article 25 of the two European Commission proposals expressly stipulated that expiry of a fixed-term contract amounted to termination. See OJ C. 56/5 of 2–3–1979.

34. Interestingly, one of the argument of Deputy Judge Alton in *Whitehead* v. *Jenks and Cattell* [1999] Eu LR 827 that termination should include expiry of a fixed-term contract was because, looking at French law, the implementing text expressly covered such an instance. In France, article L 134–12 al 1 of new commercial code stipulates that when the contract ceases, the commercial agent is compensated for the damage suffered. For additional details about the French position, see Chapter 6, especially section 6.4.1.

35. See the 1996 European Commission Report on the application of article 17 of Council Directive 86/653, p 2. See Appendix 9.

was arguably inescapable since, to only protect commercial agents who have indefinite duration contracts would have defeated the purpose of the Directive, which is to reinforce the protection of commercial agents.[36] There was therefore a strong policy argument to decide that expiry amounts to termination since, if expiry does not amount to termination, the principal can avoid the Agency Regulations by giving a series of short fixed-term contracts. On that aspect, commercial agents are therefore afforded a protection, which is similar to that of employees for whom non-renewal of a fixed-term employment contract is deemed to be a dismissal for the purposes of redundancy payments and unfair dismissal.[37]

A parallel to the offer of a suitable alternative employment principle?

We have seen, in relation to the case of *Whitehead* v. *Jenks and Cattell*[38], that the principal had offered to renew the commercial agency contract on different terms, which he knew would be unacceptable to the commercial agent. The latter refused, which he was perfectly entitled to do as the behaviour of the principal was almost certainly disloyal and contrary to his mandatory duty of good faith.[39]

This, however, raises a serious question. What happens if, before the fixed-term contract expires through effluxion of time, the principal offers the commercial agent to renew the contract on the same or even more favourable terms, but the commercial agent, who does not want to renew, refuses. In that hypothesis, has the commercial agent then himself terminated the commercial agency agreement, or does the agreement nevertheless come to an end by the effluxion of time? The question is important, since depending on the answer, the consequences will be very different.

If we consider that the commercial agent has terminated the contract, he has done so with no just cause since it cannot be justified by "circumstances attributable to the principal". The right to claim compensation or indemnity under Regulation 18(b)(i) can therefore not be triggered. If this is correct, this would seem to be similar to the English employment law principle whereby, on termination of an employment contract on grounds of redundancy,[40] the making by the employer of an offer of suitable alternative employment removes the employee's right to a statutory redundancy payment, whether the employee accepts the offer or not. This is through the operation of a statutory provision.[41]

The question is whether a similar principle can, or even needs, to be developed under the Agency Regulations, i.e. that as long as the principal offers renewal of the contract on at least the same terms, if the commercial agent refuses, then he is the one who terminates with no just cause and therefore loses the right to claim termination payments (as per Regulation 18(b)). This of course would not affect the right of the commercial agent to refuse a renewal on grounds of health, illness etc, in which case, a termination payment will be due.[42] The answer to this question has to be negative since to allow such a principle

36. See preamble of the Directive, OJ L 382/17 of 31 December 1986. See Appendix 1.
37. Sections 136(1)(b) and 95(1)(b) Employment Rights Act 1999 respectively.
38. [1999] Eu LR 827.
39. Regulation 4(1). To see what this entails, see Chapter 3, section 3.4.1.
40. Redundancy exists where the needs of an employer's business for employees to do work of a particular kind have ceased or diminished.
41. s 138 Employment Rights Act 1999.
42. Regulation 18(b)(ii) .

to apply would not only be too harsh but also against the protective stance of the Agency Regulations and therefore impossible. It would be against the mandatory nature of termination rights as defined by the European Court of Justice in the case of *Ingmar Ltd* v. *Eaton Leonard Technologies Inc.*[43]

We therefore advocate that this should not be the case; the commercial agent is under no obligation to accept renewal of a fixed-term contract on the same or even better terms proposed by the principal, and rejecting the principal's offer does not preclude him from claiming compensation or indemnity when the contract later expires. This position seems to be confirmed by the case of *Cooper, Watkins, Bartley* v. *Pure Fishing (UK) Ltd.*[44]

5.2.1.2 Unilateral termination

While the Agency Regulations expressly deal with unilateral termination of contracts of indefinite duration, they remain silent on such terminations for fixed-term contracts. This is regrettable and the two types of commercial agency contracts must therefore be considered separately.

5.2.1.2.1 Termination of indefinite period contracts: notice required

The Agency Regulations expressly stipulate that commercial agency agreements for indefinite periods can only be unilaterally terminated by the giving of proper notice.[45] Unilateral termination on notice is therefore the rule. Needless to say, this rule does not prevent either party from summarily terminating the contract when the relevant conditions are met,[46] which will be looked at later (section 5.2.1.3).

Strength of the agency regulations: consistency in the rules

By providing that notice is required for termination of indefinite-period contracts, the Agency Regulations do not significantly modify the position at common law, but they have the advantage of providing compulsory and consistent rules. In fact, at common law, when one party wishes to end the agency agreement, that party must notify the other of his intention to withdraw in order to avoid liability. However, because provision for notice is not compulsory at common law, if there is no contractual provision for such a notice, the English courts may imply a requirement to give reasonable notice. What is reasonable will depend on the facts of the case.[47]

Under the Agency Regulations, the length of the notice period will vary with the duration of the contract. The text requires a minimum notice period of one month for the first year of the commercial agency agreement, two months for the second year and a maximum of three months in the third and subsequent years.[48] The parties cannot agree on a shorter notice period.[49] The impact of such a requirement on an agreement to receive payment in lieu of notice will be considered in a little while.

43. Case C–381/98, [2001] 1 CMLR 9.
44. [2004] EWCA Civ 375, 18 March 2004. For discussion, see section 5.2.1.3.2, especially fnn 121–123 and associated text.
45. Regulation 15(1).
46. Regulation 16.
47. *Martin-Baker Aircraft Co Ltd* v. *Canadian Flight Equipment Ltd; Martin Baker Aircraft Co Ltd* v. *Murison* [1955] 2 QB 556.
48. Regulation 15(2).
49. *Ibid.*

The English government has not opted for the possibility given in the Directive to impose longer notice periods for the fourth, fifth and sixth years.[50] Yet, should the parties wish it, they may do so, providing that the notice is of the same length for each party.[51] The fact that the notice periods due have to be the same for both parties seems incongruous in the light of the protective stance of the Agency Regulations. In fact, in employment law, one of the reasons that the employer owes a longer notice period than the employee is that the latter is the weaker party, and the legislation proceeds on the assumption that it will be easier for the employer to find another employee than for the employee to find alternative employment.[52] The similarity in the notice periods for the commercial agent and the principal is nevertheless highly significant as it reinforces the symmetry of the parties highlighted by the reciprocal and mandatory obligation of good faith.[53]

Strangely, the Agency Regulations stipulate that in the silence of the parties, the end of the period of notice must coincide with the end of the calendar month.[54] The parties must therefore be cautious, because such a stipulation could add another month to their notice period if their relationship started, let us say, in the middle of the month. It is not clear what this rule aims to achieve. The rule is nevertheless important in relation to the amount of contractual damages that a commercial agent could claim in case of wrongful termination, in addition to claims for compensation or indemnity. Because the rule provided by Regulation 15 is not mandatory as such, it is therefore entirely possible for the parties to agree that the notice period should not expire at the end of the calendar month.

Even though the Agency Regulations improve the traditional common law rules, they are not perfect and raise two problems, to which we now turn separately.

Is termination of such a contract on less than the notice period required under the agency regulations nevertheless valid?

The first problem is that the Agency Regulations remain silent as to what happens if the parties do not respect the notice requirement, and it is not clear whether the common law rules apply. Considering the protective stance of the Agency Regulations, there was an argument that common law rules should be displaced and the dismissal of the commercial agent with less than the required notice by the principal should be ineffective.[55]

This very point was argued before the Scottish Court of Session in the case of *Roy* v. *MR Pearlman Ltd*.[56] In this instance, the claimant had been acting as the sole selling commercial agent of the defendant in Scotland since 1983. The contract gave either party the right to terminate by giving six months' notice (interestingly, in excess of the minimum notice period required under the Agency Regulations). On 30 June 1997, in breach of contract, the principal purported to terminate the commercial agency contract immediately and offered to pay three months' commission based on the average of the previous

50. Article 15(3) of the Directive.
51. Regulation 15(3).
52. Employment Rights Act 1999, ss 86(1) and (2).
53. Regulations 3(1) and 4(1). For more details, see Chapter 3.
54. Regulation 15(4).
55. R Bradgate *Commercial law*, (3rd edn, 2000), para 6.3.1.1, p 208.
56. [1999] 2 CMLR 1155.

12 months.[57] On 1 July 1997, the commercial agent accepted the notice of termination and issued proceedings claiming damages at common law and compensation under Regulation 17(6). However, arguing that common law rules should be displaced and that the contract was still alive, the commercial agent claimed for the commission he should have received during the correct notice period, namely six months, under Regulation 7.

Lord Hamilton, giving the judgment of the Outer House, rejected the claim that the existing domestic rules should be displaced as "unsound".[58] Looking at Regulation 15(2), Lord Hamilton noted that it prohibits the parties agreeing to any shorter periods than those prescribed but also added that the Regulation in question "makes no express provision that in the event of a wrongful termination the contract is to be treated as subsisting".[59] Remarking that in the absence of authority, such provisions could not be implied, Lord Hamilton concluded that "in such circumstances, this court must have resort to the relevant domestic principles".[60]

The impact of this case is important, as termination on less than the minimum notice period required under the Agency Regulations is nonetheless effective and, in such a case, the relevant contract law rules apply alongside the Agency Regulations. At common law, by failing to terminate the contract within the required rules, the principal commits, in contract law terms, a repudiatory breach. In principle, this wrongful termination of authority will not terminate the contract. The commercial agent must therefore accept the breach, which allows him to treat the contract as terminated before he can claim compensation or indemnity under Regulation 17(1) together with common law breach of contract damages being the loss of commission during the period of valid contractual notice. This was made clear in *Roy* v. *MR Pearlman Ltd*.[61]

Even though this appears to be correct,[62] in *Roy* v. *MR Pearlman Ltd*,[63] it was undisputed, on the facts, that the commercial agent had accepted the repudiatory breach by the principal.[64] Lord Hamilton therefore said that it was unnecessary to resolve the conflicts (if any) under domestic law as to the technical effect of a wrongful repudiation. However, would the Court of Session have reached the same decision if the right of the commercial agent to terminate the contract had been lost? The issue is most serious since the Agency Regulations do not submit the right to claim compensation or indemnity to any formal procedure.[65] A possible conflict between the two sets of rules arose in the case of *Bell Electric Ltd* v. *Aweco Appliance System GmbH & Co KG*.[66] This issue will be considered later, when dealing with summary termination.[67]

57. Sidkin remarks that whether this was meant as a payment in lieu of notice or as a payment of compensation under the Agency Regulations was not stated. See S Sidkin *Compensation for commercial agents* SJ (143) 1999, p 787.

58. [1999] 2 CMLR 1155 at para 23.

59. *Ibid*.

60. *Ibid*.

61. [1999] 2 CMLR 1155.

62. Professor Bradgate makes the point that since the notice periods apply to the commercial agent, the analysis of the court is correct. He adds that otherwise, it would be surprising if the commercial agent could purport to resign without proper notice but then argue that the resignation was ineffective and claim commission for the period of notice he should have given. See R Bradgate *Commercial law*, (3rd edn, 2000), para 6.3.1.1, p 208.

63. [1999] 2 CMLR 1155.

64. *Ibid*, at 1167, para 30.

65. Regulation 17(9) only requires the claim to be made within one year of termination.

66. [2002] EWHC 8 May 2002.

67. See section 5.2.1.3.2, especially fnn 126–135 and associated text.

Is a payment to the commercial agent effective under the Agency Regulation in lieu of notice?

The second problem is that the Agency Regulations do not expressly allow for the parties the possibility to allow payment in lieu of notice. This is regrettable since, as remarked,[68] it is usually available in commercial agency relationships at common law.[69] The issue arose in the case of *Roy* v. *MR Pearlman Ltd*[70] as to the precise form of the remedy available between damages for breach or payment in lieu of notice.[71] Counsel for the claimant tried to rely on a principle under Scottish employment law that dismissal without notice is not properly a breach but brings into operation an implied condition that payment in lieu of notice is due. Lord Hamilton refused to decide which approach was correct, arguing that in this case there was no material difference and it was better to decide as and when necessary.[72]

In the silence of the Agency Regulations on the matter, we argue that payment to commercial agents in lieu of notice should be effective for two reasons.

> First, it is possible in the light of the status of Regulation 15. It is clear that the parties may not agree on shorter notice periods than the ones prescribed in the Agency Regulations. As Regulation 15 can only be departed from if the effect is to the commercial agent's benefit, provided that payment in lieu of notice is not to the detriment of the commercial agent, it is therefore arguable that the choice should, at least, be available to the parties. Considering that the commercial agency relationship is of a personal nature, having payment in lieu of notice might in fact be a preferable option for the commercial agent, especially if he is the one who terminates the contract because of a breakdown of the relationship.
>
> Secondly, as it is accepted in the case of *Roy* v. *MR Pearlman Ltd*,[73] principles of domestic law are not displaced by the Agency Regulations. Considering that payment in lieu of notice are available as a matter of general contract law, surely, the intention of the Agency Regulations cannot be to remove that right.

5.2.1.2.2 Fixed-term contracts: the partial silence of the Agency Regulations weakens commercial agents' protection

In relation to fixed-term contracts, the impact of the Agency Regulations is mixed since the presence of some very protective rules is weakened by the silence on the issue of unilateral termination and notice.

Conversion of fixed-term contracts into indefinite period contracts

One of the strengths of the Agency Regulations in relation to fixed-term contracts is in Regulation 14, which stipulates that when a fixed-term commercial agency contract continues to be performed by both parties after the term has expired, the contract "shall be

68. Randolph and Davey, *Guide to the Commercial Agency Regulations*, (2nd edn, 2003), p 86.

69. *Llanchelian* v. *Esso Petroleum Co Ltd*, Chancery Division (Rimer J), 28 September 1998 (unreported) where the High Court held that a term giving a principal the right to terminate an agency agreement without notice, by making a specified payment to its agent in lieu of notice period otherwise required by the contract is not in breach of the Unfair Contract Terms Act 1977.

70. [1999] 2 CMLR 1155.

71. *Ibid*, at p 1168, para 33.

72. *Ibid*, at p 1169, para 37.

73. [1999] 2 CMLR 1155.

deemed converted into an agency contract for an indefinite period". Such a rule is of paramount importance for the protection of commercial agents on termination against unscrupulous principals who try to avoid the effect of the Agency Regulations by entering into a series of fixed-term contracts. Yet, it has been argued that Regulation 14 can be seen as a little harsh for principals who allow the contract to run over inadvertently or only allow a slight overrun, since, in such a situation, the relevant notice periods will apply and the earlier fixed period will be taken into consideration for its calculation.[74] As a consequence, some advise the parties to use fixed-term contracts only where they are sure that they will remember to renew.[75] Considering that the rights of commercial agents on termination are the same regardless of the duration of the relationship, it is thought that the advice would not make significant difference.

Another strength of the Agency Regulations is that Regulation 14 is complemented by Regulation 15(5), which stipulates that when a fixed-term commercial agency contract has been converted into an indefinite duration one, the earlier fixed period must be taken into consideration for the calculation of the minimum notice period. Some argue that where a fixed-term contract expires and is replaced with another fixed-term contract, the parties would not be bound by the notice period laid down in Regulation 15.[76] Considering that if there is a fixed-term contract there is no right to termination by notice unless the contract expressly so provides, this is correct.

Can Regulation 14 be derogated from?

Even though Regulation 14 is clearly protective of commercial agents with fixed-term contracts, its impact is weakened by the lack of clarity concerning its status. It is not expressly stated to be mandatory and it is therefore arguable that it could be derogated from,[77] as seems to be the case in France[78] for instance. Yet, the wording of the Agency Regulations seems to imply the contrary,[79] and allowing derogation is against the protective stance of the Agency Regulations. It has been suggested that a solution would be to look at the Italian system, which provides that the parties can insert a clause in the commercial agency contract stating that, at least the first time the contract overruns, the contract is not, for the purposes of the implementing text, to be regarded as an unlimited duration contract.[80] This is a good idea, but in the absence of a decision by an English court, the matter is uncertain.

In the light of the protective stance of the Agency Regulations and the wording of Regulation 14, it is thought that derogation is not possible.

74. Regulation 15(5).

75. S Singleton *Legal watch—Commercial Agents Regulations and IT*, IT Law Today, November 2002, lexis nexis.

76. Randolph and Davey, *Guide to the Commercial Agency Regulations*, (2nd edn, 2003), p 84.

77. Randolph and Davey on the contrary argue that since in its first proposal, the EU Commission stated that this was so, "unless otherwise agreed", by the fact that the words have been deleted, this shows that this cannot be excluded. See Randolph and Davey, *op cit,* p 84.

78. In his report during French parliamentary debates, deputy Bouquet indicated that the conversion of a fixed-term contract into an indefinite one is only a presumption, which can be rebutted by an express agreement between the parties. See Report Bouquet, No. 2026, p 23. For a similar opinion, see also JM Leloup, *Agents commerciaux*, Encyclopédie Dalloz, p 71.

79. Professor Reynolds argues that the wording seems firm to an English reader. FMB Reynolds, *Bowstead and Reynolds on Agency*, (17th edn, 2001), p 600.

80. FMB Reynolds, *op cit*, para 11–035, p 600.

Consequences of failing to comply with Regulation 14?

Some have also criticised the Agency Regulations for remaining silent as to possible remedies for non-compliance with Regulation 14. It is not clear however what kind of remedy would be appropriate. Moreover, considering the case of *Moore* v. *Piretta Ltd*,[81] where the Court of Appeal held that, when the parties enter into a string of fixed-term contracts, termination payments will be calculated according to the relationship as a whole and not merely with reference to the last commercial agency contract, the authors argue that such remedies already exist.

Termination of a fixed-term contract through notice

A further weakness of the Agency Regulations in relation to fixed-term contracts is their silence,[82] reflecting the silence of the Directive,[83] on the issue of unilateral termination. Does this silence suggest that fixed-term commercial agency agreements cannot be unilaterally terminated by notice? In the light of common law principles, this cannot be right.[84] Case law shows that fixed-term contracts do provide for unilateral termination by the giving of notice, but the issue was always overshadowed by the issue of expiration through effluxion of time.[85] The only exception was the case of *Tigana Ltd* v. *Decoro Ltd*[86] but even in this instance, the issue was dropped.[87] In the silence of the Agency Regulations on this issue, common law rules apply. As a consequence, fixed-term contracts can also be terminated by notice if the commercial agency contract provides for it. If not, there is no right to terminate such contracts by notice.

5.2.1.3 Immediate or summary termination

Even though termination by the giving of notice is the rule, immediate or summary termination, i.e. termination without the need to give notice is also possible in certain circumstances.

The way the Agency Regulations deal with immediate termination is not, as is the case in other respects, entirely satisfactory, because by simply copying the Directive to the letter, the rules provided are vague and therefore create unwelcome uncertainty.

Regulation 16 stipulates that the Agency Regulations do not affect the operation of any domestic law rules entitling either party to terminate the commercial agency agreement with immediate effect, "because of the failure of one party to carry out all or part of his obligations" i.e. a breach (Regulation 16(a)) or where "exceptional circumstances arise"

81. [1999] 1 All ER 174.

82. Regulation 15(1).

83. Article 15(1) of the Directive.

84. See the DTI comments in their 1987 Explanatory and Consultative Note, fn 4 above.

85. Interestingly, most of the reported cases suggest that the notice periods agreed in fixed-term commercial agency agreements tend to be longer than the minimum notice periods provided for in the Agency Regulations. In *Tigana Ltd* v. *Decoro Ltd* [2003] EWHC 23, [2003] Eu LR 189, the contract was entered into for an initial term of one year, the contract could be terminated by either party, upon giving 90 days' written notice. In *Whitehead* v. *Jenks & Cattell Engineering Ltd*, [1999] Eu LR 873, the contract was to run for five years with a six-months notice period. In *Bell* v. *Aweco Appliance Systems GmbH & Co*, [2002] EWHC 872 8 May 2002, the contract was to run for three years with an automatic renewal clause subject to a six months notice. In *Page* v. *CST Ltd* [1997] 3 All ER 656, the contract was entered into for five years with a 12-month notice period.

86. [2003] EWHC 23, [2003] Eu LR 189.

87. This is because the renewal had to be agreed in writing. *Ibid*, para 46.

(Regulation 16(b)). The rule is vague, as it fails to explain what amounts to such a breach or what "exceptional circumstances" entail.

As these issues have plainly been left to the different national legal systems, perhaps the vagueness is not surprising. Arguably, the lack of details can be explained by the fact that it is not within the purpose of the Directive to do so as it would interfere too much with the relevant domestic rules. Nevertheless, the express reference to domestic principles seems to indicate that national rules governing the summary termination of contract apply. Consequently, once again, the impact of the Agency Regulations must be considered in the light of the relationship between the common law rules and the Agency Regulations in order to see how the two sets of rules dovetail. The two possibilities of summary termination must be reviewed in turn.

5.2.1.3.1 Immediate termination for exceptional circumstances: Regulation 16(b)

It has been said that the expression "exceptional circumstances", in the English common law context, essentially refers to the common law concept of frustration.[88] On that issue, commercial agents appear to be better protected than employees[89] since, even when the commercial agency contract is terminated under such circumstances, termination payments will nevertheless be due, as emphasised by Bowers J in the case of *Barrett McKenzie & Company Ltd* v. *Escada Ltd*.[90] The position seems to be reinforced by the case of *Cooper, Watkins, Bartley* v. *Pure Fishing (UK) Ltd*,[91] where Tuckey LJ said that the reference to Regulation 16 in Regulation 18(a) (allowing the principal to summarily terminate and avoid having to pay compensation or indemnity) meant Regulation 16(a) only and not Regulation 16 as a whole, since in cases of frustration and *force majeure*, it is not the principal who terminates but the events which have this effect.[92] This seems very advantageous to the commercial agent and it is therefore important to see whether the term "exceptional circumstances" includes more than frustrating events. The matter will however be dealt with in more detail, in the light of the common law principles, when considering the issue of termination by operation of law.[93]

5.2.1.3.2 Immediate termination for serious breach: Regulation 16(a)

In this context, the situation is more complex, as it raises two different, yet intertwined, sets of questions. First, it is not clear what kind of breach will justify immediate termination, since Regulation 16(a) makes reference to the failure of one party to carry out "all or part of his obligation". In the light of the mention of the common law rules, which is crucial to Regulation 16, it is thought that only a serious breach will justify immediate termination. Such an interpretation is in line with the two European Commission proposals[94] and the protective stance of the Agency Regulations. Yet, the silence of the Agency Regulations raises all kinds of questions in relation to the seriousness of the

88. See FMB Reynolds, *Bowstead and Reynolds on Agency*, (17th edn, 2001), p 601.

89. Under employment law rules, the general position is that when the contract is terminated by frustration, there is no dismissal. Considering that employment claims of wrongful dismissal, redundancy payments and unfair dismissal are all based on dismissal, no claim can arise because employees are not dismissed. For details, see M Jefferson, *Principles of employment law*, (4th edn, 2000), para 7.1.2, p 221.

90. [2001] Eu LR 567, para 16.

91. [2004] EWCA Civ 375, 18 March 2004.

92. *Ibid*, para 17.

93. See section 5.2.2.1 hereof.

94. Article 27(1) of the two proposals expressly stipulate that only a serious breach will allow summary termination. See OJ C. 56/5 of 2 March 1979.

breach, such as whether the parties can by agreement, make a term a condition, the breach of which will give the victim an express right to terminate (more anon).

The second and more serious difficulty about immediate termination for serious breach is the fact that, even though Regulation 16(a) expressly allows for the possibility of immediate termination by either party, it must not be seen in isolation, as it seems to be complemented by Regulation 18 which regulates the exceptions to the commercial agent's right to claim compensation or indemnity. In fact, Regulation 18(a) stipulates that when the principal terminates the relationship because of a "default attributable to the commercial agent, which would justify immediate termination pursuant to Regulation 16", no compensation or indemnity is due. However, Regulation 18(b)(i) states that if the commercial agent himself terminates the relationship "for circumstances attributable to the principal", he can still claim compensation or indemnity, as this is a just cause for terminating the commercial agency contract.

The relationship between Regulation 16(a) and Regulation 18 raises three additional problems.

> First, it is not clear what "default attributable to the commercial agent" under Regulation 18(a) nor "circumstances attributable to the principal" under regulation 18(b)(i) mean. Do the expressions mean different things, or do they both refer to a repudiatory breach? If they do, the reference to common law rules raises questions such as how should the serious breach be assessed, whether the parties can make a term a condition, and whether the contract can contain an automatic termination clause etc.
>
> Secondly, the relationship between the two regulations is not entirely obvious because of certain discrepancies in the implementing text. Regulation 18(a) refers indirectly, by the reference to Regulation 16, to domestic law but Regulation 18(b)(i) does not. It is therefore not certain whether the process of termination itself is similar for both regulations and whether domestic rules apply to both instances.
>
> Thirdly, the Agency Regulations remain silent on the issue of damages. Consequently, it is not clear whether they are due. The three problems must be considered in turn.

(a) The meaning of Regulations 18(a) and 18(b)(i)

Regulation 18(a) refers to a serious breach

Regulation 18(a) allows the principal to summarily terminate the relationship *and* avoid having to give the commercial agent compensation or indemnity for a "default attributable to the commercial agent" providing that such a default would justify the immediate termination of the commercial agency agreement pursuant to Regulation 16. The reference to Regulation 16, which incidentally should be read as a reference to Regulation 16(a) only and not a reference to Regulation 16 as a whole,[95] seems to indicate that the word "default" in Regulation 18(a) refers to a serious breach of contract, i.e. a repudiatory breach. This analysis is confirmed by the case of *Cooper, Watkins, Bartley* v. *Pure Fishing*

95. In the case of *Cooper, Watkins, Bartley* v. *Pure Fishing (UK) Ltd*, [2004] EWCA Civ 375, Tuckey LJ stated that the reference to Regulation 16 in Regulation 18(a) could not be for Regulation 16(b) because in cases of frustration and *force majeure*, it is not the principal who terminates "but the events which have this effect". Para 17.

(UK) Ltd,[96] where Tuckey LJ said that, under Regulation 18(a), the principal is entitled to unilaterally bring the contract to an end because of "some default on the part of the agent which justifies summary termination, in other words, because the agent has committed a serious breach".[97]

So far, the Agency Regulations do not appear to significantly modify the rules of summary termination at common law.[98]

Regulation 18(b)(i) refers to a serious breach

Regulation 18(b)(i) in turn, allows the commercial agent to terminate the relationship for "circumstances attributable to the principal" and still claim a termination payment. Once again, it is not clear what "circumstances attributable to the principal" mean and since there is no reference to Regulation 16(a), it is not so obvious whether this regulation can be used by the commercial agent for summary termination. The question was raised in the case of *Bell Electric Ltd* v. *Aweco Appliance Systems GmBH & Co KG*.[99] In this instance, the claimant had been acting as the commercial agent of the defendant, a German company, for the sale of components for household electrical white goods for some years. In August 1999, a new agreement was drawn up. The contract, which was valid until the end of December 2002, was subject to an automatic renewal clause unless either party gave six months' notice. Following the continuing failure of the principal to pay the due commission, the commercial agent claimed that such a behaviour amounted to a repudiatory breach and summarily terminated the contract for "circumstances attributable to the principal" under Regulation 18(b)(i). He issued proceedings against the principal claiming damages at common law and, in the alternative, compensation under the Agency Regulations. Elias J agreed by stating that "although I would accept that a single failure to pay [the commission] would not constitute a repudiatory breach, it is now accepted that the continuing failure to pay in this case did amount to a repudiation of the contract".[100]

The fact that the High Court of England and Wales decided that the expression "default attributable to the principal" refers to a serious breach by the principal is also in line with the position at common law.[101] Interestingly, the right of the commercial agent under Regulation 18(b)(i) to summarily terminate the contract following a serious breach by the principal and still be able to claim compensation or indemnity seems reasonably similar to the rights that an employee has under the notion of constructive dismissal.

Seriousness of the breach and pre-classification of term as a condition

To decide that either party can terminate the relationship immediately upon a serious breach shows a certain symmetry between the parties. This symmetry was clearly highlighted in the case of *Bell Electric Ltd* v. *Aweco Appliance Systems GmBH & Co KG*[102] when Elias J stated that Regulations 18(a) and 18(b)(i) "ought to be seen as reverse sides

96. *Ibid*.
97. *Ibid*, para 15.
98. At common law, the principal has the right to revoke an indefinite duration contract immediately when the breach of the commercial agent is serious enough: *Campanari* v. *Woodburn* (1854) 13 CB 400.
99. [2002] EWHC 872, 8 May 2002.
100. *Ibid*, para 22.
101. At common law, the agent can terminate the agency summarily when the conduct of the principal is inconsistent with the continuation of the contract: *Nelson (E.P.) & Co* v. *Rolfe* [1950] 1 KB 139, CA.
102. [2002] EWHC 872, 8 May 2002.

of the same coin . . . the compensation is not payable if the principal terminates in circumstances which would be justifiable at common law because of the agent's conduct; but on the other hand it is payable if the commercial agent terminates in circumstances which are justifiable at common law because of the conduct of the principal".[103] Incidentally, this analysis is very close to French law.[104]

From this case, it seems clear that only a serious breach will justify summary termination and what amounts to a serious breach is governed by the relevant domestic law. At common law, a party to a contract is entitled to summarily terminate the contract on grounds of the conduct of the other party if such a conduct constitutes (i) a breach of condition, or (ii) a serious breach of contract in the *Hong Kong Fir Shipping Co Ltd* v. *Kawasaki Kisen Kaisha Ltd*[105] sense. Relying on such domestic principles, the crucial question is to know whether the principal can make a term a condition as in *Schuler* v. *Wickman*,[106] by so providing in the contract, the breach of which will give him the express right to terminate without having to pay compensation or indemnity.

In the light of the principle of freedom of contract, it is thought that this is possible. The most likely term to be entered into as a condition in a commercial agency agreement will be that of a sales quota that the commercial agent must meet. Failure to meet such sales quota will then constitute a breach of condition, thereby allowing the principal to summarily terminate the contract as per Regulation 16(a). Following Regulation 18(a), the principal terminates with a just cause, hence he can avoid paying compensation or indemnity to the commercial agent.

Even though the freedom of contract allows this, considering the civil-law rationale which underlies termination payments,[107] the right of the principal to use the breach by the commercial agent to summarily terminate the contract must nevertheless be used in the light of his obligation of good faith.[108] In practice, this means that even assuming the obligation to meet the sales quota has been made a condition in the contract, the principal would only be able to rely on the failure of the commercial agent to meet the quota as a just cause for terminating the contract by first proving that the failure to reach the target is due to the commercial agent's fault, by for instance, not doing his utmost to meet the target and consequently failing to act for the principal's interest.[109] As a result, the principal would not be able to terminate if there was a good reason outside the control of the commercial agent, for the failure to meet the target. Equally, since the right to summary termination only applies for a material breach, the principal cannot therefore use it for trivial breaches.

Finally, a more obvious example of the impact of the obligation of good faith can be seen in the case of *Cooper, Watkins, Bartley* v. *Pure Fishing (UK) Ltd*[110] where the principal who had tried to "engineer" a breach by the commercial agent in order to summarily dismiss him, and yet, failed to do so, was described as having acted in bad faith. Tuckey LJ said, obiter, that "in breach of its duty of good faith, the defendant (the

103. *Ibid*, see para 55.
104. For details, see Chapter 6, section 6.3.1.1.
105. [1962] 2 QB 26.
106. [1974] AC 235.
107. For details, see section 5.3.1.
108. Regulations 4(1).
109. Regulation 3(1).
110. [2004] EWCA Civ 375, 18 March 2004.

principal) had attempted to use its contractual rights to create a conflict of interests for the claimant".[111]

From the above, one can see that the duty of good faith in the Agency Regulations is used as a method of control over the performance of the parties' rights and obligations. Interestingly, this does not seem to add much to the existing common law principles. In domestic law, a breach of contract does not automatically bring a contract to an end.[112] This is so even when a term is classed as a condition by the parties as per *Schuler* v. *Wickman*.[113] In this case, it was a condition of the contract that the agent should visit six customers once a week. The contract was supposed to last for four years. When the agent failed to carry out one visit, the principal terminated the contract relying on the condition permitting him to summarily dismiss the agent should he miss any one visit. The House of Lords held that the contract should not be terminated merely because this term had been broken. A similar interpretation was given in the case of *Rice (trading as Garden Guardian)* v. *Great Yarmouth Borough Council*[114]: the termination clauses must be given a common sense commercial interpretation and cannot necessarily be applied literally to allow termination for any breach.

Consequences of wrongful termination

Regulations 16(a), 18(a) and 18(b)(i) apply only when there is a repudiatory breach. In the silence of the Agency Regulations, the common law principles apply. The burden of proof of the seriousness of the breach is therefore on the victim. This is important since, if the principal fails to establish that the commercial agent is guilty of a serious breach, immediate termination has no just cause and the conditions of Regulation 18(a) are consequently not fulfilled, accordingly, the commercial agent loses the right to a lump sum payment. This seems to transpire from the case *Cooper, Watkins, Bartley* v. *Pure Fishing (UK) Ltd*[115] where it was mentioned in passing that the fact that the commercial agent refused to acquiesce to the new terms of contract proposed by the principal did not constitute a breach, let alone a serious breach. However, following *Roy* v. *MR Pearlman Ltd*,[116] wrongful termination is nonetheless effective, in which case, the commercial agent will be entitled to claim compensation or indemnity together with damages for wrongful termination.

Vice versa, if the commercial agent fails to establish that the breach of the principal is sufficiently serious to warrant a termination, he is then the one who terminates without just cause as defined in Regulation 18(b) and consequently cannot claim compensation. The only right the commercial agent will have in such a situation is to claim damages for the loss suffered following the breach by the principal, such damages being evaluated following common law principles. Yet, the commercial agent being himself in breach, he can be sued for damages by the principal.

111. *Ibid*, para 9.
112. *Decro-Wall International SA* v. *Practitioners in Marketing* [1971] 1 WLR 361.
113. [1974] AC 235.
114. [2003] TCLR 1.
115. [2004] EWCA Civ 375, 18 March 2004.
116. [1999] 2 CMLR 1155.

Regulation 18(i): wider than a serious breach by the principal?

Even though a certain symmetry undeniably exists in the rights of the principal and the commercial agent provided by Regulations 18(a) and 18(b)(i) respectively, the two regulations are not identical.

We have seen that the two aforementioned regulations allow each party to summarily terminate the relationship when the other has committed a serious breach.

Regulation 18(b)(i), however, says that, where the commercial agent has terminated the agreement, so that *prima facie* under Regulation 18(b) he would have lost his right to a payment of compensation or indemnity on termination, that right is nevertheless not lost if the commercial agent's termination is "justified" by "circumstances attributable to the principal". Regulation 18(b)(i) is drafted differently from Regulation 18(a) since it does not require termination to be in circumstances where "immediate termination" would be justified as per Regulation 16(a). The scope of Regulation 18(b)(i) which helps the commercial agent therefore appears to be much wider than merely where the principal's conduct amounts to a serious breach of the commercial agency agreement.

This was confirmed in the Scottish case of *King* v. *Tunnock Ltd*,[117] where it was held that the commercial agent was entitled to terminate the relationship pursuant to Regulation 18(b)(i) and not lose his right to a termination payment even when the conduct of the principal did not amount to a breach at all. In this case, King had been acting as the commercial agent of Tunnock for over 20 years, following his father's footsteps, when the principal decided to end the production of the goods that the commercial agent was in charge of selling. The commercial agent considered such a decision to be a "circumstance attributable to the principal" and therefore, relying on Regulation 18(b)(i), summarily terminated the relationship and claimed compensation. The Court of Session agreed. In this case, the lack of written terms meant that the closure of the principal's business could not amount to a breach of contract. The case of *Page* v. *CST Ltd*[118] shows, however, that closure of business can, of course, in the right circumstances, amount to a breach.

By deciding that the expression "circumstance attributable to the principal" under Regulation 18(b)(i) allows the commercial agent to terminate the relationship and still claim compensation or indemnity even when the conduct of the principal is not a serious breach of contract, or even a breach of contract at all, the Scottish case of *King* v. *Tunnock Ltd*[119] seriously widens the scope of Regulation 18(b)(i). This interpretation is in line with the protective stance of the Agency Regulations.

Interestingly, the interpretation of the Scottish case of *King* v. *Tunnock Ltd*[120] means that commercial agents are better protected than employees, since the latter can only claim constructive dismissal when the principal has committed a serious breach.

(b) The mechanics behind summary termination under regulations 18(a) and 18(b)

Summary termination by the principal under Regulation 18(a)

As previously explained, under Regulation 18(a), the principal can summarily terminate the relationship and avoid paying compensation or indemnity to the commercial agent when the latter is guilty of a serious breach. The reference to domestic law, through the

117. [2000] Eu LR 531.
118. [1997] 3 All ER 656.
119. [2000] Eu LR 531.
120. *Ibid.*

mention of Regulation 16, seems to suggest that the common law rules relating to the *process* of summary termination of contracts will also apply.

As a matter of strict law, this means that (i) the breach by the commercial agent must be a repudiatory breach, as assessed by the English and Scottish courts, which, (ii) only once it has been accepted by the principal, doing some positive act, allows him to terminate the contract. In other words, the breach *per se* does not terminate the contract. The principal must therefore accept the breach and do something in order to be able to rely on Regulation 18(a). This point was clearly reiterated by the case of *Cooper, Watkins, Bartley* v. *Pure Fishing (UK) Ltd.*[121] In this instance, the three claimants had acted as commercial agents for the defendant principal since the mid-1980s for the sale of fishing tackle. Each claimant had the right to represent other fishing tackle manufacturers for the sale of products that did not compete with those of the defendant. In early 1999, the defendant decided to introduce a new range of products. In March 1999, when the claimants were told about this development, they objected, saying that their contracts with another principal prevented them from marketing the new proposed products for the defendant since the products were in direct competition. On 14 May 1999, the defendant alleged that the claimants' refusal to sell the new lines amounted to a material breach of contract by them, allowing him to repudiate the contract. However, the principal did not repudiate the contract, but merely appointed another commercial agent to cover such products and later wrote to each of the claimants informing them that their commercial agency contract would not be renewed when they expired. The proceedings shortly followed whereby the commercial agents claimed compensation on termination.

At first instance, His Honour Judge Kershaw QC, sitting in the Manchester District Registry of the Queen's Bench Division of the High Court, found in favour of the claimant commercial agents, on the basis that the contracts having expired by effluxion of time, there was no positive act of termination, and the commercial agents were therefore entitled to claim compensation. The principal appealed on the ground that even though he let the contracts expire by effluxion of time rather than actively terminating them, he should nevertheless be entitled to rely on the exemptions from the obligation to make a termination payment afforded by Regulation 18(a) since the word "terminated" under this regulation had the same meaning as "termination" under Regulation 17.

The Court of Appeal unanimously rejected such an analysis; Gibson LJ stated "it is in my judgment plain that Regulation 18(a) requires action by the principal to terminate the contract".[122]

The principal's lack of action, in common law terms, amounts to an affirmation of the contract, in which case, the principal loses the right under Regulation 18(a) to summarily terminate the contract for just cause, and compensation or indemnity will be due to the commercial agent, as was the case in *Cooper, Watkins, Bartley* v. *Pure Fishing (UK) Ltd.*[123] As highlighted by Professor Reynolds, the contract will also be affirmed if, close to the end of a fixed-term contract, the commercial agent commits a breach sufficiently serious to allow the principal to summarily terminate the contract, and before the principal

121. [2004] EWCA Civ 375, 18 March 2004.
122. *Ibid*, para 22.
123. [2004] EWCA Civ 375, 18 March 2004.

acts upon the breach, the commercial agent dies.[124] In such a case, the estate of the commercial agent will therefore be entitled to claim compensation or indemnity.[125]

Summary termination by the commercial agent under Regulation 18(b)(i)

The study of the mechanics of termination by the commercial agent under Regulation 18(b)(i) is more complex, because it is linked to his right to claim compensation or indemnity. As mentioned earlier, Regulation 18(b)(i) allows the commercial agent to terminate the relationship on grounds of the principal's behaviour, when his behaviour amounts to a breach of contract whether serious or not and also even when his behaviour does not amount to a breach of contract at all. Because the Agency Regulations remain silent as to the mechanics to be used under Regulation 18(b)(i), the common law rules therefore apply.

As the case of *Bell Electric Ltd* v. *Aweco Appliance Systems GmBH & Co KG*[126] shows, the commercial agent must therefore first accept the breach by the principal i.e. take some positive steps to make clear that he is terminating the contract before being able to rely on Regulation 18(b)(i). In the light of the symmetry between Regulation 18(a) and Regulation 18(b)(i) emphasised by Elias J,[127] this seems a logical conclusion.

However, on the facts of this case, there was a question whether the claimant commercial agent had lost the right to treat the contract as repudiated following an affirmation by him. Elias J had to consider the compatibility between domestic rules on repudiatory breach and a claim by a commercial agent under Regulation 18(b)(i). The issue at stake was whether the reference to domestic principles in Regulation 18(a) which incorporate Regulation 16, also applied to Regulation 18(b)(i) or not, and whether the rules of affirmation of a breach at common law (which prevent the victim from then treating the contract as repudiated) also apply to the Agency Regulations or not. Elias J responded in the affirmative "(. . .) if the agent has lost the right, for whatever reason, justifiably to bring the contract to an end at common law, then he cannot rely on Regulation 18(b)(i)".[128]

If this interpretation is correct, the risk of affirmation creates an additional exception to the right of the commercial agent to claim compensation or indemnity. Under the Agency Regulations, the commercial agent is entitled to claim compensation or indemnity if the agency relationship has ended and in one of the circumstances provided for in Regulation 18(b). If the commercial agent nevertheless affirms the contract and then subsequently terminates, he does not then terminate for a "circumstance attributable to the principal" as per Regulation 18(b)(i). Affirmation means that the principal's breach ceases to be repudiatory, in which case, common law dictates that the commercial agent loses the right to terminate the contract together with the right to claim compensation or indemnity.

124. FMB Reynolds, *Bowstead and Reynolds on Agency*, (17th edn, 2001), para 11.040, p 602.

125. Professor Reynolds however argues that the claim for indemnity under Regulation 17(3) should fail because the claim would not be equitable. See FMB Reynolds, *Bowstead and Reynolds on Agency*, (17th edn, 2001), para 11.040, p 602. Professor Reynolds is right. For details, see Chapter 6, section 6.4.1.

126. [2002] EWHC 872, 8 May 2002.

127. Elias J stated that Regulation 18(a) and 18(b)(i) "ought to be seen as reverse sides of the same coin" , at para 55.

128. *Ibid*, para 55.

Regulation 18(b)(i): the common law mechanics of summary termination should not apply

The consequences of an (inadvertent) affirmation of the commercial agency agreement highlighted by *Bell Electric Ltd* v. *Aweco Appliance Systems GmbH KG* are a significant threat to the commercial agent's protection, and therefore raise the question of compatibility between the Agency Regulations and the common law rules. They are against the protective stance of the Agency Regulations and also possibly ineffective in the light of the mandatory nature of the two termination payments.[129] The pressing question for the commercial agent is therefore to know whether it is possible to say that the common law rules regulating the mechanics of summary termination do not affect the commercial agent's right to lump sum payment on termination in instances regulated by Regulation 18(b)(i). There seem to be three arguments for the commercial agent here:

First, it is accepted that in the silence of the Agency Regulations, domestic principles only apply *when consistent with the implementing legislation.*[130] If a provision of domestic law is inconsistent with the Agency Regulations, "the domestic law will require to yield".[131] By creating an additional exception to the right of commercial agents to claim compensation or indemnity, the common law rules are inconsistent with the Agency Regulations which require no particular on termination: all that is required is that the commercial agent must claim compensation or indemnity within one year of termination.[132] The Agency Regulations should consequently prevail.

Secondly, by creating an additional exception to the commercial agent's right to claim compensation or indemnity, the common law rules reduce the protection of commercial agents. This is against the protective stance of the Agency Regulations, hence, once again, the latter should prevail. The basis for such a stance is the European origin of the Agency Regulations. In the light of the doctrine of indirect effect, the English and Scottish courts must interpret national provisions in the light of EC law.[133]

Thirdly, following the Scottish case of *King* v. *Tunnock*,[134] because it is possible to read the expression "circumstances attributable to the principal" in Regulation 18(b)(i) more widely still as not requiring a breach but allowing the commercial agent to terminate on grounds of the principal's behaviour (a) even if there is no serious breach and/or (b) even if there is no breach at all. The width of the Regulation means that an affirmation cannot bar a claim since Regulation 18(b)(i) could be applicable even if there was no breach. This argument is effectively the interpretation, which was argued, yet rejected, in a line of unfair dismissal cases starting with *Western Excavating* v. *Sharp*.[135] As a consequence, it is possible to say, because of

129. Case C–381/98 *Ingmar Ltd* v. *Eaton Leonard Technologies Inc* [2001] 1 CMLR 9.

130. *Roy* v. *MR Pearlman Ltd* [1999] 2 CLMR 1155.

131. *Ibid*, para 25 *per* Hamilton LJ.

132. Article 17(5).

133. Doctrine of indirect effect was first seen in the case 83/13 *Von Colson & Kamann* v. *Land Nordrhein-Westfalen* [1984] ECR 1891.

134. [2000] Eu LR 531.

135. [1978] 1 QB 761. It is to be noted that the position of employees has nevertheless evolved considerably since this case. Even though the conduct of the employer must amount to a serious breach for a claim of constructive dismissal to succeed, the conduct of employers can nevertheless be found in breach of the implied term of co-operation.

the scope of Regulation 18(b)(i), the procedure is not dependent on the domestic rules, in which case, the risk of affirmation disappears.

Solution: the claim for compensation or indemnity by the commercial agent amounts to acceptance

However, a much simpler solution would be to say that when the commercial agent notifies the principal of his claim for compensation or indemnity, this acts as his acceptance of any breach or other conduct amounting to a "circumstance attributable to the principal" pursuant to Regulation 18(b)(i). By accepting the breach or other conduct by the principal, the commercial agent effectively terminates the contract which satisfies the common law requirements. This also satisfies Regulation 17(1), which requires a termination before the commercial agent can claim compensation or indemnity. This right to claim can therefore only be lost when the commercial agent fails to lodge his claim within one year of the termination as per Regulation 17(9).

This solution has not been judicially tested by the courts in this country and as such is therefore somewhat uncertain.

(c) Damages for breach

The third and final problem in relation to summary termination is that the Agency Regulations remain silent on the issue of damages to be claimed by the victim of a serious breach.[136] In the light of the case of *Roy* v. *MR Pearlman Ltd*,[137] we know that the common law rules apply whenever the Agency Regulations remain silent, providing that the two sets of rules are compatible. As a consequence, damages for breach should be available to the victim. The normal common law rules of causation, mitigation etc will of course apply.[138] Such claims for damages are obviously in addition to any right that the commercial agent might have to claim compensation or indemnity. The two claims being for different losses, there is no risk of double compensation.

5.2.2 Termination by operation of law

In this context, the rules are, yet again, unsatisfactory, because of lack of detail due to the near-verbatim implementation of the Directive. The Agency Regulations expressly stipulate that they will not affect "the application of any enactment or rule of law which provides for the immediate termination of the agency contract where exceptional circumstances arise".[139] What the expression "exceptional circumstances" means is not entirely clear. Moreover, the Agency Regulations also deal with termination by operation of law, although indirectly in relation to the exceptions to the commercial agent's right to claim termination payments as per Regulation 18(b). Because the Agency Regulations do not define what "exceptional circumstances" means, the relationship between Regulations 16(b) and 18(b) is therefore not entirely clear.

136. Interestingly, an earlier draft of the Directive expressly stipulated that the party in breach should be liable for damages. F Randolph and J Davey, *Guide to the Commercial Agency Regulations*, (2nd edn, 2003), p 88.

137. [1999] 2 CMLR 1155.

138. For details, see (ed) H Beale, *Chitty on Contracts* (29th edn, 2004) Ch 26.

139. Regulation 16(b).

First, we need to see what the expression "exceptional circumstances" refers to. Secondly, when the contract is terminated by the commercial agent pursuant to Regulation 16(b), it is not clear whether the commercial agent still has the right to claim a termination payment.

5.2.2.1 Immediate termination for "exceptional circumstances": regulation 16(b)

It has been said that the expression "exceptional circumstances", in the English common law context, essentially refers to the common law concept of frustration.[140] In view of the first proposal of the European Commission, this seems correct.[141] The reference to domestic law in Regulation 16(b) means that the common law rules of contract will apply to determine whether the contract is automatically terminated or not. However, frustration is not the only event which can in English contract law terminate the agent's authority automatically. Other events must therefore also be considered.

Frustration

At common law, frustration terminates the contract automatically but it is a very narrow doctrine. A contract will effectively be discharged by frustration where, after the formation of the contract, an event occurs which renders performance of the contract, impossible, illegal or something radically different from what was contemplated by the parties when they made the contract.[142]

Frustration is a residual doctrine, and will therefore not apply where the parties have made express provisions in the contract for the risk event which occurs, e.g. use of *force majeure* clause. In the light of the reference to domestic law in Regulation 16(a), it is however, thought that the parties can agree that the commercial agency contract will be summarily terminated by *force majeure*.

Death of the commercial agent or the principal

The commercial agency relationship is of a personal nature. It is therefore terminated automatically by the death of either party.[143] This is expressly stipulated in the Agency Regulations.[144]

In relation to the principal, even though the Agency Regulations do not expressly stipulate it, in the light of the common law principles, his death would also bring the commercial agency to an end. In fact, as remarked, at common law the agent's authority is terminated automatically by events which incapacitate either principal or agent, no matter whether the authority is conferred by deed and even if it is expressed to be irrevocable.[145]

140. FMB Reynolds, *Bowstead and Reynolds on Agency*, (17th edn, 2001), p 601.

141. Article 27 (1)(b) stipulated that termination may take place "where some circumstances which make it impossible to perform the contract or which seriously prejudices its performance, or which substantially undermines the commercial basis of the contract". See OJ C. 13 of 18 January 1977.

142. It would be beyond the scope of this book to give more details as to what amounts for frustration. For more details, see the relevant chapters of Treitel, *The law of contract*, (2003).

143. This is so even where the other party has no knowledge of the death: *Campanari* v. *Woodburn* (1854) 15 CB 400.

144. Regulation 17(8).

145. Brown, *Commercial law*, (2001), p 224.

Since the commercial agent can establish himself as a legal entity and still be protected by the Agency Regulations, the issue of liquidation, dissolution etc. of a company must therefore be considered. In *Triffit Nurseries* v. *Salads Etcetera Ltd*,[146] Longmore J stated that the issue of cessation of a business was "an uncertain concept"[147] and as such, he did not consider it satisfactory to add it to the list of automatic determination of an agency relationship.

In relation to the principal, the dissolution of a limited company is generally regarded as equivalent to the death of an individual entity. On dissolution, the authority of the company's agent will therefore cease.[148] Following the case of *Triffit Nurseries* v. *Salads Etcetera Ltd*,[149] cessation of business of the principal does not in itself bring the agency to an end but it may amount to a repudiation if it makes it impossible for the principal to perform.

Insanity of the commercial agent or the principal

Similarly to death, insanity of the principal will terminate the agent's authority.[150] Insanity of the commercial agent also terminates the contract.

Bankruptcy of the commercial agent or the principal

As a general rule, bankruptcy of the principal imposes a legal incapacity and so automatically terminates the commercial agency.[151] Bankruptcy is usually regarded as analogous to death.[152]

In relation to the commercial agent, it is not clear whether his bankruptcy automatically frustrates the contract. Bankruptcy of the commercial agent would nevertheless be likely to terminate the agency since it would make the commercial agent unfit to perform his duties as commercial agent.[153]

5.2.2.2 Regulation 16(b): loss of the right to claim compensation or indemnity?

Even though common law applies to decide whether an event *automatically* terminates the contract, the second crucial question is to know whether in such cases, the commercial agent is still entitled to claim compensation or indemnity.[154] Certain events such as the death of the commercial agent are expressly covered. In such a situation, compensation or indemnity is due to his estate.[155] Insanity of the commercial agent is possibly covered by illness, in which case the Agency Regulations consider it as a just cause for termination

146. [1999] 1 Lloyd's Rep 697, aff'd [2000] 1 All ER (Comm) 737.
147. [1999] 1 Lloyd's Rep 697, at p 700.
148. *Salton* v. *New Beeston Cycle Co* [1900] 1 Ch 43.
149. [1999] 1 Lloyd's Rep 697, aff'd [2000] 1 All ER (Comm) 737.
150. Applying common law principles, the commercial agent may still be able to bind an insane principal by relying on the doctrine of apparent authority: *Drew* v. *Nunn* (1879) 4 QBD 661. Even if in this case the agent was held personally liable, this case should probably be decided upon the special fact that the agent should have known of the principal's incapacity. As the agent did not know, he was in breach of his warranty of authority: *Yongee* v. *Toynbee* [1910] 1 KB 215.
151. Poole, *Textbook on contract law*, (7th edn, 2004) p 544.
152. Brown, *Commercial law*, (2001), p 226.
153. Poole, *Textbook on contract law*, (7th edn, 2004) p 544.
154. *Barrett McKenzie & Company Ltd* v. *Escada (UK) Ltd* [2001] Eu LR 567.
155. Regulation 17(8).

such that the commercial agent's right to compensation indemnity would be preserved.[156] However, in the absence of a judicial decision, this is still uncertain.

The silence of the Agency Regulations raises problems for the other situations described earlier. In relation to the death of the principal or a cessation of the business if the principal is a legal entity, we have seen earlier that a cessation of business by the principal amounts to a "circumstance attributable to the principal", which allows the commercial agent to terminate and still claim compensation or indemnity.[157] This being the case, the Agency Regulations afford commercial agents better protection than the common law rules.[158] What if the commercial agent simply ceases trading? In the absence of any just cause (age, illness, "circumstances attributable to the principal") or a permitted assignment to a new commercial agent, he will himself have terminated the agency agreement and Regulation 18(b) will deny him any right to compensation or indemnity.

For the bankruptcy of the principal, once again, it is not clear whether compensation or indemnity are due. As seen earlier, cessation of business by the principal amounts to a "circumstance attributable to the principal", which allows the commercial agent to terminate and still claim compensation or indemnity.[159] It is thought that bankruptcy would also be covered. The Agency Regulations afford commercial agents better protection than the common law rules.[160]

If the commercial agent goes bankrupt, the situation is slightly different. If bankruptcy occurs because the commercial agent has not made "proper efforts" to comply with his commercial agency functions as per Regulation 3(2)(a), then he has not acted in the principal's interest and therefore is guilty of a serious breach, giving the principal the right to summarily terminate the relationship and avoid having to give termination payments (Regulation 18(a)). However, such a line is difficult to prove.

Finally, when the contract is frustrated, it is thought that the right to claim compensation or indemnity still exists for several reasons.

First, Regulation 16(b) stipulates that following certain domestic law principles, the contract will be summarily terminated, but says nothing about the consequences of termination.

Secondly, as mentioned earlier, there is a relationship between Regulation 16(a) and Regulation 18(a). Yet, the relationship between Regulation 18(b) and Regulation 16(b) is not immediately obvious. In fact, the grounds for excluding payment of compensation or indemnity are closely and exhaustively defined by Regulation 18. Such exceptions are essentially when the principal terminates with a just cause, i.e. a serious breach by the commercial agent (Regulation 18(a)), when the commercial agent himself terminates with no just cause to do so (Regulation 18(b)(i) and (ii) sets out what a "just cause" amounts to) or when the commercial agent assigns the commercial agency with the consent of the principal (Regulation 18(c)). In case of frustration, it is not the parties who end the contract, but the frustrating events, the conditions of Regulation 18 are therefore not

156. Regulation 18(b)(ii).

157. *King* v. *Tunnock* [2000] Eu LR 531, for details of the decision, see fn 117 and associated text.

158. Following *Triffit Nurseries (a firm)* v. *Salads Etcetera Ltd* [1999] 1 All ER (Comm) 110, aff'd [2000] 1 All ER (Comm) 737, the cessation of business by a principal does not, in itself, bring the agency to an end.

159. *King* v. *Tunnock* [2000] Eu LR 531.

160. Following *Triffit Nurseries (a firm)* v. *Salads Etcetera Ltd* [1999] 1 All ER (Comm) 110, aff'd [2000] 1 All ER (Comm) 737, the cessation of business by a principal does not, in itself bring the agency to an end.

met.[161] To stipulate that termination payments would be excluded in the event that the contract is frustrated would create an additional exception to the ones defined by Regulation 18. This is impossible, since the parties cannot derogate from such a regulation to the detriment of the commercial agent before the contract expires.[162] Moreover, to allow an additional exception would also be in breach of the mandatory nature of termination payments as defined by the European Court of Justice in the case of *Ingmar Ltd* v. *Eaton Leonard Technologies Inc*.[163]

This is important for the related issue of *force majeure*. Whereas it is not disputed that the parties can agree that the commercial agency contract will be summarily terminated by a *force majeure* event identified as such in the contract (so that the doctrine of frustration would not be relevant), it is thought that in the light of the mandatory nature of the right to termination payments, compensation or indemnity is nevertheless due in such instances.

5.3 CONSEQUENCES OF TERMINATION: COMMERCIAL AGENTS ARE ENTITLED TO CLAIM TERMINATION PAYMENTS

The significant consequence of termination is that commercial agents are entitled to receive from the principal one of two kinds of termination payments, "compensation" or "indemnity".[164] We use quotation marks here, but not in the text generally, because each concept has a very particular meaning in this context, which is not the meaning they have in normal English law parlance. It is crucial to remember that.

The entitlement to claim a termination payment is undoubtedly the most substantial enhancement of the protection of commercial agents. Prior to the implementation of the Directive, commercial agents in English law were only entitled to receive damages if, by terminating the contract, the principal was acting in breach, and normal rules of causation, mitigation etc applied.

It is now accepted that termination payments, which are civil law concepts, are very different from the common law notion of damages for breach of contract. Yet, in spite of the importance of such rights, the Directive fails to explain what such payments are for, or how they are to be calculated. This is regrettable and consequently, to this day, some significant uncertainty still surrounds termination payments.[165]

Parallels have been drawn between such payments and compensation for unfair dismissal and redundancy payments in employment law.[166] Such parallels are useful at a "high level" in order to understand, in very general terms, the nature of termination payments under the Agency Regulations. Yet, the parallel must not be over-emphasised,

161. This point was argued obiter, in a slightly different context by Tuckey LJ in *Cooper, Watkins Bartle* v. *Pure Fishing (UK) Limited*, [2004] EWCA Civ 375, at para 17.

162. Regulation 19.

163. Case C–381/98 [2001] 1 CMLR 9.

164. Regulation 17(1).

165. The confusion can be highlighted by the case of *Bell Electric* v. *Aweco Appliance Systems GmbH and Co KG*, [2002] EWHC 872 8 May 2002, where the contract itself stipulated that on cancellation by either party, the principal was to pay a twelve-month compensation to the value of the previous five years' average total earning. The principal was German, it seems therefore strange that a contractual clause appears to apply the German system but uses the French terminology.

166. See Scholes, *Agency* in (ed. Battersby), *Commercial contracts* (Legal & Commercial Publishing Co. Ltd) (2004), Vol. 1, p 1.3.1.

since termination payments are very different from compensation for unfair dismissal and redundancy payments. The differences are such that it is in fact, possible to say that commercial agents are better protected than employees.

The higher level of protection is witnessed in four areas: (1) the Agency Regulations apply from the first day of the commercial agency contract[167]; (2) the meaning of termination in the Agency Regulations is wider than that of dismissal in employment law[168]; (3) termination payments are due whether or not the principal committed a breach of contract; and finally, (4) the calculation of "compensation" and "indemnity" is carried out on a very different basis to compensation for unfair dismissal and redundancy payments.

The study of the termination payments in the Agency Regulations will be done in two steps. First, we will look at the French law rationale behind compensation and the German law rationale behind indemnity, in order to understand why commercial agents need such a level of protection (section 5.3.1). This is necessary considering the uncertainty still surrounding the purpose behind termination payments. Secondly, we will study the scope of application of the two payments, in order to see exactly when they arise and in which circumstances they can be lost (section 5.3.2). Considering the importance of the calculation of "compensation" and "indemnity", the matter will be dealt with exclusively in Chapter 6.

5.3.1 The civil law rationale behind the need to protect commercial agents on termination

Commercial agents are intermediaries whose main role is to use their skills and expertise in order to create, develop or even simply maintain a customer base (goodwill) for the goods or services of the principal, within a given territory or with a given customer group. Commercial agents are therefore used as a marketing tool by principals who primarily, but not necessarily, want to expand their businesses. Commercial agents are often compared/confused with distributors who are also used for their marketing skills, but yet do not enjoy the same level of legal protection as commercial agents do. This is because commercial agents differ from distributors in two crucial ways. First, commercial agents do not act for themselves but for the principal. As a result, they are dependent on the existence of a mandate since their only source of income, the commission,[169] will stop once the commercial agency ends. Distributors, however, act for themselves by buying and reselling products for a profit and, so the thinking goes, could more readily switch to selling another supplier's products than could a commercial agent. Secondly, in a commercial agency relationship, so the thinking goes, both parties aim at the same goal: the creation/development/upholding of a customer base for the principal's goods. This is referred to in France as *l'intérêt commun*, the common interest.

167. In employment contracts, compensation for unfair dismissal and the right to redundancy payments will only apply after one year of employment. For details, see M Jefferson *Principles of employment law* (4th edn, 2000), Chapter 12.

168. Dismissal does not include frustration.

169. See however the case of *Mercantile International Group Plc* v. *Chuan Soon Huat Industrial Group Ltd* [2001] 2 All ER 632 where it was held that commercial agents can be paid through a mark-up and still be protected by the Agency Regulations.

The French law rationale

In France, the notion of common interest is of crucial importance, since it is what differentiates commercial agency relationships from other types of agency and marketing arrangements. The French courts used the notion, as early as the 1880s, as the legal basis for compensating the commercial agent on termination.[170] In fact, the French courts considered that the power of the commercial agent to represent the principal, sometimes called a *carte*, had a certain financial value, since it not only allowed the commercial agent to receive his share of the fruits of the common interest, the commissions, but it could also be assigned to a third party or passed on to the heirs of the commercial agent in case of his death. When the contract was terminated, the loss of the *carte* caused the commercial agent to suffer a loss since he lost not only his ability to generate an income via the commissions but also his ability to assign the commercial agency to another commercial agent. The reference to the commercial agency as a "carte" shows that, in France, the commercial agency therefore has a quasi-proprietary interest. The French notion of common interest is still relevant today for the calculation of the compensation. It will therefore be reviewed in greater detail in Chapter 6 when we deal with the issue of calculation of compensation.[171]

This quasi-proprietary interest that the commercial agent has in the commercial agency is clearly present in the Directive, since the commercial agent is expressly prevented from claiming compensation or indemnity when he has assigned the commercial agency.[172] Vice versa, upon the death of the commercial agent, his estate will be entitled to claim termination payments.[173]

The German law rationale

The relationship between commercial agents and their principals is regulated by §§ 84–92 of the German Commercial Code (Handelsgesetzbuch or HGB).

Similarly to the French system, German law acknowledges that the ultimate reason for a principal to appoint a commercial agent is because the latter will create and/or expand a customer base for the principal's goods. The German notion of indemnity was originally based on the Swiss idea of compensating the commercial agent for the advantages retained by the principal.[174] However, the substantive provisions have been considerably altered by German legislation. As a result, the rationale for awarding indemnity to the commercial agent on termination is now based on the fact that the financial gains of the principal must correspond to a financial loss for the commercial agent.

When the commercial agency contract ends, the principal will continue, so the thinking goes, to benefit from the business relationships created by the commercial agent, since the principal will (it is assumed) continue to sell his goods to such customers. For such sales, the principal does not have to pay the commissions that would be due had the relationship continued, hence, the thinking is that the commercial agent suffers a loss and is therefore entitled to claim indemnity.

170. For details, see S Saintier *Commercial agency law, a comparative analysis*, (2002), pp 10–16.
171. See Chapter 6, section 6.4.1.
172. Article 18(c) of the Directive.
173. Article 17(4) of the Directive.
174. KJ Hopt, *Handelsvertreterrecht*, 2nd edn, Munich: Verlag C.H. Beck, p 15.

The English and Scottish courts understand the civil-law rationale of termination payments

After an uncertain start, it seems that the English and Scottish courts now understand it. In fact, in the case of *Moore* v. *Piretta Ltd*,[175] the Court of Appeal held that the purpose of indemnity payment is "to award the commercial agent a share in the goodwill" he helped to build, otherwise "the whole benefit of that goodwill would remain with the principal".[176] In the case of *Barrett McKenzie* v. *Escada Ltd*,[177] the High Court held that the aim of the compensation option is to compensate the commercial agent "for the loss of a quasi-proprietary right: the loss of an asset to the agent (the agency)".[178] Such a comprehension is of crucial importance, as it will help us to understand the calculation of compensation and indemnity as will be seen in Chapter 6.

5.3.2 The Agency Regulations give a choice between two termination rights

The Directive required Member States to choose between two types of termination payments: an indemnity payment based on the pre-Directive German system and a compensation payment based on the pre-Directive French system. Whilst all other Member States have chosen one or the other,[179] the government has opted for both, leaving the choice to the parties.[180] The indemnity option will only apply when it is expressly stipulated in the contract: compensation will therefore operate by default.[181] When the parties opt for the indemnity option, it must be clearly indicated in the commercial agency contract. The English and Scottish courts will clarify any confusion between the two payments that arise.[182] The two types of payment are therefore alternatives and not cumulative.[183]

The way the government has implemented the Directive is still regarded as rather unusual. Until the last minute, drafts of the Agency Regulations provided only for the compensation alternative, the view having been taken by the government (mistakenly) that "compensation" was probably no more than the equivalent of damages for breach of contract at common law.

175. [1999] 1 All ER 174. This case is analysed in detail in Chapter 6, section 6.4.2, see especially fn 316–336 and associated text.

176. [1999] 1 All ER 174, at p 177g.

177. [2001] Eu LR 567.

178. *Ibid*, see para 27.

179. France and Germany have kept their respective systems and all the other Member States have opted for the German-based system of indemnity.

180. Regulation 17(1).

181. Regulation 17(2).

182. *Hardie Polymers Ltd* v. *Polymerland Ltd* (2002) SCLR 64. In this case, the claimant was appointed to act as the commercial agent of the defendant in 1995. The contract stipulated that indemnity was available on termination. In September 1999, the defendant unilaterally terminated the contract. The claimant commercial agent brought legal action in order to obtain compensation and not indemnity on the ground that there was an ambiguity in the contract as clause 10 referred to "compensation after termination". The court rejected his claim, stating that such words meant no more than "termination payment". The court added that notwithstanding the use of the word "compensation" in clause 10, there was sufficient clarity in the contract to conclude that the intention of the parties was to provide that the commercial agent was to be indemnified and not compensated.

183. This was reiterated in the case of *Hardie Polymers Ltd* v. *Polymerland Ltd* (2002) SCLR 64 where the court held that since indemnity applied, the commercial agent was excluded from claiming compensation.

Consequently, the view was that the less departing from common law principles that took place in the Agency Regulations, the better. It is unclear why the government, at the last minute, decided to "hedge its bets" and adopt both alternatives but leave it to the parties to decide for themselves.[184] Even today, some continue to argue that the government might be in breach of its EU law obligations in having implemented the Directive in this way.[185] A reference to the ECJ for a preliminary ruling under Article 234 EC, which raised this issue was made by an English court in 1999,[186] but was subsequently withdrawn before ruling because the parties settled the main litigation out of court.

As we have emphasised throughout the book, this near-verbatim implementation makes the impact of the Agency Regulations more uncertain. It is arguable that the complexity which result from a verbatim implementation could fall foul of EU law if it violates the requirements of legal certainty. It is therefore all the more important to understand how the termination payments function. We will first introduce the rules on compensation and indemnity as they are in the Agency Regulations and then explain how they work in practice. The issue of calculation is the subject of Chapter 6.

The indemnity option

The rules on the indemnity payment are provided by Regulations 17(3) to 17(5). Following the Directive to the letter, Regulation 17(3) stipulates that the commercial agent will only be entitled to receive an indemnity on two cumulative conditions. First, the commercial agent must have brought the principal some new customers or at least must have significantly increased the volume of business with existing ones, and the principal must still derive some benefits from such customers.[187] Secondly, the payment of the indemnity must be equitable with regards to all the circumstances and in particular the commission lost by the commercial agent on the business transacted.[188]

The payment of the indemnity is capped, since payment cannot, in any event, exceed one year's remuneration, calculated taking an average over a period of five years or the entire term of the contract if the contract is less than five years old.[189] In addition, the commercial agent can claim damages at common law if the agency is terminated in breach of contract.[190] This will be the case where for instance, the principal has failed to comply with the required notice period or terminates before the expiry of the contract term. The breach in such a case is the termination without notice (in the absence of a prior breach by the commercial agent which justifies summary termination).

The compensation option

The rules on the compensation payment are provided by Regulations 17(6) and 17(7). Still following the Directive to the letter, Regulation 17(6) stipulates that the commercial agent

184. Pressure from the representatives of principals' interest has been suggested as a possible reason. See F Randolph and J Davey, *Guide to the Commercial Agency Regulations*, (2nd edn, 2003), p 93.

185. *Ibid*, p 92.

186. Case C–64/99 *Pace Airline Services Ltd* v. *Aerotrans Luftfahrtsagentur GmbH* [1999] OJ C. 121/12.

187. Regulation 17(3(a)).

188. Regulation 17(3(b)).

189. Regulation 17(4).

190. Regulation 17(5).

is entitled to compensation for the damage he suffers as a result of termination of his relations with his principal. Under Regulation 17(7), "damage" is deemed to have occurred "particularly" when termination (a) deprives the commercial agent of the commission which proper performance of the commercial agency contract would have procured for him whilst providing the principal with substantial benefits linked to the activities of the commercial agent, or (b) has not enabled the commercial agent to amortize the costs and expenses that he has incurred in the performance of the agency contract on the advice of the principal. In the case of *King* v. *Tunnock*,[191] the Scottish Court of Session stated that Regulation 17(7) is not meant to be seen as an exhaustive list of events where damage occurs; nor does it mean that the commercial agent has to demonstrate that he has suffered damage when the situations described by Regulation 17 arise.[192] Such an interpretation clearly reinforces the protective stance of the implementing legislation, rather than adopt a restrictive approach.[193] We suggest it is strongly in line with the aims of the Directive.

Even though this is not expressly stipulated in the Agency Regulations as it is for the indemnity option, a claim for compensation does not prevent commercial agents from claiming, in addition, damages for breach of contract, as for instance where the principal fails to comply with the required notice period. This was clearly understood by the Scottish courts. For instance, in the case of *King* v. *Tunnock*,[194] the Court of Session did not deduct the payment in lieu of notice from the amount of compensation due to the commercial agent since the "evaluation of the loss of the agency is made without reference to the fact that he [the commercial agent] would be entitled to statutory notice".[195] Likewise, in the case of *Roy* v. *MR Pearlman Ltd*,[196] Lord Hamilton stated that "the consequential rights and remedies arising on a purported termination without due notice of a commercial agency contract are, so far as not inconsistent with the Regulations, not displaced".[197] This seems correct. However, whether the English courts will follow the same path is another matter, and the issue is therefore not entirely settled.

It is clear that the right of commercial agents to claim compensation or indemnity on termination is at the heart of their reinforced protection. Both termination payments are based on the same premise: on termination, compensation or indemnity are due as a rule; their exclusion is the exception.

This pattern of the Directive, and therefore that of the Agency Regulations,[198] will consequently be used in order to review how termination payments work.

191. [2000] Eu LR 531.

192. *Ibid*, para 41.

193. Surprisingly, it is in line with the French implementation of the Directive. Instead of following the Directive to the letter, the French implementing text simply stipulates that "when the contract ceases, the commercial agent is compensated for the damage suffered" (article L 134–12 al 1 commercial code). The decision to depart from the Directive was taken because of the fear that having examples of damage as in the Directive could be interpreted restrictively, which would reduce the level of protection in place for a long time. See OJ of the National Assembly, session of 23 May 1991, at p 2244.

194. [2000] Eu LR 531.

195. *Ibid*, para 52.

196. [1999] 2 CMLR 1155.

197. *Ibid*, at para 24.

198. Articles 17 and 18 of the Directive and Regulation 17 is called "entitlement of the commercial agent to indemnity or compensation on termination of agency contracts" & Regulation 18 is called "grounds for excluding payment of indemnity or compensation under Regulation 17".

5.3.2.1 The rule: compensation or indemnity is due on termination

Termination is the event that allows commercial agents to be compensated or indemnified.[199] We have seen that, following the silence of the Agency Regulations as to what constitutes "termination", the notion has been widely interpreted by the English and Scottish courts so as to include expiry of a fixed-term contract whether renewal was expected or not.[200] After an uncertain start in relation to the nature of termination rights,[201] it is now clear that they are available regardless of whether the principal has committed a breach of contract in terminating.

The right of the commercial agent to claim compensation or indemnity on termination

The Agency Regulations simply stipulate that on termination, the commercial agent will be compensated or indemnified following specific rules (Regulation 17(1)). Then, the Agency Regulations give a list of grounds for excluding such claims (regulation 18). Such simplicity in the rules is to be welcomed. Yet, the rules must be considered more closely in order to see when precisely the right to claim compensation or indemnity arises.

The right of the commercial agent to claim compensation or indemnity arises in a number of situations. First, in the light of Regulation 17(1), it effectively arises whenever the principal terminates the relationship with no just cause to do so. This is wide since, as mentioned earlier, the only just cause the principal has to terminate the relationship and avoid paying compensation or indemnity is when he terminates because the commercial agent has committed a serious breach as per Regulation 18(a).

Secondly, following the quasi-proprietary nature of the two termination payments, compensation or indemnity is still due even in the event of the commercial agent's death.[202]

Thirdly, the right to claim compensation or indemnity also arises when the commercial agent himself terminates the relationship, providing he does so with a "just cause", i.e. when he is too old, ill or infirm and therefore "cannot reasonably be required to continue his activities".[203] The way Regulation 18(b)(ii) is drafted seems to suggest that in such situations, there must be no element of choice on the part of the commercial agent. This raises no difficulty in relation to illness and infirmity. The situation is however slightly different with regard to the age of the commercial agent, for which the requirement raises the question to know whether, when the commercial agent chooses to retire because he has reached a certain age, but could reasonably continue his activities, this constitutes a just cause allowing him to claim compensation or indemnity.

If, as Regulation 18(b)(ii) suggests, the commercial agent must have no choice, this would seem to indicate that, unlike employees, commercial agents do not have a right to retire upon reaching a certain age. Should a commercial agent insist on retiring upon the reaching of a certain age and yet is perfectly able to work, the way the implementing text is drafted seems to indicate that the commercial agent cannot claim compensation or

199. Regulation 17(1).

200. See section 5.2.1.1.2 above, especially fnn 15–37 and associated text.

201. The DTI seemed to have totally misunderstood the role of such payments because it said that if the principal gave the correct period of notice, this would potentially reduce the level of indemnity or compensation and that it was a matter to be decided by the courts. See DTI Guidance Notes, published in September 1994, p 19.

202. Regulation 17(8).

203. Regulation 18(b)(ii).

indemnity. However, since the rules can be derogated from to the benefit of the commercial agent,[204] the parties can therefore provide the commercial agent with the right to retire upon reaching a certain age and still be able to claim compensation or indemnity. Yet, considering that such a solution is not very beneficial to the principal, the latter is unlikely to agree to such a proposal. A better solution for both parties might be to stipulate that when the commercial agent reaches a certain age, assignment should occur.

Finally, the commercial agent is also justified in terminating the relationship and therefore able to claim compensation or indemnity if he does so "for circumstances attributable to the principal".[205] We have previously seen that this expression is very wide, since it can include a repudiatory breach by the principal allowing him to summarily terminate the relationship[206] or some lesser breach, but, also includes events that are not breaches of contract at all.[207]

How to claim compensation or indemnity

The Agency Regulations impose no formal requirement on the manner in which the commercial agent, or his estate, must exercise the right to claim compensation or indemnity. This is welcome as it provides a certain element of flexibility. All the commercial agent has to do is make his claim within one year of termination[208] by serving a notice.[209] This limitation period is mandatory; there is therefore no discretion for the English and Scottish courts to extend the period. It is not clear, though, whether the limitation period runs from the moment the principal notifies the commercial agent of termination or whether (if the termination is on notice) it runs from the date at which termination becomes effective, i.e. after the notice period. In France, it runs from the moment termination becomes effective.[210] It is thought that the same will apply in England.

The notice itself does not have to be very precise as long as the communication "conveys to the objectively reasonable reader that the agent intends to pursue claims under Regulation 17".[211] It is therefore not necessary for the commercial agent to say in the notice whether he thinks his rights are to claim compensation or to indemnity, and if he tries to do so but gets it wrong, that will not prevent him from claiming.[212]

The right for the commercial agent to be compensated or indemnified on termination is compulsory[213] and can therefore only be excluded in the circumstances defined by the Agency Regulations.

204. Regulation 19.

205. Regulation 18(b)(ii).

206. *Bell Electric* v. *Aweco Appliance Systems GmbH and Co KG*, [2002] EWHC 872, 8 May 2002.

207. *King* v. *Tunnock* [2000] Eu LR 531. For details, see section 5.2.1.3.2 above, especially fn 117 and associated text.

208. Regulation 17(9).

209. For the manner in which the notice may be served, see Regulation 22.

210. For details, see Chapter 6, section 6.3.1.

211. *Brian Hackett* v. *Advanced Medical Computer Systems Ltd* [1999] CLC 6(160) QBD.

212. See the case of *Hardie Polymers Ltd* v. *Polymerland Ltd* (2002) SCLR 64 where the commercial agent argued he should be entitled to claim compensation rather than indemnity because of an ambiguity in the contract. The court held he had no right to claim compensation but indemnity arose. For details, see footnote 182 and associated text.

213. The rules cannot be derogated from to the detriment of the commercial agent as per Regulation 19.

5.3.2.2 The exceptions to the right to claim termination payments

The Agency Regulations define specific grounds for excluding the payment of compensation or indemnity. Even though the simplicity of the format seems appealing, the lack of details nevertheless raises problems in relation to the impact of the Agency Regulations on the traditional common law rules.

THE FOUR EXCEPTIONS

First, the commercial agent loses the right to claim compensation or indemnity when the principal summarily terminates the relationship with a just cause. As already mentioned, the only such just cause is a repudiatory breach by the commercial agent.[214]

Secondly, no termination payments are due when the commercial agent himself terminates the relationship with no just cause to do so.[215] We have seen that just cause includes age, illness, infirmity, assignment and "circumstance attributable to the principal". The problem is to know whether the list of just causes is exhaustive or not, i.e. can the parties freely decide by agreement other instances when the commercial agent has a just cause for terminating e.g. to give the commercial agent the right to retire at a given age, even if he is objectively capable of continuing to act and still be entitled to claim compensation or indemnity. Considering that the rule can be derogated from to the benefit of the commercial agent,[216] it is thought that such a contractual freedom is possible.

Thirdly, in the light of the quasi-proprietary nature of the relationship, no termination payments are due when the commercial agent assigns the commercial agency to another commercial agent, with the consent of the principal.[217]

Finally, as previously mentioned, the commercial agent must make his claim for compensation or indemnity within one year of termination[218] by serving a notice.[219] Failing to do so is consequently the fourth exception to his right to claim compensation or indemnity as indirectly confirmed in the case of *Barrett McKenzie* v. *Escada*.[220]

A WATERTIGHT PROTECTION?

The Agency Regulations make it clear that the four situations we have just described are the only situations when the commercial agent loses the right to be compensated or indemnified as it is impossible for the parties to derogate from the rules to the detriment of the commercial agent "before the agency contract expires".[221]

The reference to time is somewhat puzzling. According to Advocate General Léger in the case of *Ingmar Ltd* v. *Eaton Leonard Technologies Inc*,[222] it seems that the reference to time might just have been a drafting "overlook" following some modifications of the

214. Regulation 18(a).
215. Regulation 18(b).
216. Case C–381/98 *Ingmar Ltd* v. *Eaton Leonard Technologies Inc* [2001] 1 CMLR 9.
217. Regulation 18(c). See further Chapter 6.
218. Regulation 17(9).
219. For the manner in which the notice may be served, see Regulation 22.
220. [2001] Eu LR 567, see para 14.
221. Regulation 19.
222. Case C–381/98 [2001] All ER (EC) 329.

drafts of the Directive.[223] A more obvious explanation is that the reference to time is simply present in order to prevent the principal from inserting a limitation or liquidated damages clause in the contract. Yet, the parties can enter a valid settlement agreement after the contract is terminated.

Such an interpretation is certainly in line with the ruling of the European Court of Justice in the case of *Ingmar Ltd* v. *Eaton Leonard Technologies Inc*,[224] which decided that termination rights are mandatory, hereby quashing any risk of limitation to the right of commercial agents to claim compensation or indemnity. It will be recalled that in this case, the European Court of Justice held that the Agency Regulations applied to the relationship even though a choice of law clause stipulated that the relationship was to be subject to the laws of California.[225]

In the light of such a decision, the only exceptions to the commercial agent's right to compensation or indemnity are those defined in the Agency Regulations. It is therefore impossible for the parties to agree to any other methods by which the right to compensation or indemnity can be lost such as the imposition of a probation period by the principal for instance. As seen earlier, the mandatory nature of the termination rights also seems to mean that it is impossible for the parties to include a *force majeure* clause whereby termination payments will not be due in certain circumstances.

5.3.3 Post-termination clauses

Under Regulation 20, it is possible for the parties to agree on a restraint of trade clause. Once again, in this area, the Agency Regulations replicate the Directive. This does not really raise any problems and the conditions of validity of such restrictions are straightforward. First, a restraint of trade clause is only valid if entered into in writing and if it relates to the geographical area, the group of customers entrusted to the commercial agent or the kind of goods covered by the commercial agency.[226] A restraint of trade clause cannot be valid for more than two years after the termination of the contract.[227] However, common law rules will still apply and the English and Scottish courts are therefore entitled to reduce the obligations imposed on the parties in such a clause should they see fit to do so.[228]

The issue is dealt with in more detail in Chapter 7.

5.4 CONCLUSION

Termination of the commercial agency agreement is undoubtedly the stage of the relationship where commercial agents are at their weakest and therefore their need for protection

223. See para 77 of the opinion. Advocate General Léger further stated that derogation is impossible even after the commercial agency contract has ended since the provisions on termination payments are mandatory. See § 77–91 of his opinion. Professor Reynolds remarks that it is regrettable that this comment was not taken up by the European Court of Justice in the decision as it could be important, where, for instance, the parties are in the process of renewing a fixed-term contract. FMB Reynolds, *Bowstead and Reynolds on Agency*, (17th edn, 2001), para 11.039, p 602.

224. Case C–381/98 [2001] 1 CMLR 9.

225. For a detailed discussion of this decision, see Chapter 2, section 2.4.1.2, especially fnn 101–103 and associated text.

226. Regulation 20(1).

227. Regulation 20(2).

228. Regulation 20(3).

is at its highest. In this chapter, we have seen that the Agency Regulations have met that need by providing commercial agents with their most prized level of protection: the right to claim compensation or indemnity pursuant to Regulation 17(1). Yet, we have also seen that even at this most crucial stage of the Agency Regulations, the near-verbatim implementation of the Directive, once again, jeopardises the efficiency of the level of protection it provides commercial agents.

This threat exists at two different levels. First, there are weaknesses within the Agency Regulations themselves. Because the Directive is the result of political compromise, it is not meant as a complete code regulating the relationship between the commercial agent and his principal. As a consequence, there are "holes" in the European text. Because of the near-verbatim implementation, this drawback is also present in the Agency Regulations. For instance, the Agency Regulations pose as a mandatory rule that compensation or indemnity are due on "termination" and yet, they fail to define the process by which and the circumstances in which "termination" will occur. The Agency Regulations also fail to explain why commercial agents need to be protected in such a manner and have the right to claim compensation or indemnity on termination.

In this chapter, we have seen how such flaws have been corrected by the judiciary, hence allowing the level of protection of commercial agents on termination to be significantly enhanced. This has been possible because, in their interpretation of the Agency Regulations, the English and Scottish courts have always upheld the protective stance of the implementing text. In fact, the courts held that "termination" occurs not only through a deliberate act of the parties, but also through expiry and/or non-renewal of fixed-term contracts.[229]

In relation to the nature of the two termination payments, this chapter has also shown that the English and Scottish courts now understand and accept that compensation and indemnity have a meaning which is very specific to the commercial agency relationship and must therefore not be confused with the more traditional common law concept of compensation for loss.[230] Through their interpretation of the Agency Regulations, the English and Scottish courts have at once clarified their scope of application and ensured their efficiency in protecting commercial agents.

The second level of threat to the commercial agents protection is a consequence of the first one, but is more pernicious. Because the Agency Regulations are not meant to be a complete code regulating the relationship between commercial agents and their principal, the common law rules of contract and agency still apply. Following the lack of guidelines as to how the two sets of rules cohabit, the courts held that the common law rules apply providing that they are consistent with the Agency Regulations.[231] In this chapter, we have seen that, most of the time, the two sets of rules sit easily one with another and even complement each other. For instance, we have seen that termination for non-repudiatory breach where less than the minimum notice period required under the Agency Regulations has been given is nevertheless an effective termination for the purpose of the Agency

229. *Whitehead* v. *Jenks and Cattell* [1999] Eu LR 827. For details, see section 5.2.1.1.2, especially footnotes 15–37 and associated text.

230. *Moore* v. *Piretta Ltd* [1999] 1 All ER 174, *Barrett McKenzie* v. *Escada Ltd* [2001] EU LR 567. For details, see section 5.3.1, especially fnn 175–178 and associated text.

231. *Roy* v. *MR Pearlman Ltd* [1999] CMLR 1155.

Regulations[232] and the expression "default of the commercial agent" in Regulation 18(a) allowing the principal to summarily terminate the relationship without having to pay compensation or indemnity merely refers to a serious breach.[233] On the other hand, the expression "circumstances attributable to the principal" allowing the commercial agent to terminate the relationship and still claim compensation or indemnity can also refer to a serious breach but is not confined to a serious breach or indeed, any breach at all.[234]

However, in this chapter, we have also seen that the situation is not perfect, and that problems of compatibility between the two sets of rules arise. Considering that the Agency Regulations and the traditional common law rules are based on two opposed rationales, and that the Agency Regulations introduce civil law-inspired rights, alien to common law principles, problems of compatibility were inevitable. One such problem arose in relation to the process by which the commercial agent can claim compensation or indemnity. The Agency Regulations regulate *when* the commercial agent's right to claim compensation or indemnity arises and *when* it is lost. However, in relation to *how* the commercial agent can claim compensation or indemnity, the Agency Regulations merely stipulate that all he has to do is give notice to the principal of his claim within one year of termination.[235]

This simplicity appears appealing, yet, in the silence of the Agency Regulations, domestic rules governing the termination of contract apply, which raises problems in the following circumstances. The commercial agent is entitled to terminate the relationship and still claim compensation or indemnity when he terminates for a "just cause". One such "just cause" for terminating the relationship is because of "circumstances attributable to the principal" as per Regulation 18(b)(i). Upholding the protective stance of the Agency Regulations, the courts held that this expression can include a serious breach of the principal[236] but is not restricted to a breach.[237] This is good for the protection of commercial agents.

However, the English and Scottish courts also insisted that, in such circumstances, domestic rules governing the termination of contract for breach must apply; in which case, the right of the commercial agent to terminate can be lost on the ground that the commercial agent has subsequently affirmed the contract.[238] This indirectly creates a new exception to the right of the commercial agent to claim compensation or indemnity, which seems wrong because it is against the protective stance of the Agency Regulations as well as the mandatory nature of the termination payments.[239] We have therefore proposed that in such circumstances,[240] domestic rules should not apply. We have proposed that once the commercial agent notifies the principal of his claim of compensation or indemnity, this acts as acceptance of any breach or other conduct of the principal amounting to a "circumstance attributable to the principal" pursuant to regulation 18(b)(i). This satisfies the common law requirement that the victim of a serious breach must accept it before being

232. *Roy* v. *MR Pearlman Ltd*, as above. For details, see section 5.2.1.2, especially fn 56–61 and associated text.

233. *Cooper, Watkins Bartley* v. *Pure Fishing (UK) Ltd* [2004] EWCA Civ 375. For details, see section 5.2.1.3, especially fn 97 and associated text.

234. *King* v. *Tunnock* [2000] Eu LR 531. For details, see section 5.2.1.3.2, especially footnote 117 and associated text.

235. Regulation 22.

236. *Bell Electric* v. *Aweco Appliance Systems GmbH*, [2002] EWHC 872.

237. *King* v. *Tunnock* [2000] Eu LR 531

238. *Bell Electric* v. *Aweco Appliance Systems GmbH*, as above.

239. Case C–381/98 *Ingmar Ltd* v. *Eaton Leonard Technologies Inc*, [2001] 1 CMLR 9.

240. For details, see section 5.2.1.3.2, especially footnotes 129–136 and associated text.

to repudiate the contract. It also satisfies the requirement of the Agency Regulations of the termination before the commercial agent can claim compensation or indemnity. Such a proposal, not having been tested in courts, is still uncertain, but nevertheless believed to be correct since it solves the problem highlighted and is consistent with the protective stance of the Agency Regulations.

Now that all the issues surrounding termination and the scope of application of the two termination rights are covered, it is time to turn to the other equally serious question relating to the two termination payments, that of their calculation. Considering the peculiarity of the calculation of the French-based compensation and the German-based indemnity, Chapter 6 will *inter alia* give precise examples as to how the French and the German courts calculate their respective termination payments.

CHAPTER 6

CALCULATING THE TERMINATION PAYMENTS DUE TO THE COMMERCIAL AGENT

6.1 INTRODUCTION

In Chapter 5, we have seen that termination is one of the areas where the legal protection of commercial agents has been substantially reinforced through the introduction of compulsory termination payments. It will be recalled that the Directive left the choice to Member States between two options, the German-based indemnity and the French-based compensation.[1] Whereas most Member States have chosen one or the other, the government has opted for both, leaving the choice to the parties, but if the agreement is silent compensation applies.[2] It will also be recalled that compensation and indemnity differ in two ways:

> First, the German-based indemnity concentrates on the goodwill generated by the commercial agent from which the principal still benefits after termination. The French-based compensation however concentrates on the damage suffered by the commercial agent at the stage of termination.
>
> Secondly, the German-based indemnity is capped at one year's worth of commission. The French-based compensation is not, and the French case law shows that the practice there is to award two years' worth of commission.

It is now more than ten years since the Agency Regulations came into effect. The English and Scottish courts have accepted, in principle, that compensation and indemnity are different from any common law concept. Their scope of application is reasonably well assimilated. In spite of such undeniable progress, a significant degree of uncertainty still prevails over the calculation of the two termination payments because of the silence of the Directive on that matter. By almost replicating the Directive, the Agency Regulations remain equally silent and have left the task of calculating such payments to the judiciary. The problem is that the English and Scottish courts are currently divided over the question whether they should (1) calculate compensation and indemnity in the light of the body of French and German case law or (2) rely on their own, different, methods of calculation.

The aim of this chapter is to consider this question by looking at the two alternatives, in an attempt to resolve the uncertainty surrounding the calculation of compensation and indemnity and ensure that the protection of commercial agents is indeed reinforced.

1. Article 17(1) of the Directive.
2. Regulation 17(1).

— We will first consider whether the English and Scottish courts should seek guidance from their French and German counterparts (section 6.2). To do so has the undeniable advantage of ensuring harmonisation and uniformity between Member States. For that reason, this chapter will therefore look at how the French (section 6.3) and the German courts (section 6.4) calculate their respective termination payments.
— Yet, considering that the Directive forfeited a uniform harmonisation when it gave Member States the choice between compensation and indemnity, we must therefore also consider the possibility that the English and Scottish courts should be left to calculate compensation and indemnity according to their own method of calculation, even if such a method differs from that applied by the French and German courts.

Such a possibility, in turn, raises the fundamental question as to which criteria the English and Scottish courts should use in order to calculate compensation (section 6.3.2) and indemnity (section 6.4.2).

6.2 SHOULD THE ENGLISH AND SCOTTISH COURTS SEEK GUIDANCE FROM FRANCE AND GERMANY FOR THE CALCULATION OF COMPENSATION AND INDEMNITY?

The division of the judiciary over the calculation of the two termination payments came progressively as the English and Scottish courts grew more confident with their application of the Agency Regulations.[3] In *Moore* v. *Piretta Ltd*,[4] the only reported English case to date involving indemnity, the High Court held that it was possible to look at the relevant parts of German law "for the purpose of construing the English Regulations and to use it [German law] as a guide for their application".[5]

In relation to compensation, the Scottish courts adopted a similar position. In *Roy* v. *MR Pearlman Ltd*,[6] Lord Hamilton agreed on the necessity to look at how the French courts address the question in order to assist in determining how much compensation should be awarded. In the case of *King* v. *Tunnock*[7] a compensatory award of two years' worth of gross commission was awarded by express reference to French law.

The case was not however followed by the lower courts in England and Wales. Things started to change with the case of *Ingmar Ltd* v. *Eaton Leonard Technologies Inc*[8] where the High Court of England and Wales cast a critical eye on the French system of compensation, stating that the award of two years' worth of commission could not apply in this instance as it would be "excessive and result in a considerable degree of windfall".[9] In *Duffen* v. *FraBo SpA (No 2)*[10] Hallgarten J went even further and refused to look at French

3. For an academic division over the matter, see Sidkin who is in favour of following French law ((2001) 145 SJ 431) and see Burbidge who is against ((2000) 150 NLJ 1269).
4. [1999] 1 All ER 174.
5. *Ibid*, at 177g.
6. [1999] 2 CMLR 1155.
7. [2000] Eu LR 531.
8. [2002] ECC 5.
9. *Ibid*, para 52 *per* Mr Justice Morland.
10. [2000] 1 Lloyd's Rep 180.

law when applying the compensatory award. Even though Hallgarten J recognised that French law was the direct inspiration of the award, he added that "attempting to mimic what a French court would actually have done"[11] is an impossible task for which the English courts are ill equipped. The same attitude was more recently adopted in *Tigana Ltd* v. *Decoro Ltd*,[12] where Davis J said that "I do not think what is said to be French law and practice can be used to dictate the approach to, or operation of, the assessment of compensation under Regulation 17".[13]

When the courts looked at how the French and German courts calculate their respective termination payments, it had the advantage of ensuring that the two aims of the Directive, harmonisation and a reinforced protection for commercial agents, were achieved.

However, the harmonisation argument is weak and therefore cannot be used in order to force the English and Scottish courts to follow the practices of their French and German counterparts, for the following reasons:

First, as already mentioned, by compromising and allowing the choice between the two termination rights, the Directive seriously undermines its own objective of harmonisation.

Secondly, even though France and Germany are the inspirations to the two termination payments, the other Member States are under no obligation to refer to or even follow the French and German principles when calculating the termination payments. In fact, as pointed out by Elias J in the case of *Bell Electric* v. *Aweco Appliance Systems GmbH*,[14] the European Court of Justice itself, in the case of *R* v. *Customs and Excise Commissioner ex p EMU Tabac*[15] held that "(. . .) it is clear from the case law of the court that the Community Legal order does not in principle, aim to define concepts on the basis of one or more national legal systems unless there is an express provision to that effect".[16] France and Germany are undoubtedly the inspiration for the two termination payments yet, the Directive contains no express provision that they are, hence, there is no obligation on Member States to follow the French and German judicial practices.

Incidentally, this lack of reference therefore seems to explain why the Directive imposes no method of calculation for compensation and indemnity. It also seems to explain why, in its 1996 report on the implementation of article 17,[17] the European Commission recognised the need for clarification on the calculation of the two termination payments for a more uniform interpretation, and yet did not expressly state the obligation for Member States to follow what France and Germany do. In fact, the European Commission simply remarked, without commenting, that in relation to indemnity, most Member States were not following the way the German courts calculate the award, but, instead, relied on their own, differing, methods of calculation.

The third argument is not unrelated to the second one. The fact that the Directive imposes no method of calculation for compensation and indemnity, seems to indicate that the calculation of the two termination payments does not in fact come into harmonisation. This powerful argument was used in the case of *Barrett McKenzie* v. *Escada*[18] where

11. *Ibid*, at p 198.
12. [2003] EWHC 23, [2003] Eu LR 189.
13. *Ibid*, para 98.2.
14. [2002] EWHC 872, [2002] Eu LR 443, at para 56.
15. [1998] All ER (EC) 402.
16. *Ibid*, at para 30.
17. European Commission Report, Com 96(364) published in June 1996. See Appendix 9.
18. [2001] Eu LR 567.

Bowers J said that harmonisation does not require each Member State to follow the same calculation method since "harmonisation, so far as the Directive was concerned, was as to the establishment of the right to an entitlement within the Member States generally and that the particular method of assessing the value of that entitlement can be left to the Member States to individually work out".[19] Bowers J added that such payments were not rights but remedies and as such there is no obligation on the English and Scottish courts to follow the French system of compensation since EU law leaves the national laws to find the right remedy.

Such an argument is interesting[20] as it could be used to argue that France and Germany should also look at other EU Member States, including the UK, for their interpretation of the Directive, an idea which may prove difficult to apply since France and Germany implemented the Directive so as to be in line with their legal tradition.

Finally, last but not least, to require the English and Scottish courts to follow blindly the way the French and German courts calculate their termination payments is impractical. This very point was also made by Bowers J in the case of *Barrett McKenzie* v. *Escada Ltd*[21] when he said, "the compensation principles have, in practical terms to be sufficiently UK based and developed so as to be interpreted and enforceable by UK judges without requiring in any single case (. . .) an expert in French law to determine the case".[22] Bowers J is perfectly right. Yet, case law so far shows that the attempt to apply the compensation option in a more "UK based" fashion is not, as yet successful. This is due to the conflict between the judicial practice under which compensation has evolved in France and in the English legal tradition. In fact, cases such as *Duffen* v. *FraBo SpA (No 2)*[23] and *Bell Electric* v. *Aweco Appliance Systems GmbH*[24] show that some English courts still consider compensation under the Agency Regulations as an alternative to English common law damages for breach of contract.[25] Such a position is arguably against the spirit and purpose of the Directive as it jeopardises the protection of commercial agents (more anon).

As a consequence, it is therefore necessary to look at how France and Germany apply compensation and indemnity respectively, *not* because it presupposes that they have the "right" systems of calculation,[26] but simply to cast light on civil law principles, which still puzzle English lawyers. For ease of understanding, the two termination payments must be looked at separately. For each of them, the same pattern will be followed: a look at the rules as they are applied on the continent, followed by a review of the way the English and Scottish courts apply them.

Compensation will be dealt with first, not only because, due to the way the government has implemented the Directive, most of the reported cases involve compensation[27] and in our experience, the great bulk of commercial agency agreements are consistent with that

19. *Ibid*, at para 26.

20. However, the use of the word "remedy" is not entirely correct. Compensation and indemnity are not "remedies" in the same vein as contract law damages for instance.

21. [2001] Eu LR 567.

22. *Ibid*, at para 21.

23. [2000] 1 Lloyd's Rep 180.

24. [2002] EWHC 72, [2002] Eu LR 443.

25. The two cases are discussed in more detail at section 6.3.2.1, see fnn 179–193 and associated text.

26. Absent any EU authority, there is no "right" approach. In fact, it is not inconceivable that the French approach might be "wrong" under EU law.

27. The Agency Regulations leave the choice between the two termination rights to the parties (Regulation 17(1)), but in the silence of the parties, compensation applies (Regulation 17(2)).

but also because it seems to raise more problems for the English and Scottish courts than the indemnity option.[28] We cannot, however, emphasise strongly enough that the reference to French and German decisions is only proposed as some relevant, albeit not conclusive, evidence on how to approach compensation and indemnity. We are certainly not advocating that these approaches should be slavishly followed in this country.

6.3 CALCULATING THE "COMPENSATION" DUE TO COMMERCIAL AGENTS

Under the Directive, the commercial agent is entitled to be compensated for the "damage" he suffers as a result of termination of his relations with his principal.[29] A "damage" is deemed to have occurred particularly when termination takes place in circumstances which:

(a) deprive the commercial agent of the commission which proper performance of the agency contract would have procured for him whilst providing the principal with substantial benefits linked to the commercial agent's activities, or
(b) have not enabled the commercial agent to amortise the costs and expenses that he has incurred in the performance of the agency contract on the advice of the principal.[30]

Even though such rules are inspired from the French system, they do not reflect the pre-Directive French position very accurately. The main problem is that in the first deeming provision, the Directive stipulates that compensation will arise, providing that the principal receives substantial benefits. There is no such requirement in French law as will be seen later. Moreover, in the second deeming provision, the Directive gives details of situations when damage is deemed to have occurred. The French implementing legislation however remains silent and merely stipulates that compensation is due for the damage suffered by the commercial agent.[31] The French implementing legislation therefore departs from the Directive so as to be more in line with its own pre-Directive legal tradition. The decision that the French implementing legislation should not follow the text of the Directive was reached after much debate in the French Parliament, on the ground that although the details provided in the Directive were merely examples, to adopt them might have jeopardised a system which had proved beneficial for the commercial agent for years.[32]

Interestingly, the Scottish case of *King* v. *Tunnock*[33] shows that, by applying the protective stance of the Directive, such a drastic move might not have been necessary. In this instance, the Court of Session, after looking at the wording of Regulation 17(7), stated that

28. The German-based indemnity payments are on average lower than the French-based compensation. In our experience, principals tend now to insist on the indemnity option.

29. Article 17(3) of the Directive.

30. Article 17(3) of the Directive which corresponds to Regulation 17(7).

31. Article L 134–12 al 1 French commercial code.

32. See debates in the French National Assembly, session of 23 May 1991, see the National Assembly, Official Journal 1991, p 2244.

33. [2000] Eu LR 531.

Regulation 17(7) does not "set out the exclusive circumstances giving rise to compensation"[34] and therefore is not meant to be seen as an exhaustive list of events where the damage occurs, nor does it mean that the commercial agent has to demonstrate that he has suffered a damage when these situations arise.[35]

Because of the way the government has implemented the Directive, most reported cases so far have involved compensation rather than indemnity. Yet, the concept of compensation, or *indemnité de cessation* as it is called in France, still causes problems to English lawyers for two reasons. First, it is still not entirely clear what kind of "damage" commercial agents suffer on termination.[36] Secondly, the evaluation of the "damage" by the French courts to two years' worth of commission is seen as a tariff, which does not reflect the reality of the damage suffered. In other words, it is seen as an unwarranted windfall for the commercial agent.[37] Let us therefore consider these two points separately in order to shed light on the notion, which still eludes English lawyers.

6.3.1 The French approach to compensation

In order to explain why commercial agents in France are perceived to suffer a "damage" i.e. a loss on termination, it is necessary to review, briefly, the history leading to the protection that French commercial agents have enjoyed for a long time.

In France, commercial agents have been recognised and protected as a separate class of intermediaries for over 50 years thanks to the 1958 Decree.[38] This text was the first one to recognise the special economic needs of commercial agents as a profession compared to other intermediaries and to provide them with a level of protection on termination, which was to inspire, in part, the Directive.

Even though the statutory protection came reasonably late in France, the idea that commercial agents needed protection appeared a lot earlier. Commercial agents are representatives whose main function is to act as a marketing tool for manufacturers (and other suppliers) at home and abroad. Because commercial agents are representatives, the agency rules as defined in the Civil Code governed the relationships they had with their principals.[39] However, it quickly transpired that such rules were ill-suited to the needs of the "profession"; commercial agents are mandated agents since they act on behalf of principals, but as professionals, they do so on a permanent basis and in return for payment. The Civil Code, on the other hand, adopts the Roman law conception that a mandate is a temporary and gratuitous service entered into for the sole benefit of the principal.[40]

34. *Ibid*, at para 42, *per* Caplan J.

35. *Ibid*, at para 41.

36. Looking at previous drafts of the Agency Regulations, originally, the first implementing text was in favour of compensation because at the time, it was thought that compensation was likely to prove cheaper than indemnity, merely because it was perceived to be similar to the contractual notion of damages for loss resulting from breach of contract. See *Scholes*, Agency, in (ed) Battersby, *Commercial contracts* (Legal & Commercial Publishing Co Ltd, 2004), Vol 1.

37. See comments by Mr Justice Morland in the case of *Ingmar Ltd* v. *Eaton Leonard Technologies Inc* [2002] ECC 5, para 52.

38. Decree 58–1345 of 23 December 1958, D 1959, L, 132. For an English translation, see legifrance.gouv.fr.

39. Articles 1984 to 2010 of the Civil Code. For an English translation, see www.legifrance.gouv.fr.

40. See article 1986 of the Civil Code.

As a result, under the French Civil Code, the principal can revoke the mandate immediately and at any time without incurring any liability.[41] The mandated agent however, can only terminate the mandate with due notice and for a just cause.[42] If the mandated agent acts in breach of such requirements, he has to compensate the principal for the loss caused. As early as 1885, the French Supreme Court (Cour de Cassation) considered that the ability of the principal to unilaterally terminate the relationship at a whim and without incurring any liability was not suitable for the needs of commercial agents.[43] In order to reduce such ability, the *Cour de Cassation* created the notion of the common interest mandate, *mandat d'intérêt commun,* as an exception to article 2004 CC and held that "when the contract is created in the common interest of the principal as well as that of the mandated agent, it cannot be unilaterally revoked by one or the other party, but can only be revoked by mutual consent, for a justified cause recognised by the courts or following contractual specifications".[44] Any other cause of termination invoked by the principal would be regarded as unjustified and would therefore entitle the commercial agent to claim compensation for the loss termination caused him.

This was a significant improvement for commercial agents established in France, but compensation on termination was not automatic. A commercial agent had to prove first that the mandate was indeed created for his and the principal's common interest and that compensation was not excluded by the contract.[45] The 1958 Decree lifted these burdens, by stipulating that commercial agency contracts are entered into for the common interest of the parties[46] and that unilateral termination by the principal will automatically give rise to compensation, unless justified by a breach of the commercial agent.[47] From then on, compensation for unjustified termination was the rule and its exclusion was the exception.

The notion of common interest still exists today. It is even wider than at its inception since, in addition to still being used as the rationale for compensation on termination, it now pervades and governs the commercial agency relationship as a whole.[48]

6.3.1.1. Common interest: the legal basis for awarding compensation on termination in France

As just mentioned, the French implementing legislation describes the commercial agency as "a relationship entered into for the common interest of the parties". This is because French law considers that the commercial agent and the principal aim towards the same goal, namely the creation/development/retention of a customer base, i.e. a goodwill for the principal's goods or services. As such, the relationship is seen almost as a *quasi-partnership*. In fact, in order to attain the common interest, both parties contribute to the

41. Article 2004 of the Civil Code.
42. Article 2007 of the Civil Code.
43. *Cass Civ 13 May 1885*, DP 1885, I, 350; S 1888, I, 220.
44. *Cass Civ 11 February 1891*, DP 1891, I, 197.
45. For details, see S Saintier, *Commercial agency law, a comparative analysis*, 2002, Chapter 1, pp 11–14 and pp 15–16.
46. Article 3(1) of the 1958 Decree.
47. Article 3(2).
48. Where the Directive stipulates that the parties owe each other a reciprocal duty of good faith (articles 3(1) and 4(1)), the French Commercial Code stipulates that the commercial agency contract is entered into for the common interest of the parties (article L 134-4 al 1). Once again, the French implementing legislation departs from the Directive so that the new rules can reflect the legal tradition.

relationship; the principal provides the goods or services and the commercial agent brings the necessary skills and expertise to create/develop/retain the customer base. Because both parties aim to achieve the same goal (i.e. the common interest), the whole relationship is based, or so the legal thinking in France goes, on an ethic of co-operation.

This idea of co-operation is also present in the Directive, and consequently in the Agency Regulations, through the compulsory and reciprocal obligation of good faith.[49] By helping each other to develop the common interest, the principal and the commercial agent also develop their own respective individual interests. The principal profits by selling more goods or services, which in turn benefits the commercial agent who earns more commissions. Such financial "rewards" represent the share of each party in the profit generated by the customer base (i.e. the common interest).

During the life of the commercial agency relationship, there is a perfect balance between the parties who share equally the profits generated by the common interest. However, this balance can only exist as long as the parties maintain their relationship. The mandate is therefore the instrument which allows the parties to develop and benefit from the common interest.

Any act, by either party, which jeopardises the existence of the mandate, threatens the common interest and therefore threatens the balance. Unilateral termination by the principal constitutes such an act and this is where the weakness of the commercial agents' position becomes apparent. Because commercial agents do not act for themselves, French law recognises the risk that once the customer base (i.e. the common interest) is established or developed, the principal will terminate the relationship in order to bypass having to pay commissions to the commercial agent and will start selling directly to the customers. Such an act of the principal is *a priori* unjustified, since it destroys the balance between the parties since the principal alone can benefit from the customer base that both parties worked to create, develop, or maintain. On termination, the commercial agent is deprived of the commissions on the sales, which represent his share of the benefits of the common interest. His share of the notionally jointly-owned goodwill has been taken from him, causing him a loss, for which he must be compensated. Compensation is therefore due, as the commercial agent's right, as an attempt to re-establish the lost balance and to compensate him for the loss of his share in the customer base, (the common interest); i.e. the loss of the commissions on the sales.

This is where the peculiar nature of the French notion of compensation is most clear. By defining the commercial agency relationship as entered into for the common interest of both parties and by awarding the commercial agent compensation on termination for the loss of his share in the profit generated by the common interest, compensation under French law has a *quasi-proprietary nature*.[50]

This quasi-proprietary nature of the compensation option is clearly present in the Directive/Agency Regulations. No compensation is due when the commercial agent assigns the commercial agency to a third party, with the consent of the principal.[51] The assumption in such a case is that the commercial agent will be paid by his successor, the purchaser of his right to act as commercial agent. If the principal had to pay compensation

49. Regulations 3 and 4. For more details as to what it precisely entails for each party, see Chapter 3, section 3.4.1.

50. The emphasis that it has a quasi-proprietary nature is crucial, as it shows that the customer base does not belong to the commercial agent but to the principal.

51. Article 18(c) of the Directive, Regulation 18(c).

as well, the commercial agent would be paid twice over, and when the commercial agent dies, compensation will be due to his estate.[52]

The peculiarity of the loss that the commercial agent suffers on termination, which is now accepted by the English[53] and Scottish courts[54] alike, explains why compensation for unjustified termination is the rule and its exclusion the exception.[55] The Directive/Agency Regulations follow the same pattern.[56] For the purposes of consistency, we will therefore also adopt it in order to understand its scope of application.

Under French law: compensation on termination is the rule

Under the Directive, compensation is due to the commercial agent whenever there is a "termination".[57] Here, again, France has implemented the Directive in such a way as to follow its legal tradition. Where the Directive talks of "termination", the French Commercial Code simply stipulates that compensation is due when the contract "ceases".[58] It is thought that this rather vague expression gives statutory value to the well-established judicial principle that when a fixed-term contract is not renewed, compensation is due.[59] Such an analysis was recently confirmed in a case where the French Supreme Court (the Cour de Cassation) held that "the refusal to renew a fixed-term contract, if not motivated by a serious breach by the commercial agent, gives rise to compensation".[60] On that aspect, French and English laws are similar.[61]

The rule applies very widely since the commercial agent who himself terminates the contract with a just cause to do so, can still claim compensation. Following the Directive, the notion of just cause includes age, infirmity, illness, even death of the commercial agent and also "circumstances attributable to the principal".[62]

Upon the death of the commercial agent, compensation is due to his estate automatically. For age illness and infirmity the right to compensation is not automatic since where the commercial agent wishes to rely on such circumstances to claim compensation, he must establish that as a result of one or other of those matters he cannot reasonably be required to continue his activities. In relation to the age of the commercial agent, the rule therefore seems to mean that it is not age itself, which is a just cause for termination, but the incapacity that age brings. It would therefore appear that unlike employees, commercial agents do not have the right to retire with compensation upon reaching a certain age.

52. Article 17(4) of the Directive, Regulation 17(8).

53. In *Barrett McKenzie* v. *Escada Ltd* [2001] Eu LR 567 at para 13, Bowers J stated that the aim of the compensation option is to compensate the commercial agent "for the loss of a quasi-proprietary right: the loss of an asset to the agent (the agency)".

54. *King* v. *Tunnock* [2000] Eu LR 531.

55. See articles L 134–12 and L 134–13 French Commercial Code. For an English translation, see Appendix 8.

56. Articles 17 and 18 of the Directive, Regulations 17 and 18.

57. *Ibid.*

58. Article L 134–12 al 1 French Commercial Code. For an English translation, see Appendix 5.

59. *Cass Com 21 October 1970 Sté Enema* v. *Etablissements Richard Frères*, JCP 1971, II, 16798. *Cass Com 9 October 1990, SA De Dietrich* v. *Sté de droit espagnol,* JCP E 1991, 211.

60. *Cass Com 28 May 2002 Sté Laboratoire Arkopharma et a* v. *Mlle Gravier*, Journagence, special issue to Les Annonces de la Seine, No 61 of 14 October 2002, pp 2–3.

61. See *Whitehead* v. *Jenks and Cattell Engineering Ltd* [1999] Eu LR 827 where it was held that the expiry of a fixed-term contract amounts to a termination for the purpose of the Agency Regulations. For details, see Chapter 5, section 5.2.1.1.2, especially fn 17 and associated text.

62. Article L 134–13 al 1–2 Commercial Code.

Even though this seems the logical conclusion when looking at the drafting of the French Commercial Code, the situation is currently uncertain in France because of a disagreement between two appeal courts as to the interpretation of the implementing legislation.[63]

Termination for "circumstances attributable to the principal", i.e. a serious breach

The more complicated "just cause" for termination by the commercial agent himself is when he does so because of "circumstances attributable to the principal".[64] This expression mirrors that of the Directive,[65] but is nevertheless in line with the French legal tradition since it refers to a breach of the principal, which has to be sufficiently serious to be a just cause for termination.[66] The burden of proof of the severity of the breach is on the commercial agent and the French courts will assess the severity by reference to the common interest. Interestingly, the position in English law is more protective of commercial agents, following *King* v. *Tunnock* where it was held that "circumstances attributable to the principal" does not have to be a breach (see Chapter 5).

Under French law, only a breach by the principal which negates the common interest will be regarded as sufficiently serious to allow the commercial agent to terminate the relationship with a just cause. In this context, the notion of common interest is that which governs the contract as a whole and, following a slight departure from the Directive, is akin to good faith and loyalty.[67] In the light of the common interest, one of the main obligations of the principal is to allow the commercial agent to perform his obligations.[68] Any breach of such an obligation will be regarded as serious and will therefore give the commercial agent a just cause to terminate the contract and claim compensation. The case of *Chevassus Marche* v. *Groupe Danone*[69] illustrates the point very well. In this instance, the commercial agent who was based in the Indian Ocean, had been working as the exclusive agent of the principal since 1987. In spite of the exclusivity clause, clients from the commercial agent were able to get the goods at a discount of 30 per cent by ordering directly from the manufacturer in France. The commercial agent mentioned this to the principal and asked him permission to grant similar discounts to his customers so as to be able to compete on an equal footing. The principal refused, stating that the commercial agency contract did not give him the authority to do so. The commercial agent terminated the contract for "circumstances attributable to the principal" and claimed compensation.

63. For the Versailles Court of Appeal, reaching the age of 65 gives an automatic right for the commercial agent to retire (*CA Versailles 20 January 2000 Ferreira* v. *SA Delphine*, RJDA 2000, p 863). For the Rouen Court of Appeal however, it was held that that the commercial agent must establish an inability to reasonably continue his activities (*CA Rouen, 9 March 2000*, RJDA 2000, No 12, No 1085). The latter position was recently adopted by the Paris Court of Appeal in two cases heard on the same day (*CA Paris, 12 February 2004 Sté STEP Cornillon* v. *Patrigeon*, and *Sté Exbanor* v. *Patrigeon*, D 2004, AJ 696). It is to be hoped that the Cour de Cassation will settle the difference of opinion in order to provide us with a clear position.

64. Article L 134–13 al 1 § 2 French Commercial Code. For an English translation, see Appendix.

65. Article 18(b).

66. Under the 1958 decree, compensation was due whenever termination by the principal was unjustified. The French courts extended the scope of application of compensation by granting compensation when the commercial agent himself had been forced to terminate because of the principal's conduct. This was referred to as covert termination or *résiliation détournée* by Leloup, See JM Leloup, *Les agents commerciaux, statuts juridiques, stratégies professionnelles* (5th edn, 2001), p 189.

67. Where the Directive stipulates that the parties owe each other a reciprocal duty of good faith (articles 3–4), article L 134–4 al 1 French Commercial Code stipulates that the commercial agency contract is entered into for the common interest of the parties.

68. Article L 134–4 al 3 French Commercial Code. For an English translation, see appendix

69. *Cass Com 24 November 1998,* Bull Civ 1998, IV, 232.

The French Cour de Cassation allowed his claim on the ground that by not reacting to the warnings of the commercial agent, the principal had failed to give the commercial agent the means to perform his mandate.

In the same vein, the principal's failure to pass relevant information to the commercial agent[70] or the principal's failure to pay the commercial agent his due commission[71] are also regarded as serious breaches because such failures prevent the commercial agent from performing his mandate. The French and English courts[72] seem to agree on that latter point.

However, when the failure to pay the due commission is motivated by real economic reasons, the commercial agent will not be entitled to terminate and claim compensation as illustrated by the case of *SARL Orcade* v. *SA SMAC*.[73] In this instance, following a serious decrease in his turnover, the principal failed to pay the commissions to the commercial agent. The latter used this failure to terminate the contract "for circumstances attributable to the principal" and claimed compensation. The Paris Court of Appeal however rejected the plea on the ground that, although the failure to pay the commission amounted to a breach of contract, it was motivated by the economic environment surrounding the relationship.

When the principal acts in a disloyal manner, this will also be regarded as a serious breach. This is logical since the principal who acts in a disloyal manner does not act in the common interest any more. If the principal, in breach of an exclusivity clause, appoints another commercial agent on the same territory, he will be regarded as being disloyal.[74]

It will also be regarded as a serious breach when the principal unilaterally amends certain elements in the contract that are crucial for the performance, and where this amendment destroys the equilibrium of the contract. Such an approach seems to be reasonably similar to the UK approach to breach in *Hong Kong Fir Shipping Co Ltd* v. *Kawasaki Kishen Kaisha Ltd*.[75]

A unilateral modification of commission will be regarded as a serious breach as the case of *Sté Magne* v. *Sté Azurel Equipements*[76] illustrates. In this instance, the commercial agent was entitled to a commission rate as high as 40 per cent with his best customer. The principal started to give constant significant discount on its sales prices to this very customer, which resulted in a drop of roughly 20 per cent in the commission due to the commercial agent. The commercial agent then terminated the contract for "circumstances attributable to the principal" and claimed compensation. The Cour de Cassation held that the behaviour of the principal amounted to a serious breach since it destroyed the equilibrium of the contract. Similarly, a unilateral modification of the territory by the principal will also be regarded as a serious breach, allowing the commercial agent to terminate and

70. *CA Paris, 12 July 1977, Doris-Girod* v. *Documenjou*, cited in JM Leloup, *Les agents commerciaux, statuts juridiques, stratégies professionnelles* (4th edn, 1998), p 185, note 25.

71. *Cass Com 9 January 2001,* jurisdata 98–11.313, Lamy Droit Economique, para 3960, p 1338 where held that "the breach of such an essential obligation compromised the economic balance of the agency".

72. The English courts adopted a similar position in the case of *Bell Electric* v. *Aweco Ltd* [2002] EWHC 872, [2002] Eu LR 443. For discussion, see Chapter 5, section 5.2.1.3.2, especially fnn 99–101 and associated text.

73. *CA Paris 14 February 2002*, Les Petites Affiches 2003, p 37.

74. *CA Lyon 4 February 1994* jurisdata 040489; *CA Paris, 28–31995*, Les Annonces de la Seine 1995, No 39, p 8.

75. [1962] 2 QB 26.

76. *Cass Com 11 June 2002*, Les Petites Affiches 2003, p 36.

claim compensation.[77] Once again however, when such unilateral modifications are justified for economic reasons, or by the commercial agent's own poor performance of his obligations, the principal is not at fault and no compensation is due.[78]

A final example of a serious breach by the principal is when his conduct is incompatible with the quasi-property nature of the commercial agency. This will be the case when the principal abuses his right not to allow the commercial agent to assign the contract.[79] This will also be the case when, upon the death of the commercial agent, the principal refuses the heirs of the commercial agent, their right to present a successor for no valid reason[80] or in breach of a clause allowing the heirs of the commercial agent to step in upon the death of the commercial agent, the principal contacts the clients telling them to deal with him directly[81] or appoints an employed sales representative on the territory of the deceased.[82]

From the above, termination of the commercial agency relationship is strictly regulated because, in the light of the notion of common interest, the commercial agent has a quasi-property right in the relationship. Such an interest must be protected and compensation for unjustified termination is therefore the norm. Following implementation of the Directive and to further protect the interests of the commercial agent, the norm is mandatory[83] and can therefore only be excluded in circumstances and on the conditions stipulated by the Commercial Code. Any effort to circumvent the protection (e.g. by the choice of law clause of a non-EEA country where the place of performance by the commercial agent is within the EEA) will be regarded as unlawful and ineffective.[84]

Under French law: the exclusion of the right to claim compensation is the exception

Following the Directive, French law stipulates that the commercial agent loses the right to claim compensation in four situations, specifically: (1) when termination by the principal is justified by a serious breach by the commercial agent;[85] (2) when the commercial agent himself terminates the relationship with no just cause to do so;[86] (3) when the commercial agent, with the consent of the principal, assigns the commercial agency to a third party;[87] and (4) when the commercial agent fails to claim compensation within one year following termination.[88]

The last two exceptions are reasonably straightforward and do not raise any difficulty. The fact that no compensation is due when the commercial agent assigns the commercial

77. *Cass Com 9 October 1990*, Bull Civ IV, No. 228, Lamy Droit Economique, No 3959, p 1338.

78. See for instance, *CA Paris, 21 June 1989*, D 1989, IR, p 215 where a series of breaches by the commercial agent (a failure to prospect the clients had resulted in a reduction by half of the turnover, the loss of a very important client; invoices were left unpaid etc) had left the principal with no other choice than reducing the territory entrusted to the commercial agent.

79. *Cass Com 23 May 1989*, JCP E 1989, I, 18–761.

80. *Cass Com 20 April 1967 Dame Puvis de Chavannes* v. *SOVACO*, JCP G 1968, II, 15389.

81. *Cass Com 22 May 1967 Sté Plastique Auvergne* v. *Consorts Guillemois*, JCP G 1968, II, 15389.

82. *Cass Com 12 June 1967 CGE* v. *Dame Heurtebize et autres*, JCP G 1968, II, 15389.

83. Article L 134–16 French Commercial Code. See Appendix 5.

84. Case C-381/98 *Ingmar Ltd* v. *Eaton Leonard Technologies Inc* [2001] 1 CMLR 9.

85. Article L 134–13 al 1 French Commercial Code. For an English translation, see Appendix 5.

86. Article L 134–13 al 1 § 2 French Commercial Code.

87. Article L 134–13 al 1 § 3 French Commercial Code.

88. Article L 134–12 al 2 French Commercial Code.

agency is not surprising as it is in direct line with the quasi-proprietary nature of the compensation. It must be emphasised that it is the commercial agent's rights under the commercial agency contract which can be assigned and not the customer base, which still belongs to the principal. As will be seen later, the price that the assignee has to pay to the outgoing commercial agent is usually evaluated to two years' worth of gross commissions.[89] There is therefore a consistency in the manner used by the French courts to calculate compensation.

The French Commercial Code only mentions the ability of the commercial agent to assign the commercial agency contract, but the principal can also do so. Even in this context the notion of common interest is relevant since the principal may do so only with the consent of the commercial agent.[90]

The fact that the commercial agent must bring this claim for compensation within one year of termination may seem rather short. The briefness of the period available is nevertheless generally seen as positive and in line with the common interest, since the reciprocal obligation of loyalty requires the commercial agent to claim his compensation with reasonable dispatch after termination.[91] This however only applies to claims for compensation, and not to claims for unpaid commissions or claims for contractual damages for loss suffered following breach of the required notice period,[92] for instance. In the case of *Sté Prefaest* v. *A. Huret*,[93] the French Cour de Cassation held that the limitation period starts to run when termination becomes effective, i.e. (when the termination is on notice) at the end of the notice period (provided the minimum notice periods under the Directive have been respected) and not when the commercial agent receives the letter giving him notice of termination from the principal. In relation to the manner in which the commercial agent can claim compensation, no formality is required; a simple "lettre recommandée avec accusé de reception" will therefore be sufficient.[94] Such a claim can be made by the commercial agent himself or his counsel.[95] On that aspect, the French rules are, once again, very similar to the English ones.[96]

The commercial agent will also lose the right to claim compensation if he is the one who terminates with no just cause in doing so. We have just seen that the notion of just cause includes death; age, illness and infirmity (provided that the consequence of these or any of them is that the commercial agent cannot reasonably be expected to continue to act, but not otherwise) and "circumstances attributable to the principal".

Termination for serious breach by the commercial agent

To allow the principal to terminate the relationship and avoid paying compensation because of a serious breach of the commercial agency agreement by the commercial

89. *Cass Com 15 July 1969*, *Consorts Grondier* v. *Sassermo*, D 1970, Somm 49.

90. It is argued that assignment by the principal is more frequent than assignment by the commercial agent. See JM Leloup, *Les agents commerciaux, statuts juridiques, stratégies professionnelles* (5th edn, 2001), No 933.

91. JM Leloup *Agent Commercial*, Rep Com Dalloz, 2003, § 84, p 15. Once the request has been made, the 10 year *délai de prescription* remains unchanged.

92. *Ibid.*

93. *Cass Com 11 June 2002*, JCP G 2003, suppl to No 27 of 3 July 2003, p 25.

94. NCPC ag art 651. New Code of Civil Procedure. See legifrance.gouv.fr.

95. *CA Nancy 22 September 1999 Sarl Groh* v. *Borowski*, D 2000, J, 62.

96. *Hackett* v. *Advanced medical Computer Systems Ltd* [1999] CLC 160. See Chapter 5, section 5.3.2.1, fn 211.

agent[97] is perhaps the most interesting (and difficult) exception to the principle that termination of the relationship always gives rise to a right to compensation for the commercial agent as it appears to be the mirror image to the rule allowing the commercial agent to terminate the contract and claim compensation for "circumstances attributable to the principal"[98] i.e. a serious breach of the principal. As seen in Chapter 5, this apparent symmetry of the rules between the commercial agent and the principal which is also present in the Agency Regulations was highlighted by the High Court in the case of *Bell Electric Ltd* v. *Aweco Appliance Systems GmbH & Co KG*[99] where Elias J stated that, Regulations 18(a) and 18(b)(i) were the "reverse of the same coins (. . .)."[100] Elias J added "compensation is payable if the principal terminates in circumstances which are justifiable at common law because of the agent's conduct, but on the other hand, it is payable if the commercial agent terminates in circumstances which are justifiable at common law because of the conduct of the principal".[101] However, as noted in Chapter 5, following *King* v. *Tunnock*, the expression "circumstances attributable to the principal" under Regulation 18(b)(i) allows the commercial agent to terminate even when the conduct of the principal in not a breach at all. The French position is, interestingly, more restrictive.

The fact that a serious breach by the commercial agent will serve as a just cause for the principal to terminate and therefore avoid paying compensation follows the Directive, but is also in line with the French legal tradition.[102] The French Commercial Code does not define what amounts to a serious breach. It is therefore up to the French courts but not (interestingly to an English lawyer) the parties themselves (see below) to define when a breach is sufficiently serious to allow the principal to terminate with "just cause". Similarly to the assessment of the breach by the principal, the severity of the breach by the commercial agent is assessed by the French courts in the light of the common interest; only a breach by the commercial agent, which is against the common interest will be regarded as sufficiently serious to justify termination.

As for the principal, the common interest here is that which defines the contract as a whole and is akin to good faith and loyalty. What amounts to a serious breach was more recently defined by the French Cour de Cassation in the case of *Lenne* v. *Haudebault*[103] as "a breach which jeopardises the common aim of the common interest mandate and which renders impossible the continuation of the contract".[104] This exception seems to be in line with the English notion of repudiation of the contract. Following the definition of

97. Article L 134–13 al § 1 French Commercial Code.

98. Article L 134–13 al § 2 of the French Commercial Code.

99. [2002] EWHC 872, [2002] Eu LR 443.

100. *Ibid*, *per* Justice Elias, para 54.

101. *Ibid*.

102. The 1958 Decree stipulated that compensation on termination was due unless it was justified by a breach by the commercial agent but without specifying the nature of the breach, which would justify termination. The French courts, following suggestions from academic writers (an important source of persuasive support in French litigation) (J Hémard, RTDCom 1959, p 613) decided reasonably early on that "the breach has to be sufficiently serious to justify termination": *CA Paris, 30 January 1965*, JCP 1965, IV, p 73. See also Lamy Droit Economique, para 3969, p 1341.

103. *Cass Com 15 October 2002*, No 00–18.122 in Contrats, Concurrences, Consommation, 2002, No 19, p 12. For the facts, see below.

104. *Cass Com 15 October 2002*, *Lenne* v. *Haudebault* No 00–18.122 in Contrats, Concurrences, Consommation, 2002, No 19, p 12 "la faute grave est celle qui porte atteinte à la finalité commune du mandat d'intérêt commun et rend impossible le maintien du lien contractuel".

a serious breach provided in the above case of *Lenne* v. *Haudebault*,[105] it seems that there are two kinds of serious breaches; breaches of express contractual obligations which are against the common interest and breaches, which are so serious that they render the continuation impossible.

The commercial agent who acts against the common interest: serious breach

On the common interest, the commercial agent must perform his obligations as a good professional.[106] It will therefore be regarded as a serious breach when, following the legitimate refusal by the principal to accept the proposed assignee of the commercial agency, the commercial agent refuses to continue to represent the principal until the end of the notice period.[107] It will equally be regarded as a serious breach when the commercial agent fails to inform the principal of a significant number of orders from clients, when such a failure caused clients to go to competitors, causing a serious loss of business for the principal[108] or when the commercial is in breach of his obligation to look for clients.[109] However, if a breach of the commercial agent is caused by the principal, this cannot be regarded as a serious breach.[110] This seems to be in line with the English doctrine of waiver or estoppel.[111]

An action by the commercial agent which prevents the continuation of the relation: also a serious breach

It will be regarded as a serious breach when the commercial agent verbally and physically assaults a client during an evening organised by the principal for the benefit of clients[112]; when the commercial agent acts for a competing principal without the consent of the first principal[113] or when the commercial agent purports to assign the commercial agency without the consent of the principal.[114] Some argue that when the commercial agent goes bankrupt, this is regarded as a serious breach.[115] However, in the absence of a judicial decision on this issue, the position lacks certainty.

Burden of proof

Following the symmetry of the rules applying to the principal, the burden of proof that the commercial agent committed a serious breach is on the principal. Failure to establish the severity of the breach means that the principal has no just cause to terminate and compensation will consequently be due as the case of *Lenne* v. *Haudebault*[116] illustrates. In

105. *Cass Com 15 October 2002*, No 00–18.122 in Contrats, Concurrences, Consommation, 2002, No 19, p 12.

106. Article L 134–4 al 3 French Commercial Code.

107. *Cass Com 14 March 1995 Malka* v. *Sté Kempel et Leibfried GmbH*.

108. *CA Montpellier 4 February 2003* JCP 2003, Suppl to No 27 of 3 July 2003, p 24.

109. *Cass Com 4 July 2000*, No 98–14.061 cited in Dictionnaire Permanent des Affaires 2003, § 46.

110. *Cass Com 9 February 1971*, JCP 1972 G II 17064 where the principal failed to send the new products list to the commercial agent on time and failed to pay his commissions.

111. GH Treitel, *The Law of Contract* (11th edn, 2003), pp 98–99.

112. *Cass Com 11 February 2003*, No 01–16.484 cited in Lamy Droit Economique 2003, § 3969, p 1341.

113. *CA Rennes 1 April 1998, Sté Lambert* v. *Loiret*, D 1998, IR 115.

114. *Cass Com 14 January 1997 Sté d'exploitation des établissements Hubert "Cave des Franciscains" v Sté Borie-Manoux*, D 1997, IR 33.

115. Lamy Droit Economique 2003, § 3975, p 1342.

116. *Cass Com 15 October 2002*, see fn 103.

this decision, the principal terminated the contract on the ground that the commercial agent had failed to register his commercial agency at the commercial jurisdiction of the place of their domicile as required by law and that such a failure amounted to a serious breach. The Cour de Cassation rejected such an argument and awarded compensation to the commercial agent since termination by the principal was not justified. The principal had failed to establish how the absence of registration could have such a serious impact on their relationship.[117]

Pre-classification of condition as a breach

Because the French legislation implementing the Directive does not define what amounts to a serious breach, one would have thought that it would be possible for the parties to agree in the contract that a certain behaviour of the commercial agent would amount to such a breach, allowing the principal to terminate the contract in a justified manner. In an English law contract, they could certainly do that. This was however rejected in no uncertain terms by the French Cour de Cassation in the case of *Arkopharma* v. *Melle Gravier*.[118] The court held that "in the absence of a legal definition, judges alone will be able to decide whether, on the facts, a serious breach has been committed". As a consequence, "the parties cannot decide that a certain pre-determined behaviour will be a serious breach". In this particular case, the contract stipulated that should the commercial agent not reach the agreed sales target, this would be regarded as a serious breach, allowing the principal to terminate without having to pay compensation which would have been a normal provision in an English law commercial agency agreement. Following the failure of the commercial agent to reach the target, the principal terminated for, he alleged, a just cause, refusing to pay compensation. The commercial agent successfully sued for compensation. The reasoning of this case seems close to that of the English case of *Schuler* v. *Wickman Machine Tool Sales Ltd*.[119]

The outcome of this case is logical in the light of the common interest. It is also logical in the light of the burden of proof: the non-reaching of the sales target, in itself, is not a sufficient reason for the principal to terminate the contract in a justified manner if he cannot establish that the failure to reach the target is due to a breach by the commercial agent. This is consistent case law.[120] If the principal cannot prove that there is a breach at all, then termination is not valid and compensation is due.[121]

When the commercial agent has committed a serious breach however, not only will he have no right to claim compensation but he will also have to pay damages to the principal if his breach causes the latter to suffer a loss.[122]

117. This is in line with the decision of the European Court of justice in Case C–215/97 *Barbara Bellone* v. *Yukohama SpA* [1998] ECR I–2191.

118. *Cass Com 28 May 2002*, RTDCiv 2002, p 833.

119. [1974] AC 235.

120. *CA Versailles 15 September 2000 Bertran* v. *SARL Faber Castel*, Les Petites Affiches 2001, p 12. See very recently, *CA Poitiers 17 February 2004 SA Wesper* v. *Escolle*, unreported, obtained courtesy of Maitre Leloup, avocat in Paris.

121. *T Com Paris, 15 January 2003 Sarl Serp* v. *Sté Navarti Ceramica*, Gazette du Palais 2003, No 308, p 7. In this case, the parties had not written a contract. The obligations of the commercial agents were therefore not precisely defined and the principal was unable to reproach the commercial agent the failure to comply with obligations, which were not clearly defined.

122. This is relying on article 2007 cc. *CA Versailles 26 June 1997 Ste SIOTA* v. *Mme Lecoq*, jurisdata 045912.

6.3.1.2 Calculation of the compensation by the French courts

After this unavoidably lengthy explanation of the French law thinking that lies behind the right to compensation on termination, we move to the actual calcuations.

The "rule of thumb" in French, although only a starting point, is that compensation should be a lump sum equal to two years' gross commission, payable without deduction for the expenses the commercial agent would have had to incur to earn that commission, and without any discount for the cashflow advantage of its being received as a lump sum rather than as a stream of receipts over a period. No reduction is made to take account of possible future eventualities (such as that the principal may cease to trade within two years of the termination, possible downturns in the market generally, the possibility that the commercial agent may continue to gain benefit from the principal's retained customer base by continuing to trade with them on behalf of other principals, etc). There is no expectation that the commercial agent will do anything to mitigate his loss.

Whilst the courts in Scotland (to the extent that there are reported cases, which in fairness are not numerous) have tended to be sympathetic to the French approach to compensation, the courts in England (which to date have been only the lower courts) are very sceptical, regarding the French law "rule of thumb" as providing an unmerited windfall for commercial agents.

Why two years is goss commission for compensation?

The French implementing legislation looks at the commercial agency relationship in quasi-property terms, because it is entered into for the common interest of the parties. The commercial agency contract i.e. the right for the commercial agent to represent the principal, is therefore an asset for the commercial agent since

(a) it is what allows him to obtain his share of the fruits of the common interest, the commissions; and
(b) the commercial agent may assign his rights under the contract to a third party, with the consent of the principal.

On termination, the commercial agent loses such an asset and he must be compensated for such a loss. Long-established practice[123] considers two years' worth of gross commission to be an equitable evaluation of the loss he suffers on termination.

Over the years, the French courts have used two main reasons for evaluating the loss suffered by the commercial agent to two years of gross commission: (1) two years, or so the thinking goes, is the time that it will take the commercial agent to rebuild a customer

123. The source is thought to be article 39(3) of the arrêté of 5 November 1946, D 1946, 453, which regarded two years worth of commission as an equitable amount. See V Wagner *Le nouveau statut de l'agent commercial, etude en droit français, droit européen et droit comparé* Thèse, Universitè Paris I, 1996, p 263. There is some disagreement between French academics as to whether this "practice" has in fact become a custom. As mentioned in *Ingmar Ltd* v. *Eaton Leonard Technologies Inc* [2002] ECC 5, Professor Ferrier stipulates that "this calculation is considered to be simply a practice and not a custom. The courts are therefore very careful to exclude any notion of tariff when calculating the level of compensation". Another author however states "the compensation (. . .) due on termination of the contract is customarily calculated (. . .)" in Rep Dalloz, (1996) para 87.

base similar to the one lost,[124] and (2) two years' gross commission is also seen as the estimated market value of the commercial agency when assigned to another commercial agent, i.e. it is the price that one would expect the incoming commercial agent to pay for the outgoing agent's interests in the intérêt commun.[125]

Two years' worth of commission for compensation, a tariff?

The impression which the English courts seem to have, that French judges award two years of gross commission, as to the amount of compensation, indiscriminately, may find its basis in a few decisions where the French courts have awarded two years' worth of commissions each time the parties could not establish that a higher or lower loss has actually been suffered by the commercial agent.[126] It is also true that the French courts have sometimes awarded this amount simply by treating it as a custom which, following article 1135, of the Code Civil has the force of the law.[127] It is also clear that, when reading the parliamentary debates over the implementing legislation, the intention of the French parliament was that this practice should not be changed following implementation of the Directive.[128]

Interestingly, since the implementation of the Directive, the practice to award two years' worth of gross commission as compensation seems to have come under recent criticism from some academics who think that the requirement for the commercial agent to show that he has suffered a loss is marginalised[129] and that the practice is not representative of the reality of the loss suffered. For instance, the Cour de Cassation awarded two years' worth of commission as compensation where the commercial agency agreement lasted only nine months, following the abrupt termination by the principal.[130]

124. *CA Rouen, 2ème ch, 21 April 1988, Pauwels France & Pauwels International* v. *Chevalier et Compagnie* where the court held that the evaluation to two years was justified since the effect of the termination was to prevent the commercial agent from receiving the financial benefits of his efforts spent to find clients for the principal. In *T Com Roubaix-Tourcoings, 3 October 1990*, the tribunal held that the compensation of two years of gross commission covered the investment of the commercial agent in creating a clientele for the principal. See JM Leloup, "Agents commerciaux, statuts juridiques, stratégies professionnelles" (5th edn, 2001), p 205. In *Cass Com 9 January 2001 SARL BGC Vinocor France* v. *Merlet*, Journagence, suppl to Les Annonces de la Seine, No 75 of 12 November 2001, pp 2–3, the courts used the expression "loss of the portion of the market".

125. *CA Amiens 19 December 2000 Schwartz* v. *Société Max Perles & Cie*, Journagence, special issue to Les Annonces de la Seine of 30 July 2001. More recently, see also the following three cases (unreported, obtained courtesy of Maitre Leloup, avocat in Paris): *T Com Paris, 26 April 2004, SARL Eximcom* v. *SA Parfums Lolita Lempicka*, where the court awarded two years worth of commission as compensation on the ground that termination caused the commercial agent to lose the possibility of assigning the commercial agency contract. A similar basis was adopted in *CA Paris 25 February 2004 SARL ABS Agence Baert Souillart* v. *Sté LCFH Lactalis*. The loss of the value of the commercial agency contract was also a major factor taken into consideration in *T Com Paris 8 December 2003 Kopp* v. *EURL GK Promotion*.

126. *Cass Com 28 November 1995*, Les Annonces de la Seine, Suppl to No 37 of 26 May 1997; *CA Bordeaux 24 March 1999*, Dictionnaire Permanent des Affaires 2003, § 50.

127. *Cass Com 14 October 1997 Sté Vogelsang* v. *Lacauste*, Journagence, suppl to Les Annonces de la Seine, No 75 of 12 November 2001, p 7. This decision was still under the 1958 decree. For a decision under the implementing legislation implementing the Directive, see *CA Nancy 22 September 1999*, D 2000, AJ 62.

128. Debates in the National Assembly, report of Bouquet, National Assemblies, Official Journal of 23 May 1991, p 2244.

129. Especially Fournier who says that "the situation of the commercial agent whose contract ends is abusively lucrative and enviable". F Fournier, *L'agence commerciale*, (1998), para 498, p 271. See also *Cass Com 24 March 1988* cited in D 2003 Somm 1910, where a liquidated damage clause, which awards a level of compensation equal or higher than the damage suffered, was found to be acceptable. However, the case does not seem to have been followed.

130. *CA Nancy 22 September 1999 Groh* v. *Borowski*, les Petites Affiches 2000, p 16.

It seems that the Cour de Cassation awarded such compensation in order to punish the principal for terminating so abruptly and so quickly the relationship. This is not a valid reason because it is not based on the loss that the commercial agent has suffered. As such the decision was criticised.[131] As noted, then, there is a body of respectable legal opinion in France which regards the two years' gross commission "rule of thumb" as unfairly generous to commercial agents.

The French practice of awarding two years of gross commission is nevertheless, so well established that a principal will sometimes require a potential commercial agent to pay him a pre-estimate of two years' worth of commission for the right to represent him, a sort of *droit d'entrée*. If the commercial agent cannot pay, it is apparently not unusual for the principal to lend him the required amount. Although thought to be rare and certainly not widely publicised, such practices do exist.[132] Some say that this is precisely because the principal anticipates that he will have to pay two years' worth of commission on termination.[133]

With the practice of commercial agencies being seen as marketable businesses in their own right, changing hands from one commercial agent to another (which is not a feature of commercial life in the UK) and two years' gross commission being seen by the French courts as the typical market price for such a business, it is easy to see how the idea of two years' gross commission as the benchmark for the compensation amount could become entrenched. The further practice of principals taking *droits d'entrée* of that amount in anticipation of having to pay it (or some similar sum) back to the commercial agent on termination (whenever that happens) seems only to add to the importance of the two-year figure in French thinking. After all, if the commercial agent has had to pay out the equivalent of two years' gross commission to become commercial agent to this principal in the first place (whether the previous commercial agent (if he bought that person's business) or to the principal by way, almost, of a returnable deposit), it is not unfair that he should receive back some similar sum when the relationship ends. Seen in the context of this chicken-and-egg process, the assumption that the equivalent of two years' gross commission as compensation should be the starting point, or even the default option, makes some sense. In the UK, on the other hand, where both the sale and purchase of commercial agencies as businesses and the taking by the principal of, in effect, a returnable deposit would seem very odd indeed, it is not surprising that the assumption that the equivalent of two years' gross commission is the right figure should seem to be an entirely unmerited windfall for the commercial agent. We think that a lot of misunderstanding in the UK could have been avoided if these crucial background features of French practice had been understood.

As a result of this increasing commercial pressure against the judicial practice of awarding two years of gross commission as the compensation award or termination, the French courts have more recently had to defend the accuracy of that award and prove that it is not applied as a tariff. The reaction by the French courts has taken the following forms.

First, the French courts themselves say that to award two years' worth of commission indiscriminately would be unlawful, since compensation cannot be higher than the loss

131. D 1999, AJ 62.

132. P Crahay *Les contrats internationaux d'agents et de concession de vente* (1991), § 200, p 116. Y Guyon *Droit des affaires* Tome 1, Droit commercial et des sociétés, (11th edn, 2001), § 813, p 870.

133. Revue Fiduciaire 2000, p 57.

suffered.[134] In fact, the French Cour de Cassation reiterated this recently, when it quashed a decision of a regional Court of Appeal after it had awarded two years of commission as compensation because it was customary to do so, rather than by looking at the facts.[135] The Cour de Cassation stated that compensation must be evaluated in relation to the real loss suffered in the actual case and not by reference to a custom. The Cour de Cassation will therefore check that an award of two years' worth of commission is an accurate representation of the loss suffered by the commercial agent in each case at hand. As a consequence, the French courts cannot simply refer to the custom but must look at the facts and see whether awarding two years' worth of commission covers the reality of the loss suffered.[136]

Secondly, the parties themselves cannot agree beforehand the amount of the compensation due through a liquidated damage clause or other means. This is because the loss can only be assessed when it occurs, at the moment of termination as the case of *Le Guilliec* v. *Sté Olivo*[137] illustrates. In this instance, the commercial agent was entitled to a commission of 4 per cent. The contract gave details as to how the percentage was calculated: 3.5 per cent for the remuneration of the commercial agent and 0.5 per cent by way of a payment in advance of the compensation to which the commercial agent would become entitled on termination of the agreement so that the principal would not have to pay anything on termination since the commercial agent would have received it all during the contract. The contract was terminated and, in spite of the agreement, the commercial agent claimed for compensation as termination was not justified. The French Cour de Cassation accepted his claim on the ground that to include in the remuneration, a proportion for compensation amounted to a tariff, which did not truly represent the amount of the damage suffered.

Thirdly, although two years' worth of gross commission is undeniably the most common award, it is not compulsory. The French courts will award less than two years when the principal proves that two years' worth of gross commission does not represent the loss to the commercial agent. Such will usually be the case when the relationship has lasted less than two years. For instance, only one year of commission was awarded as compensation for a commercial agency relationship which had lasted 18 months.[138] However, the reverse is also true and if the commercial agent proves that the loss suffered is greater than two years' worth of gross commission, such an amount will be awarded.[139] When the contract has a fixed-term, the courts tend to only give as compensation the gross commissions due for the time that was left for the contract to run.[140] However, in the recent decision of *International Paper* v. *Sté Labro Guidetti Inc*[141] it was held by the Cour de Cassation that when a principal terminates a fixed-term contract before the end of the term, the commercial agent can claim compensation for the loss of the share in the

134. *CA Paris 20 January 1995 de la Celle* v. *Sapaic*, D 1995, Somm p 52.

135. *Cass Com 28 May 2002, Sté Laboratoires Arkopharma et a* v. *Mlle Gravier*, JCP E 2002, I 1842, pp 2063–2067.

136. For examples of attacks against decisions on the ground that the courts were in breach of article 5 cc and 455 NCPC, see *Cass Com 17 July 2001*, No 99–11.852; *CA Poitiers 5 June 2002 ACIR Ouest* v. *Sté AEIB, T Com Nancy 10 June 2002* all cited in Dictionnaire Permanent des Affaires 2003, § 86.

137. *Cass Com 17 June 2003*, RTDCom 2004, p 149.

138. *CA Rouen 18 October 1990*, RJDA 1991, No 21.

139. Three years of gross commission was awarded in *CA Paris, 5 July 1975* Les Petites Affiches 1975, No 146, p 3 and also in *T Com Nanterre, 8 November 1991*, Les Annonces de la Seine, 1991, p 2.

140. *Cass 20 March 1972*, JCP 1973, II, 17297.

141. *Cass Com 23 April 2003,* D 2003, J 2883.

common interest and the loss of the commissions that the commercial agent would have been able to get had the contract continued to its term. Some have welcomed the decision stating that it is logical since it makes no difference when the fixed-term contract is not renewed an when it is ended before its due term.[142] Others have criticised it for mixing things.[143]

Criteria used by french courts to calculate the damage suffered

The main criterion for evaluating the loss the commercial agent suffers on termination is the loss of commissions. Using commissions as a valuation of the loss suffered is the most reliable element that the French courts have consistently used, and still do nowadays.[144] The award is calculated on all commissions due, and not merely commissions paid, over the last two years of the relationship, provided that such commissions are representative of the activities of the commercial agency. If so, they are simply added up. If the last two years are not truly representative of the activities of the commercial agent, then the commissions of the last three years are taken into consideration. For some, this is the evidence that compensation cannot be regarded as a tariff, since it is based on commissions that the commercial agent actually received.[145]

Compensation is calculated on *all* commissions earned on transactions entered into with clients, regardless of the origin of the customer base, whether the clients were existing or new ones.[146] French law therefore does not look at the financial benefit to the principal. This is a difference with the German system of indemnity. (See below, section 6.4).

Even though the loss of commission is the most reliable criterion for the calculation of the compensation, because compensation must reflect the reality of the loss suffered, other criteria are also taken into consideration, for instance, the costs incurred by the commercial agent at and as a result of termination. As a result, if the commercial agent has employees,[147] the cost of redundancy will be taken into consideration in the calculation of the compensation. Another criterion is to take into account the other kinds of remuneration earned by the commercial agent.[148] As a result, when the commission rate includes the remuneration for the transactions but also other criteria such as remuneration for collecting money or storing the goods[149] for the principal, they will be counted. A further criterion is the duration of the commercial agency relationship: the longer the commercial

142. E Chevrier, *Rupture anticipée d'un CDD d'agent commercial et cumul d'indemnité*, D 2003, Somm 162.

143. D Ferrier *L'indemnisation de l'agent commercial au terme du contrat*, D 2003, J 2883.

144. *Cass Com 29 February 2000 Snc Sélection Immobilière* v. *Mme Fanals*, No. 97–13.220, JM Leloup *Les agents commerciaux, statuts juridiques, stratégies professionnelles*, (5th edn, 2001).

145. JM Leloup, *Agent Commercial*, Rep Comm Dalloz, (2003), para 88, p 15.

146. *CA Agen 13 January 1997*, Les Annonces de la Seine 1997, Special Issue to No 37, *Cass Com 14 March 1995* No 515 and *CA Nancy 25 January 1991*, jurisdata 041572.

147. *Cass Com 14 October 1974 SA Linotype Nebiolo* v. *Veuve Facchini*. In this case, the commercial agent had employed a sales representative. When the commercial agency was terminated, she had to dismiss the sales representative, which cost her F 86.000 for the *indemnité de clientele* he was entitled to claim. The court held that this could be taken into consideration when calculating her compensation to two years worth of commission.

148. *Cass Com 22 December 1969*, Bull Civ IV, No. 395, p 365. *CA Paris 5 July 1975*, les Petites Affiches 24 December 1975, p 3.

149. *Cass Com 1 December 1981 Laiterie Coopérative de la Mélusine* v. *Sté Duponchelle et Cie*, Bull Civ 1981, No. 418. In this case, the commission of the commercial agent was of 4 per cent, calculated as follows: 3 per cent for remuneration and 1 per cent for the stock and delivery obligations of the commercial agent. The compensation was calculated on 4 per cent and not 3 per cent as the principal wanted.

agency is, the higher the damage suffered is.[150] The Cour de Cassation will also look at whether the commercial agent is bound by a non-competition clause or not.[151]

Compensation is calculated on gross commission because "compensation is not based on the income of the commercial agent but on the value of the commercial mandate, which is based on the total of the commissions".[152] For some, this is fair as the principal generally does not reimburse expenses to the commercial agent.[153] This well-established principle,[154] which was more recently reiterated[155] is in fact an essential distinction between commercial agents and employed sales representatives.[156]

Compensation is calculated at the stage of termination itself. There is therefore no duty to mitigate imposed on the commercial agent. As a result, the fact that he works for other principals will not lower the amount of compensation he receives.[157] Similarly, the compensation will not be affected if the principal ceases to trade or becomes insolvent after termination.[158]

6.3.2 Calculation of the compensation option by the English and Scottish courts: a good evolution?

Because of the manner in which the Agency Regulations have implemented the Directive, most cases involve the compensation option.[159] After an uncertain start, the assumption that compensation is merely an equivalent to damages for breach of contract seems more or less fully accepted as being erroneous, and the English and Scottish courts now appear to have grown more confident in applying this part of the Agency Regulations. Interestingly, with the accrued confidence of the courts also comes a desire to shake off and disregard the French roots of the compensation option. This is so especially from the judiciary in England and Wales, who perceive the award of two years' worth of gross commissions by way of compensation to be an unwarranted "excessive windfall"[160] for the commercial agent.

As mentioned earlier, moving away from the French origin of the option is not, *per se*, a problem since there is no obligation to follow what the French courts are doing.[161] However, there is, as yet, no clear alternative established method of calculation and some courts seem drawn to apply well-known common law principles. The confusion between

150. *CA Aix 2 May 1975 SA Laboratoire Laphal* v. *SARL Auvergne Pharma*, D 1976, J 344.

151. The existence of a non-competition clause means that the award will be higher. See *CA Paris 5 July 1975*, Les Petites Affiches No. 146 of 24 December 1975, p 3 where three years' worth of commission were awarded to the commercial agent.

152. *CA Montpellier 18 April 1985 Fromageries Paul Renard* v. *Rogalle*, unreported, cited in JM Leloup, *Agents Commerciaux, Statuts Juridiques, Stratégies Professionnelles*, (5th edn, 2001), p 220.

153. JM Leloup, *Agent Commercial*, Rep Comm Dalloz, (2003), para 88, p 15.

154. *CA Riom 8 October 1976 Sté Agemaco* v. *Sté Pomel et Eté nouvelle des Boisseaux Français*, JCP 1978, II, 18940.

155. *Cass Com 27 October 1998 Cave Coopérative Vinicole de Rauzan* v. *Beck*, les Petites Affiches 2000, p 7.

156. *CA Bordeaux 12 February 1969*, Gaz Pal 1969, II, p 288; *CA Riom 8 October 1976*, Cah Dr Entr 1977, No. 3, p 16.

157. In *CA Grenoble 5 May 1988 Huileries Réunies* v. *Coin*, the court clearly stated that "compensation is due on termination regardless of whether the commercial agent has other commercial agencies."

158. In case of insolvency of the principal, the commercial agent is regarded as an ordinary creditor.

159. Compensation is the default position pursuant to Regulation 17(2).

160. *Ingmar GB Ltd* v. *Eaton Leonard Inc* [2002] ECC 5, *per* Morland, at para 52.

161. See generally, section 6.2 above for details.

the two sets of rules stems from the lack of clarity in the Directive. The two sets of circumstances under which damage is deemed to occur, as cited under article 17(3) of the Directive, do not accurately reflect the aim of the compensatory award as applied in France. As previously mentioned, in its article 17(3), the Directive broadly reproduces the British and the French approaches which, as such, are difficult to reconcile with each other.[162]

Such confusion is undoubtedly a problem but it must not be over-emphasised, since case law in this country has evolved considerably since the Agency Regulations first came into effect.[163] It is therefore necessary to review how the English and Scottish courts apply compensation before reviewing the criteria upon which such courts could evaluate the compensation option in a more "UK-based manner" as requested by Bowers J in the case of *Barrett McKenzie* v. *Escada*.[164]

6.3.2.1 The case law on compensation

It is possible to divide the growing body of law in this area in three categories: (1) the cases where the Scottish courts calculate compensation by reference to French law; (2) the cases where the English courts seem to confuse compensation with more traditional common law principles; and (3) the cases where the English courts reject the French method of calculation but, aware of the specificity of the damage suffered by the commercial agent on termination, try to find suitable alternative methods of calculation of the compensation.

Cases where the Scottish courts follow the French method of calculation

The first Scottish case to consider the issue of compensation was that of *Roy* v. *MR Pearlman Ltd*.[165] In this instance, Hamilton LJ, relying on the French origin of the compensation option, agreed on the necessity to "have direct regard to sources of foreign law"[166] but nevertheless added that French law was not "being invoked because an issue in this court *requires* to be determined in accordance with French law".[167] For Hamilton LJ, looking at French law was only done "in the nature of a comparative law exercise".[168]

In the case of *King* v. *Tunnock*,[169] Lord Caplan had to consider whether the commercial agent was entitled to receive compensation after the principal shut down the part of business that the commercial agent represented. Lord Caplan said that he was so entitled and awarded a compensatory award of £27,144. Such a sum which represented two years' worth of commission was awarded after Lord Caplan considered French law in detail. However, to remember this case purely for awarding the commercial agent two years'

162. House of Lords Select Committee Report on European Legislation 1977.

163. We are now far from cases such as *Skingsley* v. *KJC Carpets Ltd*, Bristol County Court, 4 June 1996, (unreported) where, for a claim of compensation, the court looked at German law indemnity alternative for guidance on the calculation. An appeal was launched but was abandoned after an out of court settlement.

164. [2001] Eu LR 567, para. 21.

165. [1999] 2 CMLR 1155.

166. *Ibid*, at para 39.

167. *Ibid*, emphasis added.

168. *Ibid*.

169. [2000] Eu LR 531.

worth of commission is undoubtedly a rather superficial interpretation of the decision.[170] The main positive aspect of this case is that Lord Caplan interpreted Regulation 17(7) in the light of the protective stance of the Directive by stating that it does not restrict or qualify the right to compensation under Regulation 17(6).

In fact, as we have seen earlier, the commercial agent is entitled to claim compensation for the "damage" he suffers following termination, pursuant to Regulation 17(6). Following the near-verbatim implementation of the Directive, Regulation 17(7) stipulates that a "damage" is deemed to occur in certain circumstances, namely when termination deprives the commercial agent of the commission which (a) proper performance of the commercial agency contract would have procured him whilst providing the principal with substantial benefits, or (b) has not enabled the commercial agent to amortise the costs and expenses that he has incurred in the performance of the agency contract on the advice of the principal.[171]

Counsel for the principal in *King* v. *Tunnock* tried to argue that no compensation was due to the commercial agent since the principal did not and would not receive "substantial benefits" from the commercial agent's efforts as per Regulation 17(7)(a) since he had closed down that part of the business. Lord Caplan, applying the protective stance of the Directive, stated that Regulation 17(7) does not "set out the exclusive circumstances giving rise to compensation"[172] and therefore is not meant to be an exclusive list of events where the damage occurs nor does it mean that the commercial agent has to demonstrate that he has suffered a damage in such specific situations.

Then, accepting the quasi-proprietary aspect of the compensatory award,[173] Lord Caplan awarded two years' worth of commission as compensation to the commercial agent. Even though Lord Caplan spent a certain amount of time looking at French law and awarded two years' worth of gross commissions, that too much importance should not be attached to it. As remarked, as an appeal court, the Court of Session had limited factual evidence available and the sum of £27,144 which amounted to two years of commission had been calculated by the lower court.[174] In fact, recognising that the circumstances in question were very specific to the case at hand, Lord Caplan also added that "there may well be cases where compensation for the loss for the damage to an agent caused by termination of an agency contract will raise narrower issues".[175] After careful consideration of the specific circumstances of the case at hand, especially the fact that the commercial agent had been working for the principal since 1962 and his father before that, Lord Caplan concluded that "it is likely that the pursuer's business enjoyed considerable goodwill".[176] As a result, Lord Caplan awarded two years of commission as compensation on the ground that "it is difficult to believe that in the present case such compensation could be other than reasonable".[177]

170. SC Smith, *Death of the salesman* SLT 2000, 36, pp 289–295, at p 289.
171. Regulation 17(7).
172. [2000] Eu LR 531, at para 42.
173. Lord Caplan stated that "the French courts will regard compensation as being the reparation for the loss of the value of the terminated agency agreement". [2000] Eu LR 531, at para 44.
174. R Christou, *International Agency Distribution and Licensing Agreements,* (2003), para 3–181, p 136.
175. [2000] Eu LR 531, at para 50.
176. *Ibid*, at para 50.
177. *Ibid*.

It is therefore more accurate to say that Lord Caplan did not blindly follow the French practice but used it as a "cross-check more than a guideline".[178]

Cases where the English courts seem to confuse compensation with common law damages for breach of contract

Such cases are the most problematic ones, since they show that the English courts seem to misunderstand the aim of the compensatory award. This is most obvious with the cases of *Duffen* v. *FraBo SpA (No. 2)*[179] and *Bell Electric* v. *Aweco Appliance Systems GmbH.*[180] These two decisions share certain similarities and must therefore be reviewed together.

It will be recalled that, in the case of *Duffen v FraBo SpA (No. 2)*,[181] the claimant was appointed in August 1994 to act in the UK as the exclusive commercial agent for an Italian manufacturer. The contract was expected to last for three years but, in December 1996, following the non-payment of commissions, the commercial agent terminated the relationship, relying on a contractual clause allowing him to do so. He then proceeded to claim a sum of £27,115.81 for unpaid commissions and still relying on the contract, a payment of £100,000 under a liquidated damages clause in the contract. At first instance, Popplewell J considered that that clause was not penal and would not be invalidated by Regulation 19.

The Court of Appeal allowed the claim for unpaid commission, but held the liquidated damage clause unenforceable on the grounds that it was not a genuine pre-estimate of the loss suffered. This part of the decision does not raise any problem in relation to the Agency Regulations and is in line with the relevant contract law case law on liquidated damages clauses and penalty clauses.[182] More importantly for the purpose of the Agency Regulations, the Court of Appeal also said that the presence of the liquidated damages clause did not exclude the application of the compensation rule pursuant to Regulation 17, which is in line with the mandatory nature of the termination payments.

The case was then sent to the Central London County Court[183] where the claimant sought to recover the unpaid commission, a retainer and, relying on the Agency Regulations, compensation for the damage suffered. Somewhat strangely, the claimant was not making separate claims for damages for breach of contract and for compensation under the Agency Regulations, but wanted to know whether the Agency Regulations could be used to "augment his common law entitlement to damages". Hallgarten J, confirming the position of the Court of Appeal, said this was possible, and proceeded to look at the relevant regulation very much as if it were a question of damages for contract.

A similar position was more recently adopted in the case of *Bell Electric* v. *Aweco Appliance & Co GmbH.*[184] In this instance, the claimant had been acting continuously for the principal since 1988, selling components to manufacturers of large domestic electrical appliances. The relationship had been subject to a number of arrangements that varied over time. The dispute, however, related to an agreement entered into on 10 August 1999,

178. R Christou, op cit, para 3–185, p 137.
179. *(No. 1)* [1999] ECC 58; *(No. 2)* [2000] Lloyd's Rep 182.
180. [2002] EWHC 872, [2002] Eu LR 443.
181. *(No. 1)* [1998] 17 Tr LR 460.
182. *Dunlop Pneumatic Tyre Company Ltd* v. *New Garage and Motor Co Ltd* [1915] AC 79 followed by the Privy Council in *Phillips (Hong Kong) Ltd* v. *Attorney-General of Hong Kong* (1993) 61 BLR 49.
183. *(No. 2)* [2000] 1 Lloyd's Rep 180.
184. [2002] EWHC 872, [2002] Eu LR 443.

which was to last for at least three years. The contract could be automatically renewed subject to a notice period of six months. Following a continuous failure of the principal to pay the due commission, the commercial agent terminated the relationship pursuant to Regulation 18(b)(i) for "circumstances attributable to the principal", and claimed damages for breach of contract and compensation under the Agency Regulations. The Honourable Mr Justice Elias stated that, in this particular case, the claim under the Agency Regulations would not add anything to the common law action.[185]

The common feature of these two cases is that the parties were linked by a fixed-term contract. In both cases, following a repudiatory breach by the principal, the commercial agent terminated the contract and claimed compensation. In both cases, the claim relied first on the common law rules for breach of contract and second on the Agency Regulations. Under the common law principles, the two claimants were entitled to claim the commissions they would have received until the expiry of their respective contracts. This therefore raises the question whether, in such circumstances, it is actually better for the commercial agent to claim damages for breach of contract rather than termination payments under the Agency Regulations.

As it happens, in *Duffen* v. *FraBo SpA (No. 2)*,[186] it is true that the claim for compensation under the Agency Regulations would not have been very substantial. The relationship was not financially successful since the commissions did not even cover the expenses of the commercial agent. The commercial agent's loss was not substantial and in this particular case, it is therefore possible to say that it was better for the commercial agent to claim damages for breach at common law for the amount of commissions he should have been entitled to receive had the contract continued rather than claiming compensation under the Agency Regulations.

However, the manner in which Hallgarten J decided so is, with respect, incorrect, Hallgarten J looked at Regulation 17(7)(a) and, applying very closely the two criteria defined in this regulation, he decided that compensation would have been nominal since the "claimant did not introduce one new customer to the defendant and was less than successful in restoring the existing customers".[187] This is incorrect, since, contrary to the indemnity alternative, where the emphasis is on the improvement in the goodwill generated by the commercial agent and the lasting benefit of that to the principal, compensation alternative focuses on the loss to the commercial agent. Hallgarten J therefore seems to confuse compensation with indemnity.

In relation to *Bell Electric* v. *Aweco Appliance Systems GmbH*,[188] however, the position is different. The commercial agency relationship had been in existence since 1988 albeit under a succession of different contracts. To calculate the loss to the commercial agent purely by reference to the last contract in this series seems to go against the decision of *Moore* v. *Piretta*[189] where it was held that for the purpose of calculation of termination rights, any prior commercial agency relationship between the parties must be taken into

185. *Ibid*, at para 55.

186. *(No. 1)* [1999] ECC 58; *(No. 2)* [2000] Lloyd's Rep 180.

187. [2000] 1 Lloyd's Rep 180, at p 198.

188. [2002] EWHC 872, [2002] Eu LR 443.

189. [1999] 1 All ER 174. For discussion of this case, see section 6.4.2, especially fnn 316–338 and associated text.

consideration. In this instance, it was therefore not better for the commercial agent to claim damages for breach as opposed to compensation under the Agency Regulations, because damages would only have focussed on the current contract.

In the two cases of *Duffen* v. *FraBo SpA (No. 2)*[190] and *Bell Electric* v. *Aweco Appliance & Co GmbH*,[191] the commercial agents chose to claim under the common law rules and use the Agency Regulations as an alternative claim. The crucial question is therefore whether it is possible as a rule, for commercial agents whose fixed-term contract is terminated before the due date, to choose to claim under the common law rules of contract or compensation under the Agency Regulations and use the latter purely to top up the common law entitlement. We have seen that the right to be compensated or indemnified on termination is mandatory and cannot be excluded to the detriment of the commercial agent.[192] If, as the case of *Duffen* v. *FraBo SpA (No. 2)*[193] shows, claiming damages for breach at common law, is better for the commercial agent, in theory, nothing prevents the commercial agent from doing so. The problem is that to allow so, would really mean that compensation for the loss suffered under the Agency Regulations and compensation for breach at common law are equivalent, which is not the case.

The impact of such cases must not however be overemphasised, especially in the light of the study of later cases in the forthcoming paragraphs.

Cases where the English courts try to evaluate the French-based compensation concept by using more "UK-based" criteria

In the case of *Barrett McKenzie* v. *Escada (UK) Ltd*[194] Bowers J was asked to follow *King* v. *Tunnock*[195] and award two years' worth of commission as compensation. Bowers J clearly understood and accepted that the purpose of the compensation option is different from an entitlement to damages for breach of contract when he stated that "we have to accept, contrary to our common law instincts, that an independent agency (. . .) has a value (. . .) and it is not something which can ever be valued or assessed by using former common law principles".[196] Bowers J also accepted that under French law, "one is valuing the agency and its connections that have been established by the agent at the time or immediately before termination".[197]

However, Bowers J refused to follow the French system and award two years' worth of commission. This refusal appears to be explained by the fact that Bowers J also seems to have misunderstood how the French courts calculate the award of two years of gross commission when he said "it is either the last two years or the average of the last three multiplied by two".[198] Bowers J then said that the choice between the two possibilities

190. *(No. 2)* [2000] 1 Lloyd's Rep 180.
191. [2002] EWHC 872, [2002] Eu LR 443.
192. Regulation 19.
193. *(No. 2)* [2000] 1 Lloyd's Rep 180.
194. [2001] Eu LR 567.
195. [2000] Eu LR 531.
196. [2001] Eu LR 567, para 30.
197. *Ibid*, para 32.
198. *Ibid*, para 21.

was simply a matter for the claimant who "can go for the higher figure".[199] As we have seen earlier in the study of French law, this is not the case at all.[200]

However, a stronger explanation for the rejection of the French system is the perception of Bowers J that the French approach is a "broad brush" one which does not value "the loss of the asset which in fact had ceased to exist".[201] Bowers J therefore called for the need to evaluate the compensation by using criteria which are "sufficiently UK-based and developed".[202]

Such a call was first considered in the case of *Ingmar GB Ltd* v. *Eaton Leonard Inc*.[203] In this instance, the claimant was appointed as an exclusive commercial agent in January 1989. The contract was for the sale of equipment for the aircraft and automotive industries. Following the decision by the principal to restructure the business, the commercial agency was terminated on 1 January 1996. The commercial agent claimed, amongst other things, compensation on termination. In this instance, Morland J considered himself bound by *King* v. *Tunnock*,[204] but added that Lord Caplan did not lay down a principle of law but simply "a guideline that in many cases the two year purchase of average gross commission may be appropriate".[205]

In this instance however, Morland J refused to award two years' worth of commission as he said this would amount to "an excessive windfall to the claimant above the value of the agency on 7 July 1996".[206] Morland J nevertheless awarded £183,600 as compensation, stating that such a sum was "a fairer and more realistic result".[207] Morland J did so by taking into account the fact that the commercial agency had lasted close to eight years, that it was not profitable at the beginning and that "a high degree of engineering and sales expertise" was required for the purpose of "obtaining, nurturing and developing the customer base".[208] Interestingly, Morland J calculated the figure by reference to years 1993, 1994 and 1995 of the relationship. Morland J did not refer to the last year of the contract, 1996, as a basis for compensation as, according to him, the commissions earned during 1996 were not truly representative of the volume of sales. This aspect of the decision is close to what a French court would do.[209] What is puzzling, however, is the fact that Morland J also decided to award three times the salary and pension contribution of the commercial agent's company key sole employee and three times the management fee paid to the parent company.

The need to find "UK-based" criteria to evaluate compensation was further developed by the High Court in the more recent case of *Tigana Ltd* v. *Decoro Ltd*.[210] In this case, the parties entered into a commercial agency contract for the sale of furniture on 1 January 1999. The commercial agent was appointed for the purpose of allowing the principal to

199. *Ibid*. Bowers J also refers to article 12 of the French Civil Code as the relevant article for compensation (*ibid*, at para 19). With respect, this is not the case at all. Bowers J probably meant article L 134–12 al 1 French Commercial Code.

200. See section 6.3.1.2.

201. [2001] Eu LR 567, at para 15.

202. *Ibid*, at para 21.

203. [2002] ECC 5.

204. [2000] Eu LR 531.

205. *Ibid*, at para 45.

206. *Ibid*, at para 52.

207. *Ibid*, at para 53.

208. *Ibid*.

209. See fn 145 and associated text.

210. [2003] EWHC 23, [2003] Eu LR 189.

break into the furniture market in the UK. The contract, which was initially entered into for one year could be terminated with a 90 days' notice period. At the end of December 1999, in breach of the contractually agreed notice, the principal informed the commercial agent that the contract would not be renewed, alleging a serious breach by the commercial agent. The commercial agent sued for compensation under regulation 17.[211]

Davis J refused to look at French law by stating "I am not bound to seek to apply what is said to be French law and practice (. . .) nor, in my view, is an English court bound to enquire into French (or any other Member States') law".[212] Davis J refused to apply the two-year benchmark applied in France on the ground that it was a windfall for the commercial agent. Davis J suggests a (non-exhaustive) list of factors to assess how compensation should be applied. In the case of *Tigana Ltd* v. *Decoro Ltd*,[213] Davis J said that in order to assess compensation, even though the court necessarily had to adopt something of a broad-brush approach, "there must be some methodology to that assessment".[214] Recognising the need to define certain criteria for this methodology, Davis J then gave a list of no less than 13 factors that could be taken into consideration for the assessment of compensation as follows:

(1) the period of the agency as provided in the contract;
(2) the period for which the agency in fact lasted up to termination;
(3) the nature and history of the agency and of the particular market involved;
(4) the matters specifically mentioned in Regulation 17(7)(a)(b);
(5) the nature of the client base and of the kind of contracts anticipated to be placed, for example one-off repeats;
(6) whether the principal has appointed the agent as its exclusive or non exclusive agent;
(7) the extent to which the agent has bound himself during the agency to act exclusively for the principal and the extent to which the agent is free to act for others and whether in the same field of goods or services or not;
(8) the extent to which the principal retains after termination of the agency benefit, for example by way of enhanced trade connection or goodwill from the activities of the agent during the agency;
(9) the extent to which an agent is free, after termination, to have dealings with customers with whom he dealt during the agent (a restraint of trade clause will be relevant consideration in this context);
(10) whether there are any payments under Regulation 8 or other regulations which ought to be taken into consideration;
(11) the manner in which the agency contract is ended: for example by notice given by the principal; or by notice given by the agent, or by effluxion of time; or as the case may be;
(12) the extent to which the principal and agent respectively have contributed to the goodwill accruing during the period of agency; and finally
(13) the extent to which here may have been a loss caused by any relevant breach of contract or duty.

211. He also claimed for commission still due under Regulation 8.
212. [2003] EWHC 23, [2003] Eu LR 189 at para 100.
213. [2003] EWHC 23, [2003] Eu LR 189.
214. *Ibid*, at para 88.

The problem with such criteria is that some of them (especially numbers 5 and 8 and 12) seem closer to the way the German courts evaluate the significant benefits that the principal will receive under the indemnity alternative rather than the loss suffered by the commercial agent. Others are reminiscent of the assessment of the equitable requirement under German law and under Regulation 17(3)(b) of the Agency Regulations (especially number 8). This is reinforced by the fact that Davis J also stated that "in making that assessment, I have also asked myself, by way of a check, whether such an award is fair and proportionate: if it seemed to be *prima facie* too high (or too low) I would have reconsidered the weight I have minded to give to the various factors".[215] Davis J also stated that such factors do not represent an exhaustive list and "some may not in fact feature at all in some cases" and "the weight (if any) to be given to each of such factors will vary from case to case".[216]

Davis J awarded the sum of $452,346 for compensation. This sum represents the net remuneration earned during the agency. To the actual period of the agency, Davis J also added a period of two and a half months during which the commercial agent acted for the principal since such months were "very important in initiating some of the valuable introductions of customers to Decoro".[217] Davis J then stated that even though he regarded himself as bound to take a "two-year gross remuneration" as a starting point, he would have "unhesitatingly departed from that in all the circumstances, in particular, given that the agency here lasted for significantly less than two years, that it was non-exclusive, that there has been the award under Regulation 8(a) and that Mr Coleman the "key man" in the corporate commercial agent had free access to the customers after termination".[218]

All these cases show that (i) the English courts accept that compensation is very different from any traditional common law concepts, which therefore (ii) requires very specific criteria for calculation.

6.3.2.2 Possible criteria to calculate compensation in a more "UK-based" manner

Another very interesting aspect of the reasoning of Davis J in the case of *Tigana Ltd* v. *Decoro Ltd*[219] is the fact that, twice, Davis J compared compensation to unjust enrichment. He first said "one can discern from the Directive (and article 17 and Regulation 17 themselves) a desire to prevent the principal from, as it were, unjustly enriching itself by appropriating to itself, without recompense, the goodwill and customer connection to which the efforts of the commercial agent have contributed; and to compensate the loss to him of his agency".[220] He later added "clearly one important element, as the recitals to the Directive show, is to avoid a principal being unjustly enriched by retaining for itself without payment the entirety of the benefit of the goodwill to which the activities of the agent during the agency have contributed".[221]

The parallel between unjust enrichment as is applied under common law principles and compensation as a civil law concept is worthy of note. The justification for compensation

215. *Ibid*, at para 109.
216. *Ibid*, at para 89.
217. *Ibid*, at para 108.
218. *Ibid*, at para 110.
219. [2003] EWHC 23, [2003] Eu LR 189.
220. *Ibid*, at para 77.
221. *Ibid*, at para 90.

under the Agency Regulations has something in common with unjust enrichment as they are both assessed at the date the award is received and there is no need for mitigation.[222] We have seen that French law considers the commercial agency relationship in quasi proprietary terms. The relationship is a sort of joint-venture, the benefit of which is shared between the parties. During the commercial agency, both parties benefit from each other's efforts since the commercial agent receives more commissions and the principal benefits from increased sales of goods or services. On termination, the principal deprives the commercial agent of his legitimate share of the future profit. Davis J clearly accepted this when he stated "it seems clear that the Directive contemplates that the goodwill established by an agent for the benefit of the principal can be treated, as it were, as a quasi-proprietary right in which the agent is taken to have a share and of which he is divested on termination".[223]

By terminating the relationship, could the principal be seen as being unjustly enriched since he keeps the whole benefit of the commercial agency, i.e. his share and that of the commercial agent? The main question is whether to use unjust enrichment/restitution as a basis for compensation is legally possible under English law.

Compensation calculated on the basis of unjust enrichment/restitution

In other words, is the provision for compensation motivated by a desire to prevent unjust enrichment of the principal? Three main factors must be established for a successful plea of unjust enrichment:[224]

(1) the principal has been enriched;
(2) at the expense of the commercial agent; and
(3) that the enrichment is unjust.

The principal would be enriched in that he would be able to retain the commercial agent's share of the profit because he would not need to pay him the commissions that would have become due. The enrichment appears to be obtained at the expense of the commercial agent because, but for the termination, the commission element of the profit would be paid to the commercial agent. The problem is that although it may be morally or commercially unjust, it is doubtful "whether there is anything unjust about the principal acquiring benefits under a lawfully terminated contract".[225]

Traditionally, there are two ways to identify an unjust factor. First, through mistake, duress, undue influence or total failure of consideration. None would apply in the area of commercial agency. Secondly, crudely summarising the House of Lords" decision in the case of *Westdeutsche Landesbank* v. *Islington LBC*,[226] there is unjust enrichment if there is no legal basis for the enrichment.

Can it be said that there is no legal basis for the principal to receive the enrichment? The problem is that, arguably, the basis for the principal is that he is entitled in any event to a portion of the profits that he received from sales to the customers. Since he no longer

222. SC Smith *Death of a salesman* SLT (2000) 36, pp 289–295 at p 294.
223. [2003] EWHC 23, [2003] Eu LR 189, at para 90.
224. We are grateful to our colleague Kate Bracegirdle in the law school at the University of Sheffield for her valuable explanation on the basic principles of restitution. For additional detail, see generally Goff and Jones, *The Law of Restitution* (6th edn, 2002).
225. SC Smith *Death of a salesman* SLT (2000) 36, pp 289–295 at p 294.
226. [1996] AC 669, HL.

has any contractual obligation to pay the commission to the commercial agent, he is entitled to the money that would have gone to the commercial agent as well. It is therefore difficult to say that the principal is enriched at the expense of the commercial agent. However, looking at the French notion of *common interest*, arguably, the principal has no legal basis for getting the money that rightfully should belong to the commercial agent. If we consider that the legal basis of the relationship for both parties was the creation of the common interest, then, by terminating the contract with no just cause, the principal has no legal basis to act upon, and unjust enrichment could therefore be used as a legal basis of the relationship for compensation.

The final point is that restitution is not available only in cases of unjust enrichment. If we work on the basis that restitution is basically about remedies assessed by reference to the defendant's gain rather than the claimant's loss, this could work as a sort of "restitution in advance", i.e. a remedy assessed by reference to a gain that the principal would otherwise make.[227] The problem is that this would not work for compensation, since compensation concentrates on the loss by the commercial agent not the gain made by the principal. At first sight, this could work for the German-based indemnity, since the gain to the principal seems to be what is emphasised by the German courts. However, as will be seen, the German courts only take into consideration the benefit to the principal when this corresponds to a loss of the commercial agent.[228]

Even though unjust enrichment is unlikely to work as a legal basis for compensation, it certainly shows that the English courts are now serious about developing their own rules on compensation. It is almost seen as a challenge. As remarked by Bowers J in the case of *Barrett McKenzie* v. *Escada (UK) Ltd*,[229] the English system is not "incapable of dealing with unique challenges and changing situation or developing rules for their new right of compensation . . . the law is sufficient flexible and adaptable to deal with that".[230] Let us therefore see what other criteria could be taken into consideration to evaluate the loss to the commercial agent.

Calculation of compensation: distinction between big and small commercial agents?

The idea, which transpires from cases such as *Ingmar GB Ltd* v. *Eaton Leonard Inc*[231] and *Barrett McKenzie* v. *Escada (UK) Ltd*[232] is that the award of two years' worth of commission is too generous, especially when the commercial agent is a profitable business or part of a business rather than an individual. This therefore brings us to consider the difficult question whether the calculation of compensation should differ depending on the size of the commercial agent. The Directive is based on the civil law assumption that commercial agents are the weaker party in the relationship. Yet, as case law shows, a successful commercial agent will be earning substantial sums of money in commission and may have considerable market power. On this ground, it therefore seems difficult to agree with the statement of Staughton LJ in the case of *Page* v. *CST Ltd*[233] that commercial agents are

227. See also the interesting idea that there might be an analogy with the problem of work done in anticipation of a contract that fails to materialise. SC Smith *Death of a salesman* SLT (2000) 36, pp 289–295 at p 294.
228. See section 6.4.1.1 below.
229. [2001] Eu LR 567.
230. *Ibid*, *per* Judge Bowers, para 21.
231. [2002] ECC 5.
232. [2001] Eu LR 567.
233. [1997] 3 All ER 656.

invariably a "down trodden race who need and should be afforded protection against their principal".[234]

The question is therefore whether the award of compensation should distinguish between small and big commercial agents, giving less to the latter on the basis that they need less protection. The answer has to be negative for two reasons. First, to do so would discriminate between commercial agents, which is against the aim of the Directive. Secondly, such a difference would be very difficult to apply in practice. What criteria would be used to decide whether a commercial agent is a "big" as opposed to a "small" business? Do we consider that commercial agents who are established as legal entities are presumed to be big and those established as individual entities are presumed to be small? Do we look at the number of employees, or at the current European Commission definition of micro, small and medium sized enterprises?[235] Do we look at the amount of commission received? Considering that commission levels can vary from one month/year to another, this is not very practicable. Moreover, to distinguish between commercial agents according to their size would be equivalent to saying that highly-paid employees should receive proportionally lower redundancy package than their lower-paid colleagues. It seems difficult to see how such an idea would work in practice.

Calculating compensation as if evaluating a business

A better idea would be to calculate compensation as a valuation of a business from the commercial agent's viewpoint. Such an idea was aired in the case of *Barrett McKenzie* v. *Escada (UK) Ltd*[236] where Bowers J held that when calculating the amount of compensation due "one is valuing the agency and its connections established by the agent and it is really a question of compensating for the notional value of that agency on the open market, somewhat similar to the value of the goodwill that one might have in a business".[237]

Bowers J added that since assignment of the agency by the commercial agent is possible under the Agency Regulations, why not evaluate compensation according to how much would an incoming commercial agent have to pay for the goodwill.[238] To do so would be in line with the patrimonial aspect of the relationship. We have seen that the French courts take the possibility for the commercial agent to assign the commercial agency in consideration and consider that two years worth of commission is a fair purchase price of the commercial agency.[239] Even though in no English reported case so far, any valuation evidence appears to have been put before the court, the idea seems workable. The problem would be to ensure that the value is not assessed according to how much the commercial agent has contributed to the goodwill, otherwise, this would be too similar to the indemnity option.

Another problem with such a method of valuation is that the tendency of the courts would need to look at the future. In fact, "how can you value an agency or any business

234. *Ibid*, at p 660.
235. Commission Recommendation 2003/361/EC of 6 May 2003, OJ L. 124/36 of 20 May 2003.
236. [2001] Eu LR 567.
237. *Ibid*, at para 32.
238. Bowers J stated that the commercial agent will "receive that value from the person to whom he transfers it (the agency)". *Ibid*, at para 33.
239. See section 6.3.1.2, especially fn 125 and associated text.

without considering its future prospect".[240] This is not however how the French courts evaluate the loss suffered by the commercial agent. Yet, as we have seen earlier, the fact that the valuation by the English and Scottish courts differs from the way the French courts calculate compensation is not, *per se*, a problem. What is more serious is the fact that, by looking at the future, the calculation would be very similar to the way indemnity is calculated. We consider that recourse to the valuation principles applicable to the sale of a business would be a very fruitful way forward.

6.4 CALCULATING THE INDEMNITY TO COMMERCIAL AGENTS

The rules are provided by regulations 17(3) and 17(5). Following the Directive to the letter, Regulation 17(3) stipulates that the commercial agent will only be entitled to receive an indemnity on two cumulative conditions, namely:

(1) the commercial agent must have brought the principal new customers or at least have significantly increased the volume of business with existing customers and the principal must continue to derive substantial benefits from the business with such customers;[241] and

(2) the payment of the indemnity must be equitable with regards to all the circumstances,[242] and in particular, to the commission lost by the commercial agent on the business transacted with such customers.

The payment of the indemnity is capped, since the amount awarded cannot exceed one year's remuneration, calculated over a period of five years or the entire term of the contract if the contract is less than five years old.[243]

In addition, the commercial agent can claim damages for breach of contract.[244] This will for instance be the case where the principal has failed to comply with the required notice.

6.4.1 The German approach to indemnity[245]

Under § 89b of the German commercial code (HGB), commercial agents are entitled to receive a "reasonable compensation" (*angemessener Ausgleich*) upon "termination" of the contractual relationship. This means that the agency contract has to be terminated *de jure*. *De facto* termination is not sufficient. Termination is therefore a necessary precondition for the right to indemnity to arise as well as the decisive point in time when the

240. A Park, *Compensating commercial agents*, NLJ 2001, 1739.
241. Regulation 17(3(a)).
242. Regulation 17(3(b)).
243. Regulation 17(4).
244. Regulation 17(5).
245. We are most grateful to Merih Altay (a former student of ours, now a trainee solicitor with DLA Piper Rudnick Gray Cary (London)) and to our colleague Annette Nordhausen in the Law School at the University of Sheffield, for their invaluable contributions in this section.

right to indemnity arises. In the event of the commercial agent's death, the right to claim indemnity passes on to the commercial agent's estate.[246]

The legal basis for the indemnity: the financial gains of the principal must correspond to the loss to the commercial agent

As briefly seen in Chapter 5, German legislation was originally based on the Swiss idea of compensating the commercial agent, by way of a lump sum payment, solely on the basis that after termination the principal continues to benefit from the goodwill that the commercial agent helped to create or increase. However, German law now goes beyond this, since indemnity will only be due if the financial gains of the principal after termination correspond to a loss for the commercial agent.

The legal basis of the right for the commercial agent to claim indemnity is the commercial agency contract itself. German law recognises that the main purpose for appointing a commercial agent is only the creation of a customer base for a principal's goods. In return for creating such a customer base, the commercial agent receives commissions on the sales he generates. After termination, the principal continues to benefit from this customer base in two main ways: firstly, even after termination, he will continue to conclude transactions with the customers which the commercial agent has introduced to him. Secondly, the principal does not have to spend money on commissions that would have been due to the commercial agent had the relationship continued. Such financial gains therefore represent a loss for the commercial agent. Indemnity is due since the principal must compensate the commercial agent for the financial benefits that he retains and which he only retains following the termination of the relationship. This right of indemnity is mandatory. The commercial agent has to claim indemnity within one year from the termination of the contractual relationship.[247]

6.4.1.1 The conditions for the right to indemnity to arise

Under German law, three requirements, enumerated in § 89 b I HGB, must be satisfied for the commercial agent's claim for indemnity; specifically: (1) the principal must continue to substantially benefit from the commercial agent's efforts after termination; (2) the commercial agent, by reason of termination of the relationship, loses his right to commission on transactions concluded with customers; and (3) the payment of the indemnity is equitable with regards to all the circumstances.

Another requirement is that the indemnity claim is not explicitly excluded by law. Section 89 b III HGB enumerates the reasons for exclusion of indemnity. The claim is excluded for one or more of three possible reasons: (1) the commercial agent gives notice, unless the principal's behaviour provided the reason for the termination or, the commercial agent cannot reasonably be expected to continue due to his age or illness. (2) The principal terminates the contract due to an important reason caused by negligent conduct of the commercial agent. (3) Due to an agreement between principal and agent when a third person takes over the agency. This latter agreement can only be entered into after the

246. BGHZ (Amtliche Sammlung der Entscheidungen des Bundesgerichtshofs in Zivilsachen) 24, 214, 224 BGHZ 41, 129.

247. Section 89 b IV HGB.

termination of the contract. Such exclusions are reasonably similar to the ones provided by Regulation 18, and of course, their basis now in the Directive.

The principal must continue to benefit substantially from the customer base after termination

It is an essential requirement of German law (in marked contrast with the position in France) that the principal continues to benefit substantially after termination from the commercial agent's marketing efforts. As a consequence, where termination of the relationship is due to the principal shutting down his business or going into liquidation, the commercial agent will normally not receive any indemnity. In the Directive, this requirement is present, since the claim for indemnity arises on the double conditions that the commercial agent "has brought the principal new customers or has significantly increased the volume of business with existing customers *and* the principal continues to derive substantial benefits with such customers".[248]

German law phrases the requirement slightly differently by stating that the principal must retain significant advantages from "business relationships" with new customers. Advantages drawn from business with "old customers" are also counted in if the commercial agent increased the business relationship with an existing customer to an extent that equals a new customer economically.[249]

The requirement of continuing substantial benefits for the principal is effectively a forecast as to the prospect, for the principal, of continuing to conclude further "business relations" with such customers in the (reasonably foreseeable) future.

Forecast of significant benefits for the principal: Prognosezeitraum

In essence, the German courts have to decide how long the principal is likely to benefit from the goodwill built by the commercial agent, i.e. how long the newly acquired (and also old) customers will continue to buy the goods of the principal after termination of the agency. The forecast is made at the time the commercial agency ended and the right to indemnity arose. Accordingly, the forecast cannot be altered by circumstances that occur later on, i.e. during a court case.[250] It is an *ex ante* analysis which can only be made for a foreseeable period of time. The specific period of time for which the forecast is made depends upon the facts of the case, and is decided on a case-by-case basis. Neither the commercial agent nor the principal will be reimbursed if the forecast proves wrong or inaccurate later on.

The specific period of time for which the forecast is made depends on the facts of each case. The length of this period is determined by reference to the purposes of the goods sold, their expected lifespan but also customer migration (see the discussion of the migration rate below). Normally, a principal is expected to continue to benefit from the goodwill

248. Article 17(2)(a) of the Directive.

249. This is assessed by reference to quantitative (more products) or qualitative criteria (different products)—BGHZ (Amtliche Sammlung der Entscheidungen des Bundesgerichtshofs in Zivilsachen) 56, 242—changes in prices are irrelevant if qualitative change in products, general economic growth is not deducted or used against the commercial agent—OLG (Oberlandesgericht) Celle, BB (Betriebs-Berater) 1970, p 227.

250. BGH (Bundesgerichtshof) NJW (Neue Juristische Wochenschrift) 1998, p 75; overruling BGHZ 56, 246, WM (Wertpapier-Mitteilungen) 1991, p 1517.

created by the commercial agent for between two and three years after termination. However, this may go up to five years or more, in the case of durable goods.[251]

The principal will significantly benefit from the commercial agent's efforts after termination in two main ways: through continuing "business relationships" concluded by the commercial agent with what were then new customers or through a significant increased level of trading with "old customers", e.g. customers with whom the principal had dealings with prior to the commercial agent acting for him.

"BUSINESS RELATIONSHIPS" WITH NEW CUSTOMERS

One must distinguish between one-time or passing customers and regular customers. Only regular customers are taken into consideration in the calculation of the indemnity. Regular customers are customers who have, within a reasonably short period, concluded more than one transaction with the commercial agent or are likely to do so in the foreseeable future.[252] Usually, a customer's second purchase will suffice to classify him as a regular customer, but it is not automatically the case. The time frame for further orders from the same customer may vary depending on the goods or services in question. For instance, certain domestic appliances or pieces of industrial equipment are more durable than others, thereby necessitating a longer time frame for repeat business.[253] First-time buyers are not usually taken into consideration, but they may sometimes be viewed as having the potential of becoming regular customers.

Finally, only the customers who have actually been brought in as a result of the commercial agent's efforts will be taken into consideration. The acquisition of new customers requires causation. Causation will be lacking in the case of customers who have already decided to conclude transactions with the commercial agent or the principal before being solicited by the commercial agent.[254] However, the commercial agent need not be the sole cause for the acquisition of the new customer. Provided that customers have been solicited to some extent by the commercial agent, if the client was also attracted by the brand image of the goods, there is nevertheless causation.[255] This will however be taken into account for deduction from the amount to be awarded.[256] Causation is reasonably lax in relation, for example, to petrol station operators since it is enough for the commercial agent to keep the station open and ready to serve customers, even if the customer chose the petrol station because of its location, the brand or even the price of the petrol.[257] This represents a serious difference with English law where petrol station operators are not considered as commercial agents for the purposes of the Agency Regulations.[258]

251. BGH (Bundesgerichtshof) BB (Betriebs-Berater) 1991, p 1210 (forklift trucks, 13 years) other prevailing case law, BGHZ 135, p 19 (new cars, five years).

252. BGHZ (Amtliche Sammlung der Entscheidungen des Bundesgerichtshofs in Zivilsachen) 135, 14; NJW (Neue Juristische Wochenschrift) 1998, p 68, 73.

253. BGH (Bundesgerichtshof) NJW (Neue Juristische Wochenschrift) 1985, p 859 for furniture OLG (Oberlandesgericht) Hamm BB (Betriebs-Berater) 1978, p 1686.

254. BGH (Bundesgerichtshof) NJW (Neue Juristische Wochenschrift) 1996, p 23041 OLG (Oberlandesgericht) Karlsruhe BB (Betriebs-Berater) 1960, p 381.

255. BGHM (Bundesgerichtshof)WM (Wertpapier-Mitteilungen) 1985, p 1465, OLG (Oberlandesgericht) Karlsruhe BB (Betriebs-Berater) 1960, p 381.

256. See fn 293 and associated text.

257. Other opinion A Rittner DB (Der Betrieb) 1998, p 457.

258. *Parks* v. *Esso Petroleum Company Ltd* [2000] Tr LR 232, see Chapter 2, section 2.4.2.1.

RATE OF MIGRATION OF NEW CUSTOMERS

When calculating the forecast of the financial benefits of the principal, the German courts take into consideration the fact that a certain proportion of newly acquired customers will naturally migrate to other businesses within a given period of time (usually one year) and can therefore not be seen as regular customers for the principal.[259] The German courts will therefore deduct from the calculation of the indemnity what is referred as the migration rate. The migration rate is usually based on previous experience within the sector, or on an assumption depending on the goods or services in question, e.g. an annual rate of 20 per cent over a period of five years.[260]

Increased transactions with "old" customers

"Old customers", e.g. customers with whom the principal was dealing prior to the commercial agent standing to act for him will be treated as new customers acquired for the principal by the commercial agent provided that the commercial agent has significantly increased the volume of business transactions with them. The increase has to be to such an extent that the increase financially equates to the acquisition of new customers. The assessment of a significant increase in trade with old customers is carried out on a case-by-case basis, and may be determined on quantitative[261] or qualitative[262] criteria. An increase in the principal's turnover which is solely based on an increase/decrease in currency exchange rates is not sufficient for this purpose. However, a decrease in turnover due to a fall in sales price will not necessarily be interpreted to the detriment of the commercial agent if it can be shown that the quantity of the goods sold has gone up.[263]

Significant benefits

As we have already hinted, what matters from the principal's point of view is the prospect of making further use of the customer relations established by the commercial agent after termination of the agency agreement. The principal's benefit is therefore the prospect of further profit without having to pay the commercial agent's commission. The benefit must be derived from the business relationships with customers established by the commercial agent or those so "increased" by the commercial agent so as to be treated as new customers and the benefit must be significant. The significance of this benefit depends upon the scale and the expected regularity of the solicited new business as compared with the principal's old business (which may have increased during the duration of the agency contract without any contribution by the agent) but not with the total business of the principal.[264] An increase in turnover or sales revenue is not required[265]; a significant

259. BGH (Bundesgerichtshof) NJW (Neue Juristische Wochenschrift) 1996, p 2301.

260. BGHZ (Amtliche Sammlung der Entscheidungen des Bundesgerichtshofs in Zivilsachen) 135, 14.

261. The commercial agent sells a significantly larger amount of already supplied types of product to an old customer compared to what the customer was known to buy previously.

262. The commercial agent sells a significant amount of new products that an old customer did not previously buy.

263. Müller NJW (Neue Juristische Wochenschrift) 1987, p 343.

264. BGH (Bundesgerichtshof) BB (Betriebs-Berater) 1991, 1210; BGH (Bundesgerichtshof) NJW (Neue Juristische Wochenschrift) 1998, p 68, 74.

265. BGHZ (Amtliche Sammlung der Entscheidungen des Bundesgerichtshofs in Zivilsachen) 42, 246.

benefit can exist even where turnover or sales revenue has gone down.[266] Further, the principal's advantage may be significant even if only a part of the clientele remains with the principal.[267]

Burden of proof of significant benefit

The burden of proof regarding the principal's benefits lies on the commercial agent.[268] However, if the commercial agent has been working for the principal for a number of years, there is a rebuttable presumption that the goodwill that exists on termination was built up by the commercial agent.[269] The commercial agent can prove that he created the goodwill by presenting a list of customers or any other data enabling the courts to make an assumption. A list of customers is however unnecessary if the acquisition of new customers is clear following a rise in the principal's turnover.[270]

The requirement that the commercial agent must have lost the right to claim commissions on the business transacted by the principal with those customers

Forecasting how many customers will continue to buy the goods of the principal after termination of the commercial agent is another part of the equation. Business transactions between the commercial agent's customers and the principal after the termination of the agency contract are taken as corresponding to a loss for the commercial agent, since, had the relationship continued, the commercial agent would have earned commissions on those transactions. The calculation of the loss to the commercial agent is also a forecast. Since the loss to the commercial agent corresponds to the benefit to the principal, the two elements are usually applied in parallel following the same criteria.

Forecasting the loss to the commercial agent

The forecast of the loss is usually based on the commissions received for transactions concluded with regular customers[271] by the commercial agent in the last year prior to termination. However, this rule does not apply where the commissions earned the last year of the relationship were unusually high or unusually low, or if for instance the goods sold by the commercial agent are extremely long-lived. In such a situation, the calculation is based on an earlier year that is more representative or on average commissions calculated over a number of years.

266. BGH (Bundesgerichtshof) NJW (Neue Juristische Wochenschrift) 1990, p 2890—but a decrease in turnover may justify a lower indemnity.

267. BGH (Bundesgerichtshof) HVR (63) No 319.

268. BGHZ 55, 45.

269. OLG Düsseldorf HVR (77) Nr 504; coming to the same result BGHZ (Amtliche Sammlung der Entscheidungen des Bundesgerichtshofs in Zivilsachen) 56, 245; BGHZ 73, 104; OLG (Oberlandesgericht) Celle HVR (71) No. 436; BGH (Bundesgerichtshof) NJW (Neue Juristische Wochenschrift) 1985, p 859; BGH (Bundesgerichtshof) WM (Wertpapier-Mitteilungen) 1991, p 198.

270. OLG (Oberlandesgericht) Düsseldorf HVR (79) No 535.

271. The Bundesgerichtshof has now made clear that any customer who orders goods *at least once after the initial order* is seen as a regular customer BGHZ, Urt.v. judgment of 6 August 1997—VIII ZR 150/96, NJW (Neue Juristische Wochenschrift) 1998, p 66, 68; BGH, BGH (Bundesgerichtshof, judgment of 6 August 1997—VIII ZR 92/96, NJW (Neue Juristische Wochenschrift) 1998, pp 71, 73.

The calculation of the loss suffered by the commercial agent is influenced by two factors, a decrease in the commissions earned due to the migration of customers (*Abwanderungsquote*) and the length of time the commercial agent could reasonably be expected to earn commissions on further business from customers he has acquired (*Prognosezeitraum*). The rate of customer migration is calculated by reference to the decrease in turnover rather than by the number of customers that actually migrate to another principal. This is simply because the loss of a large number of customers might not have a high impact on the principal's turnover if such customers accounted for a small proportion of the commercial agent's commissions. By contrast, the loss of an important customer may result in a significant decrease in his commission.

In line with the expected duration of the benefits for the principal, the length of time is usually between two to three years. It can be significantly longer for longer-durable goods.

Calculation on gross commissions

The calculation of the loss is based on the expected gross commissions.[272] There is therefore no deduction for expenses (*Unkostenersatz*)[273] or VAT.[274] This is very important. A possible reason for such a calculation seems that it is in line with the usual rules for the calculation of commissions.[275]

The commissions taken into consideration are the commissions earned by the commercial agent for the negotiation and/or the conclusion of the transactions on behalf of the principal. In relation to the commission on transactions concluded, providing that such transactions are actually concluded prior to termination, the time of performance of the contract is irrelevant.[276]

In relation to commissions for the negotiation of transactions, the customers must have been solicited/acquired by the commercial agent. The mere prospect of bringing new customers does not entitle the commercial agent to commission and this prospect will have no bearing on the calculation of the indemnity.[277]

Extra commissions earned by the commercial agent for carrying additional services for the principal such as stocking or delivering the goods, are not taken into consideration and even though those may have continued to be earned post-termination, they do not form part of the loss suffered by the commercial agent.

Burden of proof

The burden of proof of the loss is on the commercial agent.[278] However, his burden of proof only applies for the commissions received for the negotiation and/or the conclusion

272. BGHZ (Amtliche Sammlung der Entscheidungen des Bundesgerichtshofs in Zivilsachen) 41, 129.

273. BGHZ (Amtliche Sammlung der Entscheidungen des Bundesgerichtshofs in Zivilsachen) 29, 92.

274. BGHZ (Amtliche Sammlung der Entscheidungen des Bundesgerichtshofs in Zivilsachen) 61, 114; BGH (Bundesgerichtshof) WM (Wertpapier-Mitteilungen) 1987, p 1465; BGH (Bundesgerichtshof) NJW (Neue Juristische Wochenschrift) 1998, p 70.

275. Another could be that it can be allowed to be taken into account on grounds of equity, but this will only happen in exceptional circumstances (W Ball in I Saenger/R Schulze (eds), Der Ausgleichsanspruch des Handelsvertreters. Beispiel für die Fortentwicklung angeglichenen europäischen Rechts, pp 17, 41).

276. The contract does not even have to be performed until after termination: BGH NJW 97, 1505.

277. BGH 24, 228, 29, 92, 34, 314.

278. BGHZ (Amtliche Sammlung der Entscheidungen des Bundesgerichtshofs in Zivilsachen) 55, 45.

of transactions. The principal bears the burden of proof in relation to the reimbursement of any expenses that may be relevant.[279]

Discount for accelerated receipt of cash: Abzinsung

Once the German courts have arrived at a certain sum, this represents the rough estimation of the indemnity to be paid. However, to that sum a deduction of unaccrued interest (*Abzinsung*) must be applied because the commercial agent effectively receives in one lump sum, the expected commission he would have got over a number of years. The indemnity must therefore be reduced in order to allow for the cash flow advantage to the commercial agent.[280] In the past, the German courts sometimes tended to compensate for the cash flow advantage by simply subtracting estimates of between 10 and 20 per cent from the indemnity.[281] There is now a respected methodology used in order to deal with this problem (see below).

The discount must be applied even where the indemnity is paid in instalments or where it is paid a long time after termination.[282] The moment when the commercial agent actually receives the indemnity has no bearing on the discount, since it still applies even if the indemnity is paid only after it has become due for payment.[283] In this repect, the approach in Germany is very different from the approach in France to the compensation alternative, where no discount for accelerated cash flow is made.

The indemnity payment must be equitable in all circumstances

This third and last condition will only apply once the previous two conditions are met. The courts are clear that the indemnity must not be determined solely in accordance with the equitable requirement without a prior determination of whether the first two requirements have been complied with.[284] However, it needs to be borne in mind that this third test is a separate requirement that exists in addition to the first two requirements. It is true that considerations of equity may be taken into account under the first two points as well, but the real "equitable" test is to be applied under the third point which may correct or adapt the results obtained earlier. All circumstances of a particular case have to be taken into account. These are normally limited to circumstances that are related to the contractual agreement; health, age and financial situation of the parties will usually not be of any relevance.[285] It is only in very exceptional cases that it will be seen as equitable to take account of circumstances that are not related to the contract.

279. BGH (Bundesgerichtshof) WM (Wertpapier-Mitteilungen) 1988, p 1204; BGH (Bundesgerichtshof), NJW (Neue Juristische Wochenschrift) 1996, p 2300.

280. BGH (Bundesgerichtshof)WM (Wertpapier-Mitteilungen) 1987, p 1465; BGH (Bundesgerichtshof), BB (Betriebs-Berater) 1991, p 368.

281. 8 per cent in BGH (Bundesgerichtshof), DB (Der Betrieb) 1991, p 1325; 10 per cent in OLG (Oberlandesgericht) Celle, BB (Betriebs-Berater) 1970, p 227; 16 per cent in OLG (Oberlandesgericht) Frankfurt, judgment of 8 December 1970—VU 1970; 20 per cent OLG (Oberlandesgericht) Köln, VersR (Versicherungsrecht) 1968, p 966.

282. BGH (Bundesgerichtshof), DB (Der Betrieb) 1991, p 1325.

283. BGHZ (Amtliche Sammlung der Entscheidungen des Bundesgerichtshofs in Zivilsachen) 29, 94; BGHZ, 55, 45; BGH (Bundesgerichtshof) NJW (Neue Juristische Wochenschrift) 1997, p 655.

284. BGHZ (Amtliche Sammlung der Entscheidungen des Bundesgerichtshofs in Zivilsachen) 43, 154 BGH (Bundesgerichtshof) NJW (Neue Juristische Wochenschrift) 1985, p 59; BGH (Bundesgerichtshof) NJW (Neue Juristische Wochenschrift) 1997, p 665.

285. Contrast BGHZ (Amtliche Sammlung der Entscheidungen des Bundesgerichtshofs in Zivilsachen) 43, 162, where circumstances not related to the contract were exceptionally taken into account.

Burden of proof

If the first two conditions are met, there is a presumption that the calculation of the indemnity is equitable. This is a simple presumption, and can be rebutted by either party for different reasons. The principal will usually use this condition in order to try to prove that certain circumstances justify a reduction of the indemnity.[286] Vice versa, the commercial agent will use this condition when he wants certain circumstances to be taken into consideration in order to avoid reduction of the indemnity.

As noted earlier, the circumstances to take into consideration in order to decide whether the indemnity is equitable are usually related only to the contract itself. However, in very extreme cases, circumstances outside the contract such as age, health, financial situations of the parties can be taken into consideration.[287]

Circumstances used to assess whether the calculation of the indemnity is equitable

Such circumstances are wide and varied, and can be used to cancel the right to claim indemnity altogether or simply to reduce the amount awarded.

Reasons for terminating the contract: the commercial agent loses his right to claim indemnity in the following circumstances: (a) when the principal terminates following a serious breach of the commercial agent himself or a serious breach of one of his employee or sub-agent[288]; (b) when the commercial agent refuses a new commercial agency contract with the principal's successor;[289] or (c) when the commercial agent refuses a contract of employment offered by the principal.[290]

Special features of the terminated contract: the commercial agent's right to claim indemnity is lost when he has assigned the commercial agency to another commercial agent.[291] The thinking behind this, as under the Directive, is that he could have been paid for the loss of future commissions by the incoming agent who is in effect buying the goodwill of the outgoing agent's business, and that, having chosen to leave the agency agreement in this way, it is up to him agent to look after himself and do his own deal with his successor and the principal has no liabilities.

The level of indemnity can be reduced if, in a given case, the commercial agent has already been rewarded for his creation of the goodwill by virtue of commissions on repeat-orders.[292] Likewise if customers are attracted to the goods of the principal because of their strong brand image.[293] On the other hand, the level of indemnity can be increased if, in a given case, the commercial agent has supported the principal financially during the agency by, for instance, relinquishing his entitlement to commission.[294]

286. BGH (Bundesgerichtshof) NJW (Neue Juristische Wochenschrift) 1990, p 2891.

287. BGHZ (Amtliche Sammlung der Entscheidungen des Bundesgerichtshofs in Zivilsachen) 43, 163; BGHZ 129, 296 where the commercial agent was responsible for a family of eight; OLG (Oberlandesgericht) Düsseldorf HVR (77) Nr 504 where the principal's business was threatened by liquidation/bankruptcy.

288. BGHZ (Amtliche Sammlung der Entscheidungen des Bundesgerichtshofs in Zivilsachen) 29, 280; BGH (Bundesgerichtshof), DB (Der Betrieb) 1981, p 1773. A single breach of contract after years of cooperation is not a sufficient reason for terminating the agreement: BGH (Bundesgerichtshof) WM (Wertpapier-Mitteilungen) 1985, p 469.

289. OLG (Oberlandesgericht) Hamm HVR (77) No. 511.

290. OLG (Oberlandesgericht) Düsseldorf HVR (56) No. 130.

291. BGH NJW 75, 1926.

292. BGH BB 57, 1161.

293. Deduction of 10 per cent in BGH NJW 82, 2820, WM 87, 1465, 94, 243, NJW 96, 2298, 2302, 97, 1506, Mü BB 94, 533. deduction of 25 per cent in Kln BB 95, 2548, cf BGH NJW 96, 2304.

294. Fbg BB 57, 561.

Duration of the contract: short-term contracts will not be interpreted to the detriment of the commercial agent.[295] Long-term contracts usually work to the advantage of the commercial agent because it shows the commercial agent's loyalty, especially when termination occurs because of his wish to retire.[296]

Total turnover: the fact that the principal's turnover decreases even though through the commercial agent's efforts he has acquired new customers may be taken into consideration to reduce the level of indemnity.[297] This is especially so if the commercial agent could have prevented the decrease. However, the loss of regular customers is not to be interpreted against the commercial agent if he has also brought new customers.[298] Interestingly, the fact that the commercial agent attracts customers by using bribes has been held not necessarily to result in the loss of the indemnity.[299]

Pension scheme: when the principal contributes to a pension scheme for the commercial agent, such contributions may be, in total or in part, deducted from the indemnity on the condition that the pension has the same practical purpose as the indemnity. This will therefore not be the case when the pension is not due within a reasonably short period of time after termination of the relationship.[300]

The commercial agent works for principal's competitors: German law considers that a commercial agent who works for more than one principal may continue after termination of his agreement with the principal to use the goodwill he has created for principal X, with his other principals. The level of indemnity in such a situation may therefore accordingly be reduced, since principal X effectively loses customers to his competitors and no longer benefits from the goodwill created or not to the same extent.[301] However, the situation depends on whether the terminated contract contains a post-termination restrictive covenant or not. If the terminated contract contains such a covenant and the commercial agent, in breach of a such a covenant, represents a principal's competitor, he will not lose the indemnity entirely[302] but his behaviour will be taken into consideration to reduce the indemnity.[303] In extreme cases, a deduction of 25 per cent was accepted.[304] However, where the terminated contract contains no post-termination restrictive covenant, the fact that after termination the commercial agent works a competing principal cannot be used to reduce the level of indemnity.[305]

Savings by the commercial agent: it is considered undeniable that the termination of a relationship will cause the commercial agent to suffer a loss. Yet, German law also considers that it is sometimes inequitable to disregard any potential savings he might make following termination. For instance, the commercial agent will save sub-commissions due to any permitted sub-agent where the latter fails to lodge his indemnity claim within the one-year limit.[306] In relation to the savings on the level of expenses normally incurred

295. BGH NJW 58, 23, NJW 97, 655, Hbg DB 63, 1214, KG HVR (70), Nr 433.
296. BGH 55, 45.
297. BGH 42, 247, NJW 90, 2891.
298. BGH NJW 90, 2891, aA BGH BB 64, 1399 (petrol station).
299. BGH NJW 77, 671.
300. BGH NJW 94 1350 (21 years), Düss NJW-RR 96, 225, Kln VersR 97, 615 (13 years). It is however different when the delay has been expressly agreed by the parties: BGH BB 84, 168 (24 years).
301. BGH BB 60, 1179, DB 81, 1173.
302. BGR VersR 60, 846.
303. BGH WM 75, 858.
304. BGH NJW 96, 2304.
305. BGH HVR (63) Nr 319.
306. KG HVR (94) Nr 811.

whilst working as a commercial agent (such as fixed and variable costs), such savings will only be taken into consideration if they are very high.[307] Savings on administrative costs, i.e. rent etc are not usually taken into consideration.

The cap of one year's worth of commission: HGB § 89 b II

In order to avoid exposing the principal to unforeseeably high payments of indemnity, the German courts cannot award an indemnity higher than one year's worth of commission,[308] to be calculated taking the average over a period of five years prior to termination or less, depending on the duration of the contract.

It must be emphasised that this limitation only applies after the three requirements under § 89 b I HGB have been used (the rough compensation ascertaining the principal's benefits, the losses to the commercial agent and whether the payment of an indemnity is equitable).

Remuneration means gross, i.e. pre-tax remuneration,[309] VAT is not to be deducted,[310] neither are business expenses[311] nor commission or remuneration for sub-agents.[312] However, this calculation is only based on commissions that have been paid for the commercial agent's actual services rendered. As a consequence, commission to reimburse expenditure such as rent for the premises of the commercial agent or money spent on the use of a car is not to be included.

Contrary to the calculation of the indemnity in relation to the "cap", there is no distinction between regular and "one-off" customers.

6.4.1.2 How indemnity is calculated in practice

HGB § 89 b I

The rough assessment: Basisprovision

As has been explained, the significant benefits to the principal must correspond to the loss of commissions of the commercial agent. The first step will therefore be to calculate the prediction of the principal's benefits which correspond to the commercial agent's loss of commission. This is usually calculated on the commissions earned by the commercial agent in the last year prior to termination, unless such a year is atypical.

The estimated period of time within which the principal is expected to benefit from the goodwill of the commercial agent (*Prognosezeitraum*) and the estimated customer migration (*Abwanderungsquote*) will determine the amount of the indemnity before the "equitable" requirement comes into play.

Let us take an example whereby the gross commission earned in the last year prior to termination amounted to £100,000. The period of time that the principal may expect to benefit from further orders from regular customers is estimated at four years due to the

307. BGH 41, 135, 56, 249 (50 per cent not seen as sufficiently high).
308. HGB § 89 b II.
309. BGH 29, 83, 56, 250, 61, 112.
310. BGH 61, 112.
311. BGH 29, 92, 41, 134.
312. BGH WM 85, 981.

loyalty of the customers in question. Past experience show that the rate of migration is on average of a cumulative 15 per cent per year. This leads to the following calculation:

The first two requirements

First year of the prognosis

£100,000 – 15% rate of customer migration (£15,000) =	£85,000

Second year

£85,000 – 15% rate of customer migration (£12,750) =	£72,250

Third year

£72,250 – 15% rate of customer migration (£10,837.50) =	£61,412.50

Fourth year

£61,412.50 – 15% rate of customer migration (£9,211.88) =	£52,200.62
Total	£270,863.12

Equitable requirement: Billigkeit

This test considers all circumstances surrounding the termination. Both parties can ask for specific circumstances related to the contract to be taken into account to lower (for the principal) or not to lower (for the commercial agent) the indemnity awarded.

Let us say that, in our example, the commercial agent promoted or sold very well-known branded goods (i.e. it was much easier for him to find customers than if the goods had been unbranded: in effect, the goods sold themselves), which would be taken to justify a deduction of 25 per cent:

Loss of commission:	£270,863.12
Less 25% discount for brand image:	£67,715.78
Total	£203,147.34

Offsetting the cash flow advantage to the commercial agent for receiving a lump sum: This is calculated according to a standard discounted cashflow methodology (*DATEV-Kapitalabzinsungstabelle*). Under such a method, an estimated interest rate of 5 per cent p.a. produces a discounted value for the stream of receipts over the 4-year period of 0.823 of their total nominal value (i.e. a discount for accelerated cash flow of about 18 per cent):

£203,147.34 × 0.823 =	£167,190.26
Total	£167,190.26

§ 89b II: maximum amount: *Höchstbetrag*

As mentioned earlier, in order to protect the principal from claims of unforeseeable profits, the indemnity is capped to the commercial agent's average annual remuneration over the five years prior to termination or the whole life of the agreement if shorter, taking into consideration all remuneration earned by the commercial agent during that time and not simply commissions on transactions negotiated and/or concluded.

Let us say that, in our example, the commercial agent had earned a grand total of £550,000 of remuneration in the last five years of the agreement. This leads to the following maximum amount:

£550,000/5 years: £110,000 per year

The above indicative indemnity of £167,190.26 is clearly higher. The commercial agent is, because of the "cap", therefore only entitled to claim an indemnity of £110,000.

Difficulties may arise when the commercial agency agreement has lasted less than 12 months. The main question is whether the commercial agent's remuneration can be added up in order to calculate a fictitious average annual remuneration. Some scholars argue that the maximum amount should be based on the remuneration that was in fact earned during the life of the relationship rather than a projected average annual remuneration. The underlying reason for this is that the maximum amount is intended to reflect the remuneration actually earned by the commercial agent during the relationship. A maximum amount based on a calculated average annual remuneration would favour the commercial agent. Accordingly, if the relationship has lasted less than 12 months, it is not necessary to project the average annual remuneration.

6.4.2 The way the English courts calculate indemnity

Under the Agency Regulations, compensation is the default position and indemnity only applies when the parties expressly opt for it.[313] For that reason, very few cases reaching the courts in this country have so far involved the indemnity option. In fact, the case of *Tamarind International Ltd and others* v. *Eastern Natural Gas Ltd* [314] was settled out of court and therefore has no precedent value. The recent Scottish decision of *Hardie Polymers Ltd* v. *Polymerland Ltd*[315] involves indemnity payments, but the main question was one of construction of the contract and not of calculation. The case of *Moore* v. *Piretta*[316] is therefore the only case to date to have considered in detail the calculation of the indemnity payment.

Although the careful analysis of German law by John Mitting QC, sitting as a deputy judge of the High Court when calculating the indemnity is an important part of this case, one other crucial aspect is also worthy of note. Mr Mitting clearly understood that the payment of the indemnity was very different from that of damages for breach of contract common law. In fact, Mr Mitting highlighted the patrimonial nature of the indemnity when he stated that the purpose of indemnity was to award the commercial agent a share in the

313. Regulation 17(2).
314. [2000] Eu LR 708.
315. (2002) SCLR 64.
316. [1999] 1 All ER 174.

goodwill he had built up otherwise "the whole benefit of the goodwill would remain with his former principal".[317]

The facts must be reviewed briefly. The claimant started to act as the commercial agent for the defendant in January 1988 when the parties entered in a fixed-term contract. The contract was renewed annually until February 1994, when a new contract was drawn in order to comply with the Agency Regulations. The new contract was for an indefinite duration and contained a six-month termination clause. The contract expressly stipulated that the commercial agent was to be indemnified on termination. In October 1994, the principal gave the commercial agent the agreed six months' notice terminating the contract. Subsequently, the commercial agent issued proceedings claiming indemnity under Regulation 17. The central contention was how much indemnity should be awarded. Three arguments of the principal raised questions of construction of the Agency Regulations and two involved the calculation of the indemnity.

In relation to matters of construction, the first argument of the principal was born out of poor drafting of Regulation 17(1) which stipulates that commercial agents are to be indemnified or compensated on termination of the "agency contract". Counsel for the principal tried to argue that since Regulation 17(1) made reference to "the agency contract", indemnity should be limited to the last contract signed by the parties. Mr Mitting rejected such an argument, deciding that the phrase "agency contract" simply meant the agency relationship and the word "contract" after agency added nothing.[318] Mr Mitting did so by looking at other regulations and stated that having a temporal restriction to Regulation 17(1) did not make sense, since no other regulation on termination had such a restriction. He also stated that having a temporal restriction would produce a "surprising and unwelcome result for principals" since "on expiry of each agency contract in an unbroken series, the agent becomes entitled to an indemnity as well as to commissions on the continuing business of customers to the principal".[319] He therefore calculated the indemnity in reference to the entire length of time the parties had been together, and not merely since 1994. Such an interpretation, in line with the protective stance of the Agency Regulations closes a potential loophole; principals cannot attempt to lower the protection of the Agency Regulations by entering into a string of fixed-term contracts. The parallel with employment law is evident.[320]

A second attempt by the principal to reduce the amount of indemnity due was by using the rules on the chronological application of the implementing legislation. The Agency Regulations apply to all commercial agency contracts entered after 31 December 1993 and to those entered into before 1 January 1994 except for rights and liabilities enforced before 1 January 1994.[321] Counsel for the principal therefore argued that the indemnity should only be calculated by reference to events which took place after 1 January 1994 as to do otherwise would give the Agency Regulations retrospective effect. Mr Mitting rejected such an argument, stating that the rules in the implementing legislation are not "truly retrospective"[322] since they simply allow the calculation of the indemnity by referring to

317. [1999] 1 All ER 174, at p 182c.
318. [1999] 1 All ER 174, at p 180a.
319. *Ibid*, at p 179j.
320. Under employment law rules, an employer cannot prevent its employees from the benefit of an indeterminate employment contract by using a string of fixed-term contracts.
321. Regulation 23(2).
322. [1999] 1 All ER 174, at p 181b.

facts, which have occurred before the entry into force of the text, commenting that "it is not an unusual concept in an analogous context, that of employment law".[323] Mr Mitting therefore stated that indemnity should be calculated by reference to the relationship as a whole.

The third argument of the principal on construction was in relation to the interpretation of the requirement that the commercial agent must have "brought new customers" as per Regulation 17(3)(a). Counsel for the principal argued that the term "brought" meant "introduced", and that the commercial agent had not satisfied such a requirement since he had only met the clients at fairs. Mr Mitting rejected such an argument, stating that to bring new customers simply meant that the commercial agent had to be "instrumental in obtaining the business of new customers".[324] Mr Mitting added that in practice, a customer can be "induced to place business with a principal by a variety of means".[325] Mr Mitting reinforced his argument by looking at the section of the 1996 report of the European Commission on the Directive which dealt with German law, which stated that a small level of involvement was sufficient and that it was enough if the commercial agent had merely contributed to bringing the new customer.[326]

The last two arguments of the principal relate to the actual calculation of the indemnity. First, counsel for the principal argued that Regulation 17(4) requires the court, in effect but not in terms, to look only at the year following the termination in order to assess the amount of indemnity due. Mr Mitting rejected such an argument stating that "one of the things that has to be assessed is the extent to which the principal continues to derive substantial benefits from the efforts of the agent. The value of the business which remains for the benefits of the principal can (. . .) be assessed by reference to periods as short as a year. But there is nothing in the regulations that requires them to be thus limited".[327] As a consequence, "if on the evidence the benefits of the agent's efforts are likely to endure for more than a year after the termination" then, "the assessment need not be limited to looking at the period of one year after termination only".[328] As we have seen earlier, this is in line with what the German courts are doing, since the benefits can last to five years or more in case of durable goods.[329]

Secondly, counsel for the principal tried to argue that the requirement whereby the indemnity "must be equitable" as per Regulation 17(3)(b), was not met in this instance. Counsel for the principal tried to argue that in relation to this requirement, although it is different from the mitigation principles under domestic contract law, something akin to what applies to wrongful dismissal cases in employment law should apply. Mr Mitting also rejected such a line of argument on the ground that the requirement of equity is only relevant in relation to the evaluation of the indemnity itself by stating that "if evidence shows that the percentage is grossly disproportionate either way to the efforts of the agent so as to produce an inequitable result, then it might be necessary to enquire into such

323. *Ibid*, at p 181c.
324. *Ibid*, at p 180f.
325. *Ibid*, at p 180d.
326. As mentioned earlier, causation in German law for this purpose is reasonably lax since it is sufficient if the efforts of the commercial agent contribute to the client buying the goods of the principal. For details, see section 6.4.1.1 especially fnn 255–258 and associated text.
327. [1999] 1 All ER 174 at p 181j.
328. *Ibid*.
329. See fn 251 above and associated text.

factors".[330] He however said that "equitable principles might require there to be taken into account such part of the goodwill as the agent was able to exploit himself (. . .) for the benefit of another principal".[331] This is, once again, a reasonably accurate representation of what happens when the German courts look at whether the calculation of indemnity is equitable when the commercial agent can work for competitors after termination of the agency relationship.[332]

In relation to the actual calculation of the indemnity, the result is generally positive. Closely following the first two German law requirements defined earlier, Mr Mitting calculated that the indemnity payable to the commercial agent was £92,000. The way he arrived at such a figure was criticised[333] on the ground that Mr Mitting calculated the figure by reference to the "value of the business of the principal",[334] as opposed to the commissions earned by the commercial agent. We disagree with this criticism for two reasons. First, as mentioned earlier, in German law, the two notions are very closely related. Secondly, looking at earlier comments by Mr Mitting as to the meaning of "value of the business of the principal", this refers to "the value to the principal of the business of new customers brought by the agent (. . .) and of existing customers whose business has been substantially increased",[335] which is the correct method used in Germany.

Some criticisms relating to the latter part of the calculation are, however, warranted. For instance, it is not clear on which basis Mr Mitting decided that the length of the benefits of the principal was 2.75 years.[336] Additionally, after applying the cap defined at Regulation 17(4), Mr Mitting decided that the final sum to be awarded was that of £64,526.33. He did not however give any detail as to how he calculated that particular sum. This is regrettable.

6.5 CONCLUSION

The most substantial improvement to commercial agents legal protection is undoubtedly their mandatory[337] right to claim compensation or indemnity on termination pursuant to Regulation 17(1). It is now well known that such rights are inspired from, respectively, French and German law, which consider that commercial agents are financially weaker than their principals and therefore need protection. This protection takes the form of a lump-sum-payment on termination in recognition of the commercial agent's efforts in creating a customer base for the principal's goods. After an uncertain start, the English and the Scottish courts now accept that the French-based compensation and the German-based indemnity are very different in their nature and rationale from any traditional common law rules. This acceptance of the civil law origin of such concepts is a positive development since it ensures that the courts in this country apply the protective stance of the Agency regulations.

330. [1999] 1 All ER 174, at p 182g.
331. *Ibid*, at p 182f.
332. See section 6.4.1.1, especially fnn 301–305 and associated text.
333. Randolph and Davey, *Guide to the Commercial Agency Regulations*, (2nd edn, 2003), p 96.
334. [1999] 1 All ER 174 at p 184j.
335. *Ibid*, at p 181f.
336. Randolph and Davey, *op cit*, p 97.
337. Case C–381/98 *Ingmar Ltd* v. *Eaton Leonard Technologies Inc* [2001] 1 CMLR 9.

The situation is however not perfect and there is still considerable disagreement as to how compensation and indemnity should be calculated. This disagreement creates uncertainty which threatens the protection of commercial agents. The situation is particularly acute in relation to the French-based compensation.

In relation to indemnity, the problems seem due, at least in part, to the fact that even if the Agency Regulations do not give precise detail as to how indemnity should be calculated, limited guidance nevertheless exists in the conditions provided by Regulation 17(3). Moreover, following Regulation 17(4), the payment is capped to one-year remuneration calculated on the commercial agent's average remuneration earned over the last five years of the relationship, or less if the relationship has not lasted so long.

In relation to the French-based compensation, no such cap exists. The Scottish courts seem in general inclined to take guidance from the French courts and two years' worth of gross commission was awarded by the Court of Session in the case of *King* v. *Tunnock*.[338] The English courts however are more reluctant to do so because they consider the award of two years worth of gross commission to be an "excessive windfall"[339] which does not "value the loss of the asset of the commercial agent"[340] . In the light of the difference in attitude between the English and the Scottish courts, this chapter has had to address the question whether it is necessary for the various courts in this country to have regard to what their French and German counterparts do in such circumstances, or whether they can calculate compensation and indemnity following their own methods. We have argued that calculating such payments by reference to French and German standards would ensure uniformity of calculation across Europe and across the UK. However, since there is no legal obligation on the English and the Scottish courts to follow what their French and German counterparts do, we therefore argue that it is perfectly possible for the courts in this country to use their own method of calculation, even if such methods might differ from those adopted in France and Germany.

Yet, this chapter has also shown that even though the courts in this country have understood not only the need for compensation and indemnity but also their rationale, certain aspects of the calculation of such payments still eludes them. For that reason, we have provided illustrations as to how the French and German courts calculate the compensation and indemnity payments. It is nevertheless necessary to reiterate once again that the illustrations of the French and German calculation of their termination payments is provided purely as some relevance and not conclusive evidence on how to approach compensation and indemnity. This is especially true in relation to the French-based compensation, since the judicial practice to award two years' worth of gross commission has come under recent criticisms from French academic writers for not being truly representative of the loss suffered by the commercial agent, and, as has been noted, there are practical ways in which businesses in France seek to circumvent this obligation of principals.

For each termination payment, the study of the French and German case law was followed by close scrutiny of the English and Scottish case law to date. Because of the way the Agency Regulations implement the Directive, most case law involve compensation. As a result, more time has inevitably been spent on the French-based option as

338. [2000] Eu LR 531.
339. *Ingmar GB Ltd* v. *Eaton Leonard Inc* [2002] ECC 5, *per* Morland J at para 52.
340. *Barrett McKenzie* v. *Escada (UK) Ltd* [2001] Eu LR 567, *per* Bowers J at para 15.

opposed to the German-based indemnity, for which *Moore* v. *Piretta*[341] is the only case to have considered in detail how indemnity should be calculated. In this case, the High Court showed a good understanding of the legal basis of indemnity, and the judge made conscious efforts to emulate how the German courts calculate indemnity. The case is not perfect, but its weaknesses are limited to the lack of precise details as to how the High Court arrived at the cap of one year's worth of remuneration.

In relation to the French-based compensation, reviewing in detail how the English courts consider this termination payment, cases such as *Duffen* v. *FraBo*[342] and *Bell Electric* v. *Aweco Appliance Systems GmbH*[343] show that the relationship between common law rules and the Agency Regulations is inevitably difficult. However, the impact of such cases must not be overemphasised, since the review of more recent cases is on the whole positive. The resistance of the English courts to look at French law for guidance on the calculation of the compensation is not *per se* a problem. Reviewing the more recent cases, we can see that the English courts are clearly aware of the acute need to devise some kind of UK-based criteria in order to calculate compensation payments in a manner which represents accurately the loss to the commercial agent. A mixed first attempt was made by Morland J in the case of *Ingmar Ltd* v. *Eaton Leonard Technologies Inc.*[344] A more considered attempt was made by Davis J in *Tigana Ltd* v. *Decoro Ltd*[345] who offered a (non-exhaustive) list of 13 criteria. We have however seen that some of these criteria show a tendency to mix French-based compensation and German-based indemnity. Following the interesting proposal of Bowers J in the case of *Barrett McKenzie* v. *Escada Ltd*,[346] to calculate compensation as if one were valuing "the goodwill that one might have in a business",[347] seems the most practical.

Even though commercial agency agreements are not traditionally regarded as being *subject* to competition law, there are nevertheless some issues to consider. Such considerations are the subject of the next chapter.

341. [1999] 1 All ER 174.
342. [2000] 1 Lloyd's Rep 180.
343. [2002] EWHC 872.
344. [2002] ECC 5.
345. [2003] EWHC 23, [2003] Eu LR 189.
346. [2001] Eu LR 567.
347. *Ibid*, para 32.

CHAPTER 7

COMPETITION LAW

In this chapter, we shall deal with the treatment of commercial agency agreements in competition law, which ought to be straightforward but, as the length of this chapter shows, is not as straightforward as one might imagine.

We shall deal first, however, with the related matter of Regulation 20 of the Agency Regulations, the specific provision about post-termination restrictive covenants accepted by the commercial agent.

7.1 POST-TERMINATION RESTRAINT OF TRADE CLAUSES ACCEPTED BY THE COMMERCIAL AGENT: REGULATION 20 OF THE AGENCY REGULATIONS

7.1.1 Generally

Regulation 20 provides as follows:

(1) A restraint of trade clause shall be valid only if and to the extent that
   (a) it is concluded in writing; and
   (b) it relates to the geographical area or the group of customers and the geographical area entrusted to the commercial agent and to the kind of goods covered by his agency under the contract.

(2) A restraint of trade clause shall be valid for not more than two years after termination of the agency contract.

(3) Nothing in this regulation shall affect any enactment or rule of law which imposes other restrictions on the validity or enforceability of restraint of trade clauses or which enables a court to reduce the obligations of the parties resulting from such clauses.

"Restraint of trade clause" is defined in Regulation 2(1) as "an agreement restricting the business activities of a commercial agent following termination of the agency contract". Regulation 20 accordingly has no bearing on any restrictions to which the commercial agent may agree which operate during the life of the commercial agency agreement (though EC competition law may do (see below)); nor does it have any bearing on any restrictions to which the principal may agree (most importantly, possible limitations on its freedom to appoint other commercial agents or other intermediaries).

While there is no express statement in the Agency Regulations that Regulation 20 is of mandatory effect, it is inconceivable, given its subject-matter, that it is not such.

7.1.2 "Concluded in writing"

The requirement that the restraint of trade clause be concluded in writing envisages something different from the memorandum of terms provided for in Regulation 13.[1] A written memorandum of an oral agreement, which would, under Regulation 13, suffice for all the other terms of the agreement, will not suffice for the restraint of trade clause. The actual restraint of trade clause must be written and signed. There is, however, no other requirement as to form (either at common law or under the Agency Regulations).

If both parties (or, conceivably, their duly authorised representatives) have signed a single document, or identical versions of the same document, the requirement will obviously be satisfied. Where, however, the principal has signed the final version of the written agreement, has sent it out to the commercial agent for signature and return, but the commercial agent begins to perform as if the agreement is in force on those terms but never physically signs the document, it would appear that the restraint of trade clause is not binding on the commercial agent because the agreement has not been "concluded in writing".[2] If the parties are not going to sign the agency agreement simultaneously in a meeting, it is essential for principals to remember to insist that commercial agents sign and return their agreements.

7.1.3 The geographical, customer and product limits in Regulation 20

The similarity between these ideas and the principles applied in English common law restraint of trade and in UK and EC competition law on the restrictions accepted by the vendor on the sale of a business is obvious. The aim is that a valid restriction should go no further than the geographical area, the types of customer and the range of products with which the commercial agent was dealing during his time as commercial agent. The drafting of Regulation 20 reflects the attitude in EC competition law at the time of enactment of the Directive to vendor restrictive covenants on the sale of a business.[3] In EC competition law, a somewhat more liberal position is now taken. A vendor restraint on sale of a business is now treated as "directly related to and necessary for" a merger[4] (so that its status will stand or fall depending on whether the substance of the merger transaction itself would "significantly impede effective competition in the common market", the substantive test of whether a concentration with Community dimension will or will not be prohibited under the EC Merger Control Regulation[5]) if it extends also to preventing the vendor from trading in areas in which it was not at the time of the sale trading but into which it was planning to move at that time,[6] provided it had already made some investment into preparing for that, and from trading in products which were not yet on the

1. See Chapter 2, section 2.4.3 above.

2. See by analogy the case law on what is now Article 23 of EC Council Regulation 44/2001 (OJ L.12/1 of 16 January 2001), the former Article 17 of the Brussels Convention on Jurisdiction and Enforcement of Judgments in Civil and Commercial Matters, where, in relation to exclusive jurisdiction clauses, there is a formal requirement for writing in terms rather more permissive than those of Regulation 20, q.v. A Layton and H Mercer (eds) *European Civil Practice* (2nd edn, 2004), paras 20.070ff.

3. Commission decision in *Reuter/BASF*, OJ L. 254/40 1976; ECJ case 42/84 *Remia* v. *Commission*, [1985] ECR 2545.

4. EC Council Regulation 139/2004, OJ L. 24/1 of 29 January 2004; see recital 21.

5. EC Council Regulation 139/2004, fn 4 above, Art 2.

6. European Commission *Notice on restrictions directly related to and necessary for concentrations*, OJ C. 56/24 of 5 March 2005, para 22.

market at the time of the business sale but were either at an advanced stage of development or were fully developed but not yet marketed.[7] This somewhat more permissive attitude is not present in Regulation 20, though if it were, it would, given the typical power of the principal in the relationship, be difficult to control effectively.

Regulation 20 refers to the geographical area and customers "entrusted to the commercial agent" and to the kind of goods "covered by his agency under the contract". The limits of the permissible restriction where the commercial agent has in practice only operated in an area or with a range of customers or products narrower than the full range entrusted to him under the commercial agency agreement is not clear.

7.1.4 The duration of the permitted restriction under Regulation 20

The words used in Regulation 20(2) are "shall be valid for not more than two years after termination of the agency contract". As the first draft of the Directive said that the restraint would be valid only if it was "limited to a period of not more than two years from termination", it has been suggested[8] that the wording finally adopted has the effect that, for example, a restraint of trade clause stated to be of four years' duration could be severed and made into a valid restraint of two years' duration, rather than failing entirely. Certainly the wording of Regulation 20(2) does not seem to prevent that being done. Whether it can actually be done, to our mind, at least where English law is the law applicable to the contract (and so governs the consequences of the contract being void) comes up against the technical limitations of the law of severance. Whilst the courts will, where they can and where it accords with public policy,[9] sever the offending parts of the contract from the good, they cannot and will not make a new contract for the parties. Accordingly, they will cross words out (the "blue pencil" test), but they will not write words into the contract to substitute a lesser restriction which they consider would be valid. In particular, if the duration of a restraint of trade clause is too long, they will not substitute a shorter period.[10] To be able to make the severance suggested will therefore only be possible where the contract contains the not uncommon "boilerplate" severance clause, to the effect that if one provision is found to be void, that is not to affect any other provision in the agreement and that the parties will attempt to agree in its place a valid and enforceable provision which achieves as closely as possible the same effect as the relevant provision.[11] Such a term is of doubtful effectiveness, an agreement to agree being in English law unenforceable,[12] though there is some limited judicial support for the idea that it at least implies an obligation on the parties to negotiate in good faith for a time.[13]

It is important to note that there have been cases where restrictive covenants for less than two years have been held, on the common law restraint of trade principles, to be invalid (particularly in the employment context). It is possible that commercial agency would be treated as akin to employment for this purpose. The extent to which there is still

7. *Ibid*, para 23.

8. Randolph and Davey, *Guide to the Commercial Agents Regulations* (2nd edn, Hart Publishing, 2003), p 105.

9. See (ed.) H Beale *Chitty on Contracts* (24th edn, 2004), paras 16–188ff.

10. *Living Design (Home Improvements) Ltd* v. *Davidson* [1994] IRLR 67.

11. See, for example, Macfarlanes, *Boilerplate* in (ed. Battersby) *Commercial Contracts* (Legal and Commercial Publishing Ltd, 2004), Vol. I, Marketing contracts and sales finance, clause 20 in the draft clauses.

12. *Walford* v. *Miles* [1992] 2 AC 128.

13. *Donwin Productions Ltd* v. *EMI Films Ltd* [1984] CLY 365.

a role for the common law restraint of trade principles, in the light of the EC competition law modernisation regulation, is considered below.

7.1.5 The relevance of the manner of termination of the commercial agency agreement

On general principles of contract law, if the principal (being the promisee of the commercial agent's post-termination restraint of trade clause) commits a repudiatory breach of contract (i.e. a breach of a major term or a breach which has very serious consequences for the other party,[14] such as to allow the commercial agent to regard that as having brought the contract to an end), then if the commercial agent accepts the repudiation, the contract is terminated, and with it the restraint of trade clause, which will not be binding on the commercial agent after termination. Such was held by the House of Lords in *General Billposting Co Ltd* v. *Atkinson*[15] to be the effect of wrongful dismissal at common law on an employee's post-termination restraint of trade clause under his contract of employment. The position under a commercial agency agreement is identical.

What, however, of a post-termination restraint of trade clause expressed to take effect upon termination of the contract "howsoever caused"? In *D.* v. *M.*,[16] such a clause was held to be in unreasonable restraint of trade and unenforceable for that reason alone, regardless of the width of the clause and of how the termination actually arose. That approach has, however, now been overruled by the Court of Appeal in *Rock Refrigeration Ltd* v. *Jones*,[17] where the court said that, in relation to a restraint of trade clause stated to operate on termination "howsoever occasioned" one has to look at how the termination took place. If the termination was a repudiatory breach by the employer which the employee accepted, the clause would become unenforceable on the employee accepting the repudiation. If, on the other hand, the employer's breach was a repudiatory breach but the employee did not accept it and carried on performing the contract of employment regardless (and only terminated some time later), or if the breach by the employer was not a repudiatory one but the employee nevertheless terminated the contract, such a restraint of trade clause (assuming it to be reasonable in terms of its width) in such circumstances would remain operative.

7.1.6 Regulation 20(3): the further requirement that the commercial agency agreement comply with applicable competition law and restraint of trade principles

This is dealt with below.

7.2 COMPETITION LAW

7.2.1 Generally

In general, commercial agency agreements ought not to give rise to competition law concerns. Indeed, often the very reason for a supplier choosing them as its preferred route

14. See, e.g. JR Bradgate, *Commercial Law* (Butterworths, 3rd edn, 2001), pp 107–109.
15. [1909] AC 118.
16. [1996] IRLR 192.
17. [1997] 1 All ER 1.

to market is that a far higher degree of control of commercial agent by principal is permitted in competition law than is possible between supplier and distributor (control of downstream selling prices, control of the commercial agent in its choice of trading areas and customers, etc).[18] Nonetheless, there are complications, as the length of the following section shows.

Until 1 May 2005 there was an important difference between EC competition law and UK competition law in their respective treatments of vertical agreements. It was accordingly important to decide whether EC competition law applied (which it would do if the agreement had an effect on trade between EU countries[19]) or if it was subject only to UK competition law (which it would be if its effects on trade were felt purely within the UK or in a part of the UK[20]). The difference was that, in UK law from 1 March 2000 (the date when the Competition Act 1998 came into force) until 30 April 2005 vertical agreements were excluded from the Chapter I prohibition under the Competition Act 1998[21] (the ban on anti-competitive agreements "cloned" from Article 81 EC) unless they provided for resale price maintenance (although they were not excluded from the possible application of the Chapter II prohibition if one of the parties was dominant). The exclusion of vertical agreements was removed with effect from 1 May 2005,[22] such that vertical agreements are now subject to the Chapter I prohibition under the 1998 Act. In the light of the similarity between Article 81 EC and the Chapter I prohibition and of the "consistency" principle in section 60 of the 1998 Act,[23] it is safe to assume (even though the current OFT published guidance on vertical agreements[24] makes no reference to them) that the position of agency agreements under the Competition Act 1998 is the same, for all practical purposes, as that under Article 81 EC.

On general principles, an agreement will only fall within Article 81 EC if (i) it is made between businesses which are independent of each other (independent "undertakings"), (ii) it affects or could affect trade between EU countries,[25] (iii) it has the object or effect of preventing, restricting or distorting competition within the EU, and (iv) (unless it contains certain restrictions of competition which are treated as anti-competitive by object and thus "hardcore") it is, when taken in context, more than insignificant.[26]

A crucial point needs to be made here, namely that a contractual restriction on the freedom of action of one or both parties does not necessarily result in a restriction of competition for competition law purposes. As a major treatise in English on competition law puts it:

> ... the concept of a restriction of competition is an economic one, and as a general proposition economic analysis is needed to determine whether an agreement could have an anti-competitive effect. A relatively small class of agreements are considered by law to have as their object the

18. See the earlier discussion in Chapter 2, section 2.2.3.
19. See the Commission *Notice on the effect on trade concept*, OJ C. 101/81 of 27 April 2004.
20. Section 2 Competition Act 1998.
21. By the *Competition Act 1998 (Land and Vertical Agreements)(Exclusion) Order 2000*, SI 2000/310.
22. By the *Competition Act 1998 (Land Agreements Exclusion and Revocation) Order 2004*, SI 2004/1260.
23. Q v. M Coleman and M Grenfell, *The Competition Act 1998: Law and Practice* (OUP, 1999), p 44ff and Freeman and Whish in Freeman and Whish (eds), *Butterworths Competition Law*, Section I, paras 1353ff (pages I/567ff).
24. OFT Competition Law Guideline *Vertical agreements: understanding competition law* (OFT 419, 2004).
25. Q.v. fn 19 above.
26. As to which aspect, see the Commission *Notice on agreements of minor importance*, OJ C. 368/11 of 22 December 2001.

restriction of competition, and even then some market analysis is required to establish that any restriction of competition is appreciable and that trade between Member States will be affected; in the case of all other agreements, anti-competitive effects must be demonstrated for there to be a breach of Article 81(1).[27]

In relation to agency agreements, though, there is a crucial preliminary point, namely whether the agreement between principal and commercial agent is an "agreement between [independent] undertakings" for Article 81 purposes at all.

7.2.2 Is a commercial agency agreement an "agreement between undertakings" for Article 81 purposes?

In substance, the question amounts to whether the commercial agent is "integrated" into the principal's business or not.

The key question is whether:

— the principal and commercial agent are sufficiently independent of each other that their commercial agency agreement qualifies as an "agreement between [independent] undertakings" under Article 81 EC at all, or

— whether they are so closely tied together that, in EC competition law, the commercial agent can be treated as part of the same economic unit as the principal, in effect an auxiliary part of the principal's business (akin to an employee or a division or a subsidiary), such that the agreement between them should be treated as an internal division of tasks within a single economic entity, and not as an "agreement between [independent] undertakings".[28]

In the latter event, Article 81 will not apply to several of the provisions in the commercial agency agreement which look to be restrictive (but may not be entirely inapplicable), because the commercial agent lacks the necessary element of independence to be able to behave as an independent player in the market.

The criteria for assessing whether a commercial agent is independent of or "integrated" within the principal's business were very uncertain in the past.

The European Commission, in its 1962 *Notice on exclusive dealing contracts with commercial agents*[29] (revoked by the 2000 *Guidelines on Vertical Restraints*[30]), said that commercial agents are auxiliaries to their principal's carrying on business and that the essential issue was whether the commercial agent assumed any "financial risk" for the sales he concluded or for the performance of the obligations to the customer.

The case law of the ECJ up to 2000

In case law in the subsequent decades, however, the ECJ plainly took the view that the emphasis in the 1962 Commission Notice on the commercial agent's bearing of "financial

27. Freeman and Whish (eds.), *Butterworths Competition Law*, Section I, para 166 (page I/105).

28. It is noteworthy, for example, that the Commission *Notice on restrictions directly related and necessary to concentrations*, OJ C. 56/24 of 5 March 2005, saying, in the context of the parties who may be bound by the vendor in the usual vendor restrictive covenant on the sale of a business, that the "the vendor may bind himself/herself, her/his subsidiaries and commercial agents", equates commercial agents with the vendor's corporate group and assumes that they have no commercial independence of their own (*ibid*, para 24).

29. OJ 139 of 24 December 1962, p 2921.

30. OJ C 291/1 of 13 October 2000, para 12, fn 7.

risk", as a proxy test for "auxiliarity", had the effect of excluding from the scope of Article 81 numbers of commercial agency agreements where the commercial agent was plainly a significant player in the market and capable of acting independently in it, in particular where the commercial agent acted for a number of unconnected principals and was not dependent on any of them. In all these cases, the companies in question were arguing that the agreements between them were not caught by Article 81 EC, on the basis (*inter alia*) that, as one party was a commercial agent and therefore supposedly dependent on the principal, they were not "agreements between undertakings".

Thus, in the European *Sugar Cartel* case[31] in the early 1970s, the ECJ held (confirming the Commission's decision on the point) that agreements between sugar producers and powerful German sugar traders which were, in terms of German commercial law, commercial agency agreements within the specific German legislation, authorising the traders to act as sales agents for the sugar producers in certain territories (although in other areas they acted as distributors), were not agency agreements for the purposes of what was then Article 85 EC. The ECJ took the view that the agents acted as commercial agents in those markets where, had they been independent distributors, they could have posed a competitive threat to the supplier, and were only allowed by the supplier to act as distributor in those markets where they could do the supplier no competitive harm. "Such an ambivalent relationship", said the court, "which in respect of the same commodity only gives the trader the opportunity of continuing to operate independently to the extent that it is in the interests of his supplier for him to do so" was not a "genuine" agency agreement in EC competition law, regardless of how national commercial law might classify the matter.[32]

In the *Flemish Travel Agents*[33] case, the ECJ similarly held that travel agents, selling holidays on behalf of a wide range of unconnected tour operator principals and where the tour operators marketed their products through numerous different travel agents, were independent undertakings in their own right and not auxiliary to the businesses of the tour operators nor any of them.[34]

In *Bundeskartellamt* v. *Volkswagen AG and VAG Leasing GmbH*,[35] the ECJ held that VW dealers who were appointed as exclusive agents for areas of Germany by a VW group vehicle leasing company, were independent undertakings in their own right. The dealers' main activity, in addition to fulfilling this role, was as authorised car dealers re-selling Audi/VW cars in their own right, and in relation to the vehicle leasing business in which they were agents they provided after-sales service on their own account and purchased vehicles from the VW group leasing company on expiry of the leases. In this case, the ECJ made the clear statement:

31. ECJ 40/73 and others *Suiker Unie* v. *Commission*, [1975] ECR 1663.

32. *Ibid*, paras 544 and 547.

33. ECJ 311/85 *Vereniging van Vlaamse Reisbureaus* v. *VZW Sociale Dienst van de Plaatselijke en Gewestelijke Overheidsdiensten*, [1987] ECR 3801.

34. Consistently with this, the European Commission, in its decision in *Virgin/British Airways*, OJ L. 30/1 of 4 February 2000, identified a market for air travel agency services to airlines in which it said BA was a dominant buyer; the CFI endorsed the Commission analysis (case T–219/99 *British Airways* v. *Commission*, 17 December 2003, [2003] ECR II–5917, saying that travel agents are "independent intermediaries carrying on an independent business of providing services" (para 93).

35. ECJ C–266/93, [1995] ECR I–3477.

Representatives can lose their character as independent traders only if they do not bear *any* of the risks resulting from the contracts negotiated on behalf of the principal *and* they operate as auxiliary organs forming an integral part of the principal's undertaking.[36] (our emphasis)

That the same agreement could be, as to parts of it, an agreement with an agent qualifying as "auxiliary" to the principal's business and, as to other parts of it, an agreement between two independent undertakings, is shown by the Commission decision in *ARG/ Unipart*.[37]

The Commission Guidelines on Vertical Restraints

Paragraph 12–20 of the Commission Guidelines on Vertical Restraints[38] are the current statement by the European Commission of its position on commercial agency agreements under Article 81, representing its distillation of the ECJ case-law, amalgamated with its earlier practice and its modern thinking on vertical agreements generally.

The determining factor in determining whether principal and commercial agent are independent of each other is (still) "whether the agent bears a significant financial or commercial risk in relation to his agency activities".[39] Paragraph 13 goes on to say that it is immaterial whether the agent acts for one or for several principals. It is noteworthy that this factor has, on the contrary, plainly been important down the years to the ECJ and, as recent case law shows, continues to be so. To this extent, Commission practice does not seem properly to reflect the case law of the ECJ (and now that of the CFI), which is best encapsulated in the passage from the ECJ judgment in *Bundeskartellamt* v. *Volkswagen* quoted above.

An agency agreement will be considered to be a "genuine" one (so that the commercial agent will not be treated as an independent business in its own right) and the obligations it imposes on the commercial agent as to the negotiation and conclusion of contracts (but not necessarily other parts of the agreement) will fall outside Article 81 EC, if the agent bears no, or only insignificant, financial and commercial risks in relation to those contracts. Where, on the other hand, the commercial agent bears such risks, he will be treated as an independent undertaking in his own right (on the basis that he is then treated as needing to remain free to decide his own marketing strategy so that he can recoup his investment[40]). In this latter event, the competition law treatment of the agency agreement will be akin to that of a distribution agreement, and consideration will generally need to be given to the possible application of the vertical agreements block exemption.[41]

There are two types of financial or commercial risks which are relevant for deciding whether the agent is a "genuine" agent for this purpose:

- those which are directly related to the contracts negotiated or concluded by the agent on behalf of the principal, e.g. as to the financing of stock or the credit risk with the customer;
- those which relate to investments specifically required for the type of selling activity and product for which the agent has been appointed by the principal, and

36. *Ibid*, para 19.
37. OJ L. 45/34, 18 February 1988.
38. OJ C. 291/1 of 13 October 2000.
39. *Ibid*, para 13.
40. *Ibid*, para 15.
41. Commission Regulation 2790/99, OJ L. 366/21 of 29 December 1999; see below.

which could not be used for other activities if the agent stops selling this type of product and conducting this particular type of activity (in effect, sunk costs[42]).

The general risks inherent in any trading activity (e.g. the liability to pay staff wages, the office rent, the risk that commission levels will fluctuate over a period) do not count as financial and commercial risks for this purpose.

The Guidelines on Vertical Restraints give the following (non-exclusive) list of examples of situations where, if the commercial agent regularly incurs one or more of the listed risks, he is likely to be treated as accepting a significant financial or commercial risk so that he would have to be treated as an independent undertaking for Article 81 purposes. The issue of risk is, however, very much a case-by-case, facts-dependent one, and the legal form which the arrangement between the parties takes is not conclusive:

— if ownership of the goods bought or sold passes to the agent;
— if the agent provides the contract services on its own account;
— if the agent does any of the following
  (i) contributes to the costs of sale or purchase of the contract goods (e.g. paying transport costs out of his own money without reimbursement of these by the principal);
  (ii) is obliged to pay out of his own resources for sales promotion, to contribute to the principal's advertising budgets etc.;
  (iii) holds stocks of the contract goods at his own expense or risk;
  (iv) provides (whether he is required by the principal to do so or not) after-sales service, repair service or a warranty service, unless it is fully reimbursed by the principal;
  (v) makes market-specific investments in equipment, premises or training of personnel (para 16 quotes the example of an agent operating a petrol filling station who pays for his own fuel storage tanks to be installed, or an insurance agent buying specific software to sell insurance);
  (vi) is liable to third parties for damage caused by the products sold;
  (vii) is liable to the principal for customers' non-performance of their contracts.

The Mercedes-Benz/DaimlerChrysler case

An example of these criteria being applied is the European Commission decision of 10 October 2001 in *Mercedes-Benz*.[43] In fining DaimlerChrysler AG €71.8m for blocking parallel trade in its passenger cars in Germany, Belgium and Spain, the Commission concluded that Mercedes-Benz's sales agents in Germany (although they were commercial agents under the German Commercial Code) had commercial freedom and assumed commercial risks similar to the position of independent traders, and were thus "undertakings" in their own right for the purposes of EC competition law. In effect, the Commission treated them as equivalent to distributors buying goods for resale on their own account. The fact than the agents were not free to sell any brand of car other than Mercedes-Benz was not relevant and (consistently with para 13 of the Guidelines on Vertical Restraints) the Commission said (at para 163) that the criterion of integration is

42. Commission Guidelines on Vertical Restraints, fn 30 above, para 15.
43. Decision COMP/36.264, OJ L. 257/1 of 25 September 2002.

not a separate test from acceptance of risk in deciding whether a commercial agent is a "genuine" one for competition law purposes or not. The conclusive factor for the Commission was that the agents, under the agency agreement (many of the terms of which were in substance (and sometimes in the drafting) identical with those of Mercedes-Benz's standard dealership agreement[44]) were, in performing their obligations as agents, obliged to bear a large number of commercial risks themselves. The relevant risks were:

— if the agent granted discounts on new car sales that were approved by Mercedes-Benz, the discounts were to come entirely out of the agent's commission (i.e. it was, according to the Commission, just like a dealer's margin);
— the cost of transport of new cars from the factory to the end-user customer was to be borne by the agent not by Mercedes-Benz, and whether and how and how much of that the agent recovered from the customer was entirely the agent's affair;
— the agent had to put significant amounts of its own resources into sales promotion, especially the purchase of demonstrator vehicles, the numbers of which Mercedes-Benz could unilaterally set if it was not agreed;
— agents had to set up and equip their workshops and offer customer and guarantee services from their own resources and keep their own spare parts stocks on their own account (i.e. as dealers);
— the agents were bound (in the normal way) to perform repair work under warranty for any Mercedes-Benz car sold by any authorised agent or dealer, but the reimbursement from Mercedes-Benz for doing this was at a standard rate, regardless of the actual cost to the agent of the parts and labour involved.

The Commission accordingly decided that "in view of the number and quantitative scope of the risks that Mercedes-Benz agents have to bear", the agents in Germany were not "genuine" commercial agents for the purposes of EC competition law. The Commission said the position would only be different if the agents could choose whether to assume those risks and if they had a choice merely to negotiate new car sales and do nothing more.[45]

The European Court of First Instance in *DaimlerChrysler AG* v. *Commission*,[46] in annulling the relevant part of the Commission decision in *Mercedes-Benz*, has recently said that the Commission had not applied all the right principles in trying to decide when a commercial agent is an undertaking independent from its principal, and that, where it had applied the right principles, it had misunderstood the facts. It had looked at the agency agreement as a document and not at what happened in practice, and overall had taken an exaggerated view of the extent of the commercial and financial risks accepted by the commercial agent. The judgment is consistent with the very "hands-on" style of judicial review which the CFI now performs in competition cases.

The CFI held that the Mercedes-Benz commercial agents in Germany were not undertakings independent of Mercedes-Benz, but, rather, were highly integrated parts of Mercedes-Benz's business with no commercial freedom to speak of, and thus akin to employees. This had the effect that the alleged agreements between Mercedes-Benz and

44. *Ibid*, para 164.
45. *Ibid*, paras 153ff.
46. T–325/01 *DaimlerChrysler AG v. Commission*, judgment of 15 September 2005.

its German commercial agents, that the latter would not deal with potential "passive" customers from outside their allocated areas, made with a view to blocking parallel trade in a new generation of Mercedes E-class car, were not agreements between undertakings for the purposes of Article 81 EC, and therefore not prohibited. The fines which the Commission had imposed on Mercedes-Benz in respect of the relevant arrangements in Germany were therefore annulled.

The CFI quotes the passage from the ECJ judgment in *Bundeskartellamt* v. *Volkswagen*[47] set out above, which emphasises that a commercial agent will be treated as not being an independent undertaking separate from his principal only if

> ***both*** he does not bear *any* of the risks resulting from the contracts negotiated on behalf of the principal
> ***and*** he operates as an auxiliary, integrated part of the principal's business.

In para 163 of the *Mercedes-Benz* decision, on the other hand, the Commission specifically says (consistently with its position taken in 1999/2000 in its *Guidelines on Vertical Restraints*, para 15) that the criterion of integration/auxiliarity is not, unlike the assumption of risk, a separate criterion for distinguishing a commercial agent from a reseller. By itself considering both aspects, the CFI rejects this proposition.

Whilst the CFI deals in detail with the Commission's treatment of the issue of acceptance of commercial risks, it appears to have been more influenced by the auxiliarity/integration/ability or not of the commercial agent to behave as an independent player in the market aspect.

The Commission had considered the integration aspect in paras 161–168 of its decision. It had decided that the various contractual obligations which Mercedes-Benz had cited in support of the proposition that the commercial agents were "integrated" were the same as those accepted by the Mercedes-Benz dealers in Spain and Belgium (the other countries relevant in the investigation) and were therefore not appropriate criteria for distinguishing an "integrated" commercial agent from an independent dealer.

To the CFI, the fact that the Mercedes-Benz dealers in Spain and Belgium had a number of similar obligations in their contracts to those of the commercial agents in Germany did not prevent the latter group being "genuine" commercial agents. The crucial thing was what the two types of intermediary actually did, and this was very different.[48] The CFI noted[49] that the German commercial agents were marketing agents and not sales agents, authorised merely to find and negotiate with potential customers but with no authority to conclude sales contracts binding on Mercedes-Benz (the decision whether, and if so at what price and on what terms, to sell to a particular customer being one for the manufacturer itself to take). Furthermore, whilst the Mercedes-Benz agents in Germany carried on servicing and spare parts distribution functions as separate traders on their own account, they were forbidden under the terms of the standard form agency agreement to sell new Mercedes-Benz cars on their own account, and could only deal in other brands of new car under specified conditions.[50] The CFI noted that this was indeed how the arrangements worked in practice. On this basis, the CFI concluded that the Mercedes-Benz commercial agents in Germany had no real commercial freedom of their own as to

47. Fn 35.
48. See paras 114–118 of the judgment.
49. Para 92 of the judgment.
50. See para 162 of the Commission decision.

the essentials of the sales transaction (to whom to sell, and on what terms). They were the equivalent of employees of Mercedes-Benz, and thus were auxiliary to/integrated in the manufacturer's business. They were "genuine" commercial agents.

On the issue of the acceptance of risks, the CFI accepted that the Commission had broadly applied the right principles, but said that it had applied them wrongly to the facts, and had failed to explain in its decision how the various obligations of the agents under the agreement which it had identified as involving the acceptance of significant financial or commercial risks or liabilities actually had that effect.

On the issue of pricing, the CFI noted the freedom of the commercial agents to agree to split their commission with customers (so as, in effect, to give a discount, but not one that would affect the sale price received by Mercedes-Benz). The CFI took the view, however, that this did not reflect any appreciable commercial risk accepted by the commercial agent. Crucial to the CFI's assessment of the position was that, unlike the Spanish and Belgian distributors (who were clearly distributors, buying in stock and re-selling it at a margin), the commercial agents in Germany were (consistent with their status as commercial agents) not obliged to buy and hold stocks of new cars at their own cost and risk. The CFI saw the buying in and holding of stock as the essence of being an independent reseller[51] (though it is a rather "classical" way of looking at distribution systems, appearing to ignore modern aspects of distribution, "just-in-time" delivery, lean supply chains, etc). The CFI reasoned that the commercial agents' freedom to agree to split their commissions with customers was, in contrast with a dealer's decision on the price at which to re-sell (and thus to split his margin), not linked to the risk of having unsold stock and the possible need to drop the price to shift it. If one of the commercial agents could not persuade a potential customer that the latter wanted to buy a new car without agreeing a significant splitting of his commission and the agent was unwilling to do that, it was always open to him (so reasoned the court) simply not to pass on the order to Mercedes-Benz at all.[52] The CFI accordingly rejected the Commission's conclusion on the facts[53] that, in having the freedom to agree to split commission, the German commercial agents were accepting a real "price risk".

Having reached this conclusion on what it saw as the main issues, the CFI looked at the other aspects of financial and commercial risk which the Commission, in its decision, had identified as significant, with a view to deciding whether the view it reached on those might lead it to change its mind on the former.

The CFI was unimpressed by the Commission's argument that the bearing by the agents of the cost of transport of cars from factory to retail customer involved a significant risk for the agents, noting that about a third of customers in Germany chose to collect their new car from the factory and the rest were willing to pay a delivery charge such that the agents were unlikely ever to make a loss on the delivery costs aspect.

As to the obligation on the commercial agent to buy, using its own resources, numbers of new vehicles for demonstration purposes (where Mercedes-Benz could unilaterally fix the number if it was not agreed), the CFI accepted there might be a risk of the agent being unable to re-sell these subsequently at a profit, so that there was some acceptance of a commercial risk there. The court took the view, on the evidence, however, that the

51. Paras 97–99 of the judgment.
52. Para 97 of the judgment.
53. In paras 155–156 of the Commission decision.

likelihood was that these would be sold by Mercedes-Benz to the agent at a very favourable price and would be very saleable by the agents as ex-demonstrator models with a few thousand kilometres "on the clock" at significant discounts to the consumer to the price of a new car.

The obligations on the commercial agent to perform repair work under warranty and servicing under warranty, which the Commission had classified as involving the acceptance of a commercial risk by the commercial agent, seemed to the CFI to be largely risk-free, as the agent had an indemnity from the manufacturer in respect of warranty work. It was true that Mercedes-Benz's reimbursement rates assumed a notional average hourly rate for labour, and that some agents' actual labour costs might be higher, but it was, by implication, up to each agent to run a tight ship.[54] That significant investment was involved in setting up a repair shop and in holding stocks of spare parts (which, under the standard commercial agency agreement, the commercial agent was obliged to do at his own expense), according to the CFI, added nothing to the degree of risk accepted by the commercial agents as they were conducting those activities on their own account in any event and on different product markets. Furthermore, the Commission had not explained in its decision how these obligations being attached to the commercial agency agreements involved serious financial risks for the agents.

In substance, then, the CFI was plainly heavily influenced by what it saw as the lack of any real commercial freedom for the commercial agents on the key aspects of the selling decision, treating them as the equivalent of employees and thus as integrated, auxiliary parts of Mercedes-Benz's business.

This reassertion of the auxiliarity/integration test of when a commercial agent is a "genuine" one for competition law purposes is consistent with the earlier case law of the ECJ. The Commission's Guidelines on Vertical Restraints specifically ignore it. That view from the Commission will probably now have to change. Interestingly, though, the CFI accepts in *DaimlerChrysler* that acceptance of a commitment by the agent to invest its own resources in the agency activity and acceptance of a limited degree of commercial risk related to the trading contracts is not inconsistent with "genuine" commercial agent status, at least as long as the agent is not liable on the essential aspects of the trading contracts with which it is involved. This is something of a relaxation of the ECJ's formulation in *Bundeskartellamt* v. *Volkswagen* that, to be a "genuine" commercial agent for competition law purposes, the agent must not accept "any" of the risks resulting from the contracts negotiated on behalf of the principal. Unless the Commission appeals the *DaimlerChrysler* judgment to the ECJ, this is in practice likely to stand.

So, in *DaimlerChrysler*, the CFI seems to give with one hand and take away with the other. The Mercedes-Benz commercial agents were marketing-only agents with, on the key commercial issues (pricing and choice of customers), next to no commercial freedom of their own. Marketing-only agents, as opposed to sales agents[55] are fairly rare in the UK. On the other hand, the acknowledgement that a commitment by the agent to invest his own resources and some limited acceptance of risk related to the sales contracts is not inconsistent with "genuine" commercial agent status in competition law is a healthy clarification and acknowledgement of commercial reality.

54. Para 111 of the judgment.
55. See Chapter 2 for the difference.

In the light of *Bundeskartellamt* v. *Volkswagen*, and now *DaimlerChrysler*, there must now be doubts about whether the Commission's statement in para 15 of the Guidelines on Vertical Restraints, that it is immaterial to the issue of "genuineness" whether the commercial agent acts for one or more than one principal, can stand. The Commission, in issuing statements of its practice is, like everyone else, bound by the interpretation of EC law as enunciated by the European courts.

Will the reassertion by the European courts of the "double-barrelled" test of "genuineness", *à la Bundeskartellamt* v. *Volkswagen*, as elaborated on in *DaimlerChrysler*, lead to more commercial agents being found to be "genuine" ones (so that the relations between them and their principals are not "agreements between [independent] undertakings" and so not caught by Article 81) than the application of the Commission's "single-strand" "significant commercial financial risk" test as set out in the Guidelines on Vertical Restraints?

We tend to think that the arrangements between Mercedes-Benz and its dealers, where the latter, being marketing agents only, had no or next to no freedom on the key selling decisions, were very specific. Many commercial agents (particularly in the UK) will have significantly more commercial freedom than that. In such cases, even if the commercial agent accepts no, or only very limited, trading risks, and is not expected to make material investment of his own resources, the application of what we take to be the CFI's test of "genuineness" would seem likely to result in the agreement being treated as one between independent traders, where an application of the Commission's single-strand "acceptance of risks" test (certainly as now relaxed slightly by the CFI) might have led to the opposite conclusion. The judgment is helpful for marketing agents (which, as we note, are not very common in the UK) but less obviously helpful for sales agents.

What is important is the emphasis which the CFI's approach places on examining all the circumstances of how the commercial agency relationship actually works in the context of the market in question, an exercise not likely to help in terms of giving legal certainty for business. If in doubt, one should assume that one's commercial agency agreements would not be seen as "genuine" in competition law terms, and should treat them, as we explain in section 7.2.6 below, as if they were distribution agreements.

7.2.3 Consequences of the agency agreement being a "genuine" one for Article 81 purposes

If the agency agreement is a "genuine" one for Article 81 purposes, all obligations imposed on the agent in relation to the contracts he negotiates or concludes on behalf of the principal will fall outside Article 81(1). This will include limitations on the territory in which the agent may negotiate or negotiate and conclude sales on the principal's behalf; restrictions on the customers with whom the agent may negotiate or negotiate and conclude sales; and restrictions as to the price or other terms and conditions on which the agent may negotiate or negotiate and conclude those contracts.[56]

The rationale behind this is that such restrictions placed upon the commercial agent are merely the principal marking out the scope of the agent's authority, and that, as the principal is the party who will be liable on the contracts to which the agent's activities give

56. Commission *Guidelines on Vertical Restraints*, para 18.

rise, the principal (and not the commercial agent) will assume the financial and commercial risk of those contracts, so it is entirely reasonable that the principal should be free to do that.[57]

Article 82 EC may be relevant even if the commercial agent is a "genuine" one, e.g. if a dominant principal discriminates in the terms offered to different commercial agents or operates pricing or commission policies designed to tie commercial agents to him.

7.2.4 Circumstances in which Article 81(1) could nevertheless apply to a "genuine" agency agreement

Other terms agreed between principal and commercial agent will need to be considered in the normal way, as if the parties were independent undertakings.

Paragraph 19 of the Commission Guidelines on Vertical Restraints refers, predictably, to exclusivity rights granted to commercial agents for particular territories, customers or types of transaction and to obligations accepted by commercial agents not to act as agent or distributor for competitors of the principal (to which it refers as "non-compete obligations"). Paragraph 19 volunteers that exclusivity rights granted to commercial agents concern only intra-brand competition (competition between dealers in the same brand of product, at the distribution level only) "and will in general not lead to anti-competitive effects". It states, on the other hand, that "non-compete obligations", including post-term non-compete obligations, concern inter-brand competition and may infringe Article 81(1) if they lead to material foreclosure on the relevant market where the contract goods are bought or sold. In other words, there may be a breach of Article 81(1) if a "non-compete obligation"[58] leads to the principal's competitors experiencing a significant denial of access of routes to customers because, for whatever reason, there are not many alternative routes to market (which will largely depend on the principal's share of the relevant market (in effect, significance) and the number of realistic alternative routes to market). Whilst Article 81(1) may apply to the restrictions on the commercial agent's handling competing products, Article 5(a) of the vertical agreements block exemption will then help (within limits) assuming the principal's market share is less than 30 per cent.[59]

Other possible problems to bear in mind would be:

— Article 81 could apply even to a "genuine" agency agreement where the agency agreement facilitates collusion, e.g. where several unconnected competing principals use the same commercial agent and exclude (whether expressly or only in practice) other suppliers from trading through that agent or through parties connected with it, or where they use the commercial agent as a means of colluding on marketing strategy or to exchange sensitive market information between each other. Such situations would instinctively strike one as unusual: one would not normally expect competitors to be using the same intermediary as their route to market, but it could happen. In such a situation, the main problem is not each agreement between individual principal and the common agent but is, rather, such horizontal agreement or understanding as there may be between the different

57. *Ibid*, para 18.
58. See further the part of Section VI of the Guidelines concerned with "single branding" restrictions, paras 138–160.
59. See below.

competing principals[60] (or possibly a collective dominance issue under Article 82 EC[61]).

— agreements made by the commercial agent with customers on the principal's behalf will, for competition law purposes, be attributed to the principal on the basis that the commercial agent is part of the same economic entity. Accordingly, if those contracts include unlawful provisions (e.g. resale price maintenance, export bans etc imposed by the agent), the principal will be liable for them;

— if a commercial agent agrees with other commercial agents or distributors acting for competitors of the principal anti-competitive horizontal arrangements (horizontal price-fixing, market sharing etc), the principal is likely, on the same basis, to be found to have taken part in such arrangements, and arguments that such acts were unauthorised are unlikely to carry much weight in enforcement proceedings;[62]

— consistently with the market definition reasoning in *British Airways* v. *Commission*[63] that there is a relevant market for the marketing services provided by travel agents separate from the market from the holiday products they sell,[64] it would seem to follow that there would be a relevant market for the services provided by commercial agents or for those provided by commercial agents and distributors taken together, perhaps differentiated to some extent by reference to the products being handled. An agreement between commercial agents as to, say, the commission they would charge to a particular principal or to principals generally would be an unlawful horizontal cartel, whether the agency agreements between principal and commercial agent gave rise to "genuine" agency in competition law terms or not.

7.2.5 The possible application of UK competition law and restraint of trade principles to "genuine" agency agreements

If the agency agreement is a "genuine" one in the sense outlined above, the key terms setting out the agent's authority will not be caught by Article 81 EC nor, because of the consistency principle,[65] by Chapter I of the Competition Act 1998, on the basis that it is not an "agreement between undertakings".

Are the common law restraint of trade principles applicable to exclusive agency appointments and "non-compete obligations" in "genuine" agency agreements, as well as

60. For which one would need to consider the provisions on joint selling between competitors in the European Commission Guidelines on Horizontal Co-operation, OJ C. 3/2 of 6 January 2001.

61. On the concept of collective dominance and the abuse of a collective dominant position, see PM Roth (ed), *Bellamy & Child: European Community Law of Competition* (5th edn., 2001), para 9–060ff, and BE Sufrin in (eds P Freeman and R Whish) *Butterworths Competition Law*, Vol. II, para VI 506ff.

62. See PM Roth (ed.), *Bellamy & Child, European Community law of competition* (5th edn, Sweet & Maxwell, 2001), para 7–034, and, by analogy, ECJ case C–310/93 *BPB Industries and British Gypsum* v. *Commission*, [1995] ECR I–865, pp 872–874.

63. See fn 34, above.

64. In the same way that, in competition law terms, retailing is treated as a service market separate from the relevant market for the products in the shop.

65. See section 7.2.1 above.

EC and UK competition law, and what if the latter do not apply to the agreement in question? It seems likely that, at least where the agency agreement can be said to have an effect on trade between EU countries, they can no longer be applied in such situations.

Article 3 of EC Council Regulation 1/2003,[66] the EC competition law "modernisation" regulation, says that, where national competition agencies and national courts apply national competition law to agreements falling within Article 81(1) (i.e. those which affect trade between EU countries[67]), they must also apply Article 81(1). It says further that national competition law cannot prohibit agreements which EC competition law regards as valid, but that this does not affect provisions of national law which "predominantly pursue an objective different from" those of Articles 81 and 82.

There are some significant differences between the common law restraint of trade principles and Article 81 EC/the Chapter I prohibition in the Competition Act 1998. Most notably, the former looks at restrictions on the freedom of conduct of the parties and not, as competition law does, at the effect of the agreement on the wider market; and one judges reasonableness under the common law principles "once and for all" at the commencement of the agreement[68] rather than on a continuing basis during the life of the agreement.[69]

Nevertheless, in *Days Medical Aids Ltd* v. *Pihsiang Machinery Manufacturing Co Ltd*[70] Langley J held that the common law restraint of trade doctrine does not "predominantly pursue an objective different from Article 81 and 82".[71] He was there dealing with an exclusive distribution agreement which he decided was, for Article 81 purposes, neither anti-competitive by object nor by effect, so that if it was to be void it would only be because of the common law restraint of trade principles. He decided that, if the common law restraint of trade principles were applicable, EC competition law would prevent him from applying them, pausing to comment[72] that he suspected "it would come as something of a surprise to many practitioners if it were the case that the common law doctrine of restraint of trade, even in the non-employment field, had been emasculated, let alone trumped, by Community competition law", as he decided was the case. Regulation 1/2003 had been adopted but was not in force at the time of the judgment: he considered he had to apply the substance of Article 3, on the basis that it merely reflected pre-existing case law of the ECJ[73] which was already binding on him.

In relation to a "genuine" agency agreement which has an effect on inter-state trade within the EU, the reason it would not be prohibited under Article 81 is not that it did not have an anti-competitive object or effect, nor that it was exempt by virtue of Article 81(3) or a block exemption (the grounds referred to in Article 3(2) of Regulation 1/2003 as those which "trump" the application of national competition law). Rather, it would be because

66. EC Council Regulation 1/2003 on the implementation of the rules on competition laid down in Articles 81 and 82 of the Treaty, OJ L.1/1 of 4 January 2003.

67. As to which see European Commission *Notice on the effect on trade concept*, above.

68. *Gledhow Autoparts Ltd* v. *Delaney* [1965] 1 WLR 1366, 1377.

69. *Apple Corps Ltd* v. *Apple Computers Inc* [1991] 3 CMLR 49, at para 113; for a curious example of the consequences of which, see *Passmore* v. *Morland* [1999] EWCA Civ 696 (2 February 1999).

70. [2004] EWHC 44, 29 January 2004.

71. Para 265 of the judgment.

72. Para 254 of the judgment.

73. C–266/93 *Bundeskartellamt* v. *Volkswagen AG and VAG Leasing GmbH*, fn 35 above.

the agreement is not an "agreement between undertakings" at all. Technically, then, it seems that Article 3(2) of Regulation 1/2003 would not operate, so that an English court, on the face of it, could apply the restraint of trade principles. It is not clear what an English court, faced with such a situation, would do, though we think it more likely than not that it would regard Article 3(2) as preventing it from applying the common law rules regardless.

In a case where a "genuine" agency agreement had no effect on inter-state trade, Article 81 EC and Article 3 of Regulation 1/2003 would not be relevant. There is no provision in English law saying that the Competition Act 1998 displaces or overrides the common law restraint of trade principles. In such a situation, therefore, the restraint of trade principles could apply to the "genuine" agency agreement as well as the Competition Act 1998. Although it is firmly established that the principle applies to restraints operating during the life of the agreement as well as to post-termination ones,[74] the overall arrangement would have to be very one-sided indeed in favour of the principal for a "non-compete obligation" accepted by the commercial agent during the life of the agreement to be realistically challengeable on this basis, particularly in the light of the traditional English law classification of the agent as fiduciary. As to the position with post-termination restraints of trade, see below.

7.2.6 The non-"genuine" agency agreement

As identified above,[75] subject to (i) in EC law the agreement having an effect on trade between EC countries, and in UK law to its having an effect on trade within the UK or in a substantial part of the UK and (ii) the agreement taken in context being more than insignificant, Article 81 or Chapter I of the Competition Act 1998 will apply to those elements of the agreement which have as their object or effect the prevention, restriction or distortion of competition.

"Insignificance" is judged by reference to the Commission Notice on Agreements of minor importance.[76] In an agreement between non-competitors (actual or potential),[77] if each party's market share on every relevant market affected by the agreement is 15 per cent or less the agreement will not, according to the Commission, appreciably restrict competition within Article 81. If there is uncertainty as to whether the parties are competitors on this basis, one should apply the lower 10 per cent market share threshold of appreciability applicable to agreements between competitors, and the lower 5 per cent threshold if the market is affected by significant cumulative foreclosure effect from parallel networks of agreements that have a similar effect in the market.[78] Paragraph 2 of the Notice comments, though, that agreements where the thresholds are exceeded may still

74. *Schroeder Music Publishing Ltd* v. *Macauley* [1974] 1 WLR 1308.

75. Section 7.2.1.

76. The current version of which is at OJ C. 368/11 of 22 December 2001, and which presupposes the correct application of the Commission's *Notice on the definition of relevant market*, OJ C. 372/5 of 9 December 1997. See also OFT guideline Market Definition, OFT 403, December 2004.

77. The notion of actual and potential competitors is dealt with in more detail in the Commission *Guidelines on Horizontal Co-operation*, OJ C. 3 of 6 January 2001, in footnotes to para 9.

78. *Ibid*, fn 62, para 8. This may well not be easy to identify.

not appreciably restrict competition and not be prohibited,[79] and paragraph 3 notes that agreements to which the only parties are small and medium-sized undertakings[80] "are rarely capable of appreciably affecting trade between Member States". By paragraph 11 of the Notice, "insignificance" does not, however, prevent agreements involving various "hardcore" restrictions (horizontal price-fixing and market sharing and the hardcore restrictions in Article 4 of Regulation 2790/99) being prohibited by Article 81.

Agreements falling within Article 81, or (subject to the possibility of severance) the offending parts of them are, of course, "automatically void" by reason of Article 81(2) or "void" under section 2(4) (but the effect is the same), unless exemptable on the basis of Article 81(3) or the equivalent provisions in section 9 if the four conditions therein can be shown to apply.[81]

The obvious way for those conditions to be satisfied is for the agency agreement to be drafted so as to fall within the protection of the vertical agreements block exemption, Commission Regulation 2790/99,[82] assuming that the background circumstances for that block exemption to apply (the 30 per cent market share cap etc) apply. If the goods with which the agency agreement is concerned are "new motor vehicles"[83] or "spare parts"[84] therefor, the applicable block exemption will not be Regulation 2790/99 but the sector-specific block exemption for motor vehicle distribution and servicing agreements, Regulation 1400/2002,[85] which takes a far more prescriptive attitude to the contents of such agreements than is the case under Regulation 2790/99. The Commission, in the Explanatory Brochure "Distribution and servicing of motor vehicles in the EU"[86] specifically confirms that a non-"genuine" agency agreement concerning those products falls within the scope of Regulation 1400/2002.[87]

While there is a Commission decision from the early 1990s about what are clearly treated as non-"genuine" agency agreements (as part of the setting up of a joint venture between two potential competitors to establish and operate a nationwide interconnected telecommunications paging system in Ireland), *Eirpage*,[88] the conclusions concerning the joint venture's proposed standard sales agency agreement are driven largely by evident Commission concerns that a number of the significant agents already sold their own paging systems, and so were already competitors of the new joint venture. There are

79. The basis of which is the CFI judgment in case T–374/94 and T–375/94 *European Night Services* v. *Commission* [1998] ECR II–3141, para 102.

80. Originally defined by reference to Commission Recommendation 96/280 (OJ L. 107/4 of 30 April 1996) but replaced, with effect from 1 January 2005, by Commission Recommendation 2003/361 (OJ L. 124/36 of 20 May 2003).

81. That the agreement (i) contributes to improving the production or distribution of goods or to promoting technical or economic progress, while (ii) allowing consumers a fair share of the resulting benefit; and that the agreement (iii) does not impose on the undertakings concerned restrictions which are not indispensable to the attainment of these objectives and (iv) does not afford the parties the possibility of eliminating competition in respect of a substantial part of the products in question.

82. OJ L. 336/21 of 12 December 1999.

83. Being "self-propelled vehicles intended for use on public roads and having three or more road wheels" (Art. 1(n) of Reg. 1400/2002).

84. Being "goods which are to be installed in or upon a motor vehicle so as to replace components of that vehicle, including goods such as lubricants which are necessary for the sue of a motor vehicle, with the exception of fuel" (Art. 1(s) of Reg. 1400/2002).

85. OJ L. 203/30 of 1 August 2002.

86. Available on the DG Competition website at europa.eu.int/comm/competition/car_sector/explanatory_brochure_en.pdf.

87. *Ibid*, fn 72, p 20.

88. Commission decision IV/32.737, OJ L. 306/22 of 7 November 1991.

accordingly significant elements of the Commission's reasoning on horizontal co-operation visible in the decision. In the normal situation, then, this will not be a helpful source of guidance.

Accordingly, one in effect has to treat a non-"genuine" agency agreement as if it were a distribution agreement.

A detailed treatment of vertical agreements in EC and UK competition law is, naturally enough, beyond the scope of this book. By way of overview, under the block exemption, vertical agreements are presumed to be lawful in the absence of one or other party (generally the supplier) having market power. A 30 per cent market share cap is used to define the existence of market power in this context, and it is generally (but not always) the supplier's market share which is relevant.[89] Where the relevant party's market share exceeds 30 per cent, the block exemption will not apply and one has to go to the somewhat more opaque economic principles set out in Section VI of the Commission Guidelines on Vertical Restraints. The definition of a vertical agreement means that the block exemption has only limited application to vertical agreements between competitors.[90] So far as the terms of the agreement are concerned, the general principle of Regulation 2790/99 applies, namely "if it is not prohibited,[91] it is permitted".[92]

Article 82 may be relevant if either party is dominant.

In the context of non-"genuine" commercial agency (and even where the principal's market share is less than 30 per cent), the following specific points should be borne in mind.

Any ban or disincentive on the commercial agent splitting his commission with customers is treated as akin to resale price maintenance (the most heinous anti-competitive arrangement that can take place in vertical agreements, born of the fundamental insistence that the buyer of goods for resale must remain entirely free to decide its own price for the downstream sale). Any such ban or disincentive will prevent the block exemption from applying to the whole agreement, and, if investigated, is likely to result in fining.[93] Accordingly, the commercial agent must be left free to lower the effective price that the customer pays without reducing the principal's turnover.[94]

The commercial agent cannot in any circumstances validly be prevented or discouraged from responding to unsolicited orders from outside the territory or customer

89. See Art. 3, reg. 2790/99, the Commission Notice on the definition of relevant market, OJ C. 372/5 of 9 December 1997, and Commission Guidelines on Vertical Restraints, paras 88–99 ("Market definition and market share calculation issues").

90. See Art. 2(4) of Reg. 2790/99.

91. See Art. 4 and 5, Reg. 2790/99.

92. See R Whish, "Regulation 2790/99: the Commission's 'new style' block exemption for vertical agreements", (2000) 37 Common Market Law Review 887.

93. Art. 4(a) of Reg. 2790/99 and Guidelines on Vertical Restraints, para 48, reflecting earlier ECJ case-law. In relation to commercial agents and the splitting of commission, see especially the *Flemish Travel Agents* case fn 33.

94. Commission decision in *Eirpage*, OJ L. 306/22 of 7 November 1999, para 5.

group which the principal has allocated to him under the commercial agency agreement.[95] This would be prohibited under Article 81(1) even if the agreement was insignificant in context[96] or if one party is an SME. Sales from a website (but not unsolicited direct e-mail advertising to individual customers or specific groups of customers) are treated as passive sales, so the agent cannot be restricted from advertising in this way.[97]

In *Eirpage*,[98] the Commission insisted, as a condition of granting individual exemption (under the pre-"modernisation" procedures), on the terms of the standard agency agreement between the joint venture and its sales agents being amended in a number of respects. We consider that these points are particular to the facts of that case, especially that the joint venture itself was between two potential competitors and that many of the sales agents appointed were already providers of competing services so that there were significant horizontal aspects to the decision which would not arise in the normal situation. We do not therefore consider *Eirpage* to be representative authority.

The principal can validly prevent or discourage the commercial agent from making active sales efforts aimed at customers from outside the territory or customer group "exclusively" allocated to him, but only insofar as the principal is seeking to close off to the commercial agent territories or customer groups where the exclusive right to make active sales efforts has either been granted by the principal to another commercial agent or distributor or has been reserved to the principal for himself.[99] In relevant circumstances, this will necessitate the principal making clear to the commercial agent where, outside the allocated sales territory/customer group, those "off limits" areas or customers are, and retaining the possibility to "close off" in the future further areas outside the territory where it does not at the date of this agreement have allocated intermediaries with "exclusive" rights to make active sales but intends to put such in place in the foreseeable future. Provided, in this latter case, the principal's intentions in this respect are made clear to the commercial agent prior to appointment, i.e. that there was never any intention that he should be allowed, for the long term, to make active sales efforts to areas outside the area allocated to him and that it is, in effect, only through an accident of timing that he is not restrained from trading in these areas from day one, one would not have thought that this could amount to a breach of the principal's duty of good faith under Regulation 4 of the Agency Regulations.

Equally, subject to the market share cap, the principal can lawfully restrain the commercial agent from handling competing products for up to a five-year fixed-term

95. Art. 4(b) of Reg. 2790/99 and Guidelines on Vertical Restraints, para 50, a fundamental principle of EC competition law on vertical agreements since the 1960s. Note now, however, the important qualification to the Commission's strictures on this subject imposed by the ECJ judgment in case C–2/01P and C–3/01P *Commission and others* v. *Bayer AG*, judgment of 6 January 2004, [2004] ECR I–23 (upholding the CFI judgment in T–41/96 *Bayer AG* v. *Commission* [2000] ECR II–3383, 26 October 2000, of which the authors of a major treatise in English on competition have said "The importance of this judgment cannot be overstated" (eds. Freeman and Whish, *Butterworths Competition Law*, Section I, para 164.1 (page I–99)), and which has been followed by the Court of Appeal in *Unipart Group Ltd* v. *O2 (UK) Ltd* [2004] EWCA Civ 1034, 30 July 2004.

96. See Commission Notice on agreements of minor importance, OJ C. 368/11 of 22 December 2001, para 11.

97. Guidelines on Vertical Restraints, para 51.

98. See fn 88 above.

99. Reg. 2790/99, Article 4(b), first indent, and see Guidelines on Vertical Restraints, paras 49–51.

period during the life of the agreement. Any ban on the commercial agent handling competing products during the life of the commercial agency agreement (a "non-compete obligation" in the terminology of Regulation 2790/99[100]) which is, by contrast, of indefinite duration or is capable of lasting for more than five years will not be block-exempt and should thus be treated as ineffective.[101] In this respect, the insistence of the Commission in *Eirpage*,[102] that the sales agent, when dealing with potential customers, had to be free to promote their own services first, or at least to give equal priority to the joint venture's services as well as to those they offered in their own right (unless the sales lead had been passed to the agent by the joint venture) reflects, as noted earlier, the unusual and powerful horizontal features of that case and is not representative. Article 5(a) of Regulation 2790/99 goes on to provide that "a non-compete obligation which is tacitly renewable beyond a period of five years is to be deemed to have been concluded for an indefinite duration". Accordingly, an agreement containing a "non-compete obligation" the duration of which is, for example, expressed to be "three years and then to continue unless and until terminated by one party on the giving of notice which it may do at any time thereafter" is capable of lasting for longer than five years and so the "non-compete obligation" is outside the protection of Article 5(a) and is thus ineffective. One must, rather, state that at the end of the five-year term the non-compete obligation will terminate but that it is open to the parties then, by positive agreement of both of them, to make a new non-compete obligation having a definite term of five years or less. There is a very limited exception to the five-year time limit, applicable "where the contract goods or services are sold by the buyer from premises and land owned by the supplier or leased by the supplier from third parties not connected with the buyer, provided that the duration of the non-compete obligation does not exceed the period of occupancy of the premises and land by the buyer".[103] That is not likely to benefit commercial agents very often. If the permitted duration of a "non-compete obligation" is, however, exceeded, it is only the non-compete obligation which is invalidated, not the whole agreement.[104] We have dealt above with the severance issues.

What is the status in competition law of a post-termination restrictive covenant accepted by the commercial agent? A literal interpretation of Article 5(b) of Regulation 2790/99 would mean that no post-termination restraint of trade clause accepted by a commercial agent would ever be block-exempt, other than in the very limited circumstances set out therein,[105] and regardless of the market share cap not being exceeded. Because such a restriction is prohibited under Article 5 and is not a "hardcore" restriction under Article 4, it could, however (assuming, if English law

100. Reg. 2790/99, Art. 1(b): note the detailed definition, which is significantly wider than what one would, in common parlance, have associated with a "non-compete obligation".

101. *Ibid*, Art. 5(a); and see Guidelines on Vertical Restraints, para 58.

102. Fn 88, above.

103. See Art. 5(a).

104. Article 5 begins "any of the following obligations contained in vertical agreements" as opposed to the Article 4 wording "shall not apply to vertical agreements . . . ".

105. That the obligation relates to goods or services which compete with the contract goods or services; that the restraint is limited to the premises and land from which the buyer has operated during the contract period, and that the restriction is indispensable to protect know-how transfer supplied by supplier to buyer, and provided that such limited restriction does not in any event exceed a period of one year from termination of the vertical agreement, although in such circumstances (but only in those circumstances) a restriction unlimited in point of time may be imposed against use or disclosure of know-how which has not entered the public domain.

is the law applicable to the contract, that the drafting permits of the application of the severance "blue pencil" test), be severed from the rest of the agreement without tainting the rest of it.

A question to which the answer is less certain is whether, being outside the protection of the block exemption, a post-termination restraint of trade clause is in breach of Article 81(1) (assuming that the parties are not SMEs, that the agreement is more than insignificant, etc). In *Eirpage*,[106] the European Commission required, as a condition of granting individual exemption to the overall joint venture arrangements, the deletion of the three-year post-termination ban on the sales agents soliciting customers who at the time of termination of the agency agreement were customers of the joint venture principal, plainly taking the view that, in the circumstances, this was a breach of Article 81(1) and not capable of exemption under the Article 81(3) criteria. As noted above, the *Eirpage* circumstances were very unusual, yet, as noted earlier (in section 7.1 of this chapter), in relation to commercial agents to whom the Agency Regulations apply, the intention of Regulation 20 is plainly that, within the limits therein set out, a post-termination restraint of trade clause should be enforceable, though that is stated in Regulation 20(3) to be subject to applicable competition law. In the light of Article 5(b) of Regulation 2790/99, can Regulation 20 of the Agency Regulations be taken at face value? It is hard to believe that the effect of the vertical agreements block exemption is to reduce Regulation 20 to being no more than a trap for the unwary. We consider that Regulation 20 can be "justified" in competition law terms along the following lines.

Where a business is being sold, it has long been accepted in EC competition law that a "normal" post-sale restrictive covenant accepted by the vendor, staying within reasonable limits as to time, geographic extent and the range of activities restrained, is not caught by the Article 81(1) prohibition, this being accepted as a necessary part of achieving the sale and purchase of the business, so that the purchaser gets the full benefit of what he has paid for, the sale of the goodwill implying a limited protection from competition by the vendor. Subject to the possible application of the EC Merger Control Regulation to "concentrations with Community dimension", it is an ancillary restraint to a legitimate commercial transaction. This was specifically accepted by the ECJ in *Remia BV* v. *Commission*.[107] The principle has been implemented in successive versions of the Commission *Notice on restrictions directly related and necessary to concentrations*[108] (previously the *Notice on ancillary restraints*) where it is limited to sales of businesses and does not extend to mere sales of assets in isolation; is limited to two years' duration if goodwill is included in the sale and to three years if there are both goodwill and know-how; is limited to territories where the vendor was trading at the time of the sale and to territories where it was about to start trading at that point, provided reasonable preparations have been made for that expansion; and is limited to products being sold by the business at that time plus products which it was about to start selling.

Given the philosophy of Regulation 17 of the Agency Regulations, that on termination of the commercial agency agreement the commercial agent will normally have

106. Fn 88 above.
107. ECJ case 42/84, [1985] ECR 2545.
108. The current version of which is at OJ C. 56/24 of 5 March 2005.

the right to a lump sum payment, by way of compensation or indemnity, being a payment to him for the notional sale of his interest in a goodwill notionally jointly owned by him and the principal,[109] and that Regulation 20 of the Agency Regulations specifically makes provision for a post-termination restraint of trade clause, it would not be unreasonable in competition law to treat the commercial agent like the vendor of a business in this respect, and for a limited restraint of trade clause not to be caught by the prohibition in Article 81(1) on the basis of reasoning akin to that in *Remia BV* v. *Commission*.[110] If, instead of the payment being made by principal to commercial agent, the lump sum payment on termination reached the outgoing commercial agent by means of a payment from the incoming commercial agent for the purchase of the outgoing agent's goodwill (as sometimes happens in France), that treatment of the matter would be natural and obvious and uncontroversial.

In the common law restraint of trade doctrine, there is authority for treating similar post-termination restrictions on sales employees in this way. In *Allied Dunbar (Frank Weisinger) Ltd* v. *Weisinger*[111] (an employer/employee case), the employment contract imposed a two-year post-termination restraint of trade clause, but the employer allowed its sales staff, on retirement, to capitalise the value of the contacts they had built up with customers by paying the employees a lump sum in respect of them. That, despite some appearances to the contrary, was held to be in substance a payment for the sale and purchase of goodwill, and the post-termination restriction was held to be valid. A similar principle has been followed in franchising cases where post-termination the franchisee is restricted from competing but is paid for transferring the goodwill of his franchise business to the franchisor: the restriction is seen as necessary for the protection of the franchisor's business.[112] Whilst these are common law restraint of trade cases not Article 81 cases, if, as *Days Medical Aids Ltd* v. *Pihsiang Machinery Manufacturing Co Ltd*[113] decides, the common law principles do not "predominantly pursue an objective different from Articles 81 and 82", then (notwithstanding the "trumping" of the common law doctrine identified by Langley J in that case) presumably they can have some persuasive value in relation to the latter.

It seems to us, then, that a strong case can be made that, in relation to commercial agency agreements, notwithstanding Article 5(b) of Regulation 2790/99, a limited post-termination restraint of trade clause within the limits of Regulation 20 of the Agency Regulations should not fall within the prohibition in Article 81(1). Any other conclusion reduces Regulation 20 to little more than a trap for the unwary. The wholesale unenforceability of restraint of trade clauses compliant with Regulation 20 would give commercial agents an unmerited windfall, given that in practice the amounts paid to them by way of compensation or indemnity will probably have taken account of the clause even though there is no requirement that it should. We are aware of no clear authority for this proposition, so it must be regarded as speculative for the moment. Given that a post-termination "non-compete obligation" is treated under Regulation 2790/99 as an Article 5 restriction and not a "hardcore" Article 4

109. See Chapter 5.
110. See fn 107 above.
111. [1988] IRLR 60.
112. See *Kall-Kwik (UK) Ltd* v. *Rush*, [1996] FSR 114.
113. Above, fn 70.

one, so that if it was found to be void it could be severed from the rest of the agreement (assuming, if English law applied, that the drafting allowed for that) without invalidating the rest of it, there would seem to be nothing for principals to lose by inserting one and taking the chance: nothing ventured, nothing gained.

The position of a non-"genuine" agency agreement under the Competition Act 1998 will in practice be the same as that under Article 81 EC. If the agency agreement benefits from regulation 2790/99, it will be protected by the parallel exemption in section 10 Competition Act 1998. Such will be the case whether the agreement has an effect on trade between EU countries or not.[114]

In relation to the common law restraint of trade principles, Article 3 of regulation 1/2003 is applicable, the position in relation to non-"genuine" agency agreements will be as set out above.

7.2.7 Agency agreements made before 9 November 1998: the continuing effects of the pre-Competition Act UK competition law

There is an exclusion from the Chapter I prohibition relevant to agreements, including agency agreements, made before 9 November 1998, which it is very easy to overlook, but which may be helpful in particular cases. Under the Restrictive Trade Practices Act 1976 (hereinafter the RTPA) (the predecessor to the Competition Act, and which was repealed by it), agreements which fell within the form-based definition of restrictive agreements under that Act had to be lodged at the OFT with a view to copies of them being placed on the public register of restrictive trading agreements and to their being subsequently referred by the Director-General of Fair Trading (as he then was) to the Restrictive Practices Court for an examination of whether they operated against the public interest.[115] Section 21(2) of the 1976 Act provided an exception to the general duty to refer an agreement to the Court: where the Secretary of State for Trade and Industry (acting on advice from the OFT, after a preliminary examination of the agreement by the latter) was of the view that the relevant restrictions in an agreement which had been duly lodged were "not of such significance as to call for investigation by the Court", the DTI would issue a direction to that effect and no reference to the court would be made. In practice, in the latter years of the RTPA at least, the great majority of those agreements which were lodged with the OFT for registration and which were found to be technically registrable were placed on the public register but a direction under section 21(2) was made in respect of them. These were, effectively, agreements technically within the criteria for registration but innocuous in their effect.

Under the transitional arrangements in the Competition Act 1998, agreements which had been the subject of section 21(2) directions under the RTPA 1976 (which agreements must have been made before 9 November 1998 and lodged with the OFT in the manner then usual and subject to the time limits then applicable) are excluded from the application of the Chapter I prohibition under the Competition Act 1998 for the whole of their

114. Section 10(2) CA 1998.

115. For a short historical view of the RTPA, see Judge CW Bellamy (as he then was), *The Europeanisation of United Kingdom competition law*, in N Green and A Robertson (eds), *The Europeanisation of UK competition law* (Hart Publishing, 1999), p 1.

duration, however long that may be.[116] The exclusion will cease to apply (so the agreement will become subject to Chapter I) if (and, if so, when) a material variation is made to the agreement[117] or if the OFT gives a direction to that effect in an individual case (the possibility of "clawback").[118] Although the loss of the exclusion in the case of a material variation is triggered by the making of a material variation to the agreement (apparently, whether the material variation has any economic effect or not[119]), the OFT has said that in practice it would consider a variation to be material only if the agreement as varied then had an appreciable effect on competition, quoting as examples of material variations the conversion of a joint marketing area into a number of partitioned markets or the addition of a significant competitor as a party to the agreement.[120] As such agreements would have been innocuous in their effects as first set up (or they would not have qualified for section 21(2) treatment in the first place), while the effect of material variations in the market will have to be judged at the time they are made, one would have thought them unlikely to result in appreciable effects on competition.

Accordingly, in relation to an agency agreement dating from before 9 November 1998 and which has not been materially varied and in respect there has been no "clawback" decision, one does not need to consider the Competition Act 1998 (though Article 81 EC may nevertheless be applicable).

On the other hand, the RTPA 1976 is still, despite its repeal, capable of delivering an unpleasant surprise in relation to other agency agreements dating from before 9 November 1998. The repeal, on general principles, does not have retrospective effect. Accordingly, if an agreement made before 9 November 1998 (the repeal date) was, when made, registrable under the RTPA (because it was made between two or more persons carrying on business in the UK in the supply of goods or the supply of services and under which relevant restrictions on conduct as defined in the Act were accepted by two or more parties) and was not lodged for registration at the OFT within the then applicable time limits, the restrictions in the agreement which made it registrable would, on the expiry of that time limit, have become void and unenforceable under the RTPA for failure to lodge. The repeal of the RTPA does not remove that problem. On the other hand, if the agreement has an effect on trade between EU countries but does not restrict competition in an Article 81(1) sense or benefits from exemption under Article 81(3) EC or is block exempt, Article 3(2) of Regulation 1/2003 would prevent that point being raised. Such issues could otherwise be raised typically by commercial agents who wish to be free of restrictions imposed on them under old agreements.

116. Schedule 3, para 2(1), CA 1998; and see OFT Guideline on the Competition Act 1998, *Transitional Arrangements* (OFT 406, March 1999), paras 4.13ff.

117. Schedule 3, para 2(2), CA 1998.

118. Schedule 3, para 2(3), CA 1998.

119. See Freeman and Whish in (eds. Freeman and Whish), *Butterworths Competition Law*, Section I, para 612, p I/263.

120. OFT Guideline on the Competition Act 1998, Transitional Arrangements (OFT 406, March 1999), para 4.16.

CHAPTER 8

GENERAL CONCLUSION

For businesses wanting to buy or sell goods using marketing or sales agents as opposed to other forms of route to market, the legal regime which we have endeavoured to describe and analyse in this book (the combination of the Agency Regulations and the pre-existing common law and equitable rules and, of course, what parties agree between themselves expressly) is the relevant one. Accordingly, what may have seemed, when the Agency Regulations were introduced in 1994, to be new, strange and peripheral has become the mainstream in this area. English law now has a special legal regime, a *lex specialis*, for commercial agents as defined, and treats them very differently from other types of agent (estate agents, insurance brokers, etc), whether or not the latter operate in what might loosely be described as a business context.

On 18 December 1986, the Council of Ministers enacted the Directive on the co-ordination of the laws of the Member States relating to self-employed commercial agents.[1] The Directive aims at reinforcing the protection of commercial agents as well as harmonising the national laws regulating the relationship between commercial agents and their principal in Europe. The Directive is based on the civil law assumption that commercial agents are the weaker party within the relationship.[2] This rationale for protecting commercial agents is however very specific to the commercial agency relationship and is therefore narrow in its basis.

The rationale finds its source in the fact that commercial agents are representatives whose main role is to create a customer base (goodwill) for a manufacturer or a trader who wants to expand his business at home and/or abroad. The commercial agent therefore does not act for himself but for the principal, which means (as one of the Scottish judges has said) that "the goodwill created by the agent is attached to the goods sold and not to the agent himself".[3] As a consequence, civil law is very sensitive to the risk that, once the commercial agent has created the customer base for the principal's goods, the principal may terminate the relationship in order to sell directly to customers. The rationale being essentially based on the economic weakness of the commercial agent on termination, the essence of the protection of commercial agents afforded by the Directive is therefore in the form of the right of the commercial agent to receive a lump sum payment on termination.

1. OJ L. 382/17 of 31 December 1986.

2. The Directive is primarily inspired from the laws of France and Germany which have formally provided a level of protection to commercial agents since 1958 (Decree 58/1345 of 25 December 1958, D 1959, L 132 and 1953 (§§ 84–92c HGB) respectively.

3. *Lloyd Gailey* v. *Environmental Waste Control* [2004] Eu LR 423 at para 24 *per* Lord Drummond Young.

In Great Britain, until the Directive was implemented, commercial agents existed under the name of manufacturers' agents but they were not recognised as a separate category from other types of agent and the common law rules of agency applied to the relationship between commercial agents and their principals. The situation was therefore very different on two counts. First, the English law of agency is of a general nature and embraces a wide range of legal areas and secondly, it is based upon the traditional assumption that because of the fiduciary nature of the agency relationship, principals need to be protected against their agents. In the light of such fundamental differences, whereas most Member States had to implement the Directive by 1 January 1990,[4] Ireland and Great Britain were granted four additional years before implementing the Directive.[5]

Regrettably, this additional implementing time was not used constructively, since the Commercial Agents (Council Directive) Regulations 1993[6] (to which we shall refer hereinafter as "the Agency Regulations") almost replicate the text of the Directive.

This near-verbatim implementation creates unwelcome uncertainty, as it causes what we have referred in this book as a *legal paradox*, which is as follows: on the one hand, the Directive and therefore the Agency Regulations are generally positive since they reinforce the protection of commercial agents by providing them with rights throughout the relationship. The most significant aspect of this reinforced legal protection comes in the form of a mandatory and reciprocal obligation of good faith[7] and the right of the commercial agent to claim compensation or indemnity on termination.[8] On the other hand, the effect of such a legal protection is severely undermined by the fact that the Directive and therefore the Agency Regulations not only fail to define what good faith means and what it entails for each party, but also fail to define what constitutes termination or how the two termination rights should be calculated. This lack of detail on crucial civil law inspired principles is however only one illustration of the legal paradox.

The uncertainty is further accentuated by the fact that the Directive and therefore the Agency Regulations are not a complete code regulating every aspect of the commercial agent/principal relationship.[9] The Agency Regulations therefore apply alongside the traditional common law rules of agency. Considering the differing rationales on which the two sets of rules are based, the relationship is not always easy, especially since the status of some regulations is not clearly defined.

The main purpose of this book was therefore to solve this legal paradox and provide as complete a guide as possible to the relationship between the commercial agent and the principal. The two essential guiding principles of the book were therefore (1) to study the Agency Regulations themselves in order to see what they mean and more importantly

4. Article 22(1) of the Directive.

5. Article 22(3) of the Directive.

6. SI 1993/3053 applies in Great Britain, i.e. England, Wales and Scotland. SI 1993/3053 was amended by SI 1993/3173 which corrected an error in SI 1993/3053 by adding the words "indemnity or" after the opening word of the first line in Regulation 17. The text was the object of a more substantial amendment in 1998 (SI 1998/2868) in order to bring the jurisdictional provisions in line with the Directive. See Appendix 2. Separate statutory instruments apply for Northern Ireland. See Appendix 3. In this book, reference to "the Agency Regulations" should be understood as a reference to the implementing text applying to Great Britain.

7. Regulation 3(1) for the commercial agent and Regulation 4(1) for the principal.

8. Regulation 17(1).

9. The two EU Commission proposals regulated the relationship more closely. However, it is not certain that the protection of commercial agents would have been better reinforced overall. For details of the difference between the text of the current Directive and the two EU Commission proposals, see Chapter 2, fn 49 and associated text.

what they entail for the relationship, and (2) to see how the Agency Regulations dovetail with the traditional common law rules of agency and contract. Such aspects were necessary, since only by understanding how and when the Agency Regulations apply can we clarify their scope of application and ensure their efficiency in protecting commercial agents. Only then can we have a complete picture of the workings of the relationship between commercial agents and their principals.

Because of the near-verbatim implementation, the legal paradox manifests itself differently in the various parts of the Agency Regulations. For this purpose, this book looks at the Agency Regulations in a chronological manner in order to cover the three crucial aspects of the commercial agency relationship, formation (and their scope of application), performance and termination.

However, given that Agency Regulations effectively create a categorisation where none existed before, it was also important to understand (1) in which circumstances they will apply and (2) to whom they apply, i.e. who commercial agents are and what kind of function they perform in order to help us define the scope of application of the Agency Regulations. This was the main purpose of Chapter 2.

In this chapter, we have seen that in relation to the first part of the scope of application of the Agency Regulations (in which circumstances they will apply), their application in point of time and in relation to the territory needed to be considered. In chronological terms, we have seen that the situation is very straightforward since the Agency Regulations apply from day one of the agreement (including to commercial agency agreements in existence before 1 January 1994 but continuing after that date) and will have an overriding effect. With regard to the territorial scope of the Agency Regulations, we have seen that it is very wide since they apply equally to purely domestic relationships where both parties are in the same Member State as well as where one of them is in another EEA Member State or even, following the European Court Justice ruling in *Ingmar Ltd* v. *Eaton Leonard Technologies Inc*,[10] where one party is outside the EU altogether, provided that the place of performance is within the EU and/or the EEA. Still in relation to the territorial scope of the implementing legislation, when the Agency Regulations first came into effect, they defined their application by reference to the place of performance.[11] Such a restriction, which was not only unclear but also inconsistent with international conventions, prompted the Agency Regulations to be amended in 1998.[12] Even though the situation is better, it is not perfect. We have therefore reviewed the situation when the parties expressly make a choice of law and when the parties remain silent on choice of law, since, in the light of conflict of law rules, the rules will differ.

With regard to the second part of the scope of application of the Agency Regulations (to whom they apply, i.e. who commercial agents are and what kind of functions they perform), thanks to the courts' interpretation, the situation is generally understood. In fact, it is clear that commercial agents are independent contractors.[13] As such, they can establish themselves as individual entities as well as legal entities and still be protected by the

10. Case C 381/98, [2001] 1 CMLR 9.

11. Regulation 1(2).

12. The Commercial Agents (Council Directive) Amendment Regulations 1998, SI 1998/2868.

13. Because of the near-verbatim implementation of the Directive, the Agency Regulations describe commercial agents as "self-employed intermediary" (Regulation 2(1)). This term is not so usual in English law parlance. Interpreting the implementing legislation in the light of the Treaty of Rome, Judge Raymond Jack QC in the case of *AMB Imballagi Plastici Srl* v. *Pacflex Ltd* [1999] 17 Tr LR 557 concluded that the expression was equivalent to the English expression "independent contractor".

Agency Regulations.[14] Such an interpretation is in line with the protective stance of the Agency Regulations. As independent contractors, commercial agents are therefore different from employees. Their independent status gives them a certain freedom as to how to run their businesses but how far this freedom goes is not defined by the Agency Regulations. Applying common law principles, Scott Baker LJ in *Smith* v. *Reliance Water Controls Ltd*[15] shows that it is essentially an issue of control, that commercial agents can conduct their business as they see fit by working by themselves or using employees or even sub-agents if the business requires. It is also clear that the independent status brings certain legal incidents for the commercial agent such as the possibility to work for other principals (at least non-competing ones) or even work for themselves apart from the commercial agency. However, it is possible, up to a point, to restrict such a freedom without risking the commercial agent being held (e.g. for employment or tax law purposes) to be an employee; even though commercial agents are independent contractors, they are first and foremost agents, i.e. they represent the interests of the principal.

Chapter 2 has also shown that, in spite of the silence of the Agency Regulations as to the meaning of the "negotiating" function of commercial agents, the courts have understood that this essentially refers to the marketing tasks of looking for clients for the goods for the principal.[16] Applying the protective stance of this implementing legislation, the courts also understand that the "negotiation threshold" is quite low, since commercial agents who merely promote the goods of the principal by soliciting orders from clients do enough to be "negotiating" for the purpose of the Agency Regulations.[17]

However, Chapter 2 has further shown that, even though so far the impact of the Agency Regulations is on the whole very positive for commercial agents, the situation is not perfect. Following the decision of *Light & Others* v. *Ty Europe Ltd*,[18] it appears that sub-commercial agents (those appointed by the "head" commercial agent to act as his agent and to market, or to market and sell, in the name of the "head" principal) are not protected by the Agency Regulations neither with rights against the "head" principal nor against the "head" agent. Furthermore, the Agency Regulations appear to cover only commercial agents who deal with goods. Consequently, the situation is not clear for commercial agents who deal with goods and services. In the Scottish case of *Lloyd Gailey* v. *Environmental Waste Control*,[19] it was decided that the answer is related to the issue of secondary activities.[20] Such an interpretation is believed to be wrong since it gives too wide an interpretation of the issue of secondary activities though the concept of secondary activities in the Agency Regulations gives rise to many other problems as well.

Following the choice left by the Directive,[21] the Agency Regulations do not apply to "persons whose activities as commercial agents are regarded as secondary under English law".[22] The Directive fails to explain what amounts to a "secondary activities": the matter

14. See cases such as *AMB Imballagi* v. *Plastici Srl* v. *Pacflex Ltd* [1999] 17 Tr LR 557, *Bell Electric Ltd* v. *Aweco Appliance System GmbH & Co* [2002] EWHC 872 (QBD, 8 May 2002).

15. [2003] EWCA Civ 1153, [2003] Eu LR 874.

16. *Parks* v. *Esso Petroleum Company Ltd* [1999] 1 CMLR 455.

17. *Tamarind International Ltd & Others* v. *Eastern Natural Gas (Retail) Ltd and Another* [2000] Eu LR 708.

18. [2004] 1 Lloyd's Rep 693.

19. [2004] Eu LR 423.

20. Lord Drummond Young stated "If the business is not predominantly one involving the sale of goods, I am of the opinion that the agent's activities are necessary secondary" at para 99.

21. Article 2.

22. Regulation 2(4).

is therefore left to each Member State. A Schedule was added to the Agency Regulations to serve that purpose.[23] This is where the problem lies; the Schedule is not only an "almost impenetrable piece of drafting"[24] but it is also unhelpful, since it does not really define what "secondary" means. As a result, it has been applied very widely by the Scottish[25] and the English[26] courts alike. Such an interpretation of the Schedule (which excludes certain commercial agents from protection under the Agency Regulations) is so wide that it risks to "remove the protection that the provisions of the Directive are intended to guarantee".[27] We have therefore advocated that a complete overhaul of the Schedule is necessary.

Chapter 3 of the book deals with the obligations of commercial agent and principal to each other while the commercial agency relationship between them is operating (other than as to the commercial agent's remuneration, which is dealt with in Chapter 4). This is now an amalgam of the express terms of the contract, terms introduced by the Agency Regulations and, to the extent not inconsistent with either of these, the implied/default common law and equitable rules.

The crucial change brought about by the Agency Regulations in this respect is the imposition of mandatory (i.e. non-excludable) mutual duties of good faith on each party towards the other. The position of these in the "architecture" of the Directive indicates that they are intended to be of major importance, and to be pervasive through all aspects of the commercial agency relationship. Yet, here again is another example of the legal paradox to which we have referred earlier: on the one hand, the introduction of these mutual duties makes the contract more evenly balanced; on the other hand, the vagueness of the Directive and the near-verbatim implementation of the Directive in the Agency Regulations leave huge uncertainty about what is meant by these principles. English law, as we have pointed out, is somewhat ambivalent about general duties of good faith in contracts. Sometimes it maintains that they are a thoroughly bad idea and that it does not have them. Sometimes, on the other hand, it says that it has something very similar, albeit that the duties have come about and exist in a piecemeal way and are called different things in different contexts. Given this starting point, the vagueness of the Agency Regulations is particularly regrettable. Yet, since the view generally held when the Agency Regulations were enacted was that the mutual duties of good faith were not intended to alter very much in English law, the vagueness is not surprising.

There has to date been only very sparse case law on these duties in the UK (and such as there has been is largely inconclusive). We are convinced that their full impact has yet to be felt.

The fact that the duties of good faith are mutual suggests to us that the Directive intends the commercial agency relationship to be something akin to the French *mandat d'intérêt commun* (common interest mandate). That would mean that each party has to look after the other's interests and co-operate for their mutual advantage (including, at the very least, refraining from taking any steps that will make performance by the other party more

23. Regulation 2(3).

24. *AMB Imballagi Plastici* v. *Pacflex Ltd* [1999] 2 All ER (Comm) 249, at p 250h, *per* Waller LJ *obiter*.

25. *Lloyd Gailey* v. *Environmental Waste Control* [2004] Eu LR 423.

26. *Tamarind International Ltd & Others* v. *Eastern Natural Gas (Retail) Ltd and Another* [2000] Eu LR 708.

27. *Tamarind International Ltd & Others* v. *Eastern Natural Gas (Retail) Ltd and Another* [2000] Eu LR 708, *per* Morison J quoting the ECJ in the case of *Barbara Bellone* v. *Yokohama* [1998] ECR I–2191.

difficult, and possibly sometimes imposing an obligation to take positive steps to help the other party perform where there is no express obligation in the contract to do so). All of that is from very different from the approach which English law has traditionally taken in relation to agents.

The imposition of a mandatory obligation of good faith on the principal is entirely new to English law. This is one of the key elements in which the Directive goes about reinforcing the position of the commercial agent, which it treats as a "down-trodden race" in need of protection.[28] We take any non-trivial breach by the principal of his obligation of good faith to be serious enough to entitle the commercial agent to bring the commercial agency agreement to an end and still have his entitlement to a lump sum payment of compensation or indemnity (on the basis that his termination was "justified by circumstances attributable to the principal").[29] So this is of some importance to principals.

We take the principal's obligation of good faith in the Agency Regulations to mean a general obligation to co-operate and to act with trust and confidence in his dealings with his commercial agent. On that basis, we have concluded that principles which the courts have developed down the years in relation to the commercial "relationship" contracts of partnership and, in particular, employment provide some very helpful sources of practical guidance for English lawyers as to what the principal's obligation consists of.

As to the level of co-operation expected of the principal, one is very much into uncharted waters. We think it likely, however, that the instincts of English courts will lead them to tend to pitch the level of co-operation etc expected of the principal fairly low, namely as an obligation not to take positive steps to make the commercial agent's position more difficult than it would otherwise be, rather than an obligation to take positive steps to help. We think that the courts will be tolerant of the idea that to a fair extent principals are free to look after their own interests. That is certainly the way in which the courts have tended to interpret express "best endeavours" and "reasonable efforts" clauses in English law contracts. It is also consistent with the idea, which is crucial in the Directive, that the duties of good faith are mutual: in acting in the interests of both parties, to further the common mandate, the principal is entitled to take account of his own interests as well as those of the commercial agent. Good faith for the principal does not mean having to favour the commercial agent's interests over his own. It is about achieving a balance, something easier said than done. To what extent the courts in the UK may interpret the need to protect the "down-trodden race" of commercial agents by pitching the threshold for principals higher than that remains to be seen.

There is, furthermore, a strand of judicial authority in English law establishing that, where one party to a contract has a discretion the exercise of which is, on the face of it, unlimited, some (admittedly fairly modest) limitations on the exercise of that discretion may be implicit. Although the courts strongly deny the analogy, the use of judicial language not dissimilar to that used in the administrative law context (*Wednesbury Corporation* unreasonableness) does not seem to be an accident. We would see the respecting of those standards as part of the principal's duty of good faith, albeit that it would seem that a principal would have to be acting dishonestly or absolutely outrageously to breach

28. *Page* v. *CST*.
29. Regulation 18(b)(ii).

them. Such has arisen already in the very sparse reported case law on the Agency Regulations.[30]

We cannot see that the principal's obligation of good faith can override key terms of the contract (e.g. to transform a marketing-only agency into a sales and marketing agency; to change the agreed rate of commission or the range of transactions on which it is to be earned; the duration of the contract: etc). But, in the exercise of apparently unlimited contractual discretions, it seems clear that one effect of the principal's duty of good faith is that commercial agency agreements may not be enforceable in all circumstances in accordance with their express terms.

Furthermore, the principal's duty of good faith applies "in his relations with the commercial agent", which we believe means both at the pre-contractual stage (so, an obligation to negotiate the commercial agency agreement itself in good faith) and post-termination, in relation to negotiations on lump-sum payments and dealing with the other consequences of termination and in the enforcement of any restraint of trade clause. Although the wording of the commercial agent's reciprocal duty of good faith is somewhat different on this aspect, we think it likely that that duty applies both in pre-contractual negotiations and post-termination.

So far as the commercial agent's position is concerned, the duty of good faith imposed by the Agency Regulations is superimposed upon whatever his express obligations may be under his commercial agency agreement and what may be implied under the general law.

The basic default obligations are, of course, the duty to perform his duties according to the terms of the contract and to obey the principal's instructions, and the duty to perform his functions with reasonable care and skill, together with the fiduciary obligations to avoid conflicts of interest (though there is a curious lack of certainty in English law as to whether a commercial agent breaches these if he acts for a competing principal without his first principal's consent) and not to make secret profits, accept bribes etc. Crucial in the commercial context to the fiduciary duties is that the terms of the contract can override what would otherwise be the fiduciary obligations implied under the general law and will be essential in establishing the extent of the fiduciary obligations, and there is significant scope for the giving of informed consent to particular transactions.

It was originally thought, when the Agency Regulations were enacted, that the commercial agent's obligations of good faith under the Agency Regulations meant about the same as the agent's implied obligations at common law and in equity. It is now clear that they mean something different from that, though quite what has yet to be fully worked out.

We take the view that the reciprocal nature of the good faith obligations, and the inspiration of these as coming from the French common interest mandate, means that (except in relation to the holding of the principal's money and property, where the commercial agent is plainly still fiduciary for the principal alone) the commercial agent's fiduciary duties are now to look, not to the interests of the principal at the expense of his own, but at the joint interests of his principal and himself rather than just at his own interests. This, we consider, is a key indicator of how far commercial agency agreements are now, in English law, different from other types of agency agreement.

30. *Ibid.*

In Chapter 4, we deal with the commercial agent's remuneration, to which a section of the Agency Regulations is devoted.[31] Even though the implementing legislation does not significantly modify the contents of the obligation of remuneration, since the Agency Regulations do not apply to unpaid commercial agents,[32] we argue that they provide a statutory obligation to pay the commercial agent the agreed commission. This is a substantial modification of the traditional common law rules of agency (and those of contract law), since the principal cannot prevent the commercial agent from earning a remuneration. This would seem to mean that the question of remuneration is therefore settled and is no longer to be decided on the matter of construction by the courts or by implication of terms as under the common law rules.[33] This position seems to be confirmed by the position of the High Court in the case of *Bell Electric* v. *Aweco Appliance Systems*,[34] where it was decided that "although I would accept that a single failure to pay [the commission] would not constitute a repudiatory breach, it is now accepted that the continuing failure to pay in this case did amount to a repudiation of the contract".[35] The generally held view is that most of the provisions of the Agency Regulations dealing with remuneration are non-mandatory and will yield to contrary agreement.

The Agency Regulations,[36] following the Directive, give the commercial agent a right to commission in respect of transactions wider than those for which he would be so entitled under the default English common law rules (where he qualifies for commission only if his involvement was the "effective cause" of the transaction), including on repeat business and even, in some circumstances, on transactions with customers of which he has never heard, let alone dealt with. They make provision for the commercial agent to be entitled to commission, in some circumstances, on transactions only concluded after termination of the commercial agency agreement, and for apportionments of commission when one commercial agent ceases to act and is succeeded by another (which rules are fairly heavily slanted in favour of the outgoing commercial agent). All of these rules are capable of exclusion or variation by the parties.

The rules which, for the commercial agent's protection, are clearly expressed to be mandatory, and which cannot be derogated from to his detriment, are those imposing the "back-stop" dates for the accrual due and payment of commission, those establishing the circumstances in which the commercial agent can lose his right to commission, and those establishing the commercial agent's right to an explanatory statement from the principal as to the calculation of his commission.

Chapters 5 and 6 deal with the two complementary aspects of termination; the right to claim termination payments[37] in Chapter 5 and the calculation of such termination payments in Chapter 6. Termination is undoubtedly the stage of the relationship where commercial agents are at their weakest and therefore their need of protection at its highest. Considering that the right to claim compensation or indemnity did not exist in English common law prior to the implementation of the Directive, it is the most crucial part of the

31. Regulations 6–12.
32. Regulation 2(2)(a).
33. Compare and contrast with the cases of *Alpha Trading Ltd* v. *Dunshaw-Patten Ltd* [1981] 1 All ER 487 and *Luxor (Eastbourne) Ltd (in liquidation) and others* v. *Cooper* [1941] 1 All ER 33.
34. [2002] EWHC QBD, 8 May 2002.
35. Para 22, *per* Elias J.
36. Regulation 4(1).
37. Regulation 17(1).

Agency Regulations. Yet, it is also the area where the legal paradox mentioned earlier is at its strongest and most complex, hence the need to spend two chapters on the issue.

In relation to the study in the right to claim compensation or indemnity, Chapter 5 shows that the legal paradox created by the near-verbatim implementation threatens the level of protection of the commercial agent in three ways. First, the Agency Regulations fail to explain why commercial agents deserve such a level of protection on termination. Secondly, the Agency Regulations provide the commercial agent with a right to claim compensation or indemnity on termination, and yet they fail to define what amounts to "termination". Thirdly, the scope of application of the right to claim compensation or indemnity and its exceptions is not always very clear.

Given the specificity of the right to claim compensation or indemnity and the alien concept of such payment, the rationale had to be explained in order to help English lawyers understand its scope of application. In fact, prior to the implementation of the Directive, commercial agents would be protected on termination only if the principal was guilty of a breach when terminating the relationship and the commercial agent suffered a loss following the breach. In Chapter 5, we see that the civil law rationale behind such payment is the fact that a commercial agent is an intermediary whose main role is to use his marketing skills to create a customer base for the principal's goods. A commercial agent does not act for himself but for his principal. Whereas a commercial agent is dependent for his source of income, the commissions, on the existence of his relationship with the principal this is not the case for the principal who, even after the end of the relationship, can still benefit from the customer base. On termination, a commercial agent has therefore a right to claim from the principal a lump-sum payment in recognition of the role he played in creating the customer base for the principal's goods.

Chapter 5 also shows that this quasi-proprietary aspect of compensation[38] and indemnity[39] is now understood by the courts in this country. It is also accepted that such a right is different from any common law concepts and it is available as a right, regardless of whether the principal has committed a breach or not.

In relation to the second problem created by the failure of the Agency Regulations to determine what "termination" means, the silence was most problematic in relation to the expiry of fixed-term contracts by effluxion of time. The question is important because the right of the commercial agent to claim compensation or indemnity arises only when the contract is "terminated". With fixed-term contracts coming to an end, they expire but do not "terminate" as such. Chapter 5 shows that the problem was resolved by the courts of this country[40] by applying, yet again, the protective stance of the Agency Regulations. In essence, the courts considered that there was a strong policy argument to decide that expiry amounts to termination since if expiry does not amount to termination, then the principal can avoid the application of the Agency Regulations by giving the commercial agent a series of fixed-term contracts.

38. In *Barrett McKenzie* v. *Escada Ltd* [2001] Eu LR 567, the court held that the aim of the compensation option is to compensate the commercial agent "for the loss of a quasi-proprietary right: the loss of an asset to the agent (the agency)", *per* Bowers J, at para 27.

39. In *Moore* v. *Piretta Ltd* [1999] 1 All ER 174 the court held that the purpose of the indemnity payment is "to award the commercial agent a share in the goodwill" he helped to create otherwise "the whole benefit of that goodwill would remain with the principal", *per* Mitting J at p 177g.

40. The first case on the issue was that of *Whitehead* v. *Jenks and Cattell* [1999] Eu LR 827, followed by *Frape* v. *Emreco* [2002] SLT 371 and *Tigana Ltd* v. *Decoro Ltd* [2003] EWHC 23, [2003] Eu LR 189.

In relation to the third and final problem, that of the scope of application of the right to claim compensation or indemnity, the rules are not very clear in relation to summary termination. This lack of clarity manifests itself in several ways. First, there is a lack of consistency between the various rules relating to summary termination. Regulation 16 specifically deals with the right of either party to summarily terminate the relationship for breach (Regulation 16(a)) or in case of "exceptional circumstances" as per Regulation 16(b). However, Regulation 18, which regulates the exceptions to the right of the commercial agent to claim compensation or indemnity, also appears to deal with summary termination. Yet, the relationship between the two regulations is not entirely clear. Regulation 18(a) stipulates that, when the principal terminates the relationship because of a "default attributable to the commercial agent which would justify immediate termination pursuant to Regulation 16", no compensation or indemnity is due. However, Regulation 18(b)(i) states that if the commercial agent himself terminates the relationship "for circumstances attributable to the principal", he will still be entitled to claim compensation or indemnity as this is a just cause for terminating the relationship, but makes no reference to Regulation 16. Chapter 5 shows that, even if Regulation 18(b)(i) fails to refer to Regulation 16 as Regulation 18(a) does, the connection is nevertheless present.[41] Chapter 5 shows that the case of *Bell Electric Ltd* v. *Aweco Appliance System GmbH & Co*[42] decided that in spite of the difference in vocabulary between Regulations 18(a) and 18(b)(i), they both refer to a serious breach allowing the victim to summarily terminate the relationship.

Chapter 5 finally shows that the case of *Bell Electric Ltd* v. *Aweco Appliance System GmbH & Co*[43] insists that in relation to the mechanics behind termination for serious breach, the common law rules should apply. We disagree since the common law rules give rise to the risk of affirmation of the contract, which represents another exception to the right of the commercial agent. In the light of the mandatory nature of termination payment,[44] this cannot be right and we therefore advocate that the simple fact that the commercial agent claims compensation or indemnity should amount to acceptance of the breach.

Chapter 6 deals with the other thorny issue on termination, that of the calculation of the termination payments. We have seen that the Agency Regulations incorporate the two termination payments, the French-based compensation and the German-based indemnity. The Agency Regulations leave the choice to the parties, but in their silence, compensation applies.[45] Because indemnity will only apply when the contract expressly states so, most cases so far have involved compensation. Only one reported case so far, that of *Moore* v. *Piretta Ltd*[46] has dealt with the indemnity. As we have explained, this case seems a fair attempt at following the way the German courts calculate the indemnity. However, considering that it is the only reported case so far on indemnity, to use this case as an assessment of the understanding of the court as to how indemnity works is therefore rather limited. Chapter 6 has shown that the problems relate to the calculation of compensation. The silence of the Directive and therefore the Agency Regulations have created a rift between the French and the Scottish courts as to how to calculate compensation. The

41. *Bell Electric Ltd* v. *Aweco Appliance System GmbH & Co* [2002] EWHC 872.
42. *Ibid.*
43. [2002] EWHC 872.
44. Case C-381/98 *Ingmar Ltd* v. *Eaton Leonard Technologies Inc*, [2001] All ER (EC) 329.
45. Regulation 17(2).
46. [1999] 1 All ER 174.

Scottish courts[47] are happy to follow the French model; the English courts, however, are reluctant to do so. As this chapter has shown, given the lack of obligation on any Member State to follow what the French or German courts do in their calculation of the compensation or indemnity payments respectively, such a reluctance by the English courts is not a problem *per se*. In fact, the English courts' rejection of the French model is based on the serious fact that they consider the calculation of the French courts of two years' worth of gross commission to be applied as a standardised tariff. Chapter 6 finally shows that the English courts are eager to find an English-based method to use in order to calculate the compensation in a way which is both practical and representative of the loss suffered by commercial agents, perhaps involving principles akin to the valuation of goodwill on sale of a business. However, no such method has, as yet, been found. Yet, considering that it is now just over 12 years since the Agency Regulations came into effect, the interpretation of this part of the Agency Regulations by the courts of this country is nevertheless remarkable.

In Chapter 7, we have gone a little off the beaten track of this book and ventured into the competition law aspects of commercial agency. The chapter begins, however, with an examination of Regulation 20 of the Agency Regulations, the specific regime for post-termination restraint of trade clauses accepted by commercial agents, the ideas behind which are driven by the same priorities as drive competition law. It bears a reassuring similarity to the common law restraint of trade principles and to the treatment of similar clauses in competition law. Inevitably, though, there are important details around the edges which are specific.

A key reason for a manufacturer/supplier to choose commercial agency as its route to market rather than some other intermediary relationship is often the greater degree of control which it is thought to allow to the manufacturer/supplier, especially as to the price of downstream sale and choice of downstream selling territories and customers.

In competition law, the crucial issue is whether the commercial agent is so closely tied into his principal's business as to lack the ability to behave as an independent player in the market and when the commercial agent is to be treated as an independent business. In the former case, the agreement will not be an agreement between independent undertakings so that, in principle, competition law will not apply to many aspects of the agreement between principal and commercial agent, though it will not be totally inapplicable. In the latter case, one applies by analogy the EC competition law regime applicable to distribution agreements.

A body of ECJ/CFI case law and European Commission practice has built up on the classification issue down the years, with Commission practice seeming not to follow the courts' case law very closely. This inconsistency of treatment as between the courts and the Commission continues in the most recent developments (the annulment, on the relevant points, by the European Court of First Instance in September 2005 in *Daimler-Chrysler* v. *Commission* of the 2001 Commission decision in *Mercedes-Benz*), which we do not consider add any clarity to the picture.

* * *

47. *King* v. *Tunnock* [2000] Eu LR 531.

If we have a concern for the future, it is that uncertainty for manufacturers and suppliers arising from the mutual good faith obligations under the Agency Regulations and understandable concern about liability for lump-sum payments on termination (the former leads into the latter, the latter being, to our mind, the principal worry for business) will lead to their using other mechanisms for getting their products to market, where a marketing or sales agency arrangement would otherwise have been their preferred option. The circumstances in which a commercial agency relationship would make the most business sense for parties are, in our experience, more numerous than one might perhaps have imagined. We are conscious, anecdotally, that much of the commercial agency work that arises for lawyers in practice concerns terminations, and our impression is that fewer new commercial agency relationships are being set up now than in the past.

If that is the case, we think it is a pity. The overall commercial "toolbox" for sales and marketing arrangements will be the poorer if commercial agency is disregarded. Some of the market practices as between principals and commercial agents in France described in Chapter 6 show ways of making the position more palatable for principals, though how transposable they are into UK commercial "culture" is not so clear. Another way, we think, may be to apply, in the calculation of the termination payments, accountancy principles on valuing goodwill on sale of a business. We have seen no evidence of that happening in reported cases so far.

Whilst the Directive is there (and we see no sign of any moves to change it), the pro-commercial agent stance of the Agency Regulations will have to remain. That said, however, the Directive leaves considerable freedom to the national legal systems of Member States to work out how to achieve that enhanced protection and, fundamentally, what degree of protection is appropriate.

We would like to think that this book will help to develop the idea (in the UK and elsewhere) that the lump-sum payments on termination are not intended to provide commercial agents with unmerited windfalls, but are, rather, intended as a reward for a job well done (and not for a job badly done) and which is likely to have long-term benefits for their principals.

APPENDIX 1

THE E.C. COMMERCIAL AGENTS DIRECTIVE: COUNCIL DIRECTIVE 86/653/EEC

(OJ L382/17 of 31st December 1986)

COUNCIL DIRECTIVE OF 18 DECEMBER 1986 ON THE COORDINATION OF THE LAWS OF THE MEMBER STATES RELATING TO SELF-EMPLOYED COMMERCIAL AGENTS

(86/653/EEC)

THE COUNCIL OF THE EUROPEAN COMMUNITIES,

Having regard to the Treaty establishing the European Economic Community, and in particular Articles 57 (2) and 100 thereof,

Having regard to the proposal from the Commission,[1]

Having regard to the opinion of the European Parliament,[2]

Having regard to the opinion of the Economic and Social Committee,[3]

Whereas the restrictions on the freedom of establishment and the freedom to provide services in respect of activities of intermediaries in commerce, industry and small craft industries were abolished by Directive 64/224/EEC;[4]

Whereas the differences in national laws concerning commercial representation substantially affect the conditions of competition and the carrying-on of that activity within the Community and are detrimental both to the protection available to commercial agents *vis-à-vis* their principals and to the security of commercial transactions; whereas moreover those differences are such as to inhibit substantially the conclusion and operation of commercial representation contracts where principal and commercial agent are established in different Member States;

Whereas trade in goods between Member States should be carried on under conditions which are similar to those of a single market, and this necessitates approximation of the legal systems of the Member States to the extent required for the proper functioning of the common market; whereas in this regard the rules concerning conflict of laws do not, in the matter of commercial representation, remove the inconsistencies referred to above, nor would they even if they were made uniform, and accordingly the proposed harmonization is necessary notwithstanding the existence of those rules;

Whereas in this regard the legal relationship between commercial agent and principal must be given priority;

1. OJ No C 13, 18.1.1977, p. 2; OJ No C 56, 2.3.1979, p. 5.
2. OJ No C 239, 9.10.1978, p. 17.
3. OJ No C 59, 8.3.1978, p. 31.
4. OJ No 56, 4.4.1964, p. 869/64.

Whereas it is appropriate to be guided by the principles of Article 117 of the Treaty and to maintain improvements already made, when harmonizing the laws of the Member States relating to commercial agents;

Whereas additional transitional periods should be allowed for certain Member States which have to make a particular effort to adapt their regulations, especially those concerning indemnity for termination of contract between the principal and the commercial agent, to the requirements of this Directive,
HAS ADOPTED THIS DIRECTIVE:

CHAPTER I

SCOPE

Article 1

1. The harmonization measures prescribed by this Directive shall apply to the laws, regulations and administrative provisions of the Member States governing the relations between commercial agents and their principals.

2. For the purposes of this Directive, "commercial agent" shall mean a self-employed intermediary who has continuing authority to negotiate the sale or the purchase of goods on behalf of another person, hereinafter called the "principal", or to negotiate and conclude such transactions on behalf of and in the name of that principal.

3. A commercial agent shall be understood within the meaning of this Directive as not including in particular:
   - a person who, in his capacity as an officer, is empowered to enter into commitments binding on a company or association,
   - a partner who is lawfully authorized to enter into commitments binding on his partners,
   - a receiver, a receiver and manager, a liquidator or a trustee in bankruptcy.

Article 2

1. This Directive shall not apply to:
   - commercial agents whose activities are unpaid,
   - commercial agents when they operate on commodity exchanges or in the commodity market, or
   - the body known as the Crown Agents for Overseas Governments and Administrations, as set up under the Crown Agents Act 1979 in the United Kingdom, or its subsidiaries.

2. Each of the Member States shall have the right to provide that the Directive shall not apply to those persons whose activities as commercial agents are considered secondary by the law of that Member State.

CHAPTER II

RIGHTS AND OBLIGATIONS

Article 3

1. In performing has activities a commercial agent must look after his principal's interests and act dutifully and in good faith.

2. In particular, a commercial agent must:
   (a) make proper efforts to negotiate and, where appropriate, conclude the transactions he is instructed to take care of;
   (b) communicate to his principal all the necessary information available to him;
   (c) comply with reasonable instructions given by his principal.

Article 4

1. In his relations with his commercial agent a principal must act dutifully and in good faith.

2. A principal must in particular:

(a) provide his commercial agent with the necessary documentation relating to the goods concerned;
(b) obtain for his commercial agent the information necessary for the performance of the agency contract, and in particular notify the commercial agent within a reasonable period once he anticipates that the volume of commercial transactions will be significantly lower than that which the commercial agent could normally have expected.

3. A principal must, in addition, inform the commercial agent within a reasonable period of his acceptance, refusal, and of any non-execution of a commercial transaction which the commercial agent has procured for the principal.

Article 5

The parties may not derogate from the provisions of Articles 3 and 4.

CHAPTER III

REMUNERATION

Article 6

1. In the absence of any agreement on this matter between the parties, and without prejudice to the application of the compulsory provisions of the Member States concerning the level of remuneration, a commercial agent shall be entitled to the remuneration that commercial agents appointed for the goods forming the subject of his agency contract are customarily allowed in the place where he carries on his activities. If there is no such customary practice a commercial agent shall be entitled to reasonable remuneration taking into account all the aspects of the transaction.

2. Any part of the remuneration which varies with the number or value of business transactions shall be deemed to be commission within the meaning of this Directive.

3. Articles 7 to 12 shall not apply if the commercial agent is not remunerated wholly or in part by commission.

Article 7

1. A commercial agent shall be entitled to commission on commercial transactions concluded during the period covered by the agency contract:
(a) where the transaction has been concluded as a result of his action; or
(b) where the transaction is concluded with a third party whom he has previously acquired as a customer for transactions of the same kind.

2. A commercial agent shall also be entitled to commission on transactions concluded during the period covered by the agency contract:
— either where he is entrusted with a specific geographical area or group of customers,
— or where he has an exclusive right to a specific geographical area or group of customers,

and where the transaction has been entered into with a customer belonging to that area or group.

Member States shall include in their legislation one of the possibilities referred to in the above two indents.

Article 8

A commercial agent shall be entitled to commission on commercial transactions concluded after the agency contract has terminated:
(a) if the transaction is mainly attributable to the commercial agent's efforts during the period covered by the agency contract and if the transaction was entered into within a reasonable period after that contract terminated; or
(b) if, in accordance with the conditions mentioned in Article 7, the order of the third party reached the principal or the commercial agent before the agency contract terminated.

Article 9

A commercial agent shall not be entitled to the commission referred to in Article 7, if that commission is payable, pursuant to Article 8, to the previous commercial agent, unless it is equitable because of the circumstances for the commission to be shared between the commercial agents.

Article 10

1. The commission shall become due as soon as and to the extent that one of the following circumstances obtains:
   (a) the principal has executed the transaction; or
   (b) the principal should, according to his agreement with the third party, have executed the transaction; or
   (c) the third party has executed the transaction.

2. The commission shall become due at the latest when the third party has executed his part of the transaction or should have done so if the principal had executed his part of the transaction, as he should have.

3. The commission shall be paid not later than on the last day of the month following the quarter in which it became due.

4. Agreements to derogate from paragraphs 2 and 3 to the detriment of the commercial agent shall not be permitted.

Article 11

1. The right to commission can be extinguished only if and to the extent that:
   — it is established that the contract between the third party and the principal will not be executed, and
   — that face is due to a reason for which the principal is not to blame.

2. Any commission which the commercial agent has already received shall be refunded if the right to it is extinguished.

3. Agreements to derogate from paragraph 1 to the detriment of the commercial agent shall not be permitted.

Article 12

1. The principal shall supply his commercial agent with a statement of the commission due, not later than the last day of the month following the quarter in which the commission has become due. This statement shall set out the main components used in calculating the amount of commission.

2. A commercial agent shall be entitled to demand that he be provided with all the information, and in particular an extract from the books, which is available to his principal and which he needs in order to check the amount of the commission due to him.

3. Agreements to derogate from paragraphs 1 and 2 to the detriment of the commercial agent shall not be permitted.

4. This Directive shall not conflict with the internal provisions of Member States which recognize the right of a commercial agent to inspect a principal's books.

CHAPTER IV

CONCLUSION AND TERMINATION OF THE AGENCY CONTRACT

Article 13

1. Each party shall be entitled to receive from the other on request a signed written document setting out the terms of the agency contract including any terms subsequently agreed. Waiver of this right shall not be permitted.

2. Notwithstanding paragraph 1 a Member State may provide that an agency contract shall not be valid unless evidenced in writing.

Article 14

An agency contract for a fixed period which continues to be performed by both parties after that period has expired shall be deemed to be converted into an agency contract for an indefinite period.

Article 15

1. Where an agency contract is concluded for an indefinite period either party may terminate it by notice.

2. The period of notice shall be one month for the first year of the contract, two months for the second year commenced, and three months for the third year commenced and subsequent years. The parties may not agree on shorter periods of notice.

3. Member States may fix the period of notice at four months for the fourth year of the contract, five months for the fifth year and six months for the sixth and subsequent years. They may decide that the parties may not agree to shorter periods.

4. If the parties agree on longer periods than those laid down in paragraphs 2 and 3, the period of notice to be observed by the principal must not be shorter than that to be observed by the commercial agent.

5. Unless otherwise agreed by the parties, the end of the period of notice must coincide with the end of a calendar month.

6. The provisions of this Article shall apply to an agency contract for a fixed period where it is converted under Article 14 into an agency contract for an indefinite period, subject to the proviso that the earlier fixed period must be taken into account in the calculation of the period of notice.

Article 16

Nothing in this Directive shall affect the application of the law of the Member States where the latter provides for the immediate termination of the agency contract:

(a) because of the failure of one party to carry out all or part of his obligations;

(b) where exceptional circumstances arise.

Article 17

1. Member States shall take the measures necessary to ensure that the commercial agent is, after termination of the agency contract, indemnified in accordance with paragraph 2 or compensated for damage in accordance with paragraph 3.

2. (a) The commercial agent shall be entitled to an indemnity if and to the extent that:

— he has brought the principal new customers or has significantly increased the volume of business with existing customers and the principal continues to derive substantial benefits from the business with such customers, and

— the payment of this indemnity is equitable having regard to all the circumstances and, in particular, the commission lost by the commercial agent on the business transacted with such customers. Member States may provide for such circumstances also to include the application or otherwise of a restraint of trade clause, within the meaning of Article 20;

(b) The amount of the indemnity may not exceed a figure equivalent to an indemnity for one year calculated from the commercial agent's average annual remuneration over the preceding five years and if the contract goes back less than five years the indemnity shall be calculated on the average for the period in question;

(c) The grant of such an indemnity shall not prevent the commercial agent from seeking damages.

3. The commercial agent shall be entitled to compensation for the damage he suffers as a result of the termination of his relations with the principal.

Such damage shall be deemed to occur particularly when the termination takes place in circumstances:

— depriving the commercial agent of the commission which proper performance of the agency contract would have procured him whilst providing the principal with substantial benefits linked to the commercial agent's activities,
— and/or which have not enabled the commercial agent to amortize the costs and expenses that he had incurred for the performance of the agency contract on the principal's advice.

4. Entitlement to the indemnity as provided for in paragraph 2 or to compensation for damage as provided for under paragraph 3, shall also arise where the agency contract is terminated as a result of the commercial agent's death.

5. The commercial agent shall lose his entitlement to the indemnity in the instances provided for in paragraph 2 or to compensation for damage in the instances provided for in paragraph 3, if within one year following termination of the contract he has not notified the principal that he intends pursuing his entitlement.

6. The Commission shall submit to the Council, within eight years following the date of notification of this Directive, a report on the implementation of this Article, and shall if necessary submit to it proposals for amendments.

Article 18

The indemnity or compensation referred to in Article 17 shall not be payable:

(a) where the principal has terminated the agency contract because of default attributable to the commercial agent which would justify immediate termination of the agency contract under national law;
(b) where the commercial agent has terminated the agency contract, unless such termination is justified by circumstances attributable to the principal or on grounds of age, infirmity or illness of the commercial agent in consequence of which he cannot reasonably be required to continue his activities;
(c) where, with the agreement of the principal, the commercial agent assigns his rights and duties under the agency contract to another person.

Article 19

The parties may not derogate from Articles 17 and 18 to the detriment of the commercial agent before the agency contract expires.

Article 20

1. For the purposes of this Directive, an agreement restricting the business activities of a commercial agent following termination of the agency contract is hereinafter referred to as a restraint of trade clause.

2. A restraint of trade clause shall be valid only if and to the extent that:
(a) it is concluded in writing; and
(b) it relates to the geographical area or the group of customers and the geographical area entrusted to the commercial agent and to the kind of goods covered by his agency under the contract.

3. A restraint of trade clause shall be valid for not more than two years after termination of the agency contract.

4. This Article shall not affect provisions of national law which impose other restrictions on the validity or enforceability of restraint of trade clauses or which enable the courts to reduce the obligations on the parties resulting from such an agreement.

CHAPTER V

GENERAL AND FINAL PROVISIONS

Article 21

Nothing in this Directive shall require a Member State to provide for the disclosure of information where such disclosure would be contrary to public policy.

Article 22

1. Member States shall bring into force the provisions necessary to comply with this Directive before 1 January 1990. They shall forthwith inform the Commission thereof. Such provisions shall apply at least to contracts concluded after their entry into force. They shall apply to contracts in operation by 1 January 1994 at the latest.

2. As from the notification of this Directive, Member States shall communicate to the Commission the main laws, regulations and administrative provisions which they adopt in the field governed by this Directive.

3. However, with regard to Ireland and the United Kingdom, 1 January 1990 referred to in paragraph 1 shall be replaced by 1 January 1994.

With regard to Italy, 1 January 1990 shall be replaced by 1 January 1993 in the case of the obligations deriving from Article 17.

Article 23

This Directive is addressed to the Member States.

Done at Brussels, 18 December 1986.

For the Council
The President
M. JOPLING

APPENDIX 2

THE U.K IMPLEMENTING LEGISLATION, EXCEPT FOR NORTHERN IRELAND: STATUTORY INSTRUMENT 1993/3053, as amended by SI 1993/3173 and SI 1998/2868

THE COMMERCIAL AGENTS 1993 (COUNCIL DIRECTIVE) REGULATIONS 1993, NO. 3053

Made	*7th December 1993*
Laid before Parliament	*8th December 1993*
Coming into Force	*1st January 1994*

ARRANGEMENTS OF REGULATIONS

PART V

Miscellaneous and Supplemental

The Secretary of State, being a Minister designated[1] for the purposes of section 2(2) of the European Communities Act 1972[2] in relation to measures relating to relations between commercial agents and their principals, in the exercise of the powers conferred by him by that section, hereby makes the following Regulations:

PART I

GENERAL

Citation, commendement and applicable law

1.—(1) These Regulations may be cited as the Commercial Agents (Council Directive) Regulations 1993 and shall come into force on 1st January 1994.

(2) These Regulations govern the relations between commercial agents and their principals and, subject to para (3), apply in relation to the activities of commercial agents in Great Britain.

(3) A court or tribunal shall:

(a) apply the law of the other member State concerned in place of regulations 3 to 22 where the parties have agreed that the agency contract is to be governed by the law of that member State;

(b) (whether or not it would otherwise be required to do so) apply these regulations where the law of another member State corresponding to these regulations enables the parties to agree that the agency contract is to be governed by the law of a different member State and the parties have agreed that it is to be governed by the law of England and Wales or Scotland.*

Interpretation, application and extent

2.—(1) In these Regulations—

"commercial agent" means a self-employed intermediary who has continuing authority to negotiate the sale or purchase of goods on behalf of another person (the "principal"), or to negotiate and conclude the sale or purchase of goods on behalf of and in the name of that principal; but shall be understood as not including in particular:

(i) a person who, in his capacity as an officer of a company or association, is empowered to enter into commitments binding on that company or association;

(ii) a partner who is lawfully authorised to enter into commitments binding on his partners;

1. S.I.1989/1327.

2. 1972 c. 68.

* The current reg. 1(3) was inserted by reg. 2(a) of the Commercial Agents (Council Directive) (Amendment) Regulations 1998, SI 1998/2868 and took effect on 16th December 1998. Reg. 1(3) as originally existing said "Regulations 3 to 22 do not apply where the parties have agreed that the agency contract is to be governed by the law of another member state."

(iii) a person who acts as an insolvency practitioner (as that expression is defined in section 388 of the Insolvency Act 1986[3]) or the equivalent in any other jurisdiction;

"commission" means any part of the remuneration of a commercial agent which varies with the number or value of business transactions;

"EEA Agreement" means the Agreement on the European Economic Area signed at Oporto on 2nd May 1992 as adjusted by the Protocol signed at Brussels on 17th March 1993;**

"member State" includes a State which is a contracting party to the EEA Agreement;**

"restraint of trade clause" means an agreement restricting the business activities of a commercial agent following termination of the agency contract.

(2) These Regulations do not apply to—

(a) commercial agents whose activities are unpaid;

(b) commercial agents when they operate on commodity exchanges or in the commodity market;

(c) the Crown Agents for Overseas Governments and Administrations, as set up under the Crown Agents Act 1979,[4] or its subsidiaries.

(3) The provisions of the Schedule to these Regulations have effect for the purpose of determining the persons whose activities as commercial agents are to be considered secondary.

(4) These Regulations shall not apply to the persons referred to in para (3) above.

(5) These Regulations do not extend to Northern Ireland.

PART II

RIGHTS AND OBLIGATIONS

Duties of a commercial agent to his principal

3.—(1) In performing his activities a commercial agent must look after the interests of his principal and act dutifully and in good faith.

(2) In particular, a commercial agent must—

(a) make proper efforts to negotiate and, where appropriate, conclude the transactions he is instructed to take care of;

(b) communicate to his principal all the necessary information available to him;

(c) comply with reasonable instructions given by his principal.

Duties of a principal to his commercial agent

4.—(1) In his relations with his commercial agent a principal must act dutifully and in good faith.

(2) In particular, a principal must—

(a) provide his commercial agent with the necessary documentation relating to the goods concerned;

(b) obtain for his commercial agent the information necessary for the performance of the agency contract, and in particular notify his commercial agent within a reasonable period once he anticipates that the volume of commercial transactions will be significantly lower than that which the commercial agent could normally have expected.

(3) A principal shall, in addition, inform his commercial agent within a reasonable period of his acceptance or refusal of, and of any non-execution by him of, a commercial transaction which the commercial agent has procured for him.

** The definitions of "EEA Agreement" and "member State" were added by reg. 2(b) of the Commercial Agents (Council Directive) (Amendment) Regulations 1998, SI 1998/2868. Their insertion took effect on 16th December 1998.

3. 1986 c. 45.

4. 1979 c. 43.

Prohibition on derogation from regulations 3 and 4 and consequence of breach

5.—(1) The parties may not derogate from regulations 3 and 4 above.

(2) The law applicable to the contract shall govern the consequence of breach of the rights and obligations under regulations 3 and 4 above.

PART II

I REMUNERATION

Form and amount of remuneration in absence of agreement

6.—(1) In the absence of any agreement as to remuneration between the parties, a commercial agent shall be entitled to the remuneration that commercial agents appointed for the goods forming the subject of his agency contract are customarily allowed in the place where he carries on his activities and, if there is no such customary practice, a commercial agent shall be entitled to reasonable remuneration taking into account all the aspects of the transaction.

(2) This regulation is without prejudice to the application of any enactment or rule of law concerning the level of remuneration.

(3) Where a commercial agent is not remunerated (wholly or in part) by commission, regulations 7 to 12 below shall not apply.

Entitlement to commission on transactions concluded during agency contract

7.—(1) A commercial agent shall be entitled to commission on commercial transactions concluded during the period covered by the agency contract—

(a) where the transaction has been concluded as a result of his action; or

(b) where the transaction is concluded with a third party whom he has previously acquired as a customer for transactions of the same kind.

(2) A commercial agent shall also be entitled to commission on transactions concluded during the period covered by the agency contract where he has an exclusive right to a specific geographical area or to a specific group of customers and where the transaction has been entered into with a customer belonging to that area or group. Entitlement to commission on transactions concluded after agency contract has terminated

8. Subject to regulation 9 below, a commercial agent shall be entitled to commission on commercial transactions concluded after the agency contract has terminated if—

(a) the transaction is mainly attributable to his efforts during the period covered by the agency contract and if the transaction was entered into within a reasonable period after that contract terminated; or

(b) in accordance with the conditions mentioned in regulation 7 above, the order of the third party reached the principal or the commercial agent before the agency contract terminated.

Apportionment of commission between new and previous commercial agents

9.—(1) A commercial agent shall not be entitled to the commission referred to in regulation 7 above if that commission is payable, by virtue of regulation 8 above, to the previous commercial agent, unless it is equitable because of the circumstances for the commission to be shared between the commercial agents.

(2) The principal shall be liable for any sum due under para (1) above to the person entitled to it in accordance with that paragraph, and any sum which the other commercial agent receives to which he is not entitled shall be refunded to the principal.

When commission due and date for payment

10.—(1) Commission shall become due as soon as, and to the extent that, one of the following circumstances occurs:

(a) the principal has executed the transaction; or

(b) the principal should, according to his agreement with the third party, have executed the transaction; or

(c) the third party has executed the transaction.

(2) Commission shall become due at the latest when the third party has executed his part of the transaction or should have done so if the principal had executed his part of the transaction, as he should have.

(3) The commission shall be paid not later than on the last day of the month following the quarter in which it became due, and, for the purposes of these Regulations, unless otherwise agreed between the parties, the first quarter period shall run from the date the agency contract takes effect, and subsequent periods shall run from that date in the third month thereafter or the beginning of the fourth month, whichever is the sooner.

(4) Any agreement to derogate from paragraphs (2) and (3) above to the detriment of the commercial agent shall be void.

Extinction of right to commission

11.—(1) The right to commission can be extinguished only if and to the extent that—

(a) it is established that the contract between the third party and the principal will not be executed; and

(b) that fact is due to a reason for which the principal is not to blame.

(2) Any commission which the commercial agent has already received shall be refunded if the right to it is extinguished.

(3) Any agreement to derogate from para (1) above to the detriment of the commercial agent shall be void. Periodic supply of information as to commission due and right of inspection of principal's books

12.—(1) The principal shall supply his commercial agent with a statement of the commission due, not later than the last day of the month following the quarter in which the commission has become due, and such statement shall set out the main components used in calculating the amount of the commission.

(2) A commercial agent shall be entitled to demand that he be provided with all the information (and in particular an extract from the books) which is available to his principal and which he needs in order to check the amount of the commission due to him.

(3) Any agreement to derogate from paragraphs (1) and (2) above shall be void.

(4) Nothing in this regulation shall remove or restrict the effect of, or prevent reliance upon, any enactment or rule of law which recognises the right of an agent to inspect the books of a principal.

PART IV

CONCLUSION AND TERMINATION OF THE AGENCY CONTRACT

Right to signed written statement of terms of agency contract

13.—(1) The commercial agent and principal shall each be entitled to receive from the other, on request, a signed written document setting out the terms of the agency contract including any terms subsequently agreed.

(2) Any purported waiver of the right referred to in para (1) above shall be void.

Conversion of agency contract after expiry of fixed period

14. An agency contract for a fixed period which continues to be performed by both parties after that period has expired shall be deemed to be converted into an agency contract for an indefinite period.

Minimum periods of notice for termination of agency contract

15.—(1) Where an agency contract is concluded for an indefinite period either party may terminate it by notice.

(2) The period of notice shall be—
(a) 1 month for the first year of the contract;
(b) 2 months for the second year commenced;
(c) 3 months for the third year commenced and for the subsequent years;
and the parties may not agree on any shorter periods of notice.

(3) If the parties agree on longer periods than those laid down in para (2) above, the period of notice to be observed by the principal must not be shorter than that to be observed by the commercial agent.

(4) Unless otherwise agreed by the parties, the end of the period of notice must coincide with the end of a calendar month.

(5) The provisions of this regulation shall also apply to an agency contract for a fixed period where it is converted under regulation 14 above into an agency contract for an indefinite period subject to the proviso that the earlier fixed period must be taken into account in the calculation of the period of notice.

Savings with regard to immediate termination

16. These Regulations shall not affect the application of any enactment or rule of law which provides for the immediate termination of the agency contract—
(a) because of the failure of one party to carry out all or part of his obligations under that contract; or
(b) where exceptional circumstances arise.

Entitlement of commercial agent to indemnity or compensation on termination of agency contract

17.—(1) This regulation has effect for the purpose of ensuring that the commercial agent is, after termination of the agency contract, indemnified in accordance with paragraphs (3) to (5) below or compensated for damage in accordance with paragraphs (6) and (7) below.

(2) Except where the agency contract* otherwise provides, the commercial agent shall be entitled to be compensated rather than indemnified.

(3) Subject to para (9) and to regulation 18 below, the commercial agent shall be entitled to an indemnity if and to the extent that—
(a) he has brought the principal new customers or has significantly increased the volume of business with existing customers and the principal continues to derive substantial benefits from the business with such customers; and
(b) the payment of this indemnity is equitable having regard to all the circumstances and, in particular, the commission lost by the commercial agent on the business transacted with such customers.

(4) The amount of the indemnity shall not exceed a figure equivalent to an indemnity for one year calculated from the commercial agent's average annual remuneration over the preceding five years and if the contract goes back less than five years the indemnity shall be calculated on the average for the period in question.

(5) The grant of an indemnity as mentioned above shall not prevent the commercial agent from seeking damages.

(6) Subject to para (9) and to regulation 18 below, the commercial agent shall be entitled to compensation for the damage he suffers as a result of the termination of his relations with his principal.

(7) For the purpose of these Regulations such damage shall be deemed to occur particularly when the termination takes place in either or both of the following circumstances, namely circumstances which—

* The word "contract" was inserted (as a correction) by reg. 2(c) of the Commercial Agents (Council Directive) (Amendment) Regulations 1998, SI 1998/2868. The original version of the 1993 Regulations said "contact" here.

(a) deprive the commercial agent of the commission which proper performance of the agency contract would have procured for him whilst providing his principal with substantial benefits linked to the activities of the commercial agent; or
(b) have not enabled the commercial agent to amortize the costs and expenses that he had incurred in the performance of the agency contract on the advice of his principal.

(8) Entitlement to the indemnity or compensation for damage as provided for under paragraphs (2) to (7) above shall also arise where the agency contract is terminated as a result of the death of the commercial agent.

(9) The commercial agent shall lose his entitlement to the indemnity or compensation for damage in the instances provided for in paragraphs (2) to (8) above if within one year following termination of his agency contract he has not notified his principal that he intends pursuing his entitlement.

Grounds for excluding payment of indemnity or compensation under regulation 17

18. The indemnity or** compensation referred to in regulation 17 above shall not be payable to the commercial agent where—

(a) the principal has terminated the agency contract because of default attributable to the commercial agent which would justify immediate termination of the agency contract pursuant to regulation 16 above; or
(b) the commercial agent has himself terminated the agency contract, unless such termination is justified—
   (i) by circumstances attributable to the principal, or
   (ii) on grounds of the age, infirmity or illness of the commercial agent in consequence of which he cannot reasonably be required to continue his activities; or
(c) the commercial agent, with the agreement of his principal, assigns his rights and duties under the agency contract to another person. Prohibition on derogation from regulations 17 and 18

19. The parties may not derogate from regulations 17 and 18 to the detriment of the commercial agent before the agency contract expires.

Restraint of trade clauses

20.—(1) A restraint of trade clause shall be valid only if and to the extent that—

(a) it is concluded in writing; and
(b) it relates to the geographical area or the group of customers and the geographical area entrusted to the commercial agent and to the kind of goods covered by his agency under the contract.

(2) A restraint of trade clause shall be valid for not more than two years after termination of the agency contract.

(3) Nothing in this regulation shall affect any enactment or rule of law which imposes other restrictions on the validity or enforceability of restraint of trade clauses or which enables a court to reduce the obligations on the parties resulting from such clauses.

PART V

MISCELLANEOUS AND SUPPLEMENTAL

Disclosure of information

21. Nothing in these Regulations shall require information to be given where such disclosure would be contrary to public policy.

** The words "indemnity or" were added (as a correction) by reg. 2 of the Commercial Agents (Council Directive) (Amendment) Regulations 1993, SI 1993/3173. The correction took effect on 1st January 1994, when the 1993 Regulations came into force.

Service of notice etc

22.—(1) Any notice, statement or other document to be given or supplied to a commercial agent or to be given or supplied to the principal under these Regulations may be so given or supplied:

(a) by delivering it to him;
(b) by leaving it at his proper address addressed to him by name;
(c) by sending it by post to him addressed either to his registered address or to the address of his registered or principal office;

or by any other means provided for in the agency contract.

(2) Any such notice, statement or document may—

(a) in the case of a body corporate, be given or served on the secretary or clerk of that body;
(b) in the case of a partnership, be given to or served on any partner or on any person having the control or management of the partnership business.

Transitional provisions

23.—(1) Notwithstanding any provision in an agency contract made before 1st January 1994, these Regulations shall apply to that contract after that date and, accordingly any provision which is inconsistent with these Regulations shall have effect subject to them.

(2) Nothing in these Regulations shall affect the rights and liabilities of a commercial agent or a principal which have accrued before 1st January 1994.

Strathclyde

Parliamentary Under-Secretary of State
Department of Trade and Industry

7th December 1993

THE SCHEDULE

Regulation 2(3).

1. The activities of a person as a commercial agent are to be considered secondary where it may reasonably be taken that the primary purpose of the arrangement with his principal is other than as set out in para 2 below.

2. An arrangement falls within this para if—

(a) the business of the principal is the sale, or as the case may be purchase, of goods of a particular kind; and
(b) the goods concerned are such that—
  (i) transactions are normally individually negotiated and concluded on a commercial basis, and
  (ii) procuring a transaction on one occasion is likely to lead to further transactions in those goods with that customer on future occasions, or to transactions in those goods with other customers in the same geographical area or among the same group of customers, and

that accordingly it is in the commercial interests of the principal in developing the market in those goods to appoint a representative to such customers with a view to the representative devoting effort, skill and expenditure from his own resources to that end.

3. The following are indications that an arrangement falls within para 2 above, and the absence of any of them is an indication to the contrary—

(a) the principal is the manufacturer, importer or distributor of the goods;
(b) the goods are specifically identified with the principal in the market in question rather than, or to a greater extent than, with any other person;
(c) the agent devotes substantially the whole of his time to representative activities (whether for one principal or for a number of principals whose interests are not conflicting);

(d) the goods are not normally available in the market in question other than by means of the agent;

(e) the arrangement is described as one of commercial agency.

4. The following are indications that an arrangement does not fall within para 2 above—

(a) promotional material is supplied direct to potential customers;

(b) persons are granted agencies without reference to existing agents in a particular area or in relation to a particular group;

(c) customers normally select the goods for themselves and merely place their orders through the agent.

5. The activities of the following categories of persons are presumed, unless the contrary is established, not to fall within para 2 above

Mail order catalogue agents for consumer goods.

Consumer credit agents.

EXPLANATORY NOTE

(This Note is not part of the Regulations)

These Regulations implement Council Directive 86/653/EEC on the co-ordination of the laws of member States relating to self-employed commercial agents (OJ No. L382, 31 December 1986, p. 17). The directive is within the scope of the Agreement on the European Economic Area by virtue of para 30 of Annex VII to that agreement.

The Regulations set out the rights and obligations as between commercial agents and their principals (regulations 3 to 5) and deal with remuneration (regulations 6 to 12), and the conclusion and termination of the agency contract (regulations 13 to 16).They contain provisions relating to the indemnity or compensation payable to a commercial agent on termination of his agency contract (regulations 17 to 19) and also to the validity of restraint of trade clauses (regulation 20).

A Compliance Cost Assessment is available, copies of which have been placed in the libraries of both Houses of Parliament. Copies are also available from the Consumer Affairs Division of the Department of Trade and Industry, Room 325, 10–18 Victoria Street, London, SW1H 0NN.

APPENDIX 3

THE NORTHERN IRELAND IMPLEMENTING LEGISLATION: STATUTORY RULE 1993 NO. 483 AND STATUTORY RULE 1999 NO. 201

COMMERCIAL AGENTS (COUNCIL DIRECTIVE) REGULATIONS (NORTHERN IRELAND)
1993 No. 483

Made	*17th December 1993*
Coming into operation	*13th January 1994*

ARRANGEMENT OF REGULATIONS

The Department of Economic Development, being a Department designated by the European Communities (Designation) Order 1989[1] for the purposes of section 2(2) of the European Communities Act 1972[2] in relation to measures relating to relations between commercial agents and their principals, in the exercise of the powers conferred on it by that section, hereby makes the following Regulations:—

PART I

GENERAL

Citation, commencement and applicable law

1.—(1) These Regulations may be cited as the Commercial Agents (Council Directive) Regulations (Northern Ireland) 1993 and shall come into operation on 13th January 1994.

(2) These Regulations govern the relations between commercial agents and their principals and, subject to paragraph (3), apply in relation to the activities of commercial agents in Northern Ireland.

(3) Regulations 3 to 22 do not apply where the parties have agreed that the agency contract is to be governed by the law of a member State of the European Communities other than the United Kingdom.

Interpretation and application

2.—(1) The Interpretation Act (Northern Ireland) 1954[3] shall apply to these Regulations as it applies to a Measure of the Northern Ireland Assembly.

(2) In these Regulations—

"commercial agent" means a self-employed intermediary who has continuing authority to negotiate the sale or purchase of goods on behalf of another person (the "principal"), or to negotiate and conclude the sale or purchase of goods on behalf of and in the name of that principal; but shall be understood as not including in particular:

(i) a person who, in his capacity as an officer of a company or association, is empowered to enter into commitments binding on that company or association;

(ii) a partner who is lawfully authorised to enter into commitments binding on his partners;

(iii) a person who acts as an insolvency practitioner (as that expression is defined in Article 3 of the Insolvency (Northern Ireland) Order 1989[4]) or the equivalent in any other jurisdiction;

1. S.J. 1989/1327.
2. 1972 c. 68.
3. 1954 c. 33 (N.I.).
4. S.I. 1989/2405 (N.I. 19).

"commission" means any part of the remuneration of a commercial agent which varies with the number or value of business transactions;

"restraint of trade clause" means an agreement restricting the business activities of a commercial agent following termination of the agency contract.

(3) These Regulations do not apply to—

(*a*) commercial agents whose activities are unpaid;

(*b*) commercial agents when they operate on commodity exchanges or in the commodity market;

(*c*) the Crown Agents for Overseas Governments and Administrations, as set up under the Crown Agents Act 1979[5], or its subsidiaries.

(4) The provisions of the Schedule have effect for the purpose of determining the persons whose activities as commercial agents are to be considered secondary.

(5) These Regulations shall not apply to the persons referred to in paragraph (4).

(6) Regulations 7 to 12 shall not apply where a commercial agent is not remunerated wholly or partly by commission.

PART II

RIGHTS AND OBLIGATIONS

Duties of a commercial agent to his principal

3.—(1) In performing his activities a commercial agent shall look after the interests of his principal and act dutifully and in good faith.

(2) Without prejudice to the generality of paragraph (1), a commercial agent shall in particular—

(*a*) make proper efforts to negotiate and, where appropriate, conclude the transactions he is instructed to take care of;

(*b*) communicate to his principal all the necessary information available to him;

(*c*) comply with reasonable instructions given by his principal.

Duties of a principal to his commercial agent

4.—(1) In his relations with his commercial agent a principal shall act dutifully and in good faith.

(2) Without prejudice to the generality of paragraph (1), a principal shall in particular—

(*a*) provide his commercial agent with the necessary documentation relating to the goods concerned;

(*b*) obtain for his commercial agent the information necessary for the performance of the agency contract, and in particular notify his commercial agent within a reasonable period once he anticipates that the volume of commercial transactions will be significantly lower than that which the commercial agent could normally have expected.

(3) A principal shall, in addition, inform his commercial agent within a reasonable period of his acceptance or refusal of, and of any non-execution by him of, a commercial transaction which the commercial agent has procured for him.

Prohibition on derogation from regulations 3 and 4 and consequence of breach

5.—(1) The parties may not derogate from regulations 3 and 4.

(2) The law applicable to the contract shall govern the consequences of breach of the rights and obligations under regulations 3 and 4.

5. 1979 c. 43.

PART III

REMUNERATION

Form and amount of remuneration in absence of agreement

6.—(1) In the absence of any agreement as to remuneration between the parties, a commercial agent shall be entitled to the remuneration that commercial agents appointed for the goods forming the subject of his agency contract are customarily allowed in the place where he carries on his activities and, if there is no such customary practice, a commercial agent shall be entitled to reasonable remuneration taking into account all the aspects of the transaction.

(2) This regulation is without prejudice to the application of any enactment or rule of law concerning the level of remuneration.

Entitlement to commission on transactions concluded during agency contract

7.—(1) A commercial agent shall be entitled to commission on commercial transactions concluded during the period covered by the agency contract—

(*a*) where the transaction has been concluded as a result of his action; or

(*b*) where the transaction is concluded with a third party whom he has previously acquired as a customer for transactions of the same kind.

(2) A commercial agent shall also be entitled to commission on transactions concluded during the period covered by the agency contract where he has an exclusive right to a specific geographical area or to a specific group of customers and where the transaction has been entered into with a customer belonging to that area or group.

Entitlement to commission on transactions concluded after agency contract has terminated

8. Subject to regulation 9, a commercial agent shall be entitled to commission on commercial transactions concluded after the agency contract has terminated if—

(*a*) the transaction is mainly attributable to his efforts during the period covered by the agency contract and if the transaction was entered into within a reasonable period after that contract terminated; or

(*b*) in accordance with the conditions mentioned in regulation 7, the order of the third party reached the principal or the commercial agent before the agency contract terminated.

Apportionment of commission between new and previous commercial agents

9.—(1) A commercial agent shall not be entitled to the commission referred to in regulation 7 if that commission is payable, by virtue of regulation 8, to the previous commercial agent, unless it is equitable because of the circumstances for the commission to be shared between the commercial agents.

(2) The principal shall be liable for any sum due under paragraph (1) to the person entitled to it in accordance with that paragraph, and any sum which the other commercial agent receives to which he is not entitled shall be refunded to the principal.

When commission due and date for payment

10.—(1) Commission shall become due as soon as, and to the extent that, one of the following circumstances occurs:

(*a*) the principal has executed the transaction; or

(*b*) the principal should, according to his agreement with the third party, have executed the transaction or

(*c*) the third party has executed the transaction.

(2) Commission shall become due at the latest when the third party has executed his part of the transaction or should have done so if the principal had executed his part of the transaction, as he should have.

(3) The commission shall be paid not later than on the last day of the month following the quarter in which it became due, and, for the purposes of these Regulations, unless otherwise agreed between

the parties, the first quarter period shall run from the date the agency contract takes effect, and subsequent periods shall run from that date in the third month thereafter or the beginning of the fourth month, whichever is the sooner.

(4) Any agreement to derogate from paragraphs (2) and (3) to the detriment of the commercial agent shall be void.

Extinction of right to commission

11.—(1) The right to commission can be extinguished only if and to the extent that—

(*a*) it is established that the contract between the third party and the principal will not be executed; and

(*b*) that fact is due to a reason for which the principal is not to blame.

(2) Any commission which the commercial agent has already received shall be refunded if the right to it is extinguished.

(3) Any agreement to derogate from paragraph (1) to the detriment of the commercial agent shall be void.

Periodic supply of information as to commission due and right of inspection of principal's books

12.—(1) The principal shall supply his commercial agent with a statement of the commission due, not later than the last day of the month following the quarter in which the commission has become due, and such statement shall set out the main components used in calculating the amount of the commission.

(2) A commercial agent shall be entitled to demand that he be provided with all the information (and in particular an extract from the books) which is available to his principal and which he needs in order to check the amount of the commission due to him.

(3) Any agreement to derogate from paragraphs (1) and (2) shall be void.

(4) Nothing in this regulation shall remove or restrict the effect of, or prevent reliance upon, any enactment or rule of law which recognises the right of an agent to inspect the books of a principal.

PART IV

CONCLUSION AND TERMINATION OF THE AGENCY CONTRACT

Right to signed written statement of terms of agency contract

13.—(1) The commercial agent and principal shall each be entitled to receive from the other, on request, a signed written document setting out the terms of the agency contract including any terms subsequently agreed.

(2) Any purported waiver of the right referred to in paragraph (1) shall be void.

Conversion of agency contract after expiry of fixed period

14. An agency contract for a fixed period which continues to be performed by both parties after that period has expired shall be deemed to be converted into an agency contract for an indefinite period.

Minimum periods of notice for termination of agency contract

15.—(1) Where an agency contract is concluded for an indefinite period either party may terminate it by notice.

(2) The period of notice shall be—

(*a*) 1 month for the first year of the contract;

(*b*) 2 months for the second year commenced;

(*c*) 3 months for the third year commenced and for the subsequent years; and the parties may not agree on any shorter periods of notice.

(3) If the parties agree on longer periods than those laid down in paragraph (2), the period of notice to be observed by the principal shall not be shorter than that to be observed by the commercial agent.

(4) Unless otherwise agreed by the parties, the end of the period of notice shall coincide with the end of a calendar month.

(5) Subject to paragraph (6) the provisions of this regulation shall also apply to an agency contract for a fixed period where it is converted under regulation 14 into an agency contract for an indefinite period.

(6) The earlier fixed period shall be taken into account in the calculation of the period of notice.

Savings with regard to immediate termination

16. These Regulations shall not affect the application of any enactment or rule of law which provides for the immediate termination of the agency contract—

(*a*) because of the failure of one party to carry out all or part of his obligation under that contract; or

(*b*) where exceptional circumstances arise.

Entitlement of commercial agent to indemnity or compensation on termination of agency contract

17.—(1) This regulation has effect for the purpose of ensuring that the commercial agent is, after termination of the agency contract, indemnified in accordance with paragraphs (3) to (5) or compensated for damage in accordance with paragraphs (6) and (7).

(2) Except where the agency contract otherwise provides, the commercial agent shall be entitled to be compensated rather than indemnified.

(3) Subject to paragraph (9) and regulation 18, the commercial agent shall be entitled to an indemnity if and to the extent that—.

(*a*) he has brought the principal new customers or has significantly increased the volume of business with existing customers and the principal continues to derive substantial benefits from the business with such customers; and

(*b*) the payment of this indemnity is equitable having regard to all the circumstances and, in particular, the commission lost by the commercial agent on the business transacted with such customers.

(4) The amount of the indemnity shall not exceed a figure equivalent to an indemnity for one year calculated from the commercial agent's average annual remuneration over the preceding five years and if the contract goes back less than five years the indemnity shall be calculated on the average for the period in question.

(5) The grant of an indemnity shall not prevent the commercial agent from seeking damages.

(6) Subject to paragraph (9) and regulation 18, the commercial agent shall be entitled to compensation for the damage he suffers as a result of the termination of his relations with his principal.

(7) For the purpose of these Regulations such damage shall be deemed to occur particularly when the termination takes place in either or both of the following circumstances, namely circumstances which—

(*a*) deprive the commercial agent of the commission which proper performance of the agency contract would have procured for him whilst providing his principal with substantial benefits linked to the activities of the commercial agent; or

(*b*) have not enabled the commercial agent to amortize the costs and expenses that he had incurred in the performance of the agency contract on the advice of his principal.

(8) Entitlement to the indemnity or compensation for damage as provided for under paragraphs (2) to (7) shall also arise where the agency contract is terminated as a result of the death of the commercial agent.

(9) The commercial agent shall lose his entitlement to the indemnity or compensation for damage in the instances provided for in paragraphs (2) to (8) if within one year following termination of his agency contract he has not notified his principal that he intends pursuing his entitlement.

Grounds for excluding payment of indemnity or compensation under regulation 17

18. The indemnity or compensation referred to in regulation 17 shall not be payable to the commercial agent where—

(*a*) the principal has terminated the agency contract because of default attributable to the commercial agent which would justify immediate termination of the agency contract pursuant to regulation 16; or

(*b*) the commercial agent has himself terminated the agency contract, unless such termination is justified—

(i) by circumstances attributable to the principal, or

(ii) on grounds of the age, infirmity or illness of the commercial agent in consequence of which he cannot reasonably be required to continue his activities; or

(*c*) the commercial agent, with the agreement of his principal, assigns his rights and duties under the agency contract to another person.

Prohibition on derogation from regulations 17 and 18

19. The parties may not derogate from regulations 17 and 18 to the detriment of the commercial agent before the agency contract expires.

Restraint of trade clauses

20.—(1) A restraint of trade clause shall be valid only if and to the extent that—

(*a*) it is concluded in writing; and

(*b*) it relates to the geographical area or the group of customers and the geographical area entrusted to the commercial agent and to the kind of goods covered by his agency under the contract.

(2) A restraint of trade clause shall be valid for not more than 2 years after termination of the agency contract.

(3) Nothing in this regulation shall affect any enactment or rule of law which imposes other restrictions on the validity or enforceability of restraint of trade clauses or which enables a court to reduce the obligations on the parties resulting from such clauses.

PART V

MISCELLANEOUS AND SUPPLEMENTAL

Disclosure of information

21. Nothing in these Regulations shall require information to be given where such disclosure would be contrary to public policy.

Service of notice etc

22.—(1) Any notice, statement or other document to be given or supplied to a commercial agent or to be given or supplied to the principal under these Reglations may be so given or supplied:

(*a*) by delivering it to him;

(*b*) by leaving it at his usual address addressed to him by name;

(*c*) by sending it by post to him addressed either to his usual or last known address or to the address of his principal place of business,

or by any other means provided for in the agency contract.

(2) Any such notice, statement or document may—

(*a*) in the case of a body corporate, be given or served on the secretary or clerk of that body;

(*b*) in the case of a partnership, be given to or served on any partner or any person having the control or management of the partnership business.

Transitional provisions

23.—(1) Notwithstanding any provision in an agency contract made before 13th January 1994, these Regulations shall apply to that contract after that date and, accordingly any provision which is inconsistent with these Regulations shall have effect subject to them.

(2) Nothing in these Regulations shall affect the rights and liabilities of a commercial agent or a principal which have accrued before 13th January 1994.

Sealed with the Official Seal of the Department of Economic Development on 17th December 1993.

(L.S.)

A. L. Brown
Assistant Secretary

SCHEDULE

Regulation 2(4)

1. The activities of a person as a commercial agent are to be considered secondary where it may reasonably be taken that the primary purpose of the arrangement with his principal is other than as set out in paragraph 2.

2. An arrangement falls within this paragraph if—

(*a*) the business of the principal is the sale, or as the case may be, purchase of goods of a particular kind; and

(*b*) the goods concerned are such that—

(i) transactions are normally individually negotiated and concluded on a commercial basis; and

(ii) procuring a transaction on one occasion is likely to lead to further transactions in those goods with that customer on future occasions, or to transactions in those goods with other customers in the same geographical area or among the same group of customers, and

that accordingly it is in the commercial interests of the principal in developing the market in those goods to appoint a representative to such customers with a view to the representative devoting effort, skill and expenditure from his own resources to that end.

3. The following are indications that an arrangement falls within paragraph 2, and the absence of any of them is an indication to the contrary—

(*a*) the principal is the manufacturer, importer or distributor of the goods;

(*b*) the goods are specifically identified with the principal in the market in question rather than, or to a greater extent than, with any other person;

(*c*) the agent devotes substantially the whole of his time to representative activities (whether for one principal or for a number of principals whose interests are not conflicting).

(*d*) the goods are not normally available in the market in question other than by means of the agent; and

(*e*) the arrangement is described as one of commercial agency.

4. The following are indications that an arrangement does not fall within paragraph 2—

(*a*) promotional material is supplied direct to potential customers;

(*b*) persons are granted agencies without reference to existing agents in a particular area or in relation to a particular group; and

(*c*) customers normally select the goods for themselves and merely place their orders through the agent.

5. The activities of the following categories of persons are presumed, unless the contrary is established, not to fall within paragraph 2—

(*a*) mail order catalogue agents for consumer goods; and

(*b*) consumer credit agents.

EXPLANATORY NOTE

(This note is not part of the Regulations.)

These Regulations implement as respects Northern Ireland Council Directive 86/653/EEC on the co-ordination of the laws of member States relating to self-employed commercial agents (OJ No. L382, 31st December 1986, p. 17). The Directive is within the scope of the Agreement on the European Economic Area by virtue of paragraph 30 of Annex VII to that Agreement.

The Regulations set out the rights and obligations as between commercial agents and their principals (regulations 3 to 5) and deal with remuneration (regulations 6 to 12), and the conclusion and termination of the agency contract (regulations 13 to 16). They contain provisions relating to the indemnity or compensation payable to a commercial agent on termination of his agency contract (regulations 17 to 19) and also to the validity of restraint of trade clauses (regulation 20).

Regulation 21 makes provision regarding disclosure of information, regulation 22 makes provision with respect to the service of notice etc and regulation 23 contains transitional provisions. The Schedule relates to persons whose activities as commercial agents are to be considered secondary.

A Compliance Cost Assessment is available, copies of which have been placed in the libraries of both Houses of Parliament. Copies are also available from the Department of Economic Development, Trading Standards Branch, 176 Newtownbreda Road, Belfast BT8 4QS.

* * * * * * * *

COMMERCIAL AGENTS (COUNCIL DIRECTIVE) (AMENDMENT) REGULATIONS (NORTHERN IRELAND) 1999, NO. 201

Made	*27th April 1999*
Coming into operation	*7th June 1999*

The Department of Economic Development, being a Department designated by the European Communities (Designation) Order 1989[6] for the purposes of section 2(2) of the European Communities Act 1972[7] in relation to measures relating to relations between **commercial agents** and their principals, in the exercise of the powers conferred on it by that section, hereby makes the following Regulations:

Citation, commencement and interpretation

1.—(1) These Regulations may be cited as the **Commercial Agents** (Council Directive) (Amendment) Regulations (Northern Ireland) 1999 and shall come into operation on 7th June 1999.

(2) The Interpretation Act (Northern Ireland) 1954[8] shall apply to these Regulations as it applies to a Measure of the Northern Ireland Assembly.

Amendment of the Commercial Agents (Council Directive) Regulations (Northern Ireland) 1993

2. The **Commercial Agents** (Council Directive) Regulations (Northern Ireland) 1993[9] shall be amended as provided in regulations 3 and 4.

3. In regulation 1, for paragraph (3) there shall be substituted the following paragraph—

"(3) A court or tribunal shall—

6. S.I. 1989/1327.
7. 1972 c. 68.
8. 1954 c. 33 (N.I.).
9. S.R. 1993 No. 483.

(a) apply the law of the other member State concerned in place of regulations 3 to 22 where the parties have agreed that the agency contract is to be governed by the law of that member State;

(b) (whether or not it would otherwise be required to do so) apply these Regulations where the law of another member State corresponding to these Regulations enables the parties to agree that the agency contract is to be governed by the law of a different member State and the parties have agreed that it is to be governed by the law of Northern Ireland.".

4. In regulation 2(2), after the definition of "commission" there shall be inserted the following definitions—

"EEA Agreement" means the Agreement on the European Economic Area signed at Oporto on 2nd May 1992 as adjusted by the Protocol signed at Brussels on 17th March 1993;
"member State" includes a State which is a contracting party to the EEA Agreement;".

Sealed with the Official Seal of the Department of Economic Development on

L.S.

A. L. Brown
Assistant Secretary
27th April 1999.

EXPLANATORY NOTE

(This note is not part of the Regulations.)

These Regulations amend the **Commercial Agents** (Council Directive) Regulations (Northern Ireland) 1993 ("the 1993 Regulations"), which implemented Council Directive 86/653/EEC on the co-ordination of the laws of member States relating to self-employed **commercial agents** (O.J. No. L382, 31.12.1986, p. 17) ("the Directive").

Following representations made by the European Commission to the effect that the 1993 Regulations did not deal with the case where the parties had expressly agreed that the law of any part of the United Kingdom was to apply to the contract between them and that a court in the United Kingdom was to have jurisdiction but the activities of the **agent** were to be carried out elsewhere in the European Communities, these Regulations seek to put the matter beyond doubt in relation to Northern Ireland.

Whether or not it would otherwise be required to do so, a court or tribunal is required to apply the 1993 Regulations in the case mentioned above, provided that the law of the other member State so permits. The 1993 Regulations already made provision for the converse case, thus permitting **agents** in Northern Ireland to agree to the application of the law of another member State. The amendment restates this provision.

The Explanatory Note to the 1993 Regulations drew attention to the fact that the Directive was within the scope of the Agreement on the European Economic Area by virtue of paragraph 30 of Annex VII to that Agreement. These Regulations take the opportunity to insert appropriate references in the 1993 Regulations.

APPENDIX 4

THE IRISH IMPLEMENTING LEGISLATION: SI 33 of 1994 and SI 31 of 1997

EUROPEAN COMMUNITIES (COMMERCIAL AGENTS) REGULATIONS, S.I. No. 33 of 1994

I, RUAIRÍ QUINN, Minister for Enterprise and Employment, in exercise of the powers conferred on me by section 3 of the European Communities Act, 1972 (No. 27 of 1972) for the purpose of giving effect to Council Directive 86/653/EEC of 18 December 1986,* on the co-ordination of the laws of the Member States relating to self-employed commercial agents, hereby make the following Regulations:

1. These Regulations may be cited as the European Communities (Commercial Agents) Regulations, 1994.

2. (1) In these Regulations:

"commercial agent" means a self-employed intermediary who has continuing authority to negotiate the sale or purchase of goods on behalf of another person, hereinafter called "the principal", or to negotiate and conclude such transactions on behalf of and in the name of the principal;

the term "commercial agent" does not include—

(*a*) a person who, in the capacity of an officer of a company or association, is empowered to enter into commitments binding on that company or association;
(*b*) a partner who is lawfully authorised to enter into commitments binding on the partners;
(*c*) a receiver, a receiver and manager, a liquidator or an examiner, as defined in the Companies Acts, 1963 to 1990, or a trustee in bankruptcy;
(*d*) a commercial agent whose activities are unpaid;
(*e*) a commercial agent operating on commodity exchanges or in the commodity market; or
(*f*) a consumer credit agent or a mail order catalogue agent for consumer goods, whose activities, pursuant to paragraph (2) of this Regulation, are considered secondary;

"the Directive" means Council Directive 86/653 EEC of 18 December 1986.*

(2) The activities of an agent of a category described in paragraph (1)(*f*) of this Regulation shall be presumed, unless the contrary is established, to be secondary for the purposes of these Regulations.

(3) The Directive shall, subject to these Regulations, apply to the relations between commercial agents and their principals from 1 January 1994.

4. In the application of Article 7(2) of the Directive, a commercial agent shall be entitled to commission on commercial transactions concluded during the period covered by the agency contract only where the agent has an exclusive right to a specific geographical area or group of customers and where the transaction has been entered into with a customer belonging to that area or group.

5. The agency contract shall not be valid unless it is evidenced in writing.

* O.J. L382/17 of 31st December 1986.

GIVEN under my Official Seal, this 21st day of February 1994.

RUAIRÍ QUINN,
Minister for Enterprise and
Employment

EXPLANATORY NOTE

(This note is not part of the Instrument and does not purport to be a legal interpretation)

These Regulations give legal effect to EU Council Directive 86/653/EEC on the Co-ordination of the LAWS of Member States relating to Self-Employed Commercial Agents. The Regulations deal with the relationship between Commercial Agents and their Principals and their respective rights and obligations. Certain categories of agent are specifically excluded.

* * * * * * * *

EUROPEAN COMMUNITIES (COMMERCIAL AGENTS) REGULATIONS, S.I. No. 31 of 1997

I, RICHARD BRUTON, Minister for Enterprise and Employment, in exercise of the powers conferred on me by section 3 of the European Communities Act, 1972 (No. 27 of 1972), for the purpose of giving effect to Council Directive No. 86/653/EEC of 18 December 1986,* on the co-ordination of the laws of the Member States relating to self-employed commercial agents, hereby make the following Regulations:

1. (1) These Regulations may be cited as the European Communities (Commercial Agents) Regulations, 1997.

(2) The European Communities (Commercial Agents) Regulations, 1994 (S.I. No. 33 of 1994) and these Regulations shall be construed as one and may be cited together as the European Communities (Commercial Agents) Regulations, 1994 and 1997.

2. It is hereby confirmed that, pursuant to Regulation 3 of the European Communities (Commercial Agents) Regulations, 1994, a commercial agent shall, after termination of the agency agreement, be entitled to be compensated for damage in accordance with Article 17(3) of the Directive subject, insofar as they are relevant to such compensation, to the provisions of that Article and of Articles 18, 19 and 20 of the Directive.

GIVEN under my Official Seal, this 7th day of January, 1997.

RICHARD BRUTON,
Minister for Enterprise and
Employment

EXPLANATORY NOTE.

(This note is not part of the Instrument and does not purport to be a legal interpretation)

These Regulations have been made in order to state expressly, for the avoidance of any possible doubt, what was done in the European Communities (Commercial Agents) Regulations 1994 (S.I. No. 33 of 1994) regarding Article 17 of the Council Directive on Commercial Agents. The Regulations confirm that, after termination of an agency agreement, a commercial agent shall be entitled to compensation under Article 17(3) of Council Directive No. 86/653/EEC of 18th December 1986.

* O.J. L382/17 of 31–12–1986.

APPENDIX 5

EXTRACT FROM THE FRENCH COMMERCIAL CODE:

(in translation following the official version on the French government legal database www.legifrance.gouv.fr)

ARTICLE L 134–1

Al 1: Commercial agents are agents who, as independent professionals not linked by contracts for services, shall be permanently entrusted with negotiating and possibly concluding sale, purchase, rental or service provision contracts for and on behalf of producers, industrialists, traders or other commercial agents. Commercial agents may be natural or legal persons.

Al 2: Agents whose representation tasks are carried out in the context of economic activities which are covered, with regard to these tasks, by special acts shall not come under the provisions of this chapter.

ARTICLE L 134–2

Each party shall be entitled, at its request, to obtain from the other party a signed document indicating the contents of the agency contract, including the contents of its riders.

ARTICLE L 134–3

Commercial agents may agree, without needing authorisation, to represent new principals. However, they may not agree to represent an undertaking competing with that of one of their principals without the latter's agreement.

ARTICLE L 134–4

Al 1: The contracts concluded between commercial agents and their principals shall be in the common interest of the parties.

Al 2: The relationships between commercial agents and principals shall be governed by an obligation of loyalty and a reciprocal duty of information.

Al 3: Commercial agents must perform their mandate in a professional manner. Principals shall make sure that the commercial agents are able to perform their mandate.

ARTICLE L 134–5

Al 1: Any element of the remuneration which varies according to the number or value of the deals concluded shall constitute a commission within the meaning of this chapter.

Al 2: Articles L.134–6 to L.134–9 shall apply when the agents are remunerated in full or in part by the commission thus defined.

Al 3: If the contract is silent on this, commercial agents shall be entitled to a remuneration in accordance with the usual practice in the sector of activity covered by their mandate and in which they carry out their activity. In the absence of any usual practice, the commercial agent shall be entitled to a reasonable remuneration which takes account of all the elements involved in the operation.

ARTICLE L 134–6

Al 1: For any commercial transactions concluded during the term of the agency contract, commercial agents shall be entitled to the commission defined in Article L.134–5 when these transactions have been concluded thanks to their intervention or when the transactions have been concluded with a third party whose custom they obtained previously for transactions of the same kind.

Al 2: When they are entrusted with a geographical sector or a specific group of persons, commercial agents shall also be entitled to the commission for any transaction concluded during the term of the agency contract with a person belonging to this sector or group.

ARTICLE L 134–7

For any commercial transactions concluded after the agency contract ceases, commercial agents shall be entitled to the commission when the transaction is mainly due to their activity during the agency contract and has been concluded within a reasonable period after the contract ceases or when, in accordance with the conditions specified in Article L.134–6, the order from the third party was received by the principal or by the commercial agent before the agency contract ceased.

ARTICLE L 134–8

Commercial agents shall not be entitled to the commission specified in Article L.134–6 if this is due, pursuant to Article L.134–7, to the previous commercial agent, unless the circumstances make it fair to share the commission between the commercial agents.

ARTICLE L 134–9

Al 1: The commission shall be acquired as soon as the principal has carried out the transaction or should have carried this out under the agreement concluded with the third party or as soon as the third party has carried out the transaction.

Al 2: The commission shall be acquired at the latest when the third party has carried out its part of the transaction or should have carried this out if the principal has carried out its own part. It shall be paid at the latest on the last day of the month following the quarter in which it was acquired.

ARTICLE L 134–10

Al 1: The right to the commission may be extinguished only if it is established that the contract between the third party and the principal will not be performed and if this is not due to circumstances attributable to the principal.

Al 2: The commission which the commercial agent has already received shall be refunded if the right relating thereto is extinguished.

ARTICLE L 134–11

Al 1: A term contract which continues to be performed by both parties after its term shall be deemed to have been converted into an open contract.

Al 2: When the agency contract is an open contract, each party may end this by giving prior notice. The provisions of this article shall apply to the term contract converted into an open contract. In this case, the calculation of the duration of the prior notice shall take account of the previous fixed term.

Al 3: The period of prior notice shall be one month for the first year of the contract, two months for the second year started and three months for the third year started and for subsequent years. In the absence of agreement to the contrary, the end of the prior notice period shall coincide with the end of a calendar month.

Al 4: The parties may not agree shorter periods of prior notice. If they agree longer periods, the prior notice period specified for the principal must not be shorter than that specified for the agent.

Al 5: These provisions shall not apply when the contract ends due to serious negligence by one of the parties or the occurrence of a case of *force majeure*.

ARTICLE L 134–12

Al 1: If their relationship with their principal ceases, commercial agents shall be entitled to an indemnity for the loss suffered.

Al 2: Commercial agents shall lose the right to this compensation if they have not notified the principal, within one year of the cessation of the contract, that they intend to use their rights.

Al 3: The legal successors of commercial agents shall also benefit from the right to compensation when the cessation of the contract is due to the death of the agent.

ARTICLE L 134–13

The compensation specified in Article L.134–12 shall not be due in the following cases:
1° The cessation of the contract is caused by the serious negligence of the commercial agent.
2° The cessation of the contract is initiated by the agent unless this cessation is justified by circumstances attributable to the principal or due to the age, infirmity or illness of the commercial agent, as a result of which the continuation of the latter's activity can no longer be reasonably required;
3° In accordance with an agreement with the principal, the commercial agent cedes to a third party the rights and obligations held under the agency contract.

ARTICLE L 134–14

Al 1: The contract may contain a non-competition clause applying after its cessation.
Al 2: This clause must be established in writing and shall cover the geographical sector and, if applicable, the group of persons entrusted to the commercial agent and the type of goods or services which the latter represents under the contract.
Al 3: The non-competition clause shall be valid only for a maximum period of two years after a contract ceases.

ARTICLE L 134–15

Al 1: When the activity of commercial agent is carried out under a written contract, signed by the parties, which is principally for another purpose, the parties may decide in writing that the provisions of this chapter do not apply to the part corresponding to the commercial agency activity.

Al 2: This renunciation shall be invalid if the performance of the contract reveals that the commercial agency activity is actually being carried out as the principal or decisive element.

ARTICLE L 134–16

Any clause or agreement contrary to the provisions of Articles L.134–2 and L.134–4, the third and fourth paragraphs of Article L.134–11 and Article L.134–15 or establishing an exception, to the detriment of the commercial agent, to the provisions of the second paragraph of Article L.134–9, the first paragraph of Article L.134–10, Articles L.134–12 and L.134–13 and the third paragraph of Article L.134–14 shall be deemed to be unwritten.

APPENDIX 6

EXTRACT FROM THE GERMAN COMMERCIAL CODE

CHAPTER 7: COMMERCIAL AGENTS

§ 84 Definition of a Commercial Agent

(1) A commercial agent is a person who is as an independent businessman continuously entrusted to procure business transactions for another businessman (the principal) or to conclude business transactions in his name. A person is independent if he is essentially free to organise his activities and to determine his hours of work.

(2) A person who, without being independent within the meaning of subsection 1, is continuously entrusted to procure business transactions for a principal or to conclude business transactions in his name, is deemed to be an employee.

(3) The principal may also be a commercial agent.

(4) The provisions of this Part are also applicable if the commercial agent's business activity does not, according to its type or scope, require a business establishment or assets equipped in the manner appropriate for a trader.

§ 85 Written Contract

Either party may require that the contents of the contract as well as any subsequent amendments thereto be contained in a document signed by the other party. This right may not be excluded.

§ 86 Duties of the Commercial Agent

(1) The commercial agent shall endeavour to procure or conclude business transactions; in doing so he shall safeguard the principal's interests.

(2) He shall communicate the necessary information to the principal, and in particular notify him without undue delay of all business transactions procured and concluded.

(3) He shall attend to his duties with the care of a prudent merchant.

(4) Agreements deviating from subsections 1 and 2 above shall be invalid.

§ 86a Duties of the Principal

(1) The principal shall place at the commercial agent's disposal the materials necessary to the performance of his activities, such as samples, drawings, price-lists, advertising material and terms of business.

(2) The principal shall give the commercial agent the necessary information. He shall notify the agent without undue delay of the acceptance or rejection of a business transaction procured by the agent or concluded by him outside the scope of his authority to represent the principal, or of the non-performance of a business transaction procured or concluded by the agent. The principal shall notify him without undue delay if it is probable that he can or intends to conclude business transactions only in a significantly smaller volume than the commercial agent could expect under normal circumstances.

(3) Agreements deviating from subsections 1 and 2 above shall be invalid.

§ 86b Del Credere Commission

(1) If a commercial agent guarantees the performance of the obligation arising out of a business transaction, he may claim a special remuneration (del credere commission). This right may not be excluded in advance. This responsibility may only be undertaken for a specific business transaction or for business transactions with specific third parties which the agent procures or concludes. This undertaking must be in writing and signed by the agent.

(2) The claim to del credere commission arises with the conclusion of the business transaction.

(3) Subsection 1 does not apply if the principal or third party has his place of business or, if none, his residence, abroad. Nor does it apply to business transactions for the conclusion and performance of which the commercial agent has unlimited authority.

§ 87 Business Transactions for which Commission is Payable

(1) The commercial agent is entitled to commission for all business transactions concluded during the contractual relationship which are attributable to his activities or concluded with third parties whom he had acquired as customers for business transactions of the same kind. He has no claim for commission if and to the extent that pursuant to subsection 3 the commission is due to the preceding commercial agent.

(2) If a specific district or specific group of customers has been assigned to the commercial agent, he is entitled to commission even for business transactions concluded without his involvement with persons in his district or from his group of customers during the contractual relationship. This does not apply if and to the extent that pursuant to subsection 3 the commission is due to the preceding commercial agent.

(3) For a business transaction concluded after termination of the contractual relationship the commercial agent is only entitled to commission if

1. he has procured or introduced and prepared the transaction in such a way that its conclusion is predominantly attributable to his activities and it is concluded within a reasonable period after termination of the contractual relationship, or
2. the third party's offer to conclude a business transaction in respect of which the commercial agent has a claim for commission pursuant to subsection 1, sentence 1 or subsection 2, sentence 1 is received by the commercial agent or the principal before termination of the contractual relationship.

The successor commercial agent shall be entitled to a proportion of the commission provided for under sentence 1 above if, by virtue of the particular circumstances, an apportionment of the commission is equitable.

(4) In addition to the claim for commission for concluded business transactions the commercial agent is entitled to a debt collection commission for amounts collected by him in accordance with instructions.

§ 87a When Commission Falls Due

(1) The commercial agent is entitled to commission as soon as and insofar as the principal has completed the transaction. An agreement to the contrary may be made; however, upon completion of the business transaction by the principal the commercial agent is entitled to a reasonable advance due not later than the last day of the following month. Irrespective of any agreement to the contrary the commercial agent is, nevertheless, entitled to commission as soon as and insofar as the third party has completed the transaction.

(2) Where it is clearly established that the third party will not perform, the claim for commission is lost; amounts already received shall be refunded.

(3) The commercial agent is also entitled to commission where it is clearly established that the principal does not carry out the business transaction in whole or in part or as agreed. Such claim shall not arise, if and to the extent that the principal's non-performance is due to circumstances for which the principal is not responsible.

(4) The claim for commission falls due on the last day of the month in which the claim is to be accounted for pursuant to § 87c, subsection 1.

(5) Agreements deviating from the provision contained in the first grammatical clause of subsection 2 and from subsections 3 and 4 to the detriment of the commercial agent are invalid.

§ 87b Amount of Commission

(1) If the rate of commission is not determined, the customary rate is deemed to have been agreed.

(2) The commission is to be calculated on the consideration payable by the third party or the principal. Discounts for cash payments are not to be deducted; the same applies to incidental costs such as freight, packaging, customs duty and taxes, unless the incidental costs are charged separately to the third party. Value added tax shown separately on an invoice solely because of tax provisions is not considered to be charged separately.

(3) In the case of fixed-term contracts for transfer of use and enjoyment the commission shall be calculated on the consideration for the term of the contract. In the case of contracts not concluded a fixed term commission shall be calculated on the consideration up to the point in time to which the third party can first give notice of termination; if the contract continues, the commercial agent is entitled to further commission calculated accordingly.

§ 87c Accounting for Commission

(1) The principal has to account on a monthly basis for the commission to which the commercial agent is entitled; the accounting period may be extended to three months at the most. The accounting shall be carried out without undue delay, at the latest by the end of the following month.

(2) When accounting takes place the commercial agent may require production of an extract from the books in respect of all business transactions for which he is entitled to commission in accordance with § 87.

(3) In addition the commercial agent may call for information concerning any matter which is material to the claim for commission, its due date and calculation.

(4) If the extract from the books is refused or if reasonable doubt exists as to the correctness or completeness of the accounting or of the extract from the books, the commercial agent may require that, at the principal's option, either he or an auditor or certified accountant of his choice shall be entitled to inspect the business books or other documents so far as is necessary to establish the correctness or completeness of the accounting or of the extract from the books.

(5) These rights of the commercial agent may not be excluded or restricted.

§ 87d Reimbursement of Expenditure

The commercial agent may only require reimbursement of expenditure incurred in the ordinary course of business if this is customary within the trade.

§ 88 Limitation of Claims

[repealed with effect from 15th December 2004]

§ 88a Right of Retention

(1) The commercial agent cannot waive his statutory rights of retention in advance.

(2) After termination of the contractual relationship the commercial agent has under the general law a right of retention over materials placed at his disposal (§ 86a subsection 1) only in respect of claims for commission which have fallen due and for reimbursement of expenditure.

§ 89 Notice to Terminate the Contract

(1) Where the contractual relationship has been entered into for an indefinite period, it may be terminated during the first year of the contract by the giving of one month's notice, during the second year of the contract by two months' notice, and during the third to the fifth year of the contract by three months' notice. After the contract has run for five years, it may be terminated by

the giving of six months' notice. Notice may only be given to the end of a calendar month, unless the parties have agreed otherwise.

(2) The periods of notice specified in subsection 1, sentences 1 and 2, may be extended by agreement; the period of notice to be given by the principal may not be shorter than that to be given by the agent. Where it has been agreed that a shorter period of notice is to be given by the principal than by the agent, the period of notice to be given by the agent shall nevertheless be deemed also to be the period of notice to be given by the principal.

(3) A contract concluded for a fixed term which is continued by both parties after expiry of such fixed term shall be deemed to have been extended for an indefinite period. The total duration of the contractual relationship shall be taken as a basis for the purposes of determining the periods of notice pursuant to subsection 1, sentences 1 and 2.

§ 89a Termination without Notice

(1) Either party may terminate the contractual relationship without notice where such termination is justified by the circumstances. This right may not be excluded or restricted.

(2) Where such termination is caused by conduct for which the other party is responsible, the latter must pay damages for loss resulting from termination of the contractual relationship.

§ 89b Claim for Compensation

(1) After termination of the contractual relationship the commercial agent may demand from the principal reasonable compensation if and insofar as:

1. substantial advantages accrue to the principal even after termination of the contractual relationship from business relations with new customers recruited by the agent, and
2. by reason of termination of the contract the commercial agent loses rights to commission which, had it continued, he would have had from business transactions already concluded or to be concluded in the future with customers recruited by him, and
3. payment of compensation is equitable taking all the circumstances into account.

A customer can be said to have been recruited if the commercial agent has so significantly increased business relations with a customer that this corresponds in commercial terms to the recruitment of a new customer.

(2) Such compensation shall amount to not more than one year's commission or other annual remuneration calculated on the basis of the average of the last five years' activities of the commercial agent; where the contractual relationship has been of shorter duration, the average during the period of activity is to be taken as the basis.

(3) Such claim shall not arise if

1. the commercial agent has terminated the contractual relationship, unless the behaviour of the principal has given good cause for such termination, or, by reason of age or illness, the commercial agent could not reasonably be expected to continue his activity, or
2. the principal has terminated the contractual relationship under circumstances justifying immediate termination by reason of fault on the part of the commercial agent, or
3. by agreement between the principal and the commercial agent a third party assumes the contractual rights and liabilities of the commercial agent in his stead; such agreement may not be concluded before termination of the contractual relationship.

(4) This claim may not be excluded in advance. It must be asserted within one year of termination of the contractual relationship.

(5) [Relates to insurance agents—not relevant.]

§ 90 Business secrets

The commercial agent shall not, either during or after the ending of the contractual relationship, exploit or disclose to others business or trade secrets entrusted to him or which have become known to him through his activities for the principal, insofar as this would, in all the circumstances, be contrary to the professional standards of a reasonable businessman.

§ 90a Non-compete clauses

(1) An agreement which restricts the commercial agent in his business activities after termination of the contractual relationship (a non-compete clause) must be in writing and a document containing the agreed terms and signed by the principal must be provided to the commercial agent. The non-compete clause will only be effective for a maximum of two years from the termination of the contractual relationship; it may extend only to the district or group of customers entrusted to the commercial agent and to the type of goods in respect of which the commercial agent was to endeavour to negotiate or conclude business for the principal. The principal is obliged to pay reasonable compensation to the commercial agent for the duration of the restriction on competition.
(2) The principal may, at any time during the termination of the contractual relationship, in writing waive the benefit of the non-compete clause. This will have the result of releasing him from the obligation to pay compensation on the expiry of six months from his declaration that he has waived that right.
(3) If one party gives notice to terminate the agency relationship for good cause on account of fault on the part of the other party, he may by giving a written declaration to the other party within one month of the termination free himself of his obligations under the non-compete clause.
(4) Other agreements to the detriment of the commercial agent may not be made.

§ 91 The commercial agent's authority

(1) Article 55 applies also to a commercial agent who has been authorized to conclude transations by a principal who is not a merchant.
(2) Even if a commercial agent is not authorized to conclude contracts on behalf of his principal, he shall be deemed to have authority to receive notices of defects in goods, declarations that goods are at the buyer's disposal and similar declarations whereby a third party assents or reserves his rights arising from an inadequate contractual performance. He may assert the principal's rights to preserve evidence. A limitation of this right will only be effective against a third party if the latter knew or ought to have known of it.

§ 91a Lack of authority

(1) If a commercial agent who has only the authority to negotiate business has concluded a transaction in the principal's name and the third party did not know of the agent's lack of authority, the transaction is to be treated as authorised by the principal unless the latter repudiates it vis-à-vis the third party without delay after being informed by the commercial agent or the third party of its conclusion and of its main contents.
(2) The same applies if a commercial agent who has the authority to conclude contracts has concluded a contract in the principal's name which he was not authorised to conclude.

§ 92 [concerns insurance agents and savings and loan association agents, and is not translated here]

§ 92a Minimum standards for working conditions

(1) As regards the contractual relationship of a commercial agent who by contract may not represent other principals or for whom, due to the manner and scope of activity required of him, this is impossible, the Federal Minister of Justice, by agreement with the Federal Minister of Economics and Labour, after hearing associations of principals and agents, may, by regulations not requiring the consent of the Federal Council, prescribe the minimum contractual duties required of a principal to ensure that the necessary social and economic needs of such commercial agents or of a particular group of them are satisfied. The duties so prescribed may not be excluded or limited by contract.
(2) [applies § 93 para. 1 to insurance agents]

§ 92b Part-time commercial agents

(1) Section 89 and section 89b do not apply to part-time commercial agents. If the contractual relationship has been entered into for an indefinite period, it may be terminated by giving one month's notice to become effective at the end of a calendar month. If a different notice period has been agreed, it must be the same for both parties. The right to claim a reasonable advance under section 87a, subsection 1, sentence 2, can be excluded.
(2) Subsection (1) may only be relied upon by a principal who has expressly entrusted the commercial agent with the negotiation or conclusion of business transactions as a part-time commercial agent.
(3) Whether the commercial agent is merely a part-time commercial agent is to be determined by reference to the expectations of persons trading in the sector.
(4) The provisions of subsections (1) to (3) apply mutatis mutandis to insurance agents and savings and loan association agents.

§ 92c Commercial agents outside the European Union; shipping agents

(1) If the activity of the commercial agent under his contract with the principal is not to be carried out within the territory of the European Union or the other contracting states of the EEA Agreement, all of the provisions of this chapter may be varied by agreement.
(2) The same is true if the commercial agent is entrusted with the negotiation or the conclusion of business whose purpose is the chartering, making ready or fitting out of ships or the booking of passengers on ships.

APPENDIX 7

HOUSE OF LORDS SELECT COMMITTEE FIFTY-FIRST REPORT

WEDNESDAY 27 JULY 1977

By the Select Committee appointed to consider Community proposals whether in draft or otherwise, to obtain all necessary information about them, and to make reports on those which, in the opinion of the Committee, raise important questions of policy or principle, and on other questions to which the Committee consider that the special attention of the House should be drawn.

Ordered to Report:—

1. R/3/77: DRAFT COUNCIL DIRECTIVE TO CO-ORDINATE THE LAWS OF THE MEMBER STATES RELATING TO (SELF-EMPLOYED) COMMERCIAL AGENTS

1. The proposed Directive deals with the legal relationship between "commercial agents" and their principals. For the purposes of the Directive a "commercial agent" is, broadly speaking, an independent person acting on a continuing basis in the name of a manufacturer or trader and negotiating or concluding contracts on his behalf for the supply of goods or services. The Directive if adopted would require standardised rules to be implied into the agency contract under which the commercial agent acts for the manufacturer or trader; in many instances departure from these standardised rules to the detriment of the commercial agent would not be permitted; the rules concern the rights and duties of the agent and of his principal, the remuneration of the agent, the agent's rights in the insolvency of the principal, and the making and cessation of the agency contract. Some of the Member States already have statutory codes, the content of which varies, concerning the legal relationship between these parties; the other Member States, including the United Kingdom, have no such code. One of the main purposes of the Directive is to introduce harmonised rules in the Member States about this kind of agency, since it is considered by the Commission that the existing differences are detrimental to the functioning of the Common Market; the other main purpose is to strengthen the position of the commercial agent *vis-à-vis* his principal by requiring the existence in all Member States of rules which favour the agents.
2. At the outset, those concerned in drafting the Directive seem to have encountered difficulty in defining the expression "commercial agent". Article 2 of the draft defines the expression to mean "a self-employed intermediary who has continuing authority for a fixed or indeterminate period to negotiate and/or to conclude an unlimited number of commercial transactions in the name and for account of another person (who is hereinafter called "the principal")." This is a wide definition, and the draftsmen seem to have been so much impressed by its width that in Article 3 they proceed to exclude from the definition two classes of persons who in any case would not have been within it. The exact area that could be covered by the definition is very indeterminate; it has been suggested that it could include such persons as travel agents, advertising agents, stockbrokers, loading brokers, and forwarding agents to the extent that they act for particular principals over a period of time. It could cover buying agents, though later articles suggest that this is not intended. Agents in the insurance and credit fields are expressly

excluded. It becomes clear, at a late stage in the draft, that it is intended to cover companies acting as agents as well as individuals so acting. Generally speaking, the Committee find the drafting of the Directive loose and uncertain.

3. The Committee take the true intended effect of the Directive to be to protect independent commercial agents who are engaged to canvass for orders for the principal's goods or services as distinct from "commercial travellers" who are employees of the persons whom they serve. The draft Directive contains rules concerning commission which considerably favour the commercial agent. Of the other detailed rules which compliance with the Directive would cause to be implicit in the agency contract, the most important would be those which would confer on the agent (*a*) the right on cessation of the contract to be paid a "goodwill indemnity" where he has brought new customers to the principal or appreciably increased the volume of business with existing customers, and as a result substantial benefits will continue to accrue to the principal (Article 30); (*b*) the right, where the commercial agent is for a period after cessation of the contract bound by an agreement restricting his business activities, to be paid remuneration during that period (Article 32); and (*c*) a right to preferential treatment in the insolvency of the principal. The inclusion in the agency contract of rights of the kind mentioned under (*a*) or (*b*) above, though required by the laws of some of the Member States, is not compulsory according to the law of the United Kingdom; in that country they are a matter for negotiation between the parties, and the inclusion of (*b*) would, it is thought, be very unusual. If the Directive were adopted in its present form these rights would, under the law in each of the Member States have to be conferred on the agent, save that the right to the goodwill indemnity could be excluded if the agent were a company with a paid-up capital exceeding 100,000 European Units of Account ("EUA") (about £67,000). It would not, however, be difficult to avoid being excluded on this ground; the company could operate on loan capital, or several companies each having a capital less than 100,000 EUA could be formed.

4. While therefore the law of the United Kingdom includes, at present, no special rules governing the relationship between commercial agents and their principals, the laws of the continental Member States do include rules for the protection of these agents, but these it appears vary very considerably from country to country. Thus the Sub-Committees (B and E) which have considered the Directive were informed in evidence that the degree of protection for agents in France goes much further than that provided for in the Directive, and had been raised so high that "principals were not interested in entering into contracts with French agents." The rules in Germany are evidently less favourable to the agents, and it is said that even after the protective law was introduced "the commercial agency was still the cheapest means of marketing goods in Germany."

5. The purpose of the present report is not to review the Directive in detail and criticize its drafting, but to consider whether there is any justification in principle for introducing a Directive on this subject at all. The justification put up by the Commission is summarised as follows in the Commission's Explanatory Memorandum at page 2.

> "Basically, the proposal has two objectives. The first is to remove the differences in law which are detrimental to the proper functioning of the common market. They affect the conditions of competition and create considerable legal uncertainty. This applies, for example, in relation to the goodwill indemnity, which is known in some Member States but not in others. It is more expensive for the principal to have an agent in those countries in which the goodwill indemnity is already compulsory by law, and this operates very much to the economic advantage of principals who are not under an obligation to pay any indemnity after the contract has terminated. The second objective is to safeguard or improve the protection that already exists for commercial agents. Although they are self-employed, most commercial agents are economically in a weak position vis-à-vis their principals. In so far as the proposal envisages minimum rules it does not affect those provisions of national law which are more favourable to the commercial agent and does not stand in the way of progress. From a more general point of view the proposal is aligned on the principles set out in Article 117 of the EEC Treaty, and, in harmonising the law, endeavours to achieve a levelling-up."

6. This statement on the part of the Commission is notable for the boldness of its assertions. It is, for example, insupportable to lay down as a general proposition that "it is more expensive for the principal to have an agent in those countries in which the goodwill indemnity is already compulsory by law, and this operates very much to the economic advantage of principals who are not under (such) an obligation . . . ". Obviously, the question whether one principal has a competitive advantage over another depends as much, if not more, on the rates of remuneration which they each pay during the period of the contract, to say nothing of the other terms of the contract. It may suit both principal and agent to dispense with a provision for goodwill indemnity in favour of a higher rate of commission during the currency of the contract. There would seem no justification for prohibiting them from making what bargain they please about this. The statement that "most commercial agents are economically in a weak position vis-à-vis their principals" appears to be simply a matter of assertion. The preamble to the Directive is couched in more cautious terms and states that "in many cases commercial agents are as a rule, though in differing degrees, economically in a weak position vis-à-vis their principals." The evidence given on the part of the Manufacturers' Agents' Association of the United Kingdom was that there are twenty thousand agents in this country. It is difficult to believe that the Commission knows the conditions under which "most" of these persons work, and their economic strength. The evidence of the Association was that "the agent used to have to get the best terms he could from his principal, today we have a form of agreement which is ever increasingly being accepted by British principals". The evidence further was that the standard form of contract "goes rather further than the directive which you are now considering, particularly in respect of the goodwill compensation clause"; and that "there is no question . . . whatever that there is now a greater demand, especially in the economic situation in which we live today, for manufacturers' agents than ever before." The Association stated in its written submission that "it is generally conceded that the commercial agent is invariably the weaker party as between himself and his principal." Dr R A Haumann, a German lawyer who gave helpful evidence about the law of that country, stated that "in general, the manufacturer's agent is in a weaker position and this weaker position is a bad thing for him. It leads to insecurity." But he went on to say that "we are not in favour of compulsory provision overall in Germany . . . there must be some compulsory provisions in agency law, but in my opinion there is a little too much in this respect in the EEC draft Directive." On the other hand, the Confederation of British Industry stated that "the realities of commercial and industrial life being what they are, it is probable that proper investigation would show that principals are very often at the mercy of commercial agents and in at least equal general need of 'protection', and that the relative economic positions (which in effect means sizes and physical or financial resources) are very frequently irrelevant in determining which party is the dominant one in practice." The Association of British Chambers of Commerce, in their submission,[1] said:

> "The guiding principle behind the Commission's proposals is that commercial agents are believed to be in a weaker negotiating position than their principals, and thus need protected and inalienable rights. The ABCC does not believe this premise is correct. The Commission claims that in countries where a preferential regime has been introduced for commercial agents (for example Belgium) there has been a resulting increase in their numbers. This is evidence of nothing more than the fact that people take advantage of a preferential status if it is offered to them. It does not mean that in the absence of this preferential status those who might otherwise act as commercial agents would be severely disadvantaged. On the contrary, the ABCC considers that an agent is frequently in a reasonably strong position and is not therefore always in need of the extended protection proposed.
>
> The Commission is particularly keen to impose protection where a principal in one country appoints a selling agent in another country. The ABCC believes that this relationship will most frequently occur when a comparatively small manufacturer wishes to break into an export market, and, having neither the resources nor the immediate sales potential for setting up a full time distributor or his own office in the country, hires an agent with

1. Memorandum, Part III printed below on page 19.

specialised and local knowledge to do the job on his behalf. In this type of situation, there is very little likelihood of the principal being in such a strong negotiating position that the agent is in need of special protection.

In the UK, at least, there exist various established trade associations, most notably the Manufacturers' Agents' Association, who protect the interests of members, and presumably provide their membership with clear advice and guidelines as to acceptable conditions of agency contracts."

7. In the result, therefore, the facts, so far as they are ascertainable at all, seem to emerge very much as might be expected. At one end of the scale it seems that there are agents who are at the mercy of their principals; at the other end, principals at the mercy of their agents; in the middle, what appears to be a substantial body of agents whose services, according to the evidence of their Association, are much in demand and who are steadily improving their position. To impose, on this variegated pattern of agencies, one body of inflexible legal rules seems to the Committee to be incapable of justification. What is needed is a flexibility which enables the parties to the agency contract to arrange terms which suit their respective needs.
8. In general, the Committee question the desirability of imposing fixed standards in these commercial matters. If terms which favour the commercial agents are imposed, then the principals will find other means of selling their goods, by employing their own travellers, by employing commission agents who act in their own names, or by forming subsidiary companies. Distortions of business are a common result of imposing inflexible rules.
9. The Commission's other justification for the Directive is that it would remove "a continuing and quite definite inequality of the conditions of competition." Here, again, the Committee feel the lack of any supporting evidence. In so far as a manufacturer wishes to sell his goods in a particular country there seems to be no room for distortion of competition. Each manufacturer will be in the same position, according to whether or not the country in question has adopted rules resembling those in the Directive. The notion that a manufacturer will be positively debarred from selling in a country where agencies are so favoured seems to the Select Committee to be fanciful.
10. It should be observed that the Directive is not intended only to govern international transactions in which the manufacturer is in one Member State and the agent in another. The Directive would apply to trade which is being carried on entirely in one Member State, so that an English manufacturer dealing through English commercial agents entirely with English customers in the domestic market would have to accord to his agents the terms laid down in the Directive. For this, the Commission relies on the proposition that "trade in goods and the provision of services should always be effected under conditions which are similar to those of a single market." The Committee do not entirely accept this far-reaching proposition; but if there is to be a single market of the size of the Community, the need for flexibility in the ways in which commercial transactions can be carried out seems to be all the greater.
11. The Committee have recently noted with concern a tendency on the part of the Commission to interfere, in ways which are not altogether judicious, with particular segments of the national legal systems. They instance, in particular, the draft Directive on liability for Defective Products[2] on which they reported in their 63rd Report of last Session,[3] and the draft Directive on Contracts negotiated away from Business Premises ("Doorstep Selling")[4] on which they are about to report. No doubt the operation of the Community requires the steady, though not hasty, development of some uniformity of general law in the commercial field throughout the Community. But caution is needed. The present Directive, for example, would, if adopted, apply to a particular and relatively small section of the field of agency, some hard and fast rules quite unknown to the general agency law of the United Kingdom. As to product liability, paragraph 8 of the Committee's 63rd Report points out that "the two legal systems of the United Kingdom, like those of the majority of the other Member States, accept as a general rule the principle that non-contractual liability for loss or damage caused to others should be based on fault—in

2. R/2237/76.
3. HL 389 (1975–76).
4. R/113/77.

the case of product liability the tort or delict of negligence. To incorporate into such a legal system a special rule whereby liability for loss or damage of a particular kind from a particular cause is made independent of all fault raises legal and practical problems of great complexity . . . ". The draft Directive on Doorstep Selling might jeopardise many sales activities in the United Kingdom which are open to abuse only to a very limited extent, and which can provide a valuable service to the consumer. The Committee are unconvinced that these interferences are, as the Commission contends, called for so as to prevent competition from being distorted. The general law of a nation is not something which has come into existence by accident; it arises from the local circumstances, habits, and sentiments of the people; changes in it must be effected only with care and where real need can be demonstrated.

Recommendation

12. The Committee are of the opinion that this draft Directive raises important questions of policy and principle. They recommend that this Report should be debated by the House.

APPENDIX 8

DEPARTMENT OF TRADE AND INDUSTRY GUIDANCE NOTES

(September 1994)

GUIDANCE NOTES ON THE COMMERCIAL AGENTS (COUNCIL DIRECTIVE) REGULATIONS 1993

CONTENTS

PART I

PART II

ANNEX

THE COMMERCIAL AGENTS (COUNCIL DIRECTIVE) REGULATIONS 1993 (S.I. 1993/3053 AS AMENDED BY S.I. 1993/3173)

PART I

(a) HISTORICAL BACKGROUND TO THE DIRECTIVE

The main purposes of the Directive were to harmonize the laws of Member States, which the Council of Ministers considered detrimental to the functioning of the Single Market, and to strengthen the position of the commercial agent in relation to his principal.

Independent commercial agents can be in a weak position when dealing with their principals, although it is acknowledged that this is not always the case. Agents have found difficulty obtaining written contracts and access to all the information they need to verify that they were being paid the correct amount of commission, and some have suffered financially because their commission has not been paid promptly and because their contracts were terminated with little or no notice.

(b) PREAMBLE TO THE DIRECTIVE

The preamble to the Directive includes the following recitals which are at the heart of the thinking behind the need for the Directive:

"Whereas the differences in national laws concerning commercial representation substantially affect the conditions of competition and the carrying-on of that activity within the Community and are detrimental both to the protection available to commercial agents vis-a-vis their principals and to the security of commercial transactions; whereas moreover those differences are such as to inhibit substantially the conclusion and operation of commercial representation contracts where principal and commercial agent are established in different Member States.

Whereas trade in goods between Member States should be carried on under conditions which are similar to those of a single market, and this necessitates approximation of the legal systems of the Member States to the extent required for the proper functioning of the common market; whereas in this regard the rules concerning conflict of laws do not, in the matter of commercial representation, remove the inconsistencies referred to above, nor would they even if they were made uniform, and accordingly the proposed harmonization is necessary notwithstanding the existence of those rules."

(c) IMPLEMENTATION OF THE DIRECTIVE

The Directive has been implemented as regards the law of England and Wales, and Scotland by Statutory Instrument No. 1993/3053 as amended by Statutory Instrument No. 1993/3173. Separate implementing provision is made in relation to Northern Ireland by the Commercial Agents (Council Directive) Regulations (Northern Ireland) 1993 (Statutory Rules for Northern Ireland No. 1993/483).

(d) PURPOSE OF THE GUIDANCE NOTES

The purpose of these notes is to assist commercial agents, principals, and their legal advisers to understand the effect of the Commercial Agents (Council Directive) Regulations 1993 by explaining why particular options for implementing the Directive were chosen and by setting out the Department's view on a number of points of difficulty. It must be emphasised that the Department's view is no more than that. As with other Community legislation, the Directive has to be interpreted uniformly throughout the Community and ultimately only the European Court can do that.

The guidance notes are in two parts. Part I continues by setting out, by regulation, the Department's general interpretation of the intention behind the Directive and hence the Regulations. Part II deals with other more specific and general points which arose during the consultation.

The notes deal only with those provisions which are novel or about which, during consultation, specific queries were raised. **IN THAT CONNECTION IT SHOULD BE NOTED THAT THE TEXT OF REGULATIONS 5, 13, 14, 15, 18, 19, 21, 22 AND 23 IS NOT PRINTED, NOR DO THESE NOTES CONTAIN ANY SPECIFIC COMMENT ON THEM.** Further issues on particular provisions may arise in the future, and the contact point is:

Christopher Farthing
Consumer Affairs Division 2a
Room 325
10–18 Victoria Street
London
SW1H ONN

Tele: 071 215 3302
Fax: 071 215 3396

The Department has taken the view that, for the most part, the substantive provisions of the Directive leave the Member States with little or no discretion as to implementation of the Directive in national law and therefore, the wording of the Regulations follows that of the Directive very closely.

(e) Details of the Regulations and the Department's Interpretation

REGULATION 1

1(1) These Regulations may be cited as the Commercial Agents (Council Directive) Regulations 1993 and shall come into force on 1 January 1994.

(2) These Regulations govern the relations between commercial agents and their principals and, subject to paragraph (3), apply in relation to the activities of commercial agents in Great Britain.

(3) Regulations 3 to 22 do not apply where the parties have agreed that the agency contract is to be governed by the law of another Member State.

INTERPRETATION

This Regulation sets out the circumstances in which the Regulations will apply to an agency contract. If the agent carries out his activities as a commercial agent in Great Britain, then the Regulations will apply *unless* the parties expressly choose the law of another Member State as the law which is to apply to the agency contract. If the law of a non-EU country is chosen then the provisions of the Regulations are intended to override that choice of law in so far as any of the activities of the commercial agent are carried out in Great Britain.

Regulation 1(2) provides that the Regulations govern relations between commercial agents and their principals and apply in relation to the activities of commercial agents *in Great Britain* (whether or not the agent is physically based in Great Britain).

The provisions of the Regulations, where the agent carries on his activities outside Great Britain, do not, however, prevent the parties from choosing the law of a part of Great Britain (for example the law of England and Wales) and incorporating in the agency agreement some or all of the provisions of the Regulations which the parties might wish to agree should apply as though the agents activities were, in fact, to be carried on in Great Britain. However, in such a case, if litigation arises, the court hearing the action may or may not:

(i) uphold the choice of law, and
(ii) accept the validity of such incorporation.

The state of the law of the other Member States relating to commercial agents will depend, in part, on the manner in which the Directive has been implemented in those States, and advice as to the relevant foreign law (both within the EU and outside) should be sought in appropriate cases.

Some examples appear in the Annex to these notes which are intended to show the application (or otherwise) of the Regulations where the principal is based in one country and his agent performs his activities in another.

The Regulations apply to *Great Britain* (Regulation 2(5)). The Directive has been implemented separately in relation to Northern Ireland by the Commercial Agents (Council Directive) Regulations (Northern Ireland) 1993 (Statutory Rules for Northern Ireland No. 1993/483).

REGULATION 2

(Articles 1 & 2 of the Directive)

2(1) In these Regulations—

"commercial agent" means a self-employed intermediary who has continuing authority to negotiate the sale or purchase of goods on behalf of another person (the "principal"), or to negotiate and conclude the sale or purchase of goods on behalf of and in the name of that principal; but shall be understood as not including in particular:

(i) a person who, in his capacity as an officer of a company or association, is empowered to enter into commitments binding on that company or association;
(ii) a partner who is lawfully authorised to enter into commitments binding on his partners;
(iii) a person who acts as an insolvency practitioner (as that expression is defined in section 388 of the Insolvency Act 1986) or the equivalent in any other jurisdiction;

"commission" means any part of the remuneration of a commercial agent which varies with the number or value of business transactions;

"restraint of trade clause" means an agreement restricting the business activities of a commercial agent following termination of the agency contract.

(2) These Regulations do not apply to—

(a) commercial agents whose activities are unpaid;

(b) commercial agents when they operate on commodity exchanges or in the commodity market;

(c) the Crown Agents for Overseas Governments and Administrations, as set up under the Crown Agents Act 1979, or its subsidiaries.

(3) The provisions of the Schedule to these Regulations have effect for the purposes of determining the persons whose activities as commercial agents are to be considered secondary.

(4) These Regulations shall not apply to the persons referred to in paragraph (3) above.

(5) These Regulations do not extend to Northern Ireland.

Interpretation

The Regulation sets out the definitions of the terms used within the Regulations and also excludes those agents where the activities are considered secondary.

The expression "self-employed" is derived from Articles 52 and 57 of the Treaty of Rome (which deal with freedom of establishment and freedom to provide services) and is consistent with Community law, to be understood as including, for example, companies as well as self-employed individuals.

If an agent is appointed for a specified number of transactions, then he would be excluded from the scope of the Regulations, owing to his lack of continuing authority.

"Goods" clearly has to be interpreted in accordance with the EC Treaty and, for that reason, the Regulations do not define the word. However, it is considered that the definition of "goods" in section 61(1) of the Sale of Goods Act 1979 as including, inter alia, all personal chattels other than things in action (e.g. shares) and money, may offer a reasonable guide, without necessarily being absolutely co-extensive with the Directive meaning.

Interpretation of the term "secondary activities" and the provisions of the Schedule to the Regulations are dealt with later in these notes.

Some agents only effect introductions between their principals and third parties. The question arises as to whether such agents are commercial agents for the purposes of the Regulations. Such agents are sometimes known as "canvassing" or "introducing" agents. As such, they generally lack the power to bind their principals and are not really agents in the true sense of the word. However, to the extent that such an agent "has continuing authority to negotiate the sale or purchase of goods" on behalf of his principal, even though, as a matter of fact, he merely effects introductions, it seems that he would fall within the definition of "commercial agent" in Regulation 2(1). It is clear that an "introducing" agent who lacks such authority falls outside the scope of the definition of "commercial agent". It may be that the courts would give a wide interpretation to the word "negotiate" and that, as a result, "introducing" agents will, in general, have the benefit of the Regulations.

It is thought that the Regulations do apply to *del credere* agents who exhibit the characteristics set out in definition of "commercial agent". The Department does not consider that the additional features of a del credere agency causes the agent to fall outside the definition. Questions can, however, arise as to whether a person is an agent at all who, in consideration of extra remuneration, guarantees to his principal that third parties with whom he enters into contracts on behalf of the principal will duly pay any sums becoming due under those contracts (and thus appears to be a del credere agent), or, whether that person is really acting on his own account.

Regulation 2(2)(b) provides that the Regulations do not apply to commercial agents when they operate on commodity exchanges or in the commodity market. A "commodity" is any tangible good. So called "commodity exchanges" deal in such goods and, to a large extent, in commodity "futures" i.e. the right to buy or sell a particular commodity at a particular price at a particular time in the future, hence e.g. "coffee futures".

REGULATION 3

(Article 3 of the Directive)

3(1) In performing his activities a commercial agent must look after the interests of his principal and act dutifully and in good faith.

(2) In particular, a commercial agent must—

(a) make proper effects to negotiate and, where appropriate, conclude the transactions he is instructed to take care of;

(b) communicate to his principal all the necessary information available to him;

(c) comply with reasonable instructions given by his principal.

Interpretation

This Regulation sets out the duties which the agent owes to the principal and, in effect, restates the duties owed at common law by an agent to his principal.

It is not certain how an agent's duty to "communicate to his principal all the necessary information available to him" is to be fulfilled where an agent is acting for several principals. However, parties to contracts of commercial agency will doubtless wish to explore the possibility of agreeing on express terms to cover that situation.

REGULATION 4

(Article 4 of the Directive)

4(1) In his relations with his commercial agent a principal must act dutifully and in good faith.

(2) In particular, a principal must—

(a) provide his commercial agent with the necessary documentation relating to the goods concerned;

(b) obtain for his commercial agent the information necessary for the performance of the agency contract, and in particular notify his commercial agent within a reasonable period once he anticipates that the volume of commercial transactions will be significantly lower than that which the commercial agent could normally have expected.

(3) A principal shall, in addition, inform his commercial agent within a reasonable period of his acceptance or refusal of, and of any non-execution by him of, a commercial transaction which the commercial agent has procured for him.

Interpretation

This Regulation deals with the principal's duties to the commercial agent. It is thought that these duties merely amplify the position at common law.

A principal is required to inform his commercial agent accordingly once the principal knows that business will decrease significantly or where an order will not be concluded.

REGULATION 6

(Article 6 of the Directive)

6(1) In the absence of any agreement as to remuneration between the parties, a commercial agent shall be entitled to the remuneration that commercial agents appointed for the goods forming the subject of his agency contract are customarily allowed in the place where he carries on his activities and, if there is no such customary practice, a commercial agent shall be entitled to reasonable remuneration taking into account all the aspects of the transaction.

(2) This Regulation is without prejudice to the application of any enactment or rule of law concerning the level of remuneration.

(3) Where a commercial agent is not remunerated (wholly or in part) by commission, Regulations 7 to 12 shall not apply.

Interpretation

This Regulation is applicable only where the parties have not agreed on the remuneration payable by the principal to the agent. In the event of a dispute as to the remuneration payable, the court would be likely to have regard to custom in the commercial area concerned. Should there be no identifiable custom in the area concerned, then it is considered that the agent would be entitled to a reasonable amount of remuneration. The position under the Regulations is thought to be similar to the position at common law.

It should be noted that where the commercial agent is not remunerated (wholly or in part) by commission, Regulations 7–12 do not apply.

REGULATION 7

(Article 7 of the Directive)

7(1) A commercial agent shall be entitled to commission on transactions concluded during the period covered by the agency contract—

(a) where the transaction has been concluded as a result of his action; or

(b) where the transaction is concluded with a third party whom he has previously acquired as a customer for transactions of the same kind.

(2) A commercial agent shall also be entitled to commission on transactions concluded during the period covered by the agency contract where he has an exclusive right to a specific geographical area or to a specific group of customers and where the transaction has been entered into with a customer belonging to that area or group.

Interpretation

This Regulation sets out the circumstances in which the agent may be considered to have earned his commission, and in that connection the view is taken that a transaction is "concluded" when the principal and the third party have entered into a contract. The provisions of (2) include so called "House Accounts" held by the principal i.e. where the principal deals directly with the third party although the agent has the rights to that area.

REGULATION 8

(Article 8 of the Directive)

Subject to Regulation 9 below, a commercial agent shall be entitled to commission on commercial transactions concluded after the agency contract has terminated if—

(a) the transaction is mainly attributable to his efforts during the period covered by the agency contract and if the transaction was entered into within a reasonable period after the contract terminated; or

(b) in accordance with the conditions mentioned in paragraph 7 above, the order of the third party reached the principal or commercial agent before the agency contract terminated.

Interpretation

This Regulation sets out when the agent is entitled to commission on commercial transactions concluded after the agency contract has come to an end. In particular where the transaction, was mainly a result of the agents efforts during the contract and the transaction was entered into within a reasonable period after the end of the agency contract.

The principal and agent may attempt to define "reasonable period" in their agreement. However, in the event of a dispute, despite any such definition, the matter would be ultimately for the decision of the court.

If the order was placed with the principal or agent before the termination of the agency contract, but the contract was not concluded until afterwards, then the principal would still be liable to pay commission.

REGULATION 9

(Article 9 of the Directive)

9(1) A commercial agent shall not be entitled to the commission referred to in Regulation 7 above if that commission is payable, by virtue of Regulation 8 above, to the previous commercial agent, unless it is equitable because of the circumstances for the commission to be shared between the commercial agents.

(2) The principal shall be liable for any sum due under paragraph (1) above to the person entitled to it in accordance with that paragraph, and any sum which the other commercial agent receives to which he is not entitled shall be refunded to the principal.

Interpretation

This Regulation deals with the apportionment of commission between a new agent and his predecessor for the same transaction.

The new agent is not entitled to commission if it is payable to the previous agent unless it is "equitable because of the circumstances" for the commission to be shared between them.

It is the principal's duty to pay commission owing to agents and where commission is paid inadvertently to one agent which was in fact owed to the other, the agent must repay it or the principal reclaim it. In either circumstance the agent entitled to the commission should receive it.

REGULATION 10

(Article 10 of the Directive)

10(1) Commission shall become due as soon as, and to the extent that, one of the following circumstances occurs:

(a) the principal has executed the transaction; or

(b) the principal should, according to his agreement with the third party, have executed the transaction; or

(c) the third party has executed the transaction.

(2) Commission shall become due at the latest when the third party has executed his part of the transaction or should have done so if the principal had executed his part of the transaction, as he should have.

(3) The commission shall be paid not later than on the last day of the month following the quarter in which it became due, and, for the purposes of these Regulations, unless otherwise agreed between the parties, the first quarter period shall run from the date the agency contract takes effect, and subsequent periods shall run from that date in the third month thereafter or the beginning of the fourth month, whichever is the sooner.

(4) Any agreement to derogate from paragraphs (2) and (3) above to the detriment of the commercial agent shall be void.

Interpretation

This Regulation sets out when the commission to be paid to an agent becomes due and when it should be paid. A transaction may be considered to be "executed" in any of the following circumstances:—

(i) when the principal has accepted or delivered the goods;

(ii) when the principal should have accepted or delivered the goods;

(iii) when the third party accepts or delivers the goods; or

(iv) when the third party pays for the goods.

It is for the two parties to agree within the terms of the contract which of these circumstances will make the commission become due. Paragraph 2 of the Regulation provides for the latest date that the commission can become due.

It is not unusual for goods to be delivered by instalments. If the agency contract does not make specific provision for the matter, the question as to when commission is due would seem to depend upon the precise nature of the sale or purchase transaction. Where each instalment delivery is the subject of a separate contract, it seems likely that a separate commission payment will be due as each separate delivery is made, or should have been made. Where a single contract applies to a number of instalment deliveries, the position is somewhat less clear. However, in view of the words "to the extent that" in Regulation 10(1) the agent may be entitled to the commission which is attributable to each particular instalment delivery.

It should be noted that paragraph (4) of Regulation 10 renders void any agreement to derogate to the detriment of the commercial agent from paragraph (2) and (3) of the Regulation.

REGULATION 11

(Article 11 of the Directive)

11(1) The right to commission can be extinguished only if and to the extent that—

(a) it is established that the contract between the third party and the principal will not be executed; and

(b) that fact is due to a reason for which the principal is not to blame.

(2) Any commission which the commercial agent has already received shall be refunded if the right to it is extinguished.

(3) Any agreement to derogate from paragraph (1) above to the detriment of the commercial agent shall be void.

Interpretation

The Regulation outlines the circumstances when the agent's right to commission is forfeited. Should a contract not be executed the principal must not be at fault for the entitlement to commission to be extinguished. Any commission already paid by the principal under these circumstances would be refunded.

REGULATION 12

(Article 12 of the Directive)

12(1) The principal shall supply his commercial agent with a statement of the commission due, not later than the last day of the month following the quarter in which the commission has become due, and such statement shall set out the main components used in calculating the amount of commission.

(2) A commercial agent shall be entitled to demand that he be provided with the information (and in particular an extract from the books) which is available to his principal and which he needs in order to check the amount of commission due to him.

(3) Any agreement to derogate from paragraphs (1) and (2) above shall be void.

(4) Nothing in this Regulation shall remove or restrict the effect of, or prevent reliance upon, any enactment or rule of law which recognises the right of an agent to inspect the books of the principal.

Interpretation

The Regulation sets out the principal's obligation to provide the agent with a statement of commission due and must set out the main components in calculating the commission. It also requires the principal to provide the agent with all *necessary* information, including extracts from his (the principal's) books, to check the commission due, should the agent request such information. N.B. the principal is only required to provide relevant extracts and *not* his full books.

REGULATION 16

(Article 16 of the Directive)

16 These Regulations shall not affect the application of any enactment or rule of law which provides for the immediate termination of the agency contract—

(a) because of the failure of one party to carry out all or part of his obligations under that contract; or

(b) where exceptional circumstances arise.

Interpretation

This Regulation preserves the common law and statutory rules of jurisdictions within Great Britain which provide for the immediate termination of an agency contract on the basis of the two matters set out in subparagraphs (a) and (b) of the Regulation. It is thought that the expression "exceptional circumstances" in paragraph (b) would include matters falling within the doctrine of frustration.

REGULATION 17

(Article 17 of the Directive)

17(1) This Regulation has effect for the purpose of ensuring that the commercial agent is, after termination of the agency contract, indemnified in accordance with paragraphs (3) to (5) below or compensated for damage in accordance with paragraphs (6) and (7) below.

(2) Except where the agency contract otherwise provides, the commercial agent shall be entitled to be compensated rather than indemnified.

(3) Subject to paragraph (9) below and to Regulation 18 below, the commercial agent shall be entitled to an indemnity if and to the extent that—

(a) he has brought the principal new customers or has significantly increased the volume of business from existing customers and the principal continues to derive substantial benefits from the business with such customers; and

(b) the payment of this indemnity is equitable having regard to all the circumstances and, in particular, the commission lost by the commercial agent on the business transacted with such customers.

(4) The amount of the indemnity shall not exceed a figure equivalent to an indemnity for one year calculated from the commercial agent's average annual remuneration over the preceding five years and if the contract goes back less than five years the indemnity shall be calculated on the average for the period in question.

(5) The granting of an indemnity as mentioned above shall not prevent the commercial agent from seeking damages.

(6) Subject to paragraph (9) and Regulation 18 below, the commercial agent shall be entitled to compensation for the damage he suffers as a result of the termination of his relations with his principal.

(7) For the purposes of these Regulations such damage shall be deemed to occur particularly when the termination takes place in either or both of the following circumstances, namely circumstances which—

(a) deprive the commercial agent of the commission which proper performance of the agency contract would have procured for him whilst providing his principal with substantial benefits linked to the activities of the commercial agent; or

(b) have not enabled the commercial agent to amortize the costs and expenses that he had incurred in the performance of the agency contract on the advice of his principal.

(8) Entitlement to the indemnity or compensation for damage as provided for under paragraphs (2) to (7) above shall also arise where the agency contract is terminated as a result of the death of the commercial agent.

(9) The commercial agent shall lose his entitlement to the indemnity or compensation for damage in the instances provided for in paragraphs (2) to (8) above if within one year following termination of his agency contract he has not notified his principal that he intends pursuing his entitlement.

Interpretation

The Regulation deals with entitlement to indemnity/compensation upon termination of the agency contract. It is for the two parties to choose which of these options they would wish to include in their contract with the backstop of compensation should no choice be indicated. There is however, nothing to preclude the two parties from agreeing to use the compensation provisions in some cases and indemnity ones in others when terminating a particular contract. The indemnity/compensation is only payable where the principal will continue to benefit from the business that the agent has brought to the principal.

It should be noted that although having fixed term contracts or giving correct periods of notice (see Regulation 15) could potentially reduce the level of indemnity/compensation it would not necessarily exclude it. The issue of whether compensation is payable on the expiry of a fixed term contract or where the contractual notice period in an indefinite term contract has been given is a matter for the courts to decide.

It is thought that in view of the terms of Regulation 19 it would be possible for the two parties to derogate from this provision **after** the termination of the agency contract.

The word "indemnity" has a rather more limited meaning than that which it normally bears in English law in that it:

(i) appears to fall short of a complete making good of the loss suffered by the principal; and

(ii) does not necessarily arise in relation to loss caused by the principal.

Its more limited nature may be inferred from Regulation 17(5) which contemplates the possibility of the agent wishing to seek damages. The amount of the indemnity is, in any event, limited by Regulation 17(4). The indemnity might appropriately be reviewed as approximating to a form of liquidated damages.

It remains to be seen how courts in Great Britain would assess amounts of indemnity, and the Department feels unable, at this stage, to offer any guidance as to the approach likely to be adopted.

Article 17.6 of the Directive requires the Commission to submit to the Council, by the end 1994, a report on the implementation of Article 17 (indemnity/compensation) and, if necessary to submit to the Council proposals for amendments.

As to the meaning of "substantial" in Regulation 17(3)(a), it is thought that word would be interpreted as meaning "material" or "not insignificant" having regard to the history of dealings between the principal and the agents and other relevant circumstances.

"Equitable" in Regulation 17(3)(b) probably means "just" or "fair" rather than necessarily based on the doctrines or principles of equity—the latter, if they exist at all in the law of every Member State, being bound to vary from State to State.

REGULATION 20

(Article 20 of the Directive)

20(1) A restraint of trade clause shall be valid only if and to the extent that—

(a) it is concluded in writing; and

(b) it relates to the geographical area or the group of customers and the geographical area entrusted to the commercial agent and to the kind of goods covered by his agency under the contract.

(2) A restraint of trade clause shall be valid for not more than two years after the termination of the agency contract.

(3) Nothing in this Regulation shall effect any enactment or rule of law which imposes other restrictions on the validity or enforceability of restraint of trade clauses or which enables a court to reduce the obligations on the parties resulting from such clauses.

Interpretation

A "restraint of trade clause" is any agreement which restricts the business activities of a commercial agent following termination of the agency contract (see the definition in Regulation 2).

The restraint of trade provisions only extend to the kind of goods that were covered in his contract. It is thought that the provisions would not extend to goods of a similar nature aimed at different types of purchasers.

THE SCHEDULE

1. The activities of a person as a commercial agent are to be considered secondary where it may reasonably be taken that the primary purpose of the arrangement with his principal is other than set out in paragraph 2 below.

2. An arrangement falls within this paragraph if—

(a) the business of the principal is the sale, or as the case may be purchase, of goods of a particular kind; and

(b) the goods concerned are such that—

(i) transactions are normally individually negotiated and concluded on a commercial basis, and

(ii) procuring a transaction on one occasion is likely to lead to further transactions in those goods with that customer on future occasions, or to transactions in those goods with other customers in the same geographical area or among the same group of customers, and

that accordingly it is in the commercial interests of the principal in developing the market in those goods to appoint a representative to such customers with a view to the representative devoting effort, skill and expenditure from its own resources to that end.

3. The following are indications that an arrangement falls within paragraph 2 above, and the absence of any of them is an indication to the contrary—

(a) the principal is the manufacturer, importer or distributor of the goods;

(b) the goods are specifically identified with the principal in the market in question rather than, or to a greater extent than, with any other person;

(c) the agent devotes substantially the whole of his time to representative activities (whether for one principal or a number of principals whose interests are not conflicting);

(d) the goods are not normally available in the market in question other than by means of the agent;

(e) the arrangement is described as one of commercial agency.

4. The following are indications that an arrangement does not fall within paragraph 2 above—

(a) promotional material is supplied direct to potential customers;

(b) persons are granted agencies without reference to existing agents in a particular area or in relation to a particular group;

(c) customers normally select the goods for themselves and merely place their orders through the agent.

5. The activities of the following categories of persons are presumed, unless the contrary is established, not to fall within paragraph 2 above—

Mail order catalogue agents for consumer goods.

Consumer credit agents.

Interpretation

The Schedule sets out the criteria for determining the persons whose activities as commercial agents are considered secondary under UK law and are excluded from the provisions of the Regulations by virtue of Regulation 2(3).

The first test is to determine whether or not a contract comes under the provisions of the Regulations. The determining factor is whether the agent is required to keep, as his own property, a considerable stock of the product.

The comparison to be made is between the agent's activities as a commercial agent and his other activities and not the relationship with the principal.

It is not possible to say which of the provisions in paragraphs 3 and 4 take priority and this will have to be determined on a case by case basis taking into account the exact nature of the agency contract.

PART II

(a) Answers to specific questions raised during the consultation exercise

Q. CAN THE PRINCIPLE OF SET-OFF CONTINUE TO APPLY?

A. The Regulations do not mention set-off. It is thought that set-off will remain available to the principal, his agent and third parties in accordance with the rules of common law.

Q. IF A PRINCIPAL EMPLOYS AN AGENT TO ACT FOR HIM IN A NUMBER OF DIFFERENT MEMBER STATES, COULD THERE BE ONE AGENCY CONTRACT GOVERNING THE RELATIONSHIP?

A. This would be possible subject to the comments made on page 5 concerning the applicability of English law to contracts outside the UK.

Q. REGULATION 17(8) EXPRESSLY ALLOWS INDEMNITY OR COMPENSATION WHERE THE AGENCY CONTRACT IS TERMINATED AS A RESULT OF THE COMMERCIAL AGENT'S DEATH. IS THE POSITION THE SAME IF THE COMMERCIAL AGENT (BEING A COMPANY) GOES INTO LIQUIDATION?

A. Where the principal or agent is a company, at common law the actual authority of the principal or agent will be determined by its winding up or dissolution. It should be noted that where the authority is irrevocable it will not be determined by such events.

Q. CAN AN AGE LIMIT BE FIXED FOR A COMMERCIAL AGENT?

A. It is thought it can. Fixed contracts are permitted and if, for example, a 40 year old agent is appointed "until he is 60" this is equivalent to a fixed contract for 20 years or until death.

Q. TO WHAT EXTENT CAN THE REGULATIONS BE DEROGATED FROM?

A. There are three different types of Regulation within the Regulations: those which cannot be derogated from; those which cannot be derogated from to the detriment of the agent; and those which make no mention of derogation.

It can be argued that where regulations mean there to be no derogation, they say so. It can also be said that if nothing is said it is to be inferred that it can be derogated from. If this is so then, for example, the agency contract could express the agent's entitlement to commission as arising where the transaction is "wholly" as a result of his action.

The Department's conclusion on this, although not a firm one, is that the terms of the agency contract can vary the events upon which the agent becomes entitled to commission, although they could not do so to an extent that it excludes the right altogether since this would conflict with Regulation 11(1).

Q. ARE SUB-AGENCY AGREEMENTS COVERED BY THE REGULATIONS?

A. Whilst the position is not clear, the Regulations are, in principle, capable of covering sub-agency agreements.

Q. IS IT POSSIBLE TO INCLUDE A LIQUIDATED DAMAGES PROVISION WITHIN THE CONTRACT?

A. Liquidated damages is a provision within a contract where one party agrees to pay to the other a specified sum of money in the event of a breach of contract.

Such clauses may be permissible provided that they represent a genuine pre-estimate of damage.

Although one object of the clause will be to limit the principal's liability, it may not be a pure limitation clause in that it forms a compromise between the parties and is intended to be enforceable whether the actual loss is greater or less than the sum agreed. Nevertheless, as against the principal, such provisions risk attack by the agent as void by virtue of Regulation 19.

Q. ARE THE REGULATIONS RETROSPECTIVE?

A. Only in the sense that they apply to all contracts as from 1 January 1994 and it is inevitable that in some respects account will have to be taken of what occurred before 1994. The Regulations do not, however, apply so as to affect the rights and liabilities of either the principal or agent if they have accrued before 1994.

Q. DO THE REGULATIONS APPLY TO AGENTS WHO SELL CHRISTMAS HAMPERS?

A. It is believed that the activities of such agents would be likely to be held as secondary, thus rendering the agents (by virtue of Regulation 2(4)) outside the scope of the Regulations.

ANNEX

(a) Examples on the application of Regulation 1

1. Principal in Great Britain, agent in France (EU Member State)

The Regulations do *not* apply, since the agent's activities are in France and therefore are not in Great Britain (see Regulation 1 (2)). However, if the parties choose English law to govern the contract between them, it is suggested that the contract could provide for the provisions of the Regulations to apply to the relations between them as though the agent's activities were in Great Britain. Although the agent is in France, if the parties choose English law to govern the agency contract, the provisions of French law implementing the Directive would not apply (unless those provisions are held to be "mandatory rules" (see Article 3 of the Rome Convention on the law applicable to contractual obligations)).

2. Principal in Great Britain, agent in Australia (non-EU Member State)

The Regulations do not apply, given that the agent's activities are in Australia and therefore not in Great Britain. However, again, it is thought that, as in the first example above, the parties could specifically adopt the provisions of the Regulations by contractual provision to that effect. Any "mandatory rules" of the relevant Australian State(s) would need to be considered in case they were capable of over-riding any provisions of the contract.

3. Principal in France, agent in Great Britain

In the absence of an express choice of French law, the Regulations would apply, given that the agent's activities are in Great Britain. If the parties choose French law, the Regulations would not apply (see Regulation 1 (3)), and the agent would have the protection of the Directive as implemented in French law.

4. Principal in USA, agent in Great Britain

If the law of a part of Great Britain is chosen by the parties to govern the agency contract, it is concluded that the Regulations will apply.

However, if the law of a State of the US is chosen, no doubt an exclusive jurisdiction clause in favour of the courts of that State would also be included in the agency contract, on the basis of which a court in Great Britain may well decline jurisdiction. In the absence of such a clause, or if a court in Great Britain nevertheless accepts jurisdiction, the court may take the view (perhaps after making an Article 177 reference to the European Court) that the Regulations constitute mandatory rules of the law of a part of Great Britain and that the Regulations should, accordingly, apply, the intention of the Directive being to afford certain protections to commercial agents operating within the European Union (but possibly only where the principal is also established within the European Union (see the recitals to the Directive referred to on page 1 of the notes under the heading "Preamble to the Directive")). Thus an agent in such circumstances would be unwise to assume that, despite operating in Great Britain, the Regulations would apply.

APPENDIX 9

EUROPEAN COMMISSION 1996 REPORT ON THE APPLICATION OF ARTICLE 17 OF COUNCIL DIRECTIVE ON THE CO-ORDINATION OF THE LAWS OF THE MEMBER STATES RELATING TO SELF-EMPLOYED COMMERCIAL AGENTS (86/653/EEC)

(COM (96) 364 final)

This Report is made under Article 17(6) of Council Directive on the co-ordination of the laws of the Member States relating to Self-Employed Commercial Agents 86/653/EEC.[1] Article 17 of Directive requires Member States to take the measures necessary to ensure that the commercial agent is, after termination of the agency contract, indemnified or compensated.

Article 17 represents a compromise between the Member States. It was therefore agreed that Member States should have the choice between the indemnity system and the compensation system and that the Commission would undertake a report to the Council on the practical consequences of the different solutions.

This report is made on the basis of responses to a questionnaire which was sent out, inter alia, to organisations representing agents and principals, chambers of commerce and federations of industry and legal practitioners specialising in agency law. The authorities of Member States were also invited to contribute with their views and experience.

THE TWO SYSTEMS

1. THE INDEMNITY SYSTEM

Under the indemnity system, the agent is entitled, after cessation of the contract, to payment of an indemnity if and to the extent that he has brought new customers to the principal or has significantly increased the volume of business with existing customers and the principal continues to derive substantial benefits from such customers after the cessation of the contract. The payment of the indemnity must be equitable having regard to all the circumstances and, in particular, the commission lost by the commercial agent on the business transacted with such customers. Finally, the Directive provides a ceiling on the level of indemnity of one year calculated from the agent's average annual remuneration over the preceding five years and if the contract goes back less than five years the maximum is to be calculated on the average for the period in question.

The indemnity represents the continuing benefits to the principal due to the efforts of the agent. The agent, however, will only have received commission during the duration of the contract, which will not typically reflect the value of the goodwill generated for the principal. It is for this reason that the payment of a goodwill indemnity is commercially justified. An indemnity will only be payable if the agent has brought to the principal new customers or increased business with existing customers. If no goodwill has been generated or there is a group of customers whom the principal can derive no benefit from, no indemnity need be paid. Therefore, a principal should not be forced to pay an unreasonable amount of indemnity.

1. O.J. L 382 p. 17 of 31.12.1986.

The indemnity system was modelled on Article 89b of the German Commercial Code which had provided for the payment of a goodwill indemnity since 1953 and concerning which a large body of case law has developed regarding its calculation. This case law and practice should provide invaluable assistance to the Courts of other Member States when seeking to interpret the provisions of Article 17(2) of the Directive.

First it is necessary to ascertain whether an agent has a right to an indemnity having regard to the circumstances in which the agency contract was terminated. An indemnity is payable on termination of the contract except where one of the circumstances in Article 18 of the Directive applies. Clearly, the indemnity is payable on the end of a fixed term contract and in principle, an indemnity or limited indemnity is payable on the bankruptcy of the principal.

Secondly, the conditions set out in Article 17(2)(a) of the Directive have to be met, namely that either the agent has brought new customers or has substantially increased the volume of business with existing customers. As regards the volume of business with old customers, the German courts look to see if the increase in volume is such that it can be considered to be economically equivalent to the acquisition of a new customer. In relation to new customers, the addition of one new customer is sufficient. However, new customers from outside his territory for which the agent is not entitled to commission are excluded as there is no loss of commission for which the agent needs to be compensated. The agent must have acquired the new client and in this respect the instrumentality of the agent is crucial. A small level of involvement is sufficient and it is enough that the agent has merely contributed to bringing the new customer. However, the agent must have played an active role and therefore the existence of a new customer who falls within the territorial scope of an exclusive agency agreement will not automatically suffice.

Thirdly, the principal must continue after the end of the agency contract to derive substantial benefits with such customers. This is presumed to be the case even if the principal sells his business or client list if it can be shown that the purchaser will use the client base.[2] If the agent continues to meet the needs of the same clients for the same products, but for a different principal, the agent is prevented from seeking an indemnity.[3] It is also possible for the court to consider a fall in the turnover of the principal's business. Fourthly, the payment of an indemnity must be equitable.

As to the actual calculation of the indemnity, it is undertaken in the following way:

STAGE 1

(a) The first stage in line with the second indent of Article 17(2)(a) is to ascertain the number of new customers and the increased volume of business with existing customers. Having identified such customers the gross commission on them is calculated for the last 12 months of the agency contract. Fixed remuneration can be included if it can be considered to be remuneration for new customers.[4] Special circumstances may justify departing from this, for example, where is a long start up period.

(b) An estimate is then made as to the likely future duration of the advantages to the principal deriving from business with the new customers and such old customers with whom the business has been significantly increased (intensified customers) which is calculated in terms of years. The aim is to predict the likely length of time the business with the new and intensified customers will last. This will involve considering the market situation at time of termination and the sector concerned. The fact that sales drop after termination of the contract does not automatically lead to a corresponding reduction in the level of indemnity as sales may decline due to lowering in quality of goods or competition.[5] The usual period is 2–3 years, but can be as much as 5 years.

(c) The next factor to consider is the rate of migration. It is acknowledged that over time customers will be lost as customers naturally move away. The rate of migration is calculated as a percentage of commission on a per annum basis and is taken from the particular

2. Case 18 U 162/76 Oberlandesgericht Hamm of 14.3.1977.
3. Case BB 605/60 Bundesgerichtshof of 25.4.1960.
4. Case VII ZR 194/63 Bundesgerichtshof of 15.2.1965.
5. Case BB 227/70 Celle of 13.11.69.

experience of the agency in question. This clearly varies, but in one case the Bundesgerichtshof held that the rate of migration was 38%.[6]

(d) The figure is then reduced in order to calculate the present value taking into account that there is an accelerated receipt of income. Such a calculation based on average interest rates is a concept found in other jurisdictions.

STAGE 2

It is at this stage that the question of equity is considered as set out in Article 17(2)(a) second indent of the Directive. The figure is rarely adjusted for reasons of equity in practice. The following factors are taken into account:

- Whether the agent is retained by other principals;
- The fault of the agent;
- The level of remuneration of the agent. For example, did the principal recently reduce the rate of commission e.g. because he felt that agent's earnings were becoming too high or pay to the agent a large amount of commission on contracts with customers which the agent did not introduce or had little to do with? Also, did the agent receive special compensation for keeping a consignment inventory, special bonuses for new clients, del credere commission, any special allowance for trade fairs or extra payments for sub-agents? Did he incur costs regarding loss of sub-agents?
- Decrease in turnover of the principal;
- Extent of the advantage to the principal;
- Payment of pension contributions by the principal;
- The existence of restraint of trade clauses. Clearly, a principal will be required to pay a higher indemnity for this.

STAGE 3

The amount calculated under Stages 1 and 2 is then compared with the maximum under Article 17(2)(b) of the Directive. This provision provides that the amount of the indemnity may not exceed a figure equivalent to remuneration for one year calculated from the commercial agent's average annual remuneration over the preceding five years and if the contract goes back less than five years the indemnity shall be calculated on the average for the period in question. The maximum is in fact therefore a final corrective, rather than as a method of calculating the indemnity.[7]

In calculating the maximum, remuneration includes all forms of payment, not just commission and is based on all customers, not only new or intensified customers.[8] If the sum under stages 1 and 2 is less than the maximum then this sum is awarded. If however, the sum exceeds the maximum, it is the maximum which is awarded. It is unusual for the maximum to be reached unless the agent has procured all or most of the customers.

6. Case VII ZR 94/93 Bundesgerichtshof of 23.2.1994.
7. Case VII ZR 47/69 Bundesgerichtshof of 19.11.1970.
8. Case VII ZR 23/70 Bundesgerichtshof of 3.6.1971.

An example of stages 1 to 3 is set out:

Commission on new customers and/or intensified customers over last 12 months of agency			50,000 ECUs
Anticipated duration of benefits is 3 years with 20% migration rate			
Year 1	50,000 – 10,000	=	40,000 ECUs
Year 2	40,000 – 8,000	=	32,000 ECUs
Year 3	32,000 – 6,400	=	25,600 ECUs
Total lost commission			97,600 ECUs
Correction to present value say 10%. This figure being equal to the actual indemnity			87,840 ECUs

This figure might be adjusted for reasons of equity (stage 2 above)

A final correction must be made should the amount exceed the maximum under Article 17(2)(b) of the Directive.

Article 17(2)(c) states that the grant of an indemnity shall not prevent the commercial agent from seeking damages. This provision governs the situation where the agent under national law is entitled to seek damages for breach of contract or failure to respect the notice period provided for under the Directive. Annex B attempts to identify these provisions.

It can thus be seen that the method of calculation of the indemnity is extremely precise and should lead to a predictable outcome. Principals should therefore be able to ascertain their risks in advance and to be able to enter into agency contracts with some degree of assurance. From the agent's perspective, clearer rights make it easier for the claim to be made and established.

2. THE COMPENSATION SYSTEM

Under Article 17(3) of the Directive, the agent is entitled to compensation for the damage he suffers as a result of the termination of his relations with his principal. Such damage is deemed to occur particularly when the termination takes place in circumstances:

- depriving the agent of the commission which proper performance of the agency contract would have procured him whilst providing the principal with substantial benefits linked to the agent's activities.
- and/or which have not enabled the agent to amortize the costs and expenses he had incurred for the performance of the agency contract on the principal's advice.

There is no maximum level of compensation.

The compensation system was based on French law, which dated from 1958 and whose aim was to compensate the agent for the loss he suffered as a result of the termination of the agency contract. As for the indemnity system in Germany, a body of case law has developed in France concerning the right and level of compensation. Various judgments of the French courts have justified the payment of compensation on the ground that it represents the cost of purchasing the agency to the agent's successor or on the ground that it represents the time it takes for the agent to re-constitute the client base which he has been forcefully deprived of.

By judicial custom the level of compensation is fixed as the global sum of the last two years commission or the sum of 2 years commission calculated over the average of last three years of the agency contract which conforms with commercial practice. However, the courts retain a discretion to award a different level of compensation where the principal brings evidence that the agent's loss was in fact less, for example, because of the short duration of the contract or where, for example, the agent's loss is greater because of the agent's age or his length of service.

The indemnity is calculated on all remuneration, not just commission. It is based on the gross figure. No distinction is made between old and new customers and it includes special commission. There is no practice to reduce for professional costs. Finally, outstanding commissions must also be included in the calculation.

The indemnity represents that part of the market lost to the agent and his loss is fixed at that moment. Accordingly, future occurrences are not taken into account, such as the principal ceasing to trade, the agent continuing to work with the same clients or developments in the market place. Similarly, the agent is not required to mitigate his loss.

The Directive has brought about a greater interest in claiming damages for failure to respect the proper notice period. The amount awarded is the highest of the period not respected calculated on commission received for the last two years or the commission received during the identical period the previous year.

Further, more specific comments on the system in France can be found in Annex B.

POSITION IN MEMBER STATES

All Member States have implemented the Directive and a list of the laws is annexed to this Report as Annex A. With the exception of France, the UK and Ireland, Member States have incorporated the indemnity option into their national law. The UK has permitted the parties to choose the indemnity option, but if they fail to do so, the agent will be entitled to compensation. Ireland has failed to make any choice at all in its legislation and accordingly the Commission has opened Article 169 proceedings. The Commission has also opened infraction proceedings against Italy for failure to implement Article 17 of the Directive correctly. Further details can be found in Annex B concerning Irish and Italian law.

In most Member States there has yet to be any reported court decision, whilst in other Member States there are only a small number of cases. This is explained by the fact that the laws in most Member States are still very new and that these laws have only applied to all contracts in operation as from 1 January 1994. In addition, in France and Germany where there are cases, many agencies are not international in nature and the law follows long established traditions.

The second reason for the lack of reported cases is the tendency for the parties to settle cases before the court hearing. Agents are not always in the financial position to pursue their claims through the courts and therefore are forced to accept settlements. In addition, the uncertainty linked to court proceedings, invariably in a different jurisdiction deters agents from pursuing their claims through the courts.

The cases in Germany and France show a continuity with the existing jurisprudence in these countries. In Portugal, where the Directive represents a change to the previous situation the case law shows an approach which is different to that of the German courts with an attempt by the judge to apply directly the principle of equity. In Italy, where there has only been one judgment under the new Article 1751 of the Civil Code, the Viterbo Magistrate Court has ruled, that having regard to the lack of criteria for calculation of the indemnity in Article 1751 of the Civil Code, it would apply the collective agreement. The collective agreement follows a system of calculation based on the duration of the agency and is not related to the number of new customers brought. Thus, it also takes a different approach to the German courts. However, this is a single judgment of the Italian courts and has yet to be confirmed. In Denmark, only three judgments have been reported. A fourth judgment is now subject to appeal. The reported cases reveal a tendency to take over and follow German jurisprudence.

Having regard to the relative lack of jurisprudence and the nature of the subject matter, the Commission in its preparation for this Report sought to ascertain the practical as well as the legal situation. An outline of the legal and practical position is set out in more detail in Annex B.

There are no statistics available in any of the Member States. The International Union of Commercial Agents and Brokers have now started to collect data. This is a helpful development, as IUCAB should be able to collect a good level of data through its member organisations in Member

States and IUCAB has offered to present these statistics periodically to the Commission. The Portuguese authorities have also established a centralised method of collecting information from all courts on the nature and outcome of cases which involve EC law or the Lugano Convention, which of course, includes the Directive on Commercial Agents.

BUSINESS PRACTICE

The Commission sought to ascertain whether, as a result of the Directive and in particular the right to an indemnity or compensation, there had been any change in business practice. The Commission also wanted to establish whether, as a result of the different options, distortions in competition had arisen. The lack of statistics makes it more difficult to reach conclusions in this regard.

Overall, the Commission found that there had not been any change in business practice. There was some evidence that principals were moving to distributorship contracts in France, Germany, Luxembourg and Belgium. This can be partially explained by the fact that on lawful termination of distributorship contracts no indemnity or compensation is payable or a reduced level. In the UK, Ireland and Sweden it was reported that principals were now considering much more carefully whether agency contracts were the most appropriate business arrangements and were therefore taking a much more cautious approach. However, principals were not always actually moving away from agency contracts.

In the UK there appears to have been a specific reaction. First prior to the coming into force of the UK Regulations implementing the Directive, principals terminated their agency contracts and on the whole re-negotiated new contracts. There were, however, occasions where new agency contracts were not entered into or the agents were taken on as employees. This reflects the fundamental change brought about by the Directive to UK law and the fear of principals of the unknown. It is too soon to determine whether there will be a permanent shift away from agency contracts in the UK.

Under French law and practice, compensation awarded in the vast majority of cases amounts to 2 years commission which is twice the legal maximum provided for under the indemnity option. This clearly makes the appointment of an agent in France under French law a much more costly enterprise. This has led some principals seeking when appointing an agent in France to seek to apply a law other than French law or to avoid entering into agency contracts altogether. There is no evidence of any widespread problems or distortions in trade as regards those Member States who have opted for the indemnity system and those who have opted for the compensation option.

REACTIONS OF PRINCIPALS AND AGENTS

It can generally be said that agents have given a positive response to the Directive as it is considered to have increased their rights. This would be the case in Austria, Denmark, Finland, Ireland, Luxembourg, Sweden and the UK. French agents continue to feel positively about the system of compensation in France and do not wish for change.

The reaction of principals has been mixed. To some extent, principals are bound to feel negative about change as they now have to grant greater rights to agents. For other principals it is not that they are against paying an indemnity on termination, but rather there is a degree of discontent in that the system lacks clarity. French principals appear to support the compensation system and have not raised any objections regarding it.

There is no tendency amongst either agents or principals in the Member States who have implemented the indemnity option to favour anything other than the indemnity system. In the UK, where the parties are able to opt in favour of payment of an indemnity, no clear preference emerges although most contracts do not contain an indemnity provision. Principals are still unclear about what the differences between the two systems are. There is a certain level of interest in the indemnity amongst some principals because of the maximum limit, but other principals prefer the compensation option as agents must prove actual loss.

DIFFICULTIES

A number of difficulties have arisen in relation to Article 17 of the Directive.

(1) INTERPRETATION DIFFICULTIES

Many commentators and lawyers have pointed to the imprecise and uncertain nature of Article 17, which causes difficulty in trying to advise clients on the extent of an agent's rights on termination. This was reported in particular in Denmark, Ireland, Italy, Spain, Sweden and the UK.

a. *Indemnity*

As regards the indemnity option, there has been a tendency in some Member States to seek reliance on the maximum figure whereas under the German system, which influenced the Directive, the maximum has no bearing on the actual method of calculation of the indemnity. It is merely used at the end of the process as a final adjuster. In some Member States attempts are made to try and establish an equitable amount taking into account various different factors, which again is not the approach taken by the German courts. Denmark and Austria appear to follow the German model but in the case of Austria, the maximum limit is often reached, whereas in Germany it is very rarely reached except when all the customers have been brought by the commercial agent.

In Italy, it appears, at the moment, that the previous system continues to apply even though a new law was introduced. This has been re-enforced in the ruling in the Pretura Viterbo case in which the court held that the provision of Article 1751 of the Italian Civil Code, which implements Article 17(2) of the Directive, was so uncertain as to the method of calculation of the indemnity, it would apply the collective agreement. The method of calculation under the collective agreement does not correspond with the German model, but is based on the length of the contract, the level of commission and the percentages set out in the collective agreement.

It therefore appears there is a divergence of approaches. However, there is of course still only a very limited jurisprudence of the courts of Member States concerning Article 17 outside Germany.

b. *Compensation*

As regards the compensation option, clearly this has not presented problems of interpretation in France where pre-existing jurisprudence has continued to be applied. However, as regards the UK which applies the compensation option in default of the choice of the parties, there is a fundamental difference in approach. At this stage, there is no UK case law but the parties in practice are attempting to apply common law principles. These common law principles are directly opposed to the well-established method of calculation of compensation in France. For example, the English system will take account of future developments after termination of the contract and this results in the need to for the injured person to mitigate his loss. Whereas, under French law, events after the termination of the agency contract have no bearing on the compensation to be awarded. Under French Law, the standard award is two years commission which represents the value of the purchase of an agency or the period it will take the agent to re-establish his client base. It is difficult to see how the UK courts will reach this figure. This, no doubt, derives from the previous legal position in the UK, that agency contracts could be terminated on notice without any payment being due. This naturally has had consequences for business practices. There was no real concept of goodwill attaching to an agency to which the agent had a right to a share in. It is not possible to predict how the UK courts will interpret the Directive, but it seems likely that they will have regard to existing common law principles.

The same difficulties are likely to arise in Ireland if Ireland opts for the compensation option.

c. *Consequences of uncertainty*

The difficulties in interpretation have had an effect on the reactions of agents and principals to the Directive. For both it has entailed increased time being spent on negotiation since rights and levels of rights are not clearly established. This benefits neither party. It has also led to different amounts being awarded. Uncertainty and divergence also lead to a reluctance to create agencies and act as a barrier to principals to take on agents in other Member States. It is important that the Directive is uniformly interpreted and leads to predictable and clear results.

(2) POSITION OF AGENTS

The Directive has led to an improvement in the position of agents vis-à-vis their principals. Nevertheless it appears that agents are not always able to enforce their rights to the full because they lack the resources to take court action. This is a problem of a general nature and not specific to the Directive. Possible remedies lie outside the remit of this Report. However, it is the view of the Commission that clarification of the provisions of the Directive and methods of calculation will be of assistance to agents and make the enforcement of rights easier.

(3) CHOICE OF LAW

Finally, certain problems have been encountered with regard to choice of law clauses in contracts and attempts have been made to avoid the application of certain laws by choice of law clauses or jurisdiction clauses. The Directive does not lay down any rules concerning private international law. The parties are therefore free to choose the law which is to govern the agency contract, subject to the rules contained in the Rome Convention 1980 on the law applicable to contractual obligations. In the Commission's opinion Articles 17 and 18 of the Directive are mandatory rules and accordingly, the courts of the Member States can apply the law of the forum in accordance with the 1980 Rome Convention and thereby ensure the application of the Directive. The 1968 Brussels Convention on jurisdiction and enforcement of judgments in civil and commercial matters will also assist in ensuring, that in so far as Community cases are concerned and the agent is carrying on his activities in the EC, that a court of a Member State will have jurisdiction.[9] Accordingly, there does not appear to be any need to amend the Directive in this regard.

CONCLUSION

The Commission notes that the indemnity option has been chosen by the vast majority of Member States and that this has received the support of agents and principals in those Member States. The Directive provides for a ceiling on the level of indemnity, but does not give precise guidance for its method of calculation. A clear and precise method of calculation would lead to greater legal certainty, which would be of advantage to both parties. As regards the compensation option, which has been maintained by France, it does not appear to have caused problems for agents and principals in France. The level of compensation in France is generally much higher than the level of indemnity. The implementation in the UK whereby the parties have the choice of the system has led to uncertainty, particularly as neither of the two options is known to the British legal system.

At this stage, there is very little jurisprudence concerning the Directive. Having regard to the information received, it appears that there is a need for clarification of Article 17. Any more further far-reaching conclusions are premature. The Commission considers that this Report, which gives detailed information, particularly concerning the method of calculation of the indemnity as it is carried out in Germany, provides further clarification of Article 17 of the Directive and secondly, by so-doing should facilitate a more uniform interpretation of Article 17 of the Directive.

9. *Arcado Sprl* v. *Haviland SA* Case No 9/87 [1988] ECR 1539 the Court held that right to compensation was contractual in nature and therefore Article 5(1) of the 1968 Brussels Convention applied thus opening the possibility of an additional basis of jurisdiction.

ANNEX A

LIST OF MEMBER STATES LAWS IMPLEMENTING THE DIRECTIVE ON COMMERCIAL AGENTS (86/653/EEC)

Expiry of implementation period: 31.12.89
(United Kingdom and Ireland: 31.12.93)
(Italy, concerning article 17: 31.12.92)

1. *Belgium* Law of 13.4.1995
published in Moniteur Belge of 2.6.1995, pg. 15621
entry into force: 12.6.1995

2. *Denmark* Law no 272 of 2.5.90
publication: Lovtidende A. 1990 p. 922
entry into force: 4.5.90
application to contracts in operation: 1.1.92

3. *Germany* Law of 23.10.89
publication: Bundesgesetzblatt 1989 I. 1910
entry into force: 1.1.90
application to contracts in operation: 1.1.94

4. *Greece* Presidential Decree no 219 of 18.5.1991
publication: OJ of the Greek government no 81 of 30.5.1991 and no 136 of 11.9.1991 as amended by Decrees no 249/93, 88/94 and 312/95.
entry into force: 30.5.1991
application to contracts in operation: 1.1.94

5. *Spain* Law 12/1992 of 27.5.1992
publication: BOE no 129 of 29.5.1992
entry into force: 19.6.1992
application to contracts in operation: 1.1.94

6. *France* Law no 91–593 of 25.6.1991
publication: OJ of the French Republic 17.6.1991 p. 8271
entry into force: 28.6.1992
Decree 92–506 of 10.6.1992
Publication: OJ of the French Republic 12.6.1992 p. 7720
entry into force: 1.1.1994
application to contracts in operation: 1.1.94

7. *Ireland* Statutory Instrument: SI No 33 of 1994 of 21.2.1994
Entry into force: 1.1.1994
application to contracts in operation: 1.1.94

8. *Italy* Legislative Decree no 303 of 10.9.1991
publication: Gazetta ufficiale no 57 of 20.9.1991.
entry into force: 1.1.1993
application to contracts in operation: 1.1.94

9. *Luxembourg* Law of 3 June 1994
publication: Memorial A-No 58 of 6.7.1994, p. 1088
application to contracts in operation: 1.1.94

10. *Netherlands* Law of 5.7.89
publication: Staatsblad 1989 no 312

entry into force: 1.11.89
application to contracts in operation: 1.1.94
Re-enacted by Law no 374 of 1993 as Articles 400–445 of Title 7 of the Burgerlijk Wetboek

11. *Austria* Federal Act of 11.2.1993
published in Federal Gazette 88
entry into force: 1.3.1993
application to contracts in operation: 1.1.1994

12. *Portugal* Decree no 178/86 of 3.7.86
publication: Diário da Républica, I série, 1986, p. 1575
entry into force: 2.8.86
application to contracts in operation: 2.8.86
amended by law No 118/93 of 13.4.93 published Diário da República No 86 p. 1818 of 13.4.93
application to contracts in operation: 1.1.94

13. *Finland* Law no 417 of 8.5.1992
published in Gesetzblatt of 14.5.1992
entry into force: 1.11.1992
application to contracts in force: 1.1.1994

14. *Sweden* Law no 351 of 2.5.1991
entry into force: 1.1.1992
application to contracts in force: 1.1.1994.

15. *UK* Statutory Instrument SI 1993 no 3053 of 7.12.93
and SI 1993 no 3173 of 16.12.1993
entry into force: 1.1.94
application to contracts in operation: 1.1.1994
Northern Ireland:
Statutory Rules of Northern Ireland 1993 no 483 of 17.12.1993
entry into force: 13.1.1994
application to contracts in operation: 13.1.1994

ANNEX B

BELGIUM

The law on Commercial Agent Contract only came into force on 12 June, 1995. Accordingly, there are no cases decided by the courts on the new law.

Article 20 of the law introduced the right to a goodwill indemnity. Prior to the new law, the right to a goodwill indemnity had been rejected by the main decisions of the Belgian courts as goodwill was considered to attach to the principal more than to the agent. Accordingly, the new law has brought about an important change to the law.

The law contains no guidance as to how the indemnity is to be calculated, but it is argued by most commentators that is for judge to determine the amount taking into account various factors such as level of commission in last years of the contract, level of development of customers, extent to which principal will continue to derive benefits, duration of contractual relations, level of involvement of the principal, existence of a pension financed by the principal or whether the agent's contract with the principal is his sole agency. One author has specifically drawn on the German method of calculation.

Practising Belgian lawyers considered that regard would be had to the law on commercial representatives and to the German experience. Under the Law on Commercial Representatives of 3 July 1978, however, the indemnity is calculated on the basis of 3 months wages for a commercial representative who has acted for the same principal for a period of one to five years. This period is increased by one month for each further five years.

Under Article 18(3) of the Belgian law, it is possible to claim damages for lack of notice, which amounts to lost commission in accordance with method of calculation set out in this Article.

Finally, under Article 21 of the Belgian law, an agent who has a right to an indemnity can claim in addition damages for the harm actually suffered. It is not clear in what circumstances is this payable and whether entitlement to an indemnity gives automatically a right to seek damages. In the view of the Commission this latter interpretation would be contrary to Article 17(1) of the Directive as the effect of such an interpretation would be that the two options would apply cumulatively.

DENMARK

With the implementation of the Directive in Denmark and the introduction of the right to an indemnity under Section 25 of Law No 272 of 2 May 1990, a new right was granted which had not existed under the previous law.

To date, only three judgments have been reported.[10] In *Lope Handel* the principal was ordered to pay losses for the failure to respect the contractual period of notice and to pay an indemnity of 1 years commission on the new customers acquired for the principal by the agent. It was proved that the new customers were lost one year after termination of the agency contract. In *S&L*, the principal was ordered to pay an indemnity equivalent to the maximum. It was proved that practically all the customers were brought by the agent. In *Cramer*, the court found that a substantial number of customers were once-only customers with whom the principal could expect no further business. The principal was ordered to pay an indemnity amounting to DKK 150,000. For comparison the maximum would have been 400,000.

In practice it appears that agents seek the maximum amount and principals try to argue the figure down. At present, although there is no set picture, there is no tendency to pay the maximum figure. Calculations appear to follow the German model.

As for other Member States, no useful statistics are available.

Section 6 of the law implements Article 17(2)(c) of the Directive and provides that if an agent or principal is in breach of his obligations to the other, the other is entitled to compensation for any damage caused thereby.

GERMANY

Article 89b of the Handelsgesetzbuch sets out the agents right to an indemnity. The method of calculation is set out in the Report itself.

In practice it appears that there has been no change in Germany as to the method of calculation of the indemnity following the implementation of the Directive in Germany as the indemnity provision of the Directive did not require change to German law. The change noted by industry was in relation to contracts with other EU countries, which prior to the Directive did not provide for an indemnity.

GREECE

The implementation of Article 17 of the Directive by Article 9 of Presidential Decree 219 of 18 May 1991 did not conform with the Directive, in particular, in that it did not implement the second indent of Article 17(2)(a) which requires that the indemnity be equitable. Greece has following correspondence with the Commission introduced a new law in 1995 which implements Articles 17(2)(a).

Article 9(1)(c) states that the right to seek an indemnity does not prevent an agent from seeking damages under the Civil Code. Damages are payable and awarded according to whether the contract was fixed term or of indefinite duration.

An agent may also seek damages for lack of proper notice.

10. *Lope Handel* v. *GE Lighting* (Commercial Court of Copenhagen of 25.9.1995); *S&L* v. *Eskimo* (High Court, Western Division of 14.11.1995); *Cramer* v. *B&B* (Commercial Court of Copenhagen of 15.12.1995).

SPAIN

Article 28 of law No 12/1992 of 27 June 1995 provides for the payment of an indemnity. Article 29 of the law provides for the award of damages if the principal unilaterally breaks an agency contract which is for an indefinite period. The Directive has filled a legal gap in Spanish law in that prior to the law implementing the Directive there was no specific law covering commercial agents or commercial agency contracts. However, Article 29 is not restricted merely to breach of contract and by virtue of this Spain has seemingly implemented both options contained in Article 17 of the Directive unless the Court interprets the scope of Article 29 narrowly.

Owing to the recent coming into force of the law there is a lack of jurisprudence in this area. The case law prior to the new law may be of relevance for the future since some of the principles may act as guidance for future judgment by the Spanish courts.

Under the old law, it was also possible to claim both damages and a goodwill indemnity and agents used to cumulate both claims. The difference between both remedies was sometimes blurred in practice. The Supreme Court has repeatedly recognised the possibility of obtaining an indemnity for goodwill. The judge is given a wide discretion to fix the level of the indemnity and in general it is calculated depending on the agent's earnings.[11] As regards damages, the courts considered a number of different matters in arriving at the award, including the level of the last commission, the nature of the activity, loss of prestige and whether the contract was exclusive or not.[12]

Finally, damages are payable for failure to respect the correct notice period which is the amount of commission the agent would have received if the notice period had been respected.[13]

However, despite these judgments it is still difficult to reach general conclusions, particularly as in Spain the level of indemnity is fixed after the hearing and the decision is not published.

FRANCE

Unlike for many other Member States, the Directive has not brought about radical change to the pre-existing law in France. Under Article 12 of Law No 91/593 of 25 June 1991, French law continues to give a right to compensation on termination of the agency contract. The change brought about relates to the circumstances in which compensation is payable and not in its calculation. The right to compensation now exists for the non-renewal of the contract and termination by the agent for reasons of old age, sickness or infirmity and on death.

Compensation is calculated as before according to the jurisprudence as neither the old law or the present law sets out the method of calculation. In the vast majority of cases it amounts to two years gross commission which is calculated from the agent's average remuneration over the preceding three years or the global sum of the last two years commission. This sum has become the customary award and is confirmed with court decisions applying the new law.[14]

The indemnity is calculated on all remuneration, not just commission. It is based on the gross figure. No distinction is made between old and new customers and it includes special commission. There is no practice to reduce for professional costs. Finally, outstanding commissions must also be included in the calculation.

The indemnity represents that part of the market lost to the agent and his loss is fixed at that moment. Accordingly, future occurrences are not taken into account, such as the principal ceasing to trade, the agent continuing to work with the same clients or developments in the market place. Similarly, the agent is not required to mitigate his loss.

The French courts do not order the payment of two years gross commission as compensation where it can be shown that the loss suffered by the agent is less, for example, because of the short duration of the contract. Similarly, the level may be increased, where, for example, an agent's loss is greater because of his age or length of the agency contract.

11. Supreme Court judgments of 22 March 1988 and 19 September 1989.

12. Judgment of Court of Appeal of Lugo of 4.6.1994; Court of Appeal Valence of 14.7.1993 and Court of Appeal Barcelona of 30.1.1995.

13. Judgment of Supreme Court of 19.9.1989.

14. See for example: Court of Appeal Toulouse 20.12.1994 Les Annonces de la Seine, No 39 1.6.1995 p.28; Court of Appeal Dijon, 16.6.1994 Les Annonces de la Seine, No 39, p.26; Court of Appeal Paris, 17.1.1995, Les Annonces de la Seine 1.6.1995, No 39, p.8.

The Directive has brought about a greater interest in claiming damages for failure to respect the proper notice period. The amount taken is the highest of the period not respected calculated on commission received for the last two years or the commission received during the identical period the previous year.

IRELAND

Ireland has not implemented this provision and therefore agents do not have either a right to compensation or an indemnity. Under the common law, an agent can seek damages for breach of contract. In a fixed term contract, this will allow the agent to claim the commission he would have received until the end of the contract, subject to the agent's duty to mitigate his loss. However, this is not sufficient for the purposes of implementing the Directive. In cases of contracts of indefinite period the claim is usually for remuneration during the notice period to be respected. In addition, in both cases, he may claim for the economic loss suffered as a result of the breach of contract.

To date there are no reported cases.

ITALY

Italy amended Article 1751 of the Civil Code by Article 4 of legislative Decree No 303 of 10 September 1991 to introduce the indemnity system set out in the Directive. However, in the view of the Commission the implementation by Italy is incorrect in that Italy has treated the two indents in Article 17(2)(a) of the Directive as alternative conditions whereas they are in fact cumulative. Accordingly the Commission has opened infraction proceedings.

It appears that the old system of collective agreements continues to apply. The Enasarco agreement of 30.10.1992 was agreed to by both principals and organisations representing agents. By doing so they have de facto re-introduced the criteria which were applicable under the previous text of Article 1751.

In its judgment of 1 December 1994, the Viterbo Magistrate Court applied the collective agreement. The court held that Article 1751 of the Civil Code could not be applied in practice as it does not fix any criteria for calculating the indemnity except the maximum. Accordingly, the court considered it appropriate to apply the collective agreement. The Court also stated that the circumstances in Article 1751 were not intended for calculating the amount of indemnity, but for determining whether an indemnity was justified if at least one of the circumstances applied. Further, the court considered that wisely the social partners, in order to avoid practically insoluble problems, had replaced the old collective agreement thereby enabling Article 1751 of the Civil Code to be applied in practice. It is not clear at this stage whether this judgment will be followed.

The system of the collective agreement is based on level of commissions and duration of the agency contract and the set percentages laid down in the agreement.

Under the collective agreement, the agent in most cases receives an amount which is much less than the maximum envisaged under the Directive.

LUXEMBOURG

Luxembourg's law implementing the Directive of 3 June 1994 applies to all contracts existing before 1 January 1994 as well as to contracts entered into force after that date. Article 19 provides for an indemnity to be paid on termination. The new law introduced a right which did not exist under the pre-existing law. It is therefore unsurprising that there courts decisions. Those consulted also thought it was too soon to develop a theory about how the law would be interpreted.

Article 23(1) sets out the right to damages for unjustified failure to give due notice and Article 23(2) provides for damages to be paid for a serious breach of contract. Article 24 states that this amounts to a sum equal to the remuneration that would have been received in the period between the breach and the normal end of the contract. To calculate this sum regard is to be had to the previous level of commissions and to other relevant matters. This sum can be reduced if the judge considers it too high in the circumstances of the case.

THE NETHERLANDS

Article 7:442 of the Civil Code provides for an indemnity to be paid on termination of the agency contract. Under Article 7:439 damages are payable for unjustified failure to respect the correct notice period and Articles 7:440 and 7:441 provide for damages to be paid for breach of contract. This covers the period from actual termination to the date on which the agency would have been terminated had proper notice been given. This amount is the amount of remuneration which would have been received and is based on the commission received prior to termination and other relevant circumstances. The judge can reduce the amount if he considers that it is too high having regard to the facts of the particular case. Under Article 7:441.3, the party can seek in place of the sum under Article 7:441.1 and 2., compensation for the actual damage suffered and he bears the burden of proving his loss.

There is not any reported case to date concerning the new law and nor are there any statistics.

AUSTRIA

The Austrian law of 11 February 1993 came into force on 1 March 1993. Under Article 24, the agent has a right to an indemnity. To date there are no reported cases concerning the amount of indemnity or damages payable on termination of an agency contract under the 1993 law. The Directive has lead to a change in the previous law and in particular to a doubling of the maximum limit. Therefore, previous case law is not useful guidance. Under the old law, there was a digressive reduction in the upper limit of compensation of aggregate amount of one year's commission calculated as a yearly average over the previous three years according to the length of the relationship.

In practice, it appears that commercial agents calculate the indemnity on the basis of the average income of the last five years taking into account the fluctuation of customers by computing a digression of income on the basis of 5 years. In most cases, this exceeds the upper limit set by law. On this basis, the parties negotiate in order to find a reasonable settlement. The method of calculation is based on German experiences.

It was considered too soon to make any judgment about the average level of indemnity paid. A claim for damages or performance of the contract can be made if a party terminates the contract prematurely without just cause under article 23. Article 23 also applies to a breach of Article 21 which is concerned with notice periods. Any other claims for damages are dealt with in accordance with the provisions of the General Civil Code and the Commercial Code.

PORTUGAL

Portugal adopted its law in 1986 which followed to a large extent the proposal for the Directive and included at Article 33 the right to an indemnity. The law came into force on 2 August 1986. It has been amended by Articles 33 and 34 of Decree No. 118/93 to bring Portugese law in conformity with Article 17 of the Directive.

In Portugal there have been a number of court judgments.[15] The courts have calculated the level of indemnity taking into account the importance of new clients, the increased development of existing customers, the advantages to the principal after the termination of the contract and the loss of commission by the agent. The courts consider the indemnity as a measure of compensation for the agent for the benefits to the principal existing at the end of the contract with the clients developed by the agent.

Under Article 32 of the law and under Articles 562–572 of the Civil Code, there is also a right to be indemnified for the damages suffered for breach of contract. Article 29 specifically provides for damages for failure to respect the notice period or alternatively to damages for lack of due notice. The agent can seek, as an alternative to damages, a sum calculated on the basis of the average monthly remuneration over the previous year multiplied by the time remaining if the contract had

15. Accórdão da Relação de Coimbra of 14.12.1993 Court of Appeal in Colectãnea de Jurisprudéncia, Year XVIII, 1993, Volume V, p. 46; Accórdão do Supremo Tribunal de Justiça of 4.5.1993 in Colectãnea de Jurisprudéncia—Accordãos do Supremo Tribunal de Justiça, Year I, Volume II, 1993, p. 78 and also same court, judgment of 27.10.1994 in Year II, Volume III, 1994, p. 101; Acórdão da Relação do Porto of 18.10.1994 in Colectãnea de Jurisprudéncia, Year XIX, Volume IV, 1994, p. 212.

continued to run. If the contract is of less than one years duration then the whole contract period is to be used.

FINLAND

Under section 28 of Act No 417 of 8 May 1992, the right to indemnity on termination of an agency contract was introduced. The Directive has brought about a change in the pre-existing law. The law came into force on 1 November 1992 and there has been no court decision to date.

In practice, it appears that agents seek the maximum amount and the principal makes a counter-offer. The negotiations result in an amount which is not based on any specific calculation, rather it is the outcome of bargaining. Generally, the indemnity is in the region of 3–6 months average commission. It was felt by the agents federation that the amount of indemnity period was slightly higher under the new law than under the old law, but no statistics are available to support this.

Under Section 9 of the law, the right to damages for harm caused by a violation of the agency contract is laid down or for when a party has neglected one of his obligations. Further, Sections 26 and 27 of the Act provide for damages where notice periods are not respected.

SWEDEN

Article 28 of Law No 351 of 2 May 1991 introduced a right to receive an indemnity which did not exist under the previous law, which only sought to ensure that an agent received commission on orders concluded after the withdrawal of the agent's authority provided that the orders were brought about through the acts of the agent during the currency of the agreement.

As for other Member States, there has yet to be any court decision. In practice agents seek the maximum amount permitted under the law and the parties negotiate on this basis to reach an equitable sum. In doing so, the parties take into account, inter alia, the duration of the contract, the agent's promotional activities, the number of new customers, orders given after termination, the possibility of a new contract for the agent and the costs incurred and investments made by the agent.

There are no statistics but the Swedish authorities estimated that awards were typically between 6 months and 1 year commission calculated as an average over the last years of the contract. This would represent an increase in the amount of compensation.

Article 34 of the law provides for damages for breach of contract.

UNITED KINGDOM

The UK has adopted its own particular system in that under Regulation 17 of Statutory Instrument No 3053 of 1993 the parties may choose whether an agent will have the right to an indemnity or compensation.[16] It is only in default of a contractual provision that the law requires compensation to be paid. This method of implementation has of itself produced uncertainty, particularly since neither of the two options are familiar to the UK legal systems.

The law has only recently come into force in the UK and has caused a certain amount of confusion as parties and lawyers attempt to apply concepts with which they are unfamiliar and which are a certain degree alien to UK traditions. Various different approaches have developed.

In relation to compensation, lawyers try to apply traditional common law principles which does not work well since under the common law, termination of a contract in accordance with its terms or at the natural end of a fixed term contract does not give rise to a damages claim. Under the common law, the court tries to put the agent in the position he would have been in if the contract had been properly performed, but the injured party is expected to mitigate his loss and the court will have regard to future events. Typically for a fixed term contract, this would give the agent the right to claim commission for the duration of the contract. In the case of a contract for an indefinite period, the agent could seek damages for the notice period amounting to the remuneration he would have received in this period. The agent could also seek compensation for costs incurred in pursuance of the agency. Lawyers therefore have difficulties in reaching a view as to the level of compensation

16. Regulation 17 of S.I No. 483 of 1993 for Northern Ireland.

where the agent has died, become ill or retired. Typical compensation payments are between 3–6 months with some payments of 15 months depending on the level of service.

Some lawyers have therefore tried to apply by analogy the law relating to unfair dismissal or redundancy which is determined by age, length of service and the weekly wage.

As regards the indemnity provision, agents claim the maximum amount and then through negotiations a smaller sum is agreed. Typical payments appear to be between 3–6 months commission based on what would have been earned rather than the average of the last 5 years.

Most contracts do not contain a provision providing for an indemnity, but this does not necessarily reflect a preference for the compensation option rather than the indemnity option.

To date, there have been no cases and parties are reluctant to litigate since lawyers are unconfident in advising what their clients' rights are and consequently what the courts will award. However, there are likely to be cases in the near future.

APPENDIX 10

EXTRACT FROM EUROPEAN COMMISSION GUIDELINES OF VERTICAL RESTRAINTS (2000)

(OJ C291/1 of 13th October 2000)

COMMISSION NOTICE

Guidelines on Vertical Restraints

(2000/C 291/01)

(Text with EEA relevance)

2. AGENCY AGREEMENTS

(12) Paragraphs 12 to 20 replace the Notice on exclusive dealing contracts with commercial agents of 1962.[1] They must be read in conjunction with Council Directive 86/653/EEC.[2]

Agency agreements cover the situation in which a legal or physical person (the agent) is vested with the power to negotiate and/or conclude contracts on behalf of another person (the principal), either in the agent's own name or in the name of the principal, for the:

— purchase of goods or services by the principal, or
— sale of goods or services supplied by the principal.

(13) In the case of genuine agency agreements, the obligations imposed on the agent as to the contracts negotiated and/or concluded on behalf of the principal do not fall within the scope of application of Article 81(1). The determining factor in assessing whether Article 81(1) is applicable is the financial or commercial risk borne by the agent in relation to the activities for which he has been appointed as an agent by the principal. In this respect it is not material for the assessment whether the agent acts for one or several principals. Non-genuine agency agreements may be caught by Article 81(1), in which case the Block Exemption Regulation and the other sections of these Guidelines will apply.

(14) There are two types of financial or commercial risk that are material to the assessment of the genuine nature of an agency agreement under Article 81(1). First there are the risks which are directly related to the contracts concluded and/or negotiated by the agent on behalf of the principal, such as financing of stocks. Secondly, there are the risks related to market-specific investments. These are investments specifically required for the type of activity for which the agent has been appointed by the principal, i.e. which are required to enable the agent to conclude and/or negotiate this type of contract. Such investments are usually sunk, if upon leaving that particular field of activity the investment cannot be used for other activities or sold other than at a significant loss.

(15) The agency agreement is considered a genuine agency agreement and consequently falls outside Article 81(1) if the agent does not bear any, or bears only insignificant, risks in relation to the contracts concluded and/or negotiated on behalf of the principal and in relation to market-specific investments for that field of activity. In such a situation, the selling or purchasing function forms part of the principal's activities, despite the fact that the agent is a separate undertaking. The

1. OJ 139, 24.12.1962, p. 2921/62.
2. OJ L 382, 31.12.1986, p. 17.

principal thus bears the related financial and commercial risks and the agent does not exercise an independent economic activity in relation to the activities for which he has been appointed as an agent by the principal. In the opposite situation the agency agreement is considered a non-genuine agency agreement and may fall under Article 81(1). In that case the agent does bear such risks and will be treated as an independent dealer who must remain free in determining his marketing strategy in order to be able to recover his contract- or market-specific investments. Risks that are related to the activity of providing agency services in general, such as the risk of the agent's income being dependent upon his success as an agent or general investments in for instance premises or personnel, are not material to this assessment.

(16) The question of risk must be assessed on a case-by-case basis, and with regard to the economic reality of the situation rather than the legal form. Nonetheless, the Commission considers that Article 81(1) will generally not be applicable to the obligations imposed on the agent as to the contracts negotiated and/or concluded on behalf of the principal where property in the contract goods bought or sold does not vest in the agent, or the agent does not himself supply the contract services and where the agent:

— does not contribute to the costs relating to the supply/purchase of the contract goods or services, including the costs of transporting the goods. This does not preclude the agent from carrying out the transport service, provided that the costs are covered by the principal;
— is not, directly or indirectly, obliged to invest in sales promotion, such as contributions to the advertising budgets of the principal;
— does not maintain at his own cost or risk stocks of the contract goods, including the costs of financing the stocks and the costs of loss of stocks and can return unsold goods to the principal without charge, unless the agent is liable for fault (for example, by failing to comply with reasonable security measures to avoid loss of stocks);
— does not create and/or operate an after-sales service, repair service or a warranty service unless it is fully reimbursed by the principal;
— does not make market-specific investments in equipment, premises or training of personnel, such as for example the petrol storage tank in the case of petrol retailing or specific software to sell insurance policies in case of insurance agents;
— does not undertake responsibility towards third parties for damage caused by the product sold (product liability), unless, as agent, he is liable for fault in this respect;
— does not take responsibility for customers' non-performance of the contract, with the exception of the loss of the agent's commission, unless the agent is liable for fault (for example, by failing to comply with reasonable security or anti-theft measures or failing to comply with reasonable measures to report theft to the principal or police or to communicate to the principal all necessary information available to him on the customer's financial reliability).

(17) This list is not exhaustive. However, where the agent incurs one or more of the above risks or costs, then Article 81(1) may apply as with any other vertical agreement.

(18) If an agency agreement does not fall within the scope of application of Article 81(1), then all obligations imposed on the agent in relation to the contracts concluded and/or negotiated on behalf of the principal fall outside Article 81(1). The following obligations on the agent's part will generally be considered to form an inherent part of an agency agreement, as each of them relates to the ability of the principal to fix the scope of activity of the agent in relation to the contract goods or services, which is essential if the principal is to take the risks and therefore to be in a position to determine the commercial strategy:

— limitations on the territory in which the agent may sell these goods or services;
— limitations on the customers to whom the agent may sell these goods or services;
— the prices and conditions at which the agent must sell or purchase these goods or services.

(19) In addition to governing the conditions of sale or purchase of the contract goods or services by the agent on behalf of the principal, agency agreements often contain provisions which concern the relationship between the agent and the principal. In particular, they may contain a provision preventing the principal from appointing other agents in respect of a given type of transaction, customer or territory (exclusive agency provisions) and/or a provision preventing the agent from

acting as an agent or distributor of undertakings which compete with the principal (non-compete provisions). Exclusive agency provisions concern only intra-brand competition and will in general not lead to anti-competitive effects. Non-compete provisions, including post-term non-compete provisions, concern inter-brand competition and may infringe Article 81(1) if they lead to foreclosure on the relevant market where the contract goods or services are sold or purchased (see Section VI.2.1).

(20) An agency agreement may also fall within the scope of Article 81(1), even if the principal bears all the relevant financial and commercial risks, where it facilitates collusion. This could for instance be the case when a number of principals use the same agents while collectively excluding others from using these agents, or when they use the agents to collude on marketing strategy or to exchange sensitive market information between the principals.

INDEX

(all references are to page number)